Initial Public Offerings

Quantitative Finance Series

Aims and Objectives

- Books based on the work of financial market practitioners and academics
- Presenting cutting-edge research to the professional/practitioner market
- Combining intellectual rigour and practical application
- Covering the interaction between mathematical theory and financial practice
- To improve portfolio performance, risk management and trading book performance
- Covering quantitative techniques

Market

Brokers/Traders; Actuaries; Consultants; Asset Managers; Fund Managers; Regulators; Central Bankers; Treasury Officials; Technical Analysts; and Academics for Masters in Finance and MBA market.

Series Titles

Return Distributions in Finance
Derivative Instruments: theory, valuation, analysis
Managing Downside Risk in Financial Markets: theory, practice & implementation
Economics for Financial Markets
Performance Measurement in Finance: firms, funds and managers
Real R&D Options
Forecasting Volatility in the Financial Markets, Second edition
Advanced Trading Rules, Second edition
Advances in Portfolio Construction and Implementation
Computational Finance
Linear Factor Models in Finance
Initial Public Offerings: an international perspective

Series Editor
Dr Stephen Satchell

Dr Satchell is the Reader in Financial Econometrics at Trinity College, Cambridge; Visiting Professor at Birkbeck College, City University Business School and University of Technology, Sydney. He also works in a consultative capacity to many firms, and edits the journal *Derivatives: use, trading and regulations* and the *Journal of Asset Management*.

Initial Public Offerings
An International Perspective

Edited by

Greg N. Gregoriou

AMSTERDAM • BOSTON • HEIDELBERG • LONDON • NEW YORK • OXFORD
PARIS • SAN DIEGO • SAN FRANCISCO • SINGAPORE • SYDNEY • TOKYO
Butterworth-Heinemann is an imprint of Elsevier

Butterworth-Heinemann is an imprint of Elsevier
Linacre House, Jordan Hill, Oxford OX2 8DP
30 Corporate Drive, Suite 400, Burlington, MA 01803

First published 2006

Library of Congress Cataloguing in Publication Data
A catalog record for this book is available from the Library of Congress

British Library Cataloguing in Publication Data
A catalogue record for this book is available from the British Library

ISBN-13: 978-0-7506-7975-6
ISBN-10: 0-7506-7975-1

For information on all Butterworth-Heinemann
publications visit our website at http://books.elsevier.com

Typeset by Macmillan India
Printed and bound in the USA

Contents

Preface

The idea for this book came about when I realized that the market for the initial public offerings (IPOs) reader was virtually nonexistent. With the cooling off of IPOs since the dot-com bubble, Google may have rekindled the fire for IPOs. This IPO text contains a collection of 25 new articles exclusive to this book by leading academics in the area, dealing with quantitative and qualitative analyses of this increasingly popular and important area of finance. The articles are intended to introduce readers to some of the new research and topics encountered by academics and professionals dealing with IPOs. The articles deal with new methods of assessing IPO performance, international IPOs, IPO evaluation, IPO underwriting, and bookbuilding. Although numerous articles are technical in nature, with econometric and statistical models, particular attention has been directed towards the understanding and the applicability of the results, as well as theoretical developments in this area. This book can assist academics, money managers, lawyer, accountants, doctoral graduates as well as undergraduate students desiring to further understand and obtain the latest cutting-edge research in this explosive field of IPOs.

Acknowledgments

I would like to thank Karen Maloney for guidance throughout the publishing process. I would also like to thank Melissa Read, Project Manager, and Geoff Crane for their editorial work. I further thank Professor of Finance Maher Kooli from the University of Quebec at Montreal for reviewing each chapter. Finally, I thank Dr Stephen E. Satchell from Cambridge University, Reader in Financial Econometrics.

About the editor

Greg N. Gregoriou is Associate Professor of Finance and coordinator of faculty research in the School of Business and Economics at the State University of New York (Plattsburgh). He obtained his Ph.D. (Finance) from the University of Quebec at Montreal and is hedge fund editor for the peer-reviewed scientific journal *Derivatives Use, Trading and Regulation* published by Henry Stewart publications (UK). He has authored over 40 articles on hedge funds and managed futures in various US, UK, and Canadian peer-reviewed publications, including the *Journal of Portfolio Management*, *Journal of Futures Markets*, *European Journal of Operational Research*, *Annals of Operations Research*, *European Journal of Finance*, *Journal of Asset Management*, etc. He has had four books published by John Wiley & Sons. This is his first book with Elsevier.

List of contributors

Joseph Aharony concluded the research that led to the contribution to this book while on leave as a Visiting Professor at the School of Accountancy, Singapore Management University. He holds a tenured position at the Faculty of Management, Tel Aviv University, Israel, where he has served twice as the Chairperson of the Accounting Department. He received his BA and MBA from the Hebrew University, Jerusalem and his Ph.D. from the Kellogg School of Management at Northwestern University. His numerous articles have appeared in such leading academic journals as *Journal of Accounting Research*, *Contemporary Accounting Research*, *Journal of Accounting and Public Policy*, *Journal of Finance*, *Journal of Business*, *Journal of Monetary Economics* and *Journal of Banking and Finance*. He has served as a Visiting Professor at the Leventhal School of Accounting, University of Southern California; Baruch College, CUNY; Anderson Graduate School of Management, UCLA; Free University of Bolzano, Italy; and Hong Kong University of Science and Technology. His research focuses on market-based accounting research and includes topics such as: value relevance of accounting information; IPOs and accounting-related issues; earnings management; corporate governance; and M&A.

Paul Ali is an Associate Professor in the Faculty of Law, University of New South Wales, Sydney, Australia. Paul was previously a corporate finance lawyer in Sydney. He was part of the core legal team that advised the Australian Mutual Provident Society, the largest Australian life company, on its demutualization and the rationalization of its group, and the IPO of a new holding company, AMP Limited, on the Australian and New Zealand Stock Exchanges in 1998 (at that time the largest IPO ever in Australia).

José Miguel Almeida has a first degree in Business Administration and an MBA from ISEG – Technical University of Lisbon, Portugal. Presently he heads the Asset Management Supervision Division at CMVM – Portuguese Securities Market Commission after having headed the Financial Intermediaries Supervision Division and the Market Department. Before joining CMVM, he worked as an asset manager in an international bank in Lisbon, Portugal. He also teaches corporate finance at ISEG – Technical University of Lisbon, Portugal.

Susana Álvarez-Otero is Associate Professor of Finance at Oviedo University, Spain. Her research includes the evaluation of corporate investment policy, analysis of mutual fund performance, initial public offerings, and privatizations.

Wolfgang Aussenegg is Associate Professor of Finance at the Vienna University of Technology, Department of Finance and Corporate Control. He has published several articles in refereed journals on initial public offerings, privatizations, capital market anomalies, and risk management issues, as well as books on asset pricing and transition economies. His research interests include privatizations in Central and Eastern European transition economies, IPOs, asset pricing, and risk management. Current working papers are posted on SSRN.

Edel Barnes, B.Comm. (NUI), M.Sc. (Finance, NUI), Ph.D.(Manc.), is currently a Senior Lecturer in Corporate Finance at University College Cork, Ireland. She completed her primary and masters degrees at UCC and studied under the supervision of Professor Martin Walker of the University of Manchester (UK) for her doctorate, which she was awarded with distinction in 2001. Her particular research interest is new securities issues, both seasoned and initial offerings. At UCC, she is program director for the B.Sc. Finance degree, has received the president's award for excellence in teaching, and is centrally involved at departmental, faculty, and college-wide levels in designing and promoting a culture of mature and lifelong learning initiatives.

Ran Barniv, Professor, Ph.D., Ohio State University. Research and teaching interests are in financial accounting and international accounting. He has published articles in capital market-based accounting research, accounting-based valuation, financial analysts, corporate governance, corporate bankruptcy and mergers, risk and uncertainty, and accounting for specific industries such as insurance and other financial institutions, and hospitals.

He has published many pieces, of which eight are single-author articles, including a feature article in the *Accounting Review*. Forthcoming articles will be published in *Contemporary Accounting Research* (CAR), *Journal of the American Taxation Association* (JATA), and the *Journal of Business Finance and Accounting* (JFBA). Previously, he has had at least two articles published in each of the *Journal of Accounting and Public Policy*, *Journal of Business Finance and Accounting*, *Journal of International Accounting Auditing and Taxation*, and the *Journal of Risk and Insurance*. He also published in the *International Journal of Accounting*, *Review of Quantitative Finance and Accounting*, *OMEGA the International Journal of Management Science*, *Journal of Macroeconomics*, *Management International Review*, *Managerial and Decision Economics*, and other journals. In recent years he has presented eight papers in Concurrent Sessions – the annual meeting of the American Accounting Association.

Prior to study for his Ph.D., Professor Barniv worked for 7 years in the industry. He served as a director of budget and planning, controller, and CFO. He also served on committees of the American Accounting Association. He teaches advanced financial accounting and international accounting, including courses in the master and doctoral programs.

Michel Boelen received a DESS from the HEC University of Liège and he is Scientific Collaborator for the Finance Department of this university. An administrator of INVESTA, he is working as Portfolio Manager and teaching business administration in the Engineering Institute of St Laurent (Liège).

Anlin Chen is Professor of Finance at National Sun Yat-Sen University, Taiwan. He received a Ph.D. from the University of Iowa, USA.

Sue L. Chiou is Associate Professor of Finance at the National Pingtung Institute of Commerce, Taiwan. She received a Ph.D. from the National Sun Yat-Sen University, Taiwan.

Steven Dolvin is an Assistant Professor of Finance at Butler University in Indianapolis, IN. He holds a Ph.D. in Finance from the University of Kentucky, and has also earned his designation as a CFA charterholder. His research primarily focuses on initial public offerings, with specific emphasis on the role of underwriters and the real cost effects on pre-existing owners. His work has been published in numerous academic journals.

João Duque is Professor of Finance at the Instituto Superior de Economia e Gestão (ISEG). He obtained his first degree in Business Administration from ISEG – Technical University of Lisbon, Portugal and completed his Ph.D. at the MBS – University of Manchester, UK. Subsequently he returned to the ISEG – Technical University of Lisbon, Portugal, where he is Professor of Finance. He teaches on financial derivatives and financial investments. Until 1998 he was the head of the Research Department at the Portuguese securities regulator, CMVM – Portuguese Securities Market Commission. His research interest lies in financial markets, financial derivatives, and portfolio management. He has recently published papers on subjects such as volatility estimators, implied volatility, volatility smiles, and financial regulation.

M. Banu Durukan studied Business Administration at the Dokuz Eylul University in Turkey and graduated in 1993 with high honors. She received an MBA from Boston University and a Ph.D. from the Dokuz Eylul University in 1995 and 1997 respectively. She has worked as a research assistant and Assistant Professor at the Dokuz Eylul University Faculty of Business since 1995. She became an Associate Professor in Finance in 2000 and is currently working at the Dokuz Eylul University Faculty of Business. She has also served as Associate Dean since 2001 and head of the Accounting and Finance Division of the Faculty of Business, Dokuz Eylul University since 1999. She has coauthored an Investment book (in English), and published articles in national and international journals. She also acts as the Associate Editor of the *Journal of Faculty of Business* and she has been a Guest Editor of *Managerial Finance*. Her research interests are behavioral finance, IPOs, and banking.

Giancarlo Giudici is Associate Professor of Finance at the Politecnico University in Milan, Italy. His research focuses on new listings and innovation financing. He has published several books and articles in international journals on initial public offerings. He is also co-editor of the book *The Rise and Fall of Europe's New Markets*.

Martin Gold lectures in the postgraduate programs of the Sydney Business School, Sydney, Australia. Martin is an experienced funds manager and investment analyst who worked for several institutional investment firms before becoming an academic in 2003. He has published in the areas of innovative financial products and the fiduciary responsibilities of fund managers.

Víctor M. González-Méndez is Associate Professor of Finance at the Oviedo University, Spain. His research includes the evaluation of corporate financial policies,

financial intermediation, insolvency, initial public offerings, privatizations, and earnings management.

Dimitrios Gounopoulos is a Lecturer in Accounting and Finance in the University of
Surrey, UK. He is near completion of his Ph.D. at the University of
Manchester/UMIST. He is holder of four Masters degrees, including an MBA from
The University of Leeds. As a researcher he is cooperating with colleagues from
Imperial College, London and the University of Warwick. In parallel he is a profes-
sional stage tutor, supporting students in various multinational firms in London,
including Deloitte and Touche, Lloyds TSB, and the DTI.

Stefan Günther has been working for HypoVereinsbank AG (Germany) since 2005.
He specializes in financial risk management for small and medium-sized companies.
He holds a Masters degree in Business Adminsitration from the University of
Bamberg, as well as an M.Sc. in Financial and Business Economics from the
University of Essex. The latter Masters degree, funded by the German Academic
Exchange Service, was awarded with a distinction.

Andreas Hack has a Ph.D. in Business Administration and is Assistant Professor of
Organization Theory at the Wissenschaftliche Hochschule für Unternehmensführung
(WHU), Vallendar, Germany's leading private business school. He has held various
positions in the financial services industry, most recently as management consultant
for Accenture. His research interests are concerned mainly with entrepreneurship,
organization theory, and marketing. He teaches organization and HRM at the WHU
and the Free University of Bolzano.

Georges Hübner holds a Ph.D. in Management from INSEAD. He is the Deloitte
Professor of Financial Management at the University of Liège and also teaches
finance at Maastricht University, EDHEC (Lille/Nice), and the Solvay Business
School (Brussels). He has taught at executive and postgraduate levels in several
countries in Europe, North America, Africa, and Asia. He has written several
books on financial management and has authored several peer-reviewed research
articles in the fields of credit risk, hedge funds, and derivatives, published in the
Journal of Empirical Finance, the *Journal of Futures Markets*, and the *Journal of
Banking and Finance*, amongst others. He was the recipient of the prestigious
2002 Iddo Sarnat Award for the best paper published in the *Journal of Banking
and Finance* in 2001. He is the coordinator of the French translation of the worldwide best-seller *Corporate Finance* (7th edition), authored by Ross, Westerfield,
and Jaffe.

Nancy Huyghebaert is Associate Professor of Finance at K. U. Leuven (Belgium),
where she obtained a Ph.D. in December 2000. Her work has been published in
*Strategic Management Journal, Journal of Corporate Finance, Journal of Business
Finance and Accounting,* and *Tijdschrift voor Economie en Management.* Her current research interests are in corporate finance. She studies the financial structure,
performance, and survival of entrepreneurial firms with a special interest in the interactions with product market characteristics. She also examines initial public offerings, privatizations, and mergers and acquisitions.

Maher Kooli is Assistant Professor of Finance at the School of Business and Management, University of Quebec in Montreal (UQAM). He holds a Ph.D. in Finance from Laval University (Quebec) and was a postdoctoral researcher in finance at the Center of Interuniversity Research and Analysis on Organizations. Maher also worked as a Senior Research Advisor for la Caisse de Depot et Placement de Quebec (CDP Capital). His current research interests include alternative investments, initial public offerings, and mergers and acquisitions.

Erik E. Lehmann studied Business and Management, and has a Ph.D in Economics. From 1999 to 2004 he held a position as an Assistant Professor at the University of Konstanz. Since 2004 he has been the Associate Director of the Entrepreneurship, Growth, and Public Policy Group at the Max Planck Institute, Jena. His main interests are financial restrictions in young and innovative firms, corporate governance, and IPO firms. He has had articles published in the *Journal of Economic Behavior and Organization, Small Business Economics, Research Policy, European Finance Review, International Journal of the Business of Economics, Economics of Innovation and New Technology, Journal of Technology Transfer, Journal of Management and Governance*, and *Empirica*, amongst others. He recently published a book titled *Entrepreneurship and Economic Growth* (Oxford University Press, 2005, with David B. Audretsch and Max Keilbach), where the impact of geographical spillovers on IPO firms is analyzed.

Chan-Jane Lin is currently a Professor at the Department of Accounting, National Taiwan University. She is now sitting on the Auditing Standards Committee, which sets the auditing standards in Taiwan. She has also served for several years on the Initial Public Offerings Review Board of the Taiwan Stock Exchange. Her research interest focuses on issues related to initial public offerings, earnings management, the impact of financial reporting regulations, and the accounting profession and audit market. She has published studies in *Contemporary Accounting Research, Journal of Accounting and Public Policy, Journal of Corporate Finance, International Journal of Accounting Studies, Chinese Accounting Review, Review of Securities and Futures*, and *Sun Yat-Sen Management Review*, amongst others.

Kojo Menyah is currently a Reader in Finance at the London Metropolitan University. His research interests, amongst others, include equity market microstructure, initial public offers, emerging capital markets, and corporate valuation. He has published in reputable academic journals such as the *Journal of Banking and Finance, Journal of Economics and Business, Journal of Financial Research, Review of Financial Economics, Journal of Business Finance and Accounting*, and *Accounting and Business Research*. He has teaching interests in corporate finance, treasury management, capital markets, and derivatives. He is the director of Ph.D. programs in the Department of Accounting, Banking and Financial Systems, and has edited a special issue of *Managerial Finance* on international cash management.

Mehmet Orhan is an Assistant Professor at the Economics Department of Fatih University, Istanbul. He is the Director of the Social Sciences Institute that is responsible from the coordination of 11 graduate programs. He received a Ph.D. from Bilkent University, Ankara, and graduated from the Industrial Engineering

Department of the same university. He had full scholarship until he obtained his Ph.D. degree. His main interests are econometrics, both theoretical and applied. He has published articles in *Economics Letters*, *International Journal of Business*, and *Journal of Economic and Social Research*. His theoretical research interests include HCCME estimation, robust estimation techniques, and Bayesian inference. He is working on IPO performance in Turkey, tax revenue estimation, and international economic cooperations as part of his applied research studies.

María J. Pastor-Llorca is Assistant Professor of Finance in the Financial Economics Department at the University of Alicante, Spain. She obtained a Ph.D. degree from the University of Alicante, and her doctoral thesis was based on the long-run performance of equity issues. Her research has been focused on different topics of corporate finance, mainly in equity offerings. She has participated in numerous international conferences and has published several papers in both national and international reviews. Her current research interest is the study of earnings management practices around primary and secondary equity offerings.

Krishna Paudyal, M.Sc., Ph.D., is a Professor of Finance and the director of the Ph.D. program at Durham Business School, University of Durham, UK. His teaching and research specializations include security analysis, international financial management, and market microstructure. Before moving into academia, he worked for the Nepal Rastra Bank, the central bank of Nepal. In 1993, Krishna made a transition to academia and joined Glasgow Caledonian University. He was promoted to a full professorship in 1996. He joined the University of Durham in 2000. He has published over 30 research publications in highly rated international journals, such as *Journal of Banking and Finance*, *Journal of International Money and Finance*, *Journal of Financial Research*, and *Journal of Business Finance and Accounting*. His contributions to the finance profession have been recognized internationally.

Francisco Poveda-Fuentes is Assistant Professor of Accounting at the Financial Economics Department of the University of Alicante, Spain. He obtained his Ph.D. from the University of Alicante and his research has focused on the empirical analysis of accounting information in capital markets. He is one of the leading experts in the study of earnings management practices in the Spanish market and has recently developed an alternative model to estimate the abnormal component of accounting results.

Peter Roosenboom is Assistant Professor of Finance at the RSM Erasmus University, the Netherlands. His research focuses on corporate finance and corporate governance. He has published articles in journals such as the *Journal of Corporate Finance*, *International Review of Financial Analysis*, *International Journal of Accounting*, and *European Financial Management Journal*. He is also coeditor of the book *The Rise and Fall of Europe's New Markets*.

Marco Rummer is currently finishing his Ph.D in Financial Economics. He has researched on IPOs for several years and has presented his work at numerous conferences, seminars, and workshops. He holds an M.Sc. in Economics and Finance from the University of York, which was funded by the German Academic Exchange

Service, and a BA in Management from the Georg-Simon-Ohm Fachhoschule, Nuremberg. His major research interests include empirical and experimental research on financial markets and corporate finance.

Josef A. Schuster is the founder of IPOX Schuster LLC, an innovative financial services company specializing in financial products design related to initial public offerings (IPOs), whose philosophy is to classify IPOs as a separate equity sector because they share unique long-run empirical dynamics. At the same time, their mission is to bring the concept of 'average IPO investing' or 'IPO indexation' to the marketplace. Before setting up IPOX Schuster LLC, he spent 7 years specializing in IPO research at the London School of Economics (LSE), where he received his Masters and Doctorate. During that time he was also a member of the Chicago Mercantile Exchange (CME), focusing on equity index arbitrage on the floor of the exchange. He holds Series 3 and 7 licences and is also a board member of the European Financial Management Association (EFMA).

Tereza Tykvová is at the Department of International Finance, Financial Management and Macroeconomics, ZEW Mannheim, Germany. After graduating from the Charles University of Prague (Economics) in 1997, she went to the University of Saarland, where she attended the postgraduate program 'European Economics' and obtained the title 'Master of Economics – Europe' with a thesis on venture capital and innovations in Germany. The thesis received the 1999 'Prof. Dr Osthoff Award'. She was a research assistant at Prof. Keuschnigg's Institute of Public Finance at the University of Saarland. In September 1999 she joined the Center for European Economic Research (ZEW) in Mannheim. Her fields of interests are venture capital, private equity, and initial public offerings. In 2004, she obtained a Ph.D. from Frankfurt University (supervisor: Prof. Uwe Walz). Her thesis focused on venture capital financing, initial public offerings, and performance of firms backed by different types of venture capitalists in Germany.

Cynthia Van Hulle is Professor of Finance at the Department of Applied Economics of the Katholieke Universiteit Leuven. She also lectures at the Vlerick Leuven Gent Management School and is Guest Lecturer at Solvay Business School. She was a Visiting Professor at the Columbia Graduate Business School (USA). She earned a Ph.D. in Applied Economics at the K. U. Leuven and has been a postdoctoral research fellow at Yale University (USA). Her primary research interests are corporate finance, corporate control, IPOs, and governance in profit and nonprofit organizations. She has published articles in the *Journal of Corporate Finance*, *Journal of Finance*, *Journal of Banking and Finance*, *International Review of Law and Economics*, *Finance*, *Health Policy*, *European Hospital*, *ASCI Journal of Management*, *European Management Journal*, *Acta Hospitalia*, and other scientific journals. Outside the university, she serves on several boards as president.

Niklas Wagner is Assistant Professor of Finance at Munich University of Technology. He received a Ph.D. in Finance from Augsburg University, Germany, and held postdoctoral visiting appointments at the Haas School of Business, UC Berkeley, and at Stanford GSB. Recent research visits led him to the Center of Mathematical Sciences, Munich University of Technology, to the Department of Applied Economics,

University of Cambridge, and to the Swiss Institute of Banking and Finance, University of St Gallen. His research interests cover the areas of applied financial econometrics, including portfolio optimization, risk management, trading strategies, and applications in behavioral finance. His research articles have been published in journals such as the *Journal of Asset Management*, the *Journal of Banking and Finance*, *Quantitative Finance*, and the *Journal of Empirical Finance*. He regularly serves as a referee to the international finance community, while he also stays in close touch with the investment community. His industry background is in quantitative asset management with HypoVereinsbank, Munich, and recently as a partner with Munich Financial Systems Consulting, mfscon.

Chinshun Wu is Professor of Finance at National Sun Yat-Sen University, Taiwan. He received a Ph.D. from the Wharton School, University of Pennsylvania, USA. He is interested in the fields of corporate finance, corporate governance, empirical methodologies, and issues in emerging markets.

Steven Xiaofan Zheng is Assistant Professor of Finance at the Asper School of Business at the University of Manitoba, where he teaches undergraduate finance courses. Steven previously taught graduate and undergraduate finance courses at SUNY at Buffalo and SUNY at Albany. He received a Ph.D. from SUNY at Buffalo. He conducts research in various areas in finance, including IPOs, seasoned equity offerings, corporate governance, and market microstructure.

Part One
Performance of IPOs

1 Nasdaq IPOs around the market peak in 2000

Niklas Wagner

Abstract

Previous evidence suggests that markets for initial public offering (IPO) stocks may reside in 'hot-issue' or 'cold-issue' regimes. Also, corporations intending to go public may initiate timing activities in order to take advantage of 'windows of opportunity' during which investors appear over-optimistic (Ritter, 1991). The peak in the recent equity market development offers a striking example of a 'hot-to-cold' market transition. Here, the Nasdaq IPOs during the pre-peak ('hot') and the post-peak ('cold') Internet bubble years 2000 to 2002 are examined. The descriptive results suggest that (i) pre-peak average initial underpricing was higher and (ii) overpricing risk was lower; i.e. IPO participation offered more favorable short-term rewards in the hot-issue market. Nevertheless, (iii) reported listing-year company profitability appears higher on average for cold issue IPOs.

1.1 Introduction

The question as to whether equity markets reside in a potential 'hot-issue' or 'cold-issue' market regime plays an essential role in the initial equity financing activity of young corporations. Given such potential market regimes, young corporations may initiate timing activities in order to influence the initial pricing of their shares and thereby entrepreneurs and venture capitalists try to take advantage of potential windows of opportunity (Ritter, 1991). We may consider the recent Nasdaq market downturn as an example. In the months before the market turned direction, i.e. before the peak around the middle of the year 2000, hardly a day went by without at least one company becoming public in the organized and the over-the-counter markets. Many of the companies belonged to the technology industry and to the Internet industry in particular. After the peak, the IPO market virtually dried up, with most of the equity markets having hit their all-time highs.

The present contribution examines Nasdaq initial public offering (IPO) stocks during the years 2000 to 2002. The period covers part of the pre-peak as well as part of the post-peak period of the recent equity markets movement – for example, it contains observations before as well as after the burst of the so-called Internet bubble. The appearance of what might be a bubble as lead by the Nasdaq market has initiated vivid discussions among practitioners and academics alike. Further, Schwert (2001) studied increased Nasdaq market volatility during the bubble period. Schwartz and Moon (2000) identified volatility of expected young corporations' sales as a factor which can drive young technology corporations' firm value. Finally, Pastor and Veronesi (2004) derived a market value to book value of equity valuation model to show that high levels of idiosyncratic volatility may justify the observed Nasdaq valuations. In the model, uncertainty about future profitability is linked to return volatility and uncertainty may hence explain both, high stock valuations as well as high return volatility.

As initial public offerings of stocks are the foremost important channel of new capital flow to young companies, the question arises why such cyclic behavior in the IPO markets occurs. IPOs play a highly important role in initial equity financing. Thus it is fascinating to see the market environment change so dramatically during relatively short periods of time. The effect of such regime changes is immediate and goes along with a vastly reduced equity financing activity of young companies. In examining the 2000 to 2002 period the differences in initial issuance market regimes are investigated and the question of how time-variation in the market for IPOs could be addressed in future work is considered.

Our descriptive empirical results suggest that the average initial underpricing was higher pre-peak, while the risk of overpricing was higher post-peak. Still, it should be emphasized that the risk of losses for first-time IPO stock buyers is generally substantial and remarkably larger during the cold-issue market. In other words, the results indicate a lower initial loss potential during the hot-market period. Furthermore, issue-year reported profitability appears to be higher on average for cold-issue IPOs, which indicates higher quality companies going public. This indication is in line with the comprehensive study by Hellwege and Liang (2002), who generally document few quality differences in hot- versus cold-issue market IPOs, but lower earnings for hot-issue IPOs on average. While earnings tend to be lower for hot issues, they may offer better future prospects. Our results show distinct non-normality of initial return distributions, which reflects uncertain future growth perspectives.

As opposed to the documented differences with respect to the issuing process in hot versus cold markets, the long-run performance for an illustrative sample of pre-peak versus post-peak issues appears very similar. In sum, the present results support the hypothesis that investors' participation in an initial listing indeed offers strikingly more short-term attractiveness during hot-issue market regimes than during cold market regimes.

The remainder of the chapter is structured as follows. The following section briefly introduces some of the literature on IPOs, including results on initial returns, aftermarket activities and returns, and long-run performance. Section 1.3 introduces the Nasdaq IPO dataset, defines a hot- and cold-issue subsample, and discusses some of the accounting characteristics of the sample Nasdaq companies. A descriptive examination of initial returns and long-run performance is given in section 1.4. The contribution ends with section 1.5.

1.2   Literature review

A vast number of empirical studies on initial equity issues in various international markets document substantial abnormal returns. Following the tradition of efficient markets, these findings pose a challenge to financial research. A recent excellent survey of the US literature on IPOs with additional references to other markets is given in Welch and Ritter (2002). Frequently, the IPO literature is categorized in research topics such as the reasons for and the timing of going public, the initial underpricing of IPO stocks, aftermarket activities, and the long-run performance of IPOs.

The initial underpricing of IPOs appears in fact substantial. Welch and Ritter (2002) and Loughran and Ritter (2004), for example, distinguish the 1980s, the 1990 to mid-1990 period, the mid-1990 to 1998 period, the Internet bubble years 1999 to 2000, and the years thereafter. For the US, average initial first-day returns are documented as follows: 7.4% for 1980 to 1989, 11.2% for 1990 to 1994, 18.1% for 1995 to 1998, 65.0% for 1999 to 2000, and 14.0% for 2001. Loughran and Ritter (2004) attribute this time-variation in part to the characteristics of the companies going public. Ljungqvist and Wilhelm (2002) found similar effects, particularly for many high-tech firms going public on Nasdaq, which accounted for a remarkable increase in the number of IPOs during the late 1990s (Welch and Ritter, 2002, p. 9).

Considering performance after the IPO, there is evidence of a difference between aftermarket and otherwise regular return behavior for IPOs in later periods. Market-maker activities and the time up to the end of the lockup period (relevant to insiders selling decisions) are potential explanations. Underwriter activities include price support (Boehmer and Fishe, 2002), which may render return behavior different from later periods. For studies on these issues see, for example, Aggarwal (2000) and Bradley et al. (2001). Other explanations for abnormal aftermarket performance could be risk considerations (Wagner, 2004). IPO performance in the longer run turns out to be mostly rather weak when measured against some market index. Ritter (1991), in his seminal paper, interpreted this poor long-run performance as an indication of cyclic over-optimism of investors with respect to the earnings potential of young growth companies. In contrast, Brav et al. (2000) found that long-run underperformance was not unique to issued companies. Eckbo and Norli (2004) found evidence that the poor performance of Nasdaq IPOs may be explainable by their risk factor model.

On the theory side, models are derived which predict many of the above empirical features. For example, Ljungqvist et al. (2003) developed a model based on sentiment investment behavior and short-sale constraints which offers testable implications with respect to initial underpricing and long-run performance, among other issues. Benninga et al. (2005) endogenized the IPO timing decision in their model and predicted, among other issues, IPO clustering and long-run performance.

1.3 The Nasdaq IPO dataset

1.3.1 Data sources

The data sources for the sample of Nasdaq IPOs for the years 2000 to 2002 were the following. The Securities Data Company (SDC) New Issues Database provided a report of all Nasdaq IPOs during the sample period. Initial prices were drawn from Nasdaq directly as made public on the market's website (www.nasdaq.com) or on other public sources, such as the financial website of yahoo (www.yahoo.com), among others. Financial statement information on the issues for the first fiscal year after initial listing was collected from the Worldscope Database. Information on aftermarket prices and returns was obtained from the Datastream Database.

1.3.2 The sample

Given the SDC filing information and the Nasdaq initial pricing information, a set with a total of 377 Nasdaq IPOs results for the given 3-year period. Figure 1.1 plots

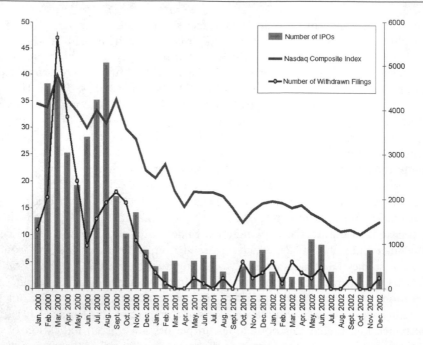

Figure 1.1 Nasdaq IPOs 2000 to 2002. Monthly number of Nasdaq IPOs in the overall sample (left scale), monthly number of withdrawn filings (left scale), and end-of-month level of the Nasdaq Composite Index (right scale). Period: 1 January 2000 to 31 December 2002

the monthly number of IPOs together with the monthly level of the Nasdaq Composite Index during our sample period January 2000 to December 2002. Additionally, Figure 1.1 shows the SDC reported number of IPO withdrawals and the month-end levels of the Nasdaq Composite Index.

Interestingly, Figure 1.1 indicates that withdrawals very much relate to the level of the stock market as well as with the IPO activity as measured by effective numbers of companies going public. The turn of the market is characterized by two peaks in withdrawals. The first and more significant peak occurred already in March 2000, while the second occurred later in September 2000. This observation does not support the hypothesis that entrepreneurs react with a time lag to investor sentiment on the equity markets.

1.3.3 Hot and cold subsamples

We now form two subsamples for the recorded Nasdaq IPOs in order to represent the hot and the cold market regimes. The first sample ('sample I') ranges from 1 January 2000 to 31 July 2000 and serves as a representative of a hot IPO market. The second sample ('sample II') represents the cold market and ranges from 1 August 2000 to 31 December 2002. Choosing the cutting point to be 31 July 2000 is admittedly a somewhat arbitrary decision. Given the data in Figure 1.1, later choices of the point may seem plausible. However, there is reason to believe that at least some substantial fraction of market participants had reduced their future market expectations already in

May 2000, when the market had experienced the first remarkable losses. Thus it seems plausible to fix a point somewhere between April and October 2000, with July being a central choice.

Table 1.1 reports a split of 197 versus 180 initial offerings for the hot and cold samples, respectively. Interestingly, while the minimum issue price was $5 for both subsamples, the maximum and average issue prices were higher during the hot market period.

1.3.4 Company characteristics

Financial statement information on the issues for the first fiscal year after initial listing was collected from the Worldscope Database. As such, the accounting information reflects the financial characteristics of the companies in the year they went public. Given our subsample choice from section 1.3.3, Tables 1.2 and 1.3 report five accounting measures for samples I and II, respectively. The measures are leverage as well as book value, cash flow, earning and sales on a per-share basis.

The accounting measures in Tables 1.2 and 1.3 do not exhibit a particular pattern with respect to differences between samples I and II. It appears that average book values per share give a fundamental valuation justification of the average issue prices of Table 1.1. Surprisingly, average book values per share are lower for the cold-market sample in Table 1.3. Sales per share with a minimum of zero indicate business activity breakdown for some companies. Average cash flow per share is negative for both samples and higher for sample II. In line with this, average earnings per share are negative

Table 1.1 Issue Price Levels

	Sample I	Sample II	Total
Minimum issue price	5	5	5
Maximum issue price	38	28	38
Mean issue price	15.79	12.79	14.36

Issue price levels for the overall sample and the two subsamples. Total sample period: January 1, 2000 to December 31, 2002.

Table 1.2 Accounting Characteristics Sample I

	Leverage	Book value per share	Cash flow per share	Earnings per share	Sales per share
Minimum	0	0.34	−120	−178	0
Maximum	16.88	392	7.94	1.32	285
Mean	0.29	10.92	−2.24	−4.98	6.41
Number of valid cases	176	175	174	170	176

First fiscal year after issuance accounting characteristics of Nasdaq IPO sample companies. As items were not available for all companies, the number of cases given is reported. Hot sample (I).

Table 1.3 Accounting Characteristics Sample II

	Leverage	Book value per share	Cash flow per share	Earnings per share	Sales per share
Minimum	0	−0.19	−60.71	−111	0
Maximum	34.06	157	12.74	1.38	79.01
Mean	0.39	5.95	−0.80	3.14	7.12
Number of valid cases	169	170	160	162	170

First fiscal year after issuance accounting characteristics of Nasdaq IPO sample companies. As items were not available for all companies the number of cases given is reported. Cold sample (II).

Table 1.4 First-day returns

	Sample I	Sample II	Total
Median %	56.3	13.6	27.6
ES %	−19.2	−26.9	−24.0
NEG %	11.4	24.7	15.8
Standard Deviation	10.7	4.0	8.4
Skewness	4.2	6.0	5.3
Kurtosis	20.4	40.5	33.3

Sample distribution of initial first-day returns of Nasdaq IPO companies for the overall sample and for the two subsamples. Expected shortfall (ES) denotes the average loss conditional on a negative first-day return realization, NEG denotes the sample fraction of negative returns. Total sample period: January 1, 2000 to December 31, 2002.

for hot-market issues and positive for cold-market issues. This indicates that cold-market issues on average show higher profitability after issuance than hot-market issues.

1.4   Nasdaq IPO returns

In this section, we study the return characteristics of our sample of Nasdaq IPOs during the 2000 to 2002 sample period. Section 1.4.1 is devoted to the initial IPO returns as reported for the first trading day following initial listing. Section 1.4.2 gives a brief glimpse into the long-run market-adjusted IPO performance.

1.4.1   Initial returns

A summary representation of the initial first-day returns for our sample, as well as for the hot-market sample (I) and for the cold-market sample (II), is given in Table 1.4. The median is used as a robust measure of location, which is only marginally influenced by single extreme return observations. The results indicate that the expected

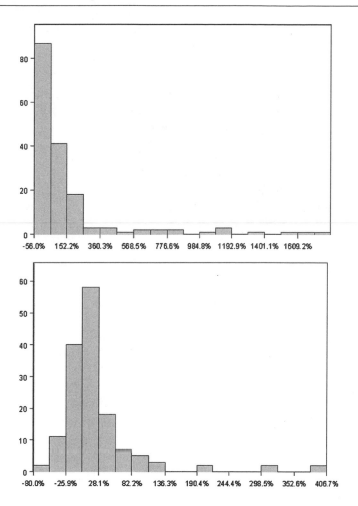

Figure 1.2 Hot- and cold-issue first-day return distributions. Truncated histograms of initial first-day IPO simple compounded returns for sample I (top) and sample II (bottom). Sample I: 1 January 2000 to 31 July 2000. Sample II: 1 August 2000 to 31 December 2002. Returns are calculated based on the offer price and the first trading day closing price as reported from Datastream. In both samples, the histograms were truncated, ignoring the 10 largest sample returns

initial IPO return drops from about 56% during the hot subsample period I to about 14% for the cold period II.

It should be noted that the initial returns of our sample IPOs spread widely, as indicated by the sample standard deviation and kurtosis measures in Table 1.4. The truncated distribution plots in Figure 1.2 indicate that the first-day return distributions are highly non-normal and show substantial positive skewness for both subsamples. As the plots demonstrate, the initial return distributions are skewed to the right and regularly exhibit extreme positive outliers on the right tail.

It appears that the remarkable spread in initial returns reflects the information asymmetry in initial IPO pricing. The distinct non-normality of the initial return distributions may reflect uncertainty with respect to the future growth perspectives of the respective IPO companies.

Participation in an IPO bears economically significant risk for first-time buyers. Table 1.4 reports that the risk of an initial loss is roughly 16% for all sample IPOs. The expected shortfall (expected loss given a loss occurred for the respective IPO) amounts to 24%. This indicates that the expected positive initial IPO returns may in part serve as a premium for large pricing uncertainty, which – given, for example, large underwriter positions in one single IPO stock – may turn out not to be fully diversifiable. Taking part in the IPO process, investors acquire positive expected initial returns and positive skewness at the expense of the risk of initial losses. For an IPO in the cold period the figures in Table 1.4 indicate that in about one out of four IPOs to which an investor subscribes they will suffer a first-day loss with an expected amount of about one-fourth on their initial investment. Thus, despite substantial initial underpricing on average, there is substantial risk involved in the IPO participation.

1.4.2 Long-run returns

This section offers a brief glance at the long-run properties of the Nasdaq sample IPO returns. We thereby refer back to the hot sample (I) and the cold sample (II), extracting the 20 last hot-sample IPOs and the first cold-sample IPOs. Figure 1.3 shows a plot of the cumulative abnormal returns in event time, i.e. after the initial listing. The returns are continuously compounded and market-adjusted based on the respective calendar-day Nasdaq Composite returns.

The performance plots in Figure 1.3 indicate that – as opposed to the documented differences with respect to the issuing returns – the long-run performance for the

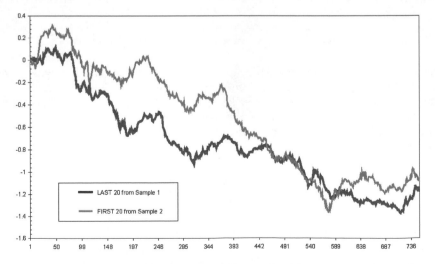

Figure 1.3 Cumulative abnormal performance of hot and cold issues. Cumulative abnormal performance of the last 20 IPOs up to 30 July 2000 and the first 20 IPOs after 30 July 2000 (continuous compounding). Lines plot the cumulative market-adjusted long-run returns during the first 750 trading days (equivalent to about three calendar years) after the issuance. The Nasdaq Composite Index serves as a market proxy in calculating market-adjusted continuously compounded returns

sample of 20 pre-peak versus 20 post-peak issues appears similar. A possible reason for this could be that our sample cut in 30 July 2000 does not represent a clear change point in the long-run performance, which may change more gradually in time. Thus, other sample selection and an examination of the full sample plus additional statistical testing would be needed to further address long-run performance.

1.5 Conclusion

The question of the present contribution addresses differences in IPO stock market regimes. In examining the 2000 to 2002 period, differences in initial issuance market regimes were investigated. At this point hypotheses and issues for further discussion may be proposed with respect to time-variation in the market for IPOs. Given the present empirical findings, the hypothesis is proposed that investors' participation in an initial listing is indeed strikingly more attractive during a hot-issue market than during a cold market. Given lower risk and higher levels of underpricing, it appears that there is more money left on the table during hot periods. This could be because over-optimistic investors are willing to pay premiums for uncertain growth opportunities or entrepreneurs are seeking a quick exit from their investments. Note that the tentative observation that the long-run performance of pre-peak versus post-peak issues is similar coincides with the paper by Helwege and Liang (2002) who, in a 5-year period, did not find much difference in the performance of firms that went public in hot and cold markets. Given such evidence, one may question which features characterize potential hot-issue markets as potential windows of opportunity. Under similar long-run overpricing of the issues, it would appear that the IPO market is efficient in the sense that – although hot and cold markets lead to differences in the conditional initial pricing and distribution of IPO stocks – aftermarket IPO performance converges to an unconditional long-run equilibrium.

Acknowledgments – I would like to thank Elisabeth Bley and Christine Sangl for valuable dataset assistance, as well as Heiko Witte of Thomson Financial for the SDC request and for his detailed explanation of the different information systems involved.

References

Aggarwal, R. (2000). Stabilization Activities by Underwriters After Initial Public Offerings. *Journal of Finance*, 55(3):1075–1103.

Benninga, S., Helmantel, M., and Sarig, O. (2005). The Timing of Initial Public Offerings. *Journal of Financial Economics*, 75(1):115–132.

Boehmer E. and Fishe R. P. H. (2002). Price Support by Underwriters in Initial and Seasoned Public Offerings. Working Paper, University of Miami, Miami, FL.

Bradley, D., Jordan, B. D., Roten, I. C., and Yi, H.-C. (2001). Venture Capital and IPO Lockup Expiration. *Journal of Financial Research*, 24(4):465–493.

Brav, A., Geczy, C., and Gompers, P. (2000). Is the Abnormal Return Following Equity Issuances Anomalous? *Journal of Financial Economics*, 56(2):209–249.

Eckbo, B. E. and Norli, O. (2004). Liquidity Risk, Leverage and Long-Run IPO Returns. Working Paper, Dartmouth College, Hanover, NH.

Helwege, J. and Liang, N. (2002). Initial Public Offerings in Hot and Cold Markets. Working Paper, Ohio State University, Columbus, OH.

Ljungqvist, A. and Wilhelm, W. (2002). IPO Pricing and the Dot-com Bubble. Working Paper, New York University, New York City, NY.

Ljungqvist, A., Nanda, V. K. and Singh, R. (2003). Hot Markets, Investor Sentiment, and IPO Pricing. Working Paper, New York University, New York City, NY.

Loughran, T. and Ritter, J. R. (2004). Why has IPO Underpricing Changed Over Time? *Financial Management*, 33(3):5–37.

Pastor, L. and Veronesi, P. (2004). Was There a Nasdaq Bubble in the Late 1990s? Working Paper, University of Chicago, Chicago, IL.

Ritter, J. R. (1991). The Long-Run Performance of Initial Public Offerings. *Journal of Finance*, 46(1):3–27.

Schwartz, E. S. and Moon, M. (2000). Rational Pricing of Internet Companies. *Financial Analysts Journal*, 56(3):62–75.

Schwert, G. W. (2001). Stock Volatility in the New Millenium: How Wacky is Nasdaq? Working Paper, University of Rochester, Rochester, NY.

Wagner, N. (2004). Time-Varying Moments, Idiosyncratic Risk, and an Application to Hot-Issue IPO Aftermarket Returns. *Research in International Business and Finance*, 18(1):59–72.

Welch, I. and Ritter, J. R. (2002). A Review of IPO Activity, Pricing and Allocation. Working Paper, Yale University, New Haven, CT.

2 Returns to style investments in initial public offerings

Kojo Menyah and Krishna Paudyal

Abstract

We extend the style investment literature by using style stock selection methods to investigate the aftermarket performance of initial public offerings (IPOs). Holding period returns for value versus growth IPOs, small-cap versus large-cap IPOs, and IPOs marketed by high-quality underwriters versus those marketed by low-quality underwriters are compared. Several conclusions emerge from the comparison of returns of these style portfolios after controlling for risk. First, value and growth IPOs do not exhibit statistically significant differences in returns for all holding periods. Second, the large-cap IPO portfolio outperforms the small-cap portfolio for up to 4-year holding periods. Third, IPOs sponsored by high-quality underwriters provide significantly higher returns than IPOs marketed by low-quality underwriters. However, after controlling for the quality of the underwriter, value and small-cap IPOs marketed by prestigious underwriters provide significantly higher and positive aftermarket returns.

2.1 Introduction

Security selection using style analysis is common practice among fund managers and individual investors. Chen et al. (2000) document that mutual funds exhibit a preference for holding small stocks, growth stocks, and momentum stocks compared to the market portfolio. Brown and Goetzmann (1997), and Wermers (2000), among others, analyzed style-based returns to mutual funds, while Kumar (2002) provided evidence of style investments at the level of individual investors. Style-based investments are not new, but their rationale derives from the perceived wisdom of practitioners and empirical evidence rather than from formal theoretical modeling. Graham and Dodd (1934) advocated the value investment style in the 1930s, while Babson (1951) suggested the growth style in the postwar period. The size style was first identified empirically in the work of Banz (1981).

The literature on style investments has, however, focused on seasoned issues and has not been tested on initial public offerings (IPOs). This belies the fact that mutual funds and individual investors include IPOs in their portfolios. Since it is well known that fund managers and individual investors use style portfolio selection methods, it is reasonable to argue that such investors will apply the same methods in the creation of aftermarket IPO portfolios. Since this is likely to be the case for a large number of investors, style portfolios can be used to gain an understanding of the aftermarket performance of IPOs. This is precisely what this chapter sets out to do. This approach contrasts with most previous IPO aftermarket studies that have tended to analyze new issues as a class rather than explicitly basing their analyses on style portfolios.

In the initial aftermarket of IPOs, the investment styles that could be used on the basis of available information would include small-cap, large-cap, value and growth stocks, as well as various combinations of these style categories. We analyze the returns associated with these aftermarket IPO investment styles. Additionally, we view the quality of the underwriter as a style category in the creation of aftermarket portfolios. This is justifiable on the grounds that the information available for the creation of an underwriter style portfolio is publicly available from published rankings of the performance of investment banks in various areas of their operations, including their corporate finance business. The construction of an IPO aftermarket portfolio based on underwriter quality is therefore analogous to the creation of value, growth, and size style portfolios from public information.

This chapter makes two major contributions to the literature. Firstly, by extending the analysis of style performance returns to new issues, we are able to isolate the styles that are appropriate for aftermarket IPO investments. Secondly, our portfolio formation method using style analysis provides a new conceptual approach for the study of the aftermarket performance of IPOs. The findings should be of interest to both investors and academics. Investors will benefit from this research by learning which style strategies are successful for making aftermarket IPO investments. Researchers gain through the introduction of a new conceptual approach to the analysis of the aftermarket performance of IPOs.

2.2 Prior studies on investment styles and their returns

Stocks with high book-to-market ratios are described as value stocks, whilst those with low book-to-market ratios are termed growth stocks. Rosenberg et al. (1985), Chan et al. (1991), and Barber and Lyon (1997), among others, have found that value stocks provide higher returns relative to growth stocks. Berk et al. (1999) developed a model in which the book-to-market ratio serves as a variable summarizing the firm's risk relative to the scale of its assets, and therefore provides a basis for characterizing the expected returns on such stocks. Brav and Gompers (1997) reported that book-to-market ratios help to predict long-run returns for up to 5 years. Strong and Xu (1997) reported that high book-to-market portfolios on the London Stock Exchange provided higher returns than growth stocks during the 1973 to 1992 period. The empirical evidence of Banz (1981) that average returns of small capitalization stocks are higher relative to those of high capitalization stocks formally introduced size as an investment style in the academic literature. Levis (1985) showed that small firms have higher returns than large firms in the UK.

The performance of value and growth style investments is, however, not stable over time. For example, Chan et al. (2000) reported that growth stocks and large stocks outperformed value and small stocks during the 1990 to 1998 period. Lucas et al. (2002) also showed that returns to value stocks generally tend to vary over time. To take account of the evidence that style returns may vary over time, we analyze style returns over different holding periods ranging from 1 to 5 years. Our analysis of value, growth, and size IPO styles focuses on the extent to which their returns are comparable to what has been documented for seasoned issues. This enables us to argue that the most effective approach to understanding the aftermarket performance of IPOs should be based on style analysis.

Theoretical and empirical work supports the view that the quality of the underwriter employed by the IPO firm to market the issue can be used to distinguish between high- and low-quality firms. Titman and Trueman (1986) developed a model which predicts that underwriters specialize by quality of offering. Beatty and Ritter (1986) provided evidence to support this proposition. Chemmanur and Fulghieri (1994) argued that investors assess the credibility of underwriters using the quality of firms they take public. Hence underwriters whose IPOs have better aftermarket performance are able to protect their reputation. Michaely and Shaw (1994) and Carter et al. (1998) provided evidence to show that IPOs marketed by high-quality underwriters suffer a smaller loss in the long run. Additionally, Jain and Kini (1999) argued that prestigious underwriters have the incentive to effectively monitor the managers of firms they take public after the IPO in order to protect their reputation and reduce the likelihood of being associated with a poorly performing firm. They also provided evidence to show that both the operating and investment performance of firms taken public by prestigious underwriters are better than those of less prestigious bankers. Dunbar (2000) documented that, where the 1-year aftermarket performance of an IPO is positive, the market share of the quality banks that take such firms public increases. Krigman et al. (2001) reported that firms that switch their underwriters to make further issues after IPOs tend to move to higher reputation underwriters. It is clear from the foregoing that underwriter reputation has some association with the aftermarket performance of IPO firms. We therefore investigate how underwriter quality helps to distinguish between the aftermarket performance of IPOs.

2.3   Data, sample, and empirical methods

2.3.1   Data

The sample covers UK IPOs from 1990 to 1998. The data were obtained from various issues of the KPMG publication, *New Issues Statistics*. This publication provided data on the direct costs of issue, issue methods, proportion of the equity of the IPO firm sold to the public, money raised for the company, market capitalization on flotation, and names of professional advisers, as well as financial and other information on issuing firms. Data on the ranking of sponsors were purchased from Consensus Research International. This provided an annual ranking of investment banks for the quality of their corporate finance services (the CRI ranking). The rankings were based on a survey of approximately 750 finance directors of listed companies. We classified the top four investment banks as high-quality underwriters for every year of our sample period. The top four banks that appeared regularly as high-quality banks included Kleinwort Benson, Lazard Brothers, Morgan Grenfell, and Schroders. These high-quality sponsors took firms public on both the main market as well as the Unlisted Securities Market, and were involved with placings as well as offers for sale. Using the number of firms taken public by underwriters during the sample period, a second method of ranking denoted as activity ranking was also developed. In the activity ranking, underwriters marketing 50 or more IPOs during 1984 to 1998, before filtering out various observations, are classified as high quality. The advantage of this method is that since active sponsors are subject to frequent evaluation of their performance in the IPO market, they can only maintain their reputation and get more business if they perform their sponsorship role very well. Share price data were collected from Datastream International.

The sample excludes investment trust issues, transfers from USM to main market, and introductory issues. A random sample of the data was cross-checked with electronic copies of prospectuses lodged with Thomson Financial Research and several news sources provided by Lexis Nexis Executive. All unusual observations that could not be corroborated by other sources were deleted. The final sample has 384 issues.

2.3.2 Characteristics of the sample

Table 2.1 records major features of the sample IPOs. The average market capitalization on flotation is £155.1 million. However, the median market value is £40.6 million, indicating that most IPOs are relatively small. An average size IPO raises £80.5 million on flotation. The average proportion of equity sold, 46%, is well above the market regulatory minimum of 25%. However, an IPO with a 5% minimum proportion sold reflects the fact that the London Stock Exchange continues to exercise its discretion in varying the minimum float, if a particular company's situation makes it appropriate. The book-to-market ratio of the sample is 42.2%. The distribution (Table 2.1) as well as the coefficient of variation (2.457) shows that this ratio varies substantially across IPOs. Although there is some annual variation in the rate of return to subscribers, the average underpricing for the sample period is 12.4%. This compares with 14.3% reported by Levis (1993) for the 1980s and 14.5% for the 1990s reported by Menyah and Paudyal (2003). It is also interesting to note that 84% of sample IPOs traded above the offer price on the first day. For all sample years, the average initial return to subscribers remained positive, with the lowest being 7.0% in 1994 and the highest 28.9% in 1990. The distribution of initial returns appears to differ by the quality of the underwriter. High-quality sponsors tend to have significantly higher initial returns than other underwriters (17.7% compared to 11.5% in CRI ranking and 17.9% vs 11.4% in activity ranking). Table 2.1 also registers the higher variability in market capitalization followed by the book-to-market ratio of the sample IPOs.

2.3.3 Composition of style portfolios

Value and growth stocks were identified using book-to-market ratios. IPOs with book-to-market ratios higher than median were classified as value stocks, whilst those with book-to-market ratios lower than or equal to the median were categorized as growth stocks. We also composed five portfolios each containing an equal number of IPOs based on book-to-market ratios to assist in further analysis of value versus growth returns. Using a similar process, IPOs were classified into two groups on the basis of their market capitalization. If the market capitalization of the IPO was higher than median it was considered as a large-cap stock, otherwise it was treated as a small-cap stock. Once again, five portfolios with equal numbers of IPOs in each were created on the basis of the market value of IPOs. The two measures of underwriter quality used in the analysis are described in section 2.3.1. We also allowed for the interaction between styles by composing two-way style portfolios (for example, value IPOs marketed by high-quality versus low-quality underwriters).

Table 2.1 Summary statistics of sample IPOs (1990 to 1998)

	N	Mean	Min	Q1	Median	Q3	Max	St. Dev.	Coeff. of variation
Offer price (pence)	384	157.4	3.0	100.0	135.0	100.0	1807.0	131.2	0.834
First day price (pence)	384	175.2	3.3	117.3	150.0	117.3	1937.5	144.3	0.824
Initial returns (%)	384	12.4	−25.0	2.1	8.2	2.1	140.0	16.0	1.290
Market value (£m)	384	155.1	1.3	21.3	40.6	21.3	5689.8	497.6	3.208
Sale proceeds (£m)	384	80.5	1.0	8.4	15.3	8.4	3088.5	259.9	3.229
Equity Sold (%)	384	46.0	5.0	32.0	41.5	32.0	100.0	21.4	0.465
Book-to-Market ratio	384	0.422	0.001	0.109	0.243	0.480	16.181	1.037	2.457

2.3.4 Empirical models

The returns used in the empirical analysis are measured in two ways. In the first measure, the excess returns of IPOs are estimated by deducting the risk free return (measured by the 3-month Treasury bill rate) from the raw aftermarket return. For the second measure, the risk-adjusted excess return is estimated using equation (2.1), which adjusts for risk factors identified in Fama and French (1996). This approach is used because conventional methods for estimating risk-adjusted excess returns, such as that of Brown and Warner (1985), require share price data for a long estimation period prior to the start of the holding period. Since IPOs lack such data, we examine the significance of risk-adjusted excess returns using Jensen's alpha, in a multi-factor asset-pricing framework. Such a model does not require parameter estimation period data. In addition, other explanatory variables, such as dummies, can be incorporated easily into the model.

$$(R_i - R_f) = \alpha + \beta_1(R_m - R_f)_i + \beta_2 SMB + \beta_3 HML + \varepsilon_i \qquad (2.1)$$

where:

$R_i - R_f$ = Excess return of IPO_i for a given holding period

R_f = Risk-free rate based on the 3-month Treasury bill rate

R_m = Return on the market portfolio (FT All Share Index) for the relevant period

SMB = The value weighted difference in the return between small market capitalization stocks and large market capitalization stocks

HML = The value weighted return differential between high book-to-market ratio stocks and low book-to-market ratio stocks.

If the return from a portfolio of IPOs consistently outperforms (underperforms) the returns predicted by the model, the value of alpha (α) will be significantly greater (less) than zero. SMB and HML are estimated using the procedure described in Fama and French (1996). All variables are calculated on the basis of buy and hold and cumulative returns for each holding period analyzed. The returns are measured with two methods in order to enable us to examine the robustness of the results to model specification. The cumulative returns strategy involves high transaction costs and therefore does not reflect the true realizable returns without adjusting for transaction costs. On the other hand, buy-and-hold returns involve small transactions costs and therefore the returns they measure are very close to realizable returns. Hence, in practice, buy-and-hold returns are better than cumulative returns. Therefore, we discuss the results based on buy-and-hold returns. However, the distribution of buy-and-hold returns is not known, and therefore the level of their significance should be viewed with caution. We report the results of cumulative returns where they differ substantially from buy-and-hold returns.

Secondly, we use both parametric (one-way analysis of variance and dummy variable regression) and nonparametric (Kruskal–Wallis) tests to compare the performance of IPO portfolios formed on the basis of style investing value versus growth, small cap versus large cap, and marketed by high-quality versus low-quality underwriters. Since the primary objective of this chapter is to present comparative performance of the portfolios of IPOs based on different styles, comparisons of excess returns of such portfolios (not adjusted for risk) should offer sufficiently meaningful inferences.

Thirdly, we examine the performance of the style portfolios within a bivariate framework to assess the returns to combination of styles. To assess the overall relevance of all style categories, we model holding period returns as a function of three risk factors and three dummy variables representing the styles of IPOs identified, within a multivariate framework.

2.4   Empirical evidence

2.4.1   Returns to value and growth styles

The estimates in Table 2.2(A) show that value portfolios gain while growth stocks suffer a loss after a year of flotation and that the excess returns between them differ significantly. However, the differences in holding period excess returns become insignificant if the portfolios are held for more than a year, especially because the value stocks' returns decline and start generating a loss after 3 years. Growth stocks generate losses for all 5-year holding periods. Kruskal–Wallis H-statistics that test for the significance of differences in the medians of two portfolios show that the excess returns from value and growth portfolios do not differ significantly except for a 5-year holding period. To get a better insight into the comparative holding period performance of value and growth IPOs, we analyze five equally weighted portfolios based on book-to-market ratios. The estimates in Table 2.2(B) show that the holding period excess returns decrease as we move from the highest value stocks to the highest growth stocks for all holding periods. The evidence that value stocks outperform growth stocks is borne out by the test of differences between extreme value (lowest) and growth (highest) stocks portfolios (see last column of Table 2.2(B)). This suggests that there is the possibility of generating excess returns by taking a long position on extreme value stocks and going short on growth portfolios of unseasoned stocks.

   To account for differences in risks and hence in required returns of value and growth stock portfolios, we estimated equation (2.1). The risk-adjusted excess returns (the values of α), show a distinctive pattern – value IPOs suffer losses while the growth IPOs show some evidence of positive returns (Table 2.2). The difference in the performance of these two portfolios – over 49% in year 4 – appears to be economically nontrivial.

   To examine the statistical significance of the differences in risk-adjusted returns, we modify equation (2.1) by including a dummy variable (DGrowth) that takes the value 1 for growth firms (lower than median book-to-market ratio) and 0 for value stocks. A significant δ coefficient (equation (2.2)) would indicate a difference in risk-adjusted excess returns from these two portfolios.

$$(R_i - R_f) = \alpha + \beta_1(R_m - R_f) + \beta_2 \text{SMB} + \beta_3 \text{HML} + \delta \text{DGrowth} \qquad (2.2)$$

The estimates (Table 2.2(A), column 'Growth dummy t-stat') show that in spite of an economically substantive difference in their returns, the performances of value and growth stocks do not differ significantly after controlling for risk. Overall, the evidence is mixed. Therefore, contrary to some evidence from seasoned stocks and results discussed above for extreme value versus growth portfolios, value IPOs do not necessarily perform significantly better than growth IPOs once returns are adjusted for risks.

Table 2.2 Aftermarket returns to value and growth IPOs

Holding period	Excess returns (%)			K–W H-stat	Risk adjusted return (%)		Growth dummy (t-stat)
	Value stocks	Growth stocks	F-stat		Value stocks	Growth stocks	
N-IPOs	192	192			192	192	
1 Year	1.82	−6.57	2.72[b]	2.29	6.280	0.579	−0.74
2 Years	1.74	−2.74	0.30	0.08	−22.128	−1.122	−0.27
3 Years	0.40	−7.09	0.59	1.08	−29.178	0.588	−0.68
4 Years	−14.30	−15.00	0.00	0.00	−27.322	21.771	0.05
5 Years	−20.80	−37.80	1.95	3.61[b]	−6.800	−24.540	−1.11

Panel A: Equally weighted excess returns $(R_i - R_f)$ of portfolios of value and growth IPOs are estimated. The cut-off for value and growth stocks is the median book-to-market ratio. Buy-and-hold returns (%) of IPOs bought on the first day of trading for various holding periods are estimated for each portfolio. Excess returns of value IPOs and growth IPOs are compared. The significance of their difference is tested with F-statistics (one-way analysis of variance) and Kruskal–Wallis (K–W) test. Risk-adjusted excess returns of both portfolios are estimated after controlling for three risk factors:

$$(R_i - R_f) = \alpha + \beta_1(R_m - R_f) + \beta_2 SMB + \beta_3 HML \tag{2.1}$$

where:

   $(R_i - R_f)$ = Excess returns on IPO_i during IPO investors' holding period
   $(R_m - R_f)$ = Market risk premium during IPO investors' holding period
   SMB = Return differential between small market capitalization stocks and large market capitalization stocks (value weighted) during the investors' holding period
   HML = Return differential between high book-to-market ratio stocks and low book-to-market ratio stocks (value weighted) during the investors' holding period
   The value of α represents risk-adjusted excess returns.
   A dummy variable $DGrowth_i$ that takes a value of 1 for growth IPOs and 0 for value IPOs is introduced into the model. The model becomes:

$$(R_i - R_f) = \alpha + \beta_1(R_m - R_f) + \beta_2 SMB + \beta_3 HML + \delta DGrowth \tag{2.2}$$

   A significant δ in equation (2.2) indicates statistically significant difference between the risk-adjusted excess returns of growth IPOs and value IPOs.

Holding period	Return on portfolios based on expected growth rates (%)						Value − growth	t-statistics
	Lowest (value)	2	3	4	Highest (growth)	All		
N-IPOs	77	77	77	77	76	384		
1 year	4.46	4.25	−9.65	6.71	−17.83	−2.37	22.29	2.84[a]
2 years	13.61	−3.71	−18.08	12.84	−7.25	−0.50	20.86	1.82[b]
3 years	20.72	−10.98	−26.64	12.10	−12.04	−3.35	32.76	2.37[a]
4 years	16.38	−30.51	−32.15	−6.13	−20.77	−14.62	37.15	2.37[a]
5 years	12.45	−35.38	−52.78	−33.91	−35.93	−29.09	48.38	3.04[a]

Panel B: Holding period excess returns $(R_i - R_f)$ of five portfolios composed on the basis of expected rate of growth (market value/book value) are estimated. The portfolios contain equal numbers of IPOs on the first day of trading. t-statistics represent the test of difference between the returns of value (lowest) and growth (highest) portfolios. [a] Significant at 5%. [b] Significant at 10%.

2.4.2 Returns to size-based style investments

The balance of evidence from seasoned equity investment suggests that portfolios of smaller firm stocks outperform those of larger firm stocks during some sample periods. The estimates in Table 2.3(A) show that the portfolios of smaller IPOs suffer a loss, while those of larger stocks gain positive excess returns $(R_i - R_f)$ up to 3 years from the date of issue. The results further show that the excess returns of these two portfolios differ significantly from each other for 3 years. However, the differences in holding period excess returns become insignificant if held for more than 3 years, when the larger IPOs also begin to show some losses. The results of the Kruskal–Wallis test, which compares the medians of two portfolios, suggests that the excess returns from small and large market capitalization portfolios become significantly different after a year of flotation, confirming the earlier evidence that larger IPOs earn higher excess returns. To get further insight into the performance of large- and small-cap IPOs, we analyzed five equally weighted portfolios based on their market capitalization. The estimates in Table 2.3(B) provide further support to the finding that holding period excess returns increase with the increase in the size of IPOs for all holding periods.

To account for any difference in the risks of small and large IPO portfolios we estimated equation (2.1). The risk-adjusted excess returns (the α values), show that small IPOs suffer losses while the large IPOs generate positive returns for up to 5-year holding periods. The differences in the performance of these two portfolios of 146% over a 4-year period appear to be economically nontrivial.

The statistical significance of the differences is examined by modifying equation (2.1) to include a dummy variable (DMcap) that captures the size category of IPOs, which gives us equation (2.3). The dummy variable takes the value 1 for large-cap IPOs (higher than median market capitalisation) or 0 for small-cap IPOs. A significant δ in equation (2.3) would indicate a significant difference in risk adjusted excess returns from these two portfolios.

$$(R_i - R_f) = \alpha + \beta_1(R_m - R_f) + \beta_2 SMB + \beta_3 HML + \delta DMcap \qquad (2.3)$$

The estimates (Table 2.3(A), column 'Firm size dummy t-stat') show that the economically substantive differences in the returns of the two portfolios are statistically significantly different as well. Large-cap IPOs gain and small-cap IPOs suffer losses. This finding is consistent with recent evidence, such as Chan et al. (2000), that large-cap style portfolios outperform small-cap stocks. To get further insight into the comparative holding period performance of large-cap and small-cap IPOs, we analyzed five equally weighted portfolios using their market capitalization on flotation. The estimates in Table 2.3(B) show that the holding period excess returns increase as we move from the smallest IPO stocks to the largest IPO stocks for all holding periods. This further confirms the above evidence that large-cap IPOs outperform small-cap IPOs in the long run.

2.4.3 Returns to underwriter quality style investments

Two equally weighted portfolios of IPOs are created on the basis of each measure of underwriter quality discussed in section 2.3.1. The estimates of returns to IPO

Table 2.3 Aftermarket returns to small-cap and large-cap IPO portfolios

Holding period	Excess returns (%)			K–W H-stat	Risk adjusted return (%)		Firm size dummy (t-stat)
	Small	Large	F-stat		Small	Large	
N-IPOs	192	192			192	192	
1 Year	−4.85	0.11	0.95	1.45	−0.502	7.502	1.21
2 Years	−10.55	9.55	6.19[a]	7.20[a]	−36.458	14.415	2.47[a]
3 Years	−15.78	9.09	6.56[a]	9.26[a]	−47.827	30.584	2.81[a]
4 Years	−22.30	−6.90	2.00	3.21[b]	−58.926	87.820	1.65[b]
5 Years	−37.20	−20.90	1.86	2.79[b]	−61.851	41.535	1.59

Panel A: Equally weighted excess returns of large- and small-cap portfolios based on market values of the IPOs at flotation. Buy-and-hold returns from the first day of trading for various holding periods are estimated for each portfolio. Excess returns of IPOs of small-cap firms (up to median) and large-cap firms (higher than median) are compared and the significance of their difference is tested with F-statistics (one-way analysis of variance) and Kruskal–Wallis (K–W) test. Risk-adjusted excess returns for both portfolios are estimated after controlling for three risk factors:

$$(R_i - R_f) = \alpha + \beta_1(R_m - R_f)_i + \beta_2 SMB + \beta_3 HML \tag{2.1}$$

where:

$R_i - R_f$ = Excess returns on IPO_i during investors' holding period
$(R_m - R_f)$ = Market risk premium during IPO investors' holding period
SMB = Return differential between small market capitalization stocks and large market capitalization stocks (value weighted) during the investors' holding period
HML = Return differential between high book-to-market ratio stocks and low book-to-market ratio stocks (value weighted) during investors' holding period
The value of α represents risk-adjusted excess returns.
A dummy variable $DMcap_i$, taking a value of 1 if the market capitalization of the IPO is higher than median and 0 otherwise, is introduced in the model to represent the level of market capitalization on flotation. The model becomes:

$$(R_i - R_f) = \alpha + \beta_1(R_m - R_f) + \beta_2 SMB + \beta_3 HML + \delta DMcap \tag{2.3}$$

A significant δ indicates a statistically significant difference between the risk-adjusted excess returns of large IPOs and small IPOs. [a] Significant at 5%. [b] Significant at 10%.

Holding period	Portfolios based on market capitalization						Smallest – largest	t-statistics
	Smallest	2	3	4	Largest	All		
N-IPOs	77	77	77	77	76	384		
1 year	−5.17	−1.13	−2.20	0.61	−3.99	−2.37	−2.80	−0.16
2 years	−16.38	−11.67	11.75	7.51	6.38	−0.50	−15.88	−1.82[b]
3 years	−21.41	−12.14	2.16	6.13	8.69	−3.35	−18.06	−1.94[b]
4 years	−29.67	−10.22	−28.45	−6.28	1.72	−14.62	−15.05	−1.82[b]
5 years	−42.38	−27.16	−49.98	−22.21	−3.41	−29.09	−13.29	−2.19[a]

Panel B: Holding period excess returns $(R_i - R_f)$ of five portfolios composed on the market capitalization of IPOs on flotation are estimated. t-statistics represent the test of difference between the returns of smallest and largest market capitalization portfolios.

portfolios marketed by high- and low-quality sponsors for various holding periods are presented in Table 2.4. For excess returns $(R_i - R_f)$, the two portfolios show no significant difference in their aftermarket performance for a year after the IPO. However, the returns to the IPO portfolio marketed by high-quality underwriters (using both measures of underwriter quality) significantly exceed that of other underwriters for 2- to 5-year holding periods. This is confirmed by Kruskal–Wallis test of differences in median returns as well. The differences also appear to be economically substantial, with 5-year holding period returns of 18.5% for high-quality underwriters (CRI ranking) compared with −37.5% for low-quality underwriters. A similar pattern is confirmed by the activity ranking of underwriters, as well as the results based on cumulative returns. The risk-adjusted results also show that IPOs marketed by high-quality sponsors generate positive excess returns, while other IPOs suffer a loss. Using the activity ranking, the excess returns of the portfolio of IPOs marketed by high-quality underwriters reaches 140%, while other IPOs suffer a loss of −47% 5 years after the flotation.

To examine the statistical significance of the differences in risk-adjusted returns from the two portfolios, we modify equation (2.1) to include a dummy variable (DSpon) to represent the quality of underwriter. In the modified equation (2.4), the dummy variable takes the value 1 for high-quality underwriters and 0 otherwise.

$$(R_i - R_f) = \alpha + \beta_1(R_m - R_f) + \beta_2\text{SMB} + \beta_3\text{HML} + \delta\text{DSpon} \tag{2.4}$$

The significance of the coefficients of the dummy variable (δ), in Table 2.4, shows that the quality of underwriters affects the performance of IPO securities held for 2–5 years. This is consistent with the evidence in Carter et al. (1998). Thus, the evidence discussed above provides support to the view that IPOs taken public by high-quality underwriters outperform those sponsored by low-quality underwriters in the long term.

2.4.4 Bivariate analysis

In this section, we investigate how the IPO styles analyzed individually in the preceding paragraphs perform when taken in combination. First, we estimate long-term excess returns $(R_i - R_f)$ when sponsor quality is combined with the other styles, one at a time. We also analyze combinations of size, growth, and value portfolios. The results presented in Table 2.5(A) show that value IPOs marketed by high-quality sponsors generate 35.91% excess returns and outperform all other groups of IPOs in 5 years. Growth IPOs marketed by low-quality underwriters suffer the highest loss (−39.83%) in 5 years. Chi-square tests confirm the significance of the differences in performance. Tests for other holding periods (1, 2, 3, and 4 years) show similar results and are not reported. This finding confirms the theoretical results that high-quality underwriters are better able to assess the future prospects of IPOs. This evidence, and the earlier evidence from the univariate style analysis, reinforce the view that value IPOs marketed by high-quality underwriters outperform other growth and underwriter quality combinations.

Table 2.5(B) reveals that small-cap IPOs marketed by high-quality sponsors outperform all other categories of IPOs. They earn a staggering 104.47% excess returns, while large-cap IPOs marketed by low-quality underwriters suffer a loss (−31.63%)

Table 2.4 Quality of sponsors and aftermarket returns

Holding period	Excess return (%)				Risk adjusted return (%)		Quality dummy (*t*-stat)
	Low quality	High quality	F-stat	K–W H-stat	Low quality	High quality	
N-IPOs	327	57			327	57	
1 Year	−3.72	5.36	1.61	0.65	3.331	4.253	0.85
2 Years	−4.45	22.18	5.49[a]	5.09[a]	−16.275[b]	12.947	2.62[a]
3 Years	−9.52	32.07	9.35[a]	8.94[a]	−13.611	27.160	3.32[a]
4 Years	−22.30	29.60	11.74[a]	9.10[a]	−10.931	49.148	3.68[a]
5 Years	−37.40	18.50	11.37[a]	7.83[a]	−47.306	140.455[a]	3.25[a]

Panel A: CRI ranking. Equally weighted portfolios are composed on the basis of the quality of underwriters (sponsors). Two measures of underwriter quality are used. The first is based on an annual survey of finance directors' views on the quality of corporate finance services provided by investment banks, which we denote as CRI ranking. These data were obtained from Consensus Research International. The top four investment banks are categorized as high-quality underwriters. The second ranking is based on the number of IPOs taken public by a sponsor in our sample, denoted as activity ranking. Sponsors marketing 50 or more IPOs during 1984 to 1998 are categorized as high-quality underwriters. Buy-and-hold returns of IPOs from the first day of trading for various holding periods are estimated for each portfolio. Excess returns of IPOs marketed by high-quality underwriters and other underwriters are compared and the significance of their difference is tested with F-statistics (one-way analysis of variance) and Kruskal–Wallis (KW) test. Risk-adjusted excess returns for both groups of IPOs are estimated after controlling for three risk factors:

$$(R_i - R_f) = \alpha + \beta_1(R_m - R_f)_i + \beta_2 SMB + \beta_3 HML \qquad (2.1)$$

where:

$R_i - R_f$ = Excess returns on IPO$_i$ during investors' holding period
$(R_m - R_f)$ = Market risk premium during IPO investors' holding period
SMB = Return differential between small market capitalization stocks and large market capitalization stocks (value weighted) during the investors' holding period
HML = Return differential between high book-to-market ratio stocks and low book-to-market ratio stocks (value weighted) during investors' holding period
The value of α represents risk-adjusted excess returns.
A dummy variable DSpon$_i$, taking a value of 1 if the sponsor quality is high and 0 otherwise, is introduced into the model to represent the quality of underwriters. The model takes the following form:

$$(R_i - R_f) = \alpha + \beta_1(R_m - R_f) + \beta_2 SMB + \beta_3 HML + \delta DSpon \qquad (2.4)$$

A significant δ indicates a statistically significant difference between the risk-adjusted excess returns from holding IPOs marketed by high-quality underwriters and those sold by other underwriters.
[a] Significant at 5%. [b] Significant at 10%.

Holding period	Excess return (%)				Risk adjusted return (%)		Quality dummy (*t*-stat)
	Low quality	High quality	F-stat	K–W H-stat	Low quality	High quality	
	328	56			328	56	
1 Year	−3.49	4.18	1.13	0.26	3.905	5.305	0.84
2 Years	−3.77	18.63	3.81[a]	4.22[a]	−14.804[b]	11.533	2.17[a]
3 Years	−9.22	31.08	8.64[a]	8.24[a]	−14.197	10.147	3.12[a]
4 Years	−21.90	27.90	10.60[a]	8.19[a]	−10.319	−3.032	3.46[a]
5 Years	−37.00	17.10	10.48[a]	7.10[a]	−44.714	71.654	3.13[a]

Panel B: Activity ranking.
[a] Significant at 5%. [b] Significant at 10%.

Table 2.5 Bivariate analysis of IPO style investments

Quality of sponsor	Growth Opportunities		All
	Low (value)	High (growth)	
Low	−33.85	−39.83	−36.99
High	35.91	−16.68	17.13
All	−20.77	−37.42	−29.09

Chi-Square = 5.352, p-value=0.021

Panel A: Quality of sponsor and value versus growth IPOs. IPOs are partitioned by the quality of underwriters and into value and growth portfolios within each under-writer category. Estimates in the tables are 5-year holding period excess returns (%). Underwriters are categorized by their quality (activity ranking). Values versus growth IPOs are identified by book-to-market ratios. A Chi-square test of the significance of the differences in the buy-and-hold excess returns $(R_i - R_f)$ for various style combinations is carried out.

Quality of sponsor	Market capitalization		All
	Small	Large	
Low	−41.03	−31.63	−36.99
High	104.47	8.57	17.13
All	−37.24	−20.95	−29.09

Chi-Square = 44.237, p-value=0.000

Panel B: Quality of sponsor and market capitalization of IPOs

Growth opportunities	Market capitalization		All
	Small	Large	
Low (value)	−34.60	−6.93	−20.77
High (growth)	−39.87	−34.97	−37.42
All	−37.24	−20.95	−29.09

Chi-Square = 0.000, p-value=1.000

Panel C: Growth opportunities and market capitalization

in 5 years. Again, this reconfirms the long-term superiority of IPOs marketed by high-quality underwriters. This finding is supported by similar tests for all holding periods from 1 to 4 years. Table 2.5(C) shows that there are no gains in designing investment strategies combining value, growth, and market capitalization simultaneously in IPO aftermarkets. IPOs of all categories based on growth and market capitalization suffer losses in 5 years. We repeated these tests for other holding periods (1, 2, 3, and 4 years) and the results remain the same. Overall, the results suggest that value IPOs marketed by quality sponsors, especially when combined with small-cap issues, offer good long-term investment opportunities.

2.4.5 Test of robustness of results

To assess the overall significance of all style categories, we model holding period returns as a function of three risk factors and three dummy variables representing the styles of IPOs identified in the univariate analysis as summarized in equation (2.5):

$$R_i - R_f = \alpha + \beta_1(R_m - R_f)_i + \beta_2 SMB + \beta_3 HML + \beta_4 DSpon_i + \beta_5 DMcap_i + \beta_6 DGrowth_i \quad (2.5)$$

All the variables are as defined before. Equation (2.5) is estimated using the OLS method and standard errors are corrected for heteroscedasticity using White's procedure. The estimates (Table 2.6) confirm the findings of the univariate and bivariate analyses and reveal further interesting features. They show that the quality of underwriter is the major factor that helps to distinguish between the aftermarket performance of IPOs over various holding periods. Its effect, however, does not appear to be significant for the first 2 years after flotation, but becomes significant from year 3 onwards and remains significant for at least up to 5 years after flotation. Size-style

Table 2.6 Factors affecting IPO style investments

	One year	Two years	Three years	Four years	Five years
Constant	2.169	−21.117[a]	−20.844	−13.896	−24.116
MKT	1.592[a]	1.390[a]	1.274[a]	0.456	0.640[b]
SMB	0.940[a]	0.348	0.503	0.485	0.760[a]
HML	−1.298[a]	−0.201	−0.883	−0.617	0.038
DSpon	2.199	16.549	26.943[a]	45.110[a]	44.148[a]
DMcap	5.078	15.996[b]	20.082[a]	6.639	7.540
DGrowth	−3.288	−1.081	−4.202	4.148	−9.870
R² (%)	16	3	4	2	4
N-Observations	384	384	384	384	384

Buy-and-hold returns (%) of IPOs bought on the first day of trading and held for a range of holding periods are estimated after controlling for the known risk factors and IPO attributes. The model is:

$$R_i - R_f = \alpha + \beta_1 (R_m - R_f) + \beta_2 SMB + \beta_3 HML + \beta_4 DSpon_i + \beta_5 DMcap_i + \beta_6 DGrowth_i \quad (2.5)$$

The value of α represents risk-adjusted return.
Where:
  $(R_i - R_f)$ = Excess returns on IPO_i during investors' holding period
  $(R_m - R_f)$ = Market risk premium during IPO investors' holding period
  SMB = Return differential between small market capitalization stocks and large market capitalization stocks (value weighted) during the investors' holding period
  HML = Return differential between high book-to-market ratio stocks and low book-to-market ratio stocks (value weighted) during the investors' holding period
  DSpon = Dummy for sponsor quality. It takes a value of 1 if the sponsor quality (activity ranking) is high, 0 otherwise.
  DMcap = Dummy for market capitalization of the IPO firm. It takes a value of 1 if the market capitalization is higher than median, 0 otherwise.
  DGrowth = Dummy for growth opportunities. It takes a value of 1 for growth IPOs and 0 for value IPOs.
  The equation is estimated using OLS and standard errors are corrected for heteroscedasticity using White's adjustment
  The value of α represents risk-adjusted returns.
  [a]Significant at 5%. [b]Significant at 10%.

portfolios also perform well for up to 3 years in the aftermarket. On the other hand, value and growth styles do not offer significant returns in the aftermarket, as shown in the univariate analysis once we control for the effects of size and sponsor quality.

2.5 Conclusion

We extend the style investing literature by using style analysis to examine the after-market performance of IPOs. Specifically, we analyze value, growth, small-cap, and large-cap style IPO portfolios, as well as combinations of these style categories. Additionally, we identify underwriter quality as a style selection criterion in the IPO market. Several interesting conclusions emerge. Unlike the seasoned equity-style litera-ture, value and growth IPOs do not exhibit significant differences in their returns after controlling for risk. In particular, neither of these two investment styles consistently generates positive returns after the first year. Second, larger IPOs provide positive returns in the aftermarket whilst smaller IPOs suffer losses. We find the differences in the performance of size-based portfolios to be economically substantive and statistically significant. Third, IPOs marketed by high-quality underwriters outperform other IPOs by a substantial margin in 2- to 5-year holding periods. The bivariate tests confirm the joint significance of some of the above styles in identifying IPOs that are likely to have better aftermarket investment returns. In general, the results indicate that value and large-cap IPOs marketed by prestigious underwriters provide significantly positive aftermarket investment returns. Within the bivariate style framework, value and small-cap IPOs marketed by prestigious underwriters provide significantly higher and posi-tive aftermarket returns.

References

Babson, D. L. (1951). The Case of Growth vs. Income Stocks on a Yield Basis. *Weekly Staff Letter*, David L. Babson and Company Inc., 17 September.

Banz, R. W. (1981). The Relationship Between Return and Market Value of Common Stocks. *Journal of Financial Economics*, 9(1):3–18.

Barber, B. M. and Lyon, J. D. (1997). Firm Size, Book-to-Market Ratio and Security Returns: A Holdout Sample of Financial Firms. *Journal of Finance*, 52(2):875–901.

Beatty, R. and Ritter, J. (1986). Investment Banking, Reputation, and the Underpricing of Initial Public Offerings. *Journal of Financial Economics*, 15(1):213–232.

Berk, J. B., Green, R.C., and Nail, V. (1999) Optimal Investment, Growth Options and Security Returns. *Journal of Finance*, 54(5):1553–1607.

Brav, A. and Gompers, P. (1997). Myth or Reality? The Long-Run Underperformance of Initial Public Offerings: Evidence from Venture and Non-venture Capital-Backed Companies. *Journal of Finance*, 52(5):1791–1821.

Brown, S. J. and Goetzmann, W.N. (1997). Mutual Fund Styles. *Journal of Financial Economics*, 43(3):373–399.

Brown, S. J. and Warner, J. (1985). Using Daily Stock Returns: The Case of Event Studies. *Journal of Financial Economics*, 14(1):3–31.

Carter, R. B., Dark, F. H., and Singh, A. K. (1998). Underwriter Reputation, Initial Returns and the Long-Run Performance of IPO Stocks. *Journal of Finance*, 53(1):285–312.

Chan, L. K., Hamao, Y., and Lakonishok, J. (1991). Fundamentals and Stock Returns in Japan. *Journal of Finance*, 46(5):1739–1789.

Chan, L., Karceski, H. J., and Lakonishok, J. (2000). New Paradigm or Same Old Hype in Equity Investing? *Financial Analysts Journal*, 56(4):23–36.

Chemmanur, T. J. and Fulghieri, P. (1994). Investment Bank Reputation, Information Production and Financial Intermediation. *Journal of Finance*, 49(1):57–79.

Chen, H.-L., Jegadeesh, N., and Wermers, R. (2000). The Value of Active Mutual Fund Management: An Examination of the Stockholdings and Trades of Fund Managers. *Journal of Financial and Quantitative Analysis*, 35(3):343–368.

Dunbar, C. G. (2000). Factors Affecting Investment Bank Initial Public Offering Market Share. *Journal of Financial Economics*, 55(1):3–41.

Fama, E. F. and French, K. R. (1996). Multifactor Explanation of Asset Pricing Anomalies. *Journal of Finance*, 51(1):55–84.

Graham, B. and Dodd, D. L. (1934). *Security Analysis*. McGraw-Hill, New York.

Jain, B. and Kini, O. (1999). On Investment Banker Monitoring in the New Issues Market. *Journal of Banking and Finance*, 23(1):49–84.

Krigman, L., Shaw, W. H., and Womack, K. L. (2001). Why Do Firms Switch Underwriters? *Journal of Financial Economics*, 60(2–3):245–284.

Kumar, A. (2002). Style Switching and Stock Returns. Working Paper, University of Cornell, Cornell, NY.

Levis, M. (1985). Are Small Firms Big Performers? *Investment Analyst*, 76, April:21–27.

Levis, M. (1993). The Long-Run Performance of Initial Public Offerings: The UK Experience. *Financial Management*, 22(1):28–41.

Lucas, A., van Dijk, R., and Kloek, T. (2002). Stock Selection, Style Rotation and Risk. *Journal of Empirical Finance*, 9(1):1–34.

Menyah, K. and Paudyal, K. (2003). IPO Decisions and the Costs of Going Public. Research Papers in Accounting, Banking and Financial Systems, London Metropolitan University, London, UK.

Michaely, R. and Shaw, W. H. (1994). The Pricing of Initial Public Offerings: Tests of Adverse Selection and Signalling Theories. *Review of Financial Economics*, 7(2):279–320.

Rosenberg, B., Reid, K., and Lanstein, R. (1985). Persuasive Evidence of Market Inefficiency. *Journal of Portfolio Management*, 11(3):9–17.

Strong, N. and Xu, X. G. (1997). Explaining the Cross-Section of UK Expected Stock Returns. *British Accounting Review*, 29(1):1–23.

Titman, S. and Trueman, B. (1986). Information Quality and the Valuation of New Issues. *Journal of Accounting and Economics*, 8(2):159–172.

Wermers, R. (2000). Mutual Fund Performance: An Empirical Decomposition into Stock-Splitting Talent, Style, Transaction Costs and Expenses. *Journal of Finance*, 55(4):1655–1703.

3 The effect of IPO characteristics on long-run performance of Taiwan's IPOs: evidence from efficiently learning markets

Anlin Chen, Sue L. Chiou, and Chinshun Wu

Abstract

Two market efficiency hypotheses are employed in this study to investigate the long-run performance puzzle of initial public offerings (IPOs) in Taiwan: the efficient markets hypothesis (EMH) and the hypothesis of an efficiently learning market (ELM). We simulate the latent true prices behind the price limits and measure the IPO expected returns using a Fama–French three-factor model under ELM. Our results show that IPO investors in Taiwan learn rationally from market information and that the IPO long-run performance puzzle is dissipated under an efficiently learning market. Furthermore, we also show that the long-run performance of Taiwan's IPOs is significantly driven by IPO underpricing and the waiting time to issue subsequent offerings. IPO method, hot-issue period, or industry do not impact on IPO long-run performance under the ELM.

3.1 Introduction

The new issue puzzle is well documented in the USA. Aggarwal and Rivoli (1990), Ritter (1991), Loughran and Ritter (1995), and Ritter and Welch (2002) showed that initial public offerings (IPOs) substantially underperform the market index. Loughran and Ritter (1995) pointed out that an investor has to spend 44% more money in the issuers than in non-issuers of the same size to have the same wealth 5 years after the offering date. Compared with the new issue problem in the USA, international evidence is less conclusive. IPOs in emerging markets such as Malaysia and Thailand have been shown to outperform rather than underperform the market in the long run (Corhay et al., 2002; Allen et al., 1999). IPOs in Finland, Germany, and South Africa have experienced poor long-run performance, as in the USA (Lee et al., 1996; Keloharju, 1993; Ljungqvist, 1997; Page and Reyneke, 1997). The above findings related to IPO long-run performance were attained based on the efficient markets hypothesis (EMH). The long-run underperformance or overperformance of IPOs is considered as a puzzle.

Note that two possible sources would bias the previous empirical results under the EMH. The first source is the asset-pricing models, which measure the appropriate expected returns. For example, Banz (1981), Rosenberg et al. (1985), Fama and French (1992), and Brav et al. (2000) demonstrated that in addition to beta risk, size and book-to-market ratio are also influential on stock returns.

The second source of bias is the strong assumption of the EMH. Fama (1976) defined the notion of market efficiency by differentiating the beliefs of returns perceived by the market on the basis of all available relevant information from the true frequencies of returns conditional on all information. Under the EMH, the market beliefs are assumed to be correct, in the sense that they coincide with the true frequencies and can be estimated from empirical frequencies. The content of beliefs can be factored into two components: a prior belief and a likelihood of all potential information. The EMH therefore requires that both are unbiased. For IPO markets, information is relatively weak and it is difficult to have unbiased prior belief.

Bossaerts (1995) and Lewellen and Shanken (2002) argued that, when investors have imperfect information about a future payoff, they must learn about the unknown parameters using whatever information is available. Thus, security prices reflect investors' beliefs about future payoffs. If the investors' beliefs are rational, the security prices should reflect all available information and hence be unpredictable. In other words, a rational market implies that the market uses Bayesian analysis to update its beliefs on the basis of the correct likelihood of information, and that a biased prior belief is allowed. By taking away unbiased priors implied in the EMH, and retaining the assumption of rationally learning through Bayesian law, Bossaerts (1995) and Bondarenko and Bossaerts (2000) derived a weak form of market efficiency and referred to it as an efficiently learning market (ELM). An ELM seems plausible for IPO markets.

Even though IPO long-run anomalies are well documented in the USA, Bossaerts and Hillion (2001) showed that under an ELM, these anomalies are no longer observed. Bossaerts and Hillion (2001) argued that once the investors efficiently learn from the market, the IPO long-run underperformance in the USA no longer holds.

US stock markets are typically considered as the most frictionless and most efficient in the world. However, there is a price limit in the Taiwan equity market. Stocks traded in Taiwan are confined within price limits. The range of such limits is calculated based on the preceding trading day's closing price. Most of the time the range is within 7% above and 7% below the preceding closing price. Nevertheless, when the market is subject to dramatic fluctuations caused by certain events, the Taiwan SEC may announce an alternative range to substitute for the 7% limits. For example, from 3 to 11 October 2000, the lower bound of price limit was temporarily revised to −3.5% of the previous closing price, with the upper bound remaining at 7% of the previous closing price. Table 3.1 summarizes the price limits in Taiwan stock markets during 1989 to 2001.

Price limits prohibit a stock on a certain day from being traded at a price outside the price limits based on its preceding closing price. The highest transaction price on a certain day equals [(1 + upper bound) × preceding closing price], while the lowest price equals [(1 + lower bound) × preceding closing price].

The regulation of price limits would increase market friction and deteriorate the investors' learning process. Under the regulation of price limits, shock will not be fully realized in a day when the closing price hits the price limit. The remaining information would spill over to the following day's price movement. Even though the price limits prohibit the stock prices to reflect their fair prices, Chen et al. (2004) show that ELM still holds even under price limits. Investors who realize the existence of price limits would manage to learn the hidden information behind the price limits to make decisions on further investments. Therefore, investors' learning behaviors under

Table 3.1 Price limits for Taiwan stock exchanges from 1989 to 2001

Period	Upper bound (%)	Lower bound (%)
11 October 1989 to 2 October 2000	7.0	−7.0
3 October 2000 to 11 October 2000	7.0	−3.5
12 October 2000 to 19 October 2000	7.0	−7.0
20 October 2000 to 7 November 2000	7.0	−3.5
8 November 2000 to 20 November 2000	7.0	−7.0
21 November 2000 to 31 December 2000	7.0	−3.5
31 December 2000 to 31 December 2001	7.0	−7.0

price limits are worth examining to figure out the asset pricing puzzles, especially for markets without abundant information such as emerging IPO markets.

This chapter explores the IPO long-run performance puzzle in Taiwan. In particular, we combine ELM, asset pricing models, and the remedy of price limits to investigate the IPO long-run performance puzzle. Both the EMH and ELM are employed to examine the long-run performance of IPOs in Taiwan. In this chapter, the expected return of an IPO is measured by the market-adjusted model and the Fama–French three-factor model. To alleviate the problem of a limitation on price variation when the closing price hits a limit, we employ a Tobit model (Tobin, 1958) to simulate the latent 'true' equilibrium return and thereby the latent true equilibrium price. We further divide the whole sample into subsamples to investigate IPO performance in more detail, considering IPO characteristics such as IPO method, underpricing, length of waiting time to issue subsequent offerings, hot-issue period, and industry. We find that ignoring investors' efficient learning process or the regulation of price limits leads to an under-reaction to market information and that positive IPO long-run performance is found. However, neglecting both investors' efficiently learning and the regulation of price limits leads to no abnormal returns of IPOs. Once we take investors' efficiently learning and the regulation of price limits into account when measuring IPO performance, we find that Taiwan's IPOs experience no abnormal returns, and no one can make a profit from IPOs, which is consistent with market efficiency.

The remaining chapter is organized as follows. The next section (3.2) describes the data sources. This is followed by an examination of the IPO performance under the efficient markets hypothesis in section 3.3. The IPO performance measured by an efficiently learning market is presented in section 3.4. Section 3.5 reports the effect of issue characteristics on IPO long-run performance, with section 3.6 summarizing the conclusions drawn.

3.2 Data

The IPO sample in this paper consists of 362 common stocks issued between 1991 and 1998 in Taiwan's stock markets. The long-run aftermarket performance is measured on a 3-year basis to be consistent with Ritter (1991). To satisfy the ELM condition, the end of the sixth trading month after the 3-year period is set as the reference point. Thus, the stock returns in this paper cover the period from January 1991 to

July 2002. IPOs issued during January 1991 to December 1998 are included in the sample. However, we use IPO aftermarket returns three and a half years after issuance to measure IPO long-run performance. To avoid possible noise in the right aftermarket, we measure the IPOs' aftermarket performance from the second trading month, where one trading month is defined as 25 trading days.

Following Bossaerts and Hillion (2001), our IPO sample is classified into a sub-sample of winners and a subsample of losers on the basis of a firm's status on the reference point to measure IPO performance under an ELM. Winners are those who survive for at least 43 trading months in the market after their offering. IPOs delisted from the exchange within 43 trading months after issuance are classified as losers and the recovery rate is assumed to be zero. The daily stock returns, market value of equity, book value of equity, and the market index (Taiwan Stock Exchange Corporation Capitalization Weighted Price Index, TAIEX) returns are collected from the *Taiwan Economic Journal* database.

3.3 Measuring IPO performance under the efficient markets hypothesis

3.3.1 Using market return as benchmark and neglecting hidden information behind price limits

In this chapter, the IPO long-run performance is measured on a 3-year basis after issuance. We follow Ritter (1991) to measure monthly returns on the basis of daily returns. One month is defined as 25 trading days in this paper, since there are six trading days a week during our empirical period. We first employ the market index return as each IPO's benchmark return. We denote $r_{m,d}$ as the return of the market portfolio at date d and $r_{i,d}$ as the return of IPO i at date d. Month 0 means the month when an IPO is issued. Accordingly, month t means the 25-day window period $t \times 25$ days after issuance. The monthly return of IPO i at month t is:

$$r_{i,t} = \left(\prod_{d=k+1}^{k+25} (1 + r_{i,d}) \right) - 1,$$ (3.1)

where $k = t \times 25$. The monthly return of market portfolio at month t is:

$$r_{m,t} = \left(\prod_{d=k+1}^{k+25} (1 + r_{m,d}) \right) - 1.$$ (3.2)

The market-adjusted monthly abnormal return is used to measure the abnormal return of IPO i at month t, which is defined as:

$$ar_{i,t} = r_{i,t} - r_{m,t}.$$ (3.3)

Given IPO abnormal return at month t, the value-weighted arithmetic average of the abnormal returns for the IPO portfolio with n IPOs is:

$$AR_t = \sum_{i=1}^{n} w_{i,t} \times ar_{i,t},$$ (3.4)

where $w_{i,t}$ is the market value of IPO i at month t divided by the total market value of all the IPOs at month t.

With the weighted average abnormal return of IPOs at month t, the cumulative abnormal return (CAR) of the IPO portfolio from month q to month s is then defined as:

$$CAR_{q,s} = \sum_{t=q}^{s} AR_{t}. \tag{3.5}$$

Equation (3.5) is typically used to investigate whether the IPO sample experiences abnormal performance under the EMH. Table 3.2 plots the 3-year cumulative abnormal returns of IPO portfolio from months 1 to 36. Table 3.2 provides overwhelming support that our IPO realized returns are not significantly different from zero during the 3-year performance evaluation period. This finding implies that the EMH holds and IPO investors in Taiwan cannot make abnormal profits.

Market-adjusted returns are used to measure abnormal IPO returns. Neglecting price limits, we use the closing prices to measure market-adjusted returns. Cumulative abnormal return (CAR) from month q to month s is the IPO performance over the period from defined month q to month s.

Table 3.2 provides convincing evidence that the Taiwan IPO market is efficient. However, since there are price limits in Taiwan's stock markets, this price constraint prevents prices from completely reflecting new information. Chu (1997) and Shiah Hou (1993) have shown that the aftermarket transaction prices of IPOs in Taiwan hit the upper bound of price limits very frequently. IPOs in Taiwan could consecutively hit the upper bound of price limits for more than 30 days. Thus, the investors can

Table 3.2 IPO performance using market return as benchmark and neglecting price limits under EMH

(q,s)	$CAR_{q,s}$	t-value	(q,s)	$CAR_{q,s}$	t-value
(1,1)	0.004	0.300	(1,19)	0.027	0.824
(1,2)	0.003	0.341	(1,20)	0.021	0.610
(1,3)	0.005	0.408	(1,21)	0.014	0.396
(1,4)	0.016	1.232	(1,22)	0.033	0.949
(1,5)	0.031	1.912	(1,23)	0.032	0.897
(1,6)	0.032	1.831	(1,24)	0.044	1.183
(1,7)	0.027	1.421	(1,25)	0.025	0.653
(1,8)	0.023	1.124	(1,26)	0.022	0.569
(1,9)	0.030	1.330	(1,27)	0.016	0.428
(1,10)	0.030	1.250	(1,28)	0.011	0.280
(1,11)	0.026	1.035	(1,29)	0.002	0.043
(1,12)	0.022	0.816	(1,30)	0.012	0.313
(1,13)	0.033	1.179	(1,31)	0.015	0.391
(1,14)	0.031	1.027	(1,32)	0.017	0.420
(1,15)	0.034	1.089	(1,33)	0.037	0.917
(1,16)	0.031	0.976	(1,34)	0.032	0.766
(1,17)	0.025	0.775	(1,35)	0.013	0.312
(1,18)	0.027	0.824	(1,36)	0.008	0.184

earn more than we measured from the realized transaction data. We therefore doubt whether the CAR pattern in Table 3.2 is disguised by the price limits.

3.3.2   Using market return as benchmark and simulating the latent 'true' prices behind price limits

To investigate whether the findings of Table 3.2 are driven by price limits, we further use the Tobit model to simulate the hidden information behind the price limits of the realized transaction prices. To relax the constraint of price limits, we treat limited moving returns as the censored variable and employ the Tobit model to estimate the latent true equilibrium returns and prices not only for issuing firms, but also for all non-issuing firms. Lee and Chung (1996) showed that today's opening price is a good proxy for the preceding day's unobserved closing price when subject to price limits. We therefore use the overnight return between these two days as one regressor to capture the remaining information behind the price limits.

The overnight return from the realized stock price for stock i at date d, $or_{i,d}$, is explicitly defined as:

$$or_{i,d} = \frac{p_{i,o,d+1} - p_{i,c,d}}{p_{i,c,d}}, \tag{3.6}$$

where $p_{i,c,d}$ is the closing price of stock i at date d and $p_{i,o,d+1}$ is the opening price of stock i at date $d + 1$.

In addition to the overnight return, the stock's mean return during the 3-year performance evaluation period, denoted as $\bar{r}_i$, is used as another regressor to capture the return level of each stock. Denoting $r_{i,d}^*$ as the latent true return for stock i at date d when the closing price hits the price limit, our Tobit model in this study is specified as follows:

$$r_{i,d}^* = \phi_i + \phi_{i,1}\bar{r}_i + \phi_{i,2}or_{i,d} + \varepsilon_{i,d}. \tag{3.7}$$

After simulating the latent true returns behind the price limits, we can calculate the plausible holding returns ($r_{i,t}^*$) at month t for stock i as follows:

$$r_{i,t}^* = \left(\prod_{d=k+1}^{k+25} (1+r_{i,d}^*) \right) - 1. \tag{3.8}$$

$r_{m,t}^*$ is the latent benchmark return, which is simply the value-weighted market return measured by all the latent returns simulated from equation (3.7) of all listed firms. The abnormal return with market return as the benchmark of IPO i at month t is calculated as:

$$ar_{i,t}^* = r_{i,t}^* - r_{m,t}^*. \tag{3.9}$$

Similar to equation (3.5), we can calculate the latent CAR over the window (q,s) for the IPOs by simulating the hidden true returns behind the price limits as:

$$CAR_{q,s}^* = \sum_{t=q}^{s} \sum_{i=1}^{n} w_{i,t} \times ar_{i,t}^*. \tag{3.10}$$

Table 3.3 IPO performance using market return as benchmark and simulating latent 'true' behind price limits under EMH

(q,s)	$CAR_{q,s}$	t-value	(q,s)	$CAR_{q,s}$	t-value
(1,1)	0.008	1.100	(1,19)	0.229	5.578*
(1,2)	0.012	1.334	(1,20)	0.239	5.618*
(1,3)	0.024	2.099	(1,21)	0.240	5.502*
(1,4)	0.050	3.080*	(1,22)	0.270	6.026*
(1,5)	0.075	3.812*	(1,23)	0.286	6.150*
(1,6)	0.088	4.111*	(1,24)	0.307	6.304*
(1,7)	0.085	3.737*	(1,25)	0.299	6.066*
(1,8)	0.092	3.722*	(1,26)	0.305	6.150*
(1,9)	0.108	4.090*	(1,27)	0.305	6.068*
(1,10)	0.111	3.958*	(1,28)	0.305	6.115*
(1,11)	0.121	4.046*	(1,29)	0.300	5.934*
(1,12)	0.126	3.934*	(1,30)	0.319	6.183*
(1,13)	0.155	4.561*	(1,31)	0.317	6.117*
(1,14)	0.166	4.669*	(1,32)	0.310	5.873*
(1,15)	0.183	4.913*	(1,33)	0.323	5.884*
(1,16)	0.193	5.081*	(1,34)	0.323	5.667*
(1,17)	0.200	5.202*	(1,35)	0.307	5.274*
(1,18)	0.216	5.294*	(1,36)	0.321	5.345*

Market-adjusted returns are used to measure IPO abnormal returns. We apply a Tobit model to simulate the 'true' market-adjusted returns behind price limits. Cumulative abnormal return (CAR) from month q to month s is the IPO performance over the period from month q to month s. * Significance level of 1%.

Table 3.3 presents the cumulative abnormal returns of IPOs by simulating the hidden true returns behind the price limits. It shows that Taiwan's IPOs experience significant positive abnormal returns within 3 years after issuance, starting from the fifth month after issuance.

Consistent with the previous findings in other emerging markets, we find that Taiwan's IPOs outperform the market when we simulate the hidden information behind the price limits. It is also known that Taiwan's IPOs experience significantly positive returns over a long period while in the aftermarket (Loughran et al., 1994). Since IPO aftermarket prices frequently hit the upper bound of price limits, the returns calculated from the realized transaction prices are underestimated. Hence, IPO returns simulated from the Tobit model are more realistic and plausible.

3.4   IPO performance under efficiently learning markets

By simulating the latent true prices behind the price limits we show that under the EMH, IPOs in Taiwan generally outperform the markets. This finding is consistent with those in emerging markets (such as Malaysia and Thailand). Nevertheless, if the market is efficient and Taiwan's IPOs outperform the markets, we are curious why investors would not learn from market prices and enter the IPO early aftermarket to make profits. There are two possible explanations for this anomaly: one is that the investor's learning process is not appropriately measured, the other that the risk level of an IPO is underestimated.

Bossaerts (2004) argues that the rationality implied in the EMH is too strict for the IPO market due to the relatively rough information of IPO firms in the aftermarket. Being relaxed but more realistic, the ELM permits investors to have wrong prior beliefs about the probability of default of an IPO stock at its offering date, but requires investors to modify these beliefs rationally. In this section, we employ the ELM to examine the long-run performance puzzle of IPOs in Taiwan.

3.4.1 Using market return as benchmark without taking the hidden information behind price limits into account

The ELM argues that investors rationally learn from the market. To evaluate the investors' learning process with market return as the benchmark, we follow Bossaerts and Hillion (2001) and define the price deflator as:

$$\kappa_{i,t} = \prod_{\tau=1}^{t}(1+r_{m,\tau}). \tag{3.11}$$

The scaled price of stock i at month t is defined as:

$$\bar{p}_{i,t} = \frac{p_{i,t}}{\kappa_{i,t}}, \tag{3.12}$$

where $p_{i,t}$ is the stock price at t. Since $\kappa_{i,t}$ is constructed from the benchmark return, the scaled price is regarded as being in a risk-neutral market and without having time value of money.

The ELM shows that a modified rate of return for stock i at $t + 1$ is:

$$\bar{r}_{i,t+1} = \frac{\bar{p}_{i,t+1} - \bar{p}_{i,t}}{\bar{p}_{i,t+1}}. \tag{3.13}$$

This modified return differs from the traditional return in that the modified rate of return uses the future (scaled) price as the basis, whereas the traditional return uses the previous price as the basis. The average modified return (denoted as AMR) of n winner IPOs for T months is:

$$AMR = \frac{1}{n}\sum_{t=1}^{n}\left(\frac{1}{T}\sum_{t=0}^{T-1}\bar{r}_{i,t+1}\right). \tag{3.14}$$

Bossaerts and Hillion (2001) argued that under the assumption of correct conditional expectations, the modified rate of return will be non-positive conditional on winners. The intuition for non-positive average modified returns for winners is as follows. For the average traditional returns calculated based on winners, a positive bias is expected if the market correctly foresees that the issuers are winners. To mitigate the positive bias, positive returns should be adjusted by a factor smaller than 1, while negative returns should be adjusted by a factor larger than 1. Since the market reacts rationally to the news that the issuers will turn out to be winners, the modified returns for winners should be non-positive.

Bossaerts (2004) and Bossaerts and Hillion (2001) further show that by using a wealth ratio on a future date, say T', as the weight, the weighted average modified return will be close to zero. The wealth ratio is defined as:

$$\overline{w}_{i,T'} = \frac{\overline{p}_{i,T'}}{\overline{p}_{i,0}} \qquad (3.15)$$

and the weighted average modified return is computed as:

$$WAMR = \frac{1}{n}\sum_{i=1}^{n}\overline{w}_{i,T'}\left(\frac{1}{T}\sum_{t=0}^{T-1}\overline{r}_{i,t+1}\right), \qquad (3.16)$$

where T' is set at 6 months after the end of the performance evaluation period. Under the efficiently learning market, WAMR should be insignificantly different from zero. The wealth ratio used to proxy for weight has an important merit. By employing stock price at the beginning of the performance evaluation period as a denominator, we regard the wealth ratio as an investment at IPO of $1 with a reinvestment of possible dividends. This process normalizes the future (scaled) price $\overline{p}_{T'}$, and further reduces the cross-sectional variation and improves the power of tests for ELM.

Table 3.4 shows that the WAMR values are positive and differ significantly from zero after issuance. Positive WAMR values imply that the ELM does not hold. That is, IPO investors do not rationally learn from the market. These positive WAMR

Table 3.4 IPO performance using market return as benchmark and neglecting price limits under ELM

(q,s)	$WAMR_{q,s}$	t-value	(q,s)	$WAMR_{q,s}$	t-value
(1,1)	0.019	2.024	(1,19)	0.033	5.293*
(1,2)	0.020	2.848*	(1,20)	0.031	5.481*
(1,3)	0.021	3.160*	(1,21)	0.031	5.621*
(1,4)	0.027	4.211*	(1,22)	0.031	5.518*
(1,5)	0.032	4.692*	(1,23)	0.032	5.208*
(1,6)	0.032	5.144*	(1,24)	0.033	5.320*
(1,7)	0.034	5.086*	(1,25)	0.029	5.123*
(1,8)	0.034	5.160*	(1,26)	0.027	4.933*
(1,9)	0.036	5.295*	(1,27)	0.027	4.721*
(1,10)	0.035	5.353*	(1,28)	0.027	4.302*
(1,11)	0.032	5.151*	(1,29)	0.029	3.568*
(1,12)	0.034	5.325*	(1,30)	0.028	3.757*
(1,13)	0.034	5.282*	(1,31)	0.028	3.754*
(1,14)	0.036	4.883*	(1,32)	0.028	3.558*
(1,15)	0.034	5.390*	(1,33)	0.030	3.494*
(1,16)	0.032	5.483*	(1,34)	0.030	3.596*
(1,17)	0.031	5.382*	(1,35)	0.030	3.489*
(1,18)	0.034	5.441*	(1,36)	0.030	3.456*

The market return is used as the benchmark deflator to calculate the weighted average modified rate of return under an ELM. Neglecting price limits, we use the closing prices to measure market returns and IPO returns. The weighted average modified returns (WAMR values) are the IPO performance under an ELM over the period from month q to month s. * Significance level of 1%.

values, however, may arise from two possible causes. The first is model misspecification. This implies that the market index returns cannot appropriately measure the expected returns of IPOs. Ibbotson (1975) showed that IPOs are riskier than average. Therefore, the beta risk of IPOs should be higher than 1. In other words, the benchmark return measured by market return is underestimated, leading to positive abnormal returns. The second cause, according to Bossaerts and Hillion (2001), is that the market underreacts to good information related to IPO firms. This suggests that investors react partially, hence barely pushing the price upwards. Therefore, is the argument valid that the market underreacts to the good information of IPOs, since IPO aftermarket prices on the Taiwan market frequently hit the upper bound of price limits, refraining the market from reacting wholeheartedly to IPO good information even though the market does fully realize good IPO information.

Therefore, market underreaction to good information might simply be a measurement problem of 'true' returns behind the price limits.

3.4.2   Using the Fama–French return as benchmark and simulating the hidden information behind the price limits

To adjust for the risk level of IPOs under an ELM, a new benchmark deflator is needed. The market return is not as good as the IPO benchmark return due to the higher risk characteristics of IPO firms. Typically, IPOs are riskier than ordinary firms.

Fama and French (1992, 1993) demonstrated that a size-related factor (SMB) and a value-related factor (HML) can improve the asset pricing model in explaining the cross-sectional variation of stock prices. Market factor, SMB, and HML are the three so-called Fama–French factors for asset pricing. Brav et al. (2000) also showed that the Fama–French three-factor model can better explain expected IPO returns than the market model.

The benchmark defactor for IPO i at month t under the Fama–French three-factor model is thus defined as:

$$FF\kappa^*_{i,t} = \left(\prod_{d=k+1}^{k+25} (1 + \alpha^*_i + \beta^*_i r^*_{m,d} + s^*_i SMB^*_d + h^*_i HML^*_d) \right) - 1, \qquad (3.17)$$

where α^*_i, β^*_i, s^*_i, and h^*_i are obtained from the time series regression of $r^*_{i,d}$ on $r^*_{m,d}$, SMB^*_d and HML^*_d. To construct SMB^*_d and HML^*_d, we mimic the procedure of forming portfolios proposed by Fama and French (1993) with simulated latent 'true' returns behind the price limits. The size-related risk premium, SMB^*, is the return on a zero investment portfolio formed by subtracting the return of a large-firm portfolio from the return of a small-firm portfolio. The value-related factor, HML^*, is defined as the return of a portfolio of high book-to-market stocks minus the return of a portfolio of low book-to-market stocks.

Using the simulated benchmark deflator of the Fama–French three-factor model, we further follow equations (3.12)–(3.16) to estimate the weighted average modified return of IPOs under an ELM. We report the weighted average modified return of IPOs under an ELM and the Fama–French model in Table 3.5. The results indicate that the weighted average modified returns are insignificantly negative at the 1%

Table 3.5 IPO performance using Fama–French return as benchmark and simulating latent 'true' behind price limits under an ELM

(q,s)	WAMRq,s	t-value	(q,s)	WAMRq,s	t-value
(1,1)	−0.005	−0.629	(1,19)	−0.017	−1.913
(1,2)	−0.016	−1.845	(1,20)	−0.014	−1.930
(1,3)	−0.012	−1.611	(1,21)	−0.016	−2.021
(1,4)	−0.009	−1.361	(1,22)	−0.018	−2.381
(1,5)	−0.004	−0.755	(1,23)	−0.017	−2.063
(1,6)	−0.004	−0.821	(1,24)	−0.017	−2.280
(1,7)	−0.004	−0.987	(1,25)	−0.017	−2.344
(1,8)	−0.005	−1.028	(1,26)	−0.019	−2.160
(1,9)	−0.003	−0.725	(1,27)	−0.019	−2.219
(1,10)	−0.006	−1.334	(1,28)	−0.024	−1.845
(1,11)	−0.006	−1.009	(1,29)	−0.019	−2.066
(1,12)	−0.008	−1.355	(1,30)	0.001	0.048
(1,13)	−0.005	−0.762	(1,31)	0.002	0.175
(1,14)	−0.006	−0.938	(1,32)	0.004	0.282
(1,15)	−0.012	−1.550	(1,33)	0.003	0.225
(1,16)	−0.015	−2.024	(1,34)	0.008	0.435
(1,17)	−0.015	−1.588	(1,35)	0.010	0.505
(1,18)	−0.014	−1.488	(1,36)	0.017	0.652

The Fama–French return estimated from the Fama–French three-factor model with simulated 'true' returns behind the price limits is used as the benchmark deflator to calculate the weighted average modified rate of return under an ELM. The weighted average modified returns (WAMR values) are the IPO performance under an ELM over the period from month q to month s.

significance level 3 years after issuance. The insignificant negative weighted average modified returns of IPOs show that the IPO market is rational in the sense that investors use the correct likelihood depending both on available information as well as non-default to infer the possibility of an IPO's future value. In other words, IPO investors learn rationally in the sense of an ELM. Our results of simulating the hidden information behind the price limits in conjunction with the Fama–French three-factor model and an ELM show that IPO investors in Taiwan use available information to distinguish the stocks' risks, leading to no abnormal performance in IPOs.

We now summarize our empirical findings. The test of the efficient markets hypothesis using the market index return as the benchmark indicates that Taiwan's IPOs experience no significant abnormal returns in the long run. This result, however, cannot be considered as a manifestation of market rationale in the sense of the efficient markets hypothesis because the realized transaction prices are subject to severe price limits. Price limits not only confine price changes, but also alter the market reaction. While using the Tobit model to simulate the hidden information behind price limits, we demonstrate that the Fama–French three-factor model improves in explaining the dynamics of the price and that IPO investors in Taiwan manage to learn efficiently from the market by simulating the latent true prices behind the price limits. Hence, investors in Taiwan earn no abnormal returns on IPOs in the long run.

3.5 Dependence of long-run performance on issue characteristics

Under an ELM Taiwan's IPOs do not experience abnormal long-run performance, implying that investors learn efficiently from IPO markets. In this section, we further split the entire IPO sample into subsamples of IPO characteristics to examine the causes for their long-run performance. The IPO characteristics we use to investigate IPO long-run performance are IPO method, IPO underpricing, the length of waiting time to issue subsequent offerings, hot-issue period, and industry.

3.5.1 Effect of IPO method on long-run performance

In Taiwan, IPOs can be issued to the market via the fixed-price method or the auction method. For fixed-priced IPOs, the IPO offer price is determined in advance by the underwriter and issuer. On the other hand, the IPO offer price is determined through an auction process for auctioned IPOs. Table 3.6 shows that, on average, IPOs distributed by competitive bidding perform better than those by fixed price. However, all the WAMR values in Table 3.6 are not significantly different from zero except for the first 7-month WAMR. This positive first 7-month WAMR implies that the market underreacts to the good information of IPOs allocated by competitive bidding with respect to those by fixed price. As time passes, more information is revealed to the market, leading to a modified underreaction, now insignificantly different from zero.

3.5.2 Effect of underpricing and length of waiting time to issue subsequent offerings on IPO long-run performance

IPO underpricing is typically measured by initial returns. We break down the entire IPO sample into two subsamples based on IPO initial returns. Since IPO aftermarket trading prices are subject to price limits, the initial return is measured from the offer price to the 25th day closing price after issuance. Therefore, the IPO initial return

Table 3.6 IPO performance under ELM categorized by IPO method

	Fixed price		Auction	
(q,s)	$WAMR_{q,s}$	t-value	$WAMR_{q,s}$	t-value
(1,6)	0.007	0.442	0.054	2.160
(1,12)	−0.058	−0.965	0.021	0.982
(1,18)	−0.045	−1.076	0.005	0.332
(1,24)	−0.005	−0.708	0.015	0.753
(1,30)	−0.022	−1.351	−0.008	−0.724
(1,36)	−0.015	−1.219	−0.007	−1.060

The Fama–French return estimated from the Fama–French three-factor model with simulated 'true' returns behind the price limits is used as the benchmark deflator to calculate the weighted average modified rate of return under an ELM. The weighted average modified returns (WAMR values) are the IPO performance under an ELM over the period from month q to month s.

consists of IPO underpricing with the market reaction during the first 25 trading days. Under the signaling model, IPO underpricing is used to signal the quality of the offering. Firms signaling their quality through underpricing will recover their losses from the subsequent offerings. That is, the waiting time to issue subsequent offerings to the public is related to the firm's quality.

IPOs are categorized into six even categories by initial return and the length of the waiting time to issue subsequent offerings. Table 3.7 shows that the market over-reacts to the information of IPOs with low initial returns, leading to negative long-run performance. Moreover, the market also overreacts to the information of those with a short waiting time to issue subsequent offerings and middle initial return.

3.5.3 Effect of hot-issue period and industry on IPO long-run performance

Ritter (1984) indicated that IPOs tend to cluster at certain hot-issue periods and that IPO underpricing is driven by certain industries. Ritter also showed that IPOs issued during the hot-issue periods experience higher initial return, referred to as the hot-issue puzzle. To examine whether IPO long-run performance is related to a hot-issue period, we divide the IPO sample into two even subsamples by monthly issuing volume. Firms issued in a month of the top 33% issuance volume are categorized as heavy issuance and denoted as 'Hot'. IPOs issued in a month of the bottom 33%

Table 3.7 IPO performance under ELM categorized by IPO underpricing and waiting time to issue subsequent offerings

Waiting time	(q,s)	Low		Middle		High	
		$WAMR_{q,s}$	t-value	$WAMR_{q,s}$	t-value	$WAMR_{q,s}$	t-value
Short	(1,6)	−0.027	−3.212*	−0.027	−1.806	0.040	1.265
	(1,12)	0.000	0.004	−0.024	−5.683*	0.028	1.022
	(1,18)	0.095	−1.122	−0.032	−1.553	0.032	1.308
	(1,24)	−0.039	−2.412*	−0.014	−3.905*	0.029	1.145
	(1,30)	−0.022	−2.027	−0.020	−4.286*	−0.024	−0.975
	(1,36)	−0.030	−1.424	−0.008	−3.285*	−0.042	−1.695
Long	(1,6)	0.002	0.076	0.013	0.570	0.044	1.771
	(1,12)	0.009	0.378	0.020	0.974	0.025	1.415
	(1,18)	−0.018	−1.112	0.009	0.735	0.021	1.372
	(1,24)	−0.018	−1.902	0.006	0.770	0.014	0.953
	(1,30)	−0.015	−2.594*	−0.001	−0.238	0.008	0.673
	(1,36)	−0.010	−2.158	0.003	0.529	0.016	0.993

The Fama–French return estimated from the Fama–French three-factor model with simulated 'true' returns behind the price limits is used as the benchmark deflator to calculate the weighted average modified rate of return under an ELM. The weighted average modified returns (WAMR values) are the IPO performance under an ELM. IPO initial return is used to measure IPO underpricing. The IPO sample is categorized into three even categories by IPO initial returns. The 'High' category includes IPOs of the top 33% initial returns, the 'Middle' category includes IPOs of the middle 34% initial returns, and the 'Low' category includes IPOs of the bottom 33% initial returns. Each category is further divided into two even subcategories on the basis of the length of the waiting time between the IPO and its first subsequent offering. * Significance level of 1%.

Table 3.8 IPO performance under ELM categorized by hot-issue period and industry

Industry	(q,s)	Cold		Middle		Hot	
		$\text{WAMR}_{q,s}$	t-value	$\text{WAMR}_{q,s}$	t-value	$\text{WAMR}_{q,s}$	t-value
Non-electronic	(1,6)	−0.063	−0.841	0.013	1.019	−0.013	−0.944
	(1,12)	−0.196	−1.022	0.004	0.434	−0.008	−0.615
	(1,18)	−0.091	−1.026	−0.003	−0.533	−0.014	−1.094
	(1,24)	−0.028	−1.241	−0.007	−1.106	−0.009	−1.238
	(1,30)	−0.048	−1.165	−0.009	−3.073*	−0.008	−1.505
	(1,36)	−0.045	−1.022	−0.011	−2.995*	−0.024	−1.440
Electronic	(1,6)	0.022	0.694	−0.023	−0.674	0.064	1.571
	(1,12)	0.025	0.928	0.010	0.444	0.060	1.877
	(1,18)	0.009	0.636	0.033	1.801	0.022	0.561
	(1,24)	0.005	0.699	0.005	0.285	0.032	1.301
	(1,30)	0.008	1.054	0.001	0.063	0.006	−0.274
	(1,36)	0.001	0.093	0.006	0.337	0.036	1.031

The Fama–French return estimated from the Fama–French three-factor model with simulated 'true' returns behind the price limits is used as the benchmark deflator to calculate the weighted average modified rate of return under an ELM. The weighted average modified returns (WAMR values) are the IPO performance under an ELM. IPO sample is categorized into three even categories by IPO issuance. The 'Hot' category includes IPOs issued in a month of the top 33% issuance, the 'Middle' category includes IPOs of the middle 34% initial returns, and the 'Cold' category includes IPOs issued in a month of the bottom 33% issuance. Each category is further divided into two subcategories by industry.

issuance volume are categorized as light issuance and denoted as 'Cold'. Furthermore, the electronics industry in the Taiwan Securities Exchange is classified as a specific group relative to firms in other industries due to its high profitability and high-risk characteristics. Thus, we classify our sample into an electronics group and a non-electronics group.

Table 3.8 reports the IPOs' WAMR values on the basis of the hot-issue period and industry grouping. We show that the hot-issue period and industry type do not have a significant effect on IPO long-run performance. Thus, the fad pattern is not present in our sample.

3.6   Conclusion

The long-run performance puzzle of IPOs has been well documented in numerous studies. It is known that IPOs experience long-run underperformance in the USA and Germany, while IPOs experience overperformance in some emerging markets. Emerging markets typically encounter more rigorous regulations and are considered less efficient than US markets. This chapter investigates the new issue puzzle in emerging markets with the example of Taiwan's IPOs.

There is an ongoing debate about whether the anomaly in IPO long-run performance is a manifestation of market inefficiency caused by the behaviors of irrational investors or whether this anomaly results from model misspecification. Two hypotheses of rationality are examined in this study: ELM and EMH. The ELM assumes that a market's likelihood of signals conditioned on available information is correct, whereas the EMH assumes not only the correct likelihood, but also unbiased prior beliefs.

There are price limits in Taiwan's stock markets and investors recognize the existence of price limits. Therefore, the transaction prices hitting the price limits do not reflect the fair prices, a fact well known by investors. Aftermarket transaction prices of IPOs in Taiwan hit the upper bound of price limits on a frequent basis. We thus employed the Tobit model to simulate the latent fair prices to examine the true returns of IPOs in Taiwan under price limits. We show that the EMH is too strong to measure the abnormal performance of IPOs for Taiwan's IPO markets. On the other hand, the ELM indicates that Taiwan's IPO markets can be considered as rational markets and that investors manage to rationally learn from the market information. Regarding the issue information, we show that IPO underpricing and length of waiting time to issue subsequent offerings are influential in IPO long-run performance.

Our results have good implications for issuers and investors. Issuers realize that IPO investors in Taiwan are rational, leading to low issuing risk in Taiwan's IPO markets. With the low issuing risk, the underwriters will charge the issuers less underwriting spreads when underwriting new issue shares. Thus, issuers are content to access the primary markets for their financial needs. On the other hand, it is also important for the investors to know that no abnormal long-run returns can be attained in Taiwan's IPO markets. Experienced speculators typically feel that they can make more money from less efficient markets or markets with fewer rational investors. Knowing that there are no abnormal returns in Taiwan's IPO markets will prevent speculators from imposing more noise on the markets. With rational investors, the capital markets will become stable, especially emerging markets.

Acknowledgments – We would like to thank Jerry Chiou and David Shyu for their helpful comments and suggestions. All the remaining errors are ours.

References

Aggarwal, R. and Rivoli, P. (1990). Fads in the Initial Public Offering Market? *Financial Management*, 19(4):45–57.

Allen, D. E., Morkel-Kingsbury, N. J., and Piboonthanakiat, W. (1999). The Long-Run Performance of Initial Public Offerings in Thailand. *Applied Financial Economics*, 9(3):215–232.

Banz, R. W. (1981). The Relationship between Return and Market Value of Common Stocks. *Journal of Financial Economics*, 9(1):3–18.

Bondarenko, O. and Bossaerts, P. (2000). Expectations and Learning in Iowa. *Journal of Banking and Finance*, 24(9):1535–1555.

Bossaerts, P. (1995). The Econometrics of Learning in Financial Markets. *Econometric Theory*, 11(1):151–189.

Bossaerts, P. (2004). Filtering Returns for Unspecified Biases in Priors When Testing Asset Pricing Theory. *Review of Economic Studies*, 71(1):63–86.

Bossaerts, P. and Hillion, P. (2001). IPO Post-Issue Markets: Questionable Predilections but Diligent Learners? *Review of Economics and Statistics*, 83(2):333–347.

Brav, A., Geczy, C. and Gompers, P. A. (2000). Is the Abnormal Return Following Equity Issuances Anomalous? *Journal of Financial Economics*, 56(2):209–249.

Chen, A., Chiou, S. L., and Wu, C. (2004). Efficient Learning under Price Limits: Evidence from IPOs in Taiwan. *Economics Letters*, 85(3):373–378.

Chu, E. L. (1997). The Honeymoon Effect of Taiwan Stock Market's Initial Public Offerings. *Review of Securities and Futures Markets*, 9(1):1–29.

Corhay, A., Teo, S., and Rad, A. T. (2002) The Long-Run Performance of Malaysian Initial Public Offerings (IPOs): Value and Growth Effects. *Managerial Finance*, 28(2):52–65.

Fama, E. F. (1976). *Foundations of Finance*. Basic Books, New York.

Fama, E. F. and French, K. R. (1992). The Cross-Section of Expected Stock Returns. *Journal of Finance*, 47(2):427–465.

Fama, E. F. and French, K. R. (1993). Common Risk Factors in the Returns on Stocks and Bonds. *Journal of Financial Economics*, 33(1):3–56.

Ibbotson, R. G. (1975). Price Performance of Common Stock New Issues. *Journal of Financial Economics*, 2(3):235–272.

Keloharju, M. (1993). The Winner's Curse, Legal Liability, and the Long-Run Price Performance of Initial Public Offerings in Finland. *Journal of Financial Economics*, 34(2):251–277.

Lee, P. J., Taylor, S. L., and Walter, T. S. (1996). Australian IPO Pricing in the Short and Long Run. *Journal of Banking and Finance*, 20(7):1189–1210.

Lee, S. B. and Chung, J. S. (1996). Price Limits and Stock Market Efficiency. *Journal of Business Finance and Accounting*, 23(4):585–601.

Lewellen, J. and Shanken, J. (2002). Learning, Asset-Pricing Tests, and Market Efficiency. *Journal of Finance*, 57(3):1113–1145.

Ljungqvist, A. P. (1997). Pricing Initial Public Offerings: Further Evidence from Germany. *European Economic Review*, 41(7):1309–1320.

Loughran, T. and Ritter, J. R. (1995). The New Issues Puzzle. *Journal of Finance*, 50(1):23–51.

Loughran, T., Ritter, J. R., and Rydqvist, K. (1994). Initial Public Offerings: International Insights. *Pacific-Basin Finance Journal*, 2(2–3):165–199.

Page, M. J. and Reyneke, I. (1997). The Timing and Subsequent Performance of Initial Public Offerings (IPOs) on the Johannesburg Stock Exchange. *Journal of Business Finance & Accounting*, 24(9–10):1401–1420.

Ritter, J. R. (1984). The 'Hot Issue' Market of 1980. *Journal of Business*, 57(2):215–240.

Ritter, J. R. (1991). The Long-Run Performance of Initial Public Offerings. *Journal of Finance*, 46(1):3–27.

Ritter, J. R. and Welch, I. (2002). A Review of IPO Activity, Pricing, and Allocations. *Journal of Finance*, 57(4):1795–1828.

Rosenberg, B., Reid, K., and Lanstein, R. (1985). Persuasive Evidence of Market Inefficiency. *Journal of Portfolio Management*, 11(3):9–16.

Shiah Hou, S. R. (1993). On the IPO Pricing in Taiwan. Unpublished Ph.D. Dissertation, National Chengchi University, Taiwan.

Tobin, J. (1958). Estimation of Relationships for Limited Dependent Variables. *Econometrica*, 26(1):24–36.

4 Short- and long-run performance of IPOs traded on the Istanbul Stock Exchange

Mehmet Orhan

Abstract

This chapter examines initial public offerings (IPOs) traded on the Istanbul Stock Exchange (ISE). The underpricing of Turkish IPO sectors grouped under three categories is examined. The returns of IPOs are calculated for different time periods to better visualize underpricing in the short, medium and long term. Chow's test is used to check for structural changes in the regression of stock returns over market returns using the Capital Asset Pricing Model (CAPM). Finally, cointegration relationships of the CAPM are investigated for several IPO returns and market returns.

4.1 Introduction

Many companies offer their shares to the public to raise capital with the intention of meeting their financial needs worldwide. The first sale of stocks to the public is called the initial public offering (IPO). There are several stages of this process. First, the company applies for registration to the Istanbul Stock Exchange (ISE). The second step is the underwriting process, whereby the company deals with financial institutions to guarantee a minimum return after the shares are traded on the stock exchange. The underwriter is usually an investment banker or a group of bankers (syndicate). Therefore, if the risk is considered too high, then it is spread among numerous bankers. The last step is the offering to the public. The company and the underwriter negotiate on the type of underwriting. There are several types of underwritings. In a best-effort underwriting arrangement, the underwriter can act as an agent to sell as much of the issue as possible. In an all-or-none underwriting, if the underwriter cannot resell the entire issue then the security is withdrawn. The issuer and the company can negotiate the price, the size, and other details typically referred to as the negotiated underwriting. Another type of arrangement requires that the highest bidder among competitive bankers underwrites the issue.

In the stand-by underwriting arrangement, the shares are first offered to existing shareholders and the remaining portion not purchased by shareholders is then offered to the public. The 'firm commitment' arrangement implies that the investment banker purchases all shares from the company first and then resells them to the public at a higher price. Finally, in the private placement all shares are sold to private investors, thereby avoiding registration fees.

On the ISE the most preferred type of underwriting arrangement is the stand-by, with a 66% share. The 'full-underwriting' and 'best-effort underwriting' have 12% and 11% shares respectively. 'Residual underwriting' constitutes a 9% share and the remainder about 2%.

The performance issue has been the main theme of many IPO studies. The vast majority of these studies have concluded that performance is high in the very short run due to their underpricing; however, conclusions for long-run performance are mixed. In other words, the initial price guarantees the marketing of all shares achieved via low or underpricing of these shares. The company and the issuer may charge a higher price to obtain a larger profit, if one can evaluate the situation as if some potential money is left by them on the table. There are several approaches explaining the reasons behind this underpricing, whereby money is left on the table (Ritter, 1984, 1998).

Since the creation of the ISE in 1986, this emerging equity market has been growing constantly both in terms of the number of firms listed and daily trading volume. Recently, Harris and Kucukozmen (2001) state that the ISE has become the 12th largest emerging market in the world, a characteristic further validated in Muradoglu (2000).

The ISE was recognized as a designated offshore securities market in 1993 by the SEC. Furthermore, in 1995 the Japan Securities Dealers Association (JSDA) indicated that the ISE was considered an appropriate foreign investment market for private and institutional Japanese investors. In addition, the ISE received similar approval from the Austrian Ministry of Finance.

The ISE currently holds memberships in many international associations, institutions, and federations similar to the World Federation of Exchanges (WFE), International Securities Services Association (ISSA), the European Capital Markets Institute (ECMI), and many others. Considered as a unique market, the ISE provides a transparent environment for both domestic and foreign issuers and traders. In 1989 a decree was passed allowing foreign traders to participate on the ISE without any restrictions. The volume of equity investment from foreign traders has been growing rapidly from $33.59 million in 1995 to $127 million in 2004. Data regarding companies, stocks, dividends, etc. that trade on the ISE are available online (www.ise.org or www.imkb.gov.tr).

The ISE has four markets: the Stock Market, the Bond and Bills Market, the International Market, and the Derivatives Market. Each of these markets has different trading hours. These four market categories include submarkets. The Stock Market, for example, is composed of the National, Regional, New Companies, and Watch-List Companies Markets, as well as the Primary Market, Official Auctions, Wholesale Market, and the Rights Coupon Market. The most prominent of all these is the National Market, where 276 stocks currently trade.

The number of companies listed on the ISE has been increasing since the first IPO launch in 1986. The average annual number of IPOs listed on the ISE during 1990 to 2000 was 24.1. However, there was a significant decrease in the number of IPOs in 1999, and particularly in 2001, as a result of the economic crisis in Turkey. Nevertheless, the number of prospective IPOs to list on the ISE is expected to increase if economic programs adopted by the government are followed.

Section 4.2 calculates the returns of IPOs for different time periods. Section 4.3 tests for structural changes in the regression equations during the financial crisis of the Turkish Economy in 2001. Finally, section 4.4 includes cointegration tests of the CAPM, and section 4.5 concludes.

4.2   IPO performance during different time intervals

There are many studies that have analyzed the underpricing and performance of IPOs over different time intervals. Many studies have concluded that in the very short run – a few days after the issue of shares – the price increases, but the results are mixed for the long-run performance of IPOs. A key paper by Ritter (1998) discussed the short-run underpricing of IPOs. Ibbotson (1975) studied IPOs of the 1960s, while Eckbo and Norli (2005) investigated the risk-return features of IPO investment strategies. Chi and Padgett (2005) explored the short-term underpricing of Chinese IPOs using data on 668 stocks. Huang and Song (2005) examined the IPOs listed in the H-Firms list in China in a similar study. Ejara and Ghosh (2004) presented a comparison and aftermarket performance of the American Depository Receipts IPOs.

Dimovski and Brooks (2004) investigated the amount of return the company owner leaves the underwriter. Underpricing in China during the 1992 to 1997 period is the subject matter of another paper by Chen et al. (2004). Leite (2004) developed a model to find the amount of underpricing and Chahine (2004) investigated the analysts' forecasts of abnormal returns in the long run.

Kooli and Suret (2004) investigated the performance of 445 Canadian IPOs during the 1991 to 1998 period. Giudici and Roosenboom (2004) studied the pricing of first-day returns of IPOs on Europe's new stock markets. Levis (1993) investigated IPOs in the UK market between 1980 and 1988, and Dawson (1987) examined Asian IPOs. Kiymaz (2000) analyzed IPO performance of Turkish stocks in various sectors during the 1990 to 1996 period. Here, Kiymaz's period is extended and the investigation continued using January 1996 to February 2005 data. A number of IPOs in this period were excluded from the data set due to bankruptcy or because of insufficient data. However, there were sufficient data to examine the short-run performance of IPOs.

We examine IPO performance using different time periods. The performance of any stock is evaluated in terms of the return calculated by:

$$R_t = \left(\frac{P_t}{P_0}\right) - 1, \tag{4.1}$$

where R_t is the return of the stock and P_t is the price of the stock, t days after its introduction to the stock market.

The abnormal returns are obtained by subtracting the market returns from stock returns:

$$AR_t = M_t - R_t, \tag{4.2}$$

where AR_t is the abnormal return of the stock and M_t the market return. We find the average abnormal sector returns by averaging over the stocks that are traded in the same sector:

$$AAR_s = \left(\frac{1}{n_s}\right)\left(\sum_i AR_i\right), \tag{4.3}$$

AAR_s is the average abnormal return of sector s, n_s is the number of stocks in sector s and AR_i is the abnormal return of the ith firm in the sector.

For the short-run evaluations we are interested in 1, 2, 3, 4, 5, 6, 8, and 10 days after the issuance of the stock. For the medium run we take 1, 2, 4, and 6 months. Each month is assumed to span 20 working days. For the long-run performance we use 1, 2, and 3 years.

The sample consists of 119 IPOs classified according to the sectors. The categorization is based on the sectors originated by the ISE. However, we merge certain sectors where the number of IPOs are too few to conduct the analyses, but an effort is made to adhere to the ISE categorization. The sectors, sector codes, coverage of these sectors, and the number of IPOs in these sectors are listed in Table 4.1. The divisions for the sectors are manufacturing, finance, and service. The original sector codes are included in Turkish to allow researchers to access the data easily. The initiation dates of the IPOs are not reported here; the reader can visit the official website of the ISE to obtain these dates.

The average short-run returns of IPOs in each sector are displayed in Table 4.2. Some sectors yield negative first-day returns that contradict previous findings when examining IPOs of other countries. This is due to several major and many minor economic crises experienced by the Turkish economy during the investigation period. During this period there were many significant changes in the interest rates, exchange rates, inflation rates, and profits of firms. Many firms requiring financial resources sought the assistance of the ISE, but investors believed that other alternatives offered much better opportunities.

During this period the government sold several bond and T-bill offerings at very high interest rates. Furthermore, the Turkish crisis impacted many firms, thereby significantly

Table 4.1 IPO codes, sectors, divisions, and number of IPOs in different sectors

Division	Code	Sector	Number of IPOs
Manufacturing	FOOD (GIDA)	Food, Beverages, Tobacco	14
	PAPE (KAGT)	Paper, Printing, Publishing	5
	CHEM (KMYA)	Chemicals, Rubber, Plastic	6
	META (MANA)	Basic Metal	2
	METB (MESY)	Metal Products, Machinery	7
	CEME (TAST)	Non-Metal Minerals	2
	TEXT (TEKS)	Textiles, Apparel, Leather	19
Financial	BANK (BANK)	Banking	4
	LEAS (FINK)	Factoring and Leasing	5
	HOLD (HOLD)	Holding and Investment Companies	6
	INSU (SGRT)	Insurance	2
	INVE (YORT)	Real Estate Investment Trusts, Investment Trusts	24
Services	INFO (BLSM)	Information Technology	4
	ENER (ELKT)	Electricity, Gas, Energy	5
	COMM (ILTM)	Communication and Transportation	2
	SPOR (SPOR)	Sports and Health	4
	MARK (TCRT)	Consumer Trade and Marketing	6
	TOUR (TRZM)	Tourism, Restaurants, Hotels	2

Table 4.2 Short-run average abnormal returns of IPOs as percentages

Sector	AAR_1	AAR_2	AAR_3	AAR_4	AAR_5	AAR_6	AAR_8	AAR_{10}
FOOD	−0.43	−0.94	1.19	2.37	4.48	4.58	2.71	5.46
PAPE	−3.81	−6.36	−7.32	−9.75	−10.28	−12.65	−12.77	−11.00
CHEM	4.18	0.52	1.49	1.30	−3.16	−1.47	−6.10	−5.52
META	−3.78	−1.72	9.11	18.27	19.93	34.93	63.26	28.69
METB	7.80	13.20	16.10	13.57	12.80	13.12	12.97	10.30
CEME	−4.55	−1.98	−1.20	−5.39	−3.22	−2.92	−4.32	−5.94
TEXT	−1.32	−2.15	−3.45	−2.87	−1.20	−1.34	−0.83	0.00
BANK	−0.77	−4.96	−5.71	−7.24	−8.06	−12.21	−11.05	−13.88
LEAS	2.84	3.89	5.12	0.88	−3.20	−3.69	−5.49	−11.84
HOLD	−0.85	−6.68	−8.93	−9.38	−8.30	−6.37	−9.49	−7.76
INSU	−1.89	−13.15	−12.22	−10.73	−12.23	−10.35	−11.49	−10.00
INVE	2.90	5.09	1.89	−0.58	3.68	4.70	4.53	6.54
INFO	6.44	9.57	6.49	4.12	3.91	2.78	−3.01	−3.34
ENER	11.28	22.28	25.66	29.04	38.10	46.17	71.30	115.03
COMM	4.93	15.80	20.69	16.86	13.09	11.47	17.95	15.76
SPOR	−1.69	−4.15	−4.89	−10.51	−8.35	−12.53	−13.58	−11.28
MARK	1.90	3.83	10.90	9.17	6.32	5.22	6.63	7.41
TOUR	9.30	17.70	30.43	45.68	63.54	43.20	44.81	41.43

Subscripts following AAR refer to the time period (days).

decreasing their dividend payments to investors. Nevertheless, there were still many cases where stocks had experienced high first-day abnormal returns.

Some firms experience oscillating returns in the very short run (the first 10 days). The largest first-day average return and largest 10-day return (approximately 115%) were attained by the energy sector (ENER).

The medium- and long-run returns are reported in Table 4.3. The table suggests that the returns in this period for many sectors are significantly higher than other periods. For example, the marketing sector's (MARK) 3-year return is approximately 761%. During this period of instability numerous Turkish firms declared bankruptcy, making the selection process more arduous for the investors. The returns in Table 4.3 display the averages of each sector. Within each sector there were companies that had high returns and companies that had declared bankruptcy, rendering the average negative.

Cumulative average abnormal returns are also included. The cumulatives are taken over T days. First, the returns for each day are calculated until T and then all those returns are averaged. One can easily calculate the cumulatives from the averages by multiplying the averages by T. This shows how the average returns of the sectors have accumulated. The cumulative average abnormal return is taken over the average returns of the stocks traded in the same sector. That is,

$$CAR_T = \left(\frac{1}{T}\right)\sum_t ART_t, \tag{4.4}$$

where CAR_T is the cumulative average return between the first day and day T for a sector. To simplify matters we do not specify the sector with the notation in equation

Table 4.3 Medium- and long-run abnormal returns of IPOs as percentages

Sector	AAR$_{20}$	AAR$_{40}$	AAR$_{80}$	AAR$_{120}$	AAR$_{240}$	AAR$_{480}$	AAR$_{720}$
FOOD	10.80	14.81	29.76	39.36	96.58	138.99	135.32
PAPE	−14.83	−13.63	−38.86	−37.56	−37.61	−4.90	8.43
CHEM	4.59	6.76	13.11	12.54	32.12	58.24	177.24
META	21.54	8.55	−9.87	−13.70	8.06	−12.00	25.86
METB	22.53	25.96	33.15	34.99	59.24	71.26	210.01
CEME	−9.86	−13.67	15.44	−2.12	−40.28	35.83	207.41
TEXT	8.86	3.56	13.62	29.99	41.76	135.58	118.44
BANK	−15.90	−23.60	−28.83	−35.25	−24.39	22.66	152.80
LEAS	−5.46	−4.82	8.99	28.15	−24.35	37.11	51.86
HOLD	−13.14	23.92	85.20	52.87	25.76	178.30	167.09
INSU	−18.10	−10.12	−8.78	−13.80	−23.84	−52.46	165.91
INVE	16.64	28.92	8.54	10.40	104.89	155.08	183.14
INFO	−0.83	−4.28	−20.30	−28.31	−63.13	−45.25	−60.49
ENER	60.68	53.94	75.72	54.74	28.42	7.70	17.84
COMM	16.80	18.42	65.63	46.01	114.00	1.25	55.12
SPOR	−10.37	−10.64	−20.30	−30.77	−31.18	−9.97	23.05
MARK	4.69	13.86	20.61	56.16	131.80	445.53	761.11
TOUR	58.49	1.54	−60.10	−64.39	−48.34	−65.51	−66.82

Subscripts following AAR refer to the time period (days).

(4.4). ART$_t$ is the average abnormal return for time t; here t is between 1 and T. The cumulative returns are similar to the returns reported in Tables 4.3 and 4.4.

4.3   Testing for the structural change of the CAPM in the 2001 economic crisis of Turkey

The behavior of the CAPM is examined at the time of the economic crisis in Turkey. This period was the harshest economic crisis the Turkish economy had faced throughout its 80-year history. February 21 was the pivotal day of the structural crisis. After meeting for 13 hours, the Turkish Cabinet announced sweeping changes whereby the economic program they suggested forced the government to change its exchange rate regime from fixed to floating. This caused the interest rate to increase to 7500% and the ISE index to fall by 18.1%, and on the following day the USD exchange rate increased by 40%. Commercial banks withdrew $US 7.5 billion from the Turkish Central Bank, making millions of dollars in profit overnight.

We verify the structural change of the CAPM (Sharpe, 1964; Lintner, 1965) and adopt the following version:

$$R_t = \alpha + \beta M_t \tag{4.5}$$

where R_t is the return of the stock at time t and M_t is the market return during the same period. We take the logarithm of the differences to account for compounding (Muradoglu et al., 2003).

Table 4.4 Cumulative abnormal returns of stocks

Sector	CAR_{10}	CAR_{20}	CAR_{60}	CAR_{120}	CAR_{240}	AAR_{480}
FOOD	2.49	5.49	11.83	23.11	40.18	70.58
PAPE	−9.12	−10.99	−14.67	−24.14	−33.46	−22.55
CHEM	−1.74	−1.52	8.40	12.05	14.86	32.52
META	27.20	25.89	12.78	1.38	−4.15	−5.81
METB	12.70	12.30	23.29	28.02	47.73	50.75
CEME	−3.87	−6.23	−7.21	5.12	−13.89	−14.94
TEXT	−1.68	−0.95	4.36	10.87	23.07	56.59
BANK	−9.18	−11.58	−21.27	−27.26	−28.70	−15.86
LEAS	1.49	−1.38	8.90	20.69	19.38	8.20
HOLD	−8.88	−11.37	19.47	57.15	62.53	77.56
INSU	−10.17	−11.59	−9.80	−6.51	−14.17	−30.96
INVE	2.67	4.70	15.11	12.74	29.44	90.16
INFO	2.25	2.50	−2.65	−13.78	−33.46	−44.47
ENER	50.34	63.19	60.14	68.95	54.65	35.14
COMM	14.83	16.11	19.36	38.00	75.04	77.71
SPOR	−15.36	−16.75	−11.55	−18.79	−29.67	−34.63
MARK	6.68	6.71	9.32	19.86	52.28	191.05
TOUR	36.94	44.43	20.54	−14.40	−24.39	−39.54

Chow's test is then used to check for structural change (Chow, 1960). There are three time periods used to confirm this structural change: the pre-crisis period, the post-crisis period, and the entire period. We test whether the intercept and slope coefficients of equation (4.5) for the pre-crisis and post-crisis periods are significantly different from each other. The null hypothesis claims that there is no such structural change – that is, α and β do not change significantly after the pivotal observation.

We run regression for the three periods specified above, namely the pre-crisis (pre), post-crises (pos), and entire (ent) time periods, and record the Residual Sum of Squares (RSS) for these, so that we get RSS_{pre}, RSS_{pos}, and RSS_{ent}. The test statistic is:

$$F\text{-stat} = ((RSS_{ent} - (RSS_{pre} + RSS_{pos}))/k)/((RSS_{pre} + RSS_{pos})/(n_1 + n_2 - 2k)). \quad (4.6)$$

Here k is the number of regressors, including the constant term, n_1 is the number of observations in the pre-crisis period, and n_2 is the number of observations in the post-crisis period.

Five stocks with sufficient observations during the pre- and post-crisis periods are selected from each of the five sectors that have experienced the crisis. To check for structural change, the regression equation model for all periods is estimated. Fifty observations before and after the crisis are used and the statistics from each period presented, including the numerical values of the coefficient estimates to indicate the differences.

The F-statistics reported reject the null hypothesis that there is no structural change at different significance levels. Indeed, the F-statistic associated with the BANK sector has a borderline significance; asterisks are added to denote significance levels. Sectors examined confirm that there has been a significant change in the CAPM relationship during the time periods examined.

The larger the *F*-statistic, the more confident one is in rejecting the null hypothesis of no structural change in the CAPM relationship. We expect the CAPM relationship to hold for time periods before and after the crisis, and indeed it does hold, but the coefficients change significantly. This is just like a break in the line indicating CAPM. For instance, the *F*-statistic = 10.796 belonging to sector TOUR in Table 4.5 indicates a significant break on the crisis day of the Turkish economy.

4.4   Long-run relationship of the CAPM

In this section we explore the long-run relationship of the CAPM using cointegration theory (Granger, 1981; Engle and Granger, 1987). Cointegration implies that some regression series may not be stationary but their linear combination may lead to a stationary series of the error term. Cointegration is mostly used to investigate long-run relationships among economic variables. As a result, even if the series of dependent and independent variables are not stationary, their cointegration designates the long-run relationship between the series. The EViews software was used to investigate the long-run relationship. The series was examined for a cointegration relationship using the CAPM regression by selecting a firm from each of the 18 modified sectors from the ISE main categorization.

The EViews results are summarized to present the cointegration coefficients. The last 50 observations of each sector were used rather than the entire data set. The results of the investigation are reported in Table 4.6. EViews first tests the null hypothesis of no cointegration relation against different alternative hypotheses of at least one cointegrating relation, or at least two cointegrating relations using the cointegration method developed by Johansen (1991, 1995). These test results are not reported, but all such tests resulted in at least one (or more) cointegrating relations. Consider the equation reported in the first line of Table 4.6, GENIND + 0.1830FOOD − 0.0038. This means in the long run the general index of the ISE and the stock from the FOOD sector have a stable relation, as indicated.

4.5   Conclusion

There are several conclusions of this study that are worth noting. The ISE is a well-disciplined milieu for all types of transparent and secured trading for both domestic

Table 4.5 Structural change test results

Sector	Pre			Post			Entire			
	α	β	RSS	α	β	RSS	α	β	RSS	*F*-stat
BANK	0.0010	0.6329	0.104	0.0078	0.2929	0.089	0.0030	0.4754	0.202	2.331***
LEAS	−0.0040	0.3112	0.121	0.0104	0.0639	0.100	0.0032	0.1915	0.239	3.884**
PAPE	−0.0017	0.6394	0.082	0.0097	0.1155	0.097	0.0028	0.3223	0.216	9.712*
META	0.0029	0.6711	0.105	0.0081	0.2938	0.079	0.0038	0.4831	0.152	6.645*
TOUR	0.0057	0.7969	0.029	0.0072	0.2879	0.086	0.0034	0.5588	0.140	10.796*

Asterisks denote significance at the 1% (*), 5% (**), and 10% (***) levels.

Table 4.6 Cointegrating coefficients for some firms from each sector of the ISE

GENIND + 0.1830 FOOD − 0.0038	Log likelihood = 258.3
GENIND − 0.4485 PAPE − 0.0044	Log likelihood = 280.9
GENIND − 0.1103 CHEM − 0.0040	Log likelihood = 266.4
GENIND + 0.7379 META − 0.0019	Log likelihood = 262.4
GENIND + 1.6855 METB − 0.0039	Log likelihood = 242.9
GENIND − 0.3552 CEME − 0.0029	Log likelihood = 242.9
GENIND − 0.0282 TEXT − 0.0038	Log likelihood = 251.4
GENIND + 0.0510 BANK − 0.0049	Log likelihood = 199.7
GENIND − 0.0378 LEAS − 0.0033	Log likelihood = 229.6
GENIND − 0.0238 HOLD − 0.0039	Log likelihood = 245.0
GENIND + 0.1395 INSU − 0.0040	Log likelihood = 248.0
GENIND − 0.0173 INVE − 0.0038	Log likelihood = 214.4
GENIND + 0.3657 INFO − 0.0045	Log likelihood = 244.3
GENIND + 0.1828 ENER − 0.0065	Log likelihood = 205.5
GENIND + 0.4137 COMM− 0.0036	Log likelihood = 230.4
GENIND + 0.4574 SPOR − 0.0044	Log likelihood = 260.6
GENIND − 0.2227 MARK − 0.0035	Log likelihood = 253.7
GENIND − 0.0922 TOUR − 0.0041	Log likelihood = 235.5

and foreign investors. This has been confirmed by numerous qualifications of the ISE granted by respected international organizations.

Contradictory to the findings of numerous studies, some sectors had experienced negative returns in the very short run after they were issued on the ISE. This is due to the lack of a legal structure in the Turkish economy. However, the crisis of 2001 forced the Turkish authorities to pass numerous laws and, as a result of these reforms, the Turkish economy managed to contain the high inflation from which it had suffered for more than 30 years. The most notable occurrences in the Turkish economy were the autonomy of the Central Bank and the introduction of banking regulation reforms.

The medium- and long-run returns of the stocks traded on the ISE were found to be more promising than the short-run returns, with the marketing sector attaining the highest returns. Tests for structural changes in the CAPM regression were partly reported and as expected the structural change occurred on the pivotal day (21 February) of the crisis, as analyzed by a version of Chow's test.

The cointegration relationships between the stock and market returns were investigated using EViews. Fortunately, such cointegration relations were found for the stocks representing their sectors. The coefficients reported offer further insight into observing the nature of the long-run relationship between stock and market returns.

The cointegrating relations are extremely valuable to the investor, since these relations explain what will happen in the long run – for instance, one can concentrate on the coefficient of a stock in the cointegrating relation. If the coefficient is −0.27, one can infer that this stock will increase by 27% if the general index increases by one unit. For the short-run and medium-run analyses we have made, there is no such statistical inference. This is true for the long-run analysis only.

References

Chahine, S. (2004). Long-Run Abnormal Return after IPOs and Optimistic Analysts' Forecasts. *International Review of Financial Analysis*, 13(1):83–103.

Chen, G., Firth, M., and Kim, J. B. (2004). IPO Underpricing in China's New Stock Markets. *Journal of Multinational Financial Management*, 14(3):283–302.

Chi, J. and Padgett, C. (2005). Short-Run Underpricing and its Characteristics in Chinese Initial Public Offering (IPO) Markets. *Research in International Business and Finance*, 19(1):71–93.

Chow, G. C. (1960). Tests of Equality between Sets of Coefficients in Two Linear Regressions. *Econometrica*, 28(3):591–605.

Dawson, S. M. (1987). Secondary Stock Market Performance of Initial Public Offers. Hong Kong, Singapore and Malaysia: 1978–1984. *Journal of Business Finance and Accounting*, 14(1):65–76.

Dimovski, W. and Brooks, R. (2004). Do You Really Ask an Underwriter How Much Money You Should Leave on the Table? *Journal of International Financial Markets*, 14(3):267–280.

Eckbo, B. E. and Norli, O. (2005). Liquidity Risk, Leverage and Long-Run IPO Returns. *Journal of Corporate Finance*, 11(1–2):1–35.

Ejara, D. D. and Ghosh, C. (2004). Underpricing and Aftermarket Performance of American Depository Receipts (ADR) IPOs. *Journal of Banking and Finance*, 28(12):3151–3186.

Engle, R. F. and Granger, C. W. J. (1987). Cointegration and Error Correction: Representation, Estimation and Testing. *Econometrica*, 55(2):251–276.

Giudici, G. and Roosenboom, P. (2004). Pricing Initial Public Offerings on Europe's New Stock Markets. *Advances in Financial Economics*, 10(3):25–59.

Granger, C. W. F. (1981). Some Properties of Time Series Data and their Use in Econometric Model Specification. *Journal of Econometrics*, 16(1):121–130.

Harris, R. D. F. and Kucukozmen, C. C. (2001). Linear and Nonlinear Dependence in Turkish Equity Returns and its Consequences for Financial Risk Management. *European Journal of Operational Research*, 134(3):481–492.

Huang, G. and Song, F. M. (2005). The Financial and Operating Performance of China's Newly Traded H-Firms. *Pacific-Basin Finance Journal*, 13(1):53–80.

Ibbotson, R. G. (1975). Price Performance of Common Stock New Issues. *Journal of Financial Economics*, 2(3):235–272.

Johansen, S. (1991). Estimation and Hypothesis Testing of Cointegration Vectors in Gaussian Vector Autoregressive Models. *Econometrica*, 59(6):1551–1580.

Johansen, S. (1995). *Likelihood-based Inference in Cointegrated Vector Autoregressive Models*. Oxford University Press, London.

Kiymaz, H. (2000). The Initial and Aftermarket Performance of IPOs in an Emerging Market: Evidence from Istanbul Stock Exchange. *Journal of Multinational Financial Management*, 10(2):213–227.

Kooli, M. and Suret, J.-M. (2004). The Aftermarket Performance of Initial Public Offerings in Canada. *Journal of Multinational Financial Management*, 14(1):47–66.

Leite, T. (2004). Excess Initial Returns in IPOs. *Journal of Financial Intermediation*, 13(3):359–377.

Levis, M. (1993). The Long-Run Performance of Initial Public Offerings. The UK Experience 1980–1988. *Financial Management*, 22(3):28–41.

Lintner, J. (1965). The Valuation of Risk Assets and the Selection of Risky Investments in Stock Portfolios and Capital Budgets. *Review of Economics and Statistics*, 47(1):13–37.

Muradoglu, G. (2000). Turkish Stock Market: Anomalies and Profit Opportunities. In: *Security Market Imperfections in Worldwide Equity Markets* (Keim, D. and Ziemba, W., eds). Cambridge University Press, Cambridge, UK.

Muradoglu, G., Zaman, A., and Orhan, M. (2003). Measuring the Systematic Risk of IPOs Using Empirical Bayes Estimates in the Thinly Traded Istanbul Stock Exchange. *International Journal of Business*, 8(3):315–334.

Ritter, J. R. (1984). The 'Hot Issue' Market of 1980. *Journal of Business*, 57(2):215–240.

Ritter, J. R. (1998). Initial Public Offerings. *Contemporary Finance Digest*, 2(1):5–30.

Sharpe, W. F. (1964). Capital Asset Prices: A Theory of Market Equilibrium under Conditions of Risk. *Journal of Finance*, 19(3):425–442.

5 Indexing the IPO sector with IPOX™ Indices

Josef A. Schuster

Abstract

Over the past years, pricing and regulatory issues surrounding initial public offerings (IPOs) have been the subject of intense professional and academic debate. In response to the fundamental developments affecting the average IPO, the family of IPOX Indices was created as Indices for value of issues of new shares, which tracks the investment performance of IPOs issued in the United States during a predetermined time in aftermarket trading. The index technology facilitates the investment decision, trading process, and analysis of risk in the IPO sector with respect to the unique institutional and market influences inherent in short- and long-run IPO aftermarket trading. Using the IPOX Indices technology also underlines the portfolio benefits of IPO indexation and average IPO investing. It aims to become the leading benchmark against which to measure aftermarket IPO performance.

5.1 Introduction

Global issuing activity in initial public offerings (IPOs) has risen over the past few years. This is being driven by the favorable long-run performance of the average US IPO. Furthermore, there have been fundamental shifts in the profile of US IPO companies with older and more mature companies going public (Figure 5.1). This development has also been associated with an increase in public scrutiny towards IPO companies following changes in the regulatory framework associated with Sarbanes-Oxley.[1] For investment professionals, the importance of gaining timely exposure into IPOs is increasingly being recognized. Russell Indices, for example, recently decided to add IPOs to their indices on a quarterly rather than an annual basis.

Through the range of the IPOX IPO Indices, the first series of investable IPO Initial Public Offerings Index Products capturing the aftermarket performance of the large universe of US IPOs (IPOX Composite Index) and the respective size Indices (IPOX-100 and IPOX-30 Indices), market participants have now an innovative opportunity to navigate the IPO market and to track the performance of the economically significant US IPO sector more accurately and comprehensively than with any other index group. IPOX Indices accomplish the systematic indexation of the aftermarket performance of the US IPO sector, while at the same time preserving the benefits of diversification into the IPO sector.

---

[1] KPMG reports that auditors' fees stemming from the Sarbanes-Oxley accounting and governance legislation should fall by between 15% and 25% in 2005. The fees resulting from auditors' review of companies' internal controls should fall because of better working practices (*Financial Times*, 25 April 2005).

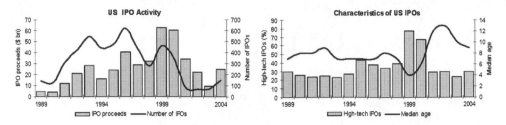

Figure 5.1 US IPO activity and characteristics of US IPOs (1989 to 2004). IPO proceeds are defined as the number of shares offered (as a percentage of the total number of shares outstanding) at the IPO date multiplied by the offering price, unadjusted for inflation and excluding over-allotment options. High-tech IPOs are defined as the fraction of high-tech IPOs based on the total number of IPOs. *Source*: IPOX Schuster LLC

The underlying rationale behind the IPOX Indices is the classification of IPOs from the rest of the market for a long period in aftermarket trading. As ample evidence from academia suggests, IPOs bear unique empirical return dynamics up to 4 years after the 'going public' event. Whether it is for the purpose of obtaining financing for growth opportunities, for enhancing a company's image and increasing its publicity and public exposure, for motivating managers and other employees or for cashing in by selling off the financial interest in the company, going public has unique and distinctive long-run impacts on the fundamental development of a company.

Due to the dynamic nature of total US IPO activity and the time-varying change of the average IPO profile (Figure 5.1) – a reflection of the growth and innovativeness of the US economy and trends in Equity Capital Markets (ECM) activity – the IPOX Indices do not make a distinction between sector, size, or style.

5.2   Why are IPOs unique? The academic perspective

A large body of academic literature has identified several empirical patterns unique to IPOs. One such pattern concerns the existence of abnormal initial returns, whereby the first market price is on average significantly higher than the offering price. Ritter and Welch (2002) found an average first-day return of 18.8% of 6240 US IPOs between 1980 and 2001. They focused on conflict of interests within the investment banking industry, which could potentially influence IPO initial returns and the dynamics in aftermarket trading. Through its three main functions – underwriting, advising, and distribution – underwriters play a crucial role in the going public process. Confronted with conflicting incentives, underwriters may face a trade-off between the costs and benefits. On one hand, for instance, underpricing an offer may lower both the risk that the issue fails as well as the efforts in marketing. On the other hand, since underwriter fees are typically proportional to gross floatation proceeds, and thus negatively related to underpricing and the value of the firm on the first day of trading, investment banks have an incentive to minimize underpricing. This conflict of interest can influence IPO initial returns, aftermarket volatility patterns, and the dynamics in aftermarket trading.

Another empirical pattern unique to IPOs relates to the hot-issue phenomenon, whereby observed issuing activity exhibits significant, recurrent, and to some extent predictable variations over time. Ritter (1984) studied initial returns for US IPOs between 1960 and 1982 and found significant autocorrelation in monthly average initial returns and in monthly IPO volume. He also observed that periods of high volume tend to follow periods of high average initial returns, with hot IPO markets concentrated in certain industries and underwriters. In a recent study, Lowry and Schwert (2002) confirmed a significant positive relation between initial returns and future IPO volume and noted that, 'increased numbers of companies go public after observing that IPOs are underpricing by the greatest amount'.

Most empirical IPO literature concentrates on aftermarket performance and returns are typically measured in event time. While the conventional view was that IPOs underperform in the long run (Ritter, 1991), it has become apparent that the performance results are sensitive to the time period chosen and methodology applied (Gompers and Lerner, 2001). This notion is underlined in Schuster (2003a), who highlighted significant cross-sectional differences in the long-run performance of a large sample of European IPOs and rejected the general notion of long-run IPO underperformance. Another facet that has attracted much interest addresses the relation between short- and long-run IPO returns. One of the first studies on these dynamics was by Stoll and Curley (1970). They found that investors in new small issues floated under Regulation A in 1957, 1959, and 1963 experienced lower long-run rates of return than if they had invested in a portfolio of large stocks represented by the Standard & Poor's 425 Industrial Average. However, short-run price appreciation of the 643 companies in the sample was considerably greater than the appreciation of large-cap stocks. Considerable short-run overperformance is also reported in Ritter (1991) and Schuster (1996, 2003b), who studied IPO performance for the US and European markets respectively. It is difficult to explain these price dynamics in the IPO aftermarket within a semi-rational setting. According to Miller (1977), the divergence of opinion about a new issue is greatest when the stock is issued, because there is uncertainty about the success of new products or the profitability of a major business expansion. As a result, short-sale constraints can lead to upward biases in stock prices, as pessimistic investors are restricted from short-selling. Over time, as a company acquires an earnings history, the marginal investor's valuation will converge towards the mean valuation and IPOs will start to underperform. Duffie et al. (2003) showed that if lendable securities are difficult to locate, then the price of the security is initially elevated and expected to decline over time.

A number of other institutional arrangements, unrelated to fundamentals, can affect aftermarket performances. Lockup agreements, for example, prohibit insider sales before a pre-specified date, usually 180 calendar days after the IPO. Since insiders often own a majority of the firm, the potential for an increase in the supply of tradable shares following lockup expiration can have a significant effect on the value of the stock (Bradley et al., 2001; Brav and Gompers, 2003; Field and Hanka, 2001). Moreover, Bradley et al. (2003) found abnormal returns in the days before the expiration of the quiet period. Furthermore, Aggarwal (2000) found that direct underwriter price support in IPOs or pure stabilization, in which an identified stabilizing bid is posted, is never done, and that aftermarket short-covering, which has no disclosure requirements, is the principal form of underwriter price support. Stabilization by short-covering can occur because the underwriter initially sells shares in excess of the original amount offered, which is then covered by exercising the over-allotment option and/or by short-covering in the aftermarket during 30 calendar days after the offering.

Teoh et al. (1998) related the analysis of aftermarket IPO performance to the type of earnings management pursued around the IPO date. They used discretionary current accruals as a proxy for earnings management and showed that companies which boost their earnings most during the IPO year also have the worst long-run performance. Luo and Schuster (2003) studied the relationship between management behavior and the subsequent market response in the German IPO market. When applying two forms of earnings management, issuers that overperform in the long run manage earnings less aggressively. Over shorter time horizons, however, companies that manage earnings more aggressively outperform. They showed that within the first 4 months of trading, IPO returns are essentially driven by factors other than fundamentals.

5.3 IPOX Index methodology[2]

The family of IPOX Indices was created to track the calendar-time investment performance of IPOs incorporated in the US during a predetermined time in aftermarket trading. All of the IPOX Indices are rules based: constituent stocks are selected based on publicly available, quantitative criteria only.

With a base date of 1 March 1989, the IPOX Composite Index acts as the basis for the investable and tradable segments of the IPOX Composite, the IPOX-100 and IPOX-30 Indices. The IPOX Composite Index is a value-weighted all-cap momentum index that is dynamically reconstituted. IPOs automatically enter the IPOX Composite on their seventh trading day after going public and automatically exit after 1000 trading days (approximately 4 years) on the stock market. Because IPO activity is fluctuating over time, the number of securities in the IPOX Composite Index does fluctuate accordingly. The IPOX Composite Index includes constituents from a broad mix of industries, including large, mature IPO companies, fast-growing and successful IPOs, as well as IPOs underperforming the market. With its 374 constituents as of 30 April 2005, the index pooled around $580bn worth of US stock market capitalization and between 7% and 15% of total daily trading volume on the US exchanges, with a total market capitalization range of between $625k (Natural Golf Inc.) and $60bn (Google Inc.). Only US-domiciled companies issuing common stock meeting minimum qualitative entrance requirements based on size, adjusted float, and initial pricing requirements initially listed on the NYSE, Nasdaq, or Amex are eligible for index membership. Closed-end funds, ADRs, Unit Investment Trusts, foreign offerings or Income Deposit Securities are excluded. Spin-Offs and Carve-Outs are included.

The IPOX-100 and IPOX-30 measure the performance of the Top 100 and Top 30 – representing around 75% and 50% of total market capitalization respectively – in the IPOX Composite Index. While the IPOX Composite Index applies a purely value-weighted capitalization scheme, the IPOX-100 and IPOX-30 Indices apply a modi-

---

[2] The IPOX Indices are calculated in real time by Standard & Poor's and available via the major data vendors, such as Bloomberg, Reuters, YAHOO Finance, or Archipelago. For ticker symbols, monthly constituent updates, and information regarding the availability of IPOX-linked financial products, visit http://www.ipoxschuster.com or contact josef@ipoxschuster.com.

fied capitalization scheme, whereby the influence of the largest index constituents is capped at 10% at the quarterly reconstitution event. The IPOX-100 and IPOX-30 Indices typically include the largest, most liquid, and best performing IPOs in the IPOX Composite Index. Unlike the IPOX Composite Index, the IPOX-100 and IPOX-30 are reconstituted quarterly to reflect changes in stock market values of IPOX Composite Index Constituents and IPO activity during the previous quarter. With their fixed numbers of constituent stocks, the IPOX-100 and IPOX-30 Indices currently pool around $400bn and $290bn worth of US stock market capitalization respectively. With median constituents market capitalizations of $1.6 bn (IPOX-100) and $4.7bn (IPOX-30) as of 29 April 2005, the indices reflect the dynamically growing and best performing universe of US companies 'going public' during the past 4 years.

5.4 IPOX Index analytics

The performance of the IPOX Indices is an important aspect when determining the effectiveness of an index as a basis for an allocation and diversification decision. As shown in Figure 5.2, the favorable historical performance comparison clearly underlines the benefits of average IPO investing and IPO indexing using the IPOX Indices technology. More specifically, the findings indicate the benefits of a systematic exposure into the IPOX Indices relative to the major US equity benchmarks.

As shown in Figure 5.2, the IPOX-100 and IPOX-30 Indices have historically produced favorable absolute and relative performance results against the major benchmark indices. These findings are confirmed when accounting for turnover in the IPOX Indexes – which is in line with the average turnover recorded by a US mutual fund – and when accounting for the slightly higher average dividend yield in non-IPOX constituent companies.

The analysis of 1-year correlation coefficients (Figure 5.3) clearly indicates the distinctive character and IPOX Index return dynamics. Between 1995 and 2000, IPO activity has been closely associated with the high-risk, high-return profile of companies in the Nasdaq. The decreasing influence of the high-tech IPO sector indicated by a sharply declining correlation with Nasdaq during the past few years is setting the IPOX Indices apart from the rest of the index universe. This development also underlines the forces behind the performance gains of the IPOX Indices in relation to the rest of the Indices universe (Figure 5.2). In addition to substantial merger and takeover activity in the IPOX Indices universe – the impact of fundamental changes associated with Sarbanes-Oxley has positively affected the profile and subsequent earnings quality of the average IPOX constituent.

Using the IPOX Indices as an IPO sector performance benchmark is consistent with findings reported in a recent string of academic IPO literature addressing the diversification benefits of using IPOs from an asset allocation perspective. Chen et al. (2005) examined whether investors can improve their investment opportunity set by adding an IPO portfolio to a set of benchmark portfolios. Using mean-variance spanning tests, they showed that adding a value-weighted IPO portfolio does lead to a statistically and economically significant enlargement of the investment opportunity set. In the cross-section of returns, they found that IPOs associated with

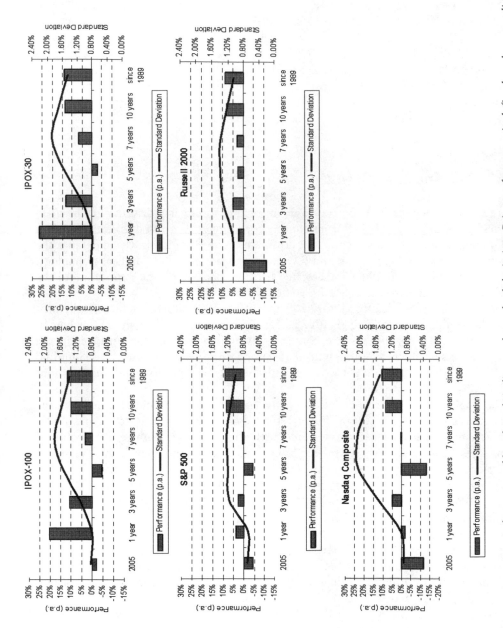

Figure 5.2 Comparative price performance of benchmark indices and standard deviation. Price performance is defined as the annualized change and excludes dividends. Standard deviation is calculated based on the change in daily closing prices over the respective time intervals. 2005 data as of 29 April 2005. *Source:* Bloomberg Analytics

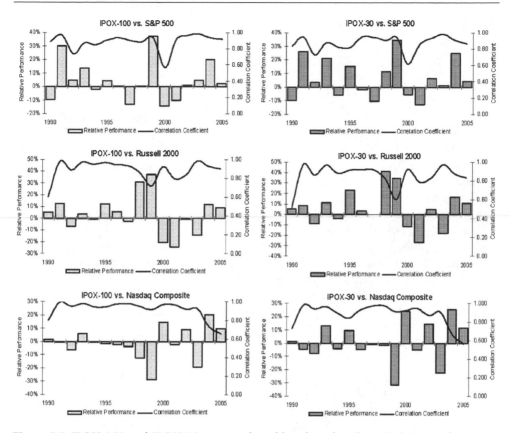

Figure 5.3 IPOX-100 and IPOX-30 versus selected benchmark indices. Relative performance is measured as the difference in annual raw returns of the respective indices (dividends not included). The rolling correlation coefficient is based on daily observations over the previous 12 months. 2005 data as of 29 April 2005. *Source*: Bloomberg Analytics

prestigious lead underwriters are the main source of this augmentation of the efficient frontier.

5.5 Conclusion

The IPOX Indices are all-cap momentum indices that provide an innovative way to make sector, size, and style decisions in equities. The IPOX-100 and IPOX-30 pool the largest and well-performing US IPOs in the IPOX Composite Index into a liquid and economically significant equity sector with unique empirical features and favorable historical performance against the major equity indices and provide average, rather than median, exposure to the long-run aftermarket performance of IPOs. The underlying empirical features in IPOs make products benchmarked against the IPOX Indices interesting for a number of market participants with varying investment horizons, including active index managers, index spreaders, basket traders, or the retail buy-and-hold return community, which seeks early, risk-controlled exposure into the

US IPO market, typically a true reflection of the trends in Equity Capital Markets and the growth and innovativeness of the US economy.

References

Aggarwal, R. (2000). Stabilization Activities by Underwriters after Initial Public Offerings. *Journal of Finance*, 55(3):1075–1103.

Bradley, D., Jordan, B., Roten, I., and Yi, H.-C. (2001). Venture Capital and IPO Lockup Expirations: An Empirical Analysis. *Journal of Financial Research*, 24(4):465–492.

Bradley, D., Jordan, B., and Ritter, J. R. (2003). The Quiet Period Goes Out With a Bang. *Journal of Finance*, 58(1):1–36.

Brav, A. and Gompers, P. (2003). The Role of Lockups in Initial Public Offerings. *Review of Financial Studies*, 16(1):1–29.

Chen, H.-C., Ho, K.-Y., and Wu, C.-H. (2005). Initial Public Offerings: An Asset Allocation Perspective. Working Paper, Yuan Zu University, Taiwan.

Duffie, D., Gârleanu, N., and Pederson, L. H. (2003). Securities Lending, Shorting and Pricing. *Journal of Financial Economics*, 66(1):307–339.

Field, L. C. and Hanka, G. (2001). The Expiration of IPO Share Lockups. *Journal of Finance*, 56(2):471–500.

Gompers, P. and Lerner, J. (2001). The Really Long-Term Performance of Initial Public Offerings: The Pre-NASDAQ Experience. *Journal of Finance*, 58(4):1355–1392.

Lowry, M. and Schwert, G. W. (2002). IPO Market Cycles: Bubbles or Sequential Learning? *Journal of Finance*, 57(3):1171–1198.

Luo, J. and Schuster, J. A. (2003). Management Behaviour and Market Response. Discussion Paper 462, Financial Markets Group, London School of Economics, London, UK.

Miller, E. M. (1977). Risk, Uncertainty, and Divergence of Opinion. *Journal of Finance*, 32(4):1151–1168.

Ritter, J. R. (1984). The 'Hot Issue' Market of 1980. *Journal of Business*, 57(2):215–240.

Ritter, J. R. (1991). The Long-Run Performance of Initial Public Offerings. *Journal of Finance*, 46(1):3–27.

Ritter, J. R. and Welch, I. (2002). A Review of IPO Activity, Pricing, and Allocations. *Journal of Finance*, 57(4):1795–1828.

Schuster, J. A. (1996). Underpricing and Crises – IPO Performance in Germany. Discussion Paper 252, Financial Markets Group, London School of Economics, London, UK.

Schuster, J. A. (2003a). The Cross-Section of European IPO Returns. Discussion Paper 460, Financial Markets Group, London School of Economics, London, UK. Working Paper, July.

Schuster, J. A. (2003b). Initial Public Offerings: Insights from Seven European Countries. Discussion Paper 461, Financial Markets Group, London School of Economics, London, UK. Working Paper, July.

Stoll, H. R. and Curley, A. J. (1970). Small Business and the New Issues Market for Equities. *Journal of Financial and Quantitative Analysis*, 5(1):309–322.

Teoh, S. H., Welch, I., and Wong, T. J. (1998). Earnings Management and the Long-Run Market Performance of Initial Public Offerings. *Journal of Finance*, 53(6):1935–1974.

6 The size effect of firms going public on the Spanish capital market

Susana Álvarez-Otero and Víctor M. González-Méndez

Abstract

The aim of this chapter is to analyze whether, for the Spanish market, the return of the companies that go public differs according to their size. To do this, we analyze not only the initial and long-term stock returns, but also the performance of the companies. The database for the study comprises all the firms that went public on the Madrid Stock Exchange between 1985 and 1997. Our analysis shows the existence of a size effect on the initial return offered by these companies and on the financial performance of the firms. Larger firms show a greater initial return to investors. Our results also provide evidence that the deterioration in the performance of the firm during the period following the issue affects all firms, though this effect is stronger for smaller companies. The results seem to be consistent with the idea of underpricing as a sign of the value of the firm.

6.1 Introduction

The academic literature that has analyzed firms going public has documented the existence of initial underpricing and long-run underperformance in the initial public offerings (IPOs). Underpricing means that the shares of firms that go public are on average offered to investors at considerably lower prices than those at which they subsequently trade on the stock market (Ritter, 1987; Levis, 1993; Ibbotson et al., 1994; Ljungqvist, 1997). On the other hand, different studies have analyzed the long-run performance of IPOs, giving rise to the second of the anomalies attributed to these offerings, which is that these usually present lower long-run returns than those of firms that have not gone public (Ritter, 1991; Levis, 1993; Loughran and Ritter, 1995; Ljungqvist, 1997; Cai and Wei, 1997). That is, relative to other quoted companies, investors appear to lose out by continuing to hold the shares of companies that have recently gone public. Likewise, other studies have shown that post-issue operating performance is also poor. Jain and Kini (1994), Mikkelson et al. (1997), Cai and Wei (1997), and Pagano et al. (1998) have documented that the post-issue profitability of IPO firms exhibits a significant decline, relative to their pre-issue levels.

In the analysis of initial underpricing, long-run performance, and operating performance, the existing empirical evidence partially documents a relationship between the size of the companies that go public and their results with regards to these three aspects. In relation to the first anomaly of IPOs, such as initial underpricing, several researchers have suggested various potential explanations for why the offer price is substantially lower than the first aftermarket price. Some studies argue that underpricing is the result of ex-ante uncertainty about the share price in the aftermarket (Rock, 1986; Beatty and Ritter, 1986; Carter and Manaster, 1990). This argument leads to the implication that the greater the ex-ante uncertainty about the value of an issue, the greater the expected underpricing. Bearing in mind that the size and the degree of establishment of the firm can be proxies for ex-ante uncertainty, different studies have tested the relation between size and the underpricing of the IPOs. For example, Ritter (1991), among others, has used the size and the degree of establishment concept to represent ex-ante uncertainty. The empirical evidence in the literature indicates that the initial returns are lower for larger, older, and better-known firms (Ritter, 1991; Barry et al., 1991; Clarkson and Merkley, 1994). Therefore, the greater the degree of establishment of an issuing firm, the lower the ex-ante uncertainty and the initial return of its IPO.

However, in relation to the anomaly of underpricing, another important explanation is also the one that considers underpricing as a sign of the quality of the firm. Taking into account the asymmetry of information among the agents participating in the IPOs, the company going public is the agent with superior information in relation to other participants (underwriters and investors). Consequently, the price discount in the initial offer is a sign of the value of the firm, and when the company decides on the price of the offer, it considers the possibility of carrying out subsequent seasoned equity offerings (SEOs).

This argument is based on papers by Allen and Faulhaber (1989), Welch (1989), and Grinblatt and Hwang (1989), and was subsequently tested in other studies as highlighted by McGuinness (1993). This last paper obtains a positive and statistically significant relationship between the market value of the firm and the level of underpricing in the initial offer. In accordance with this argument of signaling, underpricing constitutes a means of communicating the value of the shares to potential buyers. If a company is able to assume the cost of reducing the price of its shares, then it is a firm with good expectations. It will enjoy greater possibilities of obtaining future financial resources in capital markets, placing the new shares at a higher price closer to their intrinsic value.

The empirical evidence in Jegadeesh et al. (1993) established that the companies having a higher probability of carrying out successive SEOs are the larger ones. The authors propose a direct, statistically significant relationship between the probability and the level of initial underpricing of the IPO. This argument was tested by Keloharju (1993) for the Finnish stock market and by Jegadeesh et al. (1993) for the US market, obtaining favorable evidence. However, conclusive results were not obtained in other studies, like those of Michaely and Shaw (1994) and Garfinkel (1993), also for the US market. In fact, Michaely and Shaw (1994) found that firms with higher underpricing reissue less frequently and for lesser amounts than firms that underprice less. Also, firms that underprice less experience higher earnings and pay higher dividends, contrary to the predictions of the signaling models. Likewise, Garfinkel (1993) found that underpricing appears to have little incremental (signaling) effect on both the likelihood of reissue and the abnormal return to the announcement of a seasoned offering, after controlling for other variables that may affect both the probability of reissue and underpricing.

On the other hand, considering the anomaly of long-run underperformance, favorable empirical evidence exists that verifies the better long-term market return of larger companies. In this respect, Brav and Gompers (1997) verified that long-run underperformance is fundamentally due to small issuers. Additionally, Brav et al. (2000) showed that the use of weighting patterns based on the capitalization of companies reduces negative returns on the share's price by half. As for operating performance after going public, Mikkelson et al. (1997) documented that the variation in operating performance is mainly explained by the size and age of the companies and by the presence of secondary sales. Mikkelson et al. (1997) suspected that this result may be addressed by small, relatively young companies that report lower performance measures in their early years due to a low volume of sales, high initial operating costs, or an aggressive pricing strategy. However, this explanation would not justify such an influence of size on the operating performance of IPOs in Continental Europe, since IPO firms show a greater degree of establishment than those in the USA (Loughran et al., 1994).

Within this context, the aim of the present chapter is to analyze whether small firms are different in relation to these three aspects commonly studied for companies that get listed on the market. While there are studies that have analyzed the size effect on initial underpricing, long-run underperformance, and operating performance in the USA, we do not know of any papers that investigated this influence in the stock markets of Continental Europe. However, firms going public tend to be much older and larger in Europe than those going public in the USA, and do not appear to finance subsequent investment and growth.

Hence, we analyze whether the return on these companies differs – not only at the initial moment of their quotation on the Madrid Stock Exchange, but also in the long term, as well as on an operating and financial level – depending on whether the company is large or small. The database consists of companies that went public on the Madrid Stock Exchange during the period 1985 to 1997.

The rest of the chapter is structured in the following way. In section 6.2 we describe the database used in the study. The methodology and the results of the analysis of the relation between the firm's size and initial underpricing, long-run performance, and operating and financial performance, respectively, for the firms that went public on the Madrid Stock Exchange between 1985 and 1997 constitute the contents of section 6.3. The main conclusions of the study are drawn in section 6.4.

6.2 Database

The database of our study is made up of 111 firms going public on the Madrid Stock Exchange from 1985 to 1997.[1] The price data were extracted from prospectuses used to request firm listings on the Stock Exchange and were provided by the Madrid Stock Exchange for the issues between 1985 and 1989. The Spanish Securities and Exchange Commission (CNMV) provided the listings post-1989.

In order to analyze the effect of size on initial underpricing, long-term returns, and firm profitability, size is measured with two different criteria: the total assets at the end of the year prior to the date of going public and the market capitalization of the company at the end of the first day of negotiation on the stock market.

The characteristics of the database are displayed in Table 6.1 not only for the total sample, but also for small and large companies going public. The sample was divided using the median of the market value of equity at the end of the first trading day. The

---

[1] For long-term calculations the number of firms is in some cases smaller than 111, due to the lack of data.

Table 6.1 Database characteristics

	All firms		Large firms		Small firms		Diff.(p-value)
	Average	Median	Average	Median	Average	Median	
Size of the offer	61,066	14,821	107,527	33,640	13,761	8414	−4.82 (0.00)
Total assets in year −1	749,241	48,790	1453,051	114,237	32,635	21,722	−5.64 (0.00)
Age of the firm	30	22	31	21	29	23	−0.64 (0.52)
Equity in year −1	38,694	11,239	69,369	25,670	7460	5109	−5.51 (0.00)
Market value year 0	246,959	78,492	446,547	183,197	43,743	33,296	−6.07 (0.00)
Sales in year −1	194,366	34,742	356,169	66,610	29,622	21,823	−4.85 (0.00)
ROA in year −1%	11.62	9.09	10.43	5.74	12.81	10.95	2.29 (0.02)
ROE in year −1%	29.99	22.01	28.59	18.53	31.39	24.74	1.91 (0.06)
Investment rate in year −1%	70.25	8.28	34.62	3.08	104.58	9.06	0.04 (0.97)
Sales growth in year −1%	35.06	16.33	37.75	13.56	32.46	20.72	0.04 (0.97)
Book-to-market ratio	6.06	3.88	6.11	4.25	6.00	3.21	0.69 (0.49)

The table shows the characteristics of the database made up of the 111 firms that went public on the Madrid Stock Exchange between 1985 and 1997. The sample was divided taking into account the median of the market value of equity at the end of the first trading day. Size of the offer, firm's size, equity, market value, and sales are in thousand euros. Age is measured in years. For the difference between large and small firms, we show the Z-statistic and the p-value (in parentheses).

median company in our sample is about 1.2 times as large as the typical IPO in the United States in terms of sales (Loughran and Ritter, 2003). The firms that begin to quote on the Madrid Stock Exchange have high levels of profitability before the flotation of the firm, since the return on assets (ROA) in the year prior to the initial offer turns out to be 11.62%, while the return on equity (ROE) at that same moment is 30%. A similar ROA was reported by Pagano et al. (1998) for their sample of 69 IPO non-financial firms. Moreover, these are companies that have grown substantially in the year prior to the beginning of their market negotiation, not only in total volume of assets (70.25%), but also in total volume of sales (35.06%).

The average age of the established firms in the sample is 30 years, a characteristic of firms going public in Continental Europe. Vandemaele (2003) reported a median age of 28 years for 220 IPOs on the French Second Marché between 1984 and 1995. However, Loughran and Ritter (2003) reported a median age of 7 years for 6419 US IPOs from 1980 to 2000. Thus, firms going public in Continental Europe are older than those in the USA.

The sample is split up into small and large firms according to the market value of the firms after going public. This shows that large firms present higher values of offer size, total size, equity, market value of equity, and sales. However, there are no differences in the age of the firm. Small firms going public are not so young as in the USA; however, they are more profitable than large firms both in terms of return on assets and return on equity.

6.3 Effect of the firm's size on underpricing: long-term performance and the firm's performance

In this section we present the results of the empirical study of the influence of size on the initial underpricing of the companies that go public on the Spanish stock market. This is investigated over their long-term performance of 3 and 5 years after going public and over the firm's performance in a 3-year horizon after going public.

6.3.1 Initial underpricing and size

The initial underpricing of the sample firms is measured as the difference between the price obtained by the shares at the end of the first trading day and the price of the offer, with and without adjusting for the market return in that same period. The average underpricing for all the firms in the sample is 12.21% and the initial adjusted return is 11.84%. These results are in line with the existent empirical evidence at an international level. On average, the level of underpricing is 15% in industrialized countries and close to 60% in emerging markets. Ritter (1987) reported an initial return of 14.8% for the United States market, and Wethyavivorn and Koo-Smith (1991) showed a 58.1% level of underpricing for the Thai market.

To analyze the effect of the firm's size on the initial return of the companies that go public on the Spanish stock market, we split the sample according to the median of the market capitalization of the firm. The result indicates that the average adjusted initial return of large companies is 15.34%, while that of small firms is 8.40%. All these values are statistically significant at a 1% confidence level. Additionally, the Wilcoxon test shows that the difference in the underpricing between large and small firms is

Table 6.2 Differences in underpricing according to size (market value)

Underpricing	IR (%)	AIR (%)
All firms ($N = 111$)	12.21*** (4.79)	11.84*** (5.06)
Large firms ($N = 55$)	15.49*** (3.63)	15.34*** (3.95)
Small firms ($N = 56$)	8.98*** (4.66)	8.40*** (3.23)

The values in the table are average levels for the underpricing of the 111 firms that went public on the Madrid Stock Exchange during the period 1985 to 1997. IR is the initial return and AIR is the adjusted initial return. The sample was divided taking into account the median of the market value of equity at the end of the first trading day. The values in parentheses are t-statistics. Asterisks denote statistical significance at the 1% (***), 5% (**), and 10% (*) confidence levels.

Table 6.3 Underpricing and size

	IR	AIR
C	−0.57* (−1.75)	−0.556** (−1.97)
Size	0.028** (2.02)	0.028** (2.25)
Adjusted R^2 (%)	2.84	3.22
F-statistic	4.22**	4.66**

The table shows the results of the regression analysis of the initial return (IR) and the adjusted initial return (AIR). The dependent variable is measured as the natural logarithm of 1 plus the initial return or the initial market-adjusted return. Size is measured as the natural logarithm of market value of the firm at the end of the first trading day. Asterisks denote statistical significance at the 1% (***), 5% (**), and 10% (*) confidence levels.

statistically significant at almost 95% (Z-value equal to 1.89). Hence, this first result indicates that companies of greater size show a higher level of initial return (Table 6.2).

In order to analyze the effect of the firm's size on the initial underpricing of companies that go public on the Spanish stock market in more depth, we used two regressions of the initial return (IR) and the initial return adjusted by the return of the market portfolio in the same period (AIR) on the size of the company. The results of the regression analysis summarized in Table 6.3 correspond to the measure of size as the market capitalization of the firm at the end of the initial day of trading. The results of the estimations using the total assets as independent variable are of the same sign, but do not reach conventional significance levels.

From the results shown in Table 6.3, it is possible to observe a direct and statistically significant relationship at the 5% confidence level between the size of a company that goes public and the return offered to investors on the first day of trading. Not only do we consider the absolute initial return, but also the return adjusted by the yield of the market portfolio.[2]

---

[2] We repeated the estimations including control variables (firm and offer's characteristics). These variables do not affect the results presented here.

Therefore, we may affirm that the larger Spanish companies are the ones that show higher initial underpricing of shares and offer a higher initial return to the investors during the examination period. It is hence confirmed, on the basis of these results, that the size of the company going public is directly related to the return obtained by the investor on the initial offer. This relationship is contrary to results in the USA. Ritter (1991) showed that initial returns are lower for larger firms, in line with the explanation of ex-ante uncertainty. Perhaps the higher degree of establishment of firms going public in Spain compared to those in the USA may be the reason for these results.

6.3.2 Long-term performance and size

Long-run abnormal returns were calculated as the return on a buy-and-hold investment in the sample firm minus the return on a buy-and-hold investment in a reference portfolio or control firm. Thus, short-term (monthly) returns are compounded over 36 and 60 months after going public to obtain long-term returns:

$$\text{BHAR}_{iT} = \left[\prod_{t=t_i}^{T_i} (1 + R_{it}) - 1 \right] - \left[\prod_{t=t_i}^{T_i} (1 + E(R_{it})) - 1 \right] \tag{6.1}$$

where R_{it} is the return on security i in month t adjusted for dividends and seasoned offerings, T is the number of months (36 or 60), t_i is the date of the closing price on the first day of trading and $E(R_{it})$ is the expected return. We use a value-weighted (IGBM) and an equally weighted market index as benchmarks to measure the expected return.

We also create benchmark portfolios that will be assumed to represent normal returns by matching firms going public with groups of firms from the Madrid Stock Exchange based on firm characteristics. Following Fama and French (1992, 1993), we match on size and book-to-market portfolios in order to capture relevant cross-firm variation in average returns. Size and book-to-market portfolios were obtained by classifying the firms listed on the Madrid Stock Exchange during the 1987 to 1997 period according to the market value of equity in June of each year and creating size terciles. In order to avoid the portfolios being contaminated by the same firms that make up the sample, we eliminated from the portfolios the firms that went public during the 5 years following the flotation. Within each size tercile, the firms are once more classified into terciles created in terms of the book-to-market ratio in December of the previous year. Calculation of book-to-market ratios precedes their use for ranking purposes by 6 months to allow for delays in the reporting of financial statements by firms. Firms going public in the previous 5 years are allocated in July of each year to one of the nine portfolios formed and their returns are compared with those of the portfolio to obtain the abnormal return.

Finally, we used control firms of similar size and book-to-market ratio. Barber and Lyon (1997) showed that control firms of similar size and book-to-market ratio produce well-specified statistical tests in all the situations considered. We chose a control firm for each sample firm. Firms going public are placed in the appropriate size tercile based on their June market value of equity, and then we chose the firm with the book-to-value ratio closest to that of the sample firm. This process is carried out in July of each year.

To test the null hypothesis that the mean buy-and-hold abnormal return is equal to zero for the sample of firms going public, we first employ a conventional t-statistic:

$$t = \frac{\overline{AR_T}}{\sigma(AR_T)/\sqrt{n}} \tag{6.2}$$

where $\overline{AR_T}$ is the sample mean and $\sigma(AR_T)$ is the cross-sectional sample standard deviation of abnormal returns for the sample of n firms. We also use a nonparametric Wilcoxon signed rank test statistic.

The long-run abnormal returns obtained following this methodology are shown in Table 6.4. Regardless of the benchmark used, the results reveal the existence of statistically significant negative abnormal returns for 3 or 5 years. These negative abnormal returns are not a consequence of a few observations; in fact, approximately three-fourths of the sample present negative returns. These results show that, on average, the sample firms underperformed in the long run after going public. This result is consistent with the literature on long-run underperformance of IPOs in the international context. In this respect, papers have shown similar results in different countries: Ritter (1991) and Loughran and Ritter (1995) in the USA; Levis (1993) in the UK; Ljungqvist (1997) in Germany; and Cai and Wei (1997) in Japan, among others.

In order to analyze the influence of size on these results, we divided the sample according to the firm's size. We used the median market value of equity after going public to split the sample into two groups.

Table 6.4 shows that there are negative abnormal returns for large firms in the 3-year horizon that are only significant in a few cases according to the t-statistic. Five years after going public, the abnormal returns are not different from zero. Additionally, the percentage of negative returns is lower than in the whole sample. For small firms, however, there exist negative and significant abnormal returns, which vary between -29.90% and -59.54% for the 3-year period after going public. For the 5-year horizon, there are negative and significant abnormal returns regardless of the benchmark used, not only with the t-statistic but also according to the Wilcoxon test. Moreover, the percentage of negative abnormal returns is greater than in the case of large firms. However, large and small firms do not present any difference between abnormal returns according to the Wilcoxon test.

In order to lend more robustness to this analysis, we carried out the regression of the resulting return of a buy-and-hold strategy (BHAR), for 3 and 5 years after the IPO, using in both cases the four benchmarks mentioned above to estimate the return considered as normal. The results shown in Table 6.5 correspond to the measure of size as market capitalization of the company at the end of the first day of trading, bearing in mind that similar results are obtained if the total asset in the previous year of going public is used.

According to the results shown in Table 6.5, it is possible to observe a direct and statistically significant relationship between the return obtained by the company after 3 years of market trading and the size of the firm, when the benchmarks used are the IGBM and the value-weighted index. The coefficients for other benchmarks are not significant.

Likewise, the longer-term results (5 years) also confirm the existence of a direct and statistically significant relationship at levels of confidence of approximately 10% between the size and the return obtained by the firm 5 years after the beginning of

Table 6.4 Long-run return on large and small firms going public

	BHAR (%)	t-statistic	Wilcoxon test	% BHAR < 0
All firms: 36 months				
IGBM (N = 96)	−34.55	−4.28***	−5.07***	76.04
BM equally weighted index (N = 96)	−24.09	−2.88***	−3.69***	72.92
Book-to-market ratio and size portfolio (N = 96)	−45.04	−2.87***	−2.39**	61.46
Control firms (N = 96)	−46.01	−1.94*	−0.798	50.00
All firms: 60 months				
IGBM (N = 93)	−43.05	−3.48***	−5.62***	83.87
BM equally weighted index (N = 93)	−29.22	−2.18**	−4.30***	76.34
Book-to-market ratio and size portfolio (N = 93)	−51.09	−2.19**	−2.21**	61.29
Control firms (N = 93)	−69.07	−2.12**	−1.77*	59.14
Large firms: 36 months				
IGBM (N = 48)	−28.13	−2.13**	−2.85***	68.75
BM equally weighted index (N = 48)	−18.28	−1.34	−1.95**	66.67
Book-to-market ratio and size portfolio (N = 48)	−35.97	−1.71*	−1.11	56.25
Control firms (N = 48)	−32.49	−1.22	−0.57	50.00
Large firms: 60 months				
IGBM (N = 42)	−21.98	−0.87	−2.88***	78.57
BM equally weighted index (N = 42)	−3.45	−0.13	−1.82*	69.05
Book-to-market ratio and size portfolio (N = 42)	−22.19	−0.74	−0.86	57.14
Control firms (N = 42)	−22.32	−0.58	−0.62*	52.38
Small firms: 36 months				
IGBM (N = 48)	−40.96	−4.41***	−4.13***	83.33
BM equally weighted index (N = 48)	−29.90	−3.06***	−3.36***	79.17
Book-to-market ratio and size portfolio (N = 48)	−54.11	−2.31**	−2.24**	66.67
Control firms (N = 48)	−59.54	−1.51	−0.57	50.00
Small firms: 60 months				
IGBM (N = 51)	−60.41	−7.33***	−5.04***	88.24
BM equally weighted index (N = 51)	−50.46	−4.31***	−4.24***	82.35
Book-to-market ratio and size portfolio (N = 51)	−83.32	−3.17***	−2.27**	72.55
Control firms (N = 51)	−107.56	−2.15**	−1.95**	64.71

The table shows the results of a buy-and-hold strategy on firms going public 36 and 60 months from the first day of trading. Long-run returns are computed monthly up to the investment horizon considered. Returns are adjusted by the return considered normal; the Madrid Stock Exchange General Index (value-weighted index); an equally weighted index; a size and book-to-market portfolio return; and finally, control firms' return. The sample was divided taking into account the median of the market value of equity at the end of the first trading day. Asterisks denote statistical significance at the 1% (***), 5% (**), and 10% (*) levels.

Table 6.5 Long-run performance and size

	BHAR 3 IGBM	BHAR 3 Weighted Index	BHAR 3 Size-B/M	BHAR 3 Control
C	−4.27**	−4.39**	−0.92	1.04
	(−2.37)	(−2.12)	(−0.55)	(0.77)
Size (+)	0.16**	0.17**	0.037	−0.042
	(2.09)	(1.95)	(0.51)	(−0.70)
Adjusted R^2 (%)	3.63	4.14	−0.71	−0.58
F-statistic	4.81**	5.32**	0.39	0.49

	BHAR 5 IGBM	BHAR 5 Weighted Index	BHAR 5 Size-B/M	BHAR 5 Control
C	−1.52	−3.33**	−0.83	−1.09
	(−0.53)	(−2.03)	(−0.97)	(−0.71)
Size (+)	0.03	0.12*	0.06*	0.07
	(0.20)	(1.72)	(1.69)	(1.05)
Adjusted R^2	−1.25	3.05	1.85	0.20
F-statistic	0.06	3.49**	2.85*	1.20

The table shows the results of the regression analysis of the BHAR values. BHAR is defined as the differ-ence between the return on a buy-and-hold investment in the sample firm and the return on a buy-and-hold investment in an asset or portfolio. The return is adjusted by the normal return. Various benchmarks are used to measure the normal return: two market indexes (IGBM and an equally-weighted market index); size and book-to-market portfolios; and control firms. Size is measured as the natural logarithm of market value of the firm at the end of the first trading day. Asterisks denote statistical significance at the1% (***), 5% (**), and 10% (*) confidence level.

market trading, for some of the benchmarks selected. The results are statistically sig-nificant when the references are the value-weighted market index and the size and book-to-market portfolio. We repeated the estimations including control variables such as the age of the firm or the type of initial offer. These variables do not affect the results reported here.

According to the results, the larger Spanish companies that go public during the period of study are the ones that achieve better long-term performance. However, this result is not significant for all the benchmarks used.

6.3.3 Firm's performance and size

The change in performance of the sample firms from before to after going public is made by taking into account two different variables: return on assets and return on equity. On the one hand, we use the return on assets measured as the benefit before interests and taxes divided by the total assets. On the other, the return on equity is defined as the net profit over the total equity. For the two described measures of return and for each company, the change in the variable is measured as the difference between the values for the years 0, 1, 2, and 3 and the value for year −1, year 0 being the year of going public. The mean of the change is then calculated. In addition, the adjusted change according to industry is estimated in each of the return variables, comparing each company going public with companies of the same industry based on the CNAE 93 code (sectorial classification of Spanish firms). The performance of the company adjusted by industry is the difference between the change in the corresponding variable for the company and the median change in that same variable for the industry. Finally, the average of the change in the return adjusted by industry is calculated.

The change in performance of issuing firms is presented in Table 6.6, which shows the average change in return on assets (ROA) and return on equity (ROE) both before and after industry adjustment. The average changes in return on assets are 0.07%, −2.19%, −5.40%, and −6.70%, the last two values being significantly different from zero at the 0.01 level. The industry-adjusted figures show a similar decline in

Table 6.6 Performance of firms according to size

All firms	0/−1	1/−1	2/−1	3/−1
Return on assets (ROA)				
Average change (%)	0.07	−2.19	−5.40***	−6.70***
Average change adjusted by industry (%)	0.64	−0.41	−3.14***	−3.97***
Number of observations	98	98	97	84
Return on equity (ROE)				
Average change (%)	−4.60	−11.83***	−22.51***	−28.61***
Average change adjusted by industry (%)	−3.65	−9.66***	−19.97***	−23.97***
Number of observations	98	98	97	84
Large firms				
Return on assets (ROA)				
Average change (%)	0.59	−1.64	−3.81*	−5.77**
Average change adjusted by industry (%)	1.04	−0.45	−1.16	−3.38
Number of observations	49	50	47	40
Return on equity (ROE)				
Average change (%)	−4.20	−8.88	−15.69***	−21.82***
Average change adjusted by industry (%)	−3.41	−8.36	−15.17***	−19.23**
Number of observations	49	50	47	40
Small firms				
Return on assets (ROA)				
Average change (%)	−0.45	−2.76	−6.90***	−7.54***
Average change adjusted by industry (%)	0.24	−0.37	−4.99***	−4.50**
Number of observations	49	48	50	44
Return on equity (ROE)				
Average change (%)	−5.02	−14.90***	−28.92***	−34.79***
Average change adjusted by industry (%)	−3.89	−11.01**	−24.49***	−28.28***
Number of observations	49	48	50	44

The values in the table are the average changes shown as a percentage for the 111 firms that went public on the Madrid Stock Exchange between 1985 and 1997. The sample was divided taking into account the median of the market value of equity at the end of the first trading day. For the profitability variables, we measure the change in the variable for the years 0, 1, 2, and 3 in relation to the value of year −1, year 0 being the year of issue. The change is adjusted by industry with the difference for each firm's variable and the same change in the variable for industry. The test used is the Wilcoxon sign-ranked test. Asterisks denote statistical significance at the 1% (***), 5% (**), and 10% (*) levels.

operating performance. This result is in line with results reported by Jain and Kini (1994), Mikkelson et al. (1997), Cai and Wei (1997), and Pagano et al. (1998).

Return on equity follows the same trend. The industry-adjusted figures show a strong decline in the years after going public. The average changes after industry adjustment are -3.65%, -9.66%, -19.97%, and -23.97% for years 0, +1, +2, and +3 relative to the year prior to going public. The reason for this decline in ROA and ROE for firms going public has its origin in the high return prior to going public. The median firm going public has twofold ROE in the previous year to going public compared to the industry references. In fact, the average levels of ROA and ROE for firms going public decline over time, while the corresponding levels for their industry counterparts decline by a lesser amount.

The division of the sample shows that there is a size effect for the two considered variables of profitability. The smaller companies show much worse behavior, not only if we consider average values, but also if these are adjusted for industry behavior. In this respect, measuring size as the total market value of equity, large companies present average changes in their return on assets adjusted by industry of 1.04%, -0.45%, -1.16%, and -3.38% for the years 0, +1, +2, and +3 with regard to the year before going public, values that are not statistically significant. However, if we consider the smaller companies, the average changes in the return on assets adjusted by industry are 0.24%, -0.37%, -4.99%, and -4.50%, the last two values being statistically significant at the 1% and 5% levels respectively. Moreover, the differences between both subgroups are statistically significant for years 2 and 3. Similar conclusions can be obtained if we refer to the return on equity or if the size is measured as the value of the total assets. Hence, the poor post-issue performance is likely to be a consequence of small firms going public.

Moreover, the smaller companies also turn out to be more volatile in their behavior, as they tend to present greater excess return with regard to the industry in the year prior to going public than larger companies. On reaching the second or third year, they present inferior returns to the larger companies and to the industry references.

In order to analyze the influence of the size of the company on the change in performance from before to after going public, we carried out regression of the change in the return on assets and the change in the return on equity, from the year -1 to the years 0, +1, +2, and +3 (0 being the year of issue), on the size of the firm.

In Table 6.7 we present the results of the regression that correspond to the measure of size as the market value of equity of the company at the end of the first trading day. Similar results are obtained if we use the total assets of the company in the year before going public.

According to the results shown in Table 6.7, there does not exist a relationship between the firm's size and the change in the return on assets. However, the results are more conclusive when the change in the return on equity is used. These confirm the existence of a direct and statistically significant relationship, with levels of confidence that range between 5% and 10%, between the size and the change in the return on equity obtained by the firm in the same year of issue and in the successive years +1, +2, and +3 after going public.

While there is evidence that demonstrates the existence of improved operating performance for companies that have carried out privatization, we repeated the estimations including a fictitious variable that takes the value of 1 if the issue is carried out

Table 6.7 Firm's performance and size

	ROA (−1, 0)	ROA (−1, 1)	ROA (−1, 2)	ROA (−1, 3)
C	−0.11	0.04	−0.22	0.06
	(−0.76)	(0.25)	(−1.46)	(0.38)
Size (+)	0.01	−0.00	0.01	−0.00
	(0.77)	(−0.30)	(1.21)	(−0.60)
Adjusted R^2 (%)	−0.42	−0.85	−0.21	−0.67
F-Statistic	0.55	0.08	0.77	0.28
C	−0.63**	−1.25**	−1.26**	−1.21**
	(−2.04)	(−2.13)	(−2.24)	(−2.52)
Size (+)	0.03**	0.05**	0.05*	0.04**
	(1.99)	(1.99)	(1.94)	(2.13)
Adjusted R^2 (%)	1.09	2.47	1.08	1.43
F-Statistic	3.31*	3.74*	2.15	2.53

The table shows the results of the regression analysis of the change in the performance of the sample firms. The change in the return on assets (ROA) and the return on equity (ROE) is measured as the difference of the values for the years 0, 1, 2 and 3 in relation to the value for the year −1, year 0 being the year of going public. Size is measured as the natural logarithm of market value of the firm at the end of the first trading day. Asterisks denote statistical significance at the 1% (***), 5% (**) and 10% (*) confidence level.

for the privatization of the company and 0 otherwise. It does not modify the conclusions that are derived here from the results presented. We also incorporated other control variables, such as age, which did not affect the results.

In short, these results show that, among the Spanish companies that begin trading on the stock market during the period of study, the larger companies are the ones that obtain a better change in the return on assets and the return on equity. However, this fact does not seem to be clearly reflected in the market valuation of the company. It is hence confirmed, on the basis of these results, that the size of the company that goes public is directly related to the return obtained by the investor on the initial offer, as well as to financial performance, although no clear reflection on market performance is observed.

6.4 Conclusion

In this chapter we carried out a study of the existing relationship between the size of companies that go public in relation to three aspects widely analyzed in the IPO literature – initial underpricing, long-run stock return, and the firm's performance. Our aim has been to analyze whether, for the Spanish market, the return of these companies that go public differs according to their size. We have analyzed not only the initial and long-term stock returns, but also the performance (at an economic and financial level) of the companies. We used the firms that went public on the Madrid Stock Exchange between 1985 and 1997.

The analysis carried out of the companies that began trading during the mentioned period showed the existence of a size effect on the initial return offered by these companies and on the financial performance of the firms. Larger firms are the ones that show a greater initial return to investors. This result is contrary to the idea of initial underpricing being a consequence of ex-ante uncertainty. Ritter (1991), Barry et al. (1991), and Clarkson and Merkley (1994) showed that initial returns are lower for larger, older, and better-known firms. Spanish firms going public, as in other countries of Continental Europe, are well-known firms that are larger and older than US firms. The different degree of establishment of firms going public in Continental Europe and in the USA may explain this result.

Moreover, our results also afford evidence that the deterioration in the performance of the firm during the period following the issue affects all firms, though this effect is stronger for smaller companies. As for long-term market returns, larger Spanish firms that go public are the ones that obtain better long-term performance. However, this result is not significant for all the benchmarks used. The results seem to be consistent with the idea of underpricing as a sign of the value of the firm. Firms that underprice more (larger firms) perform better after going public.

References

Allen, F. and Faulhaber, G. (1989). Signaling by Underpricing in the IPO market. *Journal of Financial Economics*, 23(2):303–323.

Barber, B. and Lyon, J. (1997). Detecting Long-Run Abnormal Stock Returns: The Empirical Power and Specification of Test Statistics. *Journal of Financial Economics*, 43(3):341–372.

Barry, C., Muscarella, C., and Vetsuypens, M. (1991). Underwriter Warrants, Underwriter Compensation, and the Costs of Going Public. *Journal of Financial Economics*, 29(1):113–135.

Beatty, R. and Ritter, J. (1986). Investment Banking, Reputation, and the Underpricing of Initial Public Offerings. *Journal of Financial Economics*, 15(1–2):213–232.

Brav, A. and Gompers, P. (1997). Myth or Reality? The Long-Run Underperformance of Initial Public Offerings: Evidence from Venture and Nonventure Capital-Backed Companies. *Journal of Finance*, 52(5):1791–1821.

Brav, A., Geczy, C., and Gompers, P. (2000). Is the Abnormal Return Following Equity Issuance Anomalous? *Journal of Financial Economics*, 56(2):209–249.

Cai, J. and Wei, K. C. (1997). The Investment and Operating Performance of Japanese Initial Public Offerings. *Pacific-Basin Finance Journal*, 5(4):389–417.

Carter, R. and Manaster, S. (1990). Initial Public Offerings and the Underwriter Reputation. *Journal of Finance*, 45(4):1045–1067.

Clarkson, P. and Merkley, J. (1994). Ex-Ante Uncertainty and the Underpricing of Initial Public Offerings: Further Canadian Evidence. *Revue Canadienne des Sciences de l'Administration*, 11(1):54–67.

Fama, E. and French, K. (1992). The Cross-Section of Expected Stock Returns. *Journal of Finance*, 47(2):427–465.

Fama, E. and French, K. (1993). Common Risk Factors in the Returns of Stocks and Bonds. *Journal of Financial Economics*, 33(1):3–55.

Garfinkel, J. (1993). IPO Underpricing, Insider Selling and Subsequent Equity Offerings: Is Underpricing a Signal of Quality? *Financial Management*, 22(1):74–83.

Grinblatt, M. and Hwang, C. (1989). Signalling and the Pricing of New Issues. *Journal of Finance*, 44(2):393–420.

Ibbotson, R., Sindelar, J., and Ritter, J. R. (1994). The Market's Problems with the Pricing of Initial Public Offerings. *Journal of Applied Corporate Finance*, 7(2):66–74.

Jain, B. A. and Kini, O. (1994). The Post-Issue Operating Performance of IPO Firms. *Journal of Finance*, 49(5):1699–1726.

Jegadeesh, N., Weinstein, M., and Welch, I. (1993). An Empirical Investigation of IPO Returns and Subsequent Equity Offerings. *Journal of Financial Economics*, 34(2):153–175.

Keloharju, M. (1993). Initial IPO Returns and the Characteristics of Post-IPO Financing in Finland. Mimeograph, Helsinki School of Economics and Business Administration, Helsinki, Finland.

Levis, M. (1993). The Long-Run Performance of Initial Public Offerings: The UK Experience 1980–1988. *Financial Management*, 22(1):28–41.

Ljungqvist, A. (1997). Pricing Initial Public Offerings: Further Evidence from Germany. *European Economic Review*, 41(7):1309–1320.

Loughran, T. and Ritter, J. R. (1995). The New Issues Puzzle. *Journal of Finance*, 50(1):23–51.

Loughran, T. and Ritter, J. R. (2003). Why Has IPO Underpricing Changed Over Time? Working Paper, University of Notre Dame and University of Florida.

Loughran, T., Ritter, J. R., and Rydqvist, K. (1994). Initial Public Offerings: International Insights. *Pacific-Basin Finance Journal*, 2(2–3):165–199.

McGuinness, P. (1993). The Market Valuation of Initial Public Offerings in Hong Kong. *Applied Financial Economics*, 3(3):267–281.

Michaely, R. and Shaw, W. (1994). The Pricing of Initial Public Offerings: Tests of Adverse-Selection and Signaling Theories. *Review of Financial Studies*, 7(2):279–319.

Mikkelson, W. H., Partch, M. M., and Shah, K. (1997). Ownership and Operating Performance of Companies that Go Public. *Journal of Financial Economics*, 44(3):281–307.

Pagano, M., Panetta, F., and Zingales, L. (1998). Why Do Companies Go Public? An Empirical Analysis. *Journal of Finance*, 53(1):27–64.

Ritter, J. R. (1987). The Costs of Going Public. *Journal of Financial Economics*, 19(2):269–281.

Ritter, J. R. (1991). The Long-Run Performance of Initial Public Offerings. *Journal of Finance*, 46(1):3–28.

Rock, K. (1986). Why New Issues are Underpriced. *Journal of Financial Economics*, 15(1–2):187–212.

Vandemaele, S. (2003). Choice of Selling Mechanism at the IPO: The Case of the French Second Market. *European Financial Management*, 9(4):435–455.

Welch, I. (1989). Seasoned Offerings, Imitation Costs, and the Underpricing of Initial Public Offerings. *Journal of Finance*, 44(2):421–449.

Wethyavivorn, K. and Koo-Smith, Y. (1991). Initial Public Offerings in Thailand, 1988–89: Price and Return Patterns. In: *Pacific-Basin Capital Markets Research* (Rhee, S. G. and Chang, R. P., eds), Vol. 2. North-Holland, Amsterdam.

7 Earnings management and the long-run performance of Spanish initial public offerings

María J. Pastor-Llorca and Francisco Poveda-Fuentes

Abstract

The poor stock price performance of firms conducting initial public offerings is one of the recent puzzles in financial literature. We detect this market anomaly for Spanish initial public offering (IPO) firms and investigate whether earnings management around the time of the offering can explain these results. Consistent with this explanation, we notice that issuing firms make use of discretionary accruals to report higher earnings in the IPO year. Moreover, firms with higher levels of discretionary accruals experience more negative long-run abnormal returns. Thus, this evidence suggests that opportunistic earnings management explains, at least partially, the IPO anomaly in Spain.

7.1 Introduction

One of the most controversial topics in financial literature is the negative long-run abnormal returns in the years following initial public offerings (IPOs). Ritter (1991), Loughran (1993), and Loughran and Ritter (1995) reported this abnormal pattern in the US market. The evidence in other stock markets around the world also reveals long-run underperformance following initial equity issues: Levis (1993) and Espenlaub et al. (2000) in the UK; Ljungqvist (1997) and Stehle et al. (2000) in Germany; Lee et al. (1996) in Australia; Page and Reyneke (1997) in South Africa; and Keloharju (1993) in Finland.

One possible explanation for the poor stock price performance after the initial public offering is that investors are over-optimistic about the earnings potential of issuing firms, so the underperformance occurs as these over-optimistic expectations are gradually corrected in the post-offering period. A possible source of this investor over-optimism could be earnings management practices around the time of the issue.

Thus, directors of IPO firms could have incentives to report high earnings by adopting discretionary accounting accruals adjustments to ensure that the issue is fully subscribed and/or priced higher to garner proceeds. If the market fails to understand that the high earnings reported represent a transitory increase, negative post-offering abnormal returns would be due to a gradual correction of the initial overvaluation as earnings management reverses. Consistent with this argument, Teoh et al. (1998a, b) found that abnormal accruals are unusually high in the IPO year, and issuers with higher discretionary accruals have poorer stock returns in the subsequent years.

In the Spanish market the evidence in relation to the long-run performance following IPOs is not conclusive. On one hand, Álvarez and González (2005) analyzed a sample of 56 initial public offerings in the period 1987 to 1997 employing alternative procedures to compute and test abnormal returns, and documented that the existence of long-run abnormal returns depends on the methodology employed. On the other hand, Farinós (2001) analyzed a sample of 18 IPOs in the period 1993 to 1997 and verified that the abnormal monthly mean return of IPO firms in the post-offering period is not statistically significant.

In this context, we consider that additional research on this matter is necessary for the Spanish market in order to clarify if the IPO anomaly is also present in this stock market. Thus, our first interest is to examine, employing alternative methodological procedures, the long-run market reaction to initial public offerings in Spain with a larger and more contemporary sample than previous studies, and applying the bootstrap technique to improve the properties of our statistical tests. Secondly, our objective centers on whether managers display opportunistic behavior when revealing earnings to potential equity subscribers around initial public offerings and if these accounting practices have any relation to the post-offering return performance.

We observe that IPO firms experience a stock price underperformance in the years following the public offering. We find statistically significant negative abnormal returns in periods of up to 3 years following the offering decision. Moreover, consistent with the earnings management hypothesis, we note that issuing firms have unusually high accounting adjustments in the year of the offering. Furthermore, issuers with higher discretionary accruals have poorer stock returns in the subsequent years. Thus, this evidence implies that stock price underperformance is due, at least in part, to market inefficiency with respect to these accounting adjustments.

The chapter is organized as follows. Section 7.2 describes the sample selection procedure and data used. Section 7.3 examines the long-term stock price performance following Spanish initial public offerings. Section 7.4 discusses the measurements of earnings management. Section 7.5 studies the existence of earnings management practices by IPO firms. Section 7.6 analyzes the relationship between earnings management and post-offering stock return underperformance. Finally, our conclusions are presented in section 7.7.

7.2 Sample and data sources

To identify initial public offerings, we use the *Boletines Oficiales de la Bolsa de Madrid* and the register of the *Comisión Nacional del Mercado de Valores* (CNMV), which is the Spanish institution equivalent to the American SEC. During the period from January 1987 to December 2002, 65 initial offerings of companies listed in the *Sistema de Interconexión de las Bolsas Españolas* (SIBE) are located.[1]

The distribution of the event sample among sectors and years is illustrated in Table 7.1. Four of the sample years (1989, 1997, 1998, and 1999) are more active and cover more than 50% of the sample, with 1999 containing over 15% of the

---

[1] SIBE starts in 1989, so for years 1987 and 1988 IPO firms are listed in *Bolsa de Madrid*.

Table 7.1 Sample distribution for different years and sectors

Sector	1987	1988	1989	1990	1991	1992	1993	1994	1995	1996	1997	1998	1999	2000	2001	2002	Total
S3	0	0	1	0	1	0	0	0	0	0	0	0	0	0	0	0	2
S4	0	0	0	0	1	0	0	1	0	1	1	4	1	0	0	0	9
S5	0	0	0	1	1	1	0	1	0	0	0	0	1	0	0	0	5
S6	0	0	1	0	0	0	0	0	0	0	0	0	1	0	0	1	3
S7	0	0	0	1	1	0	2	1	0	0	1	0	0	0	1	0	7
S8	0	0	0	0	1	0	0	0	0	0	0	0	0	0	0	0	1
S9	0	0	2	0	0	0	0	0	0	0	0	0	1	0	0	0	3
S10	0	0	0	0	0	0	0	0	0	0	0	0	1	2	0	0	3
S11	0	0	0	0	0	0	0	0	0	0	1	0	0	0	0	0	1
S12	0	0	1	0	0	0	0	0	0	1	0	1	3	1	1	0	8
S15	0	1	1	0	0	0	0	1	0	0	5	3	0	1	1	0	13
S17	1	1	1	1	0	0	0	0	0	0	0	0	2	2	1	1	10
Total	1	2	7	3	5	1	2	4	0	2	8	8	10	6	4	2	65

S3: Cement, glass and construction materials; S4: Trade and other service ; S5: Construction industry; S6: Energy and water; S7: Finance and insurance; S8: Chemical industry; S9: Estate agents; S10: Communications; S11: Basic metals; S12: New technologies; S15: Other manufacturing industries; S17: Metal manufacture.

offerings. As for the distribution among sectors, more than 60% of the IPOs correspond to four sectors: trade and other services (9), new technologies (8), other manufacturing industries (13), and metal manufacture (10).

To measure long-run stock price performance, monthly returns adjusted by dividends, rights issues, and splits are employed. This information comes from the *Bolsa
de Madrid* for years 1987 and 1988, and from the SIBE for all the other years considered. To examine the existence of earnings management practices around the IPO
date, we require accounting data in CNMV for the year of the offering and the previous one, since to estimate issuing firms' accounting accruals we use variables in first
differences. As accounting data in CNMV begins in 1990, the sample for the earnings management analysis starts in 1991. Additionally, for the study of accounting
accruals it is not appropriate to include financial companies, as the nature of the
accruals of these firms is very different from that of industrial firms. Hence, the sample for the earnings management analysis is narrowed down to 47 initial public offerings.

As we will explain later, to compute IPO firms' abnormal accruals we estimate the
normal component of accruals with an estimation sample made up of non-IPO firms.
Accounting data for non-IPO firms are also obtained from the CNMV database.

Our accruals variable is reported in the fiscal year when the firm goes public.
Figure 7.1 illustrates the timing convention used. The fiscal year in which the IPO
occurs is year 0. Thus, fiscal year -1 ends before the date of the IPO, and fiscal year
0 includes both pre- and post-IPO information. Our financial statement information
is taken from fiscal year 0 for two reasons. Firstly, to estimate accounting accruals we
employ variables in first differences and pre-IPO data are not always available. So
examining abnormal accruals in the fiscal year -1 would imply a dramatic reduction
of our sample, especially due to the lack of accounting information in the CNMV
before 1990.

Secondly, IPO firms have incentives to manipulate both pre- and immediate post-
IPO earnings. That is, incentives to manage earnings are likely to persist in the
months immediately after the offering. Entrepreneurs usually cannot dispose of their
personal holdings until at least several months after the IPO. Furthermore, firms face
unusual legal and possibly reputational scrutiny in the IPO aftermath. Immediate
accounting reversals may render earnings management activities transparent enough

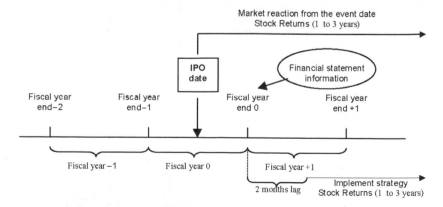

Figure 7.1 Timeline illustration

to trigger lawsuits against the firm and its management. Thus, if IPO firms decide to manage earnings, it is highly probable that they manage their first public financial statement.

In the next section, to measure the long-run market reaction to initial public offerings, as in all event studies, we analyze abnormal returns in a particular period (in our case a 3-year period) beginning on the event day – that is, the IPO date. In this way, we acquire knowledge of the stock return performance from the start of the public offering.

However, to allow investors in the market to implement a strategy based on the accrual information, this information should be available prior to the return accumulation period. Therefore, it is also appropriate to examine post-issue returns beginning after the first public financial statement, as proposed by Teoh et al. (1998a) and Rangan (1998). Since companies in Spain have 2 months after the end of the fiscal year to present financial statements to the CNMV, beginning the returns' accumulation period in the third month guarantees that accruals information is known by the market. In section 7.6 we will examine returns with this reporting lag, as well as the relation between earnings management and these abnormal returns.

7.3   Post-offering stock return performance

We measure the long-run market reaction to initial public offerings by applying two alternative procedures. Firstly, we compute abnormal returns in the years following the offering with an event time analysis and, secondly, we employ a calendar time methodology.

In the event-time analysis to measure long-run performance following the offering, we use returns net of the returns to the market value-weighted portfolio.[2] In particular, we calculate the abnormal compound return of company i in the post-offering period τ, $ACoR_{i\tau}$, as the compound return of the issuing firm i minus the compound market return:

$$ACoR_{i\tau}=\prod_{t=1}^{\tau}(1+R_{it})-\prod_{t=1}^{\tau}(1+R_{Mt}),\tag{7.1}$$

where R_{it} and R_{Mt} are the returns of firm i and the market portfolio in month t, respectively, and τ is the number of months in the post-offering period analyzed.

Abnormal compound returns are the most appropriate measure to quantify the adjusted return experienced by a stock in a period since it assesses the investor experience – that is, the value of investing in the average sample firm with respect to the benchmark over the horizon of interest. Figure 7.2 shows the mean abnormal compound return for the event sample during the 36 months following the offering decision. We observe how adjusted returns are positive up until the eighth month following the public offering, but after that abnormal returns experience a sharp decrease.

Next we test the statistical significance of this abnormal returns' performance. Addressing this topic involves the use of an appropriate methodology to minimize the specification problems that arise when testing abnormal returns in long horizon

---

[2] Results are very similar using equally weighted market portfolio returns.

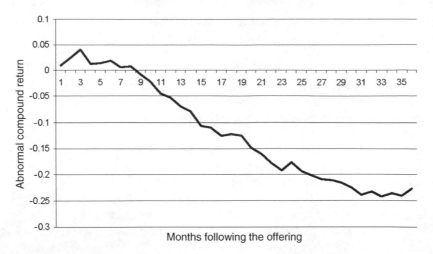

Figure 7.2 Long-run abnormal returns following the initial public offering

periods. Kothari and Warner (1997) and Lyon et al. (1999) proved that the bootstrap procedure has fewer misspecification problems and they consider it to be an
appropriate methodology to test the existence of long-run abnormal returns.
Moreover, bootstrap techniques are highly convenient in a context of small sample
sizes characteristic of a narrow market like that in Spain.

Thus, we compute traditional t-statistics but we apply the bootstrap procedure to
simulate its empirical distribution and we use this distribution to fix the acceptance
and rejection regions. The t-statistic of the event sample is computed as:

$$t = \sqrt{N}\frac{\text{AACoR}}{\hat{\sigma}}, \tag{7.2}$$

where N is the number of events in the sample, AACoR is the average abnormal compound return, and $\hat{\sigma}$ is the cross-sectional standard deviation.

In order to obtain the empirical distribution of the t-statistic, we randomly select
with replacement B subsamples with N_b events from the original sample, and for each
subsample we compute the following statistic:

$$t_b = \sqrt{N_b}\frac{\text{AACoR}_b - \text{AACoR}}{\hat{\sigma}_b}, \tag{7.3}$$

where AACoR_b and $\hat{\sigma}_b$ are the mean and standard deviation of the subsample b,
$b = 1, 2, ..., B$. Then, if B is high enough from the sample of bootstrap statistics $\{t_b:
b = 1, 2, ..., B\}$, we can obtain the empirical distribution of the t-statistic and use this
distribution to fix the acceptance and rejection regions. This methodology is applied
with $B = 10,000$ and $N_b = N$.

Table 7.2 reports average abnormal compound returns for the 1-, 2-, and 3-year
post-offering periods. As Figure 7.2 illustrated, market-adjusted returns are negative.
For the first year following the initial public offering the mean abnormal return of
IPO firms is -5.28%, becoming worse the larger the temporal horizon. In particular,
adjusted returns have a mean of -17.73% and -22.61% for the 2- and 3-year post-
issue period. Table 7.2 also shows the results of the traditional t-test applying the
bootstrap technique to compute statistical significance. Negative abnormal returns

Table 7.2 Stock return performance following the IPO

Analysis period (months)	AACoR (%)	Traditional t-statistic	Bootstrap p-value	Skewness coeff.	Skewness adjusted t	Bootstrap p-value
12	−5.28	−1.26	(0.21)	−0.29	−1.28	(0.21)
24	−17.73	−3.50	(0.00)	0.38	−3.30	(0.00)
36	−22.61	−3.32	(0.00)	0.49	−3.08	(0.00)

Panel A: Abnormal compound return for IPO firms in the 1-, 2-, and 3-year periods following the offering. This panel also reports results of traditional t-test and skewness-adjusted t-test using the bootstrap technique to evaluate statistical significance.

Analysis period (months)	$\hat{\alpha}_p$ (%)	t-statistic	p-value
12	−0.02	−0.05	(0.98)
24	−0.56	−1.99	(0.05)
36	−0.46	−1.87	(0.06)

Panel B: Abnormal monthly mean return in the post-offering period estimated with the Fama–French model in calendar-time regressions.

are not statistically significant for the 1-year post-offering period, since as we observe in Figure 7.2 in the first months following the issue mean adjusted returns are positive. However, for the 2- and 3-year post-IPO period negative abnormal returns are highly significant.

When reference portfolios are employed to estimate normal returns, in our case the market portfolio, the distribution of abnormal returns over long periods are positively skewed. We can see in Table 7.2 that skewness coefficients increase with the temporal horizon analyzed. This positive skewness over long periods could lead to misspecified t-statistics, so to avoid this problem we also calculate the skewness-adjusted t-statistic originally developed by Johnson (1978).

$$t_a = \sqrt{N}\left[\frac{AACoR}{\hat{\sigma}} + \frac{1}{3}\hat{\gamma}\left(\frac{AACoR}{\hat{\sigma}}\right)^2 + \frac{1}{6N}\hat{\gamma}\right], \qquad (7.4)$$

where $\hat{\gamma}$ is the coefficient of skewness, estimated as:

$$\frac{\sum_{i=1}^{N}(ACoR_i - AACoR)^3}{N\hat{\sigma}^3}.$$

To compute the statistical significance of the skewness-adjusted t, we also apply the bootstrap procedure. In this case, for each subsamble b, b = 1, 2, ..., B, we calculate the following statistic:

$$t_{a,b} = \sqrt{N_b}\left[\frac{AACoR_b - AACoR}{\hat{\sigma}_b} + \frac{1}{3}\hat{\gamma}_b\left(\frac{AACoR_b - AACoR}{\hat{\sigma}_b}\right)^2 + \frac{1}{6N_b}\hat{\gamma}_b\right], \qquad (7.5)$$

where $\hat{\gamma}_b$ is the skewness coefficient of the subsample b, B = 10,000, and N_b = N.

Results in Table 7.2 show that, even controlling for possible bias due to positive skewness, negative abnormal returns are highly significant for the 2- and 3-year post-offering periods. Thus, the evidence here is consistent with the IPO anomaly documented in different markets.

Several authors have documented that some biases arise when returns are accumulated over long periods (Barber and Lyon, 1997; Kothari and Warner, 1997; Lyon et al., 1999). Thus, an alternative procedure to estimate and test post-offering long-run abnormal returns is to analyze the abnormal monthly mean return by applying a calendar-time portfolio approach. This methodology analyzes the monthly return of buying the stock on the event date and holding it for τ months. In other words, this approach examines the strategy of holding a portfolio which is made up, in each calendar month, of the stocks affected by the event over the last τ months. Therefore, by studying this portfolio's return indirectly, we can analyze the return of the stocks affected by the event over the following τ months. This calendar-time methodology enables us to check the robustness of results and to avoid the problems of accumulating returns over long periods.

For the purpose of a clearer understanding of the calendar-time portfolio methodology, it is represented in Figure 7.3. The first month in our sample period where an initial public offering occurs is May 1987, so the strategy consists of buying the issue stock in this month and holding it for τ months.

In the same way if, for example, July 1987 was the next month where another initial offering occurs, we would acquire a second issue stock that month and also hold it for τ months. Similarly, if September 1987 was the next month with another IPO, so we would buy the third issue stock that month and hold it for τ months. Therefore, in September 1987 the portfolio is made up of the three stocks of the firms that made an initial public offering in May, July, and September, respectively.

Thus, we can compute the monthly return of the calendar portfolio p in each month t as:

$$R_{pt} = \frac{\sum_{i=1}^{N_{pt}} R_{jt}}{N_{pt}} \qquad t = 05/87, \ldots, 12/03, \tag{7.6}$$

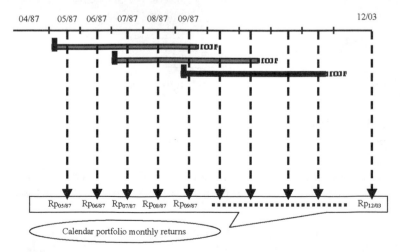

Figure 7.3 Calendar-time approach

where R_{jt} is the return of firm j in month t, N_{pt} is the number of stocks that are in the portfolio in that month t. Thus, we obtain the time series of the calendar portfolio monthly returns from May 1987 (the first IPO in our sample) to December 2003 $\{R_{p05/87} \cdots R_{p12/03}\}$.

To measure and test the portfolio's abnormal monthly mean return we apply the Fama and French (1993) three-factor model to the time series of the portfolio's monthly returns. Then, we run the following time series regression:

$$R_{pt}-R_{ft}=\alpha_p+\beta_{1p}\cdot(R_{Mt}-R_{ft})+\beta_{2p}\mathrm{HML}_t+\beta_{3p}\mathrm{SMB}_t+\varepsilon_{pt} \quad t=05/87, \ldots ,12/03, \tag{7.7}$$

where R_{ft} is the 1-month Treasury bill (risk-free) rate of return, HML_t is the difference in returns between portfolios made up of stocks with high and low book-to-market ratios, and SMB_t is the difference in returns between portfolios made up of stocks with low and high trading volumes, both variables being orthogonalized. The Jensen alpha, α_p, measures the calendar-time portfolio's abnormal monthly mean return.

This calendar-time approach, advocated by Fama (1998), corrects for possible correlations of returns across events and minimizes the skewness problem since monthly returns of portfolios are used. Furthermore, the Fama and French (1993) model takes into account the explicative power of size and book-to-market ratio in the cross-sections of stock returns. However, this procedure is not free from possible biases; several prior studies have documented that the application of the Fama–French model to test the existence of abnormal returns presents specification problems (Lyon et al., 1999; Jegadeesh, 2000; Brav et al., 2000). In addition, Loughran and Ritter (2000) argued that this factor model is less powerful in detecting abnormal returns than abnormal compound return analysis. In spite of these possible biases, the calendar-time approach provides an alternative for analyzing the post-offering abnormal long-run returns that is useful to check the robustness of results obtained in Table 7.2(A).

Table 7.2(B) reports the results of the Fama–French calendar-time regressions. We apply this methodology with a horizon τ of 12, 24, and 36 months. In this way, α_p measures the abnormal monthly mean return of IPO firms over the following 12, 24, and 36 months respectively. Given that the change in the composition of the portfolio each month could lead to heteroscedasticity problems, since the variance depends on the number of firms in the portfolio, we estimated the regression using White's covariance estimator, consistent with heteroscedasticity.

Results in Table 7.2(B) show that the intercept from the Fama–French model, α_p, is negative and significant for the 2- and 3-year horizon. Thus, this evidence indicates that the abnormal monthly mean return of IPO firms in the 2- and 3-year post-offering periods is statistically negative, which is consistent with the negative abnormal compound returns illustrated in Table 7.2(A).

7.4 Measuring earnings management

Accounting accruals are the centerpoint of earnings management tests. They are defined as the difference between earnings before extraordinary items and discontinued operations, and cash flow from operations. The accrual adjustments reflect business transactions that affect future cash flows, although cash has not currently changed hands. Under generally accepted accounting principles, firms have discretion to recognize these transactions so that reported earnings reflect the true underlying business conditions of the company. However, managerial flexibility in accruals also opens opportunities for earnings management.

Our earnings management tests are based on current accruals, which are related to non-cash working capital accounts. In order to calculate them, we use the normalized balance sheet presented in the CNMV. Specifically, in this study we utilize the standard definition of current accruals:

$$ACC_{it} = (\Delta CA_{it} - \Delta CASH_{it}) - (\Delta CL_{it} - \Delta STD_{it}), \tag{7.8}$$

where ACC_{it} are current accruals, ΔCA_{it} is the change in current assets, $\Delta CASH_{it}$ is the change in cash and cash equivalents, ΔCL_{it} is the change in current liabilities, and ΔSTD_{it} is the change in short-term debt. Subscripts i and t refer to company and period, respectively.

Observable current accruals, ACC_{it}, can theoretically be broken down into two unobservable components: the nondiscretionary or normal part, $NACC_{it}$, and the abnormal component, $AACC_{it}$, which can be used as a proxy for earnings management. Several theoretical models have attempted to obtain this breakdown by estimating the pattern of accruals in the absence of accounting discretion. In particular, these models try to explain the part of accruals due to objective reasons such as accounting rules and the firm's economic conditions. Thus, the part of accruals not explained by the model is considered discretional and used as a proxy for earnings management, since a variation in this component will represent a manager's effort to manipulate earnings more than a change in exogenous economic conditions.

In order to check the robustness of results, we apply two different models to estimate abnormal current accruals: the modified Jones model, proposed by Dechow et al. (1995), which has been used in nearly all studies about earnings management; and the model developed by Poveda (2005) which, owing to the results achieved regarding specification and power in the Spanish context, along with the different methodology used in the estimation of abnormal accruals, make it an excellent alternative to confirm if results are due to model specification or the real existence of earnings management. For the estimation of these two models, firstly we use a cross-sectional approach and secondly a panel-data estimation procedure. Additionally, all tests of abnormal accruals estimated from these models will be based on the performance matching procedure developed by Kothari et al. (2005) in order to assess a correct specification in a context where correlation exists between the analyzed event and the accounting performance of firms.

7.4.1 Cross-sectional approach

Since current accruals are not homogeneous among different activity sectors, we estimate the coefficients of each model for each activity sector and year. The estimation sample in each cluster sector–year includes exclusively non-event firms requiring a minimum of 10 observations. With these estimated coefficients clear of earnings management for each cluster sector–year, we predict the normal current accrual for issuing firms. We now describe in detail the estimation procedure of the two models.

7.4.1.1 Modified Jones model in cross-section

Dechow et al. (1995) proposed a modified version of the Jones (1991) model. Firstly, coefficients for each cluster sector–year are estimated with the original Jones model as follows:

$$\frac{ACC_{jt}}{MTA_{jt}} = \alpha_{st}\left(\frac{1}{MTA_{jt}}\right) + \beta_{st}\left(\frac{\Delta NSALES_{jt}}{MTA_{jt}}\right) + u_{jt}, \tag{7.9}$$

where j firms are non-event companies belonging to the same two-digit activity sector of issuing firm i and the subscript s refers to the activity sector which the company i belongs to. ACC_{jt} and $\Delta NSALES_{jt}$ are current accruals and the change in net sales in year t for firm j, respectively. MTA_{jt} is the mean total assets from year $t-1$ to year t for firm j. This intra-industry cross-sectional regression is estimated for each issuing firm i and year in the test period (from year 0 to +3 relative to the IPO year).

Once the coefficients are estimated, Dechow et al. (1995) suggested an adjustment in the original Jones model in order to avoid errors in the estimation of discretionary accruals when there is discretional behavior through sales. With this modification, the abnormal current accruals are estimated for issuing firms as follows:

$$AACC_{it} = \left(\frac{ACC_{it}}{MTA_{it}}\right) - \left[\hat{\alpha}_{st}\left(\frac{1}{MTA_{it}}\right) + \hat{\beta}_{st}\left(\frac{\overbrace{\Delta NSALES_{it} - \Delta TR_{it}}^{\text{adjustment}}}{MTA_{it}}\right)\right], \tag{7.10}$$

where $AACC_{it}$ is the abnormal component of current accruals and ΔTR_{it} is the change in trade receivable for the issuing company i in year t. The subscript s refers to the activity sector which firm i belongs to.

7.4.1.2 Poveda model in cross-section

Poveda (2005) proposed a new approach to estimate the abnormal component of current accruals. The main aim of this proposition is to avoid using potentially managed variables as regressors, such as sales, mitigating the simultaneity problems characteristic in accruals estimations. In addition, he suggested a desegregate estimation in order to control the possibility of a different reaction in inventory, sales, or purchases to the level of activity. With this idea, coefficients for each cluster sector–year are estimated with the following specification:

$$\left.\begin{aligned}
\frac{NSALES_{jt}}{MTA_{jt}} &= \alpha_{st} + \beta_{1st}\frac{CFS_{jt}}{MTA_{jt}} + v_{jt} \\
\frac{NP_{jt}}{MTA_{jt}} &= \gamma_{st} + \beta_{2st}\frac{CFP_{jt}}{MTA_{jt}} + \omega_{jt} \\
\frac{\Delta INVENT_{jt}}{MTA_{jt}} &= \pi_{st} + \beta_{3st}\frac{CFP_{jt}}{MTA_{jt}} + \beta_{4st}\frac{CFS_{jt}}{MTA_{jt}} + \delta_{jt}
\end{aligned}\right\}, \tag{7.11}$$

where j firms are non-event companies belonging to the same two-digit activity sector of issuing firm i and the subscript s refers to the activity sector that the company i belongs to. $NSALES_{jt}$ is the value of net sales, MTA_{jt} is the mean total assets from year $t-1$ to year t, CFS_{jt} is the cash flow generated by sales and services, NP_{jt} is the value of net purchases, CFP_{jt} is the cash flow generated by purchases and $\Delta INVENT_{jt}$ is the inventory variation, for firm j in year t. Just like with the Jones model, this cross-sectional regression is estimated for each issuing firm i and year in the test period (from year 0 to +3 relative to the IPO year).

Then, the abnormal current accrual of offering firms is estimated as follows:

$$AACC_{it} = \left[\frac{NSALES_{it}}{MTA_{it}} + \frac{NP_{it}}{MTA_{it}} + \frac{\Delta INVENT_{it}}{MTA_{it}} \right]$$

$$- \left[\hat{\alpha}_{st} + \hat{\gamma}_{st} + \hat{\pi}_{st} + (\hat{\beta}_{1st} + \hat{\beta}_{4st}) \frac{CFS_{it}}{MTA_{it}} + (\hat{\beta}_{2st} + \hat{\beta}_{3st}) \frac{CFP_{it}}{MTA_{it}} \right] \qquad (7.12)$$

The Poveda (2005) model focuses on fundamental accruals related to accelerating the recognition of credit sales, and/or postponing the accounting of purchases, and/or the overvaluation of year-end inventory. Therefore, a risk of manipulation is assumed in other working capital accounts, which is not detected by the model (Type II error). However, as the model pays attention to accounts specifically controlled by the accruals models, the probability of a Type I error is minimized – that is, the probability of detecting manipulation when there is none. We consider this aspect of the model to be highly appropriate in our context of detecting earnings management around initial public offerings.

7.4.2   Panel-data approach

In order to check the robustness of the results, we also include the estimation of the two models using panel-data analysis, thus taking into account temporal patterns that can affect accrual components. In particular, we employ as estimation sample sector-panels with non-event firms requiring temporal series with a minimum of four observations.

In addition to the simultaneity problem that arises if regressors are not orthogonal, which has been mitigated by the Poveda (2005) model by including cash flow explicative variables, we also had to bear in mind that, owing to the data employed in the area of earnings management, explicative variables would probably be correlated with regression residuals. Thus, to avoid the endogeneity problem, we introduce an unobservable heterogeneity component into the panel-data models. This component enables us to control individual characteristics that are not observable, or not identified by investors, but which could be correlated with the residual employed as a proxy for discretion. So models are estimated with a fixed effects approach.

The modified Jones (1991) model in panel data is estimated as follows:

$$\frac{ACC_{jt}}{MTA_{jt}} = \eta_j + \sum_{y=1991}^{2002} DY_y \lambda_y + \alpha_s \left(\frac{1}{MTA_{jt}} \right) + \beta_s \left(\frac{\Delta NSALES_{jt}}{MTA_{jt}} \right) + u_{jt} \qquad (7.13)$$

and the panel-data Poveda (2005) model as follows:

$$\left. \begin{array}{l} \dfrac{NSALES_{jt}}{MTA_{jt}} = \mu_j + \displaystyle\sum_{y=1991}^{2002} DY_y \rho_y + \alpha_s + \beta_{1s} \dfrac{CFS_{jt}}{MTA_{jt}} + v_{jt} \\[3mm] \dfrac{NP_{jt}}{MTA_{jt}} = \eta_j + \displaystyle\sum_{y=1991}^{2002} DY_y \lambda_y + \gamma_s + \beta_{2s} \dfrac{CFP_{jt}}{MTA_{jt}} + \omega_{jt} \\[3mm] \dfrac{\Delta INVENT_{jt}}{MTA_{jt}} = \tau_j + \displaystyle\sum_{y=1991}^{2002} DY_y \phi_y + \pi_s + \beta_{3s} \dfrac{CFS_{jt}}{MTA_{jt}} + \beta_{4s} \dfrac{CFS}{MTA_{jt}} + \delta_{j\tau} \end{array} \right\} . \qquad (7.14)$$

The variables are the same as in the cross-sectional approach, except for the introduction of the unobservable heterogeneity coefficients in each equation, and the year dummy variables $\{DY_y: y = 1991, ..., 2002\}$ to identify possible changes in mean current accruals based on the economic cycle. Once the model is estimated using samples of sector-panels clear of earnings management, coefficients are used to predict the abnormal component, as explained in the cross-sectional approach.

7.4.3 Performance-matched abnormal accruals

As pointed out in Fields et al. (2001), the most relevant problem in using abnormal accruals models to test earnings management is the specification error when sample firms have extreme financial performance. Dechow et al. (1995) examined the specification and power of abnormal accruals models, concluding that the rejection rates always exceed the nominal size of earnings management tests. Later research by Guay et al. (1996), Healy (1996), and Dechow et al. (1998) has also verified the correlation between abnormal accruals estimated by common accrual models and firm performance. The problem could be explained as a measure error econometric question using the pioneer framework proposed by McNichols and Wilson (1988). Given that the discretionary accruals are not observable by researchers, we work with an estimation based on abnormal accruals models, so we measure discretionary accruals with an error:

$$DAP_{it}^m = DA_{it} + \eta_{it}^m, \tag{7.15}$$

where DAP_{it}^m is the discretionary accrual proxy for the firm i in year t estimated using the model m; DA_{it} is the discretionary accrual for the firm i in year t; and η_{it}^m is a measure error induced by model m for the firm i in year t.

This measure error is not an uncorrelated white noise and it has been demonstrated in the above referenced papers that a correlation between this measure error and firm economic performance exists. It is this correlation that causes the serious inference problems advocated by Fields et al. (2001). As discussed in Kothari et al. (2005), to formally model accruals as a function of performance could be a solution, but doing so requires imposing a specific functional form linking accruals to performance. The alternative proposed by these authors consists of controlling for the impact of performance on estimated discretionary accruals using a performance-matched firm's discretionary accrual. Their results clearly indicate that matching on ROA provides the best specified and more powerful measures of discretionary accruals. Moreover, Kothari et al. (2005) showed that performance matching is critical to design well-specified tests of earnings management.

The procedure that we have followed to obtain the performance-matched abnormal accruals consists of matching IPO firms' abnormal accruals, estimated with the models presented in sections 7.4.1 and 7.4.2, with the closest non-IPO firm in terms of ROA in the same year and industry. The non-IPO firms have been filtered to extract from control samples any event that could be inducing earnings management, like SEOs, merges, etc. The assumption underlying this procedure, based on Kothari et al. (2005), is that the real discretionary accruals of the control firm are zero or near to zero, and the unique component of discretionary accruals proxy is due to the common measure error induced by performance:

$$\text{MDAP}^m_{\text{event firm},t} = \text{DAP}^m_{\text{event firm},t} - \text{DAP}^m_{\text{control firm},t}$$

$$\text{MDAP}^m_{\text{event firm},t} = \left(\underbrace{\text{DA}_{\text{event firm},t}}_{\substack{\text{Earnings Management} \\ => \text{DA} \neq 0}} + \eta^m_{\text{event firm},t} \right) - \left(\underbrace{\text{DA}_{\text{control firm},t}}_{\substack{\text{No Earnings Management} \\ => \text{DA} \cong 0}} + \eta^m_{\text{control firm},t} \right) \qquad (7.16)$$

$$\text{MDAP}^m_{\text{event firm},t} = (\text{DA}_{\text{event firm},t} + \underbrace{(\eta^m_{\text{event firm},t} - \eta^m_{\text{control firm},t})}_{\text{ROA matched} => \cong 0} \cong \text{DA}_{\text{event firm},t}$$

where MDAP^m_{it} is the performance-matched discretionary accruals proxy for firm i in year t estimated using the model m; DAP^m_{it} is the discretionary accruals proxy for the firm i in year t estimated using the model m; DA_{it} is the discretionary accrual for the firm i in year t; and η^m_{it} is the measure error induced by model m for the firm i in year t.

7.5 Earnings management in initial public offerings

7.5.1 ROA evolution in IPO firms

The IPO process is especially susceptible to earnings management because of the high information asymmetry at the time of the offering, when investors have little knowledge of the firm and security analysts are initiating the coverage of the company. In this context, firms have incentives to engage in opportunistic behaviors reporting high earnings to maximize the offering price. In Figure 7.4 we can observe the evolution of accounting earnings from the year of the IPO to three following years.

As illustrated in Figure 7.4(A), the return on assets (ROA) presents its maximum value at the year of the offering to revert after that in subsequent years. Moreover, this pattern is detected both for mean and medians values. In order to control for the normal amount of mean reversion in ROA, in Figure 7.4(C) we plot the performance of IPO firms' ROA in excess from their matched sector–year ROA medians of non-IPO firms. We verify how the matched ROA reproduces the same pattern in mean and medians. These results suggest an effort of IPO firms to manage upward their earnings in the event year, reverting into a clear decline in the following years. Panels B and D of Figure 7.4 show the time profile of the extraordinary and non-recurrent items (REX) of IPO firms' net income. The pattern observed for mean values is similar to that observed in ROA, before and after adjusting by the matched sector–year non-IPO firms. Nevertheless, for median values the evolution is not so clear. These results suggest that there are singular IPO firms that report unusually high REX at the event year in order to maximize the net income reported, but it is not a generalized practice between IPO firms. This is consistent with the different accounting choices for REX and ROA. The REX is clearly observable by investors, whereas earnings management practices with ROA, through discretionary accruals to influence working capital accounts, is hardly noticeable by investors.

Table 7.3 reports statistical significance of ROA performance. In panel A, we can observe a progressive decline in ROA after the offering that is significantly different from zero for the 1-, 2-, and 3-year periods. The year after the offering, IPO firms experience a decrease of 1.35%, which is statistically significant, having a p-value of

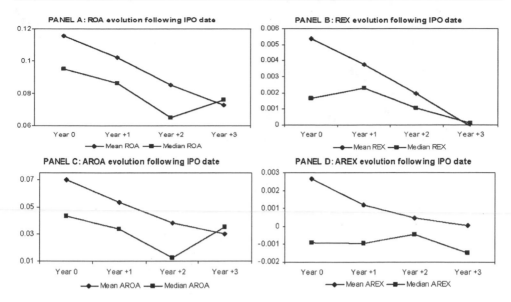

Figure 7.4 Accounting profits following initial public offerings. ROA: Return on assets; REX: Extraordinary and non-recurrent items deflated by lagged total assets; AROA: Abnormal ROA measured as the excess from the median ROA of non-IPO firms in the same sector–year cluster; AREX: Abnormal REX measured as the excess from the median REX of non-IPO firms in the same sector–year cluster

Table 7.3 ROA performance following initial public offerings

	Obs.	Mean	p-value mean	Median	p-value median
Panel A: ROA variation following IPO date					
VROA1	40	−0.013	(0.01)	−0.007	(0.01)
VROA2	40	−0.030	(0.00)	−0.024	(0.00)
VROA3	40	−0.043	(0.00)	−0.023	(0.00)
Panel B: AROA variation following IPO date					
VAROA1	40	−0.011	(0.05)	−0.005	(0.09)
VAROA2	40	−0.028	(0.00)	−0.022	(0.00)
VAROA3	40	−0.035	(0.00)	−0.013	(0.19)

VROAj: Variation in return on assets from IPO year to year j; VAROAj: Variation in abnormal ROA measured as the excess from the median ROA of non-IPO firms in the same sector–year cluster, from IPO year to year j; Obs.: Number of observations; Mean: Mean of the VROA; p-value mean: p-value of the two-sided test of the null hypothesis that Mean(VROA) = 0; p-value median: p-value of the Wilcoxon robust test of the null hypothesis that Median(VROA) = 0. Significant coefficients of at least 10% nominal size are shown in bold.

1.2%. If we extend the horizon to 2 years (3 years) after the IPO, the decline is greater than 3% (4%) and statistically significant with a near zero p-value. Focusing on median values, exactly the same pattern can be corroborated in ROA.

Focusing on Table 7.3(B), we can observe how the decline in IPO firms' ROA is significantly higher than for matched sector–year non-IPO firms. The mean decline in matched ROA for the first year after the issue is more than 1%, statistically significant with a p-value of 5%. For the 2- and 3-year periods the variation of the decrease is even greater, with p-values very close to zero. If we analyze median values for matched ROA, once again results show a decline in the 1-, 2-, and 3-year periods, although in this case the decrease for the 3-year horizon is not statistically significant.

7.5.2 Performance-matched abnormal accruals in IPO firms

Up till now, earnings management has not been tested and we can only verify that IPO firms experience abnormal reversals in their ROA levels after the event. The next stage is to test explicitly the existence of earnings management in the IPO year. To do this, we use the performance-matched abnormal accruals measures that were described in section 7.4. The main results are summarized in Table 7.4.

In Table 7.4(A) we observe how the performance-matched abnormal accruals mean for IPO firms, estimated with the modified Jones model in cross-section, is positive and significantly different from zero in the issue year, with a p-value of 6%. In subsequent years the values are not statistically different from zero, suggesting

Table 7.4 Performance-matched abnormal accruals following initial public offerings

	Obs.	Mean MDAP	p-value mean MDAP	Median MDAP	p-value median MDAP
Panel A: Performance-matched abnormal accruals from cross-section modified Jones model					
Event year	37	**0.058**	(0.06)	0.027	(0.25)
Year +1	37	−0.032	(0.39)	−0.031	(0.61)
Year +2	37	−0.035	(0.27)	−0.020	(0.18)
Year +3	37	0.026	(0.28)	0.004	(0.25)
Panel B: Performance-matched abnormal accruals from panel data modified Jones model					
Event year	39	**0.064**	(0.08)	0.033	(0.33)
Year +1	39	−0.017	(0.57)	−0.010	(0.74)
Year +2	39	**−0.071**	(0.00)	−0.049	(0.19)
Year +3	39	0.025	(0.36)	0.035	(0.33)
Panel C: Performance-matched abnormal accruals from cross-section Poveda model					
Event year	37	**0.133**	(0.00)	**0.060**	(0.07)
Year +1	37	−0.034	(0.18)	−0.020	(0.40)
Year +2	37	−0.032	(0.19)	−0.008	(0.74)
Year +3	37	0.029	(0.17)	0.040	(0.25)
Panel D: Performance-matched abnormal accruals from panel data Poveda model					
Event year	39	**0.076**	(0.01)	**0.024**	(0.00)
Year +1	39	−0.021	(0.39)	−0.009	(0.52)
Year +2	39	−0.026	(0.21)	−0.020	(0.02)
Year +3	39	0.024	(0.23)	0.017	(0.52)

Obs.: Number of observations; Mean MDAP: Mean of the matched performance abnormal accruals from the model indicated in each panel; p-value mean: p-value of the two-sided test of the null hypothesis that Mean(MDAP) = 0; p-value median: p-value of the Wilcoxon robust test of the null hypothesis that Median(MDAP) = 0; Event year: Year of IPO; Year +j: Year j relative to the IPO year. Significant coefficients of at least 10% nominal size are shown in bold.

that there are only earnings management practices in the IPO year. This pattern is also observed in medians, but without statistical significance.

When we estimate the matched abnormal accruals using the panel-data version of the modified Jones model, in Table 7.4(B), the pattern is very similar but with a more sharp reversal in the 2-year post-offering period. If we focus on the event year, again a positive and statistically significant abnormal accrual suggests that IPO firms are making an effort to report higher earnings in this year. Nevertheless, in terms of medians, statistical p-values do not allow us to corroborate this potential opportunistic behavior.

To check the results suggested by the analysis of earnings management measures based on the modified Jones model, panels C and D display the results of an alternative model that uses different variables and it is estimated by components using cash flow regressors. In Table 7.4(C), with the cross-section version of the Poveda model, we observe that, as in the IPO year, the performance-matched abnormal accruals mean is positive and statistically significant, with a p-value close to zero. In the subsequent years these abnormal accruals reverse and lose their statistical relevance. If we focus on median values, the results corroborate this pattern, with a median value in the IPO year of 0.06 and a statistical p-value of 7%.

If we move to Table 7.4(D), using another specification of the Poveda model to estimate abnormal accruals with a panel-data approach, the results are maintained and suggest the same behavior. An analysis of means reveals a positive value of performance-matched abnormal accruals in the IPO year, with a p-value of 1%. In the remainder of the years the presence of these atypical values is not observed. Practically the same pattern is detected if we focus on the median values of the performance-matched abnormal accruals. A clearly significant and positive median, with a p-value close to zero, suggests that firms are using discretionary accruals to inflate their earnings in the IPO year.

The main results presented in Table 7.4 are shown graphically in Figure 7.5, where the same pattern can be observed in all models, with the highest abnormal accrual in

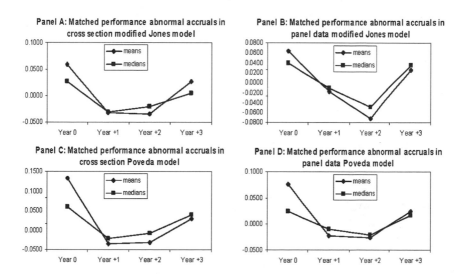

Figure 7.5 Performance-matched abnormal accruals in IPO firms

year 0, followed by a severe reversal in years +1 and +2. In year +3 a pickup in abnormal accruals occurs, but is not statistically different from zero in any case. The main conclusion from this section is that earnings management practices are detected in the IPO year, followed by a strong reversal the year after.

7.5.3   Earnings management and subsequent ROA reversals in IPO firms

Having analyzed two different models of abnormal accruals, with two different estimation procedures applied to each one, and adjusting all measures using control samples matched by ROA in the same cluster sector–year, results suggest that IPO firms implement earnings management techniques to maximize IPO prices. In this context, it is important to corroborate if the abnormal accruals detected in year 0 are related to the decline observed in ROA in the years after the IPO. For this, we estimate the equation:

$$\text{VROA}_{i\tau} = \alpha + \beta \, \text{MDAP}_i^0 + u_i, \tag{7.17}$$

where $\text{VROA}_{i\tau}$ is the variation in return on assets for firm i from IPO year to year τ, MDAP_i^0 is the matched abnormal accrual estimated for firm i in year 0, and u_i is the residual term.

It is expected to find a negative value of beta coefficient, reflecting that a higher level of positive earnings management in year 0 will imply a more pronounced decline in subsequent ROA. Furthermore, modifying the time horizon, τ, it can be determined for how long the earnings management in the IPO year is affecting subsequent results. In this sense, as we are using working capital accruals that do not include long-term components, it is expected to find a relation in the short term but not in long horizons.

In Table 7.5(A) it can be observed that the beta coefficient of equation (7.17) is negative in practically all cases, showing that the greater the artificial increase in the IPO year, the stronger the ROA reversal in subsequent periods. Using the modified Jones model (cross-section and panel data) to measure IPO year earnings management, the reversal in ROA in the year after the IPO induced by this abnormal component is negative (-0.064 and -0.043) and statistically significant, with p-values of 6%. For the 2- and 3-year periods after the IPO, the coefficients are also negative but they are not statistically significant.

If the Poveda model (cross-section and panel data) is used to estimate the amount of accruals potentially managed in the IPO year, the results are quite similar to those reported for the modified Jones model. The strong reversal in ROA produced by the year 0 abnormal accruals is detected in year +1 with a negative beta coefficient and is statistically significant, with p-values of 2% and zero. Again, the relation between year 0 abnormal accruals and ROA reversal for years +2 and +3 is not statistically significant.

As pointed out by Rangan (1998), firms that experience rapid sales growth are likely to attract new competing firms into their industries, producing an increment in competition and a decrement in subsequent profit margins. In this way, IPO firms with strong sales growth rate in year 0 will show ROA declines in subsequent years that are not related to earnings management practices. Moreover, Rangan (1998) also pointed out that for firms that invest in year 0 in projects that generate profits only from year

Table 7.5 Matched abnormal accruals in year 0 and subsequent ROA changes

	Obs.	VROA1		VROA2		VROA3	
		β MDAP	p-value β	β MDAP	p-value β	β MDAP	p-value β
mdapcs_jm	37	−0.064	(0.06)	−0.054	(0.52)	−0.058	(0.53)
mdappd_jm	39	−0.043	(0.06)	−0.014	(0.79)	−0.002	(0.96)
mdapcs_fp	37	−0.068	(0.02)	−0.035	(0.56)	0.019	(0.79)
mdappd_fp	39	−0.078	(0.00)	−0.087	(0.20)	−0.072	(0.31)

Panel A: $.\text{VROA}_{it} = \alpha + \beta \cdot \text{MDAP}_i^0 + u_i$,

	Obs.	VROA1		VROA2		VROA3	
		β^* MDAP	p-value β^*	β^* MDAP	p-value β^*	β^* MDAP	p-value β^*
mdapcs_jm	37	−0.061	(0.08)	−0.046	(0.56)	−0.048	(0.59)
mdappd_jm	39	−0.062	(0.07)	−0.044	(0.41)	0.009	(0.51)
mdapcs_fp	37	−0.052	(0.01)	−0.057	(0.46)	−0.047	(0.90)
mdappd_fp	39	−0.064	(0.00)	−0.079	(0.21)	−0.063	(0.35)

Panel B: $\text{VROA}_{it} = \alpha^* + \beta^* \cdot \text{MDAP}_i^0 + \gamma^* \cdot \text{SLGRW}_i^0 + \lambda^* \cdot \text{PPEGRW}_i^0 + u_i^*$.
VROA_{it}: variation in return on assets for firm i from IPO year to year τ; MDAP_i^0: matched abnormal accrual estimated for firm i in year 0; β: estimated coefficient for MDAP_i^0 from the regression indicated in each panel; p-value β: p-value of the two-sided test of the null hypothesis $\beta = 0$ performed with robust variances; mdapcs_jm: matched performance abnormal accruals estimated in cross-section using the modified Jones model; mdappd_jm: matched performance abnormal accruals estimated in panel data using the modified Jones model; mdapcs_fp: matched performance abnormal accruals estimated in cross-section using the Poveda model; mdappd_fp: matched performance abnormal accruals estimated in panel data using the Poveda model; Obs.: number of observations available in each estimation; SLGRW_i^0: sales growth rate for firm i in the IPO year; PPEGRW_i^0; property, plant, and equipment growth rate for firm i in the IPO year. Significant coefficients of at least 10% nominal size are shown in bold.

2 onwards, this will be reflected in systematic ROA decline in year +1. To control these normal reversals in ROA, sales growth ratio and property, plant and equipment growth ratio have been introduced as explanatory variables in equation (7.17).

Table 7.5(B) reports the beta coefficients estimated after controlling for these variables. Results are very similar to those obtained in Table 7.5(A). The coefficient on abnormal accruals remains negative and statistically significant for all measures of earning management when we focus on 1-year ROA reversal. For the 2- and 3-year periods after the IPO, the change in ROA seems to be negative related to the event year abnormal accruals, but coefficients lack statistical significance.

We can conclude that the results point to the existence of manipulative accounting practices to overstate reported earnings around the IPOs. Moreover, abnormal accruals introduced by managers in year 0 imply a reversion in IPO firms' ROA for the following year. In this context, the question arising is if these practices have any relation with the stock price underperformance suffered by IPO firms in the years following this decision. In other words, do abnormal accruals lead to issuers' overvaluation, which is gradually corrected by the market in the post-offering period, thus causing underperformance?

7.6   Earnings management and post-offering stock return underperformance

We would now like to turn our attention to the question of whether the poor post-IPO stock return performance can be explained by previous earnings management. If buyers are guided by earnings but are unaware that earnings are inflated by the generous use of accruals, they could pay too high a price. As information about the firm is revealed over time in the post-offering period, investors will gradually temper their optimism. Other things being equal, the greater the earnings management at the time of the public offering, the larger the ultimate price correction. Therefore, here we examine whether unusually abnormal accruals detected in the IPO year predict the cross-sectional variation in post-offering long-run stock return performance.

As explained previously, we use accruals data from the first public financial statement. To allow investors in the market to implement the strategy, the accrual information should be available prior to the return accumulation period. This data availability constraint on the accruals forces us to examine post-issue returns beginning the month after the first public financial statement, as proposed by Teoh et al. (1998a) and Rangan (1998). In this way, we apply the methodological procedures explained in section 3 to analyze the stock return performance of IPO firms after the publication of the IPO year financial statement.

Figure 7.6 shows the mean abnormal compound return for the IPO sample during the 36 months following the first public financial statement. As this publication is several months after the public offering, in this figure we do not observe the positive abnormal returns detected in Figure 7.2 for the first months after the IPO date. Here we observe that, from the second month, adjusted returns are negative and they experience a progressive sharp decrease till month 24. From this month abnormal returns, although still highly negative, experience a slight improvement.

Table 7.6 reports average abnormal compound returns for the 1-, 2-, and 3-year periods following the first public financial statement. Market-adjusted returns are negative and statistically significant for the three periods analyzed. In particular, for the 1-year period the mean abnormal return of IPO firms is −14.08%, with a statistical

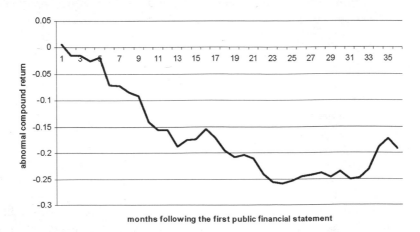

months following the first public financial statement

Figure 7.6 IPO firms' abnormal returns after the first public sector statement

Table 7.6 IPO firms' stock return following the first public financial statement

Analysis period (months)	AACoR (%)	Traditional t-statistic	Bootstrap p-value	Skewness coeff.	Skewness adjusted t	Bootstrap p-value
12	−14.08	−2.98	(0.01)	0.64	−2.69	(0.01)
24	−25.51	−4.40	(0.00)	0.90	−3.51	(0.00)
36	−24.17	−2.53	(0.02)	0.45	−2.37	(0.02)

Panel A: Mean abnormal compound returns for IPO firms in the 1-, 2-, and 3-year periods following the first public financial statement. This panel also reports results of traditional t-test and skewness-adjusted t-test using the bootstrap technique to evaluate statistical significance.

Analysis period (months)	$\hat{\alpha}_p$ (%)	t-statistic	p-value
12	−0.74	−1.86	(0.06)
24	−1.00	−3.02	(0.00)
36	−0.56	−2.14	(0.03)

Panel B: Abnormal monthly mean return in the post-offering period estimated with the Fama–French model in calendar-time regressions.

p-value of 1%. For the 2-year period, abnormal returns get worse with a mean of −25.51%, also significant at the 1% level. Finally, although abnormal returns undergo a slight recovery for the 3-year period, abnormal mean return is −24.17%, again statistically significant at the 1% level. Comparing these results with those obtained in Table 7.2, we observe that here abnormal returns are more negative for the three periods analyzed. This is due to the later accumulation period, which implies the exclusion of the first post-offerings months, where abnormal returns are positive.

In the same way as in section 7.3, we also analyze the abnormal monthly mean return estimated with the Fama and French (1993) model in calendar-time regressions. Results reported in Table 7.6(B) confirm the evidence in Table 7.6(A); the intercept from the Fama–French model, α_p, which measures the abnormal monthly mean return of IPO firms, is negative and statistically significant for the three horizons analyzed.

Our key objective is to evaluate the extent to which managed accruals have an influence on these long-run abnormal stock returns. To address this topic we first examine differences in stock returns among three tercile portfolios grouped by levels of year 0 discretionary accruals. Alternatively, we carry out a regression analysis of post-issue returns on year 0 discretionary accruals.

7.6.1 Post-IPO returns by performance-matched abnormal accruals terciles

Here we study the relation between discretionary accruals and post-IPO returns by examining the stock return performance of tercile portfolios grouped by levels of year 0 discretionary accruals. Terciles are formed by sorting sample firms based on their performance-matched abnormal accruals. All the analyses have been carried out sorting IPO firms on the basis of raw abnormal accruals with similar results.

Figure 7.7 shows the abnormal return performance for the IPO firms grouped in terciles by performance-matched abnormal accruals. We employ the four alternative models explained earlier to estimate these abnormal accounting adjustments. Figure 7.7(A) illustrates results when the modified Jones model in cross-section is employed to estimate abnormal accruals. The figure shows that IPO firms in the first conservative tercile do not underperform, the second tercile suffers from a small drift, while the third aggressive tercile underperforms dramatically. Thus, results shown as tercile returns are monotonic: the higher the discretionary accruals, the poorer the stock returns performance. Figure 7.7(B) displays results when the modified Jones model is estimated employing sector panel data. We observe the same repetitious pattern in returns among terciles.

Alternatively, we repeat the analysis estimating abnormal accruals with the model proposed by Poveda (2005). In Figure 7.7(C) we can observe the abnormal returns of IPO firms' terciles grouped on the basis of abnormal accruals estimated with the Poveda model in cross-secction. Results are qualitatively similar to those obtained with the Jones model. Abnormal returns for the first conservative tercile are near to zero. The second tercile underperforms slightly, whereas the most aggressive tercile suffers from a dramatic decrease. Figure 7.7(D) again shows this monotonic pattern when the Poveda model is used with panel data.

Table 7.7 reports abnormal compound returns and their statistical significance for the three tercile portfolios, in the 1-, 2-, and 3-year periods. Panel A displays results when the modified Jones model in cross-section is employed to estimate discretionary accruals. As Figure 7.7 illustrated, the higher the discretionary accruals, the poorer the stock returns performance. For the 1-year period the mean abnormal return for IPO firms in the first conservative tercile is 1.66%, becoming worse for the second tercile with a mean value of −4.66%. Both values are not statistically different from zero using the traditional t-test or the adjusted t-statistic. Looking at the third aggressive tercile, we observe how the mean abnormal return is much more negative with a value of −33.21%, statistically significant with a p-value of zero.

If we focus on tercile returns for the second year, we detect a very similar pattern; terciles with higher discretionary accruals experience more negative abnormal returns. In particular, the mean adjusted returns for the first and second terciles are −2.98% and −21.71% respectively, and they are not statistically significant, whereas the abnormal return for the third aggressive tercile is −37.31%, highly significant with both tests. Centering our attention on the 3-year period, once again tercile returns show the same behavior. In this case, the mean abnormal returns for the first and second terciles are 0.02% and −20.76% respectively, and they are not statistically significant; the adjusted return for the third aggressive tercile is −29.21% and is statistically significant. Thus, the results in Table 7.7(A) confirm that the post-IPO stock return underperformance is larger for companies with higher discretionary accruals. In fact, negative abnormal compound returns are only statistically significant for the aggressive accruals' tercile.

Table 7.7(B) displays results when the modified Jones model is used with sector panel data. We observe exactly the same pattern in returns among terciles. For the three temporal horizons analyzed, abnormal returns are progressively more negative for the more aggressive terciles, the negative abnormal returns being statistically significant only for the most aggressive tercile portfolio.

Panels C and D report results when the Poveda model is employed to estimate discretionary accruals, in cross-section and with panel data respectively. The same pattern

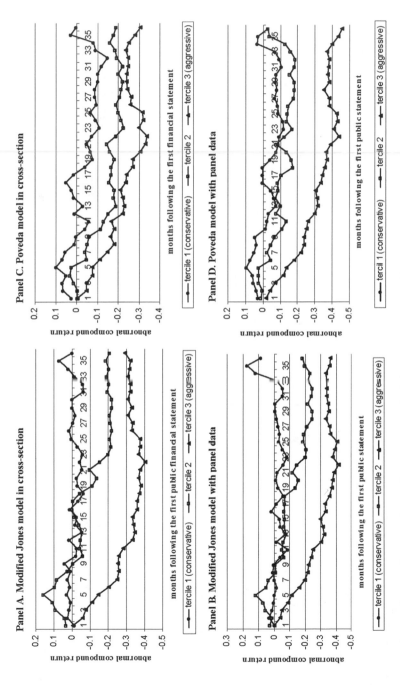

Figure 7.7 IPO firms' abnormal returns by performance-matched discretionary accruals

Table 7.7 IPO firms' stock return by performance-matched discretionary accruals terciles

Terciles	12-month period			24-month period			36-month period		
	T1	T2	T3	T1	T2	T3	T1	T2	T3
Panel A: Modified Jones model in cross-section									
AACoR (%)	1.66	−4.66	−33.21	−2.98	−21.71	−37.31	0.02	−20.76	−29.21
t-statistic	0.14	−0.49	−3.76	−0.20	−1.68	−5.64	0.00	−0.90	−2.41
Bootstr. p-value	(0.85)	(0.70)	(0.00)	(0.89)	(0.23)	(0.00)	(1.00)	(0.38)	(0.04)
Skew. adj. t	0.16	−0.44	−4.37	−0.17	−1.37	−4.11	0.02	−0.93	−1.35
Bootstr. p-value	(0.86)	(0.67)	(0.00)	(0.87)	(0.21)	(0.00)	(1.00)	(0.38)	(0.10)
Panel B: Modified Jones model with panel data									
AACoR (%)	−1.73	−5.95	−30.61	−5.85	−20.77	−39.28	8.57	−18.13	−36.53
t-statistic	−0.13	−0.69	−3.79	−0.36	−2.04	−5.23	0.34	−1.50	−1.97
Bootstr. p-value	(0.91)	(0.55)	(0.00)	(0.75)	(0.08)	(0.00)	(0.72)	(0.24)	(0.05)
Skew. adj. t	−0.11	−0.64	−3.93	−0.34	−1.55	−3.83	0.36	−1.32	−1.82
Bootstr. p-value	(0.90)	(0.53)	(0.00)	(0.74)	(0.17)	(0.00)	(0.72)	(0.21)	(0.09)
Panel C: Poveda model in cross-section									
AACoR (%)	1.24	−15.40	−22.09	−9.06	−21.59	−31.91	0.51	−19.02	−30.48
t-statistic	0.10	−1.73	−2.65	−0.70	−1.93	−2.54	0.03	−0.91	−1.42
Bootstr. p-value	(0.87)	(0.21)	(0.03)	(0.57)	(0.13)	(0.02)	(0.93)	(0.44)	(0.18)
Skew. adj. t	0.15	−1.43	−2.21	−0.63	−1.19	−1.82	0.08	−0.82	−1.46
Bootstr. p-value	(0.89)	(0.11)	(0.04)	(0.56)	(0.38)	(0.05)	(0.94)	(0.39)	(0.19)
Panel D: Poveda model with panel data									
AACoR (%)	−3.28	−7.66	−29.82	−11.60	−13.80	−43.01	−2.85	−2.61	−45.55
t-statistic	−0.30	−0.68	−4.25	−0.79	−1.23	−5.93	−0.15	−0.13	−2.39
Bootstr. p-value	(0.77)	(0.59)	(0.00)	(0.46)	(0.44)	(0.01)	(0.91)	(0.94)	(0.02)
Skew. adj. t	−0.30	−0.58	−3.95	−0.76	−0.97	−3.19	−0.14	−0.08	−2.57
Bootstr. p-value	(0.77)	(0.56)	(0.00)	(0.44)	(0.43)	(0.00)	(0.91)	(0.93)	(0.03)

This table displays the mean abnormal compound return for IPO firms' terciles based on discretionary accruals in the 1-, 2-, and 3-year periods. It also reports results of traditional t-test and skewness-adjusted t-test using the bootstrap technique to evaluate statistical significance of abnormal returns. T1 is the conservative tercile (i.e. the tercile formed by IPO firms with lower performance-matched discretionary adjusted accruals), T2 is the middle tercile, and T3 is the aggressive one, formed by firms with higher earnings management.

is observed as with the modified Jones model. Whatever the analysis period, abnormal returns are monotonically more negative for more aggressive terciles. Moreover, once again negative abnormal returns are statistically significant exclusively for the third aggressive tercile.

Alternatively, we can investigate the relation between previous earnings management and post-IPO stock returns employing the calendar-time approach. As we explained in section 7.3, this procedure analyzes the offering firms' returns over the 1-, 2-, and 3-year post-IPO period by examining the strategy of holding a portfolio which is made up, in each calendar month, of the stocks of firms that have an IPO over the last 12, 24, and 36 months, respectively.

In Table 7.6(B) we observed how the abnormal monthly mean return of the calendar portfolio was statistically negative for the 1-, 2-, and 3-year periods. To detect if there is any relationship between earnings management and these negative post-offering abnormal monthly mean returns, we apply the calendar-time approach to each accrual tercile. The results are shown in Table 7.8, applying the four alternative models to estimate discretionary accounting adjustments. Panel A displays the results obtained with the modified Jones model in cross-section. For the 1-year period, the abnormal monthly mean return, $\hat{\alpha}_p$, for IPO firms in the first conservative tercile is 0.7%, becoming worse for the second tercile with a monthly mean value of -0.28%. Anyway, both values lack statistical significance. Looking at the third aggressive tercile, we observe how the abnormal monthly mean return is much more negative with a value of -1.09%, significant with a statistical p-value of 6%.

If we focus on terciles for the second year, we detect a very similar pattern in their regression intercepts. Terciles with higher discretionary accruals experience more negative monthly abnormal returns. In particular, the intercepts from the Fama–French model for the first and second terciles are -0.34% and -0.54% respectively, and they are not statistically significant. However, the abnormal monthly mean return for the third aggressive tercile is -2.52%, significant with a statistical p-value of zero. Looking at the 3-year period, once again tercile returns show the same behavior. In this case, the abnormal monthly mean return for the first and second terciles are 0.01% and -0.27% respectively, and they are not statistically significant; the abnormal monthly return for the third aggressive tercile of -0.86% is statistically significant. Thus, results in Table 7.8(A) are consistent with those obtained with the abnormal compound return analysis and confirm that the post-IPO stock return underperformance is larger for companies with higher discretionary accruals. Moreover, and analogous to results in Table 7.7, negative monthly abnormal returns are only statistically significant for the aggressive accruals' tercile.

Table 7.8(B) shows results when the modified Jones model is used with sector panel data. We observe exactly the same monotonic pattern in the regression intercepts among terciles. For the three temporal periods, abnormal monthly returns are progressively more negative for the more aggressive terciles, the negative abnormal returns being statistically significant only for the most aggressive tercile portfolio.

Panels C and D report results when the Poveda model is used to estimate discretionary accruals, in cross-section and with panel data respectively. The results are qualitatively similar. For the three periods analyzed, monthly abnormal returns are monotonically more negative for more aggressive terciles, negative abnormal returns being statistically significant exclusively for the third tercile. Thus, the results in Table 7.8 indicate, like the previous abnormal compound return analyses,

Table 7.8 Calendar-time analysis by performance-matched discretionary accruals terciles

Terciles	12-month period			24-month period			36-month period		
	T1	T2	T3	T1	T2	T3	T1	T2	T3
Panel A: Modified Jones model in cross-section									
$\hat{\alpha}_p(\%)$	0.73	-0.28	-1.09	-0.34	-0.54	-2.52	0.01	-0.27	-0.86
t-statistic	0.99	-0.34	-1.88	-0.58	-0.86	-3.31	0.02	-0.59	-1.67
p-value	(0.32)	(0.73)	(0.06)	(0.56)	(0.39)	(0.00)	(0.99)	(0.56)	(0.09)
Panel B: Modified Jones model with panel data									
$\hat{\alpha}_p(\%)$	0.10	-1.29	-1.31	-0.30	-2.24	-2.82	0.19	-0.26	-1.28
t-statistic	0.15	-1.10	-2.07	-0.60	-1.67	-3.47	0.37	-0.31	-2.46
p-value	(0.88)	(0.27)	(0.04)	(0.55)	(0.10)	(0.00)	(0.71)	(0.76)	(0.01)
Panel C: Poveda model in cross-section									
$\hat{\alpha}_p(\%)$	0.37	-0.58	-0.91	-0.10	-0.45	-1.28	0.07	-0.23	-1.12
t-statistic	0.36	-0.77	-1.88	-0.15	-0.81	-2.06	0.15	-0.43	-2.16
p-value	(0.72)	(0.44)	(0.06)	(0.88)	(0.42)	(0.04)	(0.89)	(0.67)	(0.03)
Panel D: Poveda model with panel data									
$\hat{\alpha}_p(\%)$	0.30	-1.54	-1.38	0.31	-1.89	-2.65	0.37	-0.19	-1.20
t-statistic	0.29	-1.25	-2.28	0.36	-1.62	-3.63	0.58	-0.25	-2.42
p-value	(0.77)	(0.21)	(0.02)	(0.72)	(0.11)	(0.00)	(0.56)	(0.81)	(0.02)

This table shows the abnormal monthly mean return for IPO firms accruals' terciles in the 1-, 2-, and 3-year periods. The abnormal monthly mean return, $\hat{\alpha}_p$, is estimated as the intercept of the Fama–French model in calendar-time regressions. T1 is the conservative tercile (i.e. the tercile formed by IPO firms with lower performance-matched discretionary adjusted accruals), T2 is the middle tercile, and T3 is the aggressive one, formed by firms with higher earnings management.

that discretionary accruals in the IPO year explain the abnormal returns in subsequent years.

7.6.2   Post-IPO returns and earnings management: regression analysis

Here we employ a regression analysis to examine whether IPO year discretionary accruals can explain the subsequent poor stock price performance. With this aim, we first look at the relation between abnormal compound returns and the change in ROA following the issue by regressing the following equation:

$$ACoR_{i\tau} = \beta_0 + \beta_1 VROA_{i\tau} + \mu_{i\tau}, \tag{7.18}$$

where $ACoR_{i\tau}$ and $VROA_{i\tau}$ are the abnormal compound return and the change in return on assets of company i in period τ respectively; τ is the 1-, 2-, and 3-year period after the offering.

If the decline in stock prices after the offering is due to a gradual correction of market expectations as earnings reverse, a positive relationship between adjusted stock returns in the post-offering period and a change in ROA would be expected. So we anticipate a positive β_1 coefficient in equation (7.18). Furthermore, as shown in section 7.2, post-IPO earnings changes are partially explained by discretionary accounting accruals in the IPO year. The change in ROA is negatively related to IPO year abnormal accruals.

By substituting the expression for $VROA_{i\tau}$ in equation (7.17) into equation (7.18) we can link abnormal returns with earnings changes and IPO year discretionary accruals using a framework similar to that used by Rangan (1998) and then test if the market is surprised when earnings decline related to IPO year abnormal accruals. In this way,

$$ACoR_{i\tau} = \beta_0 + \beta_1 [\alpha_0 + \alpha_1 MDAP_i^0 + c_{it}] + \mu_{i\tau}, \tag{7.19}$$

Simplifying equation (7.18) and writing $\varepsilon_{i\tau}$ as $UE_{i\tau}$ gives us:

$$ACoR_{i\tau} = \gamma_0 + \gamma_1 UE_{i\tau} + \gamma_2 MDAP_i^0 + \mu_{i\tau}. \tag{7.20}$$

Then, abnormal compound returns in the post-offering period can be expressed as a function of two components. The first one, $UE_{i\tau}$, is the estimated residual from equation (7.17) and represents unexpected ROA variation that is not explained by the earnings management of the IPO year. The second components, $MDAP_i^0$, are performance-matched abnormal accruals for the IPO year, information that is available for investors at the beginning of the period over which abnormal returns are computed. In this context, if the market is efficient, it will react only to the unexpected earnings and not to abnormal accruals, so the γ_2 coefficient will be zero. However, if investors fail to understand the implications of these discretionary adjustments for ROA, γ_2 will be negative.

As different studies document that firm size and book-to-market ratio explain the cross-section variability in stock returns, we include the log of market capitalizations and book-to-market ratio as control variables in all regressions. However, to conserve space, we do not report coefficient estimates for these two control variables.

Table 7.9 displays the coefficient estimations of equation (7.18) as well as their p-values in parentheses. The lack of accounting information in some years entailed

Table 7.9 ROA changes and subsequent stock performance

	N	VROA$_1$		VROA$_2$		VROA$_3$	
		Coeff.	p-value	Coeff.	p-value	Coeff.	p-value
ACoR$_1$	30	**3.72**	(0.00)				
ACoR$_2$	30			**3.32**	(0.00)		
ACoR$_3$	27					**3.90**	(0.02)

This table displays coefficient estimations of equation (7.18) as well as their p-values in parentheses. ACoR$_1$, ACoR$_2$, and ACoR$_3$ are abnormal compound returns for the 1-, 2-, and 3-year post-offering periods respectively. VROA$_1$, VROA$_2$ and VROA$_3$ are the changes in return on assets for the 1-, 2-, and 3-year periods. Significant coefficients of at least 10% nominal size are shown in bold.

the reduction of the event sample. We estimate the regression for each temporal horizon with the number of events, N, with information available to compute the change in ROA.

For the 1-year post-issue period, the coefficient on VROA$_1$ is 3.72, with a zero statistical p-value. Therefore, a decrease in earnings implies a decline in abnormal returns of more than triple. When we focus on adjusted returns during the 2-year post-offering period, the coefficient of VROA$_2$ is also positive with a value of 3.32 and also highly significant, with a zero p-value. Thus, results for the 2-year post-offering period also confirm the significant positive relationship between the decline in earnings and the decrease in returns. Finally, the results obtained when analyzing abnormal compound returns for the 3-year period following the issue are also consistent with this positive relationship, with an estimated coefficient of 3.90, again statistically significant.

In general, the results of equation (7.18) indicate that there is a significant relationship between poor post-issue stock return performance and the decrease in earnings during the 1-, 2-, and 3-year periods after the offering, which is consistent with investors correcting expectations as earnings reverse.

Next, in Table 7.10, coefficient estimations of equation (7.20) and their p-values are reported. We employ the four alternative models to estimate abnormal accruals. The lack of certain information to estimate these variables entailed the reduction of the event sample. We run each regression with the number of events, N, with enough information to estimate abnormal accruals. When we focus on the 1-year post-issue period, the coefficient of matched discretionary accruals, MDAP^0, is statistically negative whatever the procedure used to estimate discretionary adjustments. Specifically, the value of this coefficient is about -1, confirming the explicative power of abnormal accruals in 1-year post-offering stock returns.

The results obtained when we analyze the 2-year post-offering period are also consistent with the negative relationship between the level of adjusted discretionary accruals and the performance in returns. The coefficient on MDAP^0 again takes a value of about -1 and is statistically significant, except with the cross-section Poveda model.

Finally, for the 3-year period following the offering, it seems that the relationship between discretionary accruals and abnormal returns is weaker. Although the coefficient on discretionary accruals is negative with three of the four estimation procedures, only with the panel-data Jones model is it statistically significant. Thus, it seems that abnormal accruals explain subsequent returns during the 1- and 2-year

Table 7.10 Adjusted abnormal accruals in year 0 and subsequent stock performance

	Panel A: Cross-section modified Jones model			Panel B: Panel data modified Jones model		
	$ACoR_1$	$ACoR_2$	$ACoR_3$	$ACoR_1$	$ACoR_2$	$ACoR_3$
N	30	30	27	30	30	27
Coeff. $MDAP^0$	**−1.02**	**−1.03**	−0.39	**−0.98**	**−0.90**	**−1.07**
p-value	(0.00)	(0.01)	(0.11)	(0.00)	(0.00)	(0.03)
Coeff. UE	**4.96**	**3.23**	**3.25**	**4.04**	**3.39**	**4.04**
p-value	(0.00)	(0.00)	(0.01)	(0.00)	(0.00)	(0.00)

	Panel C: Cross-section Poveda model			Panel D: Panel data Poveda model		
	$ACoR_1$	$ACoR_2$	$ACoR_3$	$ACoR_1$	$ACoR_2$	$ACoR_3$
N	30	30	27	30	30	27
Coeff. $MDAP^0$	**−1.08**	−0.35	1.50	**−0.84**	**−0.81**	−0.56
p-value	(0.09)	(0.56)	(0.84)	(0.00)	(0.07)	(0.11)
Coeff. UE	**5.19**	**3.19**	**3.48**	**4.81**	**3.30**	**3.56**
p-value	(0.00)	(0.00)	(0.02)	(0.00)	(0.00)	(0.01)

This table reports coefficients of equation (7.20) as well as their p-values in parentheses. $ACoR_1$, $ACoR_2$, and $ACoR_3$ are abnormal returns for the 1-, 2-, and 3-year post-offering periods respectively. $MDAP^0$ is the level of adjusted discretionary accruals in the IPO year and UE is the unexpected ROA variation. Significant coefficients of at least 10% nominal size are shown in bold.

periods, but they lose explicative power with regard to returns over the 3-year period. This is consistent with the pickup reflected in Figure 7.5 for abnormal accruals in year +3.

If we look at UE coefficients, as we have anticipated for every period and whatever the accrual model employed, there is a significant positive relation between the decrease in unexpected variation in ROA and the decline in returns. All the p-values are really close to zero, showing the robustness of this relation.

7.7 Conclusion

This chapter analyzes the long-run effect of the IPO decision in Spain. Similar to most international evidence, results show that offering companies experience negative abnormal returns in periods of up to 3 years after the public offering. We argue that this underperformance could be due to a gradual correction of an initial overvaluation induced by earnings management practices. Thus, we examined whether IPO firms manipulate earnings in order to influence market perceptions of the firm's value around the offering. We explored whether discretionary accruals are used to boost reported earnings around the offering and if these accounting practices are associated with the abnormal post-offering stock returns.

We found unusually high performance-matched abnormal accruals in the IPO year and a gradual decline thereafter. Moreover, these results are consistent even when using alternative methodological procedures to estimate the abnormal component of accruals, thus confirming that the results are not due to model specification.

We then attempted to discern if these accounting practices explain the underperformance in stock returns. We discovered that IPO terciles with higher discretionary accruals have poorer stock return performance in subsequent years. Moreover, these results are robust not only to the four different procedures used to estimate earnings management, but also to the two alternatives used to measure post-offering abnormal returns, the event-time and calendar-time approaches.

Alternatively, we also carried out a regression analysis to explore the relation between post-IPO abnormal returns and previous earnings management. Results indicate that abnormal accruals around the offering are negatively related to adjusted returns in the subsequent years, this ability of discretionary accruals to predict stock returns being robust to the different models employed to estimate managerial discretion.

Together, the results are consistent with the earnings management explanation for the IPO anomaly. Issuing firms report high earnings around the IPO date by reporting abnormal accruals aggressively. The stock market does not correctly process the implications of discretionary accruals for subsequent earnings, temporarily overvaluing IPO firms. When in the post-offering periods these accounting adjustments are reversed and previous high earnings are not maintained, the market revalues the firm down.

In spite of the potential limitations that could be associated with this chapter, the findings obtained here have great relevance for different users of financial information in capital markets. The most important information for each group of users can be summarized as follows.

On the one hand, for the academic community this study contributes to clarify the considerable debate that the IPO anomaly has generated in recent years. We verify that this anomaly is also present in the Spanish market, although its intrinsic characteristics are very different from the US market and it appears to be explained, at least in part, by opportunistic earnings management. On the other hand, for practitioners trying to value IPOs in the Spanish stock market, it would be useful to take into consideration the different measures of abnormal accruals to predict potential reversals in post-IPO stock performance. Finally, earnings management is a subject that should be taken into consideration by stock market regulators. These institutions should defend and promote the correct allocation of economic resources so any distortion by managers can be followed closely. These types of articles are useful in helping institutions like the Spanish CNMV to recognize that additional effort is necessary in seeking transparency and better quality of financial information from firms.

References

Álvarez, S. and González, V. M. (2005). The Long-Run Underperformance of Initial Public Offerings: A Methodological Problem? *Revista de Economía Aplicada*, 13(37):51–67.

Barber, B. M. and Lyon, J. D. (1997). Detecting Long-Run Abnormal Stock Returns: The Empirical Power and Specification of Tests Statistics. *Journal of Financial Economics*, 43(3):341–472.

Brav, A., Geczy, C., and Gompers, P. (2000). Is the Abnormal Return Following Equity Issuances Anomalous? *Journal of Financial Economics*, 56(2):201–249.

Dechow, P., Kothari, S., and Watts, R. (1998). The Relation Between Earnings and Cash Flows. *Journal of Accounting and Economics*, 25(2):133–168.

Dechow, P., Sloan, R. G., and Sweenney, P. (1995). Detecting Earnings Management. *Accounting Review*, 70(2):193–225.

Espenlaub, S., Gregory, A., and Tonks, I. (2000). Reassessing the Long-term Underperformance of UK Initial Public Offerings. *European Financial Management*, 6(3):319–342.

Fama, E. F. (1998). Market Efficiency, Long-Run Returns and Behavioural Finance. *Journal of Financial Economics*, 49(3):283–306.

Fama, E. F. and French, K. R. (1993). Common Risk Factors in the Returns on Stocks and Bonds. *Journal of Financial Economics*, 33(1):3–56.

Farinós, J. E. (2001). Rendimientos Anormales de las OPV en España. *Investigaciones Económicas*, 25(2):417–437.

Fields, T., Lys, T., and Vincent, L. (2001). Empirical Research in Accounting Choice. *Journal of Accounting and Economics*, 31(1–3):255–307.

Guay, W., Kothari, S., and Watts, R. (1996). A Market-Based Evaluation of Discretionary Accrual Models. *Journal of Accounting Research*, 34(Suppl.): 83–105.

Healy, P. (1996). Discussion of a Market-based Evaluation of Discretionary Accrual Models. *Journal of Accounting Research*, 34(Suppl.):107–115.

Jegadeesh, N. (2000). Long-Term Performance of Seasoned Equity Offerings: Benchmark Errors and Biases in Expectations. *Financial Management*, 29(1):5–30.

Johnson, N. J. (1978). Modified T-Tests and Confidence Intervals for Asymmetrical Populations. *Journal of the American Statistical Association*, 73(363): 536–544.

Jones, J. (1991). Earnings Management During Import Relief Investigations. *Journal of Accounting Research*, 29(2):193 228.

Keloharju, M. (1993), The Winner's Curse, Legal Liability, and the Long-Run Price Performance of Initial Public Offerings in Finland. *Journal of Financial Economics*, 34(2):251–277.

Kothari, S. P. and Warner, J. B. (1997). Measuring Long-Horizon Security Price Performance. *Journal of Financial Economics*, 43(3):301–339.

Kothari, S. P., Leone, A. J., and Wasley, C. E. (2005). Performance Matched Discretionary Accrual Measures. *Journal of Accounting and Economics*, 39(1): 163–197.

Lee, P. J., Taylor, S. L., and Walter, T. S. (1996). Australian IPO Pricing in the Short and Long Run. *Journal of Banking and Finance*, 20(7):1189–1210.

Levis, M. (1993). The Long-Run Performance of the Initial Public Offerings: The UK Experience 1980–1988. *Financial Management*, 22(1):28–41.

Ljungqvist, A. P. (1997). Pricing Initial Public Offerings: Further Evidence from Germany. *European Economic Review*, 41(7):1309–1320.

Loughran, T. (1993). NYSE vs. NASDAQ Returns: Market Microstructure or the Poor Performance of Initial Public Offerings? *Journal of Financial Economics*, 33(2):241–260.

Loughran, T. and Ritter, J. R. (1995). The New Issues Puzzle. *Journal of Finance*, 50(1):23–51.

Loughran, T. and Ritter, J. R. (2000). Uniformly Least Powerful Tests of Market Efficiency. *Journal of Financial Economics*, 55(3):361–389.

Lyon J. D., Barber, B. M., and Tsai, C. (1999). Improved Methods for Tests of Long-Run Abnormal Stock Returns. *Journal of Finance*, 54(1):165–201.

McNichols, M. and Wilson, P. (1988). Evidence of Earnings Management from the Provision for Bad Debts. *Journal of Accounting Research*, 26(Suppl.):1–31.

Page, M. J. and Reyneke, I. (1997). The Timing and Subsequent Performance of Initial Public Offerings (IPOs) on the Johannesburg Stock Exchange. *Journal of Business Finance and Accounting*, 24(9–10):1401–1420.

Poveda, F. (2005). Nuevo Enfoque en la Estimación del Componente Anormal del Resultado. *Moneda y Crédito*, No. 221, forthcoming.

Rangan, S. (1998). Earnings Management and the Performance of Seasoned Equity Offerings. *Journal of Financial Economics*, 50(1):101–122.

Ritter, J. R. (1991). The Long-Run Performance of Initial Public Offerings. *Journal of Finance*, 46(1):3–27.

Stehle, R., Ehrhardt, O., and Przyborowsky, R. (2000). Long-Run Stock of German Initial Public Offerings and Seasoned Equity Issues. *European Financial Management*, 6(2):173–196.

Teoh, S. H., Welch, I., and Wong, T. J. (1998a). Earnings Management and the Long-Run Market Performance of Inicial Public Offerings. *Journal of Finance*, 53(6):1935–1974.

Teoh, S. H., Wong, T. J., and Rao, G. R. (1998b). Are Accruals during Initial Public Offerings Opportunistic? *Review of Accounting Studies*, 3(2–3):175–208.

8 IPO initial returns on European 'new markets'

Giancarlo Giudici and Peter Roosenboom

Abstract

In this chapter we analyze a sample of 532 initial public offerings (IPOs), listed on European 'new markets' up to December 2002. 'New markets' are exchanges designed for high-growth fledging companies. We investigate the determinants of their first-day returns. We find a mean first-day return (underpricing) equal to +35.7%. Market returns, the IPO firm's risk, and price revisions in the premarket are positively related to first-day returns, whereas IPO deal flow is inversely related to underpricing.

8.1 Introduction

In 2000, more companies listed on European stock exchanges than in the United States.[1] Giudici and Roosenboom (2004) report that such increased interest in going public is largely due to the success of European 'new' stock markets designed for high-growth and high-tech fledgling companies (the French Nouveau Marché (1996), the German Neuer Markt (1997), Euro.NM Belgium (1997), the Dutch NMAX (1997) and the Italian Nuovo Mercato (1999)).

These 'new' stock markets aimed to meet the expectations of the European Commission, which has been eager to copy the success of financing high-tech and 'new economy' enterprises in the United States (European Commission, 1996). Such well-developed stock markets dedicated to high-growth firms are believed to be instrumental in creating economic growth, technological innovation, and jobs. Subrahmanyam and Titman (1999) provide theoretical support for this belief and show how jump-starting an economy's stock market can indeed improve economic efficiency. Vibrant stock markets may also increase the amount of venture capital funding available to finance young and startup companies in an economy (Jeng and Wells, 2000; Black and Gibson, 1998). European 'new' stock markets are therefore of interest to both economists and policymakers.

In this study we focus on the pricing of initial public offerings (IPOs) on five European 'new markets'. It is widely documented that companies that go public sell their shares at an offer price that is lower than the first-day closing market price. This positive first-day offer-to-close return is commonly known as underpricing. Several recent studies have investigated the underpricing phenomenon for IPOs on the main

---

[1] In particular, 727 companies listed on the New York Stock Exchange and on the Nasdaq while about 900 firms went public on European exchanges. *Source*: Federation of European Stock Exchanges (2003). Statistics exclude the United Kingdom and are adjusted for Spain, where investment funds are considered as new listings.

European stock exchanges. Ljungqvist (1997) reports an average underpricing equal to +9.2% for German IPOs from 1970 to 1993. Derrien and Womack (2003) document +9.5% underpricing in France from 1992 to 1998. Cassia et al. (2003) find that 182 Italian IPOs from 1985 to 2001 were underpriced by +21.9%, on balance. These numbers pale in comparison to the average first-day return of +35.7% of IPOs on European 'new' stock markets we report in this study.

This prompts the question: what explains the significant underpricing of IPOs on European 'new markets'? The existing literature suggests several explanations. Companies listed on 'new' stock markets tend to operate in risky entrepreneurial sectors, most notably the Internet. The information asymmetry between the issuing firm and investors is large. As a result, pricing the shares of these firms becomes more difficult and investors require underpricing to compensate them for the higher valuation uncertainty (Ritter, 1984).

Alternatively, underpricing may serve to compensate investors for their release of private information during the bookbuilding process. The bookbuilding process starts with the publication of a preliminary prospectus containing a price range for the shares. The investment bank solicits non-binding bids from institutional investors in the premarket. After gauging investors' demand in the premarket phase, the final offer price is determined. In order to reward investors for their information, underwriters only partially incorporate collected private information in the final offer price. As investors pay a lower offer price than the full information price in the secondary market, they earn high first-day returns (Benveniste and Spindt, 1989).

In this study we analyze the pricing of 532 initial public offerings (IPOs) on the French Nouveau Marché, the German Neuer Markt, Euro.NM Belgium, the Dutch NMAX, and the Italian Nuovo Mercato from March 1996 to December 2002.[2] We study the determinants of first-day returns and focus on the IPO price revisions in the premarket. These price revisions are measured as the percentage revision of the offer price from the midpoint of the file price range. We find that favorable private information released by institutional investors during the premarket phase of the bookbuilding procedure (as reflected in a greater price revision) is positively related to underpricing. We also find that first-day returns are correlated with public information available at the listing (i.e. the market returns), the IPO firm's risk, and the IPO deal flow (i.e. the number of IPOs brought to the market from 60 days before to 10 trading days after the IPO date). Consistent with the Internet hype documented in the United States, we report that Internet IPOs are more underpriced than non-Internet IPOs.

In section 8.2, we continue with an overview of the extant literature. In section 8.3 we describe the sample and summary statistics. In section 8.4 we discuss hypotheses and variable measurement. Section 8.5 provides the empirical results. We present our conclusions in section 8.6.

---

[2] These five new stock markets were members of the Euro.NM network. However, the Euro.NM initiative failed to establish operating links between the member markets. The network was disbanded on 31 December 2000, leaving full autonomy to the single national markets. Europe's new markets met with only limited success. Many markets were unable to attract sufficient numbers of listings to sustain market interest, while others suffered from inadequate rules or poor liquidity. In addition, European new stock markets were hard hit by the bursting of the Internet bubble. The market capitalization of new markets fell to record lows in 2001 and 2002. Insider trading scandals and accounting frauds tarnished the reputation of new markets. As a result, investor confidence disappeared. The most painful consequence has been the closure of Euro.NM Belgium in 2001 and the German Neuer Markt in 2003 (Giudici and Roosenboom, 2004).

8.2 Review of the literature

Pricing IPOs is a difficult task: the market is not certain about the quality of the IPO firm, while the issuing firm and its underwriter do not know the market demand for IPO shares. The disclosure of information is crucial in order to avoid mispricing. The problem facing an underwriter wanting to collect information useful to pricing an IPO is that investors have no reason to truthfully reveal their private information during the premarket phase.

Benveniste and Spindt (1989) show that, in order to induce investors to truthfully reveal their demand for IPO shares, they must be rewarded with more underpricing on deals for which there is strong demand. At the outset of the bookbuilding process, the underwriter proposes a price range for the shares. Investors express their interest for IPO shares by placing non-binding orders at different prices within the price range. When investors place their orders, they factor in their expectations about what the market price of the stock will be on the first day of trading. From these indications of interest, the underwriter can therefore learn positive and negative information that can be used when setting the final offer price of the IPO. In order to compensate investors for revealing their private information, the final offer price only partially incorporates collected private information. On average, investors earn a high first-day return by paying a lower price for the stock than the full information price in the secondary trading market.

An important prediction of the Benveniste and Spindt (1989) model is that underpricing is related to the level of interest in the premarket phase. This suggests that IPOs priced in the upper part of the price range are more likely to be heavily underpriced. Consistent with the model of Benveniste and Spindt, several US studies report a correlation between the percentage revision of the final offer price from the midpoint of the price range and first day returns. Hanley (1993), Loughran and Ritter (2002), and Lowry and Schwert (2004) report that US IPOs where the final offer price is revised upwards display higher first-day returns than those IPOs where the final offer price is revised downwards. If the private information of investors was entirely incorporated into the final offer price, then no relation between the price revision and underpricing should have been found.

Loughran and Ritter (2002) show that first-day returns on IPOs are also predictable based upon market returns in the 3 weeks prior to the IPO date. The quantitative effect is large: each 1% increase in the market during the 3 weeks before the IPO results in a first-day return which is 1.3% higher. This finding is at odds with the Benveniste and Spindt (1989) model. The model does not predict there should be partial adjustment to public information, such as market returns. Instead, public information should be fully incorporated into the final offer price.

Lowry and Schwert (2004), on the other hand, show that public information (proxied by market returns) is fully incorporated into the offer price, whereas private information is only partially incorporated. Their results suggest that negative information learned during the premarket phase is more fully incorporated into the offer price than positive information. The reason is that both underwriters and investors do not want to incur losses on overpriced issues (i.e., IPOs with negative first-day returns). In addition, Lowry and Schwert (2002) find that high-technology firms and riskier firms tend to have higher first-day returns. The higher first-day returns compensate investors for the greater valuation uncertainty associated with these deals.

Ljungqvist and Wilhelm (2003) investigate the pricing of both US and international IPOs. In line with other studies, they reported that price revisions explain underpricing. However, in contrast to Lowry and Schwert (2004), they do not find that underwriters are including negative information more fully than positive information. Another finding is that IPO deal flow has a negative effect on underpricing. A higher (expected) deal flow affords underwriters the opportunity to exclude investors from other, profitable deals as retaliation for distorting their private information. This increases the market power of underwriters and reduces the need to compensate investors for revealing their private information (Benveniste et al., 2002). The effect is large in economic magnitude, since a one-standard-deviation increase in IPO deal flow reduces underpricing from 22% to 17.2%.

8.3 Data and sample description

We analyze a sample of 532 IPOs on five European stock markets for high-growth firms (the French Nouveau Marché, the German Neuer Markt, the Euro.NM Belgium, the Dutch NMAX, and the Italian Nuovo Mercato) from March 1996 to December 2002. This number excludes transfers from other stock markets and cross-listings, financial companies, and spin-offs, but includes foreign companies that list on these markets.

Table 8.1 compares the listing requirements in the stock markets that we consider in our analysis. The minimum book value of the equity is generally equal to 1.5 million euro. The Euro.NM Belgium and the Neuer Markt require a minimum age equal to 3 years, while 1-year-old companies may list on the other markets. Companies with losses, but with an ambitious business plan and relevant growth opportunities, qualify for listing on all 'new' stock markets. The capital sold to the public must represent 20–25% of the total equity, although in some cases exceptions are tolerated. All markets require that at least 50% of the IPO shares must be newly issued. This should boost IPO firms to make new investments and grow. Lockup provisions, which prevent insiders from selling their shares immediately after the IPO, have to be implemented in most markets. Table 8.1 highlights that the listing requirements imposed by the exchanges we analyze are similar, allowing us to draw a comparison between the single national exchanges.

The sample distribution, by stock market and by industry, is reported in Table 8.2. Almost 60% of the companies we analyze went public on the German Neuer Markt and about 30% listed on the French Nouveau Marché. The Internet business (120 firms) and computer software and services (136 firms) account for 48.1% of the sample. Other industries such as electronics (12%), biotechnology (8.1%), business services (7.3%), and media (6.8%) are heavily represented as well. The industry distribution confirms that an overwhelming majority of companies going public on European 'new' stock markets operates in high-tech industries.

Table 8.3 reports summary statistics about the sample. We collect data from IPO prospectuses. Market prices are taken from Datastream. The mean market capitalization and offer size are significantly larger than the book value of total assets. The average company has an initial market capitalization that is more than 130 times its operating cash flow. Over 25% of the companies have no (or negative) operating cash flow. The IPO therefore represents an important source of capital, allowing the company to fund

Table 8.1 Listing requirements of European 'new' stock markets

Stock market	Country	Company age and size	Issue size and IPO rules	Free float	Lockup provisions
Neuer Markt	Germany	Three years; equity book value >1.5 million euro	Half of the offered shares must be newly issued; IPO proceeds >5 million euro	25% or 10% if offer size is larger than 5 million euro (at least 100,000 shares)	Insiders must lock their shares for at least 6 months
Nouveau Marché (Euronext)	France	Equity book value >1.5 million euro	Half of the offered shares must be newly issued; IPO proceeds >5 million euro	20% (at least 100,000 voting shares)	1 year (insiders must lock at least 80% of their shares
Nuovo Mercato	Italy	One year; equity book value >1.5 million euro	Half of the offered shares must be newly issued; IPO proceeds >5 million euro	20% (at least 100,000 voting shares)	1 year (insiders must lock at least 80% of their shares)
NMAX (Euronext)	The Netherlands	Equity book value >1.5 million euro	Half of the offered shares must be newly issued; IPO proceeds >5 million euro	20% (at least 100,000 voting shares)	Discretionary
Euro.NM Belgium (Euronext)	Belgium	Three years; market capitalization >2 million euro	Half of the offered shares must be newly issued; IPO proceeds >5 million euro	25% (in some cases 10%)	Not available

Table 8.2 Sample distribution

	Neuer Markt	Nouveau Marché	Nuovo Mercato	NMAX	Euro-NM Belgium	Total
Internet[a]	74	30	12	2	2	120 (22.6%)
Computer software and services[b]	91	29	7	6	3	136 (25.6%)
Electronics and instruments[c]	39	19	4	1	1	64 (12.0%)
Biotech and medical instruments[d]	25	13	2	1	2	43 (8.1%)
Business services[e]	21	15	2	1	0	39 (7.3%)
Media[f]	25	8	2	0	1	36 (6.8%)
Manufacturing[g]	17	13	1	3	2	36 (6.8%)
Retail and wholesale[h]	7	12	7	0	0	26 (4.9%)
Telecommunications[i]	8	6	1	0	0	15 (2.8%)
Other	8	6	1	0	2	17 (3.1%)
Total	315 (59.2%)	151 (28.4%)	39 (7.3%)	14 (2.6%)	13 (2.5%)	532 (100.0%)

[a] Internet companies are identified after careful reading of each firm's business description as published in the prospectus.
[b] Non-Internet companies assigned SIC codes starting with 737 (computer programming, data processing, and other computer-related services).
[c] Non-Internet companies assigned SIC codes starting with 357 (computer and office equipment), 36 (electronic and other electrical equipment), or 38 (measuring, analyzing, and controlling instruments, not 384).
[d] Non-Internet companies assigned SIC codes starting with 283 (drugs), 384 (surgical, medical, and dental instruments and supplies), 80 (health services) or assigned SIC code 8731 (commercial physical and biological research).
[e] Non-Internet companies assigned SIC codes starting with 73 (business services, not 737), 87 (engineering, accounting, research and management services, not 8731), or 89 (services, not elsewhere classified).
[f] Non-Internet companies assigned SIC codes starting with 27 (printing and publishing), 78 (motion pictures), or 79 (amusement and recreation services).
[g] Non-Internet companies assigned SIC codes starting with 20 (food and kindred products), 23 (apparel and textile products), 24 (lumber and wood products), 28 (chemicals and allied products, not 283), 30 (rubber and plastics products), 32 (stone, glass, and concrete products), 33 (primary metal industries), 34 (fabricated metal products), 35 (industrial and commercial machinery, not 357), or 37 (transportation equipment manufacturing).
[h] Non-Internet companies assigned SIC codes starting with 5 (wholesale and retail trade).
[i] Non-Internet companies assigned SIC codes starting with 48 (communications).

its future growth plans. The mean company age is equal to 12 years. This differs from previous studies of IPOs on European main exchanges (for example, Pagano et al., 1996), that show European IPO firms to be mature and established companies.

Table 8.3 Summary statistics (sample consists of 532 IPOs listed on European 'new markets' from 1996 to 2002)

	Average	Min	Percentiles			Max	Standard deviation
			25th	50th	75th		
Market capitalization (thousand euro)[a]	281,474	9054	59,200	124,800	261,498	13,252,500	839,848
Offer size (thousand euro)[b]	53,251	2541	15,051	27,159	51,959	2,700,000	149,201
Total assets (thousand euro)	27,586	6	5,124	10,483	22,028	2,311,000	108,113
Operating cash flow (thousand euro)[c]	2,107	−35,204	−182	1,185	3,162	53,497	6,114
Company age (years)	12.258	1	5	10	16	88	11.068
Underpricing (%)[d]	35.667	−25	0	10.254	42	433.333	61.693
Price revision (%)[e]	3.07	−45.455	0	6.494	8.333	72.973	10.239
Volatility (%)[f]	3.348	−1.136	2.092	3.052	4.39	11.075	1.881
Market return previous 50 days (%)[g]	4.381	−26.791	−2.699	4.18	9.748	31.872	9.7
IPO deal flow (#)[h]	46.553	0	29	44	65	98	25.184

[a] Number of shares outstanding after IPO times the closing market price on the first trading day.
[b] Number of shares sold in IPO times the final offer price.
[c] Earnings before interest, taxes, depreciation, and amortization during the most recent financial year, as disclosed in the prospectus.
[d] Initial offer-to-close return measured as: (first-day closing market price − final offer price)/final offer price.
[e] Price revision is measured as: (final offer price − midpoint of price range)/midpoint of price range. Price revisions are available for 512 firms.
[f] Standard deviation of the firm's daily stock returns during the 60-trading-day interval of 20–80 days after its IPO date minus the standard deviation of daily returns to the MSCI index for the country of listing (Germany, France, Italy, Belgium, or the Netherlands) during the same period.
[g] Return of the MSCI index of the country of listing (Germany, France, Italy, Belgium, or the Netherlands) markets from 60 trading days before to 10 trading days before the IPO date.
[h] Number of companies going public on European 'new' stock markets from 60 trading days before to 10 trading days after the IPO date.

The mean initial underpricing is equal to +35.7%, which is remarkably high if compared to first-day returns on the main stock exchanges in Europe during the same period, as reported by Derrien and Womack (2003) and Cassia et al. (2003). Yet more than 25% of the sample IPOs did not display underpricing, or are initially over-priced (for example, experience a negative first-day return).

We plot the monthly number of IPOs and the mean initial underpricing per month in Figure 8.1. We observe 'hot' issue periods, namely April 1998 to September 1998, as well as February 1999 to May 1999, and December 1999 to April 2000. These hot-issue periods are characterized by unusually high underpricing, followed by high IPO volume periods, in which the mean initial return is lower (see, for example, April 2000 to August 2000). We document a 'cold' issue period in 2001 and 2002, with only few IPOs listing on 'new markets'.

Almost all IPOs (512; 96.2%) have been priced using the bookbuilding procedure, while in 17 cases the final offer price was fixed in the prospectus and in three cases the IPO was auctioned. Considering 512 IPOs in which the final offer price is not fixed, we find that on average the final offer price is revised upwards (+3.1%) with respect to the midpoint price of the file range. However, no revision or downward revision with respect to the midpoint price is found in about 25% of the IPOs.

Table 8.4 investigates any cross-market differences. We record several marked differences among the three major markets (Nouveau Marché, Neuer Markt, and Nuovo Mercato). The German Neuer Markt leads the other markets with regard to offer size, IPO price volatility, underpricing, and percentage price revision. The French Nouveau Marché hosts smaller and less underpriced IPOs. The Italian Nuovo Mercato heads the other markets with regard to market capitalization and operating

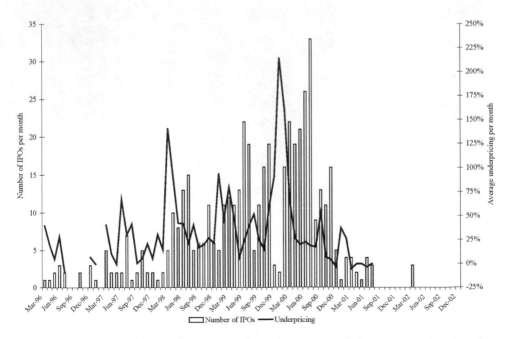

Figure 8.1 Number of IPOs and average underpricing per month for European 'new' stock markets

Table 8.4 Differences across European 'new' stock markets

	Means across markets			Test for difference					
	Neuer Markt	Nouveau Marché	Nuovo Mercato	Neuer Markt versus Nouveau Marché		Neuer Markt versus Nuovo Mercato		Nouveau Marché versus Nuovo Mercato	
				t-test	z-test[a]	t-test	z-test	t-test	z-test
Market capitalization (thousand euro)	347,997	96,752	608,484	3.437***	11.251***	1.519	1.267	3.679***	6.568***
Offer size (thousand euro)	65,472	19,166	113,645	3.41***	11.661***	1.580	1.706*	4.364***	7.002***
Total assets (thousand euro)	34,127	14,345	40,158	1.757*	2.378**	0.27	1.85*	4.456***	3.152***
Operating cash flow (thousand euro)	2051	1835	4607	0.348	1.470	2.134**	2.761***	3.521***	2.511**
Company age (years)	12.863	11.258	12.359	1.453	1.175	0.255	0.611	0.589	0.095
Underpricing (%)	47.323	16.531	22.301	5***	5.942***	2.154**	2.743***	0.821	0.124
Price revision (%)	4.162	2.777	-5.396	1.757*	4.293***	5.117***	3.039***	3.639***	2.061**
Volatility (%)	3.749	2.749	2.874	5.608***	5.34***	2.728***	3.289***	0.411	0.029
Market return previous 50 days (%)	3.542	6.134	1.360	2.675***	3.845***	1.288	0.952	3.202***	3.603***
IPO deal flow (#)	49.873	38.649	58.82	4.654***	4.870***	2.292**	2.148**	4.066***	4.063***

[a] Nonparametric Wilcoxon test. * Statistically significant at the 10% level; ** statistically significant at the 5% level; *** statistically significant at the 1% level (two-tailed).

cash flow. No differences are found concerning company age. In the next section we will investigate the effect of both market- and firm-specific characteristics on the first-day returns.

8.4   Hypotheses and variable measurement

We estimate a cross-section regression model using the first-day return (under-pricing) as the dependent variable. We investigate whether the market index return in the 50 days prior to the IPO influences first-day returns. We measure the index return by the MSCI Index of the country of listing (France, Germany, the Netherlands, Belgium, or Italy). As argued earlier, the Benveniste and Spindt (1989) model does not predict that there is partial adjustment to public information, such as market returns. Instead, public information should be fully incorporated into the final offer price. According to theory, market returns should therefore not be able to explain first-day returns.

We expect that investors require higher first-day returns to compensate them for the higher valuation uncertainty associated with risky deals. Market-adjusted volatility is used as a proxy for company risk. It is computed as the standard deviation of the firm's daily stock returns during the 60-trading-day interval of 20–80 days after its IPO date minus the standard deviation of daily returns to the MSCI index of the country of listing during that same period.[3]

We also examine whether IPO deal flow affects first-day returns. Several studies (Hoffmann-Burchardi, 2001; Loughran et al., 1994) have shown that IPO markets are subject to cycles, with 'hot' issue periods, that are characterized by high volume of IPOs and/or high first-day returns, alternating with 'cold' issue periods. 'Hot' and 'cold' markets tend to alternate and generate clustering of IPOs. The literature strongly supports the hypothesis that issuers go public during a temporary window of opportunity, and price information from past IPOs spills over to current and future offerings, affecting the decision to go public (Benveniste et al., 2003). The transition from hot to cold periods is marked by heavy volume periods in which the number of IPOs is increasing, but the typical first-day return is lower. Figure 8.1 shows the occurrence of IPO cycles during our sample period. Similar to Ljungqvist and Wilhelm (2003), we measure IPO deal flow by the number of IPOs from 60 trading days before to 10 days after the IPO date. We introduce a dummy variable for Internet IPOs. We expect Internet-related firms to be more underpriced, due to the Internet euphoria of 1999 to 2000 (Cooper et al., 2001; Ljungqvist and Wilhelm, 2003; Loughran and Ritter, 2004).

In accordance with the model of Benveniste and Spindt (1989), we hypothesize that the revision of the offer price is positively related to underpricing. Benveniste and Spindt (1989) argued that, in order to reward investors for their private information, underwriters only partially incorporate collected private information in the final offer price. The more valuable the private information is to pricing the IPO, reflected in a

---

[3] Although our risk measure is not available at the time of the IPO itself, investors clearly form opinions about the firm's risk when pricing IPOs. Following Lowry and Schwert (2004), we argue that our ex-post risk measure is an unbiased estimator of the ex-ante risk of the IPO firm.

greater price revision, the higher the first-day returns. We measure the percentage revision of the final offer price from the midpoint of the price range.

We also include four control variables in the regression models. We include the log of the book value of total assets to control for differences in size. We include company age to control for age differences. To control for differences between the national exchanges, we incorporate two dummy variables for the Neuer Markt and Nouveau Marché respectively.

8.5 Empirical results

Table 8.5 reports the results of the regression analyses. We first consider the empirical results for the full sample of 532 IPOs as shown in the first column of Table 8.5. The market index returns during the 50 days prior to the IPO are significantly related to first-day returns. A 1 percentage point increase in the market results (e.g. from 4% to 5%) results in a first-day return which is 2.1% higher. This suggests that underwriters do not fully adjust final offer prices to recent market returns. Analyzing a sample of US IPOs, Loughran and Ritter (2002) find that the market return during the 3 weeks before the IPO date displays a positive and significant relation with underpricing. Their and our results are inconsistent with the prediction of Benveniste and Spindt (1989) that public information should be fully incorporated into the final offer price.

Market-adjusted volatility is positively correlated with underpricing. This suggests that investors demand higher underpricing as compensation for the valuation uncertainty associated with risky IPOs. A one-standard-deviation increase in volatility increases the first-day return by 5.2%. This corroborates the findings of Lowry and Schwert (2004) for the United States. They also report that riskier firms have higher first-day returns.

The IPO deal flow is inversely related to underpricing. This effect is large in economic magnitude. A one-standard-deviation increase in IPO deal flow reduces the first-day return by 12.3%. One explanation for this finding may be that during periods of high IPO volume, the market power of underwriters increases (Benveniste et al., 2002). Investors are eager to buy shares in IPOs, reducing the need to compensate them for revealing their private information by high first-day returns. Alternatively, IPO deal flow may proxy for the transition from hot- to cold-issue markets. As argued earlier, this transition is characterized by an increasing number of IPOs coupled with lower first-day returns.

Other things being equal, Internet IPOs have first-day returns that are 24.3% higher than the first-day returns of non-Internet IPOs. This corresponds to the results of Lowry and Schwert (2002), who show that high-technology firms in the United States have higher first-day returns than IPOs from other industries. Interestingly, cross-market differences in first-day returns do appear, as the coefficients of the market dummies are significantly different from zero. Consistent with Table 8.4, IPOs on the German Neuer Markt are more severely underpriced, while IPOs on the French Nouveau Marché are less underpriced.

In the second column of Table 8.5 we consider 512 IPOs for which price revisions are available. We find that the price revision is significantly related to underpricing.

Table 8.5 Determinants of underpricing on European 'new' stock markets

	Full sample	Bookbuilding sample[a]	Neuer Markt sample[b]	Nouveau Marché sample[c]	Nuovo Mercato sample[d]
Market returns previous 50 days	2.062 (6.494)***	1.920 (5.693)***	2.316 (5.262)***	0.711 (2.221)**	-0.936 (-0.34)
Volatility	2.739 (2.086)**	2.772 (2.097)**	1.198 (0.789)	9.195 (3.075)***	-3.112 (-0.699)
Log (IPO deal flow)	-0.088 (-3.205)***	-0.089 (-3.171)***	-0.204 (-3.299)***	-0.044 (-1.496)	-0.116 (-0.679)
Internet dummy	0.243 (3.132)***	0.229 (2.917)***	0.162 (1.69)*	0.305 (2.575)**	0.182 (0.547)
Price revision		0.879 (3.247)***	1.637 (5.639)***	1.361 (3.766)***	0.116 (0.366)

Control variables

Log(total assets)	−0.018	−0.015	−0.044	0.032	−0.031
	(−0.983)	(−0.799)	(−1.516)	(0.866)	(−0.911)
Company age	0.003	0.003	0.004	−0.002	−0.003
	(1.093)	(1.036)	(1.098)	(−0.889)	(−0.499)
Neuer Markt dummy	0.243	0.139			
	(3.523)***	(1.930)*			
Nouveau	−0.129	−0.215			
Marché dummy	(−2.007)**	(−3.045)***			
Intercept	0.465	0.519	1.373	−0.357	1.835
	(2.227)**	(2.329)**	(3.361)***	(−1.017)	(1.676)
R^2 adjusted	0.188	0.209	0.243	0.273	−0.101
F-statistic	16.346***	16.024***	15.377***	8.71***	0.502

Cross-sectional regressions are shown, estimated by ordinary least squares with the correction for heteroscedasticity developed by White (1980). The dependent variable is underpricing. t-statistics are shown in parentheses below the estimated coefficients. * Statistically significant at the 10% level (two-tailed); ** statistically significant at the 5% level (two-tailed); *** statistically significant at the 1% level (two-tailed).

[a] 512 sample firms.
[b] 315 sample firms.
[c] 145 sample firms.
[d] 39 sample firms.

This is consistent with the theoretical model of Benveniste and Spindt (1989) and the empirical results of Loughran and Ritter (2002), Ljungqvist and Wilhelm (2003), and Lowry and Schwert (2004). A 10% increase in price revision results in a first-day return that is 8.8% higher. This suggests that investors are rewarded by higher first-day returns in exchange for their revelation of positive private information in the bookbuilding process.

We run separate regressions for the three major exchanges to investigate whether the determinants of underpricing are different across markets. The IPO valuation uncertainty (proxied by the volatility) is an important determinant of underpricing in France but not in Germany, whereas deal flow is an important determinant in Germany but not in France.

Surprisingly, we do not find significant determinants in Italy. We attribute this result to the immature nature of the Nuovo Mercato and the small sample size. Italian IPOs seem to be more influenced by the market turbulence after the Nasdaq fall in 2000. Several Italian IPOs that listed after April 2000 had a downward revision of their offer price, which was appreciated by the market as a signal of prudence, and not interpreted as a negative feedback from bookbuilding activity. This may explain why the correlation between the first-day returns and the revision of the offer price is not significant in Italy.

In additional tests we investigate whether underwriters respond differently to negative and positive information learned during the premarket phase of the bookbuilding procedure. Lowry and Schwert (2004) argued that negative information learned during the premarket is more fully incorporated into the final offer price than positive information, since investors and underwriters want to avoid losses on overpriced issues (i.e. they want to avoid buying issues with negative first-day returns). We re-estimate the regressions with an additional explanatory variable that equals the price revision if it is positive and zero otherwise. The coefficient of this variable should be significantly positive if underwriters price in positive information less fully than negative information. However, in unreported tests we do not find any evidence that underwriters incorporate positive information less fully than negative information. The coefficient is found to be 0.729 (t-statistic = 0.649).

8.6 Conclusion

This study contributes to the literature on the pricing of IPOs, which thus far has been dominated by US studies. We show that, in contrast to the evidence of main European exchanges, 'new markets' attract young and high-technology firms. We show that an average IPO on the 'new markets' displays a +35.7% first-day return, about three times larger than the first-day return of a typical IPO on the main European stock exchanges. We replicate the findings of US studies and find that similar determinants explain the high first-day returns of IPOs on 'new' European stock markets.

First, in contrast to the Benveniste and Spindt (1989) model, public information is not fully incorporated into the final offer price. This yields a positive association between market index returns (our proxy for public information) and first-day returns. Second, we find that the IPO firm's risk is positively related to underpricing.

Investors seem to demand higher first-day returns to compensate them for the higher valuation uncertainty associated with risky deals. Third, the IPO deal flow is inversely related to first-day returns. Companies that go public in a period of high IPO volume have lower first-day returns. In high IPO volume periods, the market power of underwriters may be stronger, reducing the need to compensate investors for the release of private information by means of high first-day returns. Alternatively, this result may capture the transition of a 'hot' to a 'cold' issue market, that is normally associated with an increase in the number of firms going public and a decline in the average first-day returns.

Fourth, we find that, consistent with the Internet euphoria in the United States, Internet IPOs are more underpriced than non-Internet IPOs. Fifth, the revision of the offer price with respect to the price range published in the prospectus is informative. The more optimistic the revision of the offer price, the higher the first-day returns. The higher first-day returns serve to reward investors for releasing their private information about IPO value in the premarket phase of the bookbuilding process.

References

Benveniste, L. M. and Spindt, P. A. (1989). How Investment Bankers Determine the Offer Price and Allocation of New Issues. *Journal of Financial Economics*, 24(2):343–361.

Benveniste, L. M., Busaba, W., and Wilhelm, W. J. (2002). Information Externalities and the Role of Underwriters in Primary Equity Markets. *Journal of Financial Intermediation*, 11(1):61–86.

Benveniste, L. M., Ljungqvist, A. P., Wilhelm, W. J., and Yu, X. (2003). Evidence of information spillovers in the Production of Investment Banking Services. *Journal of Finance*, 58(2):577–608.

Black, B. and Gibson, R. (1998). Venture Capital and the Structure of Capital Markets: Banks Versus Stock Markets. *Journal of Financial Economics*, 47(3):243–277.

Cassia, L., Giudici, G., Paleari, S., and Redondi, R. (2003). IPO Underpricing in Italy. *Applied Financial Economics*, 14(3):179–194.

Cooper, M., Dimitrov, O., and Rau, P. R. (2001). A Rose.com by Any Other Name. *Journal of Finance*, 56(6):2371–2388.

Derrien, F. and Womack, K. L. (2003). Auction vs. Book-Building and the Control of Underpricing in Hot IPO Markets. *Review of Financial Studies*, 16(1):31–61.

European Commission (1996). New Technology-Based Firms in Europe. EIMS Publication, 31.

Federation of European Stock Exchanges. (2003). Statistics Database, http://www.fese.be.

Giudici, G. and Roosenboom, P. (2004). *The Rise and Fall of Europe's New Stock Markets*. Elsevier, Amsterdam.

Hanley, K. W. (1993). The Underpricing of Initial Public Offerings and the Partial Adjustment Phenomenon. *Journal of Financial Economics*, 34(2):231–250.

Hoffmann-Burchardi, U. (2001). Clustering of Initial Public Offerings, Information Revelation and Underpricing. *European Economic Review*, 45(2):353–383.

Jeng, L. A. and Wells, P. C. (2000). The Determinants of Venture Capital Funding: Evidence Across Countries. *Journal of Corporate Finance*, 6(3):241–289.

Ljungqvist, A. P. (1997). Pricing Initial Public Offerings: Further Evidence from Germany. *European Economic Review*, 41(7):1309–1320.

Ljungqvist, A. P. and Wilhelm, W. J. (2003). IPO Pricing in the Dot-com Bubble. *Journal of Finance*, 58(2):723–752.

Loughran, T., Ritter, J. R., and Rydqvist, K. (1994). Initial Public Offerings: International Insights. *Pacific-Basin Finance Journal*, 2(2/3):165–199.

Loughran, T. and Ritter, J. R. (2002). Why Don't Issuers Get Upset About Leaving Money on the Table in IPOs? *Review of Financial Studies*, 15(2):413–443.

Loughran, T. and Ritter, J. R. (2004). Why Has IPO Underpricing Changed Over Time? *Financial Management*, 33(3):5–37.

Lowry, M. and Schwert, G. W. (2002). IPO Market Cycles: Bubbles or Sequential Learning. *Journal of Finance*, 57(3):1171–1200.

Lowry, M. and Schwert, G. W. (2004). Is the IPO Pricing Process Efficient? *Journal of Financial Economics*, 71(1):3–26.

Pagano, M., Panetta, F., and Zingales, L. (1996). The Stock Market as a Source of Capital: Some Lessons from Initial Public Offerings in Italy. *European Economic Review*, 40(3–5):1057–1069.

Ritter J. R. (1984). The Hot Issue Market of 1980. *Journal of Business*, 57(2):215–240.

Subrahmanyam, A. and Titman, S. (1999). The Going-Public Decision and the Development of Financial Markets. *Journal of Finance*, 54(3):1045–1082.

White, H. S. (1980). A Heteroscedastic-Consistent Covariance Matrix Estimator and a Direct Test of Heteroscedasticity. *Econometrica*, 48(4):817–838.

9 Efficiency of US IPOs: a DEA approach

Greg N. Gregoriou and Maher Kooli

Abstract

The objective of this chapter is to measure the efficiency of US initial public offering (IPO) firms, using a new approach never used in an IPO context, called Data Envelopment Analysis (DEA). We apply the basic efficiency model, the cross-efficiency model, and the super-efficiency model for our analyses. Overall, we find that efficient IPOs with a low offering price may offer a better avenue when selecting IPOs.

9.1 Introduction

In recent years, the academic community has closely examined and intensely debated the performance of initial public offerings (IPOs). More specifically, most studies on the subject focus on the initial returns, the long-run performance and operating performance of issuing firms, and present convincing empirical evidence that, on average, IPOs are underpriced and underperform in the long run (Ritter, 1991; Loughran and Ritter, 1995; Jain and Kini, 1994; Kooli and Suret, 2004, amongst others). According to Nimalendran et al. (2004), from 1993 to 2001, firms going public left more than $93.5 billion on the table, where the amount of money left on the table is defined as the product of the number of shares offered and the difference between the first-day close price and the offer price. During 1999 and 2000, the Internet bubble period, there were 803 IPOs, and the total amount of money left on the table was $63.5 billion.

On the other hand, the conclusions regarding long-term IPO abnormal performance are hotly debated and a number of reasons have been advanced. The most plausible reason is the divergence of opinion hypothesis suggested by Miller (1977). According to Miller, market IPO prices are determined by optimistic investors. As more information becomes available about a firm over time, the heterogeneous divergence of beliefs between investors will decrease, and the marginal holder will no longer be as over-optimisitic. Ritter (2003) noted that this story is consistent with the patterns in the 1999 to 2000 Internet bubble. However, Lyon et al. (1999), amongst others, have recently challenged the US findings. They found that the underperformance result is sensitive to the method used to evaluate abnormal returns, and is not exclusive to IPO firms. For academic researchers, if the aftermarket underperformance phenomenon exists, then it raises questions concerning aftermarket efficiency. For investors, it raises questions concerning the benefits of investing in firms going public.

Thus, the viability or efficiency of these firms after their IPOs is an important question. This issue is also timely as the everyday financial press reports examples of public firms that do not make it in the aftermarket.[1]

The objective of this chapter is to measure the efficiency of US IPO firms, using a new approach never used in an IPO context, called Data Envelopment Analysis (DEA). DEA is used extensively in studies on public sectors, where there is no agreed-upon performance measurement. More specifically, DEA allow us to analyze the relative efficiency and managerial performance of productive (or response) units, having the same multiple inputs and multiple outputs. We use three major DEA models: (1) the basic efficiency model (Charnes et al., 1978), (2) the cross-efficiency model (Sexton et al., 1986), and (3) the super-efficiency model (Andersen and Petersen, 1993).

Our results indicate that after the speculative Internet bubble, IPOs with a lower offer price range are efficient using DEA. It is unfortunate that we do not find Google as being efficient in any of the models, nor does it fall into the top 10 selected IPOs in terms of ranking. The rest of the chapter is organized as follows. Section 9.2 discusses the data. We then describe the methodology in section 9.3 and we present our empirical findings in section 9.4. Section 9.5 concludes.

9.2 Data

We use the http://www.ipohome.com new issues database to identify IPOs from 2002 to 2004. The summary statistics for IPOs are reported in Table 9.1. We have 354 IPOs in the 3-year sample period, of which 216 IPOs (61%) went public during 2004. The summary statistics about the whole sample and 3-year sample reported in Table 9.1 are consistent with what has been reported in the literature. These statistics indicate that IPOs as generally documented are underpriced. For instance, the mean first-day return and the mean money left on the table for the whole sample are 11.15% and

Table 9.1 Summary statistics on IPOs

	Overall	2002	2003	2004
Number of IPOs	354	70	68	216
Mean offer price ($)	14.66	15.89	15.53	13.98
Mean number of shares offered (thousands)	13744	17941	13745	12384
Mean proceeds ($ million)	230.90	338.19	223.87	198.34
Mean first-day return (%)	11.15	8.63	13.49	11.23
Mean money left on the table ($ million)	20.25	15.8	29.61	18.74

This table reports summary statistics for the IPO sample for the sample period from 2002 to 2004. The first-day return is defined as the return from the offer price to the first-day close price. Money left on the table is defined as the difference between the offer price and the first-day close price multiplied by the number of shares offered (domestic tranche only), assuming no exercise of overallotment options.

---

[1] For example, according to the article 'Paradise Lost' in *Inc.* magazine, 'Nearly two years after PRT Group's celebrated IPO, the company's stock price is under water and CEO Doug Mellinger is out of a job' (1 November 1999).

$20.25 million respectively. Note that all on the money left on the table assumes no existence of overallotment options, and the number of shares offered is measured as the domestic tranche. Table 9.2 reports the 10 biggest IPOs in our sample.

The biggest IPOs in our sample came from the financial services sector. CIT Group, a Tyco spinoff, became the fourth largest IPO in US history with its $4.6 billion offering in July. Travelers Property Casualty Corporation, a Citigroup spinoff, raised $3.9 billion in proceeds in its March IPO and became the sixth largest deal in US IPO history. The largest offerings in 2003 came from abroad. The largest was China Life Insurance (LFC), a government privatization of China's number one life insurer. Genworth (GNW), General Electric's spinoff of its life and mortgage business, was the largest IPO of 2004 with its $2.8 billion deal and Assurant (AIZ), a spinoff of Fortis' multiline insurer, was the third largest, raising $1.7 billion. Rounding out the list of largest IPOs were two semiconductor IPOs expected to benefit from the turnaround in demand for semiconductors and the Google IPO (GOOG), raising $1.7 billion.

9.3 Methodology

The application of DEA to financial analysis is a recent extension. DEA lends itself naturally to IPO efficiency because of its employment for assessing relative efficiency of IPOs using various inputs to produce outputs. In essence, DEA is an ideal method to measure efficiency relative to the best performing IPOs. This allows us to identify efficient and non-efficient IPOs and driving factors determining the efficiency of IPOs.

The inputs and outputs must correspond to the activities of IPOs for DEA. We use five variables, three for inputs and two for outputs. For inputs we use: (1) IPO price, which represents the dollar value the IPO was launched at; (2) the number of IPO shares in millions of dollars that were sold on the day the IPO went public; and (3) the deal size of the IPO, which is simply the IPO price multiplied by the IPO deal size.

For the first output (1), first-day close is used because it identifies how IPOs performed at the end of the first day of trading. The second output (2) is quarter end return for the first 3 months' performance of the IPO. This output permits us to

Table 9.2 The biggest IPOs of the period 2002 to 2004

	Company	Offer date	Proceeds ($ million)	First-day return (%)
1	CIT Group	1 July 2002	4,600.00	−4.34
2	Travelers Property Casualty	21 March 2002	3,885.00	5.72
3	China Life Insurance	11 December 2003	3,021.80	27.00
4	Genworth Financial	24 May 2004	2,827.50	0.00
5	ALCON	20 March 2002	2,301.80	3.03
6	Semiconductor Manufacturing	11 March 2004	1,803.00	−11.30
7	Assurant	4 February 2004	1,760.00	12.30
8	Google	18 August 2004	1,666.40	18.00
9	Freescale Semiconductor	15 July 2004	1,581.10	7.80
10	China Telecom	6 November 2002	1,434.20	5.37

identify the very short-run performance. Using first-day close and the quarter end close will identify which IPOs had the highest return (with the smallest) inputs.

We use an input-oriented constant returns-to-scale model to examine the efficiency of IPOs. We apply the Charnes et al. (1978) basic efficiency model, the cross-efficiency model (Sexton et al., 1986), and the super-efficiency model (Andersen and Petersen, 1993) for our analyses.

We adapt the notation from Zhu (2003) for basic efficiency, cross-efficiency, and super-efficiency models. For basic DEA, we maximize the ratio of outputs divided by inputs in equation (9.1), which forms the objective function for the particular IPO h_0^*. We denote IPOs denoted by $j = \{1, 2, ..., n\}$, which uses quantities of i inputs with $i = \{1, 2, ..., m\}$ to produce quantities of r outputs with $r = \{1, 2, ..., s\}$; furthermore, we let x_{ij} be the quantity of input i for j used to produce the quantity y_{rj} of output r. Each IPO uses a variable quantity of m different inputs ($i = 1, 2, ..., m$) to generate s different outputs ($r = 1, 2, ..., s$). In particular, IPO j uses amount x_{ij} of output i and generates y_{rj} of output r. We then presume $x_{ij} \geq 0$, $y_{rj} \geq 0$ and that each IPO has at least one positive input value and one positive output value. DEA optimization handles the observed vectors of x_j and y_j as given and selects values of output and input weights for a particular IPO. In equation (9.1) a free variable, denoted by u_0, is added in the Charnes et al. (1978) CCR model to allow for constant returns-to-scale. If an increase in an IPO's inputs produces a proportional change in its outputs, then the IPO exhibits constant returns-to-scale.

Therefore, in an input-oriented CCR model, the formulation minimizes the inputs given the outputs. We obtain the following optimization:

$$h_0^* = \max \frac{\sum_{r-1}^{s} u_r y_{r0}}{\sum_{i=1}^{m} v_i x_{i0}} \qquad (9.1)$$

subject to:

$$\frac{\sum_{r=1}^{s} u_r y_{rj}}{\sum_{i=1}^{m} v_i x_{ij}} \leq 1, \quad j = 1, 2, ...n, \qquad (9.2)$$

where:

s = number of outputs
m = number of inputs
u_r = weight of output r
v_i = weight of input i
x_{ij} = amount of i used by IPO
y_{rj} = amount of r used by IPO.

Equation (9.2) is the constraint which imposes that the equivalent weight, when implemented to all IPOs, does not allow any IPO to have an efficiency score greater than 1.0 (or less than 1). The efficiency score falls between 0 and 1.0 and an IPO is regarded as efficient upon obtaining an efficiency score of 1.0. A best practices frontier is then generated by the efficient IPOs. Therefore, each IPO will select weights to maximize its own self-efficiency with respect to the constraint in equation (9.2).

The cross-efficiency model was first seen in Sexton et al. (1986) and later in Doyle and Green (1994) and Anderson et al. (2002). It establishes the ranking procedure and computes the efficiency score of each IPO n times using optimal weights obtained via DEA models. Count n is the number of times the problem needs to be generated to differentiate the efficiency scores. Cross-efficiency adds further insight into the performance of each IPO and determines whether they have performed well in all areas according to inputs and outputs. Essentially cross-efficiency allows for all IPOs to cast their vote. A cross-efficiency matrix consists of rows and columns, each equal to the number of IPOs in the analysis. The efficiency of IPO j is computed with the optimal weights for fund k. By calculating the mean of each column, it will provide the peer appraisal score of each IPO. The cross-efficiency model (BCC model) used here is represented by equation (9.3):

$$h_{kj} = \frac{\sum\limits_{r=1}^{s} y_{rj} u_{rk}}{\sum\limits_{i=1}^{m} x_{ij} v_{ik}}, k = 1, 2,..., n, j = 1, 2,..., n, \tag{9.3}$$

where the problem is generated n times and h_{kj} is the score of IPO j cross-evaluated by the weight of IPO k. In the cross-efficiency matrix, all IPOs are bounded by $0 < h_{kj} \le 1$, and the components in the leading diagonal, h_{kk}, depict the simple DEA efficiency score, $h_{kk} = 1$ for efficient IPOs and $h_{kk} < 1$ for inefficient IPOs.

Super-efficiency (Andersen and Petersen, 1993) is used to rank the IPOs. Super-efficiency is obtained from the regular DEA model by excluding the fund under evaluation from the reference set. Super-efficiency (input-oriented) allows a highly efficient IPO to attain an efficiency score greater than 1.0 by removing the constraint $j \neq 0$ in equation (9.5).

$$h_0^* = \max \frac{\sum\limits_{r=1}^{s} u_r y_{r0}}{\sum\limits_{i=1}^{m} v_i x_{i0}} \tag{9.4}$$

subject to:

$$\frac{\sum\limits_{r=1}^{s} u_r y_{rj}}{\sum\limits_{i=1}^{m} v_i x_{ij}} \le 1, \quad j = 1,2,...n \quad \text{and} \quad j \neq 0 \tag{9.5}$$

We further compare the results of the basic efficiency and cross-efficiency models to see if the rank order of the DEA models can be used as a complementary efficiency/performance measure and if DEA can be considered as an alternative and robust ranking technique for ranking the performance of IPOs.

9.4   Empirical results

Table 9.3 provides the results of the basic efficiency and super-efficiency scores, while the cross-efficiency scores are displayed in Table 9.4. When examining the calendar

Table 9.3 Basic efficiency and super-efficiency scores of IPO launches in 2002

	Basic Efficiency	Super-Efficiency	Price Range ($)
Harrington West Financial Group	1.0000	1.68525	12–14
Jet Blue Airways	1.0000	1.22597	22–24
LeapFrog Enterprises	1.0000	1.17868	13–16
Computer Programs & Systems	1.0000	1.14661	16–18
IMPAC Medical Systems	1.0000	1.08838	15–17
Chicago Mercantile Exchange	1.0000	1.06660	31–34
SRA International	0.99860	–	16–18
Altiris	0.96762	–	10–12
MTC Technologies	0.94905	–	15–17
Hewitt Associates	0.93761	–	18–21

Table 9.4 Cross-efficiency scores of IPO launches in 2002

	Cross-Efficiency	Price Range ($)
SRA International	88.76	16–18
IMPAC Medical Systems	87.42	15–17
Computer Programs & Systems	85.62	16–18
Chicago Mercantile Exchange	84.73	31–34
LeapFrog Enterprises	84.11	13–16
Hewitt Associates	78.57	18–21
Dick's Sporting Goods	76.07	15–18
Harrington West Financial Group	75.92	12–14
Taylor Capital Group	75.56	18–20
Montpelier Re	74.93	20–22

year 2002, of the 70 IPOs[2] considered only six are deemed efficient using the basic DEA model. Furthermore, the efficient IPOs had a launching price range between $12 and $34 using the basic, cross-, and super-efficiency models in Tables 9.3 and 9.4.

This could be that small offerings in terms of issue price may be more attractive to investors. In terms of super-efficiency, the efficient IPOs displaying a score of 1.0 using the basic DEA model now have higher efficiency scores than unity, since they can now attain a score greater than unity. The IPO with the greatest super-efficiency score (Table 9.3) is Harrington West Financial Group, with 1.68525. The remaining IPOs in basic DEA that are not efficient (less than unity) keep the same efficiency score in the super-efficiency model. When examining the cross-efficiency scores (Table 9.4) we find that IPO SA International attains the highest score (88.76), closely followed by IMPAC Medical Systems (87.42).

In 2003, of the 68 IPOs examined six were found to be efficient (Table 9.5) using the basic model. The IPO with the highest super-efficiency score is Accredited Home

---

[2] We removed one offering because of unavailable data.

Lenders (1.69258). The 'suggested' offering of these efficient IPOs were in the $9–16 price range. In terms of cross-efficiency score, Ctrip.com ranked in first place (98.91; Table 9.6).

In 2004, of the 215 (total 216 minus 1 because of no information) IPOs investigated only four are efficient using the basic model (Table 9.7). The efficient IPOs in this year were in the $5.50–19 price range. Using the super-efficiency model, Valley Bancorp attained the greatest efficiency score (2.67816). When we examine the cross-efficiency scores in Table 9.8 we find that JED Oil reached a cross-efficiency score of 99.85 and had the lowest offering price range, $5.50–5.50.

When we examine IPOs during the entire period we find that only six are efficient using basic efficiency and in terms of super-efficiency we observe that Valley Bancorp (4.76807) attains the highest score (Table 9.9). In terms of cross-efficiency (Table 9.10), JED Oil attains the highest score (99.68). In all periods we find that IPOs with small offer price ranges are efficient. This is possibly due to the aftermath of the Internet bubble, whereby firms have now reduced their offer price to reflect a more realistic value of their firm rather than the high offer price ranges of many deceased dot.com IPOs.

Table 9.5 Basic efficiency and super-efficiency scores of IPO launches in 2003

	Basic Efficiency	Super-Efficiency	Price Range ($)
Accredited Home Lenders	1.00000	1.69288	9.00–11.00
Ctrip.com	1.00000	1.28830	14.00–16.00
Buffalo Wild Wings	1.00000	1.08185	14.00–16.00
RedEnvelope	1.00000	1.06891	12.00–16.00
iPayment	1.00000	1.03478	14.00–16.00
InterVideo	1.00000	1.03235	11.00–13.00
Telkom SA	0.88841	–	13.30–14.80
Digital Theater Systems	0.84393	–	14.00–16.00
Kintera	0.83325	–	8.00–10.00
China Life Insurance	0.76114	–	15.35–18.80

Table 9.6 Cross-efficiency scores of IPO launches in 2003

	Cross-Efficiency	Price Range ($)
Ctrip.com	98.91	14.00–16.00
Accredited Home Lenders	81.32	9.00–11.00
iPayment	80.41	14.00–16.00
Kintera	78.14	8.00–10.00
Buffalo Wild Wings	77.77	14.00–16.00
Digital Theater Systems	77.53	14.00–16.00
Tessera Technologies	69.11	9.00–11.00
Telkom SA	65.75	13.30–14.80
Carter's	65.27	15.00–17.00
InterVideo	64.62	11.00–13.00

Table 9.7 Basic efficiency and super-efficiency scores of IPO launches in 2004

	Basic Efficiency	Super-Efficiency	Price Range ($)
Valley Bancorp	1.00000	2.67816	17.00–19.00
JED Oil	1.00000	1.63749	5.50–5.50
51job	1.00000	1.29595	11.00–13.00
Shanda Interactive	1.00000	1.04081	13.00–15.00
Marchex	0.96601	–	6.00–7.00
Community Bancorp	0.95424	–	18.00–20.00
Crosstex Energy, Inc.	0.92920	–	16.50–18.50
Atlas America	0.86405	–	14.00–16.00
eCOST.com	0.86282	–	9.00–11.00
Cogent Systems	0.85381	–	8.50–10.50

Table 9.8 Cross-efficiency scores of IPO launches in 2004

	Cross-Efficiency	Price Range ($)
JED Oil	99.85	5.50–5.50
51job	80.10	11.00–13.00
Arbinet-thexchange	76.26	14.00–16.00
Eyetech Pharmaceuticals	75.34	18.00–20.00
Shopping.com Ltd.	74.37	14.00–16.00
MarketAxess Holdings	73.36	8.50–10.50
Las Vegas Sands	71.46	20.00–22.00
PortalPlayer	70.57	11.00–13.00
Foxhollow Technologies	70.16	12.00–14.00
Cogent Systems	69.53	8.50–10.50

Table 9.9 Basic efficiency and super-efficiency scores of IPOs combined (2002 to 2004)

	Basic Efficiency	Super-Efficiency	Price Range ($)
51job	100	1.33649	11.00–13.00
Valley Bancorp.	100	4.76807	17.00–19.00
Accredited Home Lenders	100	1.00934	9.00–11.00
JED Oil	100	1.53383	5.50–5.50
Ctrip.com	100	1.04559	14.00–16.00
Shanda Interactive	100	1.01818	13.00–15.00
Marchex	96.60	–	6.00–7.00
Community Bancorp	93.89	–	18.00–20.00
Crosstex Energy, Inc.	92.03	–	16.50–18.50
Atlas America	86.40	–	14.00–16.00

Table 9.10. Cross-efficiency scores of IPO launches in 2004

	Cross-Efficiency	Price Range ($)
JED Oil	99.68	5.50–5.50
Ctrip.com	90.99	14.00–16.00
51job	78.50	11.00–13.00
Arbinet-thexchange	76.98	14.00–16.00
Eyetech Pharmaceuticals	75.28	18.00–20.00
Shopping.com Ltd.	74.88	14.00–16.00
MarketAxess Holdings	73.82	8.50–10.50
Las Vegas Sands	71.84	20.00–22.00
PortalPlayer	71.09	11.00–13.00
Digital Theater Systems	70.84	14.00–16.00

9.5 Conclusion

An interesting finding of this new research using DEA is that efficient IPOs seem to have a low price range in all periods. It seems that efficient IPOs with a low offering price may offer a better avenue when selecting IPOs. This warrants further research to investigate this issue on a long-run basis. The results have demonstrated that DEA can be used as an alternative performance measure to examine the efficiency of IPOs. Although we only investigate the very short-run performance, we are confident that future research on long-run performance will shed light on IPOs in the US and other world markets.

Acknowledgments – We thank Wolfgang Aussenegg for assistance with the data.

References

Andersen, P. N. and Petersen, N. N. (1993). A Procedure for Ranking Efficient Units in Data Envelopment Analysis. *Management Science*, 39(1):1261–1264.

Anderson, T. R., Hollingsworth, K. B., and Inman, L. B. (2002). The Fixed Weighting Nature of a Cross-evaluation Model. *Journal of Productivity Analysis*, 17(3):249–255.

Charnes, A., Cooper, W. W., and Rhodes, E. (1978). Measuring the Efficiency of Decision Making Units. *European Journal of Operational Research*, 2(6):429–444.

Doyle, J. and Green, R. (1994). Efficiency and Cross Efficiency in DEA: Derivations, Meanings and Uses. *Journal of the Operational Research Society*, 45(5):567–578.

Jain, B. and Kini, O. (1994). The Post-Issue Operating Performance of IPO Firms. *Journal of Finance*, 49(5):1699–1726.

Kooli, M. and Suret, J.-M. (2004). The Aftermarket Performance of Canadian Initial Public Offerings. *Journal of Multinational Financial Management*, 14(1):47–66.

Loughran, T. and Ritter, J. R. (1995). The New Issues Puzzle. *Journal of Finance*, 50(1):23–51.

Lyon, J. D., Barber, B. M., and Tsai, C. (1999). Improved Methods for Tests of Long-Run Abnormal Stock Returns. *Journal of Finance*, 54(1):165–201.

Miller, E. M. (1977). Risk, Uncertainty, and Divergence of Opinion. *Journal of Finance*, 32(4):1151–1168.

Nimalendran, M., Ritter, J. R. and Zhang, D. (2004). Are Trading Commissions a Factor in IPO Allocation? Working Paper, University of Florida, Miami, FL.

Ritter, J. R. (1991). The Long-Run Performance of Initial Public Offerings. *Journal of Finance*, 46(1):3–27.

Ritter, J. R. (2003). Investment Banking and Securities Issuance. In: *Handbook of the Economics of Finance* (Constantinides, G., Harris, M., and Stulz, R., eds). North-Holland, Amsterdam.

Sexton, T. R., Silkman, R. H., and Hogan, A. (1986). Data Envelopment Analysis: Critique and Extensions. In: *Measuring Efficiency and Assessment of Data Envelopment Analysis* (Silkman, R. H., ed.), Publication No. 32, New Directions of Program Evaluation. Jossey-Bass, San Francisco, CA.

Zhu, J. (2003). *Quantitative Models for Performance Evaluation and Benchmarking*. Kluwer Academic, New York.

Part Two
IPO Underpricing: International Evidence

10 Generalizing the winner's curse hypothesis: the case of the Belgian IPO market

Michel Boelen and Georges Hübner

Abstract

This chapter examines the winner's curse hypothesis on a sample of initial public offerings (IPOs) on the Belgian stock market from 1989 to 2004. The investor is assumed to be uninformed and to systematically allocate a lump sum to an initial order. Given the very heterogeneous set of allocation rules for the various IPOs under study, the payoff structure for this uninformed investor appears to be very nonlinear. Irrespective of the reserved amount and the holding period, we find no evidence of positive abnormal return for this strategy over the period, thus confirming the winner's curse hypothesis. However, conditioning the subscription to the direction of the stock market returns can provide positive abnormal returns under some circumstances.

10.1 Introduction

Is the initial public offering (IPO) a money machine enabling investors to systematically beat the stock market? To answer this type of question, it is unfortunately not sufficient to show that the subscription price of a new company introduced on the stock market is most frequently undervalued. There can be many rational explanations concerning this subject (Ritter, 1998).

Among the most prominent explanation based on information asymmetries between informed and uninformed investors, the 'winner's curse' hypothesis put forward by Rock (1986), resting on the information asymmetry between informed and uninformed investors, is probably one of the most theoretically appealing and empirically documented. However, at the level of each national market, it is not absolutely certain that this undervaluation reveals a persistent sign of market inefficiency, exploited by a set of informed investors.

To obtain a satisfactory answer to this particular problem, an acceptable and practical way is to reproduce as well as possible the conditions of the actual market and verify in which way an uniformed investor could take advantage of this alleged undervaluation. This direct test of the winner's curse hypothesis is similar to the ones performed by Koh and Walter (1989) and Keloharju (1993) on the Singapore and Finnish markets respectively. These transparent markets differ from most market settings, where the share allocation process is related to the relationship between subscribers and investment bankers, making a 'mechanical testing' of the predictions of the winner's curse only relevant at the aggregate levels, such as in the study by Michaely and Shaw (1994), who compared homogeneous groups of IPOs.

In this chapter, we attempt to study the winner's curse hypothesis on the First Market of the Euronext Brussels stock exchange.[1] Our approach is somewhat similar to that of Koh and Walter (1989), but adapted to a setting where the heterogeneity of the share allocation process is almost unique. In several countries, such as France (Biais and Faugeron, 2002; Vandemaele, 2003), multiple mechanisms have historically been used for share allocations at IPOs. This heterogeneity can be found, to an even larger extent, in the Belgian market. Contrary to the observable tendency in the standardization amongst the Anglo-Saxon markets, the last 15 years of the market in Belgium have been marked with an almost total anarchy in the manner of price fixation at introduction and the determination of allocation mechanisms. The simulation of these real conditions is especially crucial for the case of Belgium.

Over a period of 15 years between 1989 and 2004, we simulate the impact of a systematic strategy of investment in 49 IPOs performed on the First Market of the Belgian stock exchange. Unlike the Koh and Walter (1989) setting, who assessed the performance of systematic strategies of subscribing a multiple of shares for each IPO, this study sets a fixed amount that the investor systematically commits to invest. Moreover, the investment strategy is also considered over a fixed number of trading days. This joint set of constraints – fixed amounts and fixed period – creates a two-dimensional set of possible outcomes that can be statistically tested and even optimized.

In this setting, we can decompose our sample of IPOs on the basis of market trends (bullish or bearish), price setting methodology (bookbuilding, tender, or fixed price), and type of issued stocks (only new stock or a mix of new and existing stock).

To summarize our results, we find an extremely high volatility of returns of systematic strategies involving an initial commitment to a fixed amount invested in IPOs for a given time period. Because of this variability, we obtain a very high value for the average initial return of many strategies, but none of them is statistically significant. The optimal decision rule, involving only investments in the seven IPOs designed with bookbuilding, on bull markets and mixing new and existing stocks, would have obtained an average return of more than 65% over the (optimal) 3-month horizon. Due to the very high standard deviation of these returns, we cannot conclude that it is statistically significant, but we cannot reasonably argue that such a rate of return is not economically significant.

In section 10.2 we discuss data and methodology issues. Section 10.3 summarizes our empirical results. A conclusion is provided in section 10.4.

10.2 Data and methodology

We specifically test the winner's curse hypothesis on the First Market of the Euronext Brussels Stock Exchange. We continually adopt the standpoint of an uninformed individual investor who wants to make a systematic policy of investment in the IPOs from January 1989 to March 2004. Our study is based entirely on contemporaneous

[1] We have not considered the IPOs performed on the Euro.NM (Brussels market for smaller technology stocks), as this specific and short-lived segment, organized in parallel with other European countries, has developed in a disconnected way with the rest of the market (see Ritter, 2003, for a review).

IPO and market data at the time of decision. We will evaluate the return and the risks of each proposed policy and test the strategies to find the optimal amount and the duration of the investment.

10.2.1 Data

Based on the forms extracted and manually processed from the statistical department of Euronext Brussels and an internal report from the Degroof investment bank, a sample of 63 companies introduced during the period from January 1989 to March 2004 has been constructed. This encompasses all firms that performed their IPO on the First Market of the Brussels Stock Exchange, subsequently renamed Euronext Brussels. Among those companies, the stocks of Delen, Quick Restaurants, and Le Foyer were excluded because it was impossible to determine ex-ante their allocation mechanism. Eleven real estate companies were not considered because they had been legally forced to go public by a Belgian law during a certain period, independently of the market conditions. This leaves us with a workable sample of 49 companies.[2]

Usually, financial intermediaries sort buying orders from investors as a function of the number of shares sought. When demand exceeds supply, the manager (in agreement with the emerging company) settles different classes based on quantiles of ordered shares. The allocation mode is applicable for each tranche. As we were confronted with a high degree of diversity of allocation systems, we have defined six allocation modes that were applicable to these tranches:

1. 'No allocation' – investor fully receives the number of shares ordered.
2. 'Unique percentage' – investor receives $x\%$ of ordered shares.
3. 'Percentage with a maximum limit' – investor receives $x\%$ of ordered shares with a maximum of Y.
4. 'Percentage with a minimum level' – investor receives $x\%$ of ordered shares with a minimum of Y.
5. 'Fixed allocation' – investor receives Y stocks.
6. 'Fixed allocation plus a percentage of the surplus demand' – investor who has ordered Z shares receives Y shares plus $x\%$ of $Z - Y$ $(Y \leqslant Z)$.

The stocks of Dexia and Sioen Industry do not exactly fit into these categories. Their allocation system simply guaranteed a minimum of 15 and 20 stocks respectively. We classified this procedure in the fixed allocation category.

10.2.2 Methodology

Each tested strategy is characterized by an investable sum V and an investment horizon T. This leaves us with a two-dimensional space of strategies to test. To make it workable, we set a grid where the possible investable sums are a multiple k ($k = 1, ..., K$) of a unit amount V_0. On the other hand, we consider a time window of up to T from the day of the first quotation. This leaves a set of KT strategies.

To operationalize this set of strategies, we consider that V_0 is equal to €250. Of course, this amount may seem to be extremely small, but nothing prevents the investor from organizing a simultaneous subscription of the same amount through a large number of entry points in the syndicate (either through different members, by

---

[2] See Appendix for the list of companies.

different accounts, or with different persons). The committed amount of shares for each IPO is chosen so as not to exceed the available amount set by the investor. Given that the maximum allocation provided to individual investors corresponded to an amount of € 22,250 (fees included), we have set $k = 89$.

The time unit is the business day market. This measure will only consider the opening days of the stock exchange, whose calendar is publicly known. The period of investment covers $T = 102$ business days.

First, we have to determine the real sum invested (S_{i0}) in each IPO i $(i = 1, ..., 49)$:

$$S_{i0} = (Q_{i0} \times P_{i0}) \times (1 + pf_0), \tag{10.1}$$

with Q_{i0} the number of stocks purchased under the applicable allocation mechanism, P_{i0} the introductory price of the stock, and pf_0 the proportional purchasing fees.

We then compute the return of a systematic investment policy without further trade until the investment horizon. This return is obtained for a sum $V = kV_0$ borrowed on the monetary market for a time period t, as shown in the expression below:

$$r_{i,k,t} = \frac{[(Q_{i0} \times P_{it}) \times (1-sf) - S_{i0}] - S_{i0}\left[\dfrac{I_t - I_0}{I_0}\right] + (V - S_{i0})\left[(1+l_{i0})^{\frac{c(t)}{360}}(1+b_{i0})^{\frac{c(t)}{360}}\right]}{V}, \tag{10.2}$$

with r_{ikt} the abnormal return for stock i with a committed investment of $V = kV_0$ on a period of t business days market, P_{it} the closing price for stock i after t business days, sf selling fees, I_0 the Belgian All Shares index the day before the IPO, I_t the Belgian All Shares index on the selling day of the stock, V the sum borrowed for investment, l_{i0} (b_{i0}) the 3-month lending (borrowing) interest rate loan on the day of IPO i, and $c(t)$ the number of calendar days plus one between the purchase and the sale.

Equation (10.2) simply represents the actual rate of return of the strategy minus the opportunity cost of the use of funds. This procedure is somewhat similar to the market-adjusted return used in most event studies, except that the uncertainty surrounding the effectively invested sum (S_{i0}) triggers a different treatment between funds invested in the stock market and the funds lent on the money market.

Over the number of IPOs in the sample, the return of a strategy characterized by parameters (k,t) is equalized to the average market-adjusted return obtained for each individual IPO:

$$\bar{r}_{k,t} = \frac{1}{n}\sum_{i=1}^{n} r_{i,k,t}, \tag{10.3}$$

where n represents the sample size.

Finally, we obtain the return of the optimal strategy by identifying the maximum average return in the grid of all possible values of k and t:

$$r^* = \max_{k,t}\bar{r}_{k,t}, \tag{10.4}$$

where $1 < t \leq 102$, $0 \leq V \leq 22,250$.

10.2.3 Additional assumptions

The diversity of the IPO characteristics and incompleteness of information for some operations lead us to set a certain number of assumptions:

- In many cases, two systems coexist for a single IPO – one more favorable for clients of the investment bank's members of the syndicate, and one for the other financial intermediaries. We kept the mechanisms applicable for the syndicate.
- If the investor subscribes a lower number of shares than the ones allocated in the minimum tranche, we consider that he or she obtains the total number of ordered securities.
- If the allocation is done with a percentage (e.g. each investors receives 10% of the requested amounts), we round the number of shares obtained down to the integer below, unless otherwise specified in the prospectus.
- If the issuing price is above the amount V to be invested, we stipulate that the investor does not wish to purchase this stock. It is not accounted for in the computation of the excess return. The same rule applies if the investor is simply not allocated any shares.

10.3   Empirical results

10.3.1   Raw undervaluation of IPOs

Before turning to the implementation of the proposed strategies, we check whether the common hypothesis of average underpricing of IPOs on the First Market of the Brussels Stock Exchange was fulfilled for the period under study. We simply collect the unadjusted returns of the IPOs, irrespective of the allocation systems.

Figure 10.1 reports the market-adjusted return of this systematic subscription strategy, considering purchasing fees of 0.35% and selling fees of 1.5%, the percentages being the average of transaction costs applicable during the sample period.

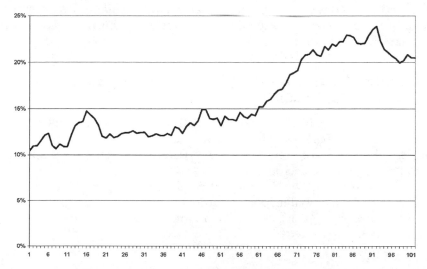

Figure 10.1 Average raw abnormal returns of 49 IPOs recorded on the First Market of the Brussels Stock Exchange, January 1989 to March 2004

Table 10.1 Descriptive statistics of the sample

Item	Value
Sample size	49
Number positive	20
Number negative	29
Range	108.92%
Minimum	−12.91%
Maximum	96.01%
Mean	10.44%
Median	2.22%
Standard deviation	22.30%
Skewness	2.36
Kurtosis	5.64

Based on the sample of 49 companies, we observe an average initial return of 10.44% on the first trading day. The returns peak on days 6 and 15, while the maximum return overall is observed for a holding period of 92 days, with an average return of 23%.

Table 10.1 describes the distribution of the returns over the first trading day for the total sample. The span of observed initial returns is quite large, as the investor could achieve differential returns of up to 108% from the worst to the best outcome. Not surprisingly, the positive skewness and high kurtosis suggest a large non-normality[3] of returns, with fat tails and right asymmetry. The mean return is thus not very symptomatic of the most likely result of systematic subscriptions, as the median return is much closer to zero. We observe a high level of standard deviation of initial returns, indicating that the mere application of the t-test would not lead to the rejection of the null hypothesis of the absence of abnormal return.

As the objective of this chapter is not the analysis of the underpricing phenomenon in general, from now on we focus on the constraints of the individual investor trying to maximize his or her profit.

10.3.2 Profitability of systematic subscription strategies over the whole period (1989 to 2004)

We first assess the effects of a policy of systematically subscribing to IPOs independently of the prevailing market conditions or the characteristics of the operation. Next, we consider the impact of conditioning the order to elements observable by the investor at the time of the decision.

Figure 10.2 displays the two-dimensional graph of average excess returns for each considered pair (V,t) of initial investment (from €250 to 22,250) and number of days in the holding period (from 1 to 102). We use the allocation mechanism corresponding to each IPO.

---

[3] The assumption of normality of the distribution of returns is rejected by the Jarque–Bera test throughout the chapter.

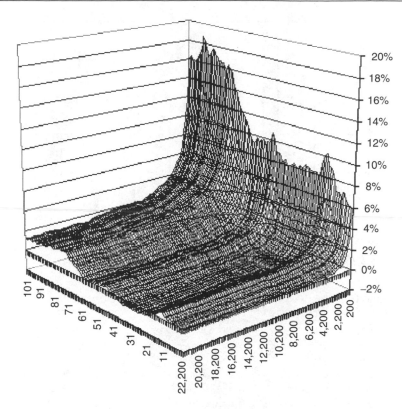

Figure 10.2 Average abnormal returns of 49 IPOs adjusted for their allocation rules for invested amounts ranging from €250 to 22,250 and holding period ranging from 1 to 102 trading days

From Figure 10.2, we can immediately observe that the policy can only be profitable for very small unit amounts. The maximum average returns arc located on the far right of the chart, implying that an uninformed investor will mostly gain from very small investments. Furthermore, the highest rate of return is achieved at the bottom of the graph, which corresponds to the longest holding period. This finding seems to contradict the common view that the highest abnormal returns can be obtained for very short time intervals.

Figure 10.3 reports the observed frequencies of abnormal returns corresponding to the 9078 (89 × 102) possible strategies.

Approximately 20% of the strategies yield a negative rate of return, while 68% give a return ranging between 0% and 3%. As a matter of fact, only 1.08% of the strategies resulted in an average return above 10%. The highest return is achieved for a strategy consisting of investing €250 for a period of 92 trading days. The relevant statistics are reported in Table 10.2.

The average abnormal return of 18.73% must be considered with caution, as it is associated with a standard deviation of more than 55%, indicating that this positive average return is very likely to be insignificant (this value alone would locate 68% of the observations in a confidence interval between −36% and +74% under the normal distribution). In particular, more than half of the stocks obtain a negative

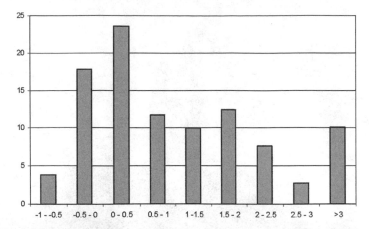

Figure 10.3 Frequency distribution of average abnormal returns for invested amounts ranging from €250 to 22,250 and holding period ranging from 1 to 102 trading days (9078 strategies)

Table 10.2 Summary statistics for the optimal strategy (t = 92, V = 250)

Item	Value
Sample size[a]	48
Number positive	19
Number negative	23
Number where no share obtained[b]	6
Range	318.39%
Minimum	−64.67%
Maximum	253.72%
Mean	18.73%
Median	0.00%
Standard deviation	55.40%
Skewness	2.45
Kurtosis	7.19

[a] One IPO has been left out as the initial price was above the investment limit of €250.
[b] In six cases, the allocation rule did not result in any share allocated for the requested amount.

abnormal return during the holding period. Removing the six stocks that the investor could not obtain does not change the results qualitatively.

As a matter of fact, the correlation coefficient between the individual returns obtained using this optimal strategy and the ones achieved irrespective of the allocation rules (Table 10.1) is equal to 97.37%, suggesting that this commitment of only investing €250 is in fact very close to experiencing the IPO abnormal returns without any particular allocation mechanism.

If the investor decided to fully invest the amount of € 250 by purchasing, at the end of the first trading, the number of shares that he or she could not obtain because of the rationing of share allocation, the average excess return under the optimal strategy would be 18.81% for a standard deviation of 55.53%. The results would not different from those where an allocation mechanism is absent, as in Table 10.1.

Our results could be somewhat improved if we decided to sell the shares that had not been rationed during the first trading day: the average abnormal return would be 19.97% for a standard deviation of 56.28%. No significant improvement can be achieved by combining the sale of undersubscribed shares and the purchase of oversubscribed stocks.

Of course, confronted with such a skewed distribution of returns, the investor would probably long for an ex-ante strategy that would only leave him or her with the more favorable outcomes. This quest is explored in the next subsection.

10.3.3 Profitability of conditional subscription strategies

10.3.3.1 Investment in bullish markets

What if the investor only relied on bullish stock market periods? Derrien (2005) showed, with a sample of French IPOs, that positive investor sentiment about the market conditions typically leads to positive excess returns in short time periods, while these IPOs tend to underperfom in the long run.

We represent this short-mindedness through the moving average of the market returns over a very short period (20 trading days).[4] If the drift is positive at the time of the IPO, the investor decides to invest, and withdraws from the IPO otherwise. This leaves us with 60% (30) of the total number of IPOs in 'bullish' market conditions.

Table 10.3 summarizes the frequency distributions of average abnormal returns for the subsamples split on the basis of market conditions.

The pattern of returns for the bull market does not look very different from that for the whole sample displayed in Figure 10.3. There are very few IPOs with negative returns, but the bulk of the returns (more than 50%) is lower than 3%. Similarly to

Table 10.3 Frequency distribution of average abnormal return for invested amounts in bull markets (30 IPOs) and bear markets (19 IPOs)

Bull market		Bear market	
Interval	Frequency (%)	Interval	Frequency (%)
[−1%,0%]	0.28	[−9%,−4%]	11.80
[0%,1%]	9.08	[−4%,−3.5%]	18.32
[1%,2%]	27.66	[−3.5%,−3%]	24.79
[2%,3%]	13.40	[−3%,−2.5%]	19.61
[3%,4%]	7.87	[−2.5%,−2%]	5.93
[4%,5%]	11.97	[−2%,−1.5%]	0.51
[5%,6%]	15.55	[−1.5%,−1%]	7.64
[6%,7%]	4.30	[−1%,−0.5%]	7.15
[7%,8%]	2.74	[−0.5%,0%]	3.59
[8%,31%]	7.16	[0%,4%]	0.67

---

[4] Alternative characterizations did not significantly alter our results.

the results obtained for the whole sample, the optimal average return of 30.16% is obtained for 91 days with an invested amount of €250.

Nevertheless, the segregation of bullish and bearish IPOs enables the investor to get rid of outcomes that are typically negative, as 'only bearish' strategies almost never achieve an average positive return. Among these strategies, the best one achieves an average return of 3.63%. It is optimal to sell the position on the very first trading day, which tends to confirm that in hard times, there seems to be a tendency of the members of the syndicate to temporarily support the quote of the newly issued stock for a couple of days before the price begins to decrease.

10.3.3.2   Investment in bookbuilding-based IPOs

The IPO market in Belgium is extremely fragmented. The three major ordering systems, namely the bookbuilding, tender (auction), and fixed price systems, have coexisted over the sample period. Figure 10.4 displays the distribution of IPOs among these three subscription systems.

Unlike on the US market, which is almost entirely dominated by the bookbuilding method, we observe a large variety of approaches on the Belgian market. Approximately half of the IPOs (24) in the sample have been performed under the tender approach. Bookbuilding (17 IPOs) and fixed price (8) share the other half.

Table 10.4 summarizes the frequency distribution of the possible systematic strategies targeting either pricing method.

The bookbuilding approach could represent an efficient way to reduce information asymmetry, and thus shrink the underpricing by several percent, provided that the underwriters can reward institutional investors with a more favorable allocation (Welch, 1992; Ritter and Welch, 2002). However, as noted by Hanley (1993) and Cornelli and Goldreich (2003), the gradual dissemination of information by informed investors most likely results in sustained underpricing. Belgian evidence confirms this view. The underpricing of IPOs in Belgium seems to be concentrated among the offerings that use this price formation system, and there is very little evidence of a winner's curse issue under this pattern. As a matter of fact, none of the strategies applied to the bookbuilding-based IPOs results in negative average returns, which is in itself a remarkable result. In contrast, the fixed price offers deliver a bitter blow to investors, as this blind method never delivers any positive mean return in the short run for systematic investment strategies. We find that the tender system is intermediate between the other two, as 95% of the outcomes provide an average return lower

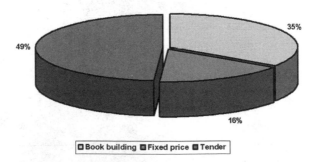

Figure 10.4 Proportions of book building, fixed price, and tender systems in the IPO sample

Table 10.4 Frequency distribution of average abnormal return for invested amounts with the bookbuilding (17 IPOs), fixed price (eight IPOs), and tender (24 IPOs) approaches

Bookbuilding		Fixed price		Tender	
Interval	Frequency (%)	Interval (%)	Frequency (%)	Interval (%)	Frequency
[0%,1.5%]	19.15	[−10%,−9%]	7.44	[−1%,−0.5%]	5.06
[1.5%,3%]	23.01	[−9%,−8%]	11.18	[−0.5%,0%]	39.81
[3%,4.5%]	11.93	[−8%,−7%]	10.80	[0%,0.5%]	36.49
[4.5%,6%]	5.49	[−7%,−6%]	10.96	[0.5%,1%]	14.44
[6%,7.5%]	8.18	[−6%,−5%]	10.35	[1%,1.5%]	1.71
[7.5%,9%]	12.83	[−5%,−4%]	0.87	[1.5%,2%]	0.67
[9%,10.5%]	6.80	[−4%,−3%]	28.24	[2%,2.5%]	0.50
[10.5%,12%]	3.17	[−3%,−2%]	14.93	[2.5%,3%]	0.37
[12%,13.5%]	2.07	[−2%,−1%]	5.11	[3%,3.5%]	0.37
[13.5%,50%]	7.37	[−1%,0%]	0.12	[3.5%,6%]	0.57

Table 10.5 Summary statistics for the optimal strategy with bookbuilding ($t = 91$, $V = 250$)

Item	Value
Sample size	17
Number positive	9
Number negative	6
Number where no share obtained	2
Range	280.14%
Minimum	−26.50%
Maximum	253.64%
Mean	48.17%
Median	2.05%
Standard deviation	79.67%
Skewness	1.41
Kurtosis	1.35

than 1%. Indeed, the bookbuilding approach outperforms the best return of 6% achieved by the tender approach in 40.3% of the simulated strategies.

As before, the optimal return for systematic strategies using the bookbuilding approach is achieved for a strategy consisting of investing €250 for a period of 91 trading days. The relevant statistics are reported in Table 10.5.

We can still not conclude on the basis of classical statistical inference that the systematic adoption of very small orders restricted to IPOs organized under the bookbuilding system delivers significant average abnormal returns. Nevertheless, the values of the skewness and kurtosis suggest that the outliers of the initial sample have been partly removed, leaving us with a more homogeneous distribution around the

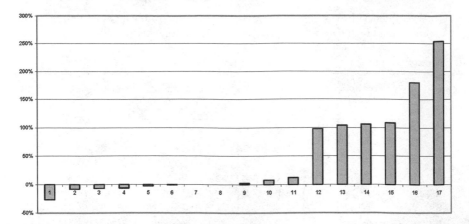

Figure 10.5 Returns of the individual IPOs organized with bookbuilding under the optimal strategy

mean. Although the results are still not statistically significant, they begin to make some sense economically.

This view is confirmed by the visual impression left by the histogram representing the individual returns of 17 IPOs organized with the bookbuilding system under this optimal strategy. This graph is reproduced in Figure 10.5.

10.3.3.3 Investment in IPOs proposing new shares

The sample displays initial offerings of new and/or existing stocks. Only four companies proposed an IPO consisting of only new shares. Among the remaining 45 operations, 19 IPOs proposed only existing shares while 26 mixed new and existing shares.

The offering of existing shares can be analyzed in the spirit of the signaling model of Leland and Pyle (1977), who showed that the proportion of retained equity kept by existing shareholders during the IPO provides a positive signal. A more formal treatment of this idea is provided by Grinblatt and Hwang (1989), who considered that a credible signal can be sent by the combination of initial underpricing and retained shares. Consistent with their hypothesis, we expect offers mixing new and existing shares to outperform those proposing only new shares. The results of splitting the sample according to this criterion are provided in Table 10.6.

Here again, the difference is revealing, as 80% of observed average returns are negative for existing shares offers, while we observe only positive average abnormal returns for offers mixing new and existing shares. This is obviously in line with Grinblatt and Hwang's (1989) conjecture that IPOs that reduce dilution provide some level of underpricing to convey their signal about the quality of the issuing firm. Unfortunately, as for the previous case, we cannot conclude that the positive outcome is statistically significant for the optimal strategy.

10.3.3.4 A combined strategy

Naturally, as we have obtained that conditioning the order to market or organizational characteristics of the IPO is likely to provide very attractive outcomes on average, we

Table 10.6 Frequency distribution of average abnormal return for invested amounts with the existing share offers (19 IPOs) and mixed offers (26 IPOs)

Existing shares		New and existing shares	
Interval	Frequency (%)	Interval	Frequency (%)
[−2%,−1.5%]	5.11	[0%,1%]	8.78
[−1.5%,−1%]	15.96	[1%,2%]	25.93
[−1%,−0.5%]	34.10	[2%,3%]	18.05
[−0.5%,0%]	25.31	[3%,4%]	6.71
[0%,0.5%]	12.19	[4%,5%]	4.99
[0.5%,1%]	2.23	[5%,6%]	13.87
[1%,1.5%]	1.08	[6%,7%]	8.24
[1.5%,2%]	0.74	[7%,8%]	4.22
[2%,2.5%]	0.67	[8%,9%]	2.36
[2.5%,9%]	2.60	[9%,32%]	6.85

are tempted to combine our criteria and to check whether we could at last achieve economically as well as statistically significant abnormal returns.

In our sample, there are seven IPOs that combine the desired features: bullish markets, bookbuilding, and mixed offers. Simply combining them and accepting the allocation rule would merely leave us with a profile of returns that closely resembles the one reported in Figure 10.1.[5] Therefore, we add one additional feature to this strategy – namely, for each IPO, we purchase the number of shares that we could not obtain because of the restriction in allocations by the underwriter. This leaves us with a fully invested sum in each of the seven IPOs. A chart plotting the observed average abnormal returns for all strategies is shown in Figure 10.6.

The visual impression is striking. Even for large invested amounts, the observed average return of this constrained strategy is above 60% at the end of the investment horizon. This seems to indicate that this strategy is likely to successfully use all relevant information to beat the winner's curse and leave the investor with the upside of underpricing. The highest return of 94.09% is again obtained for $V =$ €250 and a 91-day investment horizon. Among the 9078 strategies, only 0.9% have a negative return not exceeding −3% in absolute value. More than 75% of the occurrences experience a return higher than 20% and more than 36% exceed a 50% return.

To confirm our impression, Table 10.7 analyzes the strategy consisting of investing the maximum amount of €22,250 over the optimal investment horizon of 91 days. This choice of invested amount enables us to free ourselves from the criticism of only considering negligible investments for our analysis.

Although we cannot really consider that these results are disappointing, the small number of IPOs does not allow the mean abnormal return to be statistically significant. Nonetheless, the very high skewness of the returns distribution, the relatively small minimum (in absolute value), and the close levels of the mean and the median

---

[5] Results available upon request.

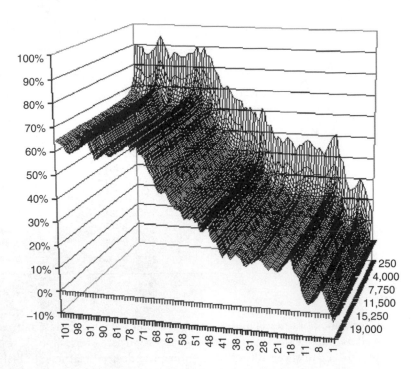

Figure 10.6 Average abnormal returns of seven IPOs performed in bullish market conditions with bookbuilding, and mixing new and existing stock, for invested amounts ranging from €250 to 22,250 and holding period ranging from one to 102 trading days

Table 10.7 Summary statistics for the strategy ($t = 91$, $V = 250$) with bull markets, bookbuilding, and mixed offers

Item	Value
Sample size	7
Number positive	5
Number negative	2
Range	248.31%
Minimum	−8.61%
Maximum	239.70%
Mean	68.38%
Median	66.43%
Standard deviation	87.21%
Skewness	1.41
Kurtosis	2.18

indicate that this strategy is more reliable as a potential value creator than any other previous one. This finding is all the more interesting in that we only picked one-seventh (7/49) of the total sample, thus reducing the number of observations and inducing more variability of the mean.

10.4 Conclusion

Based on the sample of IPOs performed on the First Market of Euronext Belgium, we consistently find evidence of underpricing that can be quite severe on average. However, taking into account the prevailing allocation systems, which can be very different from one issue to another, there is no significant evidence of the possibility of escaping the winner's curse phenomenon for an uninformed investor. Economically significant returns can be obtained for very low levels of investment, but the high volatility of observed returns over a 4-month horizon does not enable us to extract scientifically valid evidence of positive initial returns. The 'clever' attitude of picking only the IPOs that are likely to show consistent underpricing, i.e. in bullish market conditions, with the bookbuilding subscription system or with a mix of new and existing shares, leaves very appealing returns for any mix of invested amounts/investment horizon.

We are aware that the small sample size and the high non-normality of returns do not enable us to perform robust statistical inference. Instead of relying on nonparametric techniques, we have opted for a more economic view of our results. There appears to be clear indications of almost systematic IPO underpricing profits that can be booked (even) by uninformed investors. These are the economic conclusions. As researchers though, we prefer to leave the question open, as the very high range of observations does not enable us to reject the efficient market hypothesis. Probably a new batch of 15 years of data could provide us with the necessary sample size to yield undisputable results.

Acknowledgments – We thank Christelle Tremine Wilson from ARM and Bank Degroof (Belgium) for providing the data. Georges Hübner thanks Deloitte (Luxembourg) for financial support. All errors are our own.

References

Biais, B. and Faugeron, A.-M. (2002). IPO Auctions: English, Dutch, French and Internet. *Journal of Financial Intermediation*, 11(1):9–36.

Cornelli, F. and Goldreich, D. (2003). Bookbuilding: How Informative Is the Order Book? *Journal of Finance*, 58(4):1415–1443.

Derrien, F. (2005). IPO Pricing in "Hot" Market Conditions: Who Leaves Money on the Table? *Journal of Finance*, 60(1):487–521.

Grinblatt, M. and Hwang, C. Y. (1989). Signalling and the Pricing of New Issues. *Journal of Finance*, 44(2):393–420.

Hanley, K. (1993). The Underpricing of Initial Public Offerings and the Partial Adjustment Phenomenon. *Journal of Financial Economics*, 34(2):231–250.

Keloharju, M. (1993). The Winner's Curse, Legal Liability, and the Long-Run Price Performance of IPO in Finland. *Journal of Financial Economics*, 34(2):251–277.

Koh, F. and Walter, T. (1989). A Direct Test of Rock's Model of the Pricing of Unseasoned Issues. *Journal of Financial Economics*, 23(2):251–272.

Leland, H. and Pyle, D. (1977). Information Asymmetries, Financial Structures and Financial Intermediaries. *Journal of Finance*, 32(2):371–387.

Michaely, R. and Shaw, W. H. (1994). The Pricing of Initial Public Offerings: Tests of Adverse-Selection and Signaling Theories. *Review of Financial Studies*, 7(2):279–319.

Ritter, J. R. (1998). Initial Public Offerings. *Contemporary Finance Digest*, 2(1):5–30.

Ritter, J. R. (2003). Differences between European and American IPO Markets. *European Financial Management*, 9(4):421–434.

Ritter, J. R. and Welch, I. (2002). A Review of IPO Activity, Pricing, and Allocations. *Journal of Finance*, 57(4):1795–1828.

Rock, K. (1986). Why New Issues Are Underpriced. *Journal of Financial Economics*, 15(1–2):187–212.

Vandemaele, S. (2003). Choice of Selling Mechanism at the IPO: The Case of the French Second Market. *European Financial Management*, 9(4):435–455.

Welch, I. (1992). Sequential Sales, Learning, and Cascades. *Journal of Finance*, 47(2):695–732.

Appendix

Table 10.A1 List of companies in the sample

Company name	IPO date	Activity	Initial price (€)	Pricing method	Shares EN	Cycle
Société Foncière Int	10 May 89	Real estate	75.61	Tender	E	Bullish
Definance	2 Nov 89	Holding	34.58	Fixed price	N	Bearish
Desimpel	1 Jun 90	Construction	32.23	Tender	E	Bullish
Creyf's Interim	14 Jun 90	Temping services	47.72	Tender	E	Bullish
Polypal Europe	22 Jun 90	Metal	55.78	Tender	E	Bullish
A.G. 1990	4 Apr 91	Insurance	61.97	Fixed price	N	Bullish
City Hotels	10 Oct 91	Real estate	98.54	Tender	E	Bearish
Imperial Invest	6 Jan 93	Holding	27.76	Fixed price	E	Bullish
Befimmo	20 Dec 95	Sicafi	49.45	Fixed price	E	Bullish
Distrigaz	17 Jun 96	Utilities	694.10	Fixed price	E	Bullish
Sioen Industries	18 Oct 96	Textile	34.71	Fixed price	E	Bullish
Dexia/CCB	20 Nov 96	Bank	66.31	Tender	E	Bullish
Neuhaus	4 Mar 97	Food	43.38	Tender	E	Bullish
Systemat	26 Mar 97	Computer	29.13	Tender	E/N	Bullish
Real Software	10 Jun 97	Computer	37.18	Tender	E	Bullish
Brantano	16 Jun 97	Retail	27.76	Book building	E	Bullish
Hamon	23 Jun 97	Cooling systems	56.52	Tender	E/N	Bullish
GIMV	26 Jun 97	Holding	49.83	Book building	E	Bullish
IPSO-ILG	27 Jun 97	Washing machines	37.18	Book building	E/N	Bullish
Van de Velde	1 Oct 97	Apparel	39.04	Tender	E	Bullish
Resilux	3 Oct 97	Plastic packaging	30.99	Book building	E/N	Bullish
Associated Weavers	10 Oct 97	Carpet	25.41	Book building	E	Bullish
Kinépolis	9 Apr 98	Movie theaters	39.66	Book building	E/N	Bullish
Ion Beam Application	22 Jun 98	Proton therapy	59.49	Book building	E/N	Bullish
Omega Pharma	26 Jun 98	Pharma distributie	30.99	Tender	E/N	Bullish
Photo Hall	3 Jul 98	Consumer electronics	27.89	Tender	E/N	Bullish
Quest for Growth	23 Sep 98	Pricaf	25.78	Fixed price	N	Bearish

Company name	IPO date	Activity	Initial price (€)	Pricing method	Shares EN	Cycle
Miko	29 Sep 98	Coffee	33.47	Tender	E/N	Bearish
Mobistar	6 Oct 98	Telecom	30.61	Book building	E/N	Bearish
EVS	15 Oct 98	Slow motion devices	37.18	Book building	E/N	Bearish
Remi Claeys Aluminium	3 Dec 98	Aluminum	32.23	Book building	E/N	Bullish
Roularta	4 Dec 98	Media	37.18	Tender	E/N	Bullish
Ontex	11 Dec 98	Hygiene products	41.40	Book building	E/N	Bullish
Punch International	16 Mar 99	Components supplier	68.00	Book building	E/N	Bearish
VPK Packaging	9 Apr 99	Packaging	29.00	Tender	E/N	Bearish
Fountain Industries	29 Apr 99	Hot drinks	56.00	Book building	E/N	Bearish
Bureau Van Dijk	10 May 99	SAP implementation	30.00	Book building	E	Bearish
IRIS sa	18 May 99	Image recognition	34.00	Tender	E/N	Bearish
Agfa-Gevaert	1 Jun 99	Imaging	22.00	Tender	E	Bearish
Carestel sa	2 Jun 99	Food, lodging, etc.	32.00	Tender	E/N	Bearish
Vranken Monopole sa	9 Jun 99	Wine	55.00	Fixed price	E/N	Bearish
Mitiska sa	17 Jun 99	Distribution holdings	33.50	Tender	E/N	Bullish
Duvel Moortgat	22 Jun 99	Brewery	36.50	Tender	E/N	Bullish
Pinguin	25 Jun 99	Frozen vegetables	26.00	Tender	N	Bearish
ARINSO International	31 Mar 00	SAP, ERP software	40.00	Tender	E/N	Bearish
Integrated Product (IPTE)	22 May 00	Assembling and testing	22.00	Tender	E/N	Bearish
Interbrew (Inbev)	1 Dec 00	Brewery	33.00	Book building	E/N	Bearish
Docpharma	29 Jun 01	Pharma distribution	9.00	Book building	E/N	Bullish
Belgacom	22 Mar 04	Telecom	24.50	Book building	E	Bearish

11 Flipping activity in fixed offer price mechanism allocated IPOs

Dimitrios Gounopoulos

Abstract

The purpose of this chapter is to study the phenomenon of flipping (liquidation of an initial public offering (IPO) in the first 2–3 days of trading) in the immediate aftermarket. The trading behavior of all investors in 51 IPOs that took place from January 2000 to December 2000 with a fixed offer price mechanism is investigated. Electronic share settlement records are accessed for each company to investigate whether initial subscribers flip their shares during the first 2 days of trading and whether this flipping behavior relates to issuer, shareholder, underwriter, and market characteristics.

On average, flipping accounts for only 37.67% of trading volume and 24.30% of shares offered during the first 2 days of trading. Institutions do more flipping than retail investors and cold IPOs are flipped much more than hot IPOs. Firms newly listed by reputable underwriters surprisingly present high flipping at 43.5%, while less reputable banks and syndicates show 34.1% flipping activity for their IPOs.

This chapter presents a model of the flipping behavior in terms of share allocation. The model shows that institutional investors optimally choose to flip more in larger IPOs. Market classification is a factor that affects flipping activity as institutional investors prefer to flip more in IPOs of secondary (parallel) markets. In this model no significant flipping activity by retail investors is found.

11.1 Introduction

During the last decades there has been increased attention paid to studying the prior and immediate aftermarket performance of initial public offerings (IPOs). Such interest does not exist for firms that have been listed on the stock exchange for many years. The reason for this different treatment has to do with the belief that decisions during this period may affect the firm's performance for many months after the offering on the stock market.

Flipping, defined by Bayley et al. (2003) as 'the liquidation of IPO allocation in the first day of seasoning', is the easiest way to make money through an IPO by purchase of the new shares directly from the underwriter and then selling them immediately on the open market. Specifically, flipping is the reselling of a hot IPO stock in the first few days (or day) to earn a quick profit. This is not easy to do, and investors are strongly discouraged by underwriters. The reason is that underwriters want long-term investors who hold their stocks. There are no laws that prevent flipping, but the underwriter may blacklist 'bad' investors from future offerings.

Flipping has mainly negative but also positive influences. It is mainly negative for underwriters, as they risk inventory losses arising from reselling flipped shares in a declining market. Correra (1992) reported that underwriters are at 'war against IPO flippers', noting that 'the aim of the underwriters is to thwart out those nefarious types ... who buy a new issue and dump it quickly'.

Positive aspects of flipping have to do with aftermarket liquidity, which may decrease the cost of trading and lower the issuing firm's cost of capital (Amihud and Mendelsen, 1986). Ellis et al. (2000) pointed out the economic benefits that arise from flipping, while Fishe (2001) showed that underwriters can gain through covering their short position from a suppressed aftermarket price caused by flipping.

In order to avoid negative consequences (where a high level of flipping creates disappointment for the remaining investors), in many markets underwriters apply stabilization activities to prevent the stock price falling below the psychological level of the offer price. Part of this stabilization method is to allocate a higher level of underpriced IPOs to institutional investors because they are long-term investors and they will not flip in the short term. It is necessary in a few cases for investment banks to buy flipped shares in the immediate aftermarket in order to establish stability in the trading activity of some weak IPOs. Fishe (2001) reported that, in contrast to existing models of stabilization, the underwriter gains from aftermarket purchases, particularly if the contract with the issuer includes an overallotment[1] option. The overallotment option encourages a lower offer price, which may lead to underpricing.

The model used here is estimated on the basis of a sample which constitutes big investment houses and private investors. It is shown that flipping can be mainly explained by initial returns of the IPO and the reputation of the underwriter. In this approach, a unique data set is used that permits a comprehensive empirical analysis of the flipping activities by IPO customers after adjusting the allocations made to institutional and private investors.

The remainder of the chapter proceeds as follows. Section 11.2 analyzes the methodology and the data. Section 11.3 provides descriptive results on flipping activity, initial returns, type of lead underwriter, and by market categorization. Section 11.4 outlines the hypothesis which will be tested and provides the model. Section 11.5 examines the results from multivariate analysis. Section 11.6 concludes this study.

11.2 Methodology and sample description

In order to calculate flipping ratios for each IPO in the sample, the following formulae are created and summed for the total amount of IPO investors in each firm. These flipping measures are denoted by the number of shares flipped over the first 2 days.

$$STSO = \frac{\text{Shares Traded}}{\text{Shares Offered}} \times 100 \tag{11.1}$$

$$SFTV = \frac{\text{Shares Flipped}}{\text{Trading Volume}} \times 100 \tag{11.2}$$

---

[1] The underwriter and issuer set the size of the issue. The issuer grants the underwriter an overallotment option to purchase shares at the underwriter's discounted price. If the underwriter does not exercise the overallotment option, then any short position must be covered at the aftermarket price. The overallotment option allows the underwriter to avoid paying the aftermarket price when it exceeds the exercise price of the option.

$$\text{SFSO} = \frac{\text{Shares Flipped}}{\text{Shares Offered}} \times 100 \tag{11.3}$$

$$\text{SFSA} = \frac{\text{Shares Flipped by Institutions}}{\text{Shares Allocated to Institutions}} \times 100 \tag{11.4}$$

where:

STSO = Shares Traded/Shares Offered
SFTV = Shares Flipped/Trading Volume
SFSO = Shares Flipped/Shares Offered
SFSA = Shares Flipped/Shares Allocated.

First, three of these metrics will be tested at a descriptive level and then cross-sectional regression testing is carried out for the fourth. In addition, further multivariate analysis will be undertaken on the retail investors.

Table 11.1 provides several characteristics for the 51 IPOs, which will help us to study flipping activity in the Greek market. We observe that the total number of shares traded in the first 2 days as a percentage of total shares offered for IPOs listed with a fixed offer mechanism is 72.46%. The shares flipped are 37.67% of the total trading volume and 24.30% of the total shares offered.

11.3   Descriptive results on flipping

Table 11.2 reports that 37.67% of the trading volume in the first 2 days is due to shares being flipped. Only 23.65% (median 15.67%) of shares offered in the IPO are flipped on the second day; this percentage is lower on the third and fourth days of trading.

Krigman et al. (1999) noticed that one aspect of IPOs often highlighted by the financial press is the heavy first-day trading that puts many IPO firms on the list of the largest volume stocks for the day. To provide a basic understanding of the magnitude of first-day trading, we calculate the total number of shares traded on the first 2 days as a percentage of the number of shares offered in the IPO.

The variation in the flipping activity among IPO groups, classified by initial returns, is provided in Table 11.2(B). Results show that the percentage of 'shares traded as a percentage of total shares offered' is higher in the hot IPO sample. It is noticeable that during the first 2 days of trading, 90.91% of the total shares offered have been traded. This figure becomes lower as we move to less underpriced shares.

The study on flipping reveals that during the first 2 days investors chose to flip more cold IPOs. It seems that investors like to hold highly underpriced IPOs for longer while they make an effort to sell the overpriced shares. There is evidence that 58.85% of the total trading volume of the overpriced IPOs is flipped during the first 2 days. On the other hand, the flipping activity for the low underpriced IPO sample is 45.8% of the total trading volume, while for the medium and high underpriced IPOs it is 27.54% and 18.88% respectively.

The results differentiate when there is a comparison between flipping activity and total shares offered during the issue. We observe the highest flipping activity by investors in the low underpriced IPO sample, with 33.37%. It is worth noting that the flipping variance between the various categories of underpricing is much less when we use as a basis for our comparison total shares offered rather than total trading volume.

Table 11.1 Descriptive statistics for flipping activity sample

Variable	Inst. alloc.	Retail alloc.	Day 1 return	Age	Demand multiple	Syndicate size	Market classif.
Mean	65.72	34.89	54.91	21.16	135.56	15	
Median	63	37	22	19	60	14	
Proportion = 1							0.36
Min	21.67	12	−22.36	0	3	7	
Max	81.25	81	472	81	760	28	
Sample size	51	51	51	51	51	51	51

Panel A: Descriptive statistics for IPOs listed under a fixed offer price method. The table reports several characteristics for 51 IPOs listed under a fixed offer price method. Firms were listed from January 2000 to December 2000. Inst. alloc.: percentage of the IPOs allocated to institutional investors; Retail alloc.: percentage of the IPOs allocated to private investors; Day 1 return: IPO (percentage difference between the first-day returns and the offer price; Age: operating history of issuer at the time of IPO. Demand multiple: the multiple oversubscription of the issued shares; Syndicate size: denotes the number of members in the underwriting syndicate (10). Market classif.: listing in the main (primary) or the parallel (second) board of the Athens Stock Exchange – 0.36 means that 36% of shares are classified in the main market.

	Fixed price (N = 51)	
	Mean	Median
Day 1 return	60.64	22.33
Shares traded as % of total shares offered	72.46	61.83
Shares flipped as % of total trading volume	37.67	39.81
Shares flipped as % of total shares offered	24.30	18.87

Panel B: Flipping activity of IPOs. 'Shares traded as % of total shares offered' is the total number of shares traded in the first 2 days as a percentage of total shares offered. 'Shares flipped as % of total trading volume' is the total number of shares flipped on the first 2 trading days divided by the total number of shares traded on the first 2 trading days. 'Shares flipped as % of total shares offered' is the total number of shares traded on the first 2 trading days divided by the total number of shares offered in the IPO.

Test statistics and p-values indicate the level of significance different from zero using Mood's median test: *** significant at the 1% level for the two-tailed test; ** significant at the 5% level for the two-tailed test; * significant at the 10% level for the two-tailed test.

The finding of more institution flipping in cold IPOs contradicts the results of Aggarwal (2003). She reported that institutions '... do not quickly flip cold IPOs to take advantage of price support mechanism by the underwriters'. The fact that the price support mechanism applies in specific firms in Greece proves to be a demotivation for institutions, so they prefer to take out their overpriced shares.

Overall, our findings supports those of Resse (1998) in a large sample of IPOs between 1983 and 1993, that trading volume has a higher first-week trading volume for more underpriced issues. In addition, our results are consistent with those of Krigman et al. (1999), who reported a significant range of first-day adjusted trading volume within the sample, with a minimum of 1%, a median of 33%, and a maximum of 209% of shares offered.

Table 11.2 Flipping activity by filing range and initial returns

Characteristics	Mean	Median
Day 1 return (%)	60.64	22
Shares traded first day as % total shares	49.22	46.35
Shares traded second day as % total shares	23.65	15.67
Shares traded third day as % total shares	18.46	12.39
Shares traded fourth day as % total shares	10.54	6.32
Shares flipped (day 1) as % shares traded	35.9	33.84
Shares flipped (day 2) as % shares traded	44.7	41.52
Shares flipped (days 1 + 2) as % shares traded	37.67	43.56

Panel A: Descriptive statistics. The mean and median of several characteristics of IPOs offered between January 2000 and June 2002. Columns 2 and 3 report characteristics of 51 IPOs offered during that time period. Day 1 + 2 returns are the first and second day trading percentage returns to the investors. Shares traded in the first to third days as % of total shares are the total number of shares traded. Shares flipped in the first and second days as % of shares traded are the total number of shares flipped on the first and first 2 days of trading.

	Cold Day 1 return < 0 (N = 13)		Normal 0 < Day 1 return < 15 (N = 13)		Warm 15 < Day 1 return < 100 (N = 15)		Hot Day 1 return > 100 (N = 10)	
	Mean	Median	Mean	Median	Mean	Median	Mean	Median
Day 1 return	−10.36	−9.65	10.98	10.98	61.08	51.87	216.01	183.41
Shares traded as % of total shares offered	35.31	25.91	75.43	61.83	86.09	71.13	90.91	84.11
Shares flipped as % of total trading volume	58.85	58.15	45.80	45.85	27.54	32.04	18.88	17.26
Shares flipped as % of total shares offered	20.44	15.46	33.37	27.66	23.67	20.21	18.65	14.73

Panel B: Flipping activity by initial returns. A split of the sample of IPOs in four groups based on day 1 return (offer price to day close): cold, normal, warm, and hot. 'Shares traded as % of total shares offered' is the total number of shares traded in the first 2 days as a percentage of total shares offered. 'Shares flipped as % of total trading volume' is the total number of shares flipped on the first 2 trading days, divided by the total number of shares traded on the first 2 trading days. 'Shares flipped as % of total shares offered' is the total number of shares flipped on the first 2 trading days, divided by the total number of shares offered in the IPO.

11.3.1 Institutional versus individual allocation and flipping by filing range and initial returns

Next, the extent of flipping by institutions and retail customers will be studied, related to the number of shares allocated to each group. Table 11.3 shows the flipping activity of retail and institutional investors. Three variables are used for both institutions and retail investors: shares flipped as a percentage of shares allocated, shares flipped as a percentage of total shares traded, and shares flipped as a percentage of total shares offered.

Table 11.3 Institutional versus retail flipping by filing range

	Mean	Median
Shares flipped by institutions as % of shares allocated to institutions	27.06	25.58
Shares flipped by retail as % of shares allocated to retail	20.39	15.13
Shares flipped by institutions as % of total shares traded	28.3	26.57
Shares flipped by retail as % of total shares traded	9.4	7.81
Shares flipped by institutions as % of total shares offered	17.24	14.68
Shares flipped by retail as % of total shares offered	7.36	3.77

Institutional versus individual allocation and flipping by filing range. Fixed offer price ($N = 51$). Flipping activity (based on the first trading days) by institutions and individual customers partitioned by whether the final offer price was at the upper end, within or lower end at the filing range. 'Shares flipped by % of shares allocated' is the total number of shares flipped by institutions (retail investors) divided by the total number of shares allocated to institutions (retail) in the IPO. 'Shares flipped as % of shares traded' is the total number of shares flipped by institutions (retail) divided by the total number of shares traded. 'Shares flipped as % of shares offered' is the total number of shares flipped by institutions (retail) divided by the total number of shares offered in the IPO. Average size of institutional (retail) flip is the average of shares flipped in each flipping transaction. Institutional allocations is the percentage of an issue allocated to institutional investors.

It becomes clear that institutional investors flip more in all the categories. Individual observations shows that institutions flip 27.06% of total shares allocated to them, compared with 20.39% of retail flipping activity. The percentage of shares flipped by institutions as a part of total shares is more than double the percentage of shares flipped by retail investors. Similar studies show that institutional investors flip 17.24% of total shares offered to them while retail investors flip only 7.30%.

In order to study whether institutions flip more of the weak IPOs in order to benefit from underwriter's price support activities, the level of flipping activity by institutions and retail customers is examined. The hypothesis is that institutions flip less if they focus on the long term. Table 11.4 presents the results on a range of flipping transactions by the two main categories of investors. It is seen that, on average, institutions flip 19.4% (median 14.92%) of the shares allocated to them in hot IPOs and private investors flip 14.31% (median 10.52%). In the case of hot IPOs, both institutional and individual demands are high, so each institution is allocated only a small number of shares.

Aggarwal (2003) argued '… each institution must then decide what to do in the aftermarket'. There are two paths to follow. These are to buy additional shares in the aftermarket or to flip the original shares. The decision depends on the value of the IPO on the stock exchange. If the price has increased then institutions might not want to buy additional shares at a high price and might decide to flip the existing package of shares. Amihud et al. (2003) stressed the knowledge of institutional investors is a priority for investment banks, which are now very concerned about flipping in hot IPOs whose price has increased and no price support[2] is necessary.

The percentage of shares flipped for 'cold' IPOs is on average 25.29% (median 21.62%) for institutional investors and 13.83% (median 8.04%) for private investors.

---

[2] Krigman et al. (1999) argued that the cost of flipping is minimized by the underwriter's provision of after-market price support.

Krigman et al. (1999) attribute flipping in cold IPOs to uncommitted investors in these IPOs, despite the desire of investment banks for no investors in these firms to flip. Flipping in weak offerings creates selling pressure that can lower the price even below the offer price. This may force the underwriter to prevent stock prices from falling below the offer price.

Table 11.4(B) shows that institutional and retail shares flipped as a percentage of shares allocated are not significant different in the various levels of underpricing. Interestingly, there is high significance for different samples of underpricing in institutional and retail flipping as a percentage of total shares offered. The difference in the mean is significant at the 1% level but declines to 10% when we compare the 'warm' and 'hot' samples. The most striking observation here is that all the investors flip more in low underpriced IPOs than in the medium or highly underpriced samples of firms.

To summarize, the main results of the analysis are:

*   Institutions flip more than retail customers (expected because, on average, institutions are allocated larger proportions of an IPO so they have a higher proportion of flipping)
*   Institutional investors flip a higher percentage of their allocation when the IPO is cold rather than hot
*   Only a small percentage of trading volume is due to flipping by either institutional or private investors.

11.3.2 Type of lead underwriter, allocations, and flipping activity

In most cases, the lead underwriters are large investment banks with large retail operations. These banks can better manage offerings during weak market conditions or offerings that are expected to be hard to distribute. Schultz and Zaman (1994) examined the quotes of lead underwriters in the first 3 days after the IPO. They found that underwriters generally quote the highest bids and so actively support the price of less successful IPOs.

Chemmanur and Fulghieri (1994) demonstrated that the reputation of an investment bank is acquired from the capital history of the firms it underwrites. In a multiperiod setting, they showed that underwriting good quality firms enhances this reputation, while underwriting low quality firms tarnishes it. Five of the banks[3] in the sample used here have the most underwritings and highest fees in the market (and likewise are the major retail brokers in Greece, with a total share of 88% of the Greek market). These are grouped together under the heading 'reputable banks'. All others banks and securities are grouped into a second category, 'less reputable banks'. Twenty IPOs are listed as reputable banks and 31 as less reputable banks and securities.

Table 11.5(A) shows that reputable banks allocate a significantly lower proportion of IPOs to institutions, with a mean of 59.59%, as compared to less reputable banks,

---

[3] Most of the banks in Greece implemented concepts to discourage flipping because their activity creates problems by maintaining a detailed account of initial allocations. They keep notes on flipping activity by investors because the immediate reselling of shares in the aftermarket can cause downward pressure on the stock prices, mainly for weak offers. However, they do not disclose the proportion of shares allocated to institutional versus private investors and the public does not know who has flipped the shares (report by the National Bank of Greece).

Table 11.4 Institutional versus retail flipping by initial returns

	Cold Day 1 return < 0 (N = 13)		Normal 0 < Day 1 return < 15 (N = 13)		Warm 15 < Day 1 return < 100 (N = 15)		Hot Day 1 return > 100 (N = 10)	
	Mean	Median	Mean	Median	Mean	Median	Mean	Median
Shares flipped by institutions as % of shares allocated to institutions	25.29	21.26	37.22	37.59	23.84	23.21	19.42	14.92
Shares flipped by retail as % of shares allocated to retail	13.83	8.04	28.82	25.89	21.92	19.06	14.31	10.52
Shares flipped by institutions as % of total shares traded	16.64	12.35	24.53	20.13	16.10	15.10	17.14	14.06
Shares flipped by retail as % of total shares traded	6.66	2.60	11.58	9.06	8.47	6.17	11.7	10.16
Shares flipped by institutions as % of total shares offered	45.79	48.14	32.09	34.16	18.64	19.48	17.06	14.93
Shares flipped by retail as % of total shares offered	13.05	9.94	13.60	12.71	8.89	656	18.1	16.95

Panel A: Institutional versus individual allocation and flipping by initial returns. Flipping activity (based on the first trading days) by institutions and private investors who were initially allocated shares in the offering. 'Shares flipped by % of shares allocated' is the total number of shares flipped by institutions (retail investors) divided by the total number of shares allocated to institutions (retail) in the IPO. 'Shares flipped as % of shares traded' is the total number of shares flipped by institutions (retail) divided by the total number of shares traded. 'Shares flipped as % of shares offered' is the total number of shares flipped by institutions (retail) divided by the total number of shares offered in the IPO. Average size of institutional (retail) flip is the average of shares flipped in each flipping transaction. Institutional allocation is the percentage of an issue allocated to institutional investors.

t-test for difference in means   **Wilcoxon test for difference in medians**

Cold/hot	Normal/hot	Warm/hot	Cold/hot	Normal/hot	Warm/hot
0.299 (0.772)	1.634 (0.137)	0.521 (0.615)	−0.153 (0.878)	−1.580 (0.114)	−1.070 (0.285)
−0.139 (0.892)	1.576 (0.150)	1.317 (0.221)	−0.357 (0.721)	−1.376 (0.169)	−1.784 (0.074)*
−0.203 (0.844)	0.384 (0.710)	1.172 (0.275)	−0.764 (0.445)	−0.764 (0.445)	−0.899 (0.374)
1.782 (0.099)*	3.300 (0.009)***	3.380 (0.010)**	−1.988 (0.047)**	−2.701 (0.007)***	−2.547 (0.011)**
6.906 (0.000)***	5.816 (0.000)***	2.236 (0.052)*	−2.803 (0.005)***	−2.803 (0.005)***	−1.886 (0.059)
3.392 (0.008)***	5.529 (0.000)***	3.810 (0.004)***	−2.599 (0.009)***	−2.803 (0.005)***	−2.803 (0.005)***

Panel B: *t*-statistics for the difference in means and Wilcoxon test for difference in medians. Test statistics and *p*-values (in parentheses) indicate the level of significance different from zero. *** Significant at the 1% level for the two-tailed test; ** significant at the 5% level for the two-tailed test; * significant at the 10% level for the two-tailed test.

Table 11.5 Allocation and flipping by type of lead underwriter and by market

	Reputable banks (N = 20)		Less reputable banks and securities (N = 31)		Difference in mean	Difference in median
	Mean	Median	Mean	Median	t-statistic	Wilcoxon test
Offer price (€)	12	11.4	15.8	15	−2.639 (0.016)**	−2.277 (0.023)**
Issue size (€ million)	5.54	12.80	2.86	10.39	2.85 (0.035)**	1.939 (0.87)*
Day 1 return	30.8	15.8	79.7	40.6	−0.693 (0.522)	−1.046 (0.295)
Shares traded as % of total shares offered	79.1	74.6	69.1	60.1	0.460 (0.651)	−0.402 (0.687)
Shares flipped as % of total trading volume	43.5	45.6	34.1	35.3	1.175 (0.255)	−1.529 (0.126)
Shares flipped as % of total shares offered	29.9	18.6	20.9	18.3	1.325 (0.202)	−1.127 (0.260)
Shares flipped by institutions as % shares allocated to institutions	27.4	29.5	26.8	23.5	2.545 (0.019)**	−2.589 (0.010)**
Shares flipped by retail as % shares allocated to retail	20.3	15.3	20.4	14.5	2.112 (0.044)**	−2.173 (0.030)**
Institutional allocations	62.5	61.2	67.7	63.8	0.440 (0.665)	−0.684 (0.494)

Panel A: Allocation and flipping by type of lead underwriter. The sample of IPOs is partitioned into two groups based on the type of lead underwriter: reputable and less reputable.

	Main market (N = 35)		Parallel market (N = 16)		Difference in mean	Difference in median
	Mean	Median	Mean	Median	t-statistic	Wilcoxon test
Offer price (€)	15.5	12.9	13.7	11.9	0.710 (0.488)	−0.497 (0.619)
Issue size (€ million)	9.95	4.25	1.02	0.85	5.67 (0.000)***	4.184 (0.000)***
Day 1 return	46.5	5.2	67.2	31.5	−0.073 (0.943)	−0.355 (0.723)
Shares traded as % of total shares offered	44.4	39.8	88.2	83.2	−2.116 (0.050)**	−2.275 (0.023)**
Shares flipped as % of total trading volume	38.9	48.3	37.6	37.0	−1.105 (0.285)	−0.941 (0.347)
Shares flipped as % of total shares offered	17.1	15.6	28.6	26.8	−3.135 (0.006)	−2.510 (0.012)**
Shares flipped by institutions as % shares allocated to institutions	27.0	23.2	27.1	29.5	0.100 (0.921)	−0.259 (0.796)
Shares flipped by retail as % shares allocated to retail	20.8	10.3	20.2	15.3	0.334 (0.743)	−0.155 (0.877)
Institutional allocations	65.3	61.0	65.9	63.8	−0.130 (0.898)	−0.511 (0.609)

Panel B: Allocation and flipping by market classification. The sample of IPOs is split into two groups based on the type of market they are going public in.
The table provides mean and median statistics: N is the number of observations. Offer price is the initial offer price. Issue size refers to the Euro proceeds. Day 1 return is the percentage difference between the opening price on day 1 and the offer price. 'Shares traded as % of total shares offered' is the total number of shares traded in the first 2 days as a percentage of total shares offered. 'Shares offered as % of the total trading volume' is the total number of shares flipped on the first 2 trading days, divided by the total number of shares traded on the first 2 trading days. 'Shares flipped as % of total shares offered' is the total number of shares flipped on the first 2 trading days divided by the total number of shares offered in the IPO. Institutional allocation is the percentage of an issue allocated to institutional investors. Test statistics and p-values (in parentheses) indicate the level of significance different from zero using the Mood median test. *** Significant at the 1% level for the two-tailed test; ** significant at the 5% level for the two-tailed test; * significant at the 10% level for the two-tailed test.

which allocate 69.90% to institutions. Trading volume as a percentage of shares offered is marginally lower for reputable banks at 81.54% (median 65.83%) than for less reputable banks at 82.63% (median 82.63%).

Reputable banks shows a higher percentage of shares flipped as compared to total trading volume with a median of 43.5% (median 45.6%) compared with the 34.1% (median 35.3%) by less reputable banks and syndicates. The latter finding is consistent with Boehmer and Fishe's (2001b) results, that major underwriters may underprice some IPOs in order to produce a large effect of trading volume (liquidity) in the aftermarket. This creates the belief that liquidity is highly influenced by flipping.

The results of Table 11.5 show that 29.9% (median 18.6%) of shares offered in an IPO are flipped in the first 2 days of trading for reputable banks, while 20.9% (median 18.9%) of shares are flipped in IPOs for less reputable banks. The t-test for difference in means and Wilcoxon test for difference in medians do not show any significant differences between the two samples.

We have already seen that reputable banks allocate a larger percentage of IPOs to private investors than less reputable banks. This consists partly of reputable banks' plans on investor's diversification and insists on their vision for increasing liquidity and maximization of profits. On average, institutions flip 27.4% of the shares allocated to them by reputable banks. Average flipping for less reputable banks is higher at 26.8%. This result contradicts the earlier finding of higher flipping on offerings that have low initial returns. The average private flip by retail investors is 20.3% (shares allocated by reputable banks) and 20.4% (shares allocated by less reputable banks). The differences in flipping by institutional and retail investors of less reputable banks are statistically different. However, investors choose to flip more in firms that go public with reputable underwriters.

Aggarwal (2003), for the US market, reported a larger size of IPOs handled by retail banks. Compared to the results in this study, she found insignificantly higher first-day initial return for IPOs underwritten by less reputable banks. Retail (reputable) banks in the USA allocate a significantly lower proportion of an IPO to institutions. The same result is found here for the Greek market.

The findings of this study suggest that:

· Less reputable banks allocate a higher percentage of shares to institutional investors
· IPOs that go public with less reputable underwriters have higher underpricing
· Reputable underwriters list IPOs with double the size of firms issued by less reputable underwriters
· Investors flip a higher percentage of shares (over trading volume) offered to them by reputable underwriters (significant at the 5% level).

Table 11.5(B) presents the allocation and flipping based on the listing board. There are 35 IPOs listed in the main board (market) of the Athens Stock Exchange and 16 listed in the parallel market. Firms listed in the parallel market present higher day 1 initial returns of 67.2% (median 35.86%) compared with returns of 46.5% (median 41.93%) for firms listed in the main market. The difference in these results is not statistically significant.

The IPOs of the main market present higher flipping as a proportion of total trading volume, at 38.9% (median 48.3%). Flipping measured by 'shares flipped as a percentage of shares offered' is higher for IPOs listed in the parallel market, at 17.1% (median 15.6%). Finally, total institutional allocation is 65.3% (median 61%) for

IPOs listed in the main market and marginally higher at 65.9% (median 63.8%) for IPOs trading in the parallel board.

Statistical tests show that there is significantly high flipping in IPOs that succeed in listing on the parallel market of the Athens Stock Exchange. This may be the case because those firms are highly underpriced and provide good short-term returns to their investors. Moreover, investors do not seem to have the confidence to keep shares in those firms for longer periods, as they believe that they are not good long-term investments.

To summarize the findings of this study on market categorization:

* IPOs listed on the parallel market have enormous trading activity during the first 2 days (significant at the 5% level)
* Companies listed on the main market present a marginally higher percentage of shares flipped compared with the total trading volume
* Firms listed on the parallel market have a higher percentage of flipping based on shares offered (significance of 5%).

11.4   Specification of the models

The positive link between flipping activity and share allocation raises an interesting question regarding the underwriters' allocation decision. To address this, the relationship between flipping and allocation procedure is tested by running a cross-sectional multiple regression. Shares flipped by institutions as a percentage of shares allocated to institutions and retail flipping as a percentage of shares allocated to private investors are used as two separate dependent variables. The independent variables are day 1 return, the size of the issue (given by the log of the number of shares multiplied by the offer price), underwriter reputation (a dummy variable equal to 1 if the underwriter is a major bank and 0 otherwise), and market categorization (a dummy equal to 1 if the firm trades in the main market and 0 otherwise).

11.4.1   Explanation of control variables

We believe that the underpricing can partly explain the level of flipping. Numerous authors have examined flipping and its relation to underpricing. Carter et al. (1998) contended that flipping has a detrimental effect on the early price performance of IPOs. Miller and Reilly (1987) and Boehmer and Fishe (2001b) documented a positive relationship between the initial return and initial aftermarket trading volume.

H_1 Institutional flipping is higher for IPOs associated with high day 1 returns.
H_2 Retail flipping is low for IPOs associated with high initial underpricing.

Michaely and Shaw (1994) argued that larger IPOs are more difficult to market, other things being constant. Krigman et al. (1999) reported a positive and significant coefficient between large investors, flipping, and the size of a firm. They illustrated that the portfolio of lowest flipping quartile achieves the highest size-adjusted return over a period of 1 year. I believe that institutional investors will flip a lower proportion of shares in large IPOs and they will hold these shares for a longer period of time.

H_3 The percentage of institutional flipping is lower in larger firms.
H_4 The percentage of retail flipping is higher for larger companies.

Underwriters report that most IPO firms are vitally interested in placing large allocations of shares in the hands of committed institutional investors, presumably from the belief that thereby trading volatility will be minimized and value will be maximized.

Carter and Manaster (1990), Beatty and Ritter (1986), and Nanda and Yun (1997) showed reputation capital to mitigate adverse selection costs by reducing uncertainty and increasing investors' confidence.

H_5 Firms underwritten by reputable banks have a low level of institutional flipping.
H_6 Companies that choose a reputable bank to go public have a high level of retail flipping.

Mauer and Senbet (1992) showed that the issue is underpriced to compensate initial investors for the risk of purchasing stock that does not have a perfect substitute in the secondary market. Booth and Chua (1995) suggested that IPOs are underpriced to encourage a dispersed ownership structure that increases liquidity.

In the Greek context, we consider IPOs listed on the parallel market to be of higher risk to investors. An investor's indication drives underwriters to choose the market-clearing price for the IPOs. They usually set a low price that helps to create after-market trading as a result of flipping activity.

H_7 Firms listed on the main market of the ASE will have a low level of institutional flipping.
H_8 We expect higher retail flipping for IPOs listed on the main market.

The following models will be used to test institutional and retail flipping:

Institutional flipping as a percentage of shares allocated $= a + \beta_1 \text{Day 1} + \beta_2 \text{Size} + \beta_3 \text{Und} + \beta_4 \text{Market} + \ldots$ (model 1)

Retail flipping as a percentage of shares allocated $= a + \beta_1 \text{Day 1} + \beta_2 \text{Size} + \beta_3 \text{Und} + \beta_4 \text{Market} + \ldots$ (model 2).

11.5   Cross-sectional regression results

Two sets of regressions are provided. The first set studies shares flipped by institutions as a percentage of shares allocated to institutions, and the second examines shares flipped by retail customers as a percentage of shares allocated to retail customers. The results of linear regressions can be found in Table 11.6. Regression for IPOs listed with a fixed offer price method mechanism explain 17.6% and 6.1% respectively of the variation in institutional and retail flipping as a percentage of shares allocated.

The results on the coefficients of the regression model are presented in Table 11.6. The t-statistics are robust for heteroscedasticity using the White (1980) process.

Testings on day 1 returns of IPOs listed with a fixed offer price mechanism reveal significance at the 1% level. The sign is inconsistent with the hypothesis and indicates

Table 11.6 IPO allocations and flipping activity regressions

	Fixed offer price method	
	Institutional flipping as % of shares allocated (model 1)	Retail flipping as % of shares allocated (model 2)
Constant	−37.91 (−1.112)	−12.43 (0.811)
Day 1 return	−0.267 (−2.889)***	−0.053 (−0.410)
Size	0.321 (2.086)**	0.165 (0.663)
Und	0.015 (0.123)	0.031 (0.219)
Market	−0.393 (−2.736)***	−0.144 (−0.880)
Adjusted R^2	17.6	6.1
F-statistic	3.56**	0.30
Significance	0.013	0.875
N	51	51

The dummy variable 'Und' is set to 1 if the firm was underwritten by a leading investment bank (classified as reputable) and 0 otherwise. The second dummy variable we use in our testing is 'Market'. This is set to 1 if the IPO is listed and traded on the main market of the stock exchange.

A set of regressions is run: the first set uses shares by institutions as a percentage of shares allocated to institutions as the dependent variable and the second set shares flipped by retail customers as a percentage of shares allocated to retail customers. The independent variables are: the day 1 return (offer price to day 1 close), the size expressed as the log of initial proceeds, a dummy variable equal to 1 if the IPO was underwritten by a leading investment bank (classified as reputable) and 0 otherwise, and a dummy equal to 1 if the IPO trades on the main market and 0 otherwise. * Significant difference from zero at the 10% level, assuming normality and independence; ** significant difference from zero at the 5% level, assuming normality and independence; *** significant difference from zero at the 1% level, assuming normality and independence.

that institutional flipping is highly related to low initial underpricing. The findings for the second hypothesis show that retail flipping has the expected negative sign. The results are not significant. Thus, the hypothesis for low retail flipping activity in cases of highly underpriced firms can be totally rejected.

The result on institutional flipping of large firms reveals a positive sign (statistical significant at 5%). This indicates that institutional investors flip more in large firms when a fixed offer price method is widely in use. However, the results for retail flipping are consistent with Aggarwal's (2003) finding of a positive association between individual flipping and large IPOs.

Hypotheses 5 and 6 compare the underwriter's reputation with institutional and retail flipping as a percentage of shares allocated. No significant results were found for these hypotheses, though it appears positive to reputable underwriters' flipping activity.

The sign of market for firms listed on the stock market with a fixed offer price mechanism is negative and statistically significant. Thus, institutional investors choose to flip in IPOs that succeed in listing on the less demanding secondary market. This result confirms hypothesis 7. No support for hypothesis 8 was found, i.e. retail flipping is positively associated with primary market IPOs.

The results overall do corroborate Aggarwal's (2003) evidence that institutional flipping is more pronounced for shares in firms with low capital raised, whereas it contradicts high flipping in cases of high initial returns.

11.6   Conclusion

The phenomenon of excessive flipping suggests that shares are not ideally allocated, with the emphasis on buy-and-hold-oriented investors. Alternatively, low flipping can result in a lack of market liquidity.

The results suggest that the percentage of shares flipped during day 1 is 35.9% of the total shares traded during that day, increasing to 37.67% when shares flipped during days 1 and 2 are included. Study of flipping activity based on initial return of IPOs shows that overpriced new listed firms offer the highest percentage of shares flipped in comparison to trading volume, at 58.85%. The percentage of shares flipped as a percentage of total trading volume decreases the higher the level of underpricing.

Surprisingly, the results for shares flipped as a percentage of total shares offered are different. Overpriced and highly underpriced IPOs have the lowest percentage of flipping activity, with 18.65% and 20.44%, while low and medium underpriced IPOs have values of 33.37% and 23.67% respectively.

Categorization of investors into institutional and retail indicates that the shares flipped by institutions as a percentage of total shares traded is almost equal in all categories, with the overpriced IPOs having the lowest flipping and medium underpriced shares the highest. Retail investors prefer to flip more lowly underpriced IPOs, while the percentage of shares they flip in highly underpriced shares is low.

Splitting the sample into firms that were listed in the ASE with reputable and less reputable banks shows that the shares flipped as a percentage of total trading volume were higher for the reputable underwriters sample (43.5%) and lower (34.1%) for the IPOs that listed with less reputable underwriters. When flipping as a percentage of total shares offered is considered, it is observed that flipping on less reputable underwriters' IPOs is lower (20.9%) compared with IPOs listed by reputable underwriters (29.9%).

The results obtained for flipping activity based on market classification are more puzzling. The shares flipped as a percentage of total trading volume are higher for the main market sample, while the study of flipping as a percentage of total shares offered gave the opposite result.

To statistically empower these results, eight hypotheses driven by the literature were formulated to explain flipping behavior. The results show a strong link between institutional flipping and IPOs with low day 1 returns. This reveals the immediate expectation of institutional investors to reduce their participation in shares with low gains.

No support for institutional flipping in relation to underwriter's reputation was found. There is high flipping by institutions in IPOs seeking listing on the ASE's secondary market. The evidence from multivariate tests also suggests that retail investors prefer small firms for their flipping activity. This finding is inconsistent with the hypothesis that private investors flip their shares more in large firms. Finally, the results did not support retail flipping in relation to day 1 returns, underwriter's reputation, and market classification.

There is no evidence for the hypothesis that heavy trading volume during the first few days of trading in an IPO is due to flipping. It was found that, during the first few trading days, even though trading volume as a percentage of shares offered is high, high trading volume is not only due to flipping.

However, the results agree with Aggarwal's (2003) conclusion that '... the high trading volume is partly a result of other factors, such as buying and selling by investors who are not necessarily original buyers of the IPO while it is merely a result of trading activity between market makers'. These findings disagree with those of Fishe (2001), Krigman et al. (1999), Ellis et al. (2000), Boehmer and Fishe (2001a, 2003), and Bayley et al. (2003), who found that flippers pose problems to stake-holders of an IPO.

References

Aggarwal, R. (2003). Allocations of Initial Public Offerings and Flipping Activity. *Journal of Financial Economics*, 68(1):111–158.

Amihud, Y. and Mendelsen, H. (1986). Asset Pricing and the Bid-Ask Spread. *Journal of Financial Economics*, 17(2):223–249.

Amihud, Y., Samuel, H., and Amire, K. (2003). Allocations, Adverse Selection and Cascades in IPOs: Evidence from the Tel Aviv Stock Exchange. *Journal of Financial Economics*, 68(1):137–158.

Bayley, L., Lee, P., and Walter, T. (2003). IPO Flipping in Australia: Cross-Sectional Explanation. Working Paper, University of New South Wales, Sydney, Australia.

Beatty, R. and Ritter, J. (1986). Investment Banking, Reputation, and the Underpricing of Initial Public Offerings. *Journal of Financial Economics*, 15(1–2):213–232.

Boehmer, E. and Fishe, R. (2001a). Do Underwriters Encourage Stock Flipping? The Link Between Trading Profits and Pricing in IPOs. Unpublished Working Paper, University of Miami, Miami, FL.

Boehmer, E. and Fishe, R. (2001b). Equilibrium Rationing in Initial Public Offerings of Equity. Working Paper, University of Miami, Miami, FL.

Boehmer, E. and Fishe, R. (2003). Who Receives IPO Allocations? An Analysis of Equilibrium Rationing "Regular" Investors. Sixty-fifth Annual Meeting of the American Finance Association.

Booth, J. and Chua, L. (1995). Ownership Dispersion, Costly Information and IPO Underpricing. *Journal of Financial Economics*, 41(2):291–310.

Carter, B. and Manaster, S. (1990). Initial Public Offerings and the Underwriter Reputation. *Journal of Finance*, 45(4):1045–1067.

Carter, B., Dark, F., and Singh, R. (1998). Underwriter Reputation, Initial Returns and the Long Run Performance of IPO Stocks. *Journal of Finance*, 53(1):285–311.

Chemmanur, T. and Fulghieri, P. (1994). Investment Bank Reputation, Information Production and Financial Intermediation. *Journal of Finance*, 49(1):57–79.

Correra, A. (1992). Block That Sale! War on Flippers Hurts Little Guy. *Barron's*, 72(22):34.

Ellis, K., Michaely, R., and O'Hara, M. (2000). When the Underwriter is the Market Maker: An Examination of Trading in the IPO Aftermarket. *Journal of Finance*, 44(3):1039–1074.

Fishe, R. (2001). How Stock Flippers Affect IPO Pricing and Stabilisation. *Journal of Financial and Quantitative Analysis*, 37(2):319–337.

Krigman, L., Shaw, W., and Womack, K. (1999). The Persistence of IPO Mispricing and the Predictive Power of Flipping. *Journal of Finance*, 54(3):1015–1044.

Mauer, D. and Senbet, L. (1992). The Effect of Secondary Market on the Pricing of Initial Public Offerings. *Journal of Financial and Quantitative Analysis*, 27(1):55–80.

Michaely, R. and Shaw, W. (1994). The Pricing of Initial Public Offerings: Tests of Adverse Selection and Signaling Theories. *Review of Financial Studies*, 7(2):279–319.

Miller, R. and Reilly, F. (1987). An Examination of Mispricing, Returns and Uncertainty for Initial Public Offerings. *Financial Management*, 16(2):33–38.

Nanda, V. and Yun, Y. (1997). Reputation and Financial Intermediation: An Empirical Investigation of the Impact of IPO Mispricing or Underwriter Market Value. *Journal of Financial Intermediation*, 6(1):39–63.

Resse, W. (1998). IPO Underpricing Trading Volume and Investor Interest. SSRN Working Paper, www.ssrn.com.

Schultz, P. and Zaman, M. (1994). Aftermarket Support and Underpricing of Initial Public Offerings. *Journal of Financial Economics*, 35(2):199–219.

White, H. S. (1980). A Heteroscedastic-Consistent Covariance Matrix Estimator and a Direct Test of Heteroscedasticity. *Econometrica*, 48(4):817–838.

12 Getting IPO pricing right: vive la France?

Edel Barnes

Abstract

Typically, initial public offering (IPO) shares are significantly underpriced when they commence trading and frequently closing prices on the first trading day reflect substantial average initial returns to investors. The particular method chosen to effect an IPO depends both on the market environment into which the firm will sell its shares and the characteristics of the firm itself. The popularity of bookbuilding for IPOs has grown in the last decade, despite the greater costs involved. This study adds to the extant literature on new issues pricing through an examination of new issues on the French Second Marché over the 1999 to 2001 period, arguably the height of the recent hot IPO issues market. While IPO auctions are typically associated with low mean excess returns to investors and bookbuilding with substantially greater mean underpricing, it appears that French firms coming to market on the Second Marché increasingly combine the bookbuilding approach with another pricing mechanism, resulting in more efficient price setting. This hybrid approach thus works to the benefit of both issuers and investors by reducing the aggregate costs of issue associated with other IPO mechanisms.

12.1 Introduction

Globally, the late 1990s were characterized by very active markets in initial public offerings (IPOs), the mechanism whereby organizations obtain a first public listing of their shares. During the run-up to and the actual boom years of the late 1990s, activity in global IPO markets ranged from busy to frenetic. This was in part due to the huge volume of technology and Internet-related businesses that sought funding for growth opportunities, but it seems that firms in virtually every industrial and services sector were coming to the market for finance. The hype that surrounded new issues generally, together with the availability of significant amounts of investor capital seeking superior returns, ensured that demand for shares in companies coming to the market remained buoyant and that such shares traded at lofty levels only loosely related to fundamental values. Since the bursting of the Internet-related market bubble, IPOs have received global bad press and investment bankers have stood accused of dubious pricing, while investors have departed the market in droves to lick the wounds caused by the market crash and the consequent poor long-run returns from initial share offerings. Indeed, before the recent hot issues market, long-run performance of new issues has been disappointing (Ibbotson et al., 1994), which calls into question the efficiency and effectiveness of the various approaches to pricing initial public offerings of shares.

A number of methods are available to firms to conduct an IPO. The particular method chosen depends both on the market environment into which the firm will sell its shares and the characteristics of the firm itself (Chemmanur and Liu, 2003). However, the key objective from the perspective of the issuing firm is to successfully market all shares on offer and to optimize the proceeds of the sale, but therein lies a tradeoff. Typically, very little is known about startup firms and from an investor's perspective information acquisition is costly. If there is substantial uncertainty regarding a firm's activities and prospects and resolving this uncertainty is associated with significant costs, investors will either not subscribe to a new issue so that an offer fails or alternatively they will subscribe only if offered new shares at a discount, which reduces the net proceeds to the issuing firm. This offer price discount has resulted in substantial initial day returns or IPO underpricing, although typically such returns have varied across markets. Loughran et al. (1994) undertook an analysis of international IPO underpricing in 25 separate markets over a variety of periods and documented empirical evidence that illustrates this particular point, their results indicating mean excess initial returns over all markets studied of 31%, albeit with a range of 4.2–80.3%.

By definition, no prior market price is available to guide prospective investors regarding issuing firm value, and substantial uncertainty and information asymmetry will surround such new firms, about which little may be known. The problem for investment bankers who back and/or frequently underwrite such issues is to communicate true value to the market. The offer price is thus key to ensuring a successful issue, but if set too low it results in significant underpricing, whereby investors earn high initial returns but where the opportunity cost to the issuing firm of foregone share capital can be considerable. In the USA, Loughran and Ritter (2002) reported that the hot issues market of 1999 and 2000 was associated with initial day returns of 65% on average, and although returns were not so pronounced in other world markets, initial returns of the order of 20–30% were not uncommon. IPO underpricing also varies over time, a factor which Loughran and Ritter (2002) attribute to changes in the characteristics and composition of firms going public, together with changes in objectives and incentives of firm owners and prospective investors.

12.2   IPO pricing methods

The various methods of bringing new issues to market differ largely in terms of their risk of undersubscription and the costs they impose on investors in acquiring firm-specific information. Bookbuilding, fixed offer price, and auctions are the most commonly used IPO mechanisms, and while some countries are associated with the use of just one mechanism, typically firms have a choice. Generally, public information is not completely incorporated into the final offer price for IPOs and firm risk is positively related to the extent of underpricing and/or initial returns to investors.

In bookbuilding, firms hire an underwriter to certify the new issue as regards firm quality and fair pricing. The fundamental assumption underlying the use of this mechanism is that the underwriting firm has the best understanding of market conditions and access to potential investors. The underwriter will research the issuing firm; the firm and underwriter will subsequently engage in a roadshow to elicit non-binding indications of interest in the new issue from investors, many of which will be large institutions with formidable financing potential. Once this period of bookbuilding is over, the underwriter and firm will agree a final offer price and the underwriter has complete discretion in the allocation of shares once this price is set. Notwithstanding the substantial fees charged by underwriters for this service, the mechanism is utilized by the vast majority of issuing firms worldwide, perhaps because it is well understood by investors. Sherman (2002) noted that there has been a major world trend towards the use of bookbuilding at the expense of auctions for IPOs, a trend she attributed to differential public domain information regarding the issuing firm. Indeed, the bookbuilding approach is used to the virtual exclusion of other mechanisms in the USA. This is largely because it allows issuing firms to control spending on information acquisition and minimizes the risk to the issuing firm of offer failure; this risk is borne by the underwriter, typically an investment bank. The reduced risk of offer failure comes at a price; usually, IPOs conducted by the bookbuilding mechanism are associated with significant underwriting or direct costs. Incentives for underwriting investment houses to favor privileged clients in hot IPOs and to price new issues attractively to guarantee high initial returns adds to the cost to the issuing firm of utilizing the bookbuilding mechanism.

Under a fixed offer price regime, the number of IPO shares and the price at which these shares will be issued to the public is set and advertised approximately a week before the actual IPO date, this price being the result of negotiations between an issuing firm and its underwriter. Potential investors submit their orders for new shares at this fixed price and shares are allocated on a pro-rata basis. Again, underwriters incur costs of acquiring information about the issuing firm; these costs are levied on the issuing firm in the form of underwriter fees/compensation. Because the offer price is set before information regarding investor demand is known, the underwriter bears the risk of undersubscription and must buy any unsold shares, so typically the offer price will stand at a substantial discount to true value to ensure full subscription – that is, a successful offer. In consequence, fixed offer price IPOs are associated with greater underpricing than other mechanisms on average (Loughran et al., 1994), which imposes an indirect cost on the IPO firm. Because efficient price discovery requires some adjustment of offer price to demand, this fixed offer price mechanism is commonly regarded as one of the less efficient pricing mechanisms and consequently is not extensively used.

IPO firms can bring their shares to market via a Dutch auction approach (sometimes referred to as a uniform price auction), where investors are invited to submit bids indicating both the number of shares required and the price they are willing to pay. IPO shares are then sold to the highest bidders, with a uniform price set at the level of the bid of the lowest winning bidder. This standard uniform price equates supply of shares with demand by investors. Underwriters may engage in information acquisition before the offer price is set but, unlike the bookbuilding mechanism, issuing firms do not control spending on company research and investor demand determines expected issue proceeds. Auctions also carry a much higher risk of undersubscription than the alternative approaches and the offer price that clears the market is generally well below a fair value, particularly for companies and in industries that are not well established or understood. A further risk is that it may be possible for bidders to tacitly collude by placing demand functions such that the market-clearing price is very low, if aggressive bidding to gain market share were to push prices too high to yield attractive initial returns to investors. These attributes of the auction process have been cited as a rationale for the decline of this price-setting approach worldwide. Lin et al. (2003) reported a diminishing role of auctions in the

Taiwan market, for example, noting that institutional investors prefer bookbuilding, where they typically receive larger allocations than is the case with the auction process. Chemmanur and Liu (2003) similarly documented a reduction over time in the relative proportion of IPOs being conducted by auction in the US market.

In France, a variation on the Dutch auction approach, 'offre à prix minimal', is used. Here the underwriter and issuing firm set a minimal acceptable offer price approximately one week before the IPO date. On the date prior to issue, investors make price and quantity bids, which are collected and used to assess investor demand by the French market authority, the protector of investor interests. Underwriter and firm negotiate with this authority on offer maximum prices, based on this demand. The maximum price is chosen to eliminate unrealistically high bids. This collection of bids encourages investors to reveal their assessment of firm value, and shares are subsequently allocated on a pro-rata basis to bidders at a uniform offer price that lies between the acceptable minimum and maximum prices which clear the market.

12.3   IPOs and the French stock market

Three main stock markets operate in France: the Premier Marché, the Second Marché, and the Nouveau Marché. The Premier Marché is the primary French market, where securities of the largest French companies are traded. Listing requirements are stringent and typically only the largest companies are in a position to absorb the substantial costs of trading in this market. The Second Marché is a subsidiary French market that commenced trading in 1983 to allow smaller firms to obtain a listing and to go public. Listing requirements on this market are less stringent than those of the main exchange, 'la cote officielle'. The Nouveau Marché commenced trading in December 1995 and is based on the model of the US market, the Nasdaq. The aim of this market is to attract startup companies, especially those in high-technology industries.

Giudici and Roosenboom (2002) included an examination of the French Nouveau Marché in their comparative analysis of IPO underpricing in European high-technology, high-growth markets, differentiating their sample by country and approach to IPO adopted. For their sample of 482 IPOs, 96.7% were priced using the bookbuilding procedure, 2.7% utilized a fixed price offer, and just 0.6% were conducted by auction. Overall mean initial underpricing was 38%, with the French Nouveau Marché being associated with the lowest level of underpricing of 17.5% on average. These authors attributed intra-country differences in initial underpricing to differentials in institutional settings and market maturity. Derrien and Womack (2003) undertook a closer examination of the French markets, their objective being to address the issue of which IPO pricing approach, selling, and underwriting procedures might be most efficient in controlling the extent and volatility of initial mispricing. The French stock market is somewhat unique in that three basic and substantially different issuing mechanisms operate in juxtaposition: auctions, bookbuilding, and fixed offer price issues. Thus, it merits a closer examination with a view to assessing the relative efficiency of the various approaches. Derrien and Womack's (2003) sample studied 264 French IPOs, which were brought to market on the French Nouveau and Second Marchés over the period 1992 to 1998. They reported an overall average level of underpricing of 13.23% across all mechanisms for the French stock market as a whole, with average initial returns of 16.9%, 8.9%, and 6.5% being reported for bookbuilding, fixed offer price, and pure auctions respectively. This suggests that pure auctions may be optimal for issuing firms concerned with minimizing underpricing and optimizing the proceeds of issue. The French auction mechanism is market driven rather than underwriter driven, is associated with fewer frictions, and reflects investor valuations more completely in the offer price relative to other approaches. Furthermore, it was found to adjust most completely for recent market conditions in the pricing of IPOs, given that periods of high (low) IPO activity have been found to be associated with less (more) underpricing. Biais and Faugeron (2002) developed a theoretical model to analyze and compare the performance of a number of different IPO pricing mechanisms and conducted an analysis of 92 IPOs on the French Second Marché over the period 1983 to 1996, which utilized the 'offre à prix minimal' (French auction) pricing technology. They reported mean initial underpricing of 13.23% across the new issues they analyzed, which is significantly lower than initial returns earned when other pricing approaches were adopted. These authors recognized the importance of investment banks and institutional investor-driven information flows in the adjustment of offer price and concluded that the French auction approach can be structured to represent the optimal pricing mechanism. Chemmanur and Liu (2003) confirmed the finding that auctions tend to be associated with lower underpricing than other IPO methods. Derrien and Womack's (2003) study results are based on an examination of the French Nouveau and Second Marchés together, and given that the Nouveau Marché is designed to attract listings for startup and high-technology companies, one would expect underpricing to be higher for that market. Giudici and Roosenboom (2002) reported an average level of underpricing for the Nouveau Marché (17.5%) that exceeds Derrien and Womack's (2003) metric where both markets are examined together, which suggests that there may be differentials in pricing efficiency across these two markets.

12.4 Study motivations, data, and analysis

A logical question regards the type of selling and underwriting procedure that might be preferred for controlling the amount and volatility of underpricing, given that it imposes such a significant cost on firms coming initially to market by IPO. The global experience illustrates that investor gains in IPOs varied substantially across markets and by pricing mechanism chosen. The study by Loughran et al. (1994) of the international evidence on IPO underpricing indicated an average level of underpricing across all 25 countries studied of 31% over a variety of periods. Malaysia recorded the greatest underpricing due to binding governmental constraints on the setting of offer price and France reported the lowest average initial returns of 4.2%. High initial returns were generally associated with regulated markets such as Malaysia and those characterized by high marginal tax rates on income such as Sweden. Underpricing was typically greater when offer price was set before information on investor demand was known, as is the case for the fixed offer price mechanism, and lower for auction-like mechanisms, where the market-clearing approach equates demand and supply. Bookbuilding was associated with intermediate underpricing, but imposed substantial direct costs on issuing firms.

Nevertheless, in excess of 90% of IPOs adopted this approach. Despite its popularity it has been argued, and there is anecdotal evidence to this effect, that the bookbuilding approach to bringing new issues to market is inefficient largely due to the market power of underwriters and privileged investors who exercise significant control over the setting of the offer price. Underwriters may allocate shares in a hot new issue disproportionately to favored investors in exchange for commissions and/or set the offer price at a steep discount to ensure attractive initial returns to such investors.

Evidence on initial returns suggests that the auction-like approach (offre à prix minimal) utilized in France may be the most efficient in terms of minimizing underpricing. In consequence, we might expect this approach to dominate in a market where a number of diverse issuing mechanisms are simultaneously available. Is there any evidence that (a) the approach actually dominates new issue activity and (b) that French auctions represent the most efficient issue technology? The pursuit of answers to these questions, together with the differential in initial pricing across French markets documented by Derrien and Womack (2003) and Giudici and Roosenboom (2002), motivated this analysis of French IPOs in the Second Marché, where a greater variety of technologies are utilized in bringing new firms to market than is the case for the French Nouveau Marché, where bookbuilding is most typical of new issues. We also note, consistent with the empirical evidence from other world markets, that while French auctions are indeed efficient in that they are associated with few of the conflicts of interest typically associated with bookbuilding, nevertheless bookbuilding has been gaining in popularity in this market.

This study examines 55 new issues which were brought to the Second Marché during the period 1999 to 2001. Thirty-one firms came to market in 1999, 16 in 2000, and just nine in 2001. At 31 January 2001, two stocks had de-listed, but there was active trading in the remaining 53 firms' shares. Eighteen different sectors are represented with two sectors, Technology and Computer Services, each accounting for 16% of the total sample. Traditional sectors such as Food/Drink, Transport, and Retail are well represented, accounting for 13%, 15%, and 11% of the total sample respectively. Primark Global Access, which publishes prospectuses for most French new issues, was the main source of data on IPO method, while specific price data on issuing firms was obtained either from the French Stock Exchange's website or from the Datastream Advance database. The data requirements in respect of each new listing included opening and closing prices for the first day's trading and the specific mechanism utilized to determine initial price. In order to compute initial returns relative to performance of the underlying market – that is, abnormal returns – market index closing prices were obtained for days (t_{-1}, t) relative to listing date. A variety of approaches are commonly utilized to compute abnormal or excess returns, the most frequently applied methods including the Index Model, the Market Model, and the Capital Asset Pricing Model. Armitage (1995) noted that the different models produce similar but not identical results and that the Market Model is generally the most reliable in that it is at least as powerful as the next best alternative. Because historical raw returns are not available for new listings, the Index Model was chosen here to compute initial price changes for this sample, in light of Brown and Warner's (1980) conclusion that the Index Model, though simpler, performs no worse than the Market Model, and Strong's (1992) contention that accurate identification of event date is relatively more important than sophistication of the chosen model or statistical technique. Strong also notes that the main assumption underlying use of the Index Model is that ex-ante expected returns are equal for all securities and therefore equal in any period to the expected return $E(r)$ in that period. The market-adjusted or excess return metric for any given security j is therefore:

$$AR_{jt} = R_{jt} - R_{mt},$$

where

AR_{jt} = excess return for security j at time t
R_{jt} = raw return for security j at time t
R_{mt} = market return at time t.

Mean initial excess returns are simply the sum of all abnormal returns scaled by the number of firms in the sample. Wilcoxon (nonparametric) signed-rank test statistics for the hypothesis are also reported to test that median sample abnormal returns are insignificantly different from zero.

12.5 Results and discussion

Table 12.1 reports the pattern of IPO approaches utilized by the issuing firms over the period studied (1999 to 2001 inclusive), together with mean and median initial returns for each pricing mechanism.

Interestingly, just four issues used the pure auction approach and three issues utilized the pure bookbuilding method. Forty-eight firms utilized a hybrid approach and 51 issues incorporated some aspects of the bookbuilding technology. This pattern contrasts with earlier studies of the French market, where relatively substantial proportions of IPOs were conducted by auction and were associated with significantly lower underpricing than other mechanisms. Derrien and Womack (2003), for example, reported a 31% incidence of pure auctions for the sample they study (1992 to 1998) against an incidence of pure bookbuilding of 52%, and their analysis revealed average initial excess returns to investors of 17.5%, with higher mean returns being earned by investors in Nouveau Marché issues than was the case for the Second Marché. However, these authors failed to separately examine the different French markets for new issues. The Nouveau Marché is designed for startup and high-technology companies, where higher initial underpricing might be expected. Giudici and

Table 12.1 IPO mechanisms for the French Second Marché (1999 to 2001)

	Pure auction	Pure bookbuilding	80% bookbuilding 20% fixed price	80% bookbuilding 20% auction	Full sample
Total	4	3	29	19	55
% of all	7.3	5.5	52.8	34.4	100
Mean excess returns (%)	1.5	12.5	9.0	7.9*	6.3*
Median excess returns (%)	1.9**	10.2*	6.1*	5.4*	1.0*
p-value	0.035	0.01	0.001	0.001	0.001

Asterisks indicate significance at the 1% (*) and 5% (**) levels respectively.

Roosenboom (2002) documented mean initial returns for the Nouveau Marché that exceed those for the Second Marché. It is also noteworthy that new issues in the French Nouveau Marché occurred exclusively via the bookbuilding mechanism, which is associated with greater underpricing.

The analysis here clearly indicates differentials in relative pricing efficiency of the available pricing mechanisms in the French Second Marché, with the pure auction approach resulting in significantly lower initial excess returns than is the case either for the sample as a whole or for the alternative pricing methodologies, and the pure bookbuilding mechanism yielding substantially greater initial returns to investors. Despite its pricing efficiency, however, this analysis suggests that the auction mechanism seems to be losing popularity over time, to the benefit of the more costly bookbuilding-type approach and indeed to hybrid pricing methodologies. When the sample considered here is differentiated across pricing methods, it seems clear that the hybrid approach favored by French investors in the Second Marché nevertheless results in more efficient pricing from the perspective of issuing firms than is the case for the bookbuilding approach that dominates many international markets for new issues. The results indicate that, over the period of study, the French Second Marché and its associated use of hybrid pricing mechanisms continued to be associated with lower average underpricing than that documented for other markets where bookbuilding dominates. The finding also appears to be independent of technological classification – when the sample is partitioned on this basis no difference is found in mean or median excess returns, although the dispersion of excess returns across issuing firms is marginally greater for technology stocks. Neither is any meaningful difference in initial pricing methodology uncovered for technology stocks vis-à-vis non-technology firm issues. Notwithstanding the relatively small sample size, which precludes further, more rigorous analysis, it seems clear that the French Second Marché choice of hybrid pricing results in less extreme mispricing than has been documented for pure pricing approaches, yet incorporates many of the informational and transparency benefits of bookbuilding with the pricing efficiency of auctions/fixed price offers.

12.6 Conclusion

Differential initial pricing efficiency has been documented across world markets, with initial excess returns to investors, and in consequence cost of issuance to IPO firms, being influenced importantly by the mechanism adopted to determine the opening offer price. In particular, documented initial returns to investors in the French market for new issues have been significantly lower than is the case for other markets (Derrien and Womack, 2003), a finding that is reinforced here. A resolution of this seemingly new issues pricing puzzle may lie in the ability of French IPO firms to benefit from the demand-revealing attributes of bookbuilding while avoiding the costly conflicts of interest associated with underwriting–investor client relationships. Were it possible to avoid such costly conflicts, it has been argued that bookbuilding could be just as efficient a pricing mechanism as the French auction-like approach. Certainly, pure bookbuilding is an underwriter-driven mechanism and too much power in the hands of underwriters may result in substantial underpricing. It is noted here that a greater proportion of French firms enjoy relationship banking than is the case in the USA, UK, and other markets, and French IPO firms tend to choose their main creditor bank as underwriter when going public. Thus, underwriters know and understand the issuing firm prior to IPO, need to engage in considerably less information acquisition, are less likely to abuse the underwriting role with a client firm, and will both require and choose less underpricing to successfully market a new issue than in other global markets. This reduction in underpricing costs allows French firms to use hybrid issue mechanisms that incorporate both the beneficial attributes of bookbuilding (research, investor roadshows, access to potential investors) and the demand-revealing auction or fixed offer technologies, in preference to the pure auction mechanism, to attract foreign investors who are perceived to less fully understand the French auction-like approach but to better understand the bookbuilding process. This approach has resulted in average IPO underpricing of just 6.3% on the French Second Marché while the French Nouveau Marché, which utilizes only pure bookbuilding, has been characterized by underpricing of the order of approximately 17.5% on average (Giudici and Roosenboom, 2002). The inescapable implication is that the French Second Marché may be applying the bookbuilding IPO method optimally, avoiding the conflict-related costs associated with other jurisdictions and continuing to enjoy significantly lower new issue mispricing. In a period of volatile markets, dismal returns, and government privatization plans, looking forward, the evidence suggests that French investors fare only reasonably well in early IPO markets but may avoid the disappointing price reversals and consequent poor longer-run returns earned by investors in other markets. Although the age-old adage '*caveat emptor*' (let the buyer beware) still applies, the French experience of IPO markets may not be quite so unhappy as global statistics imply.

Acknowledgments – I would like to acknowledge the valuable research assistance from Derek Beatty, B.Comm., MBS (University College Cork).

References

Armitage, S. (1995). Event Study Methods and Evidence on Their Performance. *Journal of Economic Surveys*, 8(4):25–52.

Biais, B. and Faugeron, A. M. (2002). IPO Auctions: English, Dutch, French and Internet. *Journal of Financial Intermediation*, 11(1):9–36.

Brown, S. and Warner, J. (1980). Measuring Security Price Performance. *Journal of Financial Economics*, 8(3):205–258.

Chemmanur, T. J. and Liu, H. (2003). How Should a Firm Go Public? A Dynamic Model of the Choice Between Fixed-Price Offerings and Auctions in IPOs and Privatisations. Working Paper, Boston College, Newton, MA.

Derrien, F. and Womack, K. L. (2003). Auctions vs. Book-building and the Control of Underpricing in Hot IPO Markets. *Review of Financial Studies*, 16(1):31–61.

Giudici, G. and Roosenboom, P. (2002). Pricing Initial Public Offerings on New European Stock Markets. Working Paper, Tilburg University, Belgium.

Ibbotson, R., Sindelar, J., and Ritter, J. R. (1994). The Market's Problems with the Pricing of Initial Public Offerings. *Journal of Applied Corporate Finance*, 7(1):66–74.

Lin, J., Lee, Y., and Liu, Y. (2003). Why Have Auctions Been Losing Market Shares to Book-building in IPO Markets? Working Paper, Louisiana State University, Baton Rouge, LA.

Loughran,T. and Ritter, J. R. (2002). Why Has IPO Under-pricing Changed Over Time? Working Paper, University of Notre Dame and University of Florida, Miami, FL.

Loughran,T., Ritter, J. R., and Rydqvist, K. (1994). Initial Public Offerings: International Insights. *Pacific-Basin Finance Journal*, 2(2–3):165–199.

Sherman, A. E. (2002). Global Trends in IPO Methods: Book Building vs. Auctions. Working Paper, University of Notre Dame, Notre Dame, IN.

Strong, N. (1992). Modelling Abnormal Returns: A Review Article. *Journal of Business, Finance and Accounting*, 19(4):533–553.

13 Underpricing and the aftermarket performance of initial public offerings: the case of Austria

Wolfgang Aussenegg

Abstract

This study investigates the price behavior of initial public offerings (IPOs) of equities listed on the Vienna Stock Exchange during the period from 1984 to 1996. For a total sample of 67 IPOs, an average first-day return of only 6.5% is documented. The cross-section of initial abnormal returns can best be explained by the ex-ante uncertainty about the value of the issue and the existence of 'hot-issue' and 'cold-issue' periods. Till the fifth anniversary of public listing, Austrian IPOs significantly underperformed benchmark firms. This phenomenon can best be explained by cross-sectional differences in the ownership structure.

13.1 Introduction

Numerous studies have investigated unseasoned new issues, especially in the United States, but also in many other countries and financial markets. They mainly document two phenomena: the first one is that initial public offerings (IPOs) show significant positive average first-day returns. This underpricing varies from country to country and is documented as a permanent and cyclical phenomenon. Loughran et al. (1994), for example, showed that the average initial return can be as low as 4.2% for French IPOs and as high as 80% for Malaysian IPOs. Many theories and models have been developed to explain the level of underpricing and the cross-sectional differences among IPO firms. One of the best-known models was established by Rock (1986), who introduced the concept of the winner's curse in the IPO market. According to this model, a positive underpricing must exist because underpriced IPOs are rationed to a larger extent than overpriced ones and uninformed investors are, in contrast to informed investors, not able to distinguish between over- and underpriced issues.

The second phenomenon is that in the long run IPOs tend to underperform benchmark firms. Using a sample of 1526 IPOs that went public in the USA during the 1975 to 1984 period, Ritter (1991) found a significant underperformance of 29.1% in the first 3 years of public listing. Similar results for a three times larger sample of US IPOs were reported by Loughran and Ritter (1995). This long-run underperformance exists for most non-US stock markets as well. For example, Levis (1993) found evidence that UK IPOs underperform by 26.3% in the first 36 trading months of aftermarket trading. The negative long-run performance of IPOs has also been documented for

Germany (Uhlir, 1989; Ljungqvist, 1997), Finland (Keloharju, 1993), private sector IPOs in Hungary (Jelic and Briston, 1999), and Poland (Aussenegg, 2000). Also see Loughran et al. (1994) and Ritter (2003) for surveys reviewing the international empirical evidence of IPOs.

Aggarwal and Rivoli (1990) suggested that a reason for this underperformance is a possible overvaluation in early aftermarket trading. Ritter (1991) argued that issuing firms choose to go public when investors are over-optimistic about the firm's future growth potential. As Jain and Kini (1994) document, US IPOs experienced a significant decline in operating performance following the IPO for the period 1976 to 1988. They concluded that in the course of the initial issue the investors may have too high expectations with regard to the future growth in earnings, which are subsequently not fulfilled. This could finally lead to a negative performance in the aftermarket. It is puzzling that the market obviously does not account for this negative operating performance in the short-term aftermarket. Another explanation offered for the long-run underperformance is that only good information about the issuing firms is circulated when a firm goes public and that therefore the prices in the early aftermarket are distorted (Uhlir, 1989).

In contrast to the empirical findings for the initial return, the empirical evidence for the long-run aftermarket performance is not as clear. There are a few non-US studies that document a non-negative long-run aftermarket performance. Among these is the study by Kunz and Aggarwal (1994), who reported for the Swiss IPO market non-significant 2- and 3-year abnormal aftermarket performances of +1.8% and −6.1% respectively. A really extreme result was reported by Kim et al. (1995) for Korean IPOs, where a 3-year buy-and-hold abnormal performance of +91.6% was documented. This indicates that in Korea IPOs outperform benchmark firms, which is in clear contrast to the empirical evidence of a long-run underperformance in most countries. Table 13.1 provides a short summary of empirical studies measuring the performance of IPOs in different markets.

Given the above background, the present study has four major objectives. First, to record the level of first-day returns for Austrian IPOs and to investigate the cross-sectional distribution of these returns. Second, to explain the level of underpricing recorded. Several explanation models derived from the theoretical and empirical literature will be used to formulate testable hypotheses. Third, to measure the short- and long-run aftermarket performance. The aim is to detect whether it has been possible to earn significant positive abnormal returns by purchasing the issues on the first day of aftermarket trading and holding them for up to 5 years. Fourth, to give some explanations for the documented long-run aftermarket performance.

Section 13.2 describes the main features of the Austrian new issue market. Section 13.3 presents the data and section 13.4 shows the empirical results for the initial returns. After an analysis of the distribution of the initial returns and the possible effects due to rationing, several testable hypotheses to explain the level of under pricing and the cross-sectional differences in the initial returns across firms will be formulated and tested in this section. Section 13.5 describes the methodology used to calculate abnormal returns to evaluate the aftermarket performance and then documents the empirical evidence regarding the aftermarket performance of IPO firms. Explanations for the observed long-run performance conclude this section. Finally, section 13.6 will give a summary of the findings.

Table 13.1 Initial returns and aftermarket performance (exclusive of initial returns) of initial public offerings (IPOs) in different countries

Country	Study	Time period	Average initial return (%)	Three-year aftermarket performance	
				Return (%)	Wealth relative[g]
USA	Ritter (1991)[c]	1975 to 1984	+14.1	−29.1[a]	0.83
USA	Loughran and Ritter (1995)[c]	1970 to 1990	+10.0	−26.9[b]	0.80
USA	Loughran and Ritter (2004)	1980 to 2003	+18.7	n.a.	n.a.
UK	Levis (1993)[d]	1980 to 1988	+14.1	−26.3[a]	0.92
Germany	Ljungqvist (1997)[f]	1970 to 1993	+9.2	−12.1[b]	n.a.
Finland	Keloharju (1993)[d]	1984 to 1989	+8.7	−26.4[a]	0.79
Schweden	Loughran et al. (1994)[d]	1980 to 1990	+38.2	+2.0[b]	1.01
Switzerland	Kunz and Aggarwal (1994)[d]	1983 to 1989	+35.8	−6.1[a]	n.a.
Hungary	Jelic and Briston (1999)[d]	1990 to 1998	+40.0	−55.7[a,e]	n.a.
Poland	Aussenegg (2000)[d,e]	1991 to 1999	+19.8	−12.2[b,e]	0.92
Korea	Kim et al. (1995)[c]	1985 to 1989	+57.6	+91.6[a]	1.56
South Africa	Page and Reyneke (1997)[c]	1980 to 1991	n.a.	−63.5[b,f]	0.65

[a] Cumulative abnormal return.
[b] Buy-and-hold abnormal return.
[c] Matching firm adjusted.
[d] Market index adjusted.
[e] Private sector IPOs.
[f] First 4 years.
[g] The wealth relative is defined as 1 plus the buy-and-hold return of the sample of IPOs divided by 1 plus the buy-and-hold return of the corresponding benchmark firms (see also equation (13.9)).

13.2   The new issue market in Austria

The Vienna Stock Exchange (VSE) is the only stock exchange in Austria and is grouped into three market segments: the Official Market ('Amtlicher Handel'), the Semi-Official Market ('Geregelter Freiverkehr'), and the Unregulated Market ('Sonstiger Wertpapierhandel'). By the end of 1996, 118 companies were listed on the Vienna Stock Exchange: 94 in the Official Market, 12 in the Semi-Official Market, and 12 in the Unregulated Market. Firms trading in the Official Market account for about 95% of the total market value of all stocks and more than 99% of the total trading volume. The Official Market is therefore the main segment of the stock exchange, where the most liquid and the biggest Austrian stocks are listed. In contrast, stocks listed in the Semi-Official or the Unregulated Market are characterized by considerably thinner trading.

In addition to trading volume and market value, the three types of markets also differ with regard to the admission requirements for security listing. The basic listing requirements for the Official and Semi-Official Markets can be summarized as follows: (i) every company has to publish a prospectus containing all information necessary to judge its assets and liabilities, the earnings and future prospects, and their legal position; (ii) the nominal value of the total share capital has to be at least €2.9 million (about $3.9 million) for the Official Market and €0.725 million (about $0.9 million) for the Semi-Official Market; (iii) the company must have existed for at least 3 years (1 year for the Semi-Official Market) and must have published annual accounts for the most recent 3 years (1 year for the Semi-Official Market). In addition, for shares traded in the Official Market, a minimum of 25% of the share capital has to be widely scattered and investors have to be informed about the business on a regular basis. No such listing requirements exist for the Unregulated Market. Despite the fact that the listing requirements for the Official Market are the most rigorous, the vast majority of all IPOs apply for listing in this market segment. The Unregulated Market, which was not established until 1990 to reduce the requirements for admittance to the capital market for smaller companies, has not fulfilled expectations.

Till the end of the 1990s, most IPOs used a classical firm commitment contract, where the offer price and the issue volume (number of shares issued) are fixed in advance. Several weeks before the offering period starts, a preliminary prospectus containing all relevant information about the economic condition and perspectives of the firm, the offer price, and the number of shares to be sold is circulated among potential institutional as well as private investors. After having collected the state of demand for a given IPO, the final offer price and the number of shares are normally fixed just before the offering period starts. In most cases this official subscription period lasts 2–5 days. If the offer is heavily oversubscribed, the subscription period often finishes as early as at the end of the first subscription day. Since the end of the 1990s, firms are going public using a bookbuilding procedure, where in contrast to a firm commitment offering, a bookbuilding range is fixed just before the subscription period starts, whereas the offer price is fixed not before the end of the subscription period.

13.3   Data description

In 1984, after more than 18 years with only delistings, the wave of firms going public in Austria started with two initial public offerings. In the 13-year period from

1984 to 1996, the number of all firms listed on the VSE more than doubled from 58 to 118. In total, 98 companies went public during this period, 67 of which were listed on the Official Market, 11 on the Semi-Official Market, and 20 on the Unregulated Market. In order to secure a homogeneous sample of IPOs with similar listing requirements and a liquid aftermarket trading, the data sample used consists of all 67 IPOs first listed on the Official Market between 1984 and 1996 (see Table 13.2).

First-day returns are defined as the amount by which the price appreciation of the IPOs exceeds that of the Vienna Stock Exchange Share Index (WBI) for a purchase at the offering date and sale at the close of the first trading day (in percentage points), calculated using equation (13.2).

IPO firms which changed from the Semi-Official or the Unregulated Market into the Official Market are not included. Table 13.2 summarizes the distribution of the sample of 67 IPOs by year. Most firms went public after the two big bull markets in 1986 (10 IPOs) and 1990 (14 IPOs), whereas the highest total as well as average gross proceeds were earned in 1994.

One special feature of the Austrian new issues market is the distribution of the former owners or sellers of the IPO firms. Nearly 60% of all IPOs in the sample are family owned (see Table 13.3). Family-owned IPOs are defined as firms exclusively controlled by a family or by private persons before going public.

A second group of IPOs are privatizations. Thirteen out of 67 IPOs in the Official Market are former (100%) state-owned enterprises. Privatizations have taken place in almost every country where a stock market exists. The main objectives for the Austrian government to execute privatizations are (as in many other countries): (i) to raise revenue for the budget, (ii) to increase the operating efficiency of the privatized enterprise, (iii) to reduce governmental interference in the economy, (iv) to increase the portion of share ownership in the population, and (v) to introduce competition. To investigate the long-run aftermarket performance of Austrian IPOs in relation to the ownership structure, the following groups of IPOs are formed: family-owned firms, privatized enterprises, and other non family-owned firms. Other non-family-owned firms are defined as firms that are neither controlled by a family nor by private persons, nor are privatized enterprises. In most cases such firms are owned by banks or other big companies.

13.4 Initial returns

13.4.1 Research methodology

To measure the first-day return, abnormal returns are calculated for each IPO. The abnormal return for an IPO i is defined as the difference between the observed return of the IPO and the 'normal' return that can be expected from an investment in IPO i:

$$AR_i = R_i - E(R_i), \tag{13.1}$$

where AR_i is the abnormal return of IPO i, R_i is the observed return, and $E(R_i)$ is the expected return. Brown and Warner (1980, 1985) presented several alternatives to determine the ex-ante expectations. In the empirical IPO literature, the market-adjusted return method is commonly used. The initial (first-day) return for each IPO is then defined as the difference between its (observed) return and the corresponding return on the market index:

Table 13.2 Distribution of initial public offerings (IPOs) in the official market by year

Year	Number of IPOs			Gross proceeds (US$, million)		Average first-day return (%)
	All	Family owned	Non-family owned	Aggregate (inflation adjusted: prices of 1990)	Average (inflation adjusted: prices of 1990)	
1965 to 1983	0	0	0	–	–	–
1984	2	1	1	63.8	31.9	11.0
1985	2	1	1	965.8	482.9	11.1
1986	10	5	5	1570.1	157.0	3.0
1987	3	2	1	1588.6	529.5	8.5
1988	6	3	3	4227.4	704.6	−0.1
1989	6	4	2	2569.6	428.3	4.8
1990	14	11	3	7035.6	502.5	12.7
1991	8	5	3	3832.6	479.1	7.6
1992	5	3	2	2897.4	579.5	4.9
1993	1	0	1	621.6	621.6	8.9
1994	5	3	2	10,622.1	2124.4	2.9
1995	4	2	2	5985.5	1496.4	0.4
1996	1	0	1	542.8	542.8	3.4
Total	67	40	27	42,522.9	634.7	6.5

Table 13.3 Initial public offerings (IPOs) categorized by ownership, 1984 to 1996

	No. of IPOs	Gross proceeds (US$, millions)		Fraction (%)	
		Aggregate (inflation adjusted: prices of 1990)	Average (inflation adjusted: prices of 1990)	No. of IPOs	Aggregate gross proceeds
Family[a]	40	16,910.17	422.75	59.70	39.77
Priv.[b]	13	22,139.30	1703.02	19.40	52.06
Others[c]	14	3473.39	248.10	20.90	8.17
Total	67	42,522.86	634.67	100.00	100.00

[a] Former family-owned firms.
[b] Privatized enterprises.
[c] Other firms.

$$IR_{i,t} = \frac{P_{i,1} - P_{i,0}}{P_{i,0}} - \frac{I_{i,1} - I_{i,0}}{I_{i,0}} \qquad (13.2)$$

where $IR_{i,t}$ is the market index-adjusted initial return of IPO i, $P_{i,1}$ is the closing price of IPO i at the end of the first trading day, $P_{i,0}$ is the offer price of IPO i (the time index 0 refers to the first day of the subscription period), $I_{i,1}$ is the Vienna Stock Exchange Share Index (WBI) at the end of the first trading day of IPO i, and $I_{i,0}$ is the WBI on the first day of the subscription period of IPO i. Since the subscription period is very often closed prematurely, the first day of the subscription period is used for the computation of the market-adjusted returns.

13.4.2 Distribution

The first part of the empirical section investigates the question as to whether an investor who purchased every IPO of the sample issued at the offer price and sold it on the first day of public listing earned a significant average abnormal return. This implies a strategy of investing a similar amount of money in each IPO. Therefore, we test the null hypothesis that the average abnormal return is not significantly different from zero. Table 13.4 reports average first-day returns for a sample of 62 IPOs issued during the period 1984 to 1996 and the main distribution parameters. For five firms which went public using a tender procedure, no initial return is observable. Therefore, the total sample of 67 IPOs is reduced to 62 in investigating the initial return.

The average raw (unadjusted) initial return is 5.75% (with an associated t-statistic of 3.58) and the average market index-adjusted initial return (underpricing) is 6.50% (with an associated t-statistic of 3.80). The null hypothesis of no significant average abnormal initial return can therefore be rejected at the 1% significance level. This evidence indicates that Austrian IPOs, as is documented for nearly all IPO markets in different countries, are also underpriced, although their level of underpricing is lower than reported in most studies.

As the distribution of initial returns is not symmetric (positive skewness), the t-statistic must be interpreted with caution. Using a nonparametric sign test, the initial

Table 13.4 Descriptive statistics for first-day returns of 62 initial public offerings from 1984 to 1996

	Initial return	Underpricing
Mean (%)	5.75	6.50
t-value[a]	3.58	3.80
	(0.00)	(0.00)
Standard deviation (%)	12.66	13.38
Skewness	2.94	2.70
S. E.	(0.30)	(0.30)
Kurtosis	11.41	9.87
S. E.	(0.60)	(0.60)
Maximum (%)	69.16	70.26
Third quartile (%)	6.59	10.02
Median (%)	2.29	4.05
z-value[b]	4.45	3.05
	(0.00)	(0.00)
First quartile (%)	0.00	−0.95
Minimum (%)	−12.63	−14.99

The underpricing is calculated using equation (13.2).
[a] p-values in parentheses.
[b] z-values are calculated using a nonparametric sign test (p-values in parentheses).

return in both cases is also significantly different from zero at the 1% level. This supports the rejection of the null hypothesis. As in other studies – for example, Levis (1993) and Ruud (1993) – the distribution of initial returns is skewed to the right and peaked. The last column of Table 13.2 documents the fact that initial returns for Austrian IPOs are not constant over time. Especially during the first years and in the hot-issue period of 1990, the underpricing observed is above average.

13.4.3   Hypotheses to explain the level of underpricing

Many theories have been put forward to explain the underpricing of IPOs. In order to formulate hypotheses to explain the first-day return level of Austrian IPOs, the most common explanations will be examined.

13.4.3.1   Allocation (winner's curse) hypothesis

In Rock's model (1986), underpricing is a necessary equilibrium condition in a world of informational asymmetry between groups of informed and uninformed investors. Initially, all investors are uninformed about the true value of the issuing firm and its future prospects. This is termed ex-ante uncertainty. However, investors can, at a cost, acquire firm-specific information and become informed. An informed investor can distinguish between underpriced and overpriced new issues and will therefore submit purchase orders only if the offer price is less than the true value of the stock. If, on the other hand, the issue is overpriced, only uninformed investors submit purchase orders and they subsequently receive a 100% allocation. For underpriced issues, both uninformed and informed investors submit purchase orders and the allocation is subsequently rationed between the two groups. This creates a situation where the average first-day return conditional upon receiving shares is lower than the average first-day return conditional upon submitting a purchase order. Therefore, uninformed investors face a 'winner's curse': the chance of being allocated shares in overpriced new issues is greater than in underpriced issues. To keep uninformed investors participating in the IPO market, investment banks underprice to ensure them a non-negative, market-adjusted rate of return.

To test whether Rock's (1986) winner's curse hypothesis holds for the sample under investigation, it is necessary to calculate allocation-adjusted abnormal returns. This would require information of the amount of rationing. As in many other countries, there are no standardized rationing principles in Austria. The percentage allocation an investor receives depends not only on the size of the order or the average over-subscription rate, it can differ between banks and can also depend on the relationship between the customer and the investment bank. Sometimes even lotteries are used in the allocation of very oversubscribed shares. In contrast, Keloharju (1993) describes the allocation system in Finland as much more transparent. More than 30% of all Austrian IPOs are overpriced with a mean initial return of -3.70%, whereas under-priced IPOs experienced an average first-day return of $+10.94\%$.

Similar to other markets, there is a tendency in Austria for underpriced IPOs to be oversubscribed and for investors submitting purchasing orders for underpriced IPOs to receive less than the number of shares they ordered. On the other hand, overpriced IPOs are not usually oversubscribed and investors submitting purchasing orders for these IPOs are allocated up to 100%.

Therefore, the average return available to an uninformed investor who uses a simple stagging strategy (always buy at the offer price and sell on the first trading day in the aftermarket) is reduced due to rationing. This suggests that at least part of the observable unconditional abnormal return of 6.50% can be put down to the phenomenon of the winner's curse.

13.4.3.2   Ex-ante uncertainty hypothesis

One testable implication of the Rock model (1986) is that the level of underpricing required to attract uninformed investors increases with the ex-ante uncertainty about the true value of the firm. The greater the ex-ante uncertainty, the greater is the advantage of becoming an informed investor. Beatty and Ritter (1986) suggested that there should be a positive relationship between the underpricing and the non-observable ex-ante uncertainty. In order to test their proposition it is necessary to use a proxy for the ex-ante uncertainty. As recommended in the empirical literature – see, for example, Ritter (1984) and McGuinness (1992) – the volatility (standard deviation) of daily returns between the second and the 42nd day of trading (the first 2 trading months) is used as a proxy.

13.4.3.3   Underwriter reputation hypothesis

Another explanation for the level of underpricing is the reputation of the underwriter. Since an investment bank underwrites many offerings in the course of time and in their business with potential investors, an investment bank can develop a reputation and earn more on this reputation than on 'cheating' by underpricing too much or too little. A systematically too high or too low underpricing would subsequently be followed by a loss in market share. Empirical studies investigating the relationship between the underpricing level and the underwriter's reputation have found that high reputation investment banks underprice less than non-prestigious banks – see, for example, Johnson and Miller (1988). This is because high reputation underwriters issue firms with lower ex-ante uncertainty.

Carter and Manaster (1990) postulated that the prestige of an investment bank provides a signal for the market about the risk of the issue. They showed that, on average, less prestigious investment banks underwrite riskier IPOs than more prestigious banks. The less risky an issue is, the less is the incentive for investors to acquire information to become informed. If an issuing firm is less risky, the ex-ante uncertainty is lower and, according to Beatty and Ritter (1986), the underpricing should be lower. Carter and Manaster (1990) suggested that one of the reasons why prestigious investment banks issue low-risk firms is that they want to increase the expected present value of subsequent offerings. Low-risk IPO firms are more likely to survive and make subsequent offerings than high-risk IPO firms. Carter (1992) provided empirical evidence that firms with no subsequent offerings have a greater standard deviation of aftermarket returns and are therefore riskier.

To test explanations of underpricing focusing on the reputation of the underwriter, we use the logarithm of the cumulative gross proceeds of all issues an investment bank has already underwritten as lead manager since 1984. This implies that, firstly, the reputation level of an investment bank increases (in a nonlinear fashion) with the total gross proceeds of all IPOs the bank has already issued and that, secondly, the building up of reputation starts in 1984 for all banks. The latter assumption seems to be admissible because no initial public offering took place in Austria in the 18 years before 1984.

13.4.3.4   Signaling hypothesis

Studies by Allen and Faulhaber (1989), Grinblatt and Hwang (1989), and Welch (1989) suggested that underpricing may itself be a costly signal of the intrinsic value of the issuing firm. In the Welch (1989) signaling approach, for example, high-quality firms deliberately choose an offer price below the intrinsic value to signal their quality to investors. This underpricing is motivated by the possibility of achieving higher offer prices in subsequent seasoned issues. Underpricing is therefore supposed to be a sort of appetizer for subsequent issues in the aftermarket. Slovin et al. (1994), for example, reported a non-negative long-run aftermarket performance for IPOs with seasoned equity offerings. The investors know that only high-quality firms can afford the costs of underpricing. The main assumption is that low-quality firms only have the choice to imitate high-quality firms or to disclose their true quality. The former results in imitation costs and involves the danger of losing part of the imitation expenses if the true quality is recognized after the IPO but before a seasoned offering. The latter creates no imitation costs but it forgoes the possibility of achieving higher prices at the IPO and in subsequent seasoned offerings. High-quality firms (high underpricing) should therefore only offer a smaller part of their share capital at the initial issue and make subsequent issues in the aftermarket. Advocates of the signaling hypothesis argue therefore that enterprises with a high credit standing deliberately use underpricing as a means of signaling their quality to investors. If this explanation model applies, the level of underpricing should be proportional to the frequency of seasoned issues and inversely proportional to the percentage fraction issued from the share capital.

13.4.4 Regression analysis

To explain the observed underpricing of Austrian IPOs, the following hypotheses are tested:

Hypothesis H_1:   Ex-ante uncertainty hypothesis – There exists no significant relationship between the level of underpricing and the ex-ante uncertainty measured by the standard deviation (volatility) of the first 42 daily aftermarket trading returns (variable Vola).

Hypothesis H_2:   Underwriter reputation hypothesis – There exists no significant relationship between the level of underpricing and the reputation of the underwriter measured by the logarithm of the cumulative gross proceeds of issues an investment bank has already launched as lead manager since 1984 (variable Rep).

Hypothesis H_3:   Signaling hypothesis – There exists no significant relationship between the level of underpricing and the fraction of the share capital sold (variable Frac, in %) and the seasoned equity offering activity during the first 2 years of aftermarket trading (dummy variable SEO, which is coded 1 if a seasoned equity offering is made within 24 months of the IPO).

In order to examine the relationship between the state of the market and the level of underpricing, the performance of the market in the 3 months before the IPO is also considered.

Hypothesis H_4:   Market climate hypothesis – There exists no significant relationship between the level of underpricing and the performance of the stock market (Vienna Stock Exchange Share Index) in the 3-month period before the beginning of the subscription period (variable Market).

The regression equation used is:

$$UP_i = \alpha_0 + \alpha_1 \cdot Vola_i + \alpha_2 \cdot Market_i + \alpha_3 \cdot Rep_i + \alpha_4 \cdot Frac_i + \alpha_5 \cdot SEO_i + \varepsilon_i \qquad (13.3)$$

where UP_i is the average market-adjusted return between the first day of the subscription period and the close of trading on the first day (underpricing). $Vola_i$ (proxy for the ex-ante uncertainty) is the average aftermarket volatility (standard deviation) of the issuing firm, estimated on the basis of daily returns between the close of trading on the first day and the 42nd day of trading. Rep_i (proxy for the reputation (quality) of the investment bank) is the logarithm of the cumulative gross proceeds of IPOs already launched by a given bank as lead manager since 1984, and $Frac_i$ is the percentage portion (fraction) issued from the share capital. $Market_i$ (market performance prior to the issue) is the percentage change in the Vienna Stock Exchange Share Index for the 3-month period prior to the subscription period, and SEO_i (seasoned equity offering) is a dummy variable coded 1 if a seasoned issue of equities is made within 24 months of the IPO.

Table 13.5 shows the results of the multivariate regression analysis. First, a significant and positive relation can be detected between the variable UP (underpricing) and the variable Vola (ex-ante uncertainty). This supports the Beatty and Ritter

Table 13.5 Multivariate regression analysis of initial returns against several explanatory variables for 62 IPOs from 1984 to 1996

Intercept	Vola	Market	Rep	Frac	SEO	F^a	R^2adj^b	DW^c
−0.109	5.082	0.349	0.107	−0.094	−0.036	5.300	0.261	1.861
(−0.019)	(3.385)	(3.130)	(0.151)	(−1.196)	(−0.010)			
[0.985]	[0.001]	[0.003]	[0.880]	[0.237]	[0.992]	[0.000]		

The table presents the results of the model in equation (13.3). $Vola_i$ (proxy for the ex-ante uncertainty) is the aftermarket standard deviation of the issuing firm; Rep_i (proxy for the reputation [quality] of the underwriter) is the logarithm of the cumulative gross proceeds of issues already launched by a given bank as lead manager since 1984; $Frac_i$ is the percentage portion (fraction) issued from the share capital; $Market_i$ (market performance prior to the issue) is the percentage change in the Vienna Stock Exchange Share Index for the 3-month period prior to the subscription period; and SEO_i (seasoned equity offering) is a dummy variable coded 1 if a seasoned issue of equities is made within 24 months of the IPO.

^{a} The F-statistic tests the null hypothesis that the explanatory variable coefficients are equal to zero.

^{b} Adjusted R^2.

^{c} Durbin–Watson statistic.

t-values are given in parentheses and p-values in square brackets.

(1986) argument. A higher ex-ante uncertainty implies a higher underpricing. Second, the relation between UP and the variable Market (market performance prior to the issue) is also significantly positive. This finding suggests that Austrian IPOs issued after an upswing in the stock market experienced a higher underpricing than IPOs following a falling market. This finding is consistent with the existence of hot- and cold-issue markets. The positive relationship between underpricing and the market climate has also been reported for other markets – see, for example, Ritter (1984) for the USA, Uhlir (1989) for Germany, and McGuinness (1992) for Hong Kong. After the bear market of 1987 the average initial return in 1988 was −0.14%, whereas in the year after the bull market of 1989 the average initial return in 1990 was 12.72%. As the underpricing of an IPO is high following a rising market and increases with the ex-ante uncertainty, this suggests that IPOs which are unknown to investors and therefore more difficult to evaluate (higher ex-ante uncertainty) are more frequently issued following a rising stock market.

Third, there is no significantly negative relationship between the underpricing level and the reputation of the investment bank (no significant association between UP and Rep), which is in clear contrast to the reputation hypothesis. In Austria only three banks launched more than five issues from 1984 to 1996. They were, however, responsible for more than three-fourths of all the IPOs and had an average underpricing of 7.92%. All other banks launched less than five issues in the period considered and jointly accounted for less than one-fourth of the IPOs. Surprisingly, their underpricing level averaged 1.86%. It could be that the rejection of the reputation hypothesis for the Austrian IPO market is due to the fact that the market structure is oligopolistic and thus not very competitive.

Fourth, no significant relationship can be detected between the underpricing and the fraction of the share capital sold (Frac), which is in contrast to the suggestion of the signaling hypothesis that high quality (equals high underpricing) firms sell less at the initial offering and more in the aftermarket. In addition, the dummy variable SEO, which controls for seasoned equity offerings in the first 2 years following the IPO, is neither positive nor significantly related to the underpricing level. This implies that the view cannot be supported that firms making secondary offerings in the 24 months following an IPO underprice initial public offerings significantly more than others. This evidence for Austrian IPOs is in line with the findings by Espenlaub and Tonks (1998) for UK IPOs. On balance, their empirical results reject existing IPO underpricing signaling models.

13.5 Aftermarket performance

13.5.1 Research design

To measure the abnormal performance of IPOs in the aftermarket it is first necessary to specify appropriate benchmarks. This task is of particular importance because it can affect the measured aftermarket performance. One possibility is to use a matching firm adjustment procedure, in which for each IPO firm a non-IPO firm of approximately similar size and the same industry is chosen – see, for example, Ritter (1991), Loughran and Ritter (1995), and Kim et al. (1995). Another possibility, which is used for markets in which the number of potential benchmark firms is low, is to use one or more indices, e.g. a market index, as a benchmark – see, for example, Keloharju (1993) for the Finnish IPO market and Kunz and Aggarwal (1994) for the Swiss IPO market. To account for the fact that the Austrian stock market is small and the average number of IPO firms is about the same as for non-IPO firms, a market index is not used as a benchmark. Otherwise IPOs would be compared with a portfolio of IPOs and non-IPOs and a measured abnormal performance would be biased. Instead, portfolios of only non-IPO firms (all firms listed in the Official Market of the VSE exclusive of IPOs for their first 5 years after going public) are formed.

Starting with 1984, all non-IPO firms listed at the beginning of each calendar year are sorted by their market capitalization as of the last trading day of the prior calendar year and grouped into three reference portfolios, each containing an equal number of non-IPO firms. If a non-IPO firm is delisted before the end of the calendar year, its last price before delisting is used till the end of the year. Dependent on its market capitalization at the end of the first trading day, each IPO firm is then assigned to one of these three reference portfolios. On the first trading day of each calendar year, this assignment procedure is repeated to account for size changes in the IPO firms and the firms in the reference portfolios. This procedure ensures that IPO firms are compared with a portfolio of non-IPO firms of approximately similar size. Classifying the reference portfolios by industries is not done because the overall number of non-IPOs is small and only a few publicly traded companies are available in most industries.

The bases for the evaluation of the aftermarket performance of Austrian IPOs are the following ex-ante implementable trading strategies: (a) purchase each IPO on its first aftermarket trading day; (b) purchase each IPO's corresponding reference portfolio on the IPO's first aftermarket trading day; and (c) sell each IPO and its corresponding reference portfolio on the earlier of the last day before the IPO's delisting and (1) the 22nd (i.e. after 1 month of aftermarket trading), (2) the 125th (after 6 months), (3) the 251st (after 12 months), (4) the 751st (after 3 years), and (5) the 1251st trading day (after 5 years). As the number and size of future IPOs is ex-ante unknown, it is assumed that an equal amount of money is invested in each IPO and each corresponding reference portfolio.

To measure the aftermarket performance for each IPO and its corresponding reference portfolio, buy-and-hold returns are calculated. In contrast to cumulative returns, buy-and-hold returns have the advantage that they are based on a realistic ex-ante trading strategy. The methodology used is similar to equation (1) in Loughran and Ritter (1995). The buy-and-hold return for IPO i ($BHR_T^{IPO\,i}$) is defined as:

$$BHR_T^{IPO\,i} = \left[\prod_{t=1}^{\min(T,\text{delisting})} (1 + R_{i,t}) \right] - 1, \tag{13.4}$$

where $R_{i,t}$ is the return of IPO i in period t, $t = 1$ indicates the first trading day in the aftermarket, T is the aftermarket trading day number 22, 125, 251, 751, or 1251 respectively, and $\min(T,\text{delisting})$ is the earlier of the last day before delisting and T. The buy-and-hold return for the corresponding reference portfolio of IPO i ($BHR_T^{RPF\,i}$) is defined as:

$$BHR_T^{RPF\,i} = \left[\prod_{t=1}^{\min(T,\text{delisting})} (1 + R_{RPF\,i,t}) \right] - 1, \tag{13.5}$$

where $R_{RPF\,i,t}$ is the return of the reference portfolio of IPO i in period t, $t = 1$ indicates the first trading day of IPO i in the aftermarket, T is the aftermarket trading day number 22, 125, 251, 751, or 1251 of IPO i respectively, and min(T, delisting) is the earlier of the last day before delisting of IPO i and T. Therefore, buy-and-hold returns over identical intervals are calculated for each IPO and its corresponding reference portfolio. This procedure introduces no survivorship bias or look-ahead bias. The average buy-and-hold return for a sample of n IPOs (BHR_T^{IPO}) and corresponding reference portfolios (BHR_T^{RPF}) is then measured as:

$$BHR_T^{IPO} = \frac{1}{n} \sum_{i=1}^{n} BHR_T^{IPO\,i} \tag{13.6a}$$

$$BHR_T^{RPF} = \frac{1}{n} \sum_{i=1}^{n} BHR_T^{RPF\,i}, \tag{13.6b}$$

where n is the number of IPOs. To measure the abnormal performance for the above-described trading strategies, buy-and-hold abnormal returns are calculated for each IPO i as:

$$BHAR_T^{IPO\,i} = BHR_T^{IPO\,i} - BHR_T^{RPF\,i}, \tag{13.7}$$

where $BHR_T^{IPO\,i}$ is the buy-and-hold return of IPO i and $BHR_T^{RPF\,i}$ is the buy-and-hold return of the corresponding reference portfolio of IPO i. Then, the average buy-and-hold abnormal return is given by:

$$BHAR_T = \frac{1}{n} \sum_{i=1}^{n} [BHAR_T^{IPO\,i}]. \tag{13.8}$$

A positive (negative) average buy-and-hold abnormal return can be interpreted as an outperformance (underperformance) of the IPO sample relative to the reference portfolios. Following Ritter (1991), the relative aftermarket performance is also evaluated using wealth relatives. The wealth relative for a portfolio of n IPOs for the described trading strategies is defined as:

$$WR_T = \frac{1 + BHR_T^{IPO}}{1 + BHR_T^{RPF}}, \tag{13.9}$$

where BHR_T^{IPO} is the average buy-and-hold return of n IPOs and BHR_T^{RPF} is the average buy-and-hold return of the corresponding reference portfolios. A wealth relative greater than (below) 1 indicates that the IPO sample has outperformed (underperformed) a portfolio of benchmark firms.

Another important point in measuring the long-horizon abnormal performance of security prices is the usage of appropriate test statistics. As the simulation results of Kothari and Warner (1997), Barber and Lyon (1997), and Lyon et al. (1999) show, conventional tests of long-run abnormal security returns are often misspecified. They found that conventional parametric test statistics often indicate a long-run abnormal performance when none is present (i.e., p-values are too high and the null hypothesis of no abnormal performance is too often rejected). They mention especially three main reasons for potential misspecifications: (a) survival-related biases, which occur if failing firms are excluded; (b) rebalancing biases, which arise if cumulative return procedures are used; and (c) biases because long-run abnormal performance measures are typically skewed.

To minimize the first two sources of misspecification, this study also includes all firms delisted on the VSE during the investigation period and uses buy-and-hold returns to calculate the long-run performance. In addition, to account for the skewness bias, a skewness-adjusted t-statistic with bootstrapped p-values (as suggested by Lyon et al., 1999) and a nonparametric sign test are used to test the null hypothesis of no abnormal long-run performance. As a result of their simulation analyses concerning the long-horizon security price performance, Kothari and Warner (1997) recommended using nonparametric and bootstrap tests to reduce misspecification.

Cumulative abnormal returns (CARs) have the disadvantage that they are not based on a practical ex-ante trading strategy. In contrast to BHRs, cumulative returns (CRs) and CARs contain the implicit assumption of periodic portfolio weight adjustments. In addition, especially when used to measure the performance over longer periods (for example, several years), CRs and CARs do not necessarily reflect the correct economic performance. The example in Table 13.6 presents this effect.

After 14 periods the IPO as well as the benchmark both reach the original price level of 100. The economically correct absolute as well as abnormal performance of the IPO is therefore zero. The BHRs, BHARs, and WRs reflect this fact. On the other hand, both CR measures and the CARs (+106%) are well above zero and therefore create a performance that does not exist.

13.5.2 Short-run performance

As the underpricing of Austrian IPOs is relatively low compared to other markets, an explanation for this could be that the price adjustment process did not finish at the end of the first trading day. If this is true, a significant abnormal performance should be observable during the first days of aftermarket trading. For example, Kim et al. (1995) documented for 169 Korean firms that went public from 1985 to 1989 a significant and huge matching firm-adjusted average buy-and-hold return of more than 31% during the first month of trading in the aftermarket (excluding the first-day return). Table 13.7 reports the aftermarket performance for the total sample of Austrian IPOs excluding the initial return.

The first three columns show that the short-run aftermarket performance is neither significantly negative nor significantly positive. At the first anniversary, for example, 36 out of 66 IPOs have a negative and 30 a positive buy-and-hold abnormal return. This evidence suggests that, at least for the short term, the average initial return does not disappear and that the tendency for full price adjustment to occur on the first trading day is apparent for the Austrian IPO market. This is in line with other studies – for example, Miller and Reilly (1987) for the USA, Finn and Higham (1988) for Australia, Uhlir (1989) for Germany, and Kunz and Aggarwal (1994) for Switzerland.

13.5.3 Long-run performance

Besides the initial return and the short-run performance of unseasoned new issues, the long-run aftermarket return is also important for underwriters, issuing firms, and investors. Significant abnormal returns in the long run would suggest that IPOs are not priced at true values in the early aftermarket. This would call into question the aftermarket efficiency in valuing newly listed firms. The last two columns of Table 13.7 report the long-run performance for the first 36 and 60 months following the

Table 13.6 Cumulative returns and CAR versus BHR and BHAR: an example

t	IPO			Benchmark (B)					BHR_IPO	BHR_B	BHAR	WR
	Price	Return	CR	Price	Return	CR	AR	CAR				
1	100			100								
2	95	−5.00	−5.0	98	−2.00	−2.0	−3.00	−3.00	−5	−2	−3	0.969
3	90	−5.26	−10.3	100	2.04	0.0	−7.30	−10.30	−10	0	−10	0.900
4	80	−11.11	−21.4	95	−5.00	−5.0	−6.11	−16.42	−20	−5	−15	0.842
5	70	−12.50	−33.9	85	−10.53	−15.5	−1.97	−18.39	−30	−15	−15	0.824
6	60	−14.29	−48.2	88	3.53	−12.0	−17.82	−36.20	−40	−12	−28	0.682
7	50	−16.67	−64.8	75	−14.77	−26.7	−1.89	−38.10	−50	−25	−25	0.667
8	40	−20.00	−84.8	50	−33.33	−60.1	13.33	−24.76	−60	−50	−10	0.800
9	30	−25.00	−109.8	35	−30.00	−90.1	5.00	−19.76	−70	−65	−5	0.857
10	20	−33.33	−143.2	20	−42.86	−32.9	9.52	−10.24	−80	−80	0	1.000
11	10	−50.00	−193.2	25	25.00	−07.9	−75.00	−85.24	−90	−75	−15	0.400
12	10	0.00	−193.2	15	−40.00	−47.9	40.00	−45.24	−90	−85	−5	0.667
13	50	400.00	206.8	55	266.67	118.7	133.33	88.09	−50	−45	−5	0.909
14	100	100.00	306.8	100	81.82	200.6	18.18	106.27	0	0	0	1.000

This table compares cumulative returns (CR) and cumulative abnormal returns (CAR) with buy-and-hold returns (BHR) and buy-and-hold abnormal returns (BHAR). Other variables used in this table are abnormal returns (AR) and the wealth relative (WR). All returns are given as percentages.

Table 13.7 Aftermarket performance (excluding initial return)

	Month relative to IPO				
	Short-run aftermarket			Long-run aftermarket	
	1	6	12	36	60
Average BHR$_{IPOs}$ (%)[a]	2.09	4.11	16.23	26.02	31.42
Geometric mean p.a. (%)				8.01	5.62
Average BHR$_{Ref\,PF}$ (%)[b]	1.33	5.12	18.85	73.44	105.38
Geometric mean p.a. (%)				20.15	15.48
Wealth relative[c]	1.01	0.99	0.98	0.73	0.64
Average BHAR (%)[d]	0.76	−1.02	−2.62	−47.42*	−73.95*
t-value[e]	(0.45)	(−0.25)	(−0.29)	(−3.64)	(−3.14)
Median BHAR (%)	−0.59	−1.28	−5.28	−18.75*	−42.42*
z-value[f]	(−1.10)	(−0.25)	(−0.74)	(−2.78)	(−3.78)
No. of positive BHARs	29	32	30	18	12
No. of negative BHARs	38	34	36	39	39
No. of IPOs (total)	67	66	66	57	51

* Significantly different from zero at the 1% level.
[a] Average buy-and-hold return for the sample of IPOs.
[b] Average buy-and-hold return for the corresponding reference portfolios.
[c] Wealth relative for the sample of IPOs, calculated using equation (13.9).
[d] Average buy-and-hold abnormal return for the sample of IPOs, calculated using equations (13.7) and (13.8).
[e] Bootstrapped skewness-adjusted t-statistics (as suggested by Lyon et al., 1999).
[f] z-values are calculated using a nonparametric sign test.

first day of public trading. Fifty-seven (51) firms, which went public during the period 1984 to 1993 (1984 to 1991), are utilized in measuring the 3-year (5-year) performance.

Focusing first on the 3-year performance, an investor purchasing each IPO for an equal amount of money on its first aftermarket trading day would have earned a mean return of 26.02% (or an average annual return of 8.01%) holding these IPOs until the third anniversary of public trading. An alternative investment in the corresponding reference portfolio would have yielded a much higher average return of 73.44% (or an average annual return of 20.15%) over the same time interval. The mean and median buy-and-hold abnormal return of −47.42% and −18.75% respectively are both significantly different from zero at the 1% level. The difference in the mean and median values reflects the skewness in the distribution of the buy-and-hold abnormal returns. The null hypothesis of no abnormal 3-year performance therefore has to be rejected. The wealth relative of 0.73 implies that an investor would have had to invest 37% more in each IPO than in each corresponding reference portfolio to achieve the same wealth after 3 years of public trading.

Column 5 of Table 13.7 shows the results based upon 5-year holding periods. The performance of IPOs continues to be poor in years 4 and 5, with significantly negative mean and median buy-and-hold abnormal returns of −73.95% and −42.42% respectively. Only 23% of the sample of 51 IPOs experienced a positive buy-and-hold abnormal return on their fifth anniversary. The wealth relative of 0.64 also documents a severe underperformance of the average Austrian IPO.

This finding, which is in contrast to the observation of a non-negative long-run aftermarket performance for Swiss IPOs (Kunz and Aggarwal, 1994) and Korean IPOs (Kim et al., 1995), is in line with the empirical evidence for the IPO markets in the USA (Ritter, 1991; Loughran and Ritter, 1995), in Finland (Keloharju, 1993), in Germany (Ljungqvist, 1997), in the UK (Levis, 1993), and with the evidence for private sector IPOs in Hungary (Jelic and Briston, 1999).

13.5.4 Possible explanations for the observed long-run performance

As mentioned in section 13.3, about 60% of all Austrian IPOs are firms that are exclusively controlled by a family or by private persons before going public. On the other hand, about 20% of all Austrian IPOs are enterprises owned by the state before going public. One main difference between these two groups is that in state-owned companies ownership and management are separated, whereas in family-owned firms this is not the case. In the latter the owners are also the managers and in most cases sell part of their company to the public, mainly to raise money for their own pocket. The mean fraction issued from the share capital by family-owned firms is 31.1%. The crucial question which arises is: does the long-run aftermarket performance of an IPO depend on its pre-issue ownership structure?

The ownership structure of family-owned firms going public might fit into one implication of the agency theory: as managerial ownership in a firm is reduced, the managers' incentives to maximize the firms' value decreases. As a consequence, the operating performance after going public should be poor. In this respect, Jain and Kini (1994) documented a significant operating underperformance for a sample of (non-privatized) US IPOs. In contrast to their findings, Megginson et al. (1994) analyzed the operating performance of privatized firms. They compared the operating performance of 61 companies from 18 countries before and after privatization over the period 1961 to 1991, and documented that the profitability and operating efficiency as well as real sales and capital investment spending increased significantly after privatization. Similar results were reported by D'Souza and Megginson (1999) for a sample of 85 companies from 28 industrialized countries, and by Boubakri and Cosset (1998) for a sample of 78 companies from 21 developing countries. This raises the question as to whether a positive operating performance after going public might lead to a non-negative or perhaps positive long-run aftermarket performance of former state-owned enterprises. This would imply at least a better long-run aftermarket performance for privatized enterprises in comparison to family-owned firms.

Table 13.8 reports the 5-year abnormal performance of family-owned IPOs, privatized firms, and the group of other IPOs. Several interesting findings can be observed: first, by implementing a trading strategy to invest an equal amount of money in each family-owned IPO on the first trading day in the aftermarket, investors would not only have experienced a poor performance in relation to the alternative strategy of investing in corresponding reference portfolios, they would also actually have lost money. The average buy-and-hold return on the fifth anniversary is −19.69% or −4.29% on an annual basis (see Figure 13.1(A)).

Table 13.8 Five-year aftermarket performance: first trading day till the fifth anniversary (exclusive of initial return) for all issues, family-owned issues (family), privatized firms (privatized), and other issues (others), 1984 to 1991

	All	Family	Privatized	Others
Average BHR_{IPO} (%)[a]	31.42	−19.69	152.03	88.36
Geometric mean p.a. (%)	5.62	−4.29	20.31	13.50
Average $BHR_{Ref\ PF}$ (%)[b]	105.38	98.92	102.17	122.51
Geometric mean p.a. (%)	15.48	14.75	15.12	17.35
Wealth relative[c]	0.64	0.40	1.25	0.85
Average BHAR (%)[d]	−73.95*	−118.60*	49.85	−34.15
t-value[e]	−3.14	−6.12	0.86	−0.62
Median BHAR (%)	−42.42*	−51.56*	28.90	−25.88
z-value[f]	−3.78	−4.13	0.38	−1.39
No. of positive BHARs	12	4	4	4
No. of negative BHARs	39	27	3	9
No. of IPOs (total)	51	31	7	13

Family-owned IPOs are defined as firms exclusively controlled by a family or by private persons before going public; privatized firms are former (100%) state-owned enterprises; and other firms are firms exclusively controlled by a bank or another big company (i.e. not controlled by a family).
* Significantly different from zero at the 1% level.
[a] Average buy-and-hold return for the sample of IPOs.
[b] Average buy-and-hold return for the corresponding reference portfolios.
[c] Wealth relative for the sample of IPOs, calculated using equation (13.9).
[d] Average buy-and-hold abnormal return for the sample of IPOs, calculated using equations (13.7) and (13.8).
[e] Bootstrapped skewness-adjusted t-statistics (as suggested by Lyon et al., 1999).
[f] z-values are calculated using a nonparametric sign test.

Panel A: Family-owned IPOs and their benchmark.

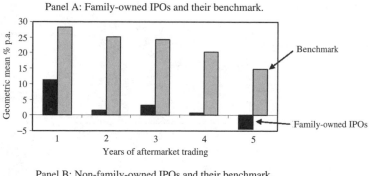

Panel B: Non-family-owned IPOs and their benchmark.

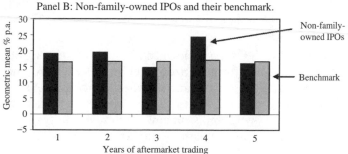

Figure 13.1 Average annualized aftermarket performance for family-owned IPOs, non-family-owned IPOs, and their corresponding benchmarks

This clear evidence of extremely poor performing family-owned IPOs also shows up in the average and median buy-and-hold abnormal returns of −118.60% and −51.56% respectively (both are significantly different from zero at the 1% level). Only four of 31 IPOs managed to outperform non-IPOs; in other words, 87% of all family-owned IPOs underperformed their corresponding benchmark firms over the first 5 years of seasoning. The wealth relative of 0.40 implies the necessity for an investor to invest 150% more in family-owned IPOs than in non-IPOs of approximately similar size to have the same wealth on the fifth anniversary after going public.

In clear contrast to these findings is the evidence for the two other groups. Privatized firms managed to outperform their benchmark firms on average by +49.85% (median value +28.90%) with a wealth relative of 1.25, whereas the group of other IPOs underperform by −34.15% (average buy-and-hold abnormal return) and −25.88% (median buy-and-hold abnormal return) respectively, with a wealth relative of 0.85. Neither the overperformance of privatized enterprises nor the underperformance of the group of other IPOs are significantly different from zero (also see Figure 13.1(B)). Similar results for a sample of Hungarian IPOs were documented by Jelic and Briston (1999). They reported that Hungarian privatizations significantly outperform their private sector counterparts. Further details on the special characteristics of privatizations are provided in Megginson (2005) and Megginson and Netter (2001). Figure 13.2 compares the development of the WR over time for the different groups of Austrian IPOs till the fifth anniversary.

At least three main conclusions can therefore be drawn from these findings. First, there is evidence that the main reasons for the underperformance of Austrian IPOs is

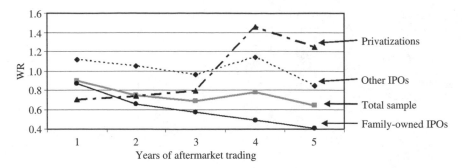

Figure 13.2 Wealth relative (WR) over time for different groups of Austrian IPOs: Total sample, family-owned IPOs, privatizations, and other IPOs

due to one particular class of IPOs: family-owned IPOs. Second, no significant under-performance can be documented for privatized and other IPOs. Third, the conclusion that privatized enterprises outperform family-owned firms in the long run (fifth anniversary of IPO) seems to be appropriate. This evidence shows that in the case of the Austrian IPO market the ownership structure is an important reason for the over-all underperformance, which is in line with the expectations formulated above.

13.5.5 Regression analysis

To get further information about possible explanations for the long-run underper-formance of Austrian IPOs, a cross-sectional regression analysis is conducted. The estimated model is:

$$\text{BHAR}_T^{\text{IPO}\,i} = \alpha_0 + \alpha_1 \cdot \text{Vola}_i + \alpha_2 \cdot \text{Market}_i + \alpha_3 \cdot \text{Rep}_i + \alpha_4 \cdot \text{Family}_i + \varepsilon_i \qquad (13.10)$$

where $\text{BHAR}_T^{\text{IPO}\,i}$ is the average buy-and-hold abnormal return from the closing price of the first trading day till the fifth anniversary of IPO i measured using equation (13.7), Vola_i is the aftermarket standard deviation of the issuing firm, estimated on the basis of daily returns between the close of trading on the first day and the 42nd day of trading, and Market_i (market performance prior to the issue) is the percentage change in the Vienna Stock Exchange Share Index for the 3-month period prior to the subscription period. Rep_i (proxy for the reputation [quality] of the underwriter) is the logarithm of the cumulative gross proceeds of issues already launched by a bank as lead manager since 1984 and Family_i is a dummy variable coded 1 if IPO i is family owned prior to the issue and 0 otherwise.

The variable Vola_i is included to test whether higher price fluctuations in the short-term aftermarket are associated with a worse long-run performance as the heteroge-neous expectation hypothesis would imply (Jenkinson and Ljungqvist, 2001, p. 149). The variable Market_i is used to test the windows of opportunity hypothesis. This hypothesis states that firms time their IPO and go public when investors are over-optimistic. The latter is mostly the case after stock market booms. About 50% of all Austrian IPOs are cumulated after the two stock market booms in 1985 and in 1989/1990.

The results presented in Table 13.9 confirm in essence the above results for the long-run underperformance of Austrian IPOs. Whilst the variable Vola has no

Table 13.9 Multivariate regression analysis of 5-year buy-and-hold abnormal returns $(BHAR_T)$ against several explanatory variables, all issues from 1984 to 1991 (51 IPOs)

Intercept	Vola	Market	Rep	Family	F[a]	R^2adj[b]	DW[c]
−117.098	20.699	−2.649	19.054	−161.026		0.235	2.135
(−2.243)	(1.060)	(−1.834)	(2.646)	(−3.624)	4.842		
[0.030]	[0.295]	[0.073]	[0.011]	[0.001]	[0.002]		

[a] The F-statistic tests the null hypothesis that the explanatory variable coefficients are equal to 0.
[b] Adjusted R^2.
[c] Durbin–Watson statistic.
t-values are given in parentheses and p-values in square brackets.
The table presents the results of the model in equation (13.10). $Vola_i$ is the aftermarket standard deviation of the issuing firm; $Market_i$ (market performance prior to the issue) is the percentage change in the Vienna Stock Exchange Share Index for the 3-month period prior to the subscription period; Rep_i (proxy for the reputation [quality] of the underwriter) is the logarithm of the cumulative gross proceeds of issues already launched by a bank as lead manager since 1984; and $Family_i$ is a dummy variable coded 1 if an IPO is family-owned prior to the issue and 0 otherwise.

explanatory power, it is shown that the long-run performance is worse the better the stock market performance prior to the issue. This would testify for the windows of opportunity hypothesis, but we have to consider that the variable market is only significantly different from zero at the 10% level.

More pronounced are the results for the reputation and the ownership structure hypotheses: first, the higher the reputation of the underwriter, the better the long-run performance (and vice versa). This is in line with the findings of Nanda et al. (1995), who observed significant differences in the average long-run performance of US IPOs based on the reputation of the underwriter (lead manager). They showed that the long-run underperformance is a phenomenon primarily associated with IPOs done by less established underwriters with lower reputation. In addition, they documented that those underwriters whose IPOs experienced the poorest long-run performance suffered a significant loss of market share. On the other hand, IPOs underwritten by investment banks with a high reputation do not experience a long-run underperformance. Second, the very poor performance of family-owned IPOs is also confirmed by the regression results. The variable $Family_i$ is significantly different from zero at the 1% level and has a negative sign.

13.6 Conclusion

This study examines the price behavior of 67 Austrian IPOs going public on the Official Market of the Vienna Stock Exchange (VSE) over the period 1984 to 1996. After more than 18 years with only delistings, in every year of the 13-year investigation period firms went public. In accordance with the findings for other markets, the average initial returns of Austrian IPOs are significantly positive. At an average level of 6.5%, however, the initial returns are lower than for most other IPO markets. More than 30% of all IPOs are overpriced, with negative initial returns.

Several hypotheses to explain the observed underpricing of Austrian IPOs have been tested. The empirical findings only show support for the ex-ante uncertainty and the market climate hypotheses. The underpricing level is significantly positive in relation to the return standard deviation in the short-term aftermarket and to the stock market performance in the last 3 months prior to the IPO. This supports both the Beatty and Ritter (1986) argument that the underpricing increases with the ex-ante uncertainty and the existence of hot-issue and cold-issue periods. On the other hand, the underwriter reputation and signaling hypotheses do not explain the cross-sectional differences in the level of underpricing. An additional explanation for the observed underpricing could be Rock's (1986) winner's curse hypothesis. Although it is not possible to directly test this hypothesis due to the lack of a standardized rationing procedure, there is a tendency for the allocation to be lower for underpriced issues than for overpriced ones, so that the allocation-adjusted average initial return should be smaller than the unadjusted 6.5%.

In contrast to the findings for the Swiss and Korean IPO markets (Kunz and Aggarwal, 1994; Kim et al., 1995), but in line with the evidence for the USA (Loughran and Ritter, 1995), Finland (Keloharju, 1993), the UK (Levis, 1993) and Germany (Ljungqvist, 1997), Austrian IPOs significantly underperform in the long run. An investor purchasing each IPO for an equal amount of money on its first aftermarket trading day would have earned a mean buy-and-hold return of 31.42% till the fifth anniversary, whereas an alternative investment in corresponding reference portfolios of non-IPO firms of approximately similar market capitalization would have yielded a much higher average buy-and-hold return of 105.38% over the same time interval. The mean buy-and-hold abnormal return of -73.95% is significantly different from zero and the wealth relative amounts to 0.64.

The main explanation for the observed severe long-run underperformance are cross-sectional differences in the ownership structure of Austrian IPOs: nearly 60% of all IPOs are firms that are exclusively controlled by a family or by private persons (family-owned IPOs), whereas privatized and other non-family-owned firms account for around 20% each. In state-owned and non-family-owned companies, ownership and management are separated, whereas in family-owned firms this is not the case. In the latter the owners are also the managers and in most cases sell part of their company to the public, mainly to raise money for their own pockets. In addition, their going public is clustered after stock market booms, which suggests that they are best able to time an IPO and take advantage of windows of opportunity.

For family-owned firms going public, the average 5-year buy-and-hold return is -19.69%, which implies that an investor with a simple (ex-ante implementable) trading strategy to purchase only family-owned IPOs would have lost money over the first 5 aftermarket trading years. The wealth relative of 0.40 implies the necessity for an investor to invest 150% more money in family-owned IPOs than in non-IPOs of (approximately) similar size to have the same wealth at the fifth anniversary after going public. In contrast to this extreme underperformance, no significant positive or negative abnormal performance can be detected for privatized enterprises or other non-family-owned IPOs.

Acknowledgments – I would like to thank Jos van Bommel, Martin Holmen, Roger M. Kunz, Alexander Ljungqvist, Hans Reitbauer, Jay R. Ritter, Laura O. Robinson, and Helmut Uhlir, as well as seminar participants at the University of Graz and the Vienna Institute of Advanced Studies, for helpful comments.

References

Aggarwal, R. and Rivoli, P. (1990). Fads in the Initial Public Offering Market? *Financial Management*, 19(4):45–57.

Allen, F. and Faulhaber, G. R. (1989). Signalling by Underpricing in the IPO Market. *Journal of Financial Economics*, 23(2):303–323.

Aussenegg, W. (2000). Privatization Versus Private Sector Initial Public Offerings in Poland. *Multinational Finance Journal*, 4(1–2):69–99.

Barber, B. M. and Lyon, J. D. (1997). Detecting Long-Run Abnormal Stock Returns: The Empirical Power and Specification of Test Statistics. *Journal of Financial Economics*, 43(3):341–372.

Beatty, R. P. and Ritter, J. R. (1986). Investment Banking, Reputation, and the Underpricing of Initial Public Offerings. *Journal of Financial Economics*, 15(1–2):213–232.

Boubakri, N. and Cosset, J.-C. (1998). The Financial and Operating Performance of Newly Privatized Firms: Evidence from Developing Countries. *Journal of Finance*, 53(3):1081–1110.

Brown, S. J. and Warner, J. B. (1980). Measuring Security Price Performance. *Journal of Financial Economics*, 8(3):205–258.

Brown, S. J. and Warner, J. B. (1985). Using Daily Stock Returns. The Case of Event Studies. *Journal of Financial Economics*, 14(1):3–31.

Carter, R. B. (1992). Underwriter Reputation and Repetitive Public Offerings. *Journal of Financial Research*, 15(4):341–354.

Carter, R. B. and Manaster, S. (1990). Initial Public Offerings and Underwriter Reputation. *Journal of Finance*, 45(4):1045–1067.

D'Souza, J. and Megginson, W. L. (1999). The Financial and Operating Performance of Privatized Firms During the 1990s. *Journal of Finance*, 54(4):1397–1438.

Espenlaub, S. and Tonks, I. (1998). Post-IPO Directors' Sales and Reissuing Activity: An Empirical Test of IPO Signalling Models. *Journal of Business Finance and Accounting*, 25(9):1037–1079.

Finn, F. J. and Higham, R. (1988). The Performance of Unseasoned New Equity Issues-Cum-Stock Exchange Listings in Australia. *Journal of Banking and Finance*, 12(3):333–351.

Grinblatt, M. and Hwang, C. Y. (1989). Signalling and the Pricing of New Issues. *Journal of Finance*, 44(2):393–420.

Jain, B. A. and Kini, O. (1994). The Post-Issue Operating Performance of IPO Firms. *Journal of Finance*, 49(5):1699–1726.

Jelic, R. and Briston, R. (1999). Hungarian Privatisation Strategy and Financial Performance of Privatised Companies. *Journal of Business Finance and Accounting*, 26(9):1319–1357.

Jenkinson, T. and Ljungqvist, A. (2001). *Going Public – The Theory and Evidence on How Companies Raise Equity Finance*, 2nd edition. Oxford University Press, New York.

Johnson, J. M. and Miller, R. E. (1988). Investment Banker Prestige and the Underpricing of Initial Public Offerings. *Financial Management*, 17(1):19–29.

Keloharju, M. (1993). Winner's Curse, Legal Liability, and the Long-Run Price Performance of Initial Public Offerings in Finland. *Journal of Financial Economics*, 34(2):251–277.

Kim, J., Krinsky, I., and Lee, J. (1995). The Aftermarket Performance of Initial Public Offerings in Korea. *Pacific-Basin Finance Journal*, 3(4):429–448.

Kothari, S. P. and Warner, J. B. (1997). Measuring Long-Horizon Security Price Performance. *Journal of Financial Economics*, 43(3):301–339.

Kunz, R. M. and Aggarwal, R. (1994). Why Initial Public Offerings are Underpriced: Evidence from Switzerland. *Journal of Banking and Finance*, 18(4):705–723.

Levis, M. (1993). The Long-Run Performance of Initial Public Offerings: The UK Experience 1980–1988. *Financial Management*, 22(1):22–41.

Ljungqvist, A. P. (1997). Pricing Initial Public Offerings: Further Evidence from Germany. *European Economic Review*, 41(7):1309–1320.

Loughran, T. and Ritter, J. R. (1995). The New Issues Puzzle. *Journal of Finance*, 50(1):23–51.

Loughran, T. and Ritter, J. R. (2004). Why Has IPO Underpricing Changed Over Time? *Financial Management*, 33(3):5–37.

Loughran, T., Ritter, J. R., and Rydqvist, K. (1994). Initial Public Offerings: International Insights. *Pacific-Basin Finance Journal*, 2(2–3):165–199.

Lyon, J. D., Barber, B. M. and Tsai, C. L. (1999). Improved Methods for Tests of Long-Run Abnormal Stock Returns. *Journal of Finance*, 54(1):165–201.

McGuinness, P. (1992). An Examination of the Underpricing of Initial Public Offerings in Hong Kong 1980–90. *Journal of Business Finance and Accounting*, 19(2):165–186.

Megginson, W. L. (2005). *The Financial Economics of Privatization*. Oxford University Press, New York.

Megginson, W. L. and Netter, J. (2001). From State to Market: A Survey of Empirical Studies on Privatization. *Journal of Economic Literature*, 39(2):321–389.

Megginson, W. L., Nash, R. C., and Van Randenborgh, M. (1994). The Financial and Operating Performance of Newly Privatized Firms: An International Empirical Analysis. *Journal of Finance*, 49(2):403–452.

Miller, R. E. and Reilly, F. K. (1987). An Examination of Mispricing, Returns, and Uncertainty for Initial Public Offerings. *Financial Management*, 16(1):33–38.

Nanda, V., Yi, J.-H., and Yun, Y. (1995). IPO Long Run Performance and Underwriter Reputation. Working Paper 95-22, School of Business Administration, University of Michigan, Ann Arbor, MI.

Page, M. J. and Reyneke, I. (1997). The Timing and Subsequent Performance of Initial Public Offerings (IPOs) on the Johannesburg Stock Exchange. *Journal of Business Finance and Accounting*, 24(9):1401–1420.

Ritter, J. R. (1984). The "Hot Issue" Market of 1980. *Journal of Business*, 57(2):215–240.

Ritter, J. R. (1991). The Long-Run Performance of Initial Public Offerings. *Journal of Finance*, 46(1):3–27.

Ritter, J. R. (2003). Investment Banking and Securities Issuance. In: *Handbook of the Economics of Finance* (Constantinides, G., Harris, M., and Stulz, R., eds). Elsevier Science, Amsterdam.

Rock, K. (1986). Why New Issues Are Underpriced. *Journal of Financial Economics*, 15(1–2):187–212.

Ruud, J. S. (1993). Underwriter Price Support and the IPO Underpricing Puzzle. *Journal of Financial Economics*, 34(2):135–151.

Slovin, M. B., Sushka, M. E., and Bendeck, Y. M. (1994). Seasoned Common Stock Issuance Following an IPO. *Journal of Banking and Finance*, 18(1):207–226.

Uhlir, H. (1989). Going Public in the F.R.G. In: *A Reappraisal of the Efficiency of Financial Markets* (Guimarães, R.M.C., Kingsman, B. G. and Taylor, S. J., eds), pp. 369–393. Springer, Berlin.

Welch, I. (1989). Seasoned Offerings, Imitation Costs, and the Underpricing of Initial Public Offerings. *Journal of Finance*, 44(2):421–449.

14 The hot-issue period in Germany: what factors drove IPO underpricing?

Stefan Günther and Marco Rummer

Abstract

This chapter focuses on the hot-issue market in Germany, which was characterized by a high number of initial public offerings (IPOs) and extreme levels of underpricing. In particular, using different cross-sectional regressions we show that investor sentiment and agency conflicts were the determinants of high underpricing as opposed to traditional explanations with regard to ex-ante uncertainty. Our results confirm recent studies by Cornelli et al. (2004) and Derrien (2005). Additionally, using a VAR(4) model, we illustrate that more firms tend to go public following months of high underpricing. Finally, analyzing the descriptive statistics we suggest that the higher the underpricing, the poorer the subsequent performance of the IPO, supporting the leaning against the wind hypothesis.

'Not to be absolutely certain is, I think, one of the essential things in rationality.'
(Bertrand Russell, 1947)

14.1 Introduction

Since the phenomenon of initial public offering (IPO) underpricing was first documented in the 1970s, an enormous amount of research has been produced on IPOs, confirming underpricing in nearly every market and attempting to explain the apparent contradiction with market efficiency. More recently, Ritter (2001) predicted that 'the Internet bubble of 1999 will be to IPO researchers what the Great Depression of the 1930s is to macroeconomists'. And indeed, IPO research has become even more vibrant since the burst of the bubble. Research has mainly been driven by the existence of three apparent anomalies: issuing activity, underpricing, and long-run underperformance.

The first anomaly concerns the time-series behavior of first-day returns and IPO volume – for example, the number of IPOs. The 1997 to 2001 period exhibited a unique wave of firms going public in the traditionally bank-financed German financial system. The Frankfurt Stock Exchange became during this time period the most important stock market in Europe in terms of issue activity and market capitalization of new economy stocks (Ritter, 2003). Periods of higher than average issuing activity are referred to as hot-issue markets (Ritter, 1984; Ibbotson et al., 1994). This period of high issuing activity coincided with an unprecedented stock market boom, leading to the bursting bubble in 2000. Apparently, firms respond to favorable investor sentiment by issuing equity. Using a VAR(4) model we show that average underpricing positively influences future issuing activity, determining hot IPO markets.

The most extensively documented empirical regularity is the initial underpricing phenomenon. The first day trading prices typically exceed the price at which the shares were offered to the investors. The majority of explanations for IPO underpricing are based on asymmetric information in terms of ex-ante uncertainty. In the light of the dot-com bubble, however, traditional rationalizations do not seem to be the primary determinant. As Ritter and Welch (2002) pointed out, 'nonrational explanations and agency explanations will play a bigger role in the future research agenda'. Under agency explanations, though mostly based on asymmetric information as well, the cited authors summarized allocation and trading-related explanations. Ljungqvist et al. (2003) showed that the underpricing puzzle can be explained by the presence of sentiment investors. The notion of sentiment characterizes irrational investors showing strong interest towards IPO. Therefore, this study analyzes what factors drove the severe IPO underpricing during the dot-com bubble in Germany: ex-ante uncertainty, agency explanations, or investor sentiment. Using cross-sectional regressions estimated by ordinary least squares, we can confirm that investor sentiment was a driving factor of IPO underpricing. Moreover, we support the view that agency conflicts are a determinant of underpricing.

Finally, a more recent empirical anomaly is the poor long-run performance of IPOs. The immediate gain that investors typically make as a result of the underpricing tends to be associated with poor relative performance in the long run. Economists are captivated by the apparent anomalies, as they violate the fundamental principle of no arbitrage. If the observations were correct, systematic trading rules – for example, selling allocated shares on the first trading day – could be derived. However, the very existence of profitable trading rules implies a violation of the informational efficiency of stock markets. Using descriptive statistics, we find support for the leaning against the wind hypothesis in Germany. Underwriters might value the firm with its long-run value in mind. We illustrate that the higher the first-day initial return, the lower might be the subsequent performance.

The chapter proceeds as follows. In section 14.2 we discuss the literature on the IPO puzzle and set up the methodology for this study. Section 14.3 presents the essential features of the German market and describes the dataset. In section 14.4, we describe the firm and transaction characteristics. Additionally, we present results of average initial returns with regard to industry sectors, market segments, issuing activity, and long-run performance. Finally, we combine the discussed theory and the results of the previous subsections in a cross-sectional regression for underpricing. The last section summarizes and concludes.

14.2 Related research and methodology

After introducing selected aspects of the IPO process and outlining hitherto existing empirical evidence of IPO underpricing, we examine related theory concerning the IPO puzzle pattern of issuing activity, underpricing, and long-run underperformance. For alternative research see the other chapters of the book in hand. For a comprehensive survey of the large theoretical and empirical literature, see Jenkinson and Ljungqvist (2001), Ritter and Welch (2002), and Ljungqvist (2004). Concurrently, we state what methods will be used in this study in order to analyze the anomalies during the 1997 to 2001 period in Germany.

14.2.1 The basics of IPOs, bookbuilding, and underpricing

If a firm is issuing equity to the public for the first time, it is conducting an initial public offering (IPO). In Germany not only small and medium-sized companies go public, but also subsidiary companies (carve-out) and companies of the public sector in the context of privatizations. Firms go public for various reasons. First, at the public markets firms may be able to gain better access to capital at more attractive terms. Additionally, original shareholders gain liquidity. The stock of a publicly traded firm may be considered a more attractive form of compensation than the stock of a private firm; therefore, an IPO is seen as a measure to attract highly skilled employees. Moreover, the original owners can diversify while keeping control by means of a broad distribution of the shares. In addition, going public might be good publicity. Besides increased attention of the media and analysts, the listing requirements and follow-up obligations may improve the firm's credibility with its customers, employees, and suppliers. Finally, Ritter (1991) suggested that managers try to exploit the temporary overvaluation of firms within specific industry groups.

Taking a company public is a process that usually requires several months. The bookbuilding process is the most common procedure for pricing and selling a new issue. After registering and marketing the issue, the underwriter and issuer decide how many shares to offer within the bookbuilding range and the bookbuilding period. Subsequently, investors' purchase offers are collected. The final issue price is determined after receiving these offers. A major difference to the fixed price method, an alternative pricing method which was predominant until the mid-1990s in the German IPO market, is the higher transparency in the pricing process, as well as the consideration of the demand pattern and of the current capital market condition. However, one of the controversial features of bookbuilding is that underwriters might allocate shares to investors on the basis of favoritism.

Obviously, the process of going public is quite expensive. An apparent expense is the underwriter's fee. Total direct costs of taking a firm public are about 11% of the proceeds (Grinblatt and Titman, 2002). Once public, follow-up obligations, the loss of confidentiality, and public pressure cause additional costs on a publicly listed company. Additionally, and equally important as the direct costs, is the degree of underpricing, i.e. the money left on the table. Though, as firms often raise only small amounts of money in the IPO, the cost as a fraction of the firm's total value is generally smaller.

Empirical evidence suggests that the first-day trading price usually exceeds the final offer price, which is referred to as IPO underpricing. IPO underpricing is measured by the initial return. Initial return equals the difference between the offer price of an IPO, i.e. the underwriters' valuation of the firm, and the secondary market's valuation, expressed as the first trading day closing price. Analytically, initial return (IR) is calculated as:

$$\frac{P_1 - P_{\text{offer}}}{P_{\text{offer}}},$$

where P_1 is the first-day closing price and P_{offer} the offer price. Prior to the dot-com bubble, empirical evidence suggested an average underpricing in developed countries between 10% and 15%. In emerging markets, rates of above 60% have been identified, which can be ascribed to political factors (Jenkinson and Ljungqvist, 2001; Ritter 2003).

Studies of the German market revealed diverse initial returns. Analyzing a sample of 180 IPOs between 1970 and 1993, Ljungqvist (1997) found an average under-pricing of 9.2%. For a sample of 407 IPOs from 1978 to 1999, the rate increased to 27.7% (Ritter, 2003). Considering merely public offerings on the Neuer Markt ('New Market'), a newly established secondary market for young growth companies from 1997 to 2001, Gerke and Fleischer (2001) reported an average underpricing of 50% (examining 319 IPOs), whereas Kiss and Stehle (2002) reported a first-day initial return of 49.04% for the period from 1997 to 2001 (325 IPOs).

14.2.2 The hot-issue period

The differences in the reported levels of underpricing can be attributed to differing periods of time, selection criteria, and distinguished methods of computation. Ritter (1984) and Ibbotson et al. (1994) showed that the issue market is extremely cyclical. Evidently, in the late 1990s the market was characterized by higher-than-average issue activity, which is referred to as a hot-issue market.

There are basically two explanations for this cyclical nature of the IPO market. On the one hand, there are periods when a large number of firms have investment projects that need to be funded. On the other hand, there might be periods when investors have a lot of money to invest or might be specifically optimistic. The latter is supported by Loughran and Ritter (1995), who suggested that the long-run performance of firms that go public in hot-issue periods is quite poor.

Though the cyclical behavior of the number of issues as well as the high average initial return has been documented for a long time, the understanding of the relationship between the two series is scanty. Recently, Lowry and Schwert (2002) reported that IPO volume, i.e. the monthly number of issues, and average initial return are highly autocorrelated. The authors noted that IPO volume is influenced positively following periods of especially high returns. It appears puzzling why an increased number of firms go public after observing high levels of underpricing. Assuming firms prefer to raise as much money as possible, the reverse behavior would seem reasonable. As a justification the authors suggested that the level of under-pricing at the time when a company decides to go public does not explain the eventual underpricing. Hence, due to investment bankers' learning process and investor sentiment, companies can even raise more money subsequent to periods of high underpricing.

Lowry (2003) also proposed that not only firms' demand for capital, but also investor sentiment is an important determinant of IPO volume. Since more firms go public when investor sentiment is high and, accordingly, the cost of going public is low, issuers apparently time their IPOs in order to take advantage of the 'window of opportunity' of excessive optimism.

Following Lowry and Schwert (2002), vector autoregressive (VAR) models allow testing of the incremental predictive ability of lagged initial returns to predict future volume, and vice versa. Hence, in order to examine the cyclical behavior and the relation between the initial return and the IPO volume during the hot-issue period in Germany, a VAR(4) model of monthly averages is employed in section 14.4.3.

14.2.3 Underpricing

Transaction costs and the assumption of risk aversion can plausibly explain a limited amount of underpricing. Beyond this, most of the theoretical work on IPOs has attempted to rationalize persistent underpricing as an equilibrium outcome, in a large part by introducing asymmetric information. However, the extreme underpricing during the period from 1997 to 2001 calls for alternative explanations. As Ljungqvist and Wilhelm (2003) highlight, 'it strains belief that even collectively this body of theory [informational frictions] can account for the profound change in market behavior'. Hence, most recent research suggests other explanations to be the primary determinant of the excessive underpricing during the late 1990s.

One way to distinguish asymmetric information-based models is to categorize them on the basis of where heterogeneous information arises between market participants. Assuming investors to be differentially informed suggests that investors fear a winner's curse or that issuers fear a negative cascade (Rock, 1986; Welch, 1992). IPO signaling models (Allen and Faulhaber, 1989; Grinblatt and Hwang, 1989; Welch, 1989) presumed that the issuing firms are better informed than the investors. Alternatively, Ibbotson (1975) assumed that issuers pursue a two-stage sale. In a separating equilibrium high-quality firms want 'to leave a good taste in investors' mouths', so that future underwritings from the same issuer can be sold at attractive prices (Ibbotson, 1975). Since low-quality firms cannot level the costly signal of underpricing in a following issue, the signal is credible.

Whereas mostly the underwriter is assumed to be an invisible intermediary, Benveniste and Spindt (1989) developed a model in which the main task of the investment bank is to obtain information from better informed investors: Underpricing is the monetary reward for truthfully revealing their private information. If strong demand prevails, the underwriter will set a higher offer price. Moreover, the authors show that the bookbuilding procedure can be such a mechanism; thus, models in this focus are labeled bookbuilding models.

Since ex-ante uncertainty with respect to the firm value is mainly determined by asymmetric information, all models of asymmetric information have one key implication in common: with increasing asymmetric information, both ex-ante uncertainty and, consequently, underpricing amplifies. Although it is reasonable that informational frictions happened to be more severe during the dot-com bubble, it has to be analyzed whether the theory can explain the profound change in market behavior and the extreme underpricing during the hot-issue period.

An alternative and promising stream in IPO research is based on the allocation and trading of IPO shares, leading to agency conflicts. Even though they could also be allocated to asymmetric information theories, in accordance with Ritter and Welch (2002) we explore these newer theories separately, since different implications can be derived. Among others, Ljungqvist and Wilhelm (2003) supposed that the incentives of insiders and firms' key decision makers in bargaining over the offer price and reducing underpricing are influenced by their involvement in the transaction and wealth effects of IPOs for (insider) shareholders. They claimed that declining pre-IPO insider ownership stakes, falling CEO investment, and an increasingly fragmented ownership along with directed share programs (DSPs) amplified this agency conflict.

Habib and Ljungqvist (2001) argued that the level of underpricing is influenced by the extent of insider selling. Owners do care more about underpricing, when they sell a great amount of shares. Taking the same line of argument, Loughran and Ritter (2002) proposed a prospect theory model that focused on the covariance of the money left on the table and the owners' wealth changes. In contrast, Wasserfallen and Wittleder (1994) found that underpricing decreases in the insider retention rate. By retaining more equity the original owners signal their commitment to the company and therefore reduce the perceived risk. Especially, during the analyzed period of the hot-issue market, one might presume that original owners retaining a higher fraction are not interested in cashing out within the window of opportunity. Instead of being involved in the hottest IPO ever and getting a high media exposure, they are motivated to accumulate a fair deal for the company having the long run in mind. On the other hand, DSPs also became increasingly famous during the hot-issue period in Germany. These programs, most often called family and friends, might increase initial returns as they create an incentive to underprice in order to benefit the targeted clients.

Baron and Holmström (1980) and Baron (1982) were the first to take into consideration the role of the underwriter and the arising agency problems between issuing firm and underwriter. In these models, the underwriter is better informed with respect to the demand and price than the issuing firm. On the one hand, the underwriter has an incentive to underprice the issue to limit the marketing and distributing costs. On the other hand, the underwriter fees are usually linked to the proceeds. This trade-off between the costs and benefits leads to some initial returns in equilibrium. More prestigious underwriters are supposed to have greater experience and the capability to better price an issue, resulting in them leaving less money on the table. In contrast, recent studies found an inverse relationship. The suggested change was reported by Loughran and Ritter (2002). In the dot-com bubble, investment bankers in particular benefit from underpricing as a result of lower marketing costs and rent-seeking behavior on the part of potential investors.[1]

As the initial returns are more excessive in periods with high issuing activity, investor sentiment and climate effects may not only determine the issuing activity, as mentioned before, but also influence the level of underpricing in the IPO market. Ritter and Welch (2002) argued that overenthusiasm among retail investors may explain the pattern of high initial returns. Ljungqvist et al. (2003) and Oehler et al. (2005), along with Derrien (2005), claimed that it was not ex-ante uncertainty but investor sentiment that drives underpricing in the hot-issue period. Therefore, the third strand of research analyzed below focuses on behavioral finance and bounded rationality in order to explain the pattern of time variance and persistence of initial returns. The idea is supported by the fact that the Nemax50 index was highest when underpricing peaked. This index included the 50 shares of the Neuer Markt, which are ranked highest according to both market capitalization and turnover within the last 60 trading days. Hence, two reasons are commonly offered in order to explain the extreme underpricing during the bubble: the Internet euphoria and the media hype around new offerings during this period, leading to strong and mostly irrational interest towards IPOs. In Germany, the Neuer Markt was the symbol of the new economy, covering primarily Internet and high-technology stocks. By means of descriptive statistics and a cross-sectional regression on industry groups, we explore this issue in more depth in section 14.4.2. It might be

---

[1] The role and significance of the (lead) underwriter is not only affected by pre-IPO decisions, but also by its price support and participation in the aftermarket. See Ruud (1993).

assumed that the Neuer Markt attracted the highest levels of media coverage, thus amplifying market optimism and boosting underpricing.

The midpoint of the bookbuilding range is assumed to reflect the expected offer price before launching the bidding period. Price revisions measure the percentage adjustment from the expected offer price to the final offer price. Based on the Benveniste and Spindt (1989) partial adjustment model, price revision reflects the effects of information learned during the subscription period from investors. Hanley (1993) and Lowry and Schwert (2002) showed that initial returns are significantly related to the price update. Loughran and Ritter (2002) revealed that short-run market returns prior to the IPO are positively related to the subsequent underpricing. Another novelty makes this very interesting for the analysis of the underpricing phenomenon. IPOs can only be priced outside the indicative price range in Germany if the underwriter cancels the actual offering and re-offers the IPO, therefore stating a new price range. This expected offer price thus has to be set with greater care in Germany.

With this body of theory in mind, we will test what factors drove IPO underpricing in Germany during the hot-issue period in the section 14.4.5. Using cross-sectional regressions estimated by ordinary least squares (OLS), we will therefore explore whether ex-ante uncertainty, investor sentiment, or agency conflicts were the main determinants for the excessively high initial returns.

14.2.4 Long-run underperformance

Though evidence is less definitive than for underpricing, many studies have observed the long-run underperformance of IPOs. No abnormal return in the long run would indicate that the stock market efficiently values IPO shares once trading begins and no further abnormal returns than the initial return can be earned. However, long-run underperformance has been reported for most markets. Even though studies for the German stock market by Ljungqvist (1997) and Stehle et al. (2000) (6% for the 3-year post-offering period) suggested less underperformance than reported for the US market by Loughran and Ritter (1995) (7–8% in 3 years), the anomaly seems to be present.

All these results have to be interpreted with caution. As Jenkinson and Ljungqvist (2001) pointed out, the apparent underperformance could be a result of the inability to measure long-run performance precisely. This is mostly due to problems in controlling for risk correctly, or in implementing statistical significance tests properly. Obviously, long-run performance is measured relative to some benchmark. Therefore, long-run performance studies are especially sensitive to the chosen benchmark, sample period, and econometric methodology.

Firms that go public during periods of positive investor sentiment obviously would like to take advantage of the 'window of opportunity'. Hence, one crucial question in IPO theory is why there are still high initial returns even though firms want to take advantage of over-optimistic investors. Why don't issuers and their chosen underwriters take full advantage of investors' over-optimism by raising offer prices? Curiously, the media (still) associates a large initial price rise with a successful IPO, namely a hot IPO. Selling an object at a fraction of its market value usually is not considered to be a good thing.

One explanation might be what Loughran and Ritter (2002) call the 'leaning against the wind' theory. Underwriters, well aware of over-optimistic investors in an overreacting IPO market, price the IPO with the long-run value in mind. They know that the temporary exuberance will eventually vanish and the decreased value from the offering price could lead to severe losses to the opening investors. Hence, the underwriters set a lower offer price in order to avoid the possible embarrassment and lawsuits that may follow if the offer was priced to take full advantage of the positive investor sentiment. Despite the fact that the legal insurance hypothesis cannot account for the high level of underpricing in Germany, leaning against the wind might prevent even more serious damage to private investors.[2] This theory predicts that there should be a negative correlation between initial returns and subsequent long-run performance. Consistent with this idea, Puranandam and Swaminathan (2004) reported that IPOs which are overvalued at the offer price display particularly high initial returns and particularly low returns in the long run. Conversely, subsequent to IPOs, investment banks regularly issued 'buy' recommendations for shares whose market prices were already far above the original offer price. These analysts' recommendations encouraged overvaluations during the bubble and disagreed with the proposed leaning against the wind hypothesis.

Of the underpricing models based on asymmetric information, only the signaling and the bookbuilding theories have prognostic power about long-run performance. Both theories anticipate positive aftermarket returns. Following the first theory, the share price has to increase for a multiple-stage sale strategy to be beneficial. Hence, a testable implication emerges in such a way that the greater the quality of the firm, the more equity capital is retained by initial owners at flotation and the better they perform; thus, long-run returns increase the retention rate. The bookbuilding theory predicts positive abnormal returns due to partial adjustment of the offer price. Consequently, long-run performance will correlate positively with the initial price revision.

Since this study focuses mainly on the underpricing puzzle, we do not conduct a detailed long-run performance study. However, in the section 14.4.4, we do present categorized, descriptive statistics for long-run total returns in absolute prices and relative to the benchmark of the Nemax50. This breakdown will shed light on the stated hypotheses and the subsequent hypotheses that emerge while analyzing IPO underpricing.

14.3 The dataset

14.3.1 German market features

As compared to Anglo-Saxon countries, publicly listed firms represent only a small fraction of all firms in Germany. However, in the decade ending in 2000, Germany, as well as continental Europe, experienced an all-time boom in the number of firms going public. Though stock trading in Germany is segmented in eight regional exchanges, the market is dominated by the Frankfurt Stock Exchange (Frankfurter Wertpapierbörse), run by the Deutsche Börse Group. Hence, this analysis focuses on the Frankfurt markets, covering more than 90% of the German equity market.

Towards the end of the 1990s, the Frankfurt markets mainly consisted of four market segments. The Official Market (Amtlicher Handel, AH) for most liquid stocks was

---

[2] Though the syndicated bank, together with the issuer, accepts liability for the statement made in the sales prospectus, the risk of being sued in Germany is economically not significant (see Jenkinson and Ljungqvist, 2001, p. 113).

complemented by the Regulated Market (Geregelter Markt, GM) for small and medium-sized firms. In 1997, on the model of the US Nasdaq, Germany's New Market (Neuer Markt, NM) was founded as a secondary market for young and high-growth firms. The Neuer Markt had the strongest listing requirements and follow-up obligations of all segments. Additionally, in April 1999, the 'SMAX' was created for small caps from the old economy. Listing requirements were lower than in the Neuer Markt, but higher than in the Geregelter Markt. In this study, however, firms listed on the SMAX are ranked among the listings on the latter segment.

Due to the bursting bubble and changes in German stock exchange regulations, the Deutsche Börse restructured the segments in 2002 and 2003. 'General' and 'Prime Standard', designed for issuers aiming at basic and international requirements respectively, were created, while the Neuer Markt was shut down. This chapter analyzes the period from March 1997 to July 2001, while the Neuer Markt symbolized the new economy and the dot-com bubble.

The bookbuilding process was the dominant offering mechanism in the primary market for issues in recent years. In German IPOs the price range, usually between 10% and 20% relative to the midpoint, is generally wider than in the USA. However, once the bookbuilding period is over, the final offer price is set in-between the prior range. Contrary to US practice, there are no price revisions above the maximum and rarely any below.[3] During the analyzed period, IPOs were typically severely oversubscribed. For an overview of the differences between European and American IPO markets, see Ritter (2003); for more details of the German institutional background, refer to Theissen (2003).

14.3.2 Data sources

The dataset consists of firms completing an IPO on the Frankfurt Stock Exchange between March 1997 and July 2001. Companies being traded nationally or internationally before going public on the Frankfurt Stock Exchange have been excluded. Eight IPOs not applying the bookbuilding procedure have also been removed. Data for some explanatory variables – for instance, the foundation year – used in the cross-sectional analysis were not available for seven companies. Moreover, Datastream, the source we used to compile data on, does not include data for 52 companies. Hence, though the sample universe consists of 424 firms, the regression sample applied in this analysis covers 366 firms.

The list of companies that went public and the data on the IPO are taken mainly from the Frankfurt Stock Exchange web pages, the yearly 'Deutsches Aktieninstitut' (DAI) Factbooks, and are double-checked with the online IPO database of OnVista and the company's homepage. Information about the bookbuilding price range, the offer price, the number of issued stocks, the issuing volume, the market segment, directed share programs (DSPs), and the information about the leading underwriter is taken from the same sources.

Datastream provided the secondary market prices, the total number of stocks, and the market valuation, given by the total number of shares multiplied by the price. However, first-day closing prices were double-checked for plausibility with the first

---

[3] Only two companies were priced below the initial price range: Charles Voegele AG and Neue Sentimental Film AG.

trading price given in the Frankfurt Exchange web pages. Though most of the first prices given in Datastream represent the first-day closing prices, some prices describe the offer price. Identified by the jump to the subsequent trading price, which equals the initial return, we adjusted the discrepancies concerning the first-day closing price, the initial return, and the market value. Since the long-run performance is measured by the total return of the firm's share from the first day's closing price, also taken from Datastream, the data had to be adjusted for the same reason.

The industry classification is taken from the Frankfurt Stock Exchange (All Share Index), OnVista, or the DAI Factbook. The 18 sector indices are based on a total of 62 industry groups, which are aligned to the industry groups of STOXX, thus allowing for international comparison. The business climate index (adjusted) and the total return index of the Nemax50 are taken from Datastream.

Unfortunately, we were not able to identify the reason why some companies were missing from Datastream. The explanation could be delistings, mergers, or new names. However, since Datastream also contains dead series, and most missing companies are still active, the analyzed sample should not be subject to survivorship bias.

14.4 Empirical analysis

14.4.1 Descriptive statistics

Table 14.1 characterizes the IPO firms and transactions for each year and the whole sample period. The analysis covers the 1997 to 2001 period for firms listed for the first time at one of the segments of the Frankfurt Stock Exchange, consisting of 366 firms. The number of admissions per year shows a positive trend until 2000. The peak of issue activity is given in 1999 and the first half of 2000. For the year 2000, the year the bubble started to burst in March, it is noteworthy that the majority of firms went public until July 2000. Apparently, market participants needed some time to finally realize the change of sentiment.

In the sample period the average issuing company was approximately 17 years old, while Ljungqvist (1997) reported an average age at issue of 52 years. In 1997, the average issuer was nearly 40 years old versus 12.5 years in 2000. Hence, the age at issue declined not only compared to earlier studies, but also within the hot-issue period. The median age was around 11 years over the whole period, depicting a right-skewed distribution. The results suggest that the majority of firms are relatively young companies, in line with data reported by the recent US studies of Ljungqvist and Wilhelm (2003) and Loughran and Ritter (2002).

Mean gross proceeds are reported with €122.79 million for the sample period, but the distribution is highly skewed (median €38.52 million) because of some big offerings. Whereas the smallest offer was OAR Consulting with €4.3 million in 1998, the largest IPO in terms of proceeds was Deutsche Post AG in November 2000 with €5842 million, 1358 times bigger. Gross proceeds peaked in 2000 due to big offerings in the second half of the year.

The money left on the table (€ million) is defined as the number of shares offered multiplied by the first-day capital gain, measured from the offer price to the first-day closing price. Since the distribution is heavily right skewed, most of the money left comes from a minority of IPOs. Though these figures do not appear on the income statement,

Table 14.1 Descriptive firm and transaction characteristics

	Total	1997	1998	1999	2000	2001
No. of IPOs	366	17	53	149	130	17
(missing)	(58)	(7)	(11)	(18)	(20)	(2)
Age (years)						
Mean	17.38	39.73	18.98	18.06	12.54	21.10
Median	10.66	13.31	15.26	10.05	10.02	16.28
Min	1	3	3	1	1	7
Max	160	147	132	160	100	77
Gross proceeds (€ million)						
Mean	122.79	126.85	53.93	80.42	195.32	150.07
Median	38.52	37.63	28.12	37.80	46.13	22.50
Min	4.29	8.28	4.29	6.00	8.09	6.50
Max	5842.20	644.23	394.44	1540.00	5842.20	1072.05
SD	466.87	215.63	75.63	177.79	741.51	325.52
Money left (€ million)						
Mean	48.00	25.80	48.88	21.74	85.99	7.01
Median	8.11	6.71	13.53	5.60	10.91	0.13
Min	−49.00	−4.70	−1.74	−49.00	−32.20	−19.74
Max	5366.16	205.80	1030.20	281.75	5366.16	122.57
SD	293.03	50.41	148.51	44.56	478.35	30.75
Market value (€ million)						
Mean	727.50	510.23	237.54	306.22	1471.45	475.65
Median	181.24	131.61	180.47	164.26	221.66	72.38
Min	5.36	38.04	25.71	12.16	5.36	26.51
Max	43,045.66	3653.46	1232.09	2982.00	43,045.66	3688.20
SD	3592.91	994.36	216.15	425.06	5928.95	1093.44
Price revision (%)						
Mean	3.78	7.04	6.77	4.05	2.58	−2.06
Median	6.98	7.72	7.09	6.98	6.82	−3.85
MIn	−35.14	−1.23	−8.58	−35.14	−28.89	−17.65
Max	20.55	11.09	13.59	20.55	17.07	14.29
SD	8.59	2.89	3.85	8.30	9.83	11.04
Bookbuilding range (%)						
Mean	17.81	16.71	15.79	17.81	18.20	22.18
Median	16.87	16.76	15.38	16.47	17.14	22.61
Min	4.88	8.70	8.00	8.00	4.88	14.29
Max	70.27	24.00	27.20	70.27	45.45	35.29
SD	6.38	3.61	4.18	6.82	6.64	6.13
Retention rate (%)						
Mean	0.68	0.64	0.65	0.68	0.70	0.68
Median	0.70	0.70	0.70	0.70	0.71	0.70
Min	0.00	0.00	0.00	0.01	0.31	0.37
Max	0.96	0.87	0.96	0.91	0.96	0.83
SD	0.14	0.20	0.19	0.13	0.09	0.10

(Continued)

Table 14.1   (*Continued*)

	Total	1997	1998	1999	2000	2001
Initial return (%)						
Mean	45.76	34.83	65.00	41.99	48.97	5.32
Median	19.43	15.65	39.99	14.00	20.20	1.43
Min	−30.00	−12.50	−8.33	−17.50	−30.00	−28.40
Max	444.44	124.27	403.50	355.56	444.44	83.57
SD	70.61	41.67	76.65	69.71	73.92	24.78
Negative	58	1	4	27	20	6
Performance Nemax50 (%)	127.62	97.91	224.95	56.63	−43.63	−59.91

Min = minimum, Max = maximum, SD = standard deviation.

they should be regarded as indirect costs for the issuing firm. Some young growth Internet firms left more money in the IPO than they had total revenues in 1 year.

The market value (€ million) gives a better proxy for the firm's size than the issuing volume, since it also covers shares retained by the issuers not in the free float. The numbers confirm that the biggest companies went public in 2000 and 2001, Infinion with €43,045.66 million being the highest valued company. This pattern might suggest that big firms react slowly in response to an IPO boom.

Price revision is measured as the percentage change of the expected offer price, i.e. the midpoint of the bookbuilding range, reflecting the information learned from investors during the subscription period. Obviously, in times of high underpricing price revisions are highest, whereas at the end of the analyzed period the acquired information led to several negative price revisions. The bookbuilding range represents the spread between lower and upper limits relative to the midpoint. While the average is 17.81%, it seems to be smaller when the IPO boom peaks. However, as mentioned before, the range is wider than in the USA, but there are no price revisions above the maximum and rarely any below (for an analysis of this phenomenon, see Jenkinson et al., 2004). This again leads to lower price revisions.

The average fraction of retained shares is persistently around 70%. Though the retention rate is slightly lower during the beginning of the IPO boom, no profound changes can be seen from this statistic.

Mean initial returns amount to 45.76% for the sample period. Throughout the chapter we do not adjust for market movements, like most recent studies, in reporting initial returns, since market movements are small in comparison (Loughran and Ritter, 2002). The first-day returns are again heavily right skewed, with extreme positive outliers increasing over time both in frequency and size, but suggesting that only a fraction of companies suffer from severe underpricing. In 2001, and in the second half of 2000, underpricing is considerably reduced. The highest underpricing of 444.44% was reported for Biodata Information Technology in February 2000, the highest negative initial return of −30.00% for Brainpower in September 2000. The high fraction of firms closing at the offer price can be attributed to stabilization activities of the underwriter.

The Nemax50 crashed in 2000. The index peaked at 9631.53 on 10 March 2000, having increased 89.23% in the preceding 2 months, but during the rest of the year lost 86.86% of its value. Interestingly, the maximum is observed when underpricing is at its highest. The results emphasize the fact that underpricing depends crucially on the underlying period. Though the sample is dominated by the dot-com bubble, the inclusion of the pre- and post-IPO boom years 1997 and 2001 respectively controls for different market conditions.

14.4.2 Underpricing by sectors and segments

The statistics in Table 14.2 are based on the current sector index classification of the Frankfurt Stock Exchange in June 2004. Since the sample period covers the dot-com bubble, the majority of IPOs can be classified as firms belonging to the 'new economy', namely the sectors Media, Pharma and Healthcare, Software (including Internet), Technology, and Telecommunication, representing 71.6% of the total sample. This observation is in line with the well-known fact that firms of the same industry tend to go public at the same time.

IPOs of the new economy account not only for the most excessive underpricing, but also for the highest negative first-day returns. Moreover, the sectors of the new economy display the highest standard deviation, which may represent the higher ex-ante uncertainty of these sectors in the traditional view of ex-ante uncertainty. The distributions of initial returns are right skewed for all sectors with more than one IPO. All sectors register IPOs yielding zero or even negative returns.

Table 14.3 summarizes initial returns by market segments. Underpricing of firms listed on the Neuer Markt was considerably higher than the other two segments. Though expected from the previous discussion, this result may be puzzling. Since the Neuer Markt had the strongest listing requirements of the three segments considered, one may suspect less ex-ante uncertainty. On the other hand, especially young growth companies, which tend to be more risky, chose this segment. Despite the fact that the highest negative initial returns were also reported within this segment, the Neuer Markt apparently boosted the underpricing. In contrast, the Neuer Markt had been the center of attention by investors and nearly all IPOs going public on this market segment were heavily oversubscribed. This leads to the conclusion that investor sentiment and demand influences the increase between the offer price and the first-day closing price. Thus, another goal of our analysis is to differentiate if ex-ante uncertainty of investor sentiment influences the initial return.

For further analysis we run diverse cross-sectional regressions, estimated by ordinary least squares (OLS), using the different industry and stock market dummies as explanatory variables. Heteroscedasticity in the residuals is adjusted by the methodology of White (1980). The dependent variable ln(IR) is defined as $\ln(P_1/P_{offer})$, where P_1 is the first-day closing price and P_{offer} the offer price. In line with recent findings in the USA, regressions (1), (2) and (3) in Table 14.4 show that IPOs belonging to the 'new economy' exhibit higher first-day returns compared to other industry groups. While interpreting the results, the reader has to be aware of the low explanatory power of the regressions.

Table 14.2 Underpricing by industry sectors

	No. of IPOs	Mean	Median	Min	Max	Standard deviation	IR negative	t-value[a]
Total	366	45.76	19.43	−30.00	444.44	70.61	58	12.40***
Automobile	5	22.30	7.27	6.00	75.92	30.23	0	1.65
Banks	1	43.14	43.14	43.14	43.14	n/a	0	n/a
Basic resources	1	2.82	2.82	2.82	2.82	n/a	0	n/a
Chemicals	1	−3.18	−3.18	−3.18	−3.18	n/a	1	n/a
Construction	1	1.10	1.10	1.10	1.10	n/a	0	n/a
Consumer	5	6.32	0.00	−5.00	40.63	19.31	2	0.73
Financial services	17	38.07	13.55	−8.33	155.53	53.86	2	2.91**
Food and beverages	1	1.38	1.38	1.38	1.38	n/a	0	n/a
Industrial	52	31.79	9.19	−8.82	171.41	44.41	7	5.16***
Media	46	61.53	19.84	−21.54	355.56	88.48	10	4.72***
Pharma and healthcare	31	32.86	9.58	−9.30	245.56	54.42	4	3.36***
Retail	11	30.30	0.00	−20.67	165.79	67.23	4	1.50
Software	123	58.66	30.37	−30.00	352.17	75.04	18	8.67***
Technology	48	41.60	19.46	−17.50	444.44	75.18	7	3.83***
Telecommunication	14	47.13	21.27	−28.40	403.50	106.03	2	1.66
Transp. and logistics	8	25.87	10.19	−0.57	76.13	31.58	1	2.32**
Utilities	1	0.19	0.19	0.19	0.19	n/a	0	n/a

[a] The t-value was computed for the test that the underpricing in the sector equals zero.
Asterisks denote significance at the 10% (*), 5% (**), and 1% (***) levels (two-tailed test).

Table 14.3 Underpricing by markets segments

	Number of IPOs	Mean	Median	Minimum	Maximum	Standard deviation	IR negative	t-value[a]
Total	366	45.76	19.43	−30.00	444.44	70.61	58	12.40***
NM	288	54.21	28.62	−30.00	444.44	75.61	40	12.17***
AH	56	13.60	1.17	−15.86	149.38	30.67	12	3.32***
GM	22	17.04	2.02	−16.67	155.53	38.43	6	2.08**

[a] The t-value was computed for the test that the underpricing in the segment equals zero.
Asterisks denote significance at the 10% (*), 5% (**), and 1% (***) levels (two-tailed test).

As regressions (4)–(6) illustrate, the dummy variable Neuer Markt has a significant positive influence on underpricing. These results confirm the intuitive findings that the investor optimism was strongly linked to this market segment. We ascribe this fact to the media coverage of the Neuer Markt during the IPO boom and the brand 'Neuer Markt' interacting with the positive investor sentiment. The results support the incorporation of the dummy variable 'Neuer Markt' in the final cross-sectional regression.

14.4.3 *Average underpricing and issuing activity*

IPO activity seems to be time dependent. Figure 14.1 shows no clear lead-lag relationship between average quarterly initial returns, calculated using equal weights, and the number of IPOs per quarter. Initial returns seem to be highest in the first quarter of the year. In contrast to the findings of Lowry (2003), issue activity does not seem to be lower at the beginning of each year. Oehler et al. (2005) found that issuing activity in Germany was highest in the second quarter, supporting a proposed lead-lag relation between initial returns and IPO volume.

With the intention of testing the incremental predictive ability of lagged initial returns to predict future volume and vice versa, the Granger causality statistics, as well as the VAR(4) models, are shown in Table 14.5. Monthly mean initial returns (IR), defined as in section 14.2, are calculated using equal weights. NIPO is defined as the number of IPOs per month. The lag length has been chosen using the Akaike Information Criteria.

These tests confirm that there is a positive relation between initial returns and future number of IPOs. The Granger F-test rejects the hypothesis that four lags of initial returns have no explanatory power for the IPO activity at the 1% level, with a p-value of 0.0022 (not reported). Hence, the test supports the proposition that past initial returns have a significant positive effect on future issue activity. On the contrary, the hypothesis that higher IPO activity is associated with lower initial returns cannot be confirmed. Though the variables $NIPO_{t-3}$ and $NIPO_{t-4}$ have a negative sign, the relation is not significant at conventional levels, with a p-value of 0.3756 using the Granger F-test. Therefore, it cannot be assumed that past IPO volume has the power to predict future initial returns and therefore we do not consider a proxy for this effect in the final cross-sectional regression.

Table 14.4 Industry and market segment regression

	(1) OLS ln(*IR*)	(2) OLS ln(*IR*)	(3) OLS ln(*IR*)	(4) OLS ln(*IR*)	(5) OLS ln(*IR*)	(6) OLS ln(*IR*)
Automobile	0.037 (0.032)					-0.019 (0.033)
Consumer	-0.004 (0.031)					-0.003 (0.031)
Financial services	0.067* (0.035)					0.051 (0.038)
Industrial	0.052** (0.024)**					0.011 (0.023)
Media	0.096 (0.030)***	0.051 (0.025)**				0.039 (0.030)
Pharma and healthcare	0.050 (0.026)*	0.005 (0.021)				-0.009 (0.028)
Retail	0.032 (0.052)					-0.012 (0.053)
Software	0.098 (0.023)***	0.053 (0.016)***				0.029 (0.026)
Technology	0.064 (0.026)**	0.019 (0.020)				0.001 (0.029)

	(1)	(2)	(3)	(4)	(5)	(6)
Telecommunication	0.051 (0.038)	0.006 (0.034)				−0.015 (0.040)
Transp. and logistics	0.043 (0.032)					0.008 (0.035)
New economy			0.038 (0.013)***			
NM				0.069 (0.019)***	0.073 (0.018)***	0.074 (0.020)***
AH				0.001 (0.021)	0.000 (0.020)	0.004 (0.021)
Constant	1.022 (0.019)***	1.067 (0.010)***	1.067 (0.010)***	1.035 (0.018)***	1.037 (0.017)***	1.019 (0.026)***
F-statistic	2.81***	2.76**	8.53***	11.40***	17.10***	4.22***
Adjusted R^2	0.01	0.02	0.02	0.05	0.05	0.04
Observations	366	366	366	366	366	366

Robust standard errors are given in parentheses.
Asterisks denote significance at the 10% (*), 5% (**), and 1% (***) levels.

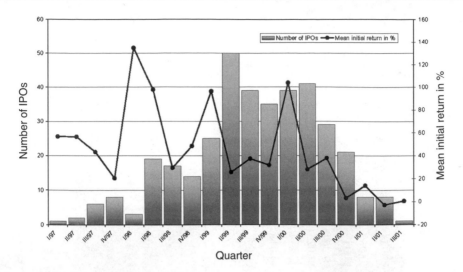

Figure 14.1 Time pattern of underpricing and quarterly IPO activity

Table 14.5 VAR(4) model for initial returns and number of IPOs

| | (7) | | (8) | |
| | Monthly IR$_t$ | | Monthly NIPO$_t$ | |
	Coefficient	Standard error	Coefficient	Standard error
NIPO$_{t-1}$	0.911	−1.756	0.171	−0.163
NIPO$_{t-2}$	3.038*	−1.818	0.154	−0.169
NIPO$_{t-3}$	−1.322	−1.841	−0.137	−0.171
NIPO$_{t-4}$	−1.943	−1.669	0.680***	−3.74
IR$_{t-1}$	0.616***	−0.192	0.010	−0.178
IR$_{t-2}$	−0.129	−0.216	0.033*	−0.02
IR$_{t-3}$	−0.014	−0.192	0.017	−0.018
IR$_{t-4}$	−0.241	−0.166	0.025	−0.015
Constant	32.138	20.763	−2.851	1.928
R^2	0.3453		0.6171	
Granger F-test:				
Lagged NIPO	4.231			
Lagged IR			16.758***	
Sample size	31		31	

Standard errors are given in parentheses.
Asterisks denote significance at the 10% (*), 5% (**), and 1% (***) levels.

Figure 14.2 allows for a closer look at the dynamics of past initial returns and IPO activity on future issue activity, as it plots the respective impulse response functions of regression (8).

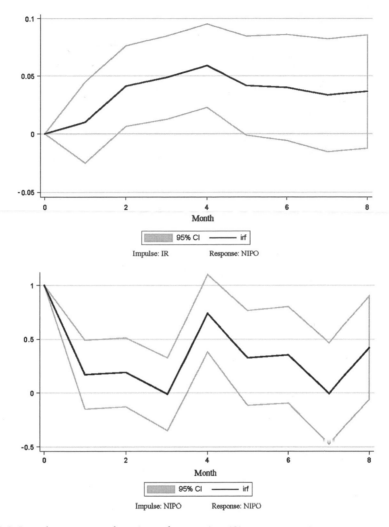

Figure 14.2 Impulse response function of regression (8)

14.4.4 Underpricing and long-run underperformance

Long-run underperformance studies are very sensitive to the benchmark and the sample constitution. In addition, post-IPO periods have a high overlap. Hence, the individual observations of the long-run abnormal returns are not statistically independent as assumed in the standard significance tests and cannot be applied. Though these figures are descriptive in nature and one must be cautious in drawing conclusions, present patterns might shed some light on the testable empirical implications concerning the relationship between long-run performance and underpricing, stated in section 14.2 above.

After categorizing our sample vertically by initial return, as well as horizontally by prior market movement, retention rate, and price revisions, respectively, Tables 14.6–14.8 present four quantities for each category. The top one is the sample size.

Table 14.6 Long-run performances categorized by initial returns and 10 days prior market performance

| Pre-market performance | Initial return | | | |
	Negative	0–60	>60	All
Performance <0%	45	112	36	193
Mean 3-year return	−62.94	−65.89	−66.79	−65.38
Three-year market return	−70.14	−43.40	−57.14	−52.20
Abnormal return	7.20	−22.49	−9.65	−13.18
Middle range	5	43	18	66
Mean 3-year return	−75.97	−62.52	−83.92	−69.38
Three-year market return	−85.59	−57.43	−35.03	−53.45
Abnormal return	9.62	−5.09	−48.89	−15.93
Performance >5%	8	55	42	105
Mean 3-year return	−53.88	−69.53	−76.39	−71.08
Three-year market return	−86.23	−67.63	−55.06	−64.02
Abnormal return	32.35	−1.90	−21.33	−7.06
All	58	210	96	364
Mean 3-year return	−62.85	−66.15	−74.20	−67.75
Three-year market return	−73.69	−52.08	−52.08	−55.83
Abnormal return	10.84	−10.84	−22.12	−11.91

Four quantities are reported for each category in Tables 14.6–14.8. The top one is the sample size. The second is the mean 3-year buy-and-hold return of the IPOs. The third is the average total market return over the same 3-year periods, quantified by the Nemax50 Index as benchmark. The bottom value in each category is the abnormal return, calculated as the difference between the IPO's buy-and-hold return and the return of the benchmark. The ranges are purposely chosen to control for excessive observations in each category. We excluded Mobilcom and EM TV, with abnormal returns of 2637 and 8822, respectively. Two of the high fliers during the dot-com bubble until 2000, they collapsed badly afterwards. Hence, the reported figures are extremely time dependent. As they were part of the Nemax50 they boost its performance and their exclusion might bias the results for the whole sample. However, as they would dominate specific cells, but an exclusion does not alter the shown patterns, we eliminated both IPOs with these enormous, but time-dependent, positive abnormal returns.

The second is the mean 3-year buy-and-hold return of the IPOs. The third is the average total market return over the same 3-year periods, quantified by the Nemax50 Index as benchmark. The bottom value in each category is the abnormal return, calculated as the difference between the IPO's buy-and-hold return and the return of the benchmark.

To separate the underpricing phenomenon and the long-run performance, it seems important to consider the performance of IPOs from the first day's closing price. If the closing price is an unbiased measure of the firm's true market value then there should be no abnormal returns in the long run. Hence, the 3-year return is measured from the first-day closing price to the 3-year anniversary or the delisting date, whichever is earlier. The Nemax50, covering solely new listings, may not be an accurate benchmark for a performance study. However, in order to detect some patterns within new listings, it seems to be a reasonable point of reference. We eliminated two extreme

Table 14.7 Long-run performances categorized by initial returns and the fraction of shares retained by the original owners

Retention rate	Initial return			All
	Negative	0–60	>60	
Retained <0.65	24	51	26	101
Mean 3-year return	−45.91	−55.94	−64.16	−55.67
Three-year market return	−58.65	−34.73	−0.42	−31.58
Abnormal return	12.74	−21.21	−63.74	−24.09
Middle range	19	102	44	165
Mean 3-year return	−66.79	−73.55	−86.70	−76.28
Three-year market return	−80.28	−62.20	−82.03	−69.57
Abnormal return	13.49	−11.35	−4.67	−6.71
Retained >0.75	15	57	26	98
Mean 3-year return	−84.96	−62.04	−63.09	−65.83
Three-year market return	−89.39	−51.49	−53.08	−57.71
Abnormall return	4.43	−10.55	−10.01	−8.12
All	58	210	96	364
Mean 3-year return	−62.85	−66.15	−74.20	−67.75
Three-year market return	−73.69	−52.08	−52.08	−55.83
Abnormal return	10.84	−10.84	−22.12	−11.91

outliers, changing the overall result in the bottom right cell notably. Hence, the conclusion that an underperformance of nearly 12% is reported might be misleading.

The leaning against the wind hypothesis suggests a negative correlation between initial returns and subsequent long-run performance. Table 14.6 explores this suggestion by categorizing for initial returns and controlling for prior market returns over the last 10 days before the offer date.Consequently, the underwriter can only set the final offer price within this indicative price range, and therefore might not be able to include the prevailing short-run investor sentiment into the initial pricing. An examination of Table 14.6 reveals several patterns, confirming the proposition of a negative correlation. In contrast to the finding of no pattern by Loughran and Ritter (2002), long-run performance in our sample seems to be poorer for highly underpriced firms. IPOs with initial returns above 60% have a negative abnormal return exceeding 20% (−22.12%), whereas IPOs with negative initial returns tend to exhibit positive abnormal returns (10.84%).

Moreover, as discussed above, the pre-market performance influences, firstly, initial returns, but additionally long-run performance. If the market return during the bookbuilding period was negative, leading to a decrease in investor sentiment, initial returns were low as well. As the long-run return is commonly measured from the first-day closing price, the 3-year performance seems to be superior.

These results have several implications. First, the illustrated pattern backs the leaning against the wind hypothesis. Second, the market sentiment seems to be determined by the very recent past. Hence, the inclusion of market sentiment proxies as explanatory variables for underpricing in the cross-sectional analysis is supported. Finally, in contrast

Table 14.8 Long-run performances categorized by initial returns and the final offer price relative to the expected offer price

| Price revision | Initial return | | | |
	Negative	0–60	>60	All
Price revision ≤0	32	55	1	88
Mean 3-year return	−57.90	−74.11	−99.82	−68.51
Three-year market return	−65.84	−83.54	−90.10	−77.18
Abnormal return	7.94	9.43	−9.72	8.67
Middle range	13	86	54	153
Mean 3-year return	−66.68	−57.04	−78.29	−65.36
Three-year market return	−80.98	−28.62	−65.28	−46.01
Abnormal return	14.30	−28.42	−13.01	−19.35
Price revision >8%	13	69	41	123
Mean 3-year return	−71.18	−71.17	−68.2	−70.18
Three-year market return	−85.71	−57.88	−33.78	−52.79
Abnormal return	14.53	−13.29	−34.42	−17.39
All	58	210	96	364
Mean 3-year return	−62.85	−66.15	−74.20	−67.75
Three-year market return	−73.69	−52.08	−52.08	−55.83
Abnormal return	10.84	−10.84	−22.12	−11.91

Four quantities are reported for each category in Tables 14.6–14.8. The top one is the sample size. The second is the mean 3-year buy-and-hold return of the IPOs. The third is the average total market return over the same 3-year periods, quantified by the Nemax50 Index as benchmark. The bottom value in each category is the abnormal return, calculated as the difference between the IPO's buy-and-hold return and the return of the benchmark. The ranges are purposely chosen to control for excessive observations in each category. We excluded Mobilcom and EM TV, with abnormal returns of 2637 and 8822, respectively. Two of the high fliers during the dot-com bubble until 2000, they collapsed badly afterwards. Hence, the reported figures are extremely time dependent. As they were part of the Nemax50 they boost its performance and their exclusion might bias the results for the whole sample. However, as they would dominate specific cells, but an exclusion does not alter the shown patterns, we eliminated both IPOs with these enormous, but time-dependent, positive abnormal returns.

to the efficient market hypothesis, the offer price might be a better proxy for the true value of a company than the market valuation during the first day, emphasizing the importance of the underwriter. However, whether the leaning against the wind hypothesis can indeed be affirmed will be discussed further in the next subsection.

Signaling models suggest that the greater the quality of the firm, the more equity initial owners retain at flotation and the better they perform. Thus, long-run returns increase the retention rate. An inspection of Table 14.7 discloses some minor patterns. IPOs during which the initial owners retained less than 65% of the outstanding shares show a poor long-run performance, with −24.09%. The performances tend to be better with a higher fraction of shares retained. The results might be influenced from outliers, as they have a great influence on the smaller sample sizes. Considering the previous results of the likely negative correlation between underpricing and long-run performance, as well as evaluating the cells with respect to both categorizations, retained shares might have a negative influence on underpricing.

These results back the discussed commitment hypothesis. Therefore, we incorporate the variable 'retention rate' as an explanatory variable in the final cross-sectional regression for underpricing.

Table 14.8 reports long-run performances of IPOs categorized by initial returns and price revisions, calculated as the mean of the final offer price relative to the expected offer price. The distribution of the price revisions is right skewed, suggesting that underwriters are reluctant to price below the expected offer price. The book-building theory predicts positive abnormal returns due to a partial adjustment of the offer price. Consequently, long-run performance will correlate positively with the initial price revision. The lack of any reliable pattern is inconsistent with this hypothesis. In contrast, due to the mentioned partial adjustment problem and the suggestion that higher underpricing leads to poorer long-run performances, the inverse relation might be proposed. These results endorse the incorporation of price revision as an explanatory variable in the cross-sectional analysis for the German market. Moreover, the outcomes support the proposition that investor sentiment might drive initial return.

14.4.5 Cross-sectional regression

In this section we evaluate the relationship between underpricing, calculated as the log of first-day returns (ln(IR)), and different explanatory variables through means of cross-sectional regressions estimated by ordinary least squares (OLS). Heteroscedasticity in the residuals is adjusted by the methodology of White (1980). The explanatory variables as proxies for ex-ante uncertainty, investor sentiment, and agency conflicts are listed in Table 14.9. Table 14.10 summarizes the regression results. Regressions (9) and (10) focus solely on the proxies for ex-ante uncertainty and investor sentiment respectively. Regressions (11) and (12) take into consideration the discussed agency conflicts. Regression (13) combines all variables for an overall impression and therefore gives a first indication about the robustness of our results.

14.4.6 Ex-ante uncertainty

In regression (9), all integrated traditional proxies for ex-ante uncertainty are highly significant. However, only the issuing firm's age and the aftermarket volatility show the signs expected according to the asymmetric information models. As suggested by Ritter (1984) and Beatty and Ritter (1986), a new issue incorporates a high degree of uncertainty about its fundamentals. Especially during the hot-issue market analyzed, many small growth companies with short operating histories went public, consistent with the view that ex-ante uncertainty about the true value of an IPO drives the level of underpricing; older firms seem to be valued more accurately, displaying less initial return. This conclusion is not only encouraged by implied ex-ante uncertainty, but also by the fact that the most severely underpriced IPOs can be allocated to the group of high-technology companies, which are inherently young companies. In line with Wasserfallen and Wittleder (1994), the aftermarket volatility is used as a risk measure and is found to be highly significant in all regressions. Though this variable might suffer from a lack of exogeneity, as Ljungqvist (1997) pointed out, it has been widely used across different studies. In our sample it supports the proposition that underpricing is related to uncertainty about the value of the shares.

Table **14.9** Definition of explanatory variables

Variable	Definition	Expected sign
Ex-ante uncertainty proxies		
Age	Issuing firm's age, calculated as the difference between the IPO and the year of foundation	−
ln(Market value)	Log of the market value, calculated as the total number of shares multiplied by the first closing price	−
BBW	Width of the bookbuilding range, calculated as the spread between lower and upper limit relative to the midpoint	+
Volatility	Aftermarket volatility, calculated as the standard deviation of daily closing prices in the first 15 trading days subsequent to the IPO	+
Investor sentiment proxies		
NM	A dummy coded 1 if listed on the Neuer Markt, and zero otherwise	+
B-climate	The value of the business climate index of the pricing month	+
Bubble	A dummy coded 1 for the bubble period from the quarters I/1999 to II/2000, and zero otherwise	+
Pre-market	Pre-market performance of the Nemax50 10 trading days prior to the IPO	+
Price revision	Price revision is measured as the percentage change of the expected offer price, i.e. the midpoint of the bookbuilding range	+
Agency conflicts proxies		
Retention rate	The fraction of share capital retained by insiders	−
DSP (>5%)	A dummy coded 1 if the DSP was higher than 5% of the total offering, and zero otherwise	+
Underwriter	A dummy coded 1 if the lead underwriter belongs to the highest of three quantiles, and zero otherwise. The ranks are taken from the overall results of the ranking of underwriters by Gerke et al. (2001)	−

The log of the market value, as well as the width of the bookbuilding range, shows the oppositee sign to that expected by ex-ante uncertainty theory. Following Hanley (1993) and Jenkinson et al. (2004), the width of the bookbuilding range is seen as a signal for the ex-ante uncertainty, a positive relationship being expected. In the traditional ex-ante uncertainty view, market value could be used as a proxy for firm size. Consequently, since smaller firms inherit a higher degree of risk, a negative relationship is suggested by asymmetric information theory. In a market determined by investor sentiment and great media exposure, large firms get more press and media coverage, pushing the demand. Hence, it is plausible to expect a negative relationship in contrast to the traditional asymmetric information hypothesis. This is also consistent with the increase in mean and median issue size in the US IPO market in the 1990s documented by Ljungqvist and Wilhelm (2003).

In line with this argument, underwriters, knowing hot IPOs to be highly oversubscribed, might be able to reduce the bookbuilding range and, as Oehler et al. (2005)

Table 14.10 OLS underpricing regressions

	(9) OLS ln(IR)	(10) OLS ln(IR)	(11) OLS ln(IR)	(12) OLS ln(IR)	(13) OLS ln(IR)	(14) 2SLS ln(IR)
Age	-0.001		-0.001		-0.000	
	(0.000)***		(0.000)***		(0.000)**	
ln(Market value)	.025		0.029		0.024	
	(0.005)***		(0.006)***		(0.005)***	
BBW	-0.308		-0.297		-0.105	
	(0.080)***		(0.079)***		(0.089)	
Volatility	0.004		0.005		0.003	
	(0.001)***		(0.001)***		(0.001)***	
NM		0.066		0.062	0.049	0.050
		(0.012)***		(0.013)***	(0.015)***	(0.015)***
B-climate		0.001		0.001	-0.002	0.002
		(0.002)		(0.002)	(0.002)	(0.003)
Bubble		0.001		-0.002	-0.013	-0.002
		(0.011)		(0.011)	(0.011)	(0.015)
Pre-market		0.003		0.003	0.003	0.003
		(0.001)***		(0.001)***	(0.001)***	(0.015)
Price revision		0.004		0.004	0.003	0.007
		(0.001)***		(0.001)***	(0.001)***	(0.003)*
Retention rate			-0.078	-0.002	-0.076	-0.012
			(0.045)*	(0.040)	(0.043)*	(0.050)
DSP (>5%)			0.029	0.020	0.019	0.028
			(0.012)**	(0.012)	(0.012)*	(0.015)*
Underwriter			-0.029	-0.019	-0.030	0.060
			(0.012)**	(0.011)*	(0.011)***	(0.072)
Constant	0.991	0.925	1.020	0.951	1.131	0.848
	(0.034)***	(0.185)***	(0.042)***	(0.187)***	(0.187)***	(0.285)***
F-Statistics	23.29***	31.09***	14.72***	20.76***	15.77***	10.64***
Adjusted R²	0.16	0.23	0.19	0.23	0.29	0.11
Observations	366	366	366	366	366	366

Robust standard errors are given in parentheses.
Asterisks denote significance at the 10% (*), 5% (**), and 1% (***) levels.

pointed out, shorten the subscription period. Moreover, one could argue that this negative relation affirms the underwriters' claim of pricing 'against the wind'; though knowing an IPO will be exceedingly subscribed in an over-optimistic market, they do not price the firm too much above the true market value. However, in most cases even the valuation at the offer price was ex-post by far too high a margin.

14.4.7   Investor sentiment

Regression (10) includes the investor sentiment proxies. It confirms the prior findings of a demand-driven market, showing a higher explanatory power than regression (9) with an adjusted R^2 of 0.23. The business climate index, included as a proxy of the macroeconomic conditions (see Ljungqvist, 1997), and the bubble dummy, incorporated in order to control for the 'hottest' period, are highly insignificant. It should be noted that both variables might be too broadly defined. On the contrary, the variables Neuer Markt, pre-market, and price revision are highly significant in all regressions involved. The latter two variables add explanatory power for the initial return, by revealing information not known before the indication of the initial price range. At the same time, these market-related variables are proxies for the investor sentiment. The regressions show that the investors are specifically optimistic after prior, positive short-run (10 days) market performances, confirming a demand-driven market. Moreover, as hypothesized, the 'brand' Neuer Markt, attracting young, high-technology firms as well as catching much media attention, boosts investor awareness and, accordingly, initial return.

   As a matter of fact, underwriters are not able to include this fact in the initial pricing. As documented by Ljungqvist and Wilhelm (2003), underpricing is directly related to the magnitude of price revisions. Our results in regressions (10) and (12) do support this hypothesis. However, allowing for possible asymmetries by including a dummy à la Lowry and Schwert (2002), no significance can be reported (not stated). Since in Germany the offer price cannot be updated above the initial price range, just comparing both results would lead to biased results.

14.4.8   Agency conflicts

Regressions (11) and (12) add variables for testing the agency conflicts described in section 14.2. Unfortunately, no database in Germany provides detailed information on IPO ownership structure. Hence, in this analysis the 'retention rate' is used as proxy in order to control for post-IPO ownership structure. Moreover, a dummy variable is included to test the significance of DSPs, being 1 if the DSP was higher than 5% of the total offering, and 0 otherwise.

   The results confirm the earlier noted presumption of a negative relation between underpricing and the retention rate; the greater the fraction of shares originally kept by owners, the lower the underpricing. However, the significance is not very high. Only in interaction with the less significant ex-ante uncertainty proxies and in the overall regression is the variable significant at the 10% level. Though the outcome backs the earlier hypothesis of Wasserfallen and Wittleder (1994), it is contrary to recent findings in the USA. Using more detailed data on pre- and post-IPO ownership structure and selling behavior, Ljungqvist and Wilhelm (2003) found that, according to classical agency theory, the less CEOs and pre-IPO owners are involved, the less bargaining and monitoring effort the agents display respectively. As underpricing might be seen as implicit costs for the firm and implicit benefits for the underwriter, the less the original owners have to bear the costs, the greater the underpricing. However, when commitment can be signaled through the retention rate, original owners not only want to keep as much control, but also try to reduce the money left on the table.

In contrast, the positive relationship between DSPs and initial returns supports the findings of the cited authors. In order to let clientele of the friends and family program benefit, and to most likely leave a good taste in the friends' mouth, the firms' key decision makers show less effort to reduce underpricing. However, again, significant differences are only found in interaction with the ex-ante uncertainty proxies in regressions (11) and (13).

When key decision makers have a purpose to control for underpricing, we assume them to get involved with a top-ranked investment bank, since signaling can also be accomplished through the choice of underwriter (Allen and Faulhaber, 1989). This assumption is confirmed by the significant negative influence, which shows that the greater the reputation of the investment bank, the lower the initial returns. This finding is in contrast to recent studies, documented by Loughran and Ritter (2002), which suggest a positive relationship during the hot-issue period. However, it supports the well-known hypothesis that more experienced underwriters are capable of better valuing a company, better extracting information from potential investors during the roadshow, and therefore leaving less money on the table. Moreover, top-ranked underwriters have the option of choosing which firm to accompany in the going public process and which to deny. In the ex-ante uncertainty view, this may lead to a negative sign, as more uncertain firms have to employ a lower-ranked investment bank. On the other hand, the negative sign might contrast the leaning against the wind hypothesis. It is precisely the underwriters with a high reputation who should have the strength not to take advantage of temporary over-optimistic investor sentiment.

14.4.9 Robustness

The regressions (12) and (13) treat both underwriter rank and the degree of price revisions as exogenous. Following Ljungqvist and Wilhelm (2002), the choice of underwriter might be treated as endogenous. Hence, we estimate a Two-Stage Least Squares (2SLS) model that treats both underwriter reputation and price revision as endogenous. Therefore, underwriter as well as price revision are estimated by BBW, ln(market value), age, NM, bubble, pre-market, volatility, B-climate, retention rate, and DSP (>5%) in the first stage. Comparing the OLS coefficients in (12) and the 2SLS coefficients in (14) reveals little change, so the previous results seem to be robust. However, similar to Ljungqvist and Wilhelm (2002), the underwriter reputation switches sign, when treated as potentially endogenous. However, allowing for the effect of the underwriter reputation to have changed during the period, we find a negative and significant ($p = 0.003$) relation during the bubble period, and a positive but insignificant relation otherwise (not reported). These results are in direct contrast to the given results of the mentioned authors and Loughran and Ritter (2002). German underwriters conceivably acted differently than their US counterparts.

All regressions in Table 14.10 assume that the effects of the explanatory variables can be separately identified. Consistent with this assumption, the highest pairwise correlation between the variables can be reported for the width of the bookbuilding range and the price revision (0.35), which is not surprising and does not alter the results. A possible omitted variable bias is conceivable. However, considering earlier studies, the specification of the firms' characteristics seems to be adequate. Other variables should not alter the results as a whole.

14.5 Conclusion

From 1997 to 2001, there was a high volume of IPOs and extremely high initial returns, especially at the 'new markets'. This study investigated the IPO puzzle pattern of issuing activity, long-run underperformance, and, in particular, underpricing during this hot-issue period in Germany.

The time-series relationship between the number of issues and the average initial return was analyzed using a VAR(4) model. We show that past initial returns have a significant positive effect on future issue activity. On the contrary, IPO volume obviously has no power to predict future initial returns.

Concerning the long-run underperformance, we apply descriptive statistics to detect specific patterns in the data. Firstly, we find some support that underwriters might price IPOs having the long-run value in mind. The higher the initial returns, the poorer the subsequent performance. Secondly, the results propose that investors' (over-)optimism was a driving force of underpricing. Finally, consistent with standard signaling theory, long-run returns might increase the retention rate. The greater the quality of the firm, the more shares initial owners retain at flotation and the better they perform. Concomitantly, retained shares might have a negative influence on underpricing.

Taking these findings into account, we use cross-sectional regressions to identify whether ex-ante uncertainty, investor sentiment, or agency conflicts may have been the determinants of IPO underpricing during the period studied. Due to the extreme underpricing, solely ex-ante uncertainty cannot explain the reported pattern. Instead, the investor sentiment was a driving force, affirmed by the strong significance and the explanatory power of the variables Neuer Markt and pre-market performance, as well as the reversed signs of two of the proxies for ex-ante uncertainty. Since IPOs were pushed to media events, and the media associate a large price increase with a successful IPO, some companies were indeed interested in high underpricing in order to draw the public's attention. Consequently, underpricing could be considered as a branding event designed to increase consumer awareness of the Internet company. Though an extremely expensive way of advertising, this fraction of firms was specifically interested in the hottest IPO ever, leaving the lion's share of money on the table. Moreover, agency conflicts may have played a major role. Interestingly, the regressions affirm the intuitive suggestion and recent findings in the USA that directed share programs, having become popular among issuing firms, might have reduced the incentive to control for underpricing by the issuers. In contrast to the USA, original owners seem to signal their commitment to the company by retaining a higher fraction of shares, not cashing out in the window of opportunity. On their behalf, top-ranked underwriters might have reduced underpricing in order to obtain equity at lower cost. Considering the findings of the ownership structure as explanatory variables, this string of research is very encouraging. Unfortunately, detailed information for Germany is not available.

This study suggests that the reported extreme underpricing is more likely to be explained with models emphasizing agency conflicts and nonrational explanations rather than the basis of ex-ante uncertainty. Possibly, neither model can fully explain investor behavior during this period. As Ritter (2003) points out, 'even if these questions are answered, however, new questions will develop, since financial markets evolve rather than remaining unchanged'.

Acknowledgments – This chapter benefited from discussions with Philipp Federspieler, Andreas Oehler, Eric Smith, and Peter N. Smith. Any remaining errors are our own.

References

Allen, F. and Faulhaber, G. R. (1989). Signalling by Underpricing in the IPO Market. *Journal of Financial Economics*, 23(2):303–323.

Baron, D. P. (1982). A Model of the Demand for Investment Banking Advising and Distribution Services for New Issues. *Journal of Finance*, 37(4):955–976.

Baron, D. P. and Holmström, B. (1980). The Investment Banking Contract for New Issues under Asymmetric Information: Delegation and the Incentive Problem. *Journal of Finance*, 35:955–976.

Beatty, R. P. and Ritter, J. R. (1986). Investment Banking, Reputation, and the Underpricing of Initial Public Offerings. *Journal of Financial Economics*, 15(2):213–232.

Benveniste, L. M. and Spindt, P. A. (1989). How Investment Bankers Determine the Offer Price and Allocation of New Issues. *Journal of Financial Economics*, 24(2):343–361.

Cornelli, F., Goldreich, D., and Ljungqvist, A. (2004). Investor Sentiment and Pre-Issues Market. Working Paper, CEPR Discussion Paper No. 4448 (http://ssrn.com/abstract=569662).

Derrien, F. (2005). IPO Pricing in "Hot" Market Conditions: Who Leaves Money on the Table? *Journal of Finance*, 60(1):487–521.

Gerke, W. and Fleischer, J. (2001). Die Performance der Börsengänge am Neuen Markt. *Zeitschrift für betriebswirtschaftliche Forschung*, 53(8):827–839.

Gerke, W., Bank, M., and Ehrlich, F. (2001). Ranking der Emissionsbanken 1999 und 2000. Working Paper, University of Nuremberg-Erlangen, Numermeber, Germany.

Grinblatt, M. and Hwang, C. Y. (1989). Signalling and the Pricing of New Issues. *Journal of Finance*, 44(2):393–420.

Grinblatt, M. and Titman, S. (2002). *Financial Markets and Corporate Strategy*. McGraw-Hill, Boston.

Habib, M. A. and Ljungqvist, A. P. (2001). Underpricing and Entrepreneurial Wealth Losses in IPOs: Theory and Evidence. *Review of Financial Studies*, 14(2):433–458.

Hanley, K. W. (1993). The Underpricing of Initial Public Offerings and the Partial Adjustment Phenomenon. *Journal of Financial Economics*, 34(2):231–250.

Ibbotson, R. G. (1975). Price Performance of Common Stock New Issues. *Journal of Financial Economics*, 2(3):235–272.

Ibbotson, R. G., Ritter, J. R., and Sindelar, J. (1994). The Market's Problems with the Pricing of Initial Public Offerings. *Journal of Applied Corporate Finance*, 7(1):66–74.

Jenkinson, T. and Ljungqvist, A. P. (2001). *Going Public*, 2nd edition. Oxford University Press, Oxford.

Jenkinson, T. J., Morrison, A., and Wilhelm, W. (2004). Why are European IPOs so Rarely Priced Outside the Indicative Price Range? Working Paper, University of Oxford, Oxford, UK.

Kiss, I. and Stehle, R. (2002). Underpricing and Long-Term Performance of Initial Public Offerings at Germany's Neuer Markt, 1997–2001. Working Paper, Humboldt University of Berlin, Germany.

Ljungqvist, A. P. (1997). Pricing Initial Public Offerings: Further Evidence from Germany. *European Economic Review*, 41(7):1309–1320.

Ljungqvist, A. P. (2004): IPO Underpricing. In: *Handbook of Empirical Corporate Finance* (Eckbo, B. E., ed.). North-Holland (forthcoming).

Ljungqvist, A. P. and Wilhelm, W. J. (2002). IPO Allocations: Discriminatory or Discretionary? *Journal of Financial Economics*, 65(2):167–201.

Ljungqvist, A. P. and Wilhelm, W. J. (2003). IPO Pricing in the Dot-com Bubble. *Journal of Finance*, 58(2):723–752.

Ljungqvist, A. P., Nanda, V., and Singh, R. (2003). Hot Markets, Investor Sentiment, and IPO Pricing. Working Paper, NYU Stern School of Business, New York, NY.

Loughran, T. and Ritter, J. R. (1995). The New Issues Puzzle. *Journal of Finance*, 50(1):23–51.

Loughran, T. and Ritter, J. R. (2002). Why Don't Issuers Get Upset About Leaving Money on the Table in IPOs? *Review of Financial Studies*, 15:413–443.

Lowry, M. (2003). Why Does IPO Volume Fluctuate so Much? *Journal of Financial Economics*, 67(1):3–40.

Lowry, M. and Schwert, W. (2002). IPO Market Cycles: Bubbles or Sequential Learning. *Journal of Finance*, 57(3):1171–1200.

Oehler A., Rummer, M., and Smith, P. N. (2005). IPO Pricing and the Relative Importance of Investor Sentiment – Evidence from Germany. Working Paper, University of Bamberg, Bamberg, Germany.

Puranandam A. K. and Swaminathan, B. (2004). Are IPOs Really Underpriced? *Review of Financial Studies*, 17(3):811–848.

Ritter, J. R. (1984). The "Hot Issue" Market of 1980. *Journal of Business*, 57(2): 215–241.

Ritter, J. R. (1991). The Long-Run Performance of Initial Public Offerings. *Journal of Finance*, 46(1):3–27.

Ritter, J. R. (2001) Foreword to *Going Public*, 2nd edition, by Jenkinson and Ljungqvist. Oxford University Press, Oxford.

Ritter, J. R. (2003). Differences between European and American IPO Markets. *European Financial Management*, 9(4):421–434.

Ritter, J. R. and Welch, I. (2002). A Review of IPO Activity, Pricing, and Allocations. *Journal of Finance*, 57(4):1795–1828.

Rock, K. (1986). Why New Issues Are Underpriced. *Journal of Financial Economics*, 15(1–2):187–212.

Ruud, J. S. (1993). Underwriter Price Support and the IPO Underpricing Puzzle. *Journal of Financial Economics*, 34(2):135–151.

Theissen, E. (2003). Organized Equity Markets in Germany. CFS Working Paper 2003/17, Centre for Financial Studies.

Stehle, R., Ehrhardt, O., and Przyborowsky, R. (2000). Long-Run Performance of German Initial Public Offerings and Seasoned Equity Issues. *European Financial Management*, 6(2):173–196.

Wasserfallen, W. and Wittleder, C. (1994). Pricing Initial Public Offerings: Evidence from Germany. *European Economic Review*, 38(7):1505–1517.

Welch, I. (1989). Seasoned Offerings, Imitation Costs, and the Underpricing of Initial Public Offerings. *Journal of Finance*, 44(2):421–449.

Welch, I. (1992). Sequential Sales, Learning, and Cascades. *Journal of Finance*, 47(2):695–732.

White, H. (1980). A Heteroscedasticity-Consistent Covariance Matrix Estimator and a Direct Test of Heteroscedasticity. *Econometrica*, 48(4):817–838.

15 Reassessing Canadian IPO underpricing: evidence from common share, Capital Pool Company, and unit offerings

Maher Kooli

Abstract

Evidence of underpricing of initial public offerings (IPOs) has spawned considerable theoretical literature that attempts to explain the apparent contradiction to market efficiency. In this chapter, I examine not just common shares Canadian IPOs, but also unit and junior stock IPOs from the period 1991 to 1998. This study shows that the IPO market in Canada is good only for large offerings, and that the underpricing is huge for Capital Pool Company (CPC) IPOs. It is also found that unit IPOs are more underpriced than common share IPOs. A number of possible explanations for the high initial return of Canadian issuing firms are entertained. It is found that underpricing is significantly related to the prestige of the underwriter, to the period of the issue, and to whether or not the IPO is a CPC.

15.1 Introduction

The existence of the underpricing phenomenon in initial public offerings (IPOs) is well documented by the finance literature, and seems to be a common characteristic in most international markets. Recently, with high-tech and Internet stock offerings making huge gains on their market debuts, investors, analysts, and researchers have again focused their attention on the IPO market. Why are some IPOs more underpriced than others?

Underpricing represents a cost to the issuing company because if securities are underpriced, relatively more money is left on the table for the IPO buyers and relatively less is available as proceeds for the issuing company. This also means that owners of the firm prior to the IPO suffer a higher dilution of their ownership and have a lower level of wealth than if the issue had been priced at market. Furthermore, underpricing of IPOs contradicts the assumption of market efficiency. If markets were efficient, issuers should generally receive market value for the shares issued and investors should not regularly be able to purchase IPOs at a discount to their market value. Given the importance of this phenomenon to the economy in general, and to investors and entrepreneurs in particular, it is important to be aware of the level of underpricing. This research makes two main contributions to the IPO literature. First, previous Canadian studies are few (compared to US ones) and suffer from one caveat: they are restricted to firms that qualified for listing on the Toronto Stock Exchange (TSE). Although the TSE is Canada's largest exchange, results drawn from it do not necessarily apply to what smaller companies experience. A reassessment of the market conditions of Canadian IPOs seems warranted. Second, the institutional characteristics of the Canadian market allow for an independent test of the best-known anomaly in the IPO literature (focusing mainly on the USA). Therefore, the aim of this research is to provide out-of-sample evidence and to use a large, contemporaneous sample of Canadian IPOs in order to update the previous results and clarify the role of the underpricing determinants. Additionally, the short-term behavior of three types of unseasoned issues is examined: common stock issues, unit issues, and junior stock issues. Although units stocks represent an important source of financing for many small Canadian firms, they have received little attention in the finance literature. Lee et al. (2000, p. 3) pointed out that: '... although practitioner explanations for unit IPOs may seem unsatisfactory, there is relatively little analytical or empirical evidence on their use.' How and Howe (2001) also documented that evidence on unit IPOs is needed. This chapter will attempt to fill this gap and improve our understanding of such particular offerings by examining their short-term behavior.

Using a wide sample of 971 Canadian IPOs from the period of 1991 to 1998, it is found that the average initial return for common share IPOs (excluding junior stocks) was 20.57% (22.57% with a market-adjusted measure). However, the degree of underpricing depends on the type of issue. Unit IPOs are more underpriced than common share IPOs. Furthermore, Capital Pool Company (CPC) IPOs, typical Canadian offerings, are more underpriced than common share IPOs. This is the first study to document such a result. This analysis suggests that the IPO market in Canada is good only for large offerings. Moreover, mining, oil and gas, real estate, and technology IPOs are more underpriced than IPOs from other sectors. A number of possible explanations for the high initial return of Canadian issuing firms are considered and it is found that the underpricing is significantly related to the prestige of the underwriter, to the period of the issue, and to whether or not the IPO is a CPC.

The remainder of this chapter is organized as follows. Section 15.2 underlines some of the causes of this phenomenon and addresses the hypotheses. Section 15.3 contains a discussion of the data and the methodology used in the empirical investigation. The results are presented in Section 15.4. Section 15.5 summarizes the findings and provides concluding remarks.

15.2 Background and hypothesis development

Many past studies have indicated that common share IPOs have often been notably undervalued in the primary market, with some movement towards a security's intrinsic value observed in secondary trading. This short-run phenomenon has been experienced in every country with a stock market, although the degree of underpricing varies from country to country.[1] Table 15.1 summarizes the findings of previous Canadian studies of underpricing. At first glance, we notice that the degree of underpricing decreases over time, which is good news.

---

[1] See Ritter (2003) for a review of IPO underpricing across countries.

Table 15.1 Historical underpricing in Canadian studies

Study	Period studied	Average underpricing (%)
Jog and Riding (1987)	1971 to 1983	9.96
Jog and Srivastava (1994)	1971 to 1992	7.87
Jog (1997)	1984 to 1992	7.89
Clarkson and Merkley (1994)	1984 to 1987	6.44
Kryzanowski and Rakita (1996)	1984 to 1993	4.18
Ursel and Ljucovic (1998)	1987 to 1994	3.64
Ursel (2000)	1997 to 1999	7.06
Jog and Wang (2002)	1990 to 1999	12.00

However, these studies only examined stock issued on the Toronto Stock Exchange (TSE). Although the TSE is Canada's largest exchange, a reassessment of the phenomena for all Canadian public equity offerings, including junior offerings, is needed. The structure of Canadian exchanges is discussed further in section 15.3.

Next, the sources of underpricing will be conceptually examined, in order to define the theoretical backdrop for the empirical results. Several hypotheses[2] have been proposed that focus on one or more players in the IPO process (the current owner of the firm, the underwriter, and the potential new shareholders). Generally, these theoretical explanations are not mutually exclusive. Ritter (1998) pointed out that all the explanations for the underpricing phenomenon can be criticized on the grounds of either the extreme assumptions that are made or the unnecessarily convoluted stories involved. Nonetheless, most of the explanations have some element of truth in them and invariably state that the degree of underpricing should be increasing in the ex-ante uncertainty of the issue (Beatty and Ritter, 1986), where ex-ante uncertainty is defined as the uncertainty about the offering's value once it starts trading. By implication, there should be a relation between the degree of underpricing and the gross proceeds of the firm or of the issue, the choice of the underwriter, and the market conditions.

15.2.1 Size and underpricing

A substantial body of literature examines the effect of size on the initial return of IPOs. Overall, the empirical evidence suggests that a smaller IPO is riskier than a larger IPO, all other things being equal. Therefore, a smaller IPO is more underpriced than a larger IPO. Carter and Manaster (1990) documented that, in maximizing the value of their information acquisition, the informed investors (the institutions) will take into account not only the degree of uncertainty in a given issue, but also its size. Thus, the bigger the IPO, the greater the potential gains from acquiring information about the issue.

---

[2] These hypotheses include the winner's curse hypothesis, the market feedback hypothesis, the bandwagon hypothesis, the investment banker's monopsony power hypothesis (Chalk and Peavy, 1990), the lawsuit hypothesis, the signaling hypothesis (Allen and Faulhaber, 1989; Welch, 1989), and the ownership dispersion hypothesis. See Ritter (1998) for a review of these explanations.

15.2.2   Role of the underwriter and underpricing

Underwriters provide a wide range of services: they act as intermediaries between the firm and investors in marketing and distributing the shares, in timing the IPO, and in fixing the price and the volume of the offer. Rock (1986) developed a model in which there are two classes of investors: informed investors and uninformed investors. Informed investors are able to determine the investment quality of a particular IPO and will attempt to purchase a large amount of the underpriced IPOs and a lesser amount of the overpriced IPOs. The uninformed investors are unable to differentiate between the types of IPO and will ultimately purchase a higher percentage of the overpriced IPOs and a lower percentage of the underpriced IPOs. Therefore, uninformed investors face a winner's curse: the greater probability of being allocated shares of overpriced new issues than underpriced issues. To keep uninformed investors participating in the IPO market, underwriters underprice to ensure a non-negative rate of return and to cover their losses on the overpriced IPOs. Beatty and Ritter (1986) suggested that underwriters will enforce the IPO underpricing to maintain their reputation. However, a systematically too high or too low underpricing would subsequently be followed by a loss in their market share. The underwriters thus underprice a strong issue by as much as they can get away with without damaging their reputation. Carter and Manaster (1990), and Carter et al. (1998), among others, found that high-reputation underwriters underprice less than non-prestigious underwriters. This is because high-reputation underwriters issue firms with lower ex-ante uncertainty. However, Ljungqvist (1997) analyzed US IPOs during the 1990s and found that more prestigious underwriters are associated with higher underpricing. He postulated that this result may be explained by a possible conflict of interest between venture backers and entrepreneurs. Overall, a positive relation between underpricing and the underwriter's reputation is expected.

15.2.3   IPO market conditions and underpricing

Many researchers have found that issuers or underwriters are able to successfully time their offerings when the market is optimistic about IPOs in general and when the demand for IPOs is high, in order to achieve a smooth distribution of shares and raise a large amount of capital. Derrien and Womack (2000) suggested that current market conditions play an important role in determining an IPO's underpricing. Indeed, in euphoric or hot markets, investors may be overly optimistic about a firm's prospects, causing the aftermarket equilibrium price to be greater than in normal conditions. Furthermore, market conditions not only affect the number of successful offerings, but also the amount and the variability of IPO underpricing. For example, when the market is hot, the level of underpricing may double or even triple. In contrast, if the market is cold, the level of underpricing would be much lower. Loughran and Ritter (2002) pointed out that underpricing is a form of indirect compensation to underwriters to gain favorable allocations on hot issues. How et al. (1995) analyzed the Australian IPO market and confirmed that the level of underpricing is high during hot periods and low during cold periods. Stoughton et al. (2001) suggested that the clustering of IPOs may be explained by the revelation of a common value factor of one firm, which serves as a feedback mechanism for other IPOs.

Helwege and Liang (2004) contended that 575 firms went public in the hot-issue year of 1993, whereas during the cold-issue year of 1988 only 143 firms went public.

Furthermore, the level of underpricing averaged 14.6% in 1983 and 6.6% in 1988. Ljungqvist (1997) reported that a positive macroeconomic climate raises the average amount of underpricing. Lowry and Schwert (2000) found that initial returns are significantly negatively correlated with past IPO volume and significantly positively correlated with future IPO volume. They pointed out that if high average initial returns indicate that the sentiment is especially high or market conditions are better than expected, then more companies are likely to go public. As more firms go public, the uncertainty surrounding the true value of these firms decreases, thus causing average initial returns to decrease.

The relations reviewed above between underpricing and the size of the issue, the underwriter reputation, and the market conditions have motivated the formulation of the following hypotheses. First, a negative relation between the level of underpricing and the ex-ante uncertainty measured by the size of the issue is expected. Second, a negative relation between the level of underpricing and the reputation of the underwriter is expected. Finally, it is hypothesized that IPOs issued during an upswing in the stock market will experience a higher underpricing than IPOs issued during a falling market.

In the next section, the data and the methodology used to measure the level of underpricing are discussed. The hypotheses are tested in section 15.4.

15.3 Data and methodology

Before 1999, Canadian stock markets included four markets and the OTC (over-the-counter) market. Of these markets, the Toronto Stock Exchange (TSE) is Canada's premier market for senior equities, accounting for approximately 95% of all equity trading in Canada.

In 1999, the TSE, along with the Montreal, Vancouver, and Alberta exchanges, was restructured, which brought the competition that once existed among the Canadian exchanges to an end, although the competition between exchanges and markets worldwide has never been greater. The TSX Venture Exchange was created in 1999 through the merger of the Vancouver and Alberta exchanges, creating a national junior market in Canada with offices in Calgary, Vancouver, Winnipeg, and Toronto. The Montreal exchange continues to service the needs of the Quebec junior markets through an affiliation with the TSX Venture Exchange.

One of the particular characteristics of the Canadian market IPOs is the existence of the Capital Pool Company (CPC) program (formerly named the Junior Capital Pool program) that was initiated in November 1986. This program, introduced in Alberta, is similar to the blind pool programs that were implemented in the 1980s in the USA to help startup firms raise equity. Unfortunately, the experience of US investors with blind pools has been poor (Stern and Bornstein, 1985).

The CPC process comprises three steps from its initial incorporation to the completion of its major transaction. The first step of the CPC process consists of incorporating the shell company, selecting directors and a management team, and injecting seed capital. The management and directors are required to contribute a minimum of $100,000 as founders' seed capital. The second step involves the filing and clearing of a prospectus through the TSX Venture Exchange and the listing of the company's shares on the TSX Venture Exchange. The total equity capital raised, including the founders' seed capital, cannot exceed $500,000 and cannot be less than $200,000. In addition, the offering price (including those shares issued through seed capital) cannot be less than 10 cents per share. At least 70% of the proceeds from the sale of all common shares (including proceeds from sales of common shares prior to the offering) is required to be used in pursuit of its major transaction and not for general and administration expenses, including compensation of officers or directors. Also, all the shares issued as a result of the founders' capital are subject to escrow restrictions.

The first and second steps of the CPC process generally take approximately 75 days to complete and cost approximately $35,000, plus what is generally a 10% commission and 10% option to the agent. The third and final step involves the completion of a major transaction within 18 months of listing on the TSX Venture Exchange. A major transaction is defined as a transaction in which a CPC issues securities representing more than 25% of its securities issued and outstanding immediately prior to the issuance, in consideration for the acquisition of assets or securities of an operating company. At this point, if the CPC firm has an operating business looking for access to the public markets, this major transaction could be conducted between the shell company and the operating business.

One of the most significant requirements of the major transaction is that the company or assets acquired must be based in Canada. The third step generally takes approximately 80–110 days to complete and the costs can vary depending on the business or assets acquired. The major transaction also requires the approval of the company's shareholders. A significant number of major transactions are done by way of a reverse takeover, whereby control of the combined companies passes to the shareholders of the acquired company. Until the completion of the major transaction, the CPC cannot carry on any business other than the identification and evaluation of assets or businesses in connection with the potential major transaction.

If a CPC does not complete its major transaction within 18 months, it is delisted by the TSX Venture Exchange. It is possible that this 18-month period will force some outside shareholders to make suboptimal investment decisions near the end of the period if they are concerned about the company being delisted. The TSX Venture Exchange has resolved this potential problem by allowing the CPC to become reinstated if they complete a major transaction after the 18-month period. In its early years, the CPC primarily listed oil and gas firms. Over time, it has diversified its listings to include the manufacturing, services, and high-technology sectors. Overall, the CPC program provides an interesting alternative to the more traditional IPO. It offers a practical and cost-effective solution for growth-oriented companies searching for new capital to finance their operations and seeking to go public.

The primary source of data is the 'Record of New Issues: Annual Report by the Financial Post Datagroup', which reports offering dates, offering prices, issue size, and the name of the underwriter. The sample used here includes 971 IPOs[3] between January 1991 and December 1998: 878 common share IPOs (including 433 CPC IPOs) and 93 unit IPOs. Table 15.2 presents the distribution of the sample by industry,[4] both in terms

---

[3] Closed-end fund and real estate investment trust companies are excluded from the sample.
[4] This segmentation by industry is based on the classification of the System for Electronic Document Analysis and Retrieval (SEDAR), available at www.sedar.com.

Table 15.2 Distribution of Canadian IPOs by industry

Industry or sector	Common share IPOs	Gross proceeds ($ million)	Unit IPOs	Gross proceeds ($ million)	Full sample	Gross proceeds ($ million)
Mining	102	1644.1	23	67.8	125	1711.9
Oil and gas	54	1604.55	23	90.44	77	1695
Production	84	3927.98			84	3927.9
Technology	86	2838.06	12	28.39	98	2866.45
Financial services	18	590.12	6	682.17	24	1272.3
Real estate	11	537.38	4	398.23	15	935.6
Biotech/pharmaceutical products	22	423.1	2	50	24	473.1
Communications and media	17	1254.38	3	67.93	20	1322.3
Merchandising	14	445.06	13	333.03	27	778.1
Film production	6	134.92	2	3.61	8	138.5
Other[a] (include CPC)	31 + 433	1258.08 + 308.8	5	15.55	469	1582.4
Total	878	14,966.75	93	1737.17	971	16,703.9

The sample consists of 971 Canadian IPOs by firms subsequently listed on the Canadian exchanges from January 1991 to December 1998.
[a] The 'Others' category comprises the following sectors or industries: public services, transport, agriculture, conglomerates, film production, Capital Pool Company (CPC) starting without a primary activity, and others.

of the number of offers and the gross proceeds. Table 15.2 shows that the sample also covers different industries.

To measure the level of underpricing, previous studies have used the conventional method where the initial return available to the subscribers is given by:

$$\text{Initial return}_i = \frac{(P_m - P_e)}{P_e}, \tag{15.1}$$

where P_m = first-day price and P_e = offer price.

15.4 Results

15.4.1 The underpricing phenomenon in Canada

Table 15.3 contains descriptive statistics of the degree of underpricing for a sample of 971 Canadian IPOs for the period of 1991 to 1998. The average initial return for common share IPOs (excluding CPC IPOs) was 20.57%, with a t-value of 7.65. In line with previous studies, it is concluded that traditional Canadian IPOs are, on average, underpriced, as are most IPOs worldwide.

Table 15.3 also reveals that CPC IPOs are more underpriced than non-CPC IPOs. The average initial return is huge (135.41%). The t-value on the difference in average initial return between CPC and non-CPC IPOs is significant at the 1% level. The

Table 15.3 Underpricing of Canadian IPOs

	Common share IPOs (CPC excluded)	CPC IPOs	Common share IPOs (with CPC)	Unit IPOs	Full sample
Number	445	433	878	93	971
Mean (%)	20.57	135.41 [P(N)]	77.20	40.06 [P(N)]	73.65
Standard error	0.56	1.73	1.40	1.46	1.41
Skewness coefficient	2.15	3.66	4.29	3.66	4.17
Kurtosis coefficient	7.82	19.55	29.20	15.52	27.32
t-statistic	7.65	16.21	16.25	2.63	16.2
Median (%)	5	100	30	1	30

The sample consists of 971 Canadian IPOs by firms subsequently listed on the Canadian exchanges from January 1991 to December 1998. Capital Pool Company (CPC) IPOs are included. The degree of under-pricing (UND) is measured as follows: (mean closing price of the first 5 days of listing − offer price)/offer price. [P] t-test for differences in average initial returns between the subgroups 'common share IPOs excluding CPC IPOs versus CPC IPO' and 'common share IPOs excluding CPC IPOs versus unit IPOs' significant at the 1% level. [N] Kruskal–Wallis and Mann–Whitney t-tests for differences in average initial returns between subsamples significant at the 1% level.

high level of underpricing for CPC IPOs may be explained by the characteristics of the securities (for example, risk and return) and their low issue prices, which are usually set at between 10 and 20 cents. Furthermore, the CPC program was transitory and a CPC firm has a deadline of 18 months in which to complete a major transaction, otherwise it is delisted. Thus, this deadline increases the risk of the CPC IPO. Robinson (1997) analyzed CPC IPOs and obtained a non-adjusted average initial return of 248% for the period of 1987 to 1988 and a non-adjusted average initial return of 68% for the period of 1988 to 1992. He concluded that the dramatic reduction in the degree of underpricing may be explained by the fact that Canadian investors became accustomed to the characteristics of the CPC program. However, the results in this study suggest that the investor's attitude has not changed and the reduction in underpricing observed by Robinson is principally related to the market conditions during the period of analysis. It is important to note that 1991 and 1992 were cold-issue periods in Canadian markets.

Overall, for those who claim that the CPC program simplifies the process for raising equity and filing a public offering, bear in mind that it is not without its inherent costs, such as high underpricing.

Furthermore, Table 15.3 reveals that unit IPOs are more underpriced than common share (excluding CPC) IPOs. The average initial return was 40.59%. The t-value on the difference in average initial return between unit and non-unit IPOs is significant at the 1% level. The results of this study are consistent with those of Schultz (1993) and How and Howe (2001). For a sample of 797 US IPOs from 1986 to 1988, Schultz (1993) documented that 167 firms making unit offerings are typically smaller, younger, and riskier than those making common share offerings. In contrast, for a sample of 394 Australian IPOs from 1979 to 1990, How and Howe (2001) found underpricing of 68.57% for unit IPOs and 40.64% for common share IPOs.

The high percentage of underpricing for unit IPOs and CPC IPOs may be partly explained by the small size of the offerings. This relation is tested in the next section.

Table 15.4 reveals that the distribution of the degree of underpricing is not stationary. In 1991, common share IPOs (excluding CPC) are slightly overpriced (UND $=-4.85\%$). In 1992, the degree of underpricing increased, but this is due to two outliers: Primo Gold Limited (UND $= 300\%$) and Quest Technologies Inc. (UND $= 350\%$). If we eliminate these two IPOs, the degree of underpricing for 1992 would be 6.22%. In 1993 and 1994, the average initial return increased, while in 1995 it decreased. In 1996, the underpricing level increased by 107.31% according to the 1995 average initial return. In 1997, the degree of underpricing reached a maximum of 39.30%. It is important to note that 1997 was a hot-issue period with a maximum of $3328.5 million collected through IPOs. In 1998, the number of IPOs and the degree of underpricing decreased. Ibbotson and Jaffe (1975) showed that a hot period is usually characterized by a high volume of issues and a high average initial return followed by a decrease in the level of underpricing. The same pattern is observed for unit IPOs and CPC IPOs.

15.4.2   Cross-sectional patterns[5]

Below, a cross-sectional analysis of the short-run behavior of IPOs will be performed. This section sheds some light on the determinants of underpricing. More specifically, the relation between underpricing and the size of the issue, the role of the underwriter, the industry of the issuer, and the market conditions is examined.

15.4.3   Size

Table 15.4 presents underpricing results for the sample partitioned on the basis of the size of the issue. The results in Table 15.4 suggest that small IPOs (gross proceeds less than $1 million) and excluding CPC firms are more underpriced (52.94%) than large IPOs. More interestingly, CPC IPOs are more underpriced than small common share IPOs, and IPOs with gross proceeds of more than $20 million are slightly overpriced (-1.36%). The difference in the average initial return between the two subgroups is significant at 1%. This confirms the existing evidence, which indicates a high ex-ante uncertainty associated with small offerings. The underpricing would be essentially a small issue phenomenon.

15.4.4   Industry

When the sample is segmented by industry (Table 15.5), the underpricing of Canadian IPOs varies widely in different industries. For example, mining, real estate, oil and gas, and technology IPOs are more underpriced than production and film production IPOs (35.71%, 16.9%, 29.04%, and 19.77%, respectively, versus

---

[5] A multivariate analysis was also performed and confirmed the basic conclusions drawn from the univariate analysis. Further, structural adjustment tests (available upon request) were performed and found that the impact of the coefficients of the independent variables (the size of the issue, the market condition, the prestige of the underwriter, and the industry of the issuer) on the degree of underpricing (the dependent variable) is the same regardless of whether or not the IPO is a CPC.

Table 15.4 Distribution of Canadian IPOs by year of issue

Year	Common share IPOs excluding CPC IPOs		CPC IPOs		Common share IPOs including CPC IPOs		Unit IPOs		Full sample	
	Number	UND (%)	Number	UND (%)	Number	UND (%)	Number	UND (%)	Number	UND (%)
1991	11	−4.85	2	0.55	13	−4.01	6	34.29	19	8.07
1992	25	31.72***	8	85.42**	33	44.74*	5	−29.87	38	34.92**
1993	78	15.87**	55	159.54*	133	75.29*	14	118.46	147	79.40*
1994	70	17.85*	55	127.79*	125	66.22*	16	54.34	141	64.88*
1995	41	16.87**	52	53.73*	93	37.48*	8	10.43	101	35.34*
1996	85	13.25*	68	68.41*	153	37.76*	9	10.27	162	36.24*
1997	88	39.30*	96	194.23*	184	120.13*	25	18.10	209	107.93*
1998	47	13.79*	97	165.49*	144	115.98*	10	51.23	154	111.78*
1991 to 1998	445	20.57*	433	135.41*	878	77.20*	93	40.59*	971	73.64*

The sample consists of 971 Canadian IPOs by firms subsequently listed on the Canadian exchanges from January 1991 to December 1998. CPC: Capital Pool Company.
Asterisks denote significance at the 1% (*), 5% (**), and 10% (***) levels.

Table 15.5 Distribution of Canadian IPOs by sector

Sector	Common share IPOs		Unit IPOs		Full sample	
	Number	UND (%)	Number	UND (%)	Number	UND (%)
Biotechnology /pharmaceutical products	22	17.03	2	−18	24	14.11
Communications and media	17	−4.66	3	−49.7**	20	−11.42
Financial services	18	1.31	6	−22.33*	24	−4.59
Film production	6	4.05	2	−8.33	8	0.9*
Merchandising	14	−1.9	13	41.10	27	18.80
Mining	102	35.71*	23	108.7*	125	49.14*
Oil and gas	54	29.04*	23	12.23	77	24.02*
Production	84	11.11**			84	11.11**
Technology	86	19.77*	12	58.03	98	24.46*
Real estate	11	16.9	4	6.13	15	14.07
Other	31	25.92*	5	4.88	101	35.34*
CPC starting without a primary activity	433	135.41*			433	135.41*
Total	878	77.20*	93	40.59*	971	73.64*

The sample consists of 971 Canadian IPOs by firms subsequently listed on the Canadian exchanges from January 1991 to December 1998. CPC: Capital Pool Company.
Asterisks denote significance at the 1% (*), 5% (**), and 10% (***) levels.

11.11% and 4.05%, respectively). These results confirm the findings of Ritter (1991). A plausible explanation for the technology IPOs is given by Hand (2000), who suggests that since technology IPOs are generally smaller than the old economy IPOs, the supply of shares is very low compared with the demand; this may cause high initial returns. Wen (1999) documented that investors are willing to buy, in general, new economy stocks in order to diversify their portfolios and reduce systematic risk. Arosio et al. (2000) pointed out that the huge initial returns of high-tech IPOs are basically explained by three factors: investor's euphoria for the new economy; the quality of the private information; and publicly available information from the prospectus. These factors may explain the Canadian results presented here. Moreover, it is found that communications and media, and merchandising IPOs are overpriced (−4.66% and −1.9% respectively) and financial services IPOs are slightly underpriced (1.31%). The same patterns are observed for unit IPOs and for the entire sample.

15.4.5 Underwriter reputation

The value of the underwriter's reputation depends not only on its activity in the IPO market, but on the entire array of activities with which it is involved. The *Financial Post* provides the ranking of the top 25 underwriters, according to the value of IPOs raised by each underwriter as a leader and a syndicate member as a proxy for its reputation. Given this ranking, the sample in this study was divided into two groups, prestigious and less prestigious underwriters. Underwriters that appeared in the *Financial Post* rankings are considered as prestigious. The average underpricing for the sample partitioned on the basis of underwriter reputation is presented in Table 15.5. For common share IPOs excluding CPC, the degree of underpricing is 31.13% when the IPO is raised by a non-prestigious underwriter and 9.37% when a prestigious underwriter helps the company to go public. The difference between the two groups is significant at the 1% level. These results can be interpreted as follows. The reputation of the underwriter resolves some of the uncertainty about the quality of the IPO. The greater the underwriter prestige, the less risky the IPO and the lower the required initial return. Prestigious underwriters avoid the smaller firms for several reasons. First, they are concerned about the reputation of their firms being affected if they begin to participate in the underwriting of smaller firms. For example, the average proceeds for common share IPOs (excluding CPC) underwritten by prestigious underwriters was $52.48 million, versus $14.5 million for IPOs underwritten by less prestigious underwriters. Second, the underwriting commission is typically a function of the issue size.

The same pattern is observed for CPC IPOs and unit IPOs. Moreover, the difference between the two groups for CPC IPOs is smaller but significant at the 1% level. This result may be explained by the fact that CPC IPOs are generally raised by less prestigious underwriters. Indeed, in Alberta a number of regional brokerage firms have taken advantage of the CPC program to carve out a profitable underwriting and trading niche. MacIntosh (1994) pointed out that national investment dealers have shown little interest in serving the IPO market for offerings of less than $25 million.

15.4.6 Market conditions

The average underpricing for the sample partitioned on the basis of market conditions[6] is presented in Table 15.6. For common share IPOs excluding CPC, we find that the degree of underpricing is 22.03% when the IPO market is hot and 16.77% when the IPO market is cold. The difference in average initial returns between hot issues and cold issues is not significant at the conventional level. The same pattern is found for unit IPOs and CPC IPOs. As confirmed by previous studies, the market conditions may underpin the decision to go public for many issues. At the same time, investors are willing to compensate underwriters indirectly in order to gain favorable allocations on hot deals, by paying above the offer price. As issuers desire to offer their securities at the highest possible prices, it is important to examine whether they can expect to obtain higher prices in a hot or a cold market. Loughran and Ritter (2002) documented that issuers care about the change in their wealth rather than the level of wealth, and they do not bargain hard for an offer price increase when the market goes up. However, Loughran and Ritter's application of prospect theory fails to explain why issuers choose underwriters with a history of severe underpricing. The relation between the degree of underpricing and the hot issues market is still a puzzle.

---

[6] Taking into account the IPO gross proceeds of each period, 1993, 1994, 1996, and 1997 are considered as hot Canadian IPO periods, and 1991, 1992, 1995, and 1998 as cold Canadian IPO periods.

Table 15.6 Distribution of Canadian IPOs by role of underwriters and market conditions

	Common share IPOs excluding CPC IPOs		CPC IPOs		Common share IPOs with CPC		Unit IPOs		Full sample	
	Number	UND (%)	Number	UND (%)	Number	UND (%)	Number	UND (%)	Number	UND (%)
High-prestigious underwriters	216	9.37*P(N)	126	127.81*P(N)	342	53.01*P(N)	36	19.27*P(N)	378	49.79*P(N)
Low-prestigious underwriters	229	31.13*	307	138.53*	536	92.64*	57	53.18*	593	88.85*
Hot market	321	22.03*	274	142.70*	595	77.60*	64	48.02*	659	74.73*
Cold market	124	16.77*	159	122.84*	283	76.36**	29	22.49	312	71.13*
Total	445	20.57*	433	135.41*	878	77.20*	93	40.59*	971	73.64*

The sample consists of 971 Canadian IPOs by firms subsequently listed on the Canadian exchanges from January 1991 to December 1998. CPC: Capital Pool Company.

Asterisks denote significance at the 1% (*), 5% (**), and 10% (***) levels. ^{P} t-test for differences in average initial returns between the subgroups 'high-prestige underwriters versus low-prestige underwriters' and 'hot market versus cold market' significant at the 1% level. ^{N} Kruskal–Wallis and Mann–Whitney t-tests for differences in average initial returns between the subgroups significant at the 1% level.

15.5   Conclusion and policy implications

This study has examined the relation between degree of underpricing, for a wide sample of 971 Canadian IPOs, and ex-ante uncertainty for the period 1991 to 1998. The average initial return for common share IPOs (excluding CPC) was 20.57% (22.57% with a market-adjusted measure). Thus, there appears to be no major difference between the degree of underpricing of Canadian IPOs and previous international evidence, yet the results here differ from those of previous Canadian studies that include only TSE IPOs. Moreover, the degree of underpricing depends on the type of issue. Unit IPOs are more underpriced than common share IPOs, which is consistent with the findings of Lee et al. (2000) and How and Howe (2001). Furthermore, CPC IPOs, typical Canadian offerings, are more underpriced than common share IPOs. This is the first study to document such a result. Thus, for those who claim that the CPC program simplifies the process for raising equity and filing a public offering, bear in mind that it is not without its inherent costs, such as high underpricing.

The empirical analysis performed in this study suggests that, as expected, the IPO market in Canada is good only for large offerings. Further, oil and gas, real estate, and technology IPOs are more underpriced than IPOs from other sectors. It is also found that the underpricing is related to the prestige of the underwriter and to the period of the issue.

One important aspect of a firm's decision to go public is that of receiving a proper price for its common shares. If IPOs are significantly underpriced, many eligible firms would be reluctant to choose an IPO as a means of raising equity capital. This study shows a major pricing problem for Canadian small offerings, which raises the following question: why is underpricing not contracted ex-ante? For example, by fixing a threshold for the underpricing, the underwriter should pay a penalty to the issuer if the initial returns are beyond this level. This question certainly merits further investigation.

References

Allen, F. and Faulhaber, G. (1989). Signaling by Underpricing in the IPO Market. *Journal of Financial Economics*, 23(2):303–323.

Arosio, R., Guidici, G., and Paleari, S. (2000). What Drives the Initial Market Performance of Italian IPOs? An Empirical Investigation on Underpricing and Price Support. Working Paper, Universita di Bergamo, Bergamo, Italy.

Beatty, R. and Ritter, J. (1986). Investment Banking, Reputation and the Underpricing of Initial Public Offerings. *Journal of Financial Economics*, 15(1–2):213–232.

Carter, R. and Manaster, S. (1990). Initial Public Offerings and Underwriter Reputation. *Journal of Finance*, 45(4):1045–1068.

Carter, R., Dark, F., and Singh, A. (1998). Underwriter Reputation, Initial Returns, and the Long-Run Performance of IPO stocks. *Journal of Finance*, 53(1):285–311.

Chalk, A. and Peavy, J. (1990). Understanding the Pricing of Initial Public Offerings. *Research in Finance*, 8(2):203–240.

Clarkson, P. and Merkley, J. (1994). Ex-Ante Uncertainty and the Underpricing of Initial Public Offering: Further Canadian Evidence. *Canadian Journal of Administrative Sciences*, 11(1):54–67.

Derrien, F. and Womack, K. (2000). Auctions Versus Book-Building and the Control of Underpricing in Hot Markets. Working Paper, Dartmouth University, Hanover, NH.

Hand, J. (2000). Profits, Losses and the Non-Linear Pricing of Internet Stocks. Working Paper (www.ssrn.com).

Helwege, J. and Liang, N. (2004). Initial Public Offerings in Hot and Cold Markets. *Journal of Financial and Quantitative Analysis*, 39(3):541–567.

How, J. and Howe, J. (2001). Warrants in Initial Public Offerings: Empirical Evidence. *Journal of Business*, 74(3):433–457.

How, J., Izan, H., and Monroe, G. (1995). Differential Information and the Underpricing of Initial Public Offerings: Australian Evidence. *Accounting and Finance*, 35(1):87–106.

Ibbotson, R. and Jaffe, J. (1975). Hot Issue Markets. *Journal of Finance*, 30(4):1027–1042.

Jog, V. (1997). The Climate for Canadian Initial Public Offerings. In: *Financing Growth in Canada* (Halpern, P., ed.), pp. 357–401. University of Calgary Press.

Jog, V. and Riding, A. (1987). Underpricing in Canadian IPOs. *Financial Analysts Journal*, 43(6):48–55.

Jog, V. and Srivastava, A. (1994). Underpricing in Canadian IPOs 1971–1992: An Update. *FINECO*, 4(1):81–87.

Jog, V. and Wang, L. (2002). Aftermarket Volatility and Underpricing of Canadian Initial Public Offerings. *Canadian Journal of Administrative Sciences*, 19(3):231–248.

Kryzanowski, L. and Rakita, I. (1996). The Short-Run Intraday Behaviour of Canadian IPOs (Tannous, G. F., ed.). *Administrative Science Association of Canada Proceedings Finance*, 17(1):41–50.

Lee, M., Lee, P., and Taylor, S. (2000). Unit Initial Public Offerings: Staged Equity or Signalling Mechanism? *Accounting and Finance*, 43(1):63–85.

Ljungqvist, A. (1997). Pricing Initial Public Offerings: Further Evidence from Germany. *European Economic Review*, 41(7):1309–1320.

Loughran, T. and Ritter, J. R. (2002). Why Don't Issuers Get Upset About Leaving Money on the Table in IPOs? *Review of Financial Studies*, 15(2):413–433.

Lowry, M. and Schwert, G. (2000). IPO Market Cycles: An Explanatory Investigation. Working Paper, Social Sciences Research Network (www.ssrn.com).

MacIntosh, J. (1994). Legal and Institutional Barriers to Financing Innovative Enterprise in Canada. Working Paper, Queen's University, Kingston, ON.

Ritter, J. R. (1991). The Long-Run Performance of Initial Public Offerings. *Journal of Finance*, 46(1):3–27.

Ritter, J. R. (1998). Initial Public Offerings. *Contemporary Finance Digest*, 2(1):5–30.

Ritter, J. R. (2003). Investment Banking and Securities Issuance. In: *Handbook of the Economics of Finance* (Constantinides, G., Harris, M., and Stulz, R., eds). Elsevier Science, Amsterdam.

Robinson, M. (1997). Raising Equity Capital for Small and Medium-Sized Enterprises Using Canada's Public Equity Markets. In: *Financing Growth in Canada* (Halpern, P., ed.), pp. 659–709. University of Calgary Press.

Rock, K. (1986). Why New Issues are Underpriced. *Journal of Financial Economics*, 15(1–2):187–212.

Schultz, P. (1993). Unit Initial Public Offerings – A Form of Staged Financing. *Journal of Financial Economics*, 15(2):187–212.

Stern, R. L. and Bornstein, P. (1985). Why New Issues Are Lousy Investments. *Forbes*, 2 December:152–154.

Stoughton, N., Wong, K., and Zechner, J. (2001). IPO and Product Quality. *Journal of Business*, 74(3):375–408.

Ursel, N. D. (2000). Hot Issue Markets in Canada. Working Paper, University of Windsor, Windsor, ON.

Ursel, N. and Ljucovic, P. (1998). The Impact of Bank Ownership of Underwriters on the Underpricing of IPOs. *Canadian Journal of Administrative Sciences*, 15(1):15–20.

Welch, I. (1989). Seasoned Offerings, Imitation Costs and the Underpricing of Initial Public Offerings. *Journal of Finance*, 44(2):421–449.

Wen, K. (1999). Residual Risk, Investor Heterogeneity, and Participation Restriction: Explaining Long-Run Underperformance of Initial Public Offerings. Working Paper (www.ssrn.com).

16 IPO underpricing and ownership structure: evidence from the Istanbul Stock Exchange

M. Banu Durukan

Abstract

The present study aims to investigate the influence of ownership structure on initial public offering (IPO) underpricing within the context of the Istanbul Stock Exchange (ISE) in Turkey, an emerging market. The present study provides evidence from an emerging market (the ISE) and a civil law country (Turkey) which possess different characteristics than the developed markets and common law countries that have been extensively investigated by the majority of the existing studies in the IPO underpricing literature. The findings of the study, as a whole, can be interpreted to conclude that the relationship between ownership structure and underpricing, if there is one, is weak. The results may be interpreted as a reflection of Turkey being a civil law country where the focus on the stock market and the corporate control provided by the stock market is quite negligible. As a result, the IPO does not act as a means of change in the control mechanisms of firms, hence control and monitoring concerns do not influence the level of underpricing.

16.1 Introduction

One of the intriguing areas of research in finance is underpricing of initial public offerings (IPOs). The IPO underpricing phenomenon is well documented throughout world markets (Ritter, 2003). Even though there is an immense literature and evidence on the existence of this global anomaly, researchers are still looking for the reasons behind it. A myriad of explanations have been put forth by researchers to this end; however, the debate has still not been laid to rest, since none can explain the changing underpricing patterns.

As Ritter and Welch (2002) suggested in their review of the theoretical explanations of IPO underpricing, that theories on the reasons of underpricing are conventionally grouped under two main headings: (i) those based on asymmetric information and (ii) those based on corporate control or allocation of shares. Theories under the first heading emphasize the asymmetry of information possessed by investors and issuers, and accordingly argue that underpricing helps reduce the existence of asymmetric information. One line of the theories of asymmetric information directs attention to the issue of investors having differential information. That is, the investors are assumed to possess information to which the issuers do not have access. On the basis of such a premise, Rock (1986) and Barry and Jennings (1993) put forward the argument that informed investors are rewarded for purchasing the securities and revealing private information by underpricing of IPOs, which leads to abnormal initial returns.

Complementing the above argument, Benveniste and Spindt (1989), on the other hand, pointed out that bookbuilding as a flotation method enables the investment bankers to extract information from the investors regarding the value of the securities. This, in turn, puts them in an advantageous position to set the offer price more accurately, leading to less underpricing (Loughran et al., 1994; Ritter, 1998). However, it must be noted that the investment bankers partially adjust the offer price to the acquired information in order to reward those investors who provide it. Moreover, these investors are also favored with preferential allocation of underpriced shares (Benveniste and Spindt, 1989; Cornelli and Goldreich, 2001). Derrien (2005), by producing evidence to support the above argument, claimed that positive initial returns following IPOs are a cost paid by issuers in order to obtain private information from investors. Derrien (2005) further argued that even though issuers leave money on the table, those who buy IPO shares on the aftermarket may also do the same thing if the shares are overpriced by over-optimistic investors at the time of the offering, as suggested by Aggarwal and Rivoli (1990) and Aggarwal et al. (1993).

The other line of theories of asymmetric information advances the argument that the issuers have differential information and thus signal quality through underpricing (Allen and Faulhaber, 1989; Welch, 1989). That is, when the pre-IPO owners, at some future date, sell the shares that they have retained at the IPO, they aim to recover the losses associated with underpricing. This argument is called the IPO underpricing signaling hypothesis, for which there exists mixed evidence in the IPO literature (Garfinkel, 1993; Espenlaub and Tonks, 1998; Ritter and Welch, 2002).

On the other hand, another group of researchers, notably Booth and Smith (1986) and Carter and Manaster (1990), stated that firms, instead of signaling by underpricing, can benefit from the certification role of reputable investment banks or backing by large block shareholders (or venture capitalists). Lin (1996) and Hamao et al. (2000) presented empirical evidence that backing signals reduce the magnitude of underpricing. Such evidence, however, is contradicted by Loughran and Ritter (2004), who found that recently issuers have accepted higher underpricing levels by reputable investment bankers in exchange for wider analyst coverage. Cliff and Denis (2004) produced evidence to support that underpricing acts as compensation for investment banks for the research coverage they provide and, consequently, the issuers are not upset about the underpricing of their shares. Within this context, Habib and Ljungqvist (2001) argued that underpricing can substitute marketing activities and, in turn, reduce marketing expenditures of the IPO process. Additionally, Loughran and Ritter (2004) drew attention to the point that underpricing may still be too large, thereby leading to excessive underwriter compensation.

Although theories based on asymmetric information can explain the reasons for IPO underpricing, they lack the power to explain the differences in the levels of IPO underpricing (Ritter and Welch, 2002). Hence, corporate control mechanisms, namely the ownership structure, should be taken into consideration. Stated differently, the ownership structure of a firm influences the level of IPO underpricing, which leads to changes in this structure. Even though researchers agree on this argument in general terms (Booth and Chua, 1996; Brennan and Franks, 1997; Stoughton and Zechner, 1998), there is an ongoing debate on the nature of such an influence.

In light of the above explanations, the present study aims to investigate the influence of ownership structure on IPO underpricing within the context of the Istanbul Stock Exchange (ISE) in Turkey, an emerging market. As stated by Lins (2003), emerging markets are important in the valuation effects of ownership structure literature because of their general characteristics of pyramid ownership structures, poor investor protection, and underdeveloped markets for corporate control. Within this context, firms listed on the ISE appear to have similar characteristics, confirmed by La Porta et al. (1998), Yurtoğlu (2000), Demirağ and Serter (2003), and Kula (2005). Moreover, the theoretical and empirical work on IPO underpricing and ownership structure focuses mostly on common law countries, which are characterized as market-based economies with the emphasis on capital markets as the main source of financing and dispersed ownership structures (La Porta et al., 1999, 2000). Turkey, on the other hand, is a civil law country where (i) the main source of financing is banks, (ii) the capital markets have a limited role in the economy, and (iii) there is concentrated ownership. The foregoing discussion provides a convenient framework to cite the present study's contribution toward resolving the discussion of IPO underpricing by providing evidence from an emerging market (the ISE) and a civil law country (Turkey), which possess different characteristics than the developed markets and common law countries that have been extensively investigated by the majority of the existing studies in the IPO underpricing literature.

The rest of the chapter proceeds as follows. Section 16.2 provides the theoretical framework of the relationship between ownership structure and IPO underpricing. Section 16.3 presents sample and data characteristics. The empirical findings are presented and discussed in section 16.4. The final section (16.5) summarizes the findings of the study and concludes.

16.2   Theoretical background

The question why pre-IPO shareholders do not seem to be upset about leaving money on the table has received considerable research attention. Many theories, none of which are mutually exclusive, have been put forward to explain the reasons for IPO underpricing.[1] Even though it is relatively simple to calculate underpricing, the relationship between underpricing and factors associated with it is not straightforward. It should be noted that the underpricing phenomenon, being a preferred or welcomed outcome of the IPO process, is a complex and controversial issue (Ritter and Welch, 2002).

As stated by Marshall (1998), Ritter (1998), and Daily et al. (2003), the factors accounted for by the theories of asymmetric information are inadequate to explain this anomaly. Therefore, ownership structure, a significant explanatory factor suggested by the literature, must be taken into consideration. A firm going public experiences a change in its ownership structure. The motivation of the pre-IPO owners in terms of control and the changes in the ownership structure as an internal control mechanism may influence the IPO process. The role of the targeted ownership structure in the

---

[1] See Ritter (1998), Loughran and Ritter (2002), Ritter and Welch (2002), Daily et al. (2003), and Loughran and Ritter (2004) for reviews of the theories on underpricing.

decision to go public and the impact of the ownership structure on the firm's value are two important issues examined in the finance literature. Consequently, the association between the ownership structure and underpricing appears to be another research issue to be investigated.

The research on this issue has lead to contradictory views on the nature of the relationship between ownership structure and IPO underpricing, even though there is consensus on the existence of the relationship itself. The diversity in the views is based on the fact that different ownership structures come with their costs and benefits. On the one hand, Burkart and Gromb (1997), La Porta et al. (1999), Claessens et al. (2000), and Lins (2003) have acknowledged that the use of pyramidal ownership structures and cross-holdings allows insiders to exercise effective control over a firm and to monitor effectively the manager's reducing agency conflicts. Within this context, concentrated ownership coincides with lack of investor protection, because owners who are not protected will seek protection by becoming controllers themselves (Shleifer and Vishny, 1997; La Porta et al., 1998, 2000; Denis and McConnell, 2003). On the other hand, Dyck and Zingales (2004) argued that the large shareholders may also act to maximize the private benefits of control, which has the effect of exposing minority shareholders to a conflict of interest. Based on how the large shareholders prefer to act, the firm's value can be negatively or positively affected (Holderness, 2003). The firm's value and the existence of large shareholders have a positive relationship if the large shareholders use their power of monitoring to achieve shared benefits of control. In cases where the large shareholders act to extract private benefits of control, the firm's value is influenced negatively (Lemmon and Lins, 2003).

In light of the above arguments, Pagano and Röell (1998) and Pagano et al. (1998) indicated that the decision to go public by the owners is strongly influenced by the pre-IPO and post-IPO ownership structures. The motive of the controlling shareholders will depend on the tradeoff between the costs and benefits of going public, which results in transfer of control to some external shareholders. Based on the arguments on concentrated ownership and private benefits of control, the reduced monitoring hypothesis put forward by Brennan and Franks (1997) argues that owners or insiders who value independence and control of a firm take steps to ensure that they will retain their private benefits of control after the IPO. Accordingly, they underprice the securities to attract many shareholders and ration the securities so that the outside ownership is dispersed. In other words, to retain control, which brings private benefits, the initial owners aim to encourage oversubscription by underpricing. In the share allocation process, the small shareholders are favored to achieve greater dispersion which, in turn, reduces the incentive to monitor the existing management and increases the cost for new blockholders to accumulate large stakes.

The level of underpricing is also dependent upon whose shares are sold. Booth and Chua (1996) stated that directors trade-off two effects on their wealth that arise from underpricing. These effects are the immediate cost of underpricing and later benefits of being able to sell shares at a price that is higher because of the greater liquidity brought about by a more diffuse shareholding. As Brennan and Franks (1997) found, the selling shareholders tend to be non-directors rather than directors. Therefore, the costs of underpricing fall more heavily on the selling shareholders because the dilution effect hurts them more (Habib and Ljungqvist, 2001). The shareholders retaining their shares maintain control as well as having the opportunity to sell their shares at a higher price, since the liquidity provided by disperse ownership reduces the required rate of return, thereby increasing the equilibrium price of the shares (Booth and Chua, 1996; Loughran and Ritter, 2002).

It should be noted that ownership structures are fluid and there is no guarantee that the disperse ownership structure achieved by underpricing will prevail. Field and Sheehan (2004) provided evidence that casts doubt on the ability of the pre-IPO owners to achieve the expected outcomes from the investors who are allocated shares at the time of IPO. They discovered that underpricing has little or no apparent effect on outside blockholding. However, they suggested that if the effect exists, it supports the argument of Brennan and Franks (1997), but it is neither reliable nor large.

As a substitute to underpricing, firms can issue nonvoting shares that enable the managers to control the firm in the long run. Dual-class structures compared to underpricing can therefore offer a less costly or more effective means of preserving control. Smart and Zutter (2003), who provide support to Brennan and Franks' (1997) argument, showed that dual-class firms experience less underpricing, have slightly higher institutional ownership, and hand over control through acquisitions less frequently than single-class firms. Brennan and Franks (1997) also contended that dual-class firms underprice less because they have no need to create ownership dispersion to retain control. Issuing nonvoting shares to avoid monitoring reduces the control motivation for underpricing. Field and Karpoff (2002) also support these arguments that IPO managers aim to maintain their independence and control, thereby using takeover defenses to insulate themselves from the market for control as well.

Booth and Chua (1996), Kothare (1997), and Field and Sheehan (2004) argued that the excess demand, hence dispersed to outside shareholders, created by underpricing should be evaluated based on the relationship between control and liquidity. As Maug (1998) explained, liquid stock markets have two opposing effects on the exercise of corporate control by large shareholders. High liquidity enables large shareholders to exercise corporate control to correct managerial failure. At the same time, it may also reduce the willingness of large shareholders to monitor, since it enables them to dispose of their shares before experiencing any decline in the prices due to managerial failure. Thus, the key idea is to provide large shareholders the incentive to monitor the firms going public.

Cornelli and Goldreich (2001) and Aruğaslan et al. (2004) provided evidence which raises grave concerns for the validity of the above arguments, and claimed that both control and liquidity issues are not considered by shareholders in the IPO process. They further add that institutional shareholdings in firms immediately after their IPO are driven by firm size and not by their underpricing or dual-class status. On the contrary, Fernando et al. (2004) hypothesized that firms choose an IPO price consistent with the institutional intensity of their preferred ownership structure. That is, they relate the post-IPO ownership structure to IPO underpricing and the firm's subsequent performance. They documented a U-shaped relationship between underpricing and offer price, and suggested that the IPO offer price contains information about the post-IPO ownership structure. They further state that lower offer prices are chosen to discourage institutional investors.

The international evidence on the above arguments has been provided by Pham et al. (2003) for Australia, Su (2004) for China, Sullivan and Unite (2001) for the Philippines, and Kiymaz (2000) for Turkey. These studies provide supporting evidence that ownership structure has a significant influence on underpricing.

16.3   Sample and data

The primary source for the IPOs and related data were the Istanbul Stock Exchange (ISE) IPO database, yearbooks, and website. The dataset includes initial public offerings from 1 January 1994 to 31 December 2003. The information on IPOs is retrieved from the IPO files provided through the website of the ISE (http://www.ise.org.tr). However, the data provided were not uniform for all the years, which put some limitations on some of the variables that could be used.

Since the information on the allocation of shares was not provided for IPOs before 1994, and also it was not possible to access information on the ownership structures of these firms in detail, the IPOs before 1994 were excluded from the sample. The original sample included 182 firms that completed an IPO from 1994 to 2003. Following Loughran and Ritter (2004), the best effort companies were not included. The financial service firms (for example, closed-end mutual funds, banks) were excluded from the sample. The firms that had missing data were also eliminated. The final sample covers 112 firms that have offered shares through initial public offerings. Table 16.1 provides descriptive statistics for the sample. It shows the mean and standard deviation of IPO first-day returns, aggregate proceeds in dollars (USD), proportion of secondary and new shares offered, the age of the sample firms, and the percentage of firm offered.

As Table 16.1 indicates, the mean initial return – that is, the first-day return of the IPOs – is 7.05% for the sample firms. The fraction of shares offered ranges from 5% to 45.15%, with a mean of 20.86%. This shows that the pre-IPO owners continue to retain the majority of the shares. The proportion of secondary shares sold at the IPO is 6.59%, which is only 31.52% of all the shares offered. Hence, the firms go public by issuing new shares, which may imply that they go public to raise funds for the firm.

Table 16.1 Descriptive statistics for the sample IPOs, 1994 to 2003

	N	Minimum	Maximum	Mean	Standard deviation
Initial return (%)	112	−18.26	25.00	7.05	11.27
Gross proceeds ($ million)	112	1083	1,780,000,000	21,400,975	168,408,333
Fraction of shares offered (%)	112	5.00	45.15	20.86[a]	8.28
Fraction of secondary shares offered (%)	106	0.00	38.50	6.59	9.43
Fraction of new shares offered (%)	106	0.00	45.00	13.97	11.03
Age	109	1	66	18.88	12.59

[a] 20.86 = 6.59 + 13.97.

Initial return is calculated by dividing the difference between the offer price and the first trading day closing price by the offer price. 'Gross proceeds' is the total proceeds received from the sale of the issues offered. 'Fraction of shares' offered is the percentage of shares offered to the public. 'Fraction of secondary shares offered' is the percentage of shares offered by the pre-IPO owners at the IPO. 'Fraction of new shares offered' is the new shares issued to be offered at the IPO. Age is found by subtracting the year of establishment of the firm from the year of the IPO.

Table 16.2 Ownership structure of the sample firms

	Max	Mean	Standard deviation
Pre-IPO			
Corporate stakes	100.00	74.19	23.54
Individual blocks	100.00	56.77	32.73
Foreigners stakes	35.06	28.05	3.97
Post-IPO			
Corporate stakes	92.99	60.90	22.81
Individual blocks	83.00	46.95	25.44
Foreigners stakes	40.00	31.02	9.69

Corporate stake is the fraction of shares of the firm that other corporations hold. Individual block is the total percentage of the shares held by individuals who are reported to own more than 10% of total shares by themselves. Foreigner stake is the fraction of shares held by foreigners, mainly investment funds.

The data on the ownership structures of the firms were collected from the ISE Yearbook of Companies for the years 1994 to 1997 and from the files of companies retrieved from the ISE website for the years 1998 to 2003. The pre-IPO ownership structure was not available for the firms whose data were collected from the year-books. Table 16.2 shows comparative information on the sample firms whose pre-IPO and post-IPO ownership structure data were available.

As the pre-IPO and post-IPO ownership structures denote, the Turkish firms have concentrated ownership structures. Even though the corporate stakes are associated with one corporation, the individual stakes are individuals who are reported to own more than 10% of the shares of the firm. These individuals are mostly either the founders or a member of the founding family, who act as directors or have a seat on the board. These findings are consistent with those of Demirağ and Serter (2003) and Kula (2005). The share of the corporate stakes and individual blocks decline after the IPO; however, they still control the majority of the shares. Table 16.2 points out that, after the IPO, the firms experience an increase in foreign ownership. The foreigners who purchase the IPO shares are mostly foreign investment funds, which are interested in investing in Turkey to receive high returns.

16.4 Empirical findings

The aim of the study is to investigate the relationship between ownership structures and underpricing. As a first step, Table 16.3 was prepared to provide information on the distribution of firms based on their ownership structures after the IPO, the type of selling owner, and the allocation of shares.

As is seen from the table, its content is separated to show the details of the sale of shares, the allocation of these shares, and post-IPO ownership structure for the firms that underprice and for the whole sample. An examination of the table reveals the following:

1   The firms that underprice are the ones that have positive initial returns in the first trading day. Thus, 67.86% of sample firms have underpriced their shares.

2   35.71% of the sample firms underprice and issue new securities. On the other hand, 17.86% of all underpricing firms sell only secondary shares. This implies that the existing shareholders of the underpricing firms do not sell their shares at the IPO.
3   Among the selling shareholders, the corporate shareholders have the higher proportion (20.54%) compared to the individual blockholders (12.50%) for the underpricing firms.
4   Allocation of shares both to corporations and to new blocks is much higher compared to the allocations to the individuals and employees. The majority of the sample firms underprice and they also allocate their shares to institutional investors, mainly to foreigners.
5   The new blocks are foreign investment funds, which are interested in investing in Turkey as an emerging market that provides profitable opportunities.
6   Even though the proportion of firms with corporate blocks is 68.75% for the whole sample, only 22.32% of sample firms that underprice have corporate stakes. The same is true for individual blocks. This can be interpreted as underpricing firms having less post-IPO blockholders compared to the whole sample.

As a second step, following Field and Sheehan (2004), conditional probabilities are calculated to examine further the relationship between the ownership structure measures and underpricing. These probabilities are presented in Table 16.4.

The conditional probabilities are nearly equal to the unconditional probability of underpricing. Thus, the chi-square statistic also yields the same conclusion. The only probability that stands out as different from the conditional probability of underpricing is the case of the existence of the post-IPO corporate block. In this case, the probability declines. That is, the probability of underpricing declines if the firms have a post-IPO corporate block.

Table 16.3 Selling owners, allocation of shares sold, and post-IPO ownership

	Underpricing firms		All firms	
	Number of firms	%	Number of firms	%
Sale of shares				
New shares	40	35.71	63	56.25
Secondary shares	20	17.86	30	26.79
Both new and secondary	16	14.29	19	16.96
Corporate stakes	23	20.54	32	28.57
Individual blocks	14	12.50	19	16.96
Pre-emptive rights	28	25.00	44	39.29
Allocation of sales				
New blocks	40	35.71	57	50.89
To corporations	40	35.71	62	55.36
To individuals	19	16.96	32	28.57
To employees	22	19.64	33	29.46
To foreigners	50	44.64	76	67.86
Post-IPO ownership				
Corporate block	25	22.32	77	68.75
Individual block	38	33.93	56	50.00
Sample size	76	67.86	112	100

Table 16.4 Unconditional and conditional probabilities of underpricing

	Probability
p(Underpricing)	0.6786
p(Underpricing|New shares)	0.6349
p(Underpricing|Secondary shares)	0.6667
p(Underpricing|Both new and secondary)	0.8421
p(Underpricing|Corporate stakes)	0.7188
p(Underpricing|Individual blocks)	0.7368
p(Underpricing|Pre-emptive rights)	0.6364
p(Underpricing|New blocks)	0.7018
p(Underpricing|To corporations)	0.6452
p(Underpricing|To individuals)	0.5938
p(Underpricing|To employees)	0.6667
p(Underpricing|To foreigners)	0.6579
p(Underpricing|Corporate block)	0.3247
p(Underpricing|Individual block)	0.6786

Table 16.5 Unconditional and conditional probabilities:
underpricing as a condition

	Probability
p(New blocks)	0.5089
p(New blocks|Underpricing)	0.5263
p(To corporations)	0.5536
p(To corporations|Underpricing)	0.5263
p(To individuals)	0.2857
p(To individuals|Underpricing)	0.2499
p(To employees)	0.2946
p(To employees|Underpricing)	0.2894
p(To foreigners)	0.6786
p(To foreigners|Underpricing)	0.6579
p(Corporate block)	0.6875
p(Corporate block|Underpricing)	0.3289
p(Individual block)	0.5000
p(Individual block|Underpricing)	0.4999

It is worth calculating the reverse conditional probabilities of the measures related to post-IPO ownership structure and allocation of shares based on the condition that the IPO is underpriced. Table 16.5 presents these probabilities.

The conditional probabilities in Table 16.5 indicate that the probability of a post-IPO corporate blockholder is low if there is underpricing. However, the same does not apply to individual blocks. The other conditional probabilities are not significantly different from the unconditional probabilities as confirmed by the chi-square tests. All probability calculations in Tables 16.4 and 16.5 indicate that the association between underpricing and ownership-related measures is quite low.

All the above findings are inconsistent with the findings of the existing empirical studies, verifying an association between ownership structure of firms and underpricing. However, before coming to any conclusions, more in-depth analysis must be carried out. To examine if there is a difference between firms underpricing and not underpricing in terms of the measures of ownership structure, equivalence of means is tested as the third step. The test results are presented in Table 16.6.

Consistent with the findings of both Brennan and Franks (1997) and Stoughton and Zechner (1998), the underpriced firms are expected to be different in terms of ownership measures compared to the firms that do not underprice. However, as can also be seen from Table 16.6, this argument is not supported for the sample under investigation. The differences of the means are very small and not significant. The only exception is that more shares are allocated to foreigners when they are underpriced (28.77% compared to 18.80%). These results are consistent with those of Field and Sheehan (2004).

As a fourth step, the role of underpricing in new block formation for IPO firms is analyzed by grouping the firms based on the sale of shares to new blocks. New blocks are identified as the reported sale of more than 5% of firm shares to one shareholder at the IPO. The information required for the analysis is presented in Table 16.7.

As seen in Table 16.7, 70% of the firms that underprice yield to new block formations. However, the test of equality carried out for the means of new block and no new block subsamples indicates the difference is not significant. This is also consistent with Field and Sheehan's (2004) argument that if there are already blocks in place at the time of the IPO, which is true for most firms in the sample, it is easier to form new blocks in cases where the pre-IPO blockholders sell their shares. The results presented in Table 16.7 support the evidence in Table 16.2. As was noted, the proportion of the corporate and individual blockholders generally decline after the IPO, whereas foreign shares increase. Since the foreigners are the institutional investors,

Table 16.6 Difference between underpricing and non-underpricing firms based on share sales, allocation, and post-IPO ownership structure of firms

	Underpricing firms	Non-underpricing firms	p-value
Sale of shares			
Total sold (%)	20.99	20.61	0.819
Secondary shares (%)	6.88	5.99	0.651
New shares (%)	13.92	14.05	0.955
Allocation of shares			
To corporations	11.37	9.43	0.794
To individuals	9.55	11.74	0.536
To employees	2.68	2.81	0.901
To foreigners	28.77	18.80	0.028
Post-IPO ownership			
Corporate block	40.61	41.09	0.942
Individual block	23.31	22.53	0.894

they become new blockholders of the firms whose shares they purchase, together with the pre-IPO blockholders.

At the fifth stage, following Smart and Zutter (2003) and Aruğaslan et al. (2004), the sample is divided into two groups based on the type of shares that the firm has outstanding. That is, the firms that issued different classes of shares giving different rights to their holders are grouped under the heading of multi-class firms. These shares provide either more than one voting right or privileges in the determination of the board of directors. Thus, these shares may influence the underpricing level of firms since the control of the firm is maintained by the pre-IPO owners through these shares. The second group is the single-class firms, which issue only one type of shares. Table 16.8 presents the relationship between these two groups of firms and underpricing.

As seen from Table 16.8, there is no significant relationship between mean initial returns of multi-class and single-class firms, even though the mean initial return is higher for the single-class firms. This result implies that multi-class firms underprice more compared to the single-class firms. However, the number of firms that underprice is almost the same for both classes of firms.

As the final step, the relationship between the underpricing and ownership structure is analyzed by employing the regression method, in which initial returns are regressed on firm and IPO characteristic variables and ownership structure-related variables. The firm and IPO characteristic variables are the size of firm, age, gross proceeds, multi-class shares, percentage of firm sold, and number of investors. The ownership variables that are put into the regression equation interchangeably are new block formation, post-IPO corporate stakes, post-IPO individual blockholder, size of sale of new issues, size of sale of secondary shares, and allocation of shares to corporations. However, most of the ownership-related variables were found to be non-significant in the regression equations which are not reported.

Table 16.9 reports the results of the regression analysis, which yielded significant results. As can be seen from the table, underpricing is found to be significantly negatively

Table 16.7 New block formation and underpricing

	New block	No new block	
Number of firms	57	55	Total = 112 firms
Mean initial return	7.82	6.26	p-value = 0.473
Underpricing firms	40	36	Total = 76 firms
Non-underpricing firms	17	19	Total = 36 firms

Table 16.8 Multi-class firms and single-class firms

	Multi-class	Single-class	
Number of firms	48	56	Total = 104 firms
Mean initial return	8.22	6.62	p-value = 0.477
Underpricing firms	35	37	
Non-underpricing firms	13	19	

Table 16.9 Multiple regression analysis

Variables	
Constant	10.994** (2.401)
Secondary shares sold	3.529 (0.449)
Pre-emptive rights	−10.157** (2.376)
Percentage of firm sold	−0.016 (0.077)
Number of investors	0.042** (2.499)
Age	1.281 (0.643)
Gross proceeds	−4.719*** (3.405)
Multi-class share	2.760 (0.953)
Percentage sold to foreigners	0.138* (1.888)
Post-IPO blockholdings	−0.0155 (0.175)
R^2	0.339
Adj. R^2	0.189
F-value	2.265**

The dependent variable in the regression analysis is the initial return (the first-day closing price relative to the offer price). The secondary shares sold is the percentage of secondary shares sold. Pre-emptive rights is the pre-emptive rights that are sold in the IPO process. Percentage of firm sold is the proportion of total shares outstanding sold at the IPO. Number of investors is the total number of different types of investors who are allocated shares. Age is the natural logarithm of 1 + age. Gross proceeds is the natural logarithm of dollar value of total proceeds received from the IPO. Multi-class share is a dummy variable which takes the value of 1 if the firm has more than one type of shares outstanding. Percentage sold to foreigners is the percentage of shares sold to foreign investors. Post-IPO blockholdings is the sum of the post-IPO corporate stakes in the company >5% and post-IPO blocks (>5%) held by individuals. Asterisks denote significance at the 10% (*), 5% (**), and 1% (***) levels.

related to pre-emptive rights sales, and positively significantly associated with number of investors and percentage sold to foreigners as ownership structure-related measures. However, the coefficients on these variables are not large, thus indicating low influence on the initial return of the IPO. These regression results are in line with the findings of the previous steps. Therefore, the conclusion reached by this study can be stated as follows: ownership structure variables are not strongly associated with underpricing of IPOs. It should immediately be added that this conclusion appears to confirm the results presented by Field and Sheehan (2004) and Aruğaslan et al. (2004).

16.5 Conclusion

IPO underpricing is a global phenomenon that awaits explanation. Even though there have been many studies on underpricing and many theories put forward, none can fully explain it. The changing levels of underpricing based on time periods and different conditions make it even more difficult to explain. The theories based on information asymmetry between issuers and investors have been successful in explaining the reasons for IPO underpricing. However, they were not adequate to explain the differences in levels of underpricing. Thus, Booth and Chua (1996), Brennan and Franks (1997), Mello and Parsons (1998), and Stoughton and Zechner (1998) put forward the argument that the ownership structure of a firm may play an important role in the underpricing of shares.

The ownership structure is found to affect firm value and the decision to go public by researchers. Thus, pre-IPO owners of the firm may choose to underprice to increase subscription and then allocate the shares based on their expectations of the monitoring that will be provided by the new investors. Consequently, two conflicting views emerge from this argument. One suggests that underpricing is used for achieving disperse ownership structure to avoid monitoring by new shareholders, whereas the other indicates that underpricing is used to attract institutional investors to benefit from their monitoring services.

The present study aims to investigate the role of ownership structure on influencing IPO underpricing within the context of the Istanbul Stock Exchange (ISE) in Turkey, an emerging market. Firms listed on the ISE appear to have pyramid ownership structures. Turkey, on the other hand, is a civil law country where (i) the main source of financing is banks, (ii) the capital markets have a limited role in the economy, and (iii) there is concentrated ownership. The present study contributes to the unresolved discussion of IPO underpricing by providing evidence from an emerging market (the ISE) and a civil law country (Turkey), which possess different characteristics than the developed markets and common law countries that were extensively investigated by the majority of existing studies in the IPO underpricing literature.

The findings of the study, as a whole, can be interpreted to conclude that the relationship between ownership structure and underpricing is weak, if there is any. This conclusion may be due to the low proportion of ISE firms being offered and the pre-IPO ownership structure being maintained even after the IPO. That is, the pre-IPO owners and managers are not threatened by the monitoring of new post-IPO investors or losing any private benefits of corporate control. The pyramidal ownership structure makes the corporate shareholders the main monitors of the firms. Moreover, these corporate shareholders continue to hold their proportion of shares after the IPO. In summary, the results may be interpreted as a reflection of Turkey being a civil law country, where the focus on the stock market and corporate control provided by the stock market is quite negligible. As a result, the IPO does not act as a means of a change in the control mechanisms of firms, hence control and monitoring concerns do not influence the level of underpricing.

Acknowledgments – The detailed and insightful comments of Mehmet A. Civelek are gratefully acknowledged.

References

Aggarwal, R. and Rivoli, P. (1990). Fads in the Initial Public Offering Market. *Financial Management*, 19(4):45–57.

Aggarwal, R., Leal, R., and Hernandez, F. (1993). The Aftermarket Performance of Initial Public Offerings in Latin America. *Financial Management*, 22(1):42–53.

Allen, F. and Faulhaber, G. (1989). Signaling by Underpricing in the IPO Market. *Journal of Financial Economics*, 23(2):303–323.

Aruğaslan, O., Cook, D. O., and Kieschnick, R. (2004). Monitoring as a Motivation for IPO Underpricing. *Journal of Finance*, 59(5):2403–2420.

Barry, C. B. and Jennings, R. H. (1993). The Opening Price Performance of Initial Public Offerings of Common Stock. *Financial Management*, 22(1):54–63.

Benveniste, L. M. and Spindt, P. A. (1989). How Investment Bankers Determine the Offer Price and Allocation of New Issues. *Journal of Financial Economics*, 24(2):343–361.

Booth, J. R. and Chua, L. (1996). Ownership Dispersion, Costly Information, and IPO Underpricing. *Journal of Financial Economics*. 41(2):291–310.

Booth, J. R. and Smith, R. (1986). Capital Raising: Underwriting and the Certification Hypothesis. *Journal of Financial Economics*, 15(1–2):261–281.

Brennan, M. J. and Franks, J. (1997). Underpricing, Ownership and Control in Initial Public Offerings of Equity Securities in the UK. *Journal of Financial Economics*, 45(3):391–413.

Burkart, M. and Gromb, D. (1997). Large Shareholders, Monitoring, and the Value of the Firm. *Quarterly Journal of Economics*, 112(3):693–728.

Carter R. and Manaster, S. (1990). Initial Public Offerings and Underwriter Reputation. *Journal of Finance*, 45(3):1045–1067.

Claessens, S., Djankov, S., and Lang, L. H. P. (2000). The Separation of Ownership and Control in East Asian Corporations. *Journal of Financial Economics*, 58(1–2):81–112.

Cliff, M. T. and Denis, D. J. (2004). Do Initial Public Offering Firms Purchase Analyst Coverage with Underpricing? *Journal of Finance*, 59(6):2871–2901.

Cornelli, F. and Goldreich, D. (2001). Bookbuilding and Strategic Allocation. *Journal of Finance*, 56(6):2337–2370.

Daily, C. M., Certo, S. T., Dalton, D. R., and Roengpity, R. (2003). IPO Underpricing: A Meta-Analysis and Research Synthesis. *Entrepreneurship Theory and Practice*, 27(3):271–294.

Demirağ, I. and Serter, M. (2003). Ownership Patterns and Control in Turkish Listed Companies. *Corporate Governance*, 11(1):40–51.

Denis, K. D. and McConnell, J. J. (2003). International Corporate Governance. *Journal of Financial and Quantative Analysis*, 38(1):1–36.

Derrien, F. (2005). IPO Pricing in "Hot" Market Conditions: Who Leaves Money on the Table. *Journal of Finance*, 60(1):487–521.

Dyck, A. and Zingales, L. (2004). Private Benefits of Control: An International Comparison. *Journal of Finance*, 59(2):537–600.

Espenlaub, S. and Tonks, I. (1998). Post-IPO Directors' Sales and Reissuing Activity: An Empirical Test of IPO Signaling Models. *Journal of Business Finance and Accounting*, 25(9–10):1037–1080.

Fernando, C. S., Krishnamurthy, S., and Spindt, P. A. (2004). Are Share Price Levels Informative? Evidence from the Ownership, Pricing, Turnover and Performance of IPO Firms. *Journal of Financial Markets*, 7(4):377–403.

Field, L. C. and Karpoff, J. M. (2002). Takeover Defenses of IPO Firms. *Journal of Finance*, 57(5):1857–1890.

Field, L. C. and Sheehan, D. P. (2004). IPO Underpricing and Outside Blockholdings. *Journal of Corporate Finance*, 10(2):263–280.

Garfinkel, J. A. (1993). IPO Underpricing, Insider Selling and Subsequent Equity Offerings: Is Underpricing a Signal of Quality? *Financial Management*, 22(1):74–83.

Habib, M. A. and Ljungqvist, A. P. (2001). Underpricing and Entrepreneurial Wealth Losses in IPOs: Theory and Evidence. *Review of Financial Studies*, 14(2):433–458.

Hamao, Y., Packer, F., and Ritter, J. R. (2000). Institutional Affiliation and the Role of Venture Capital: Evidence from Initial Public Offerings in Japan. *Pacific-Basin Finance Journal*, 8(5):529–558.

Holderness, C. G. (2003). A Survey of Blockholders and Corporate Control. *FRBNY Economic Policy Review*, Spring:51–64.

Kiymaz, H. (2000). The Initial and Aftermarket Performance of IPOs in an Emerging Market: Evidence from Istanbul Stock Exchange. *Journal of Multinational Financial Management*, 10(2):213–227.

Kothare, M. (1997). The Effects of Equity Issues on Ownership Structure and Liquidity: A Comparison of Rights and Public Offerings. *Journal of Financial Economics*, 43(1):131–147.

Kula, V. (2005). The Impact of the Roles, Structure and Process of Boards on Firm Performance: Evidence from Turkey. *Corporate Governance*, 13(2):265–277.

La Porta, R., Lopez-de-Silanes, F., Shleifer, A., and Vishny, R. (1998). Law and Finance. *Journal of Political Economy*, 106(6):1113–1155.

La Porta, R., Lopez-de-Silanes, F., Shleifer, A. (1999). Corporate Ownership Around the World. *Journal of Finance*, 54(2):471–517.

La Porta, R., Lopez-de-Silanes, F., Shleifer, A., and Vishny, R. (2000). Investor Protection and Corporate Governance. *Journal of Financial Economics*, 58(1–2):3–27.

Lemmon, M. L. and Lins, K. V. (2003). Ownership Structure, Corporate Governance, and Firm Value: Evidence from the East Asian Financial Crisis. *Journal of Finance*, 58(4):1445–1468.

Lin, T. H. (1996). The Certification Role of Large Blockholders in Initial Public Offerings: The Case of Venture Capitalists. *Quarterly Journal of Business and Economics*, 35(2):55–65.

Lins, K. V. (2003). Equity Ownership and Firm Value in Emerging Markets. *Journal of Financial and Quantitative Analysis*, 38(1):159–184

Loughran, T. and Ritter, J. R. (2002). Why Don't Issuers Get Upset About Leaving Money on the Table in IPOs. *Review of Financial Studies*, 15(2):413–443.

Loughran, T. and Ritter, J. R. (2004). Why Has IPO Underpricing Changed Over Time? *Financial Management*, 33(3):5–37.

Loughran, T., Ritter, J. R. and Rydqvist, K. (1994). Initial Public Offerings: International Insights. *Pacific-Basin Finance Journal*, 2(2–3):165–199.

Marshall, A. P. (1998). Discussion of Post-IPO Directors' Sales and Reissuing Activity: An Empirical Test of IPO Signaling Models. *Journal of Business Finance and Accounting*, 25(9–10):1081–1088.

Maug, E. (1998). Large Shareholders as Monitors: Is There a Trade-Off between Liquidity and Control? *Journal of Finance*, 53(1):65–98.

Mello, A. S. and Parsons, J. E. (1998). Going Public and the Ownership Structure of the Firm. *Journal of Financial Economics*, 49(1):79–109.

Pagano, M. and Röell, A. (1998). The Choice of Stock Ownership Structure: Agency Costs, Monitoring, and the Decision to Go Public. *Quarterly Journal of Economics*, 113(1):187–225.

Pagano, M., Panetta, F., and Zingales, L. (1998). Why Do Companies Go Public? An Empirical Analysis. *Journal of Finance*, 53(1):27–64.

Pham, P. K., Kalev, P. S., and Steen, A. B. (2003). Underpricing, Stock Allocation, Ownership Structure and Post-Listing Liquidity of Newly Listed Firms. *Journal of Banking and Finance*, 27(5):919–947.

Ritter, J. R. (1998). Initial Public Offerings. *Contemporary Finance Digest*, 2(1):5–30.

Ritter, J. R. (2003). Differences between European and American IPO Markets. *European Financial Management*, 9(4):421–434.

Ritter, J. R. and Welch, I. (2002). A Review of IPO Activity, Pricing, and Allocations. *Journal of Finance*, 57(4):1795–1828.

Rock, K. (1986). Why New Issues are Underpriced. *Journal of Financial Economics*, 15(1–2):187–212.

Shleifer, A. and Vishny, R. (1997). A Survey of Corporate Governance. *Journal of Finance*, 52(2):737–783.

Smart, S. B. and Zutter, C. J. (2003). Control as a Motivation for Underpricing: A Comparison of Dual- and Single-Class IPOs. *Journal of Financial Economics*, 69(1):85–110.

Stoughton, N. M. and Zechner, J. (1998). IPO-Mechanism, Monitoring and Ownership Structure. *Journal of Financial Economics*, 49(1):47–77.

Su, D. (2004). Leverage, Insider Ownership, and the Underpricing of IPOs in China. *International Financial Markets, Institutions and Money*, 14(1):37–54.

Sullivan, M. J. and Unite, A. A. (2001). The Influence of Group Affiliation and the Underwriting Process on Emerging Market IPOs: The Case of the Philippines. *Pacific-Basin Finance Journal*, 9(5):487–512.

Welch, I. (1989). Seasoned Offerings, Imitation Costs, and the Underpricing of Initial Public Offerings. *Journal of Finance*, 44(1):421–450.

Yurtoğlu, B. B. (2000). Ownership, Control and Performance of Turkish Listed Firms. *Empirica*, 27(2):193–222.

Part Three
Corporate Structure and IPO Evaluation

17 IPOs and earnings management in Germany

Tereza Tykvová

Abstract

Managers of companies shift reported income among fiscal periods for various reasons. Several recent papers (Teoh et al., 1998a) have shown that companies are more aggressive in pushing earnings upwards around their initial public offering (IPO) date than in any other period. They argue that, due to large information asymmetries between investors and issuers, companies have incentives to manipulate earnings upwards in order to support high stock prices after the offering.

This chapter offers one of the first investigations of earnings management and IPOs in a European country. The study examines earnings management by companies in Germany measured by the level of their discretionary current accruals. Firstly, I investigate the hypothesis that companies manage their earnings upwards in the fiscal year when they go public. Secondly, I test whether the level of discretionary current accruals around the offering date has an impact on stock performance. In general, the evidence is consistent with managers who use upward earnings management in the fiscal year when the firm went public. The upward earnings manipulation around the offering date has a negative impact on performance.

17.1 Introduction

Empirical research has uncovered the manipulation of earnings by managers who shift reported income among fiscal periods. As early as the 1980s and the beginning of the 1990s, papers have been written about the active management of earnings. Healy (1985) documented that managers whose compensation was tied to reported earnings tended to manipulate earnings in order to receive a bonus. DeAngelo (1988) concluded that managers whose incumbency was threatened by a proxy contest tended to overstate earnings during the contest. Jones (1991) showed that managers made income-decreasing accruals during import relief investigations. In these papers, the reason for such opportunistic behavior by managers is to mislead the uninformed outsiders about the true profitability of a company (Fields et al., 2001).

Some authors reject this explanation and suggest an alternative scenario. In their opinion, managerial discretion improves the ability of earnings to reflect fundamental value. Subramanyam (1996) showed that discretional accruals communicated information about future firm profitability rather than being used in order to opportunistically manipulate reported earnings. Liberty and Zimmerman (1986) did not find any indication that managers of firms engaged in union negotiations systematically understated earnings in attempts to reduce wage concessions. DeAngelo's (1986) evidence does not support the hypothesis that managers systematically understated earnings before the management buyout. She argues that her results and those of Liberty and Zimmerman (1986) may be explained by the careful examination of firms' financial statements for evidence of income-reducing accounting techniques by those potentially affected by the manipulation.

Recent papers (Teoh et al., 1998a; Roosenboom et al., 2003) have shown that companies are more aggressive in pushing earnings upwards around their initial public offering (IPO) date than in any other period. They argue that, due to large information asymmetries between investors and issuers, companies have incentives to use upward earnings management in order to support high stock prices after the offering. Investors are unable to understand the full extent to which IPO firms engage in earnings management. This situation leads to a negative long-run post-IPO stock performance.

This chapter examines earnings management by companies in Germany measured by the level of their discretionary current accruals. The study offers one of the first investigations of earnings management and IPOs in a European country.[1] It deals with the 'Neuer Markt', a segment for young innovative companies in Germany launched in 1997. As far as the author knows, it is the first study dealing with earnings management by firms on the Neuer Markt. Earnings manipulation or aggressive accounting has been highlighted in the German press (see, for example, *Frankfurter Allgemeine Zeitung*, 25 August 2004) as the key explanation for the failure of this market segment and deserves an empirical evaluation. Another reason why this particular segment has been chosen for the investigation of earnings management around the IPO date in Germany is that there were not nearly as many IPOs in other market segments and in other periods.

The study focuses on two issues. Firstly, I investigate the hypothesis that companies in Germany manage their earnings upwards in the fiscal year when they go public. Secondly, I test whether the level of discretionary current accruals around the offering date has an impact on stock performance. It can be expected that earnings management is even more pronounced in the German IPO market where, in general, the potential new investors are less experienced than in the USA. In order to pursue these goals, I create a unique dataset encompassing all German IPOs which have occurred on the Neuer Markt. This dataset is compiled from several databases, some of which were hand collected. In general, the evidence is consistent with managers using upward earnings management in the fiscal year when the firm went public. The upward earnings manipulation around the offering date has a negative impact on the performance.

The rest of the chapter is organized as follows. Section 17.2 tenders a short historical and structural overview of the Neuer Markt. In this setting, the dataset is described and some descriptive statistics are given. Section 17.3 deals with the methodology of accrual measurement. In section 17.4 discretionary current accruals by fiscal years are analyzed. The relationship between earnings management and post-IPO stock performance is discussed in section 17.5. Section 17.6 states the conclusions.

---

[1] Most previous studies analyze the US market.

17.2 Data

One of the prime characteristics of the German IPO market is that its main development occurred rather recently. The average number of IPOs between 1949 and 1982 was only 3.3 per year. Beginning in 1983 this number increased, reaching an average of 19.5 companies between 1983 and 1996 (Franzke et al., 2003). The situation with the IPO market in Germany changed quite drastically with the establishment of the Neuer Markt in 1997, a segment for young growth companies. Its introduction was celebrated as a huge innovation for German IPO markets. This market segment started in 1997, with 11 initial public offerings, and went through an unprecedented growth period. Forty-one IPOs in 1998 were followed by 130 IPOs in 1999. This number was even exceeded in 2000, the peak of the market, with 133 IPOs. Many companies were rushed into the market in 1999 and 2000, even if they were too young for an IPO. More than 80% of all IPOs on the Neuer Markt took place within these 2 years.

In the second half of 2000, market conditions deteriorated and market valuations decreased, making IPOs more and more difficult. This was reflected by the drastic slow-down in the number of IPOs: in 2001, only 11 firms went public. In 2002, the situation became even more extreme, with only a single firm making it onto the Neuer Markt. This was the last firm with an IPO on the Neuer Markt. The brand disappeared in June 2003 after several cases of fraud and a massive reduction in market valuation. Earnings manipulation or aggressive accounting has been highlighted as the main reason for this failure. In this sense, this chapter analyzes whether companies were aggressive around their IPO in order to increase their valuation and whether the level of this aggressiveness influenced their post-IPO performance.

The Neuer Markt was more demanding in regards to listing, reporting, and disclosure requirements compared to other German segments. Firms on the Neuer Markt had to use IAS or US GAAP. Compared to firms listed in other segments and former IPOs, which were rather well-established companies in mature industries, firms going public on the Neuer Markt were substantially smaller and younger.

My analysis is based on a unique hand-collected database of IPOs on Germany's Neuer Markt. Only real IPOs were considered. Thus, firms that were listed on a different exchange when going public on the Neuer Markt were excluded. Using this approach, 327 IPOs were identified. The data were extracted from several sources. From the 'Deutsche Börse AG', I received the date of the IPO, the issue size, and the offer price. The information on the firm's age (AGE), size, and the book value at IPO was collected from the listing prospectuses of the companies. With these data I calculated market value (MV), the book-to-market ratio (BTM) at the IPO, and the issue size in euros based on the offer price (SIZE). When they went public on the Neuer Markt, the firms were 13 years old and their market value was nearly 250 million euros on average (Table 17.1).

Table 17.1 Summary statistics for the sample firms (means)

AGE (days)	BTM (10^6)	MV (euro, millions)	SIZE (euro, millions)	RETURN (BHR, 1 year)
4758.0	2921.3	247.4	53.2	−0.39

The NEMAX All Share Index returns and the individual stock prices and dividends came from the 'Bloomberg' database. A few companies were not found in Bloomberg, therefore Thomson Financial Datastream was used as well. One particular outlier, EM.TV, was excluded from the calculations on performance.[2] The market return (MARKET$_i$) is the buy-and-hold return on the NEMAX All Share Index computed separately for each firm i in the corresponding period between 1 and 2 years after its IPO (closing prices). The return of firm i (RETURN$_i$) is the buy-and-hold raw return during the period between 1 and 2 years after its IPO (closing prices); dividends during this 1-year period are included. The median return is −61% and the mean reaches −39% (Table 17.1).

The accounting data are based on information from the Hoppenstedt Bilanzdatenbank. This is a database consisting of German companies, which includes detailed data from annual reports of more than 6000 non-financial German companies. The final IPO sample consists of non-financial German companies that went public on the Neuer Markt and were found in the Hoppenstedt Bilanzdatenbank. As a result, there are 250 IPOs in the sample.

Data from consolidated accounts are used. Dummy variables are also employed for different accounting methods. The year of the first annual report as a listed company is labeled year 0 (Teoh et al., 1998b). For 187 companies, information on current accruals in year 0 is available. The reason why the first report after the IPO is used is that old investors cannot sell their shares immediately after the IPO but have to retain them for a certain period of time (lockup). On the Neuer Markt in Germany, this period lasted for a minimum of 6 months. Due to data restrictions, I concentrate only on years −1 through +2. For other years, the number of available observations drops substantially. For example, for the calculation of accruals in year −2 data from year −3 are needed in order to ascertain changes. This information is available in Hoppenstedt Bilanzdatenbank for only 49 firms of the 250 IPOs in my sample. All financial data before 1999 were converted into euros.

Moreover, data were collected on the quality and experience of lead underwriters and designated sponsors.[3] The rank of an underwriter (UNDRANK$_i$) depended on his or her activities as the lead underwriter, namely the number of new issues on the Neuer Markt and their volume in the previous year. The rank of a designated sponsor (DSRANK$_i$) was assigned quarterly and based equally on the number of mandates on the Neuer Markt and on the rating with the Deutsche Börse AG in the preceding period. The reputation measures were designed in the following way: the lower the number, the better the rank (thus, 1 indicates the best rank).

17.3 Methodology of accrual measurement

Reported earnings are determined by cash flows from operations plus accruals. In order to investigate earnings management, I focus on current accruals (CAs), since

---

[2] This firm shows impressive returns in the 2-year post-IPO period, but from then on it turns out to be one of the most widely discussed cases of fraud on the Neuer Markt. Since EM.TV extremely outperforms all other firms, it would clearly dominate the estimations. In order to exclude this particular influence, I decided to eliminate EM.TV from my sample.

[3] Each share on the Neuer Markt had to have at least two designated sponsors. Their main task was to provide liquidity for the trading of this security.

managers have greater flexibility and control over current than over long-term accruals. CAs are computed from balance sheets. This approach is used by the majority of studies dealing with earnings management (Teoh et al., 1998b; Bartov et al., 2001; Dechow et al., 1995; Hochberg, 2003; Rangan, 1998; Sloan, 1996). Alternatively, Hribar and Collins (2002) argued that computing accruals directly from the statement of cash flows is superior to a balance sheet approach under certain circumstances. In particular, if mergers and acquisitions take place, the balance sheet approach may lead to estimation errors. However, the cash flow statement is not available in Hoppenstedt Bilanzdatenbank.

Thus, current accruals in this chapter are measured as:

CA = Δ (current assets − cash) − Δ (current liabilities − current maturity of long-term debt).

CAs can be broken up into non-discretionary and discretionary parts. Whereas non-discretionary current accruals (NDCAs) are constrained by rules, firm, and industry conditions, discretionary current accruals (DCAs) are subject to management. It is assumed that managers of the issuing firm can raise reported earnings by altering discretionary accruals. The investigation is based on the underlying assumption that earnings management arising from incentives other than opportunistic earnings manipulation due to the IPO event is not systematically different for the sample and the control firms.

However, it is difficult to infer how much of the accruals are discretionary and what adjustments are necessary in order to reflect the business conditions. There are several ways to specify a model for the estimation of DCAs (for the evaluation of the relative performance of the different models see Bartov et al., 2001; Dechow et al., 1995). However, it is still an open empirical question whether these discretionary accruals models are able to separate accruals into discretionary and non-discretionary components properly and detect earnings management (Fields et al., 2001; Guay et al., 1996). Therefore, in contrast to the existing literature where typically only one measure of DCAs is used, I employ several measures in order to check the robustness of the outcomes.

In the first model that is used in this chapter, the change in CAs (divided by lagged total assets) is analyzed (DeAngelo, 1986). Here, NDCAs are equal to lagged relative CAs. Thus:

$$\text{DCA}_{i,t} = \frac{\text{CA}_{i,t}}{\text{TA}_{i,t-1}} - \frac{\text{CA}_{i,t-1}}{\text{TA}_{i,t-2}}. \tag{17.1}$$

This model is labeled as 'Change in CA' (Model A).

However, firms may be managing earnings in both years. So, more sophisticated approaches for the estimation of DCAs have been developed in the literature. One method used in previous research was to estimate firm-specific coefficients (Jones, 1991) using past values of the firm's current accruals (CAs), total assets (TA), and revenues (REV) in a time-series setting. For the purposes of this study, the time-series approach is not applied since the firms in this sample are very young. Thus, there are typically only a few observations for each single firm.

An alternative approach used in this chapter is cross-sectional estimation, following Bartov et al. (2001) and Subramanyam (1996), who pointed out that the cross-sectional version of the modified Jones model is superior, ex-ante, to the time-series version. First, by not requiring lengthy historical data, the cross-sectional model is less subject to survival bias and allows the inclusion of firms with short histories. Second, the number of observations used in each estimation is considerably higher in the cross-sectional version, which increases the accuracy of the resulting coefficient estimates. Third, non-stationarity is much less of a concern for the cross-sectional version than it is for the time-series version.

The most popular choice in the literature for estimating DCAs is, for each sector j and year t, the estimation of the following model (Hochberg, 2003), using data from annual reports of all firms k in that sector in that year (the issuer is excluded):

$$\frac{CA_{jk,t}}{TA_{jk,t-1}} = \alpha_{j,t,0} \frac{1}{TA_{jk,t-1}} + \alpha_{j,t,1} \frac{\Delta REV_{jk,t}}{TA_{jk,t-1}} + \varepsilon_{jk,t}. \tag{17.2}$$

Then, the NDCAs of firm i in sector j in year t are determined using the estimated sector- and year-specific coefficients:

$$NDCA_{ji,t} = \hat{\alpha}_{j,t,0} \frac{1}{TA_{ji,t-1}} + \hat{\alpha}_{j,t,1} \frac{\Delta REV_{ji,t} - \Delta TR_{ji,t}}{TA_{ji,t-1}}. \tag{17.3}$$

The change in trade receivables (ΔTR) is subtracted from the revenue growth (modified Jones model). The reason is that the issuer might manipulate credit sales in order to obtain high sales prior to the offering by allowing generous credit policies (Dechow et al., 1995). The DCA of firm i in sector j and year t are calculated as:

$$DCA_{ji,t} = \frac{CA_{ji,t}}{TA_{ji,t-1}} - NDCA_{ji,t}. \tag{17.4}$$

In a large number of the sectors based on two-digit NACE codes, there are only a few firms in Hoppenstedt Bilanzdatenbank. Therefore, instead of using sector (and performance) matched samples I employ pooled samples. Here, two alternatives based on the modified Jones model for the estimation of the coefficient's set are used:

1   A single regression for all German firms (pooling of all sectors j) within each single year (year-specific, but not sector-specific coefficients, as in, for example, Roosenboom et al., 2003); this model is labeled 'DCA, Years' or Model B.
2   A single regression for all Neuer Markt firms within each single year (year-specific, but not sector-specific coefficients); this model is labeled 'DCA, Neuer Markt' or Model C.

Furthermore, I re-estimate all models using dummy variables indicating the accounting rules used. The results of all additional models with dummy variables for the different accounting methods are very similar to those without these dummy variables. Therefore, the results are not reported within the chapter.

The findings may vary among different models because each of them relies on a different set of assumptions that are unlikely to hold for all firms. Thus, each model has its advantages and disadvantages. This fact can quickly be demonstrated for one issue, namely the appropriate benchmark for the measurement of NDCAs. The advantage of Model A is that for the calculation of earnings management I do not need other firms that might be very different from the firms listed on the Neuer Markt and thus be an inappropriate benchmark for the estimation of NDCAs.

However, firms may manage earnings in both years. The advantage of Model C is that firms on the Neuer Markt are similar. Thus, an appropriate estimation sample for the discretionary accruals parameter is used. On the other hand, this sample is quite limited in size, which is a disadvantage of this approach. Moreover, there is a large fraction of IPOs in this sample, particularly in the years 1999 and 2000.

17.4 Earnings management by fiscal years

Earnings management shifts the recognition of transactions and events to periods other than those in which the related cash flow occurs. Therefore, over the long run, accruals will total zero since, throughout the life of the business, the sum of earnings must equal the sum of cash flows. As a consequence of excessive upward earnings management, negative accruals in the following or precedent year(s) must occur.

In this section I examine DCAs by fiscal years. I want to analyze whether companies manage their earnings upwards by concealing poor performance or exaggerating good performance around the IPO date. The investigation is built on the arguments made by Teoh et al. (1998a) and Roosenboom et al. (2003) that companies have incentives to use high accruals around the offering date in order to support high stock prices after the IPO. In particular, I look at whether companies have positive DCAs in the IPO year and whether those are equalized in the years preceding and following the IPO. I expect an increase between year −1 and year 0 that should serve as a positive signal for new potential investors who ultimately increase their demand for shares. Thus, old investors can get higher prices for their old shares when the lockup period expires.

Roosenboom et al. (2003) documented large significant positive DCAs in year 0 and large significant negative DCAs in year +1, whereas Teoh et al. (1998a) reported significant negative values no earlier than in year +5; for the years 0 through +4 they are positive. Due to data restrictions, in this study only 1 year before the IPO and 2 years thereafter are considered.

Hypothesis 1: discretionary current accruals in year 0 are positive and reach the largest level (within the timespan year −1 through year +2). There is an increase (decrease) between years −1 and 0 (years 0 and +1).

I can detect significant differences in DCAs during different fiscal years. The results using alternative models for the determination of DCAs (see section 17.3) are shown in Table 17.2. This table reports on the mean, median, standard deviation, maximum, minimum, and percentage of positive values of DCAs in different fiscal years (−1, 0, +1, and +2). All DCA-values are expressed as a fraction of lagged total assets. Managers of IPO firms from the Neuer Markt employed large DCAs in the first fiscal year ending after the offering (year 0). Since the sample contains huge outliers, I concentrate on the comparison of medians (z-values). The medians of DCAs in years −1, +1, and +2 were highly statistically significant and negative (with only one exception). In year 0 the medians were positive.

This upward earnings management in the IPO year was equalized in the subsequent and previous years. The changes in DCAs between fiscal years were large and statistically significant. Prior to the offering, between the years −1 and 0, the level of DCAs increased significantly in all three models. On the contrary, it declined significantly between years 0 and +1, as expected.

Table 17.2 Discretionary current accruals by fiscal years

	Year −1	Year 0	Year +1	Year +2
Model A: Change in CA				
Mean DCA	19.33	2.72	2.78	−2.10
t-value	1.00	1.69*	1.02	−1.46(*)
Median DCA	0.08	0.44	−0.33	−0.05
z-value	1.21	6.51***	−5.86***	−2.78***
St. dev.	128.8	17.0	35.5	19.5
Max DCA	854.1	174.2	328.8	4.1
Min DCA	−3.6	−5.6	−172.6	−246.5
No. of obs.	44	111	171	183
% positive	65.9	76.6	27.5	42.1
Between years		*−1 and 0*	*0 and +1*	*+1 and +2*
t-value		−1.34	0.02	−1.61(*)
z-value		3.73***	−8.68***	5.03***
Model B: DCA, Years				
Mean DCA	−0.86	21.42	0.12	−0.43
t-value	−3.39***	0.88	0.10	−1.14
Median DCA	−0.24	0.04	−0.08	−0.12
z-value	−5.42***	0.35	−3.93***	−7.01***
St. dev.	2.7	330.9	17.3	5.3
Max DCA	14.3	4499.6	167.9	35.3

	−1 and 0	0 and +1	+1 and +2
Min DCA	−12.8	−144.8	−49.1
No. of obs.	118	218	200
% positive	28.8	39.4	24.5
Between years	*−1 and 0*	*0 and +1*	*+1 and +2*
t-value	0.73	−0.95	−0.43
z-value	**4.54***	**−2.33**	**−1.50(*)**

Model C: DCA, Neuer Markt

	−1 and 0	0 and +1	+1 and +2
Mean DCA	−7.15	0.07	−0.86
t-value	**−5.21***	0.04	−1.15
Median DCA	−0.23	−0.05	−0.12
z-value	**−5.10***	**−2.54***	**−6.20***
St. dev.	1.9	30.3	10.6
Max DCA	2.5	311.8	35.4
Min DCA	−7.3	−287.5	−136.3
No. of obs.	118	218	200
% positive	33.1	43.6	28.0
Between years	*−1 and 0*	*0 and +1*	*+1 and +2*
t-value	−0.96	1.33	−0.41
z-value	**4.65***	**−2.60***	**−1.96**

t-value is the value of the parametric *t*-test (two-sample *t*-test for the comparison between years) for the means and *z*-value is the value of the Wilcoxon signed-ranks test (Wilcoxon rank-sum test for the comparison between years) for the medians. Asterisks denote significance at the 10% (*), 5% (**), and 1% (***) levels. An asterisk in parentheses indicates significance at the 15% level.

Depending on the model, the difference between the share of firms with positive DCAs in year 0 and in year -1 amounted to values between 10.7 (Model A) and 24.7 (Model C) percentage points. These results are broadly consistent with my assumptions about earnings manipulation in year 0 and findings from former studies on pre- and post-IPO earnings management.

17.5 Earnings management and stock performance

Several recent empirical papers, based mostly on US data, investigated earnings management and demonstrated the impact of accruals on future firm performance. Rangan (1998) documented that upward earnings management in the IPO year predicted not only the stock performance, but also earnings changes in the subsequent year. Teoh et al. (1998a, b) provided evidence for the underperformance of initial public and seasoned equity offerings with high DCAs respectively and argued that investors naively extrapolated previous earnings without fully adjusting for the potential manipulation of reported earnings. Bhojraj and Swaminathan (2003) showed that the same story held for bond markets: corporate bonds of firms with high accruals underperformed corporate bonds of firms with low accruals. Thus, securities of firms with high accruals typically are overvalued. Bradshaw et al. (2001) provided evidence that sell-side analysts and independent auditors did not alert investors to the (predictable) future earnings problems associated with high accruals. They showed that these predictable earnings declines were not incorporated in the forecasts of analysts and auditors. Teoh and Wong (2002) demonstrated that analysts were overly optimistic about firms with large past accruals. This credulity about large positive accruals explains investor mispricing of stocks with high accruals.

In this section, an analysis is performed to determine whether DCAs in the IPO year predicted the post-IPO underperformance of firms on the Neuer Markt. The upward earnings management around the IPO date might be misunderstood by market participants and therefore may lead to a negative long-run post-IPO stock performance (Sloan, 1996; Teoh et al., 1998a). According to Mashruwala et al. (2004), mispricing may result from the nonexistence of close substitutes for stocks with extremely high accruals. My key objective is to investigate whether managed accruals in year 0 have a negative impact on the post-IPO performance on the Neuer Markt. The hypothesis is that investors either are not sophisticated enough to discount for earnings management and/or do not have close substitutes for stocks with very high accruals.

This investigation requires an appropriate measure for long-run returns. To analyze post-IPO performance time series, three-factor models designed by Fama and French (1993) are commonly used, where portfolio returns are regressed on the market (beta) factor, size, and book-to-market effects. Some studies consider additional factors, e.g. leverage and liquidity (Eckbo and Norli, 2005), or the previous return (Brav et al., 2000). Due to a short timespan and lack of data on factors for Germany, I do not perform factor model analysis. Instead, I employ an event–time cross-section analysis analogous to Ritter (1991) and Tykvová and Walz (2005), with DCA as an additional explanatory variable. I use buy-and-hold returns as these are the most relevant for an investor. A similar approach has already been used by Roosenboom et al. (2003), Luo and Schuster (2002), and Teoh et al. (1998a).

One-year buy-and-hold returns in the period between 1 and 2 years after the IPO are used. Thus, aftermarket returns are typically calculated beginning several months after the fiscal year ends. The reason is that the accrual information should be available prior to the return cumulation period. Thus, I start 12 months after the IPO (see Figure 17.1). Due to the dataset and the specific situation of the German market, I concentrate on this timespan. Since the bulk of all IPOs took place in 2000 and the Neuer Markt ceased to exist in 2003, a longer time period would exclude a large number of IPOs. Thus, I deviate from the convention of researchers using US data to look at 3- or even 5-year returns (Ritter, 1991). Thus:

$$RETURN_i = \frac{P_{i,t+2} + D_{i,t+2} - P_{i,t+1}}{P_{i,t+1}} \qquad (17.5)$$

with $P_{i,t+1}$ ($P_{i,t+2}$) being the share price of the firm i 1 year (2 years) after the IPO. Additionally, the dividends during this 1-year period ($D_{i,t+2}$) are taken into account.

Hypothesis 2: initial public offerings with large discretionary current accruals in year 0 experience poor stock price performance.

First, I look at this issue using a univariate approach. I divide the firms into quartiles based on their 1-year buy-and-hold abnormal returns (with the NEMAX All Share Index as a benchmark):

$$BHAR_i = RETURN_i - MARKET_i$$

The median DCAs for the lowest and the highest performance quartiles are depicted in Table 17.3. All DCA-values are expressed as a fraction of lagged total assets. The median DCAs in the lowest performance quartile were always larger than those in the highest performance quartile, as expected. The difference in two cases (Models B and C) was highly statistically significant. Thus, firms with high abnormal returns had lower DCAs in year 0. Moreover, DCAs in the lowest performance quartile were always statistically significant and positive, whereas in the highest performance quartile they were positive in only one case.

In the next step, I analyze the issue of underperformance using a multivariate approach. To control the influence of DCAs on performance, I expand the set of independent variables used in traditional cross-section models (Ritter, 1991). Thus, 1-year buy-and-hold raw firm returns (RETURN) are regressed on the respective market return in this period (MARKET), various control variables (MV, BTM, AGE, DSRANK, UNDRANK), and finally DCA in a cross-section. The results are shown in Table 17.4. Since there are large outliers, I perform robust regression. After an

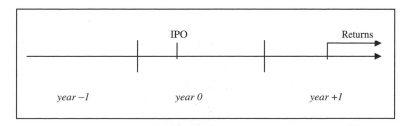

Figure 17.1 Timeline: fiscal years, IPO and returns

Table 17.3 Median DCAs for the lowest and the highest performance quartiles

	Model A		Model B		Model C	
	Median DCA	z-value	Median DCA	z-value	Median DCA	z-value
Lowest BHAR quartile	0.70	2.86***	0.19	1.56(*)	0.10	1.68*
Highest BHAR quartile	0.38	2.60***	−0.16	−1.29	−0.00	−0.82
z-value (difference)	0.85		1.88*		1.74*	

z-value in the columns is the value of the Wilcoxon signed-ranks test; z-value in the last row is the value of the Wilcoxon rank-sum test for the comparison between groups. Asterisks denote significance at the 10% (*), 5% (**), and 1% (***) levels. An asterisk in parentheses indicates significance at the 15% level.

Table 17.4 Robust regressions of post-IPO returns (%)

	Model A	Model B	Model C
MARKET	110.12***	104.26***	109.34***
MV	−0.03***	−0.02**	−0.02**
BTM	27.21	32.05	31.86
AGE (years)	0.10	0.10	0.10
DSRANK	−0.14	−0.06	−0.15
UNDRANK	0.61	−0.16	−0.24
DCA	0.09	−0.39(*)	−0.14***
No. of obs.	102	172	173
F-value	6.99***	11.02***	14.49***

Asterisks denote significance at the 5% (**) and 1% (***) levels. An asterisk in parentheses indicates significance at the 15% level.

initial screening based on Cook's distance >1, gross outliers are eliminated prior to calculating starting values. Then, as suggested by Li (1985), Huber iterations are performed followed by biweight iterations (Hamilton, 1991).

In two of the three models depicted in Table 17.4, DCA had a significant negative impact on post-IPO returns. Upwards earnings management in the IPO year resulted in underperformance. Moreover, larger firms had significantly lower returns. Furthermore, the market return in the respective period was highly statistically significant. The results remain similar if time and sector dummies are included (not reported here).

There are two main reasons why these results should be interpreted with caution. First, long-run returns are sensitive to the computation method (Barber and Lyon, 1997; Kothari and Warner, 1997). Thus, another measurement method could deliver different results. Secondly, due to data restrictions, I concentrated on a 1-year timespan. However, 1 year may be too short for the investigation of long-run returns.

17.6   Conclusion

This chapter examines earnings management by companies on the Neuer Markt, measured by the level of their discretionary current accruals. This issue is of interest not only to academics, but also to practitioners and regulators. One of the key contributions of this study is its focus on the German market. Whereas nearly all other investigations consider the US market, this chapter investigates whether the same mechanisms of upward earnings management around the initial public offering date and its negative impact on stock performance can be found in the German market as well. It is one of the first studies dealing with initial public offerings and earnings management in a European country.

Using different models for the estimation of discretionary current accruals, evidence shows that managers of German companies use earnings management around the offering date in a similar way as their US counterparts. They use large positive discretionary current accruals in the fiscal year when the firm goes public (year 0). Also, they become significantly negative in the subsequent 2 years. In particular, the increase in the level of discretionary current accruals between years −1 and 0, as well as the decrease between years 0 and +1, are highly statistically significant. So, earnings in the IPO year are typically manipulated upwards.

The level of discretionary current accruals around the IPO influences the stock price performance. A negative impact of upward earnings management on the long-run returns is found. Thus, investors are unable to understand the full extent to which IPO firms engage in earnings management.

However, the results must be interpreted with care since the sample is small and the time period under review is very specific, with a huge rise and fall in stock prices and IPO activities. Moreover, the results sometimes hold only for some and not for all models of discretionary current accruals. In addition, the consequences of the potential error embedded in estimated discretionary current accruals using the balance sheet approach are ignored. Furthermore, it is assumed that the motive for upward earnings management is the IPO event and that other incentives that may induce manipulation of earnings are not systematically different between sample and control firms. Despite these limitations, hopefully the results remain interesting.

Acknowledgments – Financial support by the German Research Foundation (DFG) is gratefully acknowledged. Christian Schwab, Engin Celebi, and Waldemar Rotfuß did substantial work in data collection and organization. I am grateful for the helpful comments provided by the participants of the 2004 Meeting of the German Finance Association (DGF) in Tübingen and of the 2005 Royal Economic Society Annual Conference in Nottingham.

References

Barber, M. B. and Lyon, J. D. (1997). Detecting Long-Run Abnormal Stock Returns: The Empirical Power and Specification of Test Statistics. *Journal of Financial Economics*, 43(3):341–372.

Bartov, E., Gul, F., and Tsui, J. (2001). Discretionary-Accruals Models and Audit Qualifications. *Journal of Accounting and Economics*, 30(3):421–452.

Bhojraj, S. and Swaminathan, B. (2003). How Does the Corporate Bond Market Value Capital Investments and Accruals? Discussion Paper, Cornell University.

Bradshaw, M., Richardson, S., and Sloan, R. (2001). Do Analysts and Auditors Use Information in Accruals? *Journal of Accounting Research*, 39(1):45–74.

Brav, A., Geczy, C., and Gompers, P. A. (2000). Is the Abnormal Return Following Equity Issuances Anomalous. *Journal of Financial Economics*, 56(2): 209–249.

DeAngelo, L. E. (1986). Accounting Numbers as Market Valuation Substitutes: A Study of Management Buyouts of Public Stockholders. *Accounting Review*, 61(3):400–420.

DeAngelo, L. E. (1988). Managerial Competition, Information Costs, and Corporate Governance: The Use Accounting Performance Measures in Proxy Contests. *Journal of Accounting and Economics*, 10(1):3–36.

Dechow, P., Sloan, R., and Sweeney, A. (1995). Detecting Earnings Management. *Accounting Review*, 70(2):193–225.

Eckbo, B. E. and Norli, O. (2005). Liquidity Risk, Leverage, and Long-Run IPO Returns. *Journal of Corporate Finance*, 11(1–2):1–35.

Fama, E. F. and French, K. R. (1993). Common Risk Factors in the Returns of Stocks and Bonds. *Journal of Financial Economics*, 33(1):3–55.

Fields, T., Lys, T., and Vincent, L. (2001). Empirical Research on Accounting Choice. *Journal of Accounting and Economics*, 31(1–3):255–307.

Frankfurter Allgemeine Zeitung (25 August 2004). Eine Kette von Skandalen.

Franzke, S., Grohs, S., and Laux, C. (2003). Initial Public Offerings and Venture Capital in Germany. Discussion Paper 2003/26, Center for Financial Studies, Franfurt, Germany.

Guay, W., Kothari, S., and Watts, R. (1996). A Market-Based Evaluation of Discretionary Accruals Models. *Journal of Accounting Research*, 34(1): 83–105.

Hamilton, L. C. (1991). How Robust is Robust Regression? *Stata Technical Bulletin*, 2(2):21–26.

Healy, P. M. (1985). The Effect of Bonus Schemes on Accounting Decisions. *Journal of Accounting and Economics*, 7(1–3):85–107.

Hochberg, Y. (2003). Venture Capital and Corporate Governance in the Newly Public Firm. Discussion Paper, Cornell University.

Hribar, P. and Collins, D. W. (2002). Errors in Estimating Accruals: Implications for Empirical Research. *Journal of Accounting Research*, 40(1):105–134.

Jones, J. (1991). Earnings Management During Import Relief Investigations. *Journal of Accounting Research*, 29(2):193–228.

Kothari, S. P. and Warner, J. B. (1997). Measuring Long-Horizon Security Price Performance. *Journal of Financial Economics*, 43(3):301–339.

Li, G. (1985). Robust Regression. In: Exploring *Data Tables, Trends, and Shapes* (Hoaglin, D. C., Mosteller, F. and Tukey, J. W., eds), pp. 281–340. John Wiley, New York.

Liberty, S. and Zimmerman, J. (1986). Labor Union Contract Negotiations and Accounting Choices. *Accounting Review*, 61(4):692–712.

Luo, J. and Schuster, J. (2002). Management Behaviour and Market Response. Discussion Paper, London School of Economics.

Mashruwala, C., Rajgopal, S., and Shelvin, T. (2004). Why is the Accrual Anomaly Not Arbitraged Away? Discussion Paper, University of Washington.

Rangan, S. (1998). Earnings Management and the Performance of Seasoned Equity Offerings. *Journal of Financial Economics*, 50(1):101–122.

Ritter, J. R. (1991). The Long-Run Performance of Initial Public Offerings. *Journal of Finance*, 46(1):3–27.

Roosenboom, P., der Goot, T. V. and Mertens, G. (2003). Earnings Management and Initial Public Offerings: Evidence from the Netherlands. *International Journal of Accounting*, 38(3):243–266.

Sloan, R. (1996). Do Stock Prices Fully Reflect Information in Accruals and Cash Flows About Future Earnings? *Accounting Review*, 71(4):289–315.

Subramanyam, K. (1996). The Pricing of Discretionary Accruals. *Journal of Accounting and Economics*, 22(1–3):249–281.

Teoh, S. H., Welch, I., and Wong, T. J. (1998a). Earnings Management and the Long-Run Market Performance of Initial Public Offerings. *Journal of Finance*, 53(6):1935–1974.

Teoh, S. H., Welch, I., and Wong, T. J. (1998b). Earnings Management and the Underperformance of Seasoned Equity Offerings. *Journal of Financial Economics*, 50(1):63–99.

Teoh, S. H. and Wong, T. J. (2002). Why New Issues and High-Accrual Firms Underperform: The Role of Analysts' Credulity. *Review of Financial Studies*, 15(3):869–900.

Tykvová, T. and Walz, U. (2005). Are IPOs of Different VCs Different? RICAFE Working Paper No. 019.

18 Signaling and the valuation of IPOs: regression tests

Steven Xiaofan Zheng

Abstract

Downes and Heinkel (1982) and Ritter (1984) tested the signaling model in Leland and Pyle (1977) and found evidence supporting it. I examine the regression model they use and find a possible bias. Simulations show that their regression model leads to highly significant results even when randomly generated inputs are used. An alternative regression model is suggested. Using the alternative model, I find evidence supporting the Leland and Pyle (1977) signaling model. Additional tests also provide evidence favoring the signaling model.

18.1 Introduction

Downes and Heinkel (1982) and Ritter (1984) tested the signaling model in Leland and Pyle (1977) and found evidence supporting it. I examine the regression model they used and find a possible bias. Simulations show that their regression model leads to highly significant results even when randomly generated inputs are used. An alternative regression model is suggested. Using the alternative model, I find evidence supporting the Leland and Pyle (1977) signaling model. Additional tests also provide evidence favoring the signaling model.

Downes and Heinkel (1982) and Ritter (1984) are two influential papers trying to test the signaling model in Leland and Pyle (1977). They found that the value of initial public offering (IPO) firms is positively related to the proportion of shares retained by entrepreneurs. This can be interpreted as evidence supporting the model. However, the regression model they use may be subject to a spurious correlation bias. I find that their regression model is similar to an accounting identity. Theoretically, the model can generate significant results even when no theoretical relation exists between firm value and share retention. In simulations, the model leads to highly significant results even when the signaling relation does not exist. A small change to the model avoids the spurious correlation. Empirical tests using the refined model do show a positive relation between share retention and the equity value of IPO firms. This is consistent with the signaling model. Additional tests try to distinguish the signaling model from other possible explanations. The results are most favorable to the signaling model. However, other explanations cannot be completely ruled out.

The organization of the rest of this chapter is as follows. Section 18.2 shows the simulation tests of the correlation bias. An alternative regression model and the tests using this model are described in section 18.3. Section 18.4 explores other possible explanations to the test results in section 18.3. Section 18.5 concludes this chapter.

18.2   Regression model misspecification

In their classic paper, Leland and Pyle (1977) constructed a firm valuation model in which the current value of a firm is a function of the fraction of equity retained by the entrepreneur. They assumed that the entrepreneur knows the expected future cash flow of the firm and that potential investors do not. It is costly for entrepreneurs to retain a significant ownership interest in their firms because by doing so they forgo diversification of their personal portfolios. Therefore, they will retain a significant ownership interest only if they expect the future cash flows to be high relative to their firms' current value, so that rational investors see α, the fraction of equity retained by the entrepreneur, as a signal of firm value. Specifically, Leland and Pyle (1977) showed that in the context of the CAPM the value of the firm will be given by:

$$V(\alpha) = -\frac{bZ}{1+r}[\log(1-\alpha) + \alpha] + K, \tag{18.1}$$

where V is the market value of the firm, r is the riskless interest rate, b is the risk aversion parameter in the entrepreneur's utility function, K is the amount of capital outlay, and Z is a constant related to the variance of market return, the variance of the firm's cash flow, and the covariance between market return and cash flow. In this model, the market value of the firm is positively related to the fraction of equity retained by entrepreneurs.

Based on Leland and Pyle (1977), Downes and Heinkel (1982) and Ritter (1984) examined the empirical relation between IPO firm value and pre-IPO owners' retention of shares using regressions. Their regression models can be simplified to the following:

$$V_{Ej} = b_0 + b_1 F_j + b_2 \alpha_j + u_j, \tag{18.2}$$

where, for firm j, V_E is the total market value of equity after IPO, calculated as the product of offer price, P, and shares outstanding after the IPO, N. Downes and Heinkel (1982) and Ritter (1984) noted that their results did not change if market price is used instead of offer price. F is the amount of funds raised in the IPO, calculated as the product of P and the number of primary shares in the initial offer, N_p. In Downes and Heinkel (1982) and Ritter (1984), F is used to account for capital outlay K. α is the proportionate ownership retained by the entrepreneurs, calculated as $(N_0 - N_s)/N$, where N_0 is the number of shares owned by pre-IPO shareholders before the IPO and N_s is the number of secondary shares offered by pre-IPO shareholders. In both Downes and Heinkel (1982) and Ritter (1984), earnings is also included as an explanatory variable. It is not relevant to the analysis here and thus is excluded. It is included later in alternative models. In Downes and Heinkel (1982), $\hat{\alpha}$, which is equal to $\alpha + \log(1-\alpha)$, is used instead of α. $\hat{\alpha}$ is negatively related to α. Both Downes and Heinkel (1982) and Ritter (1982) found that V_E is positively related to α in their regression results. Downes and Heinkel (1982) interpreted this as evidence supporting Leland and Pyle (1977). Ritter (1984) suggested that the results are also consistent with an agency hypothesis and a wealth effect hypothesis.

However, regression model (18.2) may be subject to a correlation bias, which may cause a spurious positive relationship between V_E and α even when no signaling effect exists. Specifically, we can express firm value V as:

$$V_E = NP = N_pP + N_0P = F + (N\alpha + N_s)P \Rightarrow V_E = \frac{F + N_sP}{1 - \alpha} \qquad (18.3)$$

This expression shows that V_E can always be expressed as a function of F and α. In other words, it seems market value of equity is always positively related to the amount of funds raised and the proportion of shares retained, irrespective of the validity of Leland and Pyle's signaling model. Any correlation detected by model (18.2) may be just the result of the arithmetic relation between the variables instead of the correlation predicted by Leland and Pyle (1977). And this will not change if we replace offer price by market price. To some extent, estimating regression model (18.2) is like regressing $1/(1 - x)$ on x: The regression coefficient will always be highly significant and the R-square will always be very high.

This issue can be addressed from another angle. In Leland and Pyle (1977)'s signal model, V, the market value of firm, includes both V_E and the market value of debt, V_D. For most IPO firms, we can assume that V_D is very close to the book value of debt. K, the capital outlay, actually includes not only F, the new capital raised, but also the capital invested by entrepreneurs. We can use A_b, total assets before IPO, to represent the capital invested by entrepreneurs. So equation (18.1) can be rearranged as:

$$V_E + V_D = -\frac{bZ}{1+r}[\log(1 - \alpha) + \alpha] + A_b + F \Rightarrow V_{Eb} - B_E$$

$$\qquad (18.4)$$

$$= -\frac{bZ}{1+r}[\log(1 - \alpha) + \alpha].$$

In this equation, V_{Eb} is the market value of entrepreneur's equity (including both the equity retained and the secondary equity sold). B_E is the book value of equity before IPO. Thus, Leland and Pyle (1977)'s signal model actually suggests a positive relation between $V_{Eb} - B_E$, the value added on entrepreneur's equity, and α.

Now, assume that the model does not hold – that is, the correlation between $V_{Eb} - B_E$ and α is zero. Because Leland and Pyle (1977)'s signaling model does not assume any relationship between α and B_E, zero correlation between $V_{Eb} - B_E$ and α implies that $SV_{Eb,\alpha}$, the covariance between V_{Eb} and α, is zero. The proportion of primary shares among all shares offered, $N_p/N_p + N_s$, is denoted by β. Then V_E, the market value of equity, can be expressed as:

$$V_E = \frac{V_{Eb}}{1 - (1 - \alpha)\beta}.$$

F, the amount of funds raised, can be expressed as:

$$F = \frac{V_{Eb}(1 - \alpha)\beta}{1 - (1 - \alpha)\beta}.$$

To simplify our analysis, first assume that β is not correlated with V_{Eb} or α. Obviously, $S_{V_E,\alpha} < 0$; $S_{V_{Eb},F} > 0$.

If we regress V_E on F and α, like in regression (18.2), b_2, the coefficient of α, can be expressed as:

$$\frac{S_{V_E,\alpha} S_{F,F} - S_{F,\alpha} S_{V_E,F}}{S_{\alpha,\alpha} S_{F,F} - S_{F,\alpha} S_{F,\alpha}},$$

where the S values are variances and covariances. Because $V_E = V_E + V_{Eb} + F$ and $S_{V_{Eb},\alpha} = 0$, $S_{V_E,\alpha} = S_{F,\alpha}$ and $S_{V_E,F} = S_{V_{Eb},F} + S_{F,F}$. So

$$b_2 = -\frac{S_{V_E,\alpha} S_{V_{Eb},F}}{S_{\alpha,\alpha} S_{F,F} - S_{F,\alpha} S_{F,\alpha}}.$$

Because $S_{V_E,\alpha} < 0$, $S_{V_{Eb},F} > 0$, and $S_{F,F} S_{\alpha,\alpha} - S_{F,\alpha} S_{F,\alpha} > 0$,[1] $b_2 > 0$. So, although we assume that Leland and Pyle (1977)'s signal model does not hold, we still get a positive coefficient on α when we estimate regression (18.2). Intuitively, once α and V_{Eb} are given, F and V_E will be restricted to specific ranges (because β is in the range of 0 to 1) and they will be mechanically correlated with α and V_{Eb}. As long as β is not correlated with V_{Eb} or α, the arithmetic relation between V_E and α will lead to a positive coefficient for α when F is controlled for in a regression.

18.3   Simulated regressions

The analysis above assumes that β is not correlated with V_{Eb} or α. In real IPO samples, β is usually correlated with V_{Eb} and α. It is possible that these correlations may offset the correlation caused by the arithmetic relation between V_E and α, thus making the regression between V_E and α less biased. This conjecture can be best addressed by simulated regressions. In simulated regressions we can use randomly generated inputs while allowing β to be correlated with V_{Eb} and α. If the arithmetic correlations are not offset by these correlations, simulated regressions will show that regression (18.2) produces significant results even when Leland and Pyle (1977)'s signaling model does not hold, as long as the random inputs satisfy expression (18.3).

To make the simulation as realistic as possible, I start from actual IPO data. The initial sample of IPO firms is collected from the Securities Data Company (SDC) database. Given that the valuation of IPOs changed substantially over time, I use a relatively short sample period from 1990 to 1996. Unit issues, depository issues, closed-end funds, and real estate investment trusts (REITs) are all excluded. Each offering firm should have offer price, the number of primary shares offered, and the number of secondary shares offered available. All IPOs with offer price below \$8.00 per share are excluded. These firms should have positive pre-offering book value of equity and positive post-offering book value of equity. In addition, these firms must

[1] $S_{F,F} S_{\alpha,\alpha} - S_{F,\alpha} S_{F,\alpha} > 0$ as long as α and F are not perfectly correlated. Here α and F are not perfectly correlated because

$$F = \frac{V_{Eb}(1 - \alpha)\beta}{1 - (1 - \alpha)\beta}$$

and $S_{V_{Eb},\alpha} = 0$.

have post-offering shares outstanding available from the University of Chicago Center for Research in Security Prices (CRSP) database. If all of an IPO firm's equity comes from the offering – that is, its number of post-offering shares outstanding is the same as its number of primary shares – then the IPO is also excluded. The final sample includes 1114 firms. A simple sample analysis shows that the correlation between α and β is positive. This increases $S_{V_E,\alpha}$ and tends to offset the arithmetic correlation in regression (18.2).

In the first step, I estimate regression (18.2) using actual historical IPO data. Like in previous studies, I do both ordinary least squares (OLS) and weighted least squares (WLS) regressions. When WLS is used, V_E and all explanatory variables are deflated by both post-offering book value of equity (Downes and Heinkel, 1982) and pre-offering book value of equity (Ritter, 1984). I also use another method: taking the log of both V_E and F, to correct for heteroscedasticity.

The results from actual data are reported in Table 18.1. They are very similar to those in Downes and Heinkel (1982) and Ritter (1984). Table 18.1 shows that the coefficients of α are highly significant. They have t-values of 27.20 in OLS, 25.79 in the first WLS, 29.69 in the second WLS, and 42.45 in the log OLS. The coefficients of K are also highly significant in all the regressions. In addition, it seems that the log regression does a much better job in correcting for heteroscedasticity – it has a much higher R-square.[2]

As indicated earlier, all these could be due to the arithmetic relation between V_E, F, and α. So, in the second step, I conduct simulation regressions to test the misspecification. For each IPO firm, V_{Eb}, the actual market value of entrepreneur's equity, is calculated as the product of offer price and the number of shares held by pre-IPO shareholders before IPO. Then, three methods are used to generate simulated inputs for α, β (the proportion of primary shares among all shares offered), V_E and F.

In method 1, for each IPO firm, simulated α and β are independently randomly drawn from the sample. They have the same individual distributions as the actual α and β. Because they are randomly drawn, they are not correlated with the actual V_{Eb} or the actual $V_{Eb} - B_E$. This makes sure that Leland and Pyle (1977)'s signaling model does not hold for the simulated data. It also precludes other hypotheses relating share retention to firm value, such as the wealth hypothesis in Ritter (1984). Because simulated α and β are drawn independently, they are not correlated with each other. This is consistent with the assumption we made in part 18.2. Later we will drop this assumption. Using simulated α and β, simulated V_E is calculated as:

$$V_E = \frac{V_{Eb}}{1 - (1 - \alpha)\beta};$$

simulated F is calculated as:

$$F = \frac{V_{Eb}(1 - \alpha)\beta}{1 - (1 - \alpha)\beta}.$$

---

[2] The R-squares reported for the OLS regression and the Log OLS regression cannot be compared directly because they have different dependent variables. But additional tests computing comparable R-squares show that Log OLS regression does give a much better fit.

Table 18.1 Regression between firm value and proportion of shares retained

Type	Weight	Intercept	Funds raised, F	Proportion of shares retained, α	Adj. R-square
OLS		-2.01×10^8	3.41	3.30×10^8	0.695
		(-22.94)	(45.23)	(27.20)	
WLS	Post-IPO book value of	-1.34×10^8	3.59	2.14×10^8	0.705
	equity (POBE)	(-22.62)	(46.51)	(25.79)	
WLS	Pre-IPO book value of	-1.19×10^8	3.38	1.89×10^8	0.751
	equity (PRBE)	(-26.02)	(53.17)	(29.69)	
Log		1.14	0.92	2.44	0.855
OLS		(5.13)	(71.98)	(42.45)	

Regression (18.2): $V_{Ej} = b_0 + b_1 F_j + b_2 \alpha_j + u$.

In method 2, pairs of simulated α and β are randomly drawn from the sample. Because they are drawn in pairs, they have the same joint distribution and positive correlation as the actual α and β. However, they are not correlated with the actual V_{Eb} or the actual $V_{Eb} - B_E$. So again Leland and Pyle (1977)'s signaling model does not hold for the simulated data. Using simulated α and β, simulated V_E and simulated F are calculated using the same formulas as in method 1.

In method 3, simulated α is randomly drawn from the sample. It has the same individual distribution as the actual α, but it is independent from all other variables. So Leland and Pyle (1977)'s signaling model does not hold for the simulated data either. Simulated V_E and simulated F are calculated using simulated α, actual V_{Eb}, and actual β. If there is any correlation between V_{Eb} and β, it will continue to exist among simulated inputs.

For each of the three simulation methods, I estimate regression (18.2) using the simulated V_E, the simulated F, and the simulated α. Because log transformation was shown to be the most effective in reducing heteroscedasticity, I employ log OLS regression. Simple OLS and WLS regressions are not used because they suffer from serious heteroscedasticity problems when using simulated V_E and simulated F. Some extreme observations will dominate the simple OLS and WLS regressions. This procedure is repeated 1000 times for each of the three methods. If regression (18.2) is not biased, the coefficients of α should be positive and significant at the 5% level for about 25 times.

The distributions of the coefficients of α and their t-values are reported in Table 18.2. The results of regressions using inputs from simulation method 1 are quite consistent with the analysis in part I. The coefficients of α are positive and significant at the 5% level in all 1000 cases. Actually, all the regressions produce t-values above 25. The coefficients fall in the range of (1.84, 2.52), which covers 2.44, the coefficient of α estimated using actual data. So, if α and β are independent of each other, the level of the arithmetic correlation between V_E and α will be close to the correlation estimated using real data and regression (18.2).

When the correlation between α and β is maintained, as in simulation method 2, the level of arithmetic correlation between V_E and α is offset by just a little. In 1000 simulated regressions, the range of coefficients for α becomes (1.69, 2.37). This is still close to the result we get using actual data. All the t-statistics are above 24. It seems the correlation between α and β does not significantly reduce the effect of the arithmetic correlation.

The correlation between V_{Eb} and β actually increases the effect of the arithmetic correlation. In 1000 simulated regressions using method 3, the range of coefficients for α is (2.03, 2.63), which covers 2.44 again. All t-statistics are above 29. So, it seems the arithmetic correlation dominates even after we allow β to be correlated with α and V_{Eb}.

Because of the way we generate simulated inputs, it is highly unlikely that the significant results in simulated regression are caused by any signaling effect. Instead, they are consistent with the following explanation: regression (18.2) is actually a test of expression (18.3), which holds like an accounting identity even when no signaling effect exists. The results are the same if first-day market closing price is used to replace offer price in the regressions. Thus, the empirical results based on regression (18.2) (Downes and Heinkel, 1982; Ritter, 1984) are more or less biased.

Table 18.2 Regression simulation results

Range of coefficient	<1.69	1.69–1.84	1.84–2.03	2.03–2.37	2.37–2.52	2.52–2.63	>2.63
Method 1	0	0	46	899	55	0	0
Method 2	0	43	448	509	0	0	0
Method 3	0	0	0	710	269	21	0

Panel A: Distribution of coefficients of α after 1000 simulations of regression (18.2) (V_E, F, and α are based on inputs randomly drawn from the sample).

Range of t-values	<24	24–25	25–29	29–36	36–38	38–40	>40
Method 1	0	0	50	920	18	2	0
Method 2	0	3	142	838	17	0	0
Method 3	0	0	0	1000	0	0	0

Panel B: Distribution of t-statistics for coefficient of α after 1000 simulations of regression (18.2) (V_E, F, and α are based on inputs randomly drawn from the sample).

18.4   Correcting the misspecification

So, more than 25 years after Leland and Pyle (1977), we still do not have an un-biased test of their model. Thus, it is necessary for this chapter to provide an alternative. Due to the ex-ante accounting relation between α, V_E, and F, it is difficult to test the predicted relationship between α and V_E in Leland and Pyle (1977). However, as shown earlier, Leland and Pyle (1977) can be transformed into a model about the relationship between α and V_{Eb} or $V_{Eb} - B_E$. There is no accounting relationship between α and V_{Eb} or $V_{Eb} - B_E$. So a regression between α and V_{Eb} or $V_{Eb} - B_E$ should avoid the arithmetic correlation bias.

Based on this rationale, I estimate two regressions. One regression uses the log of $V_{Eb} - B_E$ as dependent variable and α is the only explanatory variable. The other regression uses the log of V_{Eb} as the dependent variable. α and the log of B_E are used as explanatory variables. The regression results are reported in Table 18.3.

Table 18.3 shows a positive relation between α and firm valuation. The coefficients of α are positive and highly significant in both of the two regressions. In addition, it seems α explains a significant portion of the variation in V_{Eb}. Consistent with our intuition, the coefficient of B_E is positive and significant when B_E is included as an explanatory variable in the regression.

Previous research shows that several accounting variables, including earnings, sales, and EBIT, are important in IPO valuation. The regressions above omit these variables and could have omitted-variable biases. So I collect these data from the Compustat database for the year prior to IPO and include the log of these variables in the regression. For consistency, book value of equity from SDC is also replaced by data from Compustat (Data item 60). Additional tests show that the results are not affected by this step. In this process, IPO firms with negative earnings are excluded and the sample is reduced to 661 IPOs. The new regression results are also reported in Table 18.3.

Table 18.3 Regressions without the arithmetic correlation bias

	Dependent variable	Proportion of shares retained, α	Log of B_E, book value of equity before IPO	Log of earnings	Log of sales	Log of EBIT	Number of obs.	Adj. R-square
OLS	Log of $V_{Eb} - B_E$	4.46 (23.34)					1114	0.501
OLS	Log of V_{Eb}	3.72 (28.60)	0.18 (13.04)				1087	0.334
OLS	Log of V_{Eb}	3.59 (24.41)	0.05 (2.57)	0.07 (2.87)	0.04 (1.20)	0.16 (3.86)	661	0.568
2SLS	Log of V_{Eb}	3.34	0.06	0.08	0.03	0.16	661	0.566

Table 18.3 shows that the positive correlation between share retention and firm valuation is not affected by the inclusion of additional control variables. The value of coefficient of α does not change much and its significance does not change much either. Consistent with the literature, firm value is positively related to its earnings and EBIT.

18.4.1 Alternative explanations

The regression results appear to be quite consistent with Leland and Pyle (1977). However, the results are also consistent with the agency hypothesis and the wealth hypothesis in Ritter (1984). The agency hypothesis suggests that entrepreneurs have better incentive to work hard and add value to the firm when they retain more shares. The wealth hypothesis suggests that when firms are valued higher, they can issue fewer shares to meet their capital needs. This implies that higher valuation causes higher retention, not the other way around. Following Ritter (1984), I use simultaneous equations to try to distinguish these hypotheses.

To specify a simultaneous equation system, we need a theory (other than the wealth hypothesis) about the factors affecting share retention. In their IPO prospectus, most IPO firms suggest that their primary use of IPO proceeds is General Corporate Purpose or Retiring Debt. So the level of capital expenditure and the level of debt may be related to the decision of share retention. I conjecture that IPO firms with higher capital expenditure tend to issue more shares and have lower retention ratio. Firms with higher debt level may also tend to issue more shares and have lower retention ratio. In addition, the decision about retention may also be related to the ownership structure of the IPO firm. For example, IPO firms backed by venture capital may have a different retention ratio. So I specify a simultaneous two-equation system as below:

$$V_{Eb} = b_0 + b_1\alpha + b_2B_E + b_3(\text{Earnings}) + b_4(\text{Sales}) + b_5(\text{EBIT}) + u \tag{18.5}$$

$$\alpha = c_0 + c_1V_{Eb} + c_2\beta + c_3(\text{Dept}) + c_4(\text{Assets}) + c_5(\text{EBIT})$$
$$+ c_6(\text{Capital Expenditure}) + c_7(\text{Venture}) + v \tag{18.6}$$

Equation (18.5) alone has already been estimated using OLS in Table 18.2. The whole simultaneous equation system can be estimated using two-stage least squares regression (2SLS). Both the signaling hypothesis and the agency hypothesis predict that the 2SLS regression will have a positive and significant coefficient on α in equation (18.5). The wealth hypothesis predicts that the 2SLS regression will produce a positive and significant coefficient of V_{Eb} in equation (18.6). In addition, according to Ritter (1984), if the wealth hypothesis is true, then the OLS regression of equation (18.5) will be subject to simultaneous equation bias and the 2SLS regression will have a coefficient on V_{Eb} closer to zero. If the agency hypotheses are true, then an OLS regression of equation (18.6) will be subject to simultaneous equation bias and the 2SLS regression will have a coefficient on α closer to zero.

I estimate the 2SLS regressions using the log of equity value and the log of most financial variables. The exogenous variables are used as instrumental variables. The results are reported at the end of Table 18.3 and the end of Table 18.4. The beginning of Table 18.4 also reports the results of a separate OLS regression on equation (18.6).

Table 18.4 Regressions with proportion of shares retained as dependent variable

	Log of V_{Eb}	Proportion of primary offering	Log of debt	Log of assets	Log of EBIT	Log of capital expenditure	Venture	Number of obs.	Adj. R-square
OLS	0.14 (25.99)	0.16 (7.48)	0.01 (1.39)	-0.04 (-3.28)	-0.01 (-1.21)	-0.00 (-3.15)	0.00 (0.47)	661	0.529
2SLS	0.11 (3.05)	0.15 (5.78)	0.00 (0.09)	-0.03 (-1.29)	-0.00 (-0.08)	-0.00 (-1.76)	0.01 (0.86)	661	0.510

Consistent with the signaling hypothesis and the agency hypothesis, the 2SLS regressions report a positive and significant coefficient of α in equation (18.5). The wealth hypothesis is also supported because the 2SLS regressions also report a positive and significant coefficient of V_{Eb} in equation (18.6). If we compare the estimates of equation (18.5) in 2SLS with the results of a separate OLS regression on equation (18.5), we notice that, consistent with the wealth hypothesis, the coefficient of α is closer to zero in the 2SLS regressions. However, the difference in the magnitude of the coefficient is not significant. If we compare the 2SLS estimates of equation (18.6) with those of separate OLS regression on equation (18.6), the 2SLS estimate of the coefficient on V_{Eb} is closer to zero. This is consistent with the signaling and agency hypotheses. However, again the difference in the level of the coefficient is not significant. In the 2SLS regressions, both of the two equations have adjusted R-square above 0.5, suggesting that the instrumental variables perform reasonably well. So, the insignificant difference is probably not due to bad instrument variables. Actually, the coefficients of Assets and Capital Expenditure in the OLS regression of equation (18.6) are quite consistent with my conjecture about the factors affecting share retention.

Ritter (1984) includes the growth rate of sales as one of the explanatory variables for α. It is not used in my equation system here because only 83 IPO firms have historical sales growth rate available. For those firms with historical sales growth rate, both the OLS regressions and the 2SLS regressions are estimated. The results are similar. Many other specifications of the simultaneous equation system are also tried. They usually have lower explanatory power. But most of them show similar results for the coefficients of α and V_{Eb}.

In the tests above, offer price is used to calculate firm value. Some people may argue that market price is a better measure. So I repeated all the regressions above using firm value calculated from first-day market price. The results are all similar.

Overall, it seems that the evidence does not allow us to exclude any of the three hypotheses. Specifically, when we examine the level of relevant coefficients in both the OLS and the 2SLS regressions, we do not see the significant difference predicted by the wealth hypothesis or the agency hypothesis. So the evidence does not support any claim that the positive relation between share retention and firm value is 100% caused by either the wealth effect or the agency effect. The evidence is probably most favorable to the signaling hypothesis of Leland and Pyle (1977). An explanation solely based on the signaling hypothesis is still consistent with the regression results. However, we cannot completely rule out the wealth hypothesis and the agency hypothesis.

18.5   Conclusion

I examine the possible correlation bias in Downes and Heinkel (1982) and Ritter (1984). I find that the regression model they use leads to significant results even when no theoretical relation exists. A new regression model is suggested to avoid the bias. The regression results show a positive relation between share retention and IPO firm valuation. This positive relation can be caused by a positive impact from share retention to firm valuation. It can also be caused by a positive impact from firm valuation to share retention. 2SLS estimates of simultaneous equations suggest that both of the two impacts exist. The evidence is most consistent with the signaling model in Leland and Pyle (1977), but the agency hypothesis and the wealth hypothesis in Ritter (1984) cannot be ruled out.

References

Downes, D. H. and Heinkel, R. (1982). Signaling and the Valuation of Unseasoned New Issues. *Journal of Finance*, 37(1):1–10.

Leland, H. E. and Pyle, D. H. (1977). Informational Asymmetrics, Financial Structure, and Financial Intermediaries. *Journal of Finance*, 32(2):371–388.

Ritter, J. R. (1984). Signaling and the Valuation of Unseasoned New Issues: A Comment. *Journal of Finance*, 39(4):1231–1237.

19 The role of venture capitalists in IPO performance: empirical evidence from German IPO data

Andreas Hack and Erik E. Lehmann

Abstract

This chapter examines empirically the impact of venture capitalists on initial public offering (IPO) performance in Germany. In particular, we analyze whether IPO performance is influenced by the different ownership structures, especially banks, firms, and venture capitalists. Based on a unique and hand-collected dataset of all German IPOs during 1997 and 2002, our study shows that IPO performance could not be explained by ownership-variables. In contrast, the results confirm the finding of Ritter (1991) that in IPO waves the quality of the firms brought to the stock market decreases over time.

19.1 Introduction

Venture capitalists play a crucial role in the economy for at least two reasons. Firstly, they incubate new and small firms by supplying them with equity capital (Gohrman and Sahlman, 1989). Secondly, they bring firms to public and thus increase their equity base to finance their future growth (Cumming and MacIntosh, 2003; Kaplan and Stroemberg, 2004; Hellmann and Puri, 2002). Theoretical and empirical studies thus emphasize the advantages of venture capitalists in financing high-tech firms compared to other sources of finance (Hellmann, 1998; Berger and Udell, 1998; Sahlman, 1990; Audretsch and Lehmann, 2004). This chapter presents an empirical analysis of the impact of venture capitalists and other major shareholders on firm performance as measured by first-day initial public offering (IPO) returns.

Unlike the USA or UK, Germany suffers from having a less developed capital market and a less vibrant venture capital industry. Although being the third largest economy in the world (behind the USA and Japan), Germany is associated with considerably lower growth rates per capita and of total factor productivity. The USA and the UK appear to be better able to cope with such economic problems as the radical and rapid process of structural change from mass production of the industrial sector to the service sector and the increasing importance of the new industries like biotechnology, telecommunication, software, and others (Audretsch and Thurik, 2001; Rajan and Zingales, 2000). According to Gompers and Lerner (2001), the vibrant venture capital industry is seen as one of the cornerstones of America's leadership in the commercialization of technological innovation.

Thus, the lack of a developed venture capital industry to finance young and high-risk firms is one explanation for low growth rates in Germany in the past 10 years. The historical advantage of the German bank-based system now turns into a structural and institutional disadvantage. In contrast to banks, equity providers like venture capitalists are more able to overcome the problems of asymmetric information associated with the high risk and thus foster such innovative firms (Hellmann, 1998).

Gompers and Lerner (2001) have identified the important role that venture capital plays in financing young and innovative firms in the USA. However, virtually nothing is known about whether this role is the same or different in a bank-based country such as Germany. In fact, there are some reasons to doubt that the role of venture capital is invariant between countries with bank-based systems and those with more specialized markets (Black and Gilson, 1997). On the one hand, Germany has a long tradition of specific regional and national financial institutions financing the German Mittelstand, or small and medium-sized enterprises. On the other hand, a new generation of venture capitalists has emerged that provides finance to highly innovative firms.

One necessary condition is a well-functioning and liquid stock market (Black and Gilson, 1997). Active and liquid stock markets make IPOs affordable for companies and attractive for investors. The American experience with the Nasdaq, which provides an equity market for high-tech companies where most of them are backed by venture capitalists, is suggestive in this respect.

Although it is proclaimed to be the largest venture capital market in continental Europe (Bottazi and Da Rin, 2002), there is only scarce empirical evidence about the role of venture capitalists in Germany. The history of the venture capital industry in Germany dates back to the mid-1960s (Becker and Hellmann, 2001) – in contrast to the USA, where it dates back to the 1940s (Gompers and Lerner, 2001). German venture capitalists also differ from those in the USA by their lack of experience (Dittmann et al., 2001; Schefczyk and Gerpott, 2001) and in their organizational form (Becker and Hellmann, 2001; Bascha and Walz, 2001). Audretsch and Lehmann (2004) showed that venture capitalists are reluctant to invest in firms with high amounts of debt. They also showed that survival rate of firms listed on the stock market decreases significantly with the amount of equity held by venture capitalists (Audretsch and Lehmann, 2005). Lehmann (2005) provided evidence that venture capital syndication leads to higher growth rates as measured by employees. However, none of these papers analyzes the impact of venture capitalists on first-day IPO performance of German IPOs.

Using a sample of US IPOs from 1996 to 2000, Ljungqvist and Wilhelm (2003) found a significant and negative effect for pre-IPO stakes of venture capitalists on underpricing. While Megginson and Weiss (1991) found that venture capital-backed firms are associated with a lower underpricing in 1983 to 1987, Barry et al. (1990) could not confirm this result for the period 1978 to 1987 and Benveniste et al. (2003) cannot find such association in 1985 to 2000. Thus, the impact of venture capitalists as one of the major shareholders of IPO firms is rather mixed.

The remainder of this chapter is as follows. In the next section we describe the role of large shareholders of high-tech firms in a bank-based country like Germany. Section 19.3 provides the data and how the variables are measured. The descriptive statistics, econometric analysis, and empirical results are presented in section 19.4. Section 19.5 concludes.

19.2   Venture capitalists as shareholders and IPO returns

Ever since Berle and Means (1932) stated that in the modern corporation hired managers have enough discretion for corporate plundering, the issue of separating ownership from control and its resulting impact on firm performance has been placed high on the agenda of economists. A prime element of corporate governance is the alignment of shareholders' interests with the interests of managers hired to run the firm.

In the literature on managerial discretion and agency costs it has been argued that the presence of a large shareholder reduces agency costs because a high stake in the firm makes it in the shareholder's interest to control the executive managers hired to run the firm. Ownership concentration thus may be the key to effective corporate governance and shareholder value maximization (Frick and Lehmann, 2005; Lehmann and Weigand, 2000; Lehmann et al., 2004a; for Germany).

Thus, potential investors anticipate the benefits of large shareholders which should be shown in abnormal IPO rents. However, if capital markets are perfect, the costs and benefits of large shareholders are anticipated by the market and thus neither the type of shareholders nor the amount of equity held by them should have any significant impact on IPO returns.

As in Ljungqvist and Wilhelm (2003), we use the pre-IPO ownership structure as the explanatory variables to explain first-day IPO returns. In particular, we identify five different groups of shareholders, namely venture capitalists, banks, industrial firms, CEOs, friends and family members.

Venture capitalists are seen to play a pivotal role in controlling young and innovative firms. Firms in a knowledge-based economy are associated with a high degree of uncertainty, which emanates from asymmetric information about the management quality of the entrepreneur and actions, and from the fact that the firm's operations are highly complex and the optimal space of the management team is hard to specify (Audretsch et al., 2005). Otherwise, uncertainty might also be the result of external sources that are not under the control of managers, such as uncertainty about market demand, supply, and competition. As a consequence, the resulting conflicts between entrepreneurs and their investors cannot be easily solved by traditional financial intermediaries like banks, but by specialized financial intermediaries like venture capitalists (Gompers and Lerner, 2001). They mitigate these problems by collecting information before they decide to invest, by monitoring them once the project is under way, and by designing and controlling the financial contracts that provide the incentives for the entrepreneur to behave optimally (Hellmann, 1998; Gompers, 1995).

To cover the high cost of information collection and monitoring, venture capitalists need high returns from their investments to make money and attract investors. The most profitable way is to turn their non-liquid stakes in those companies into realized returns by an initial public offering. This makes venture capitalists the most prominent investors in small and highly innovative firms (Gompers and Lerner, 2001).

Although there is overwhelming evidence that banks, as financial intermediaries, play a major role in the reduction of agency costs (Diamond, 1984; Lehmann and Neuberger, 2001; Lehmann et al., 2004b), they may fail in providing debt when the degree of asymmetric information is too high. In this case, a profit-maximizing bank cannot capture the expected costs of debt by the interest rates of the loan (Stiglitz and Weiss, 1981).

Aghion and Bolton (1992) showed that the double moral hazard problem in financing young entrepreneurs arises especially in high-technology and science-based industries. As the relationship between the financer and the entrepreneur develops over time, eventualities arise that could not easily have been foreseen or planned for in an initial contract. Due to the disutility of effort neither the entrepreneur nor the venture capitalist may undertake first-best actions in order to enhance the expected outcome of the project. This creates a two-sided moral hazard problem where the entrepreneur as well as the venture capitalist has to be induced to undertake effort (Gompers, 1995, 1996; Kaplan and Stroemberg, 2003, 2004; Lehmann, 2005).

However, the very nature of entrepreneurship prevents start-ups and their financiers from writing complete contracts where the obligations are specified in all relevant conceivable future contingents (Hart and Moore, 1998). Thus, optimal contracts between entrepreneurial firms in high-technology and science-based industries and their financiers differ between venture capitalists and banks.

Firstly, venture capitalists take an equity-linked stake in the firms they finance, sharing in both upside and downside risks. Secondly, they are also assumed to have a higher technological expertise, which allows them both to better identify projects than banks and to undertake the projects without the original entrepreneur (Berglöf, 1994; Udea, 2003). This creates the double moral hazard problem. Banks, however, cannot credibly commit themselves to run the firm instead of the entrepreneur. In contrast, venture capitalists with their experts frequently replace the original founders as CEOs (Hellmann and Puri, 2000; Gohrman and Sahlman, 1989; Lerner, 1994). Thirdly, the role played by venture capital in staging the investments is to reduce agency and verifiability problems (Bergemann and Hege, 1998; Gompers, 1995). After their initial investment, venture capitalists provide entrepreneurs with access to consultants, accountants, and play an active role as monitors (Lerner, 1995) and provide information for other stakeholders of the firm. Finally, they take an active part in guiding the exit decision either by selling their shares directly to other firms or investors or by an initial public offering (IPO) (Lerner, 1994; Gompers, 1995; Cumming and MacIntosh, 2003).

Since providing equity by venture capitalists is associated with ownership, they play a major role in the governance structure of those firms, although they may receive only few private benefits of their control (Kaplan and Stroemberg, 2004). Ownership by venture capitalists may increase their incentive to invest in information collection and monitoring activities. They may also be more likely to strengthen the management teams as their control rights via ownership increase.

Summing up, we formulate the hypotheses that the presence of venture capitalists as shareholders would positively influence the IPO returns. If venture capitalists sell all their equity stakes at the time of the initial public offering, they would send a negative signal to the market. We will test this hypothesis against the null hypothesis that capital markets are efficient and thus we would not see any significant effect in our results.

As noted above, we also include other types of shareholders. As mentioned in the literature, banks play a pivotal role in the governance of firms in Germany (Frick and Lehmann, 2005; Lehmann and Weigand, 2000; Lehmann et al., 2004a; for Germany). However, their impact on firm performance is ambiguous since they often act in their own interest, which contradicts the interests of other shareholders (Lehmann and Weigand, 2000). Furthermore, German law protects the interests of banks as debt holders against equity owners. However, the presence of banks could also be seen as a signal of quality of the firm. Thus, the impact of banks as shareholders is ambiguous.

Besides venture capitalists and banks, entrepreneurial firms could receive equity from several other sources like other firms, friends, and family members or by the entrepreneur himself. However, the impact of these types of shareholders on IPO returns is ambiguous. Managerial ownership could be seen as an incentive mechanism that helps to internalize the costs of managerial behavior. This follows directly from the famous work by Jensen and Meckling (1976). Otherwise, managerial ownership may lead to entrenchment effects by lowering the probability of takeovers.

Equity provided by friends or family members can serve as a signal that the entrepreneur is not able to attract financial resources from banks or venture capitalists. But strong ties from family members may also serve as a signal for the quality of the firm. Other firms may invest in young and high-technology firms to benefit from future profits or innovations. On the other hand, they can use their voting power to extract benefits at the cost of minority shareholders.

As noted by Demsetz (1983), a perfect capital market should anticipate the costs and benefits created by the shareholders. Thus, ownership structure is endogenous and has no impact on future returns. Then, IPO rents reflect the difference between the valuation of the firm by the major shareholders and the capital markets.

19.3   Data, measurement, and estimation methods

To conduct this study, we use a hand-collected dataset of firms listed on the Neuer Markt in Germany from 1997 until 2002. This market segment for young and highly innovative firms is the German equivalent of the Nasdaq and allowed venture capitalists and other equity holders to earn profits by selling their shares. The unique dataset consists of 341 firms listed on the Neuer Markt from 1997 until 2002. From those 341 we dropped all firms located outside Germany, holding companies, banks, firms with a double listing, and non-IPO firms. This leads to a set of 285 firms. The data are collected by combining individual balance sheet data from IPO prospects with information from the Deutsche Boerse AG, Datastream, and OnVista.

We take first-day IPO returns as the endogenous variable. We measure these returns using the bookbuilding price of a firm's share and the first market price:

$$[(Market\ Price) - (Bookbuilding\ Price)]/(Bookbuilding\ Price)] \qquad (19.1)$$

Our major explanatory variables are the different major groups of shareholders before IPO. We identified five important groups of shareholders: venture capitalists, banks, large firms, friends and family, and the board of management.

As control variables we include firm age (AGE) and size (SIZE). Firm age is measured in years and size in the number of employees, both before IPO. These variables could influence the IPO returns, since both variables are correlated with firm risk. Firstly, younger and smaller firms are associated with a higher degree of asymmetric information for outside financiers. Gathering information is very costly and thus may give an incentive to share these costs and risk with multiple venture capitalists. Secondly, an overwhelming amount of empirical studies shows that younger and smaller firms have the highest rates of failure (Caves, 1998; Audretsch, 1995) and thus are associated with a higher firm risk.

To control for time effects, we include the IPO date as a dummy variable for the years 1997 to 2001. Ritter (1991), Ljungqvist and Wilhelm (2003), and Loughran and Ritter (2001), among others, showed that the quality of firms decreases during IPO waves. If this holds also for this IPO wave, this trend should be reflected by the IPO dummies. We further include dummy variables for the following industries: software (SOFT-WARE), e-services (SERVICE), e-commerce (ECOMMERCE), computer and hardware (COMPUTER), telecommunication (TELOCOM), biotechnology (BIOTECH), medicine and life science (MEDTEC), media and entertainment (MEDIA), and technology (TECHNOLOGY).

We use the following equation to test the impact of venture capitalists and other major shareholders on IPO returns:

$$Y \text{ (IPO returns)} = f(\text{Governance Structure, Size, Age, Industry, IPO Year}) + u. \quad (19.2)$$

Figure 19.1 shows the distribution of first-day IPO returns (emrendit) for all German IPOs in the dataset. It can be seen that the dependent variable is highly skewed. The heavily right-skewed distribution of first-day IPO returns was also reported by Ljungqvist and Wilhelm (2003) and seems to be typically for first-day IPO returns.

Thus, OLS estimation is not an appropriate estimation technique. Thus, we follow the example in the labour market literature by using the method of quantile regression estimation. This semi-parametric technique provides a general class of models in which the conditional quantiles have a linear form. In its simplest form, the least absolute deviation estimator fits medians to a linear function of covariates. The method of quantile regression is potentially attractive for the same reason that the median or other quantiles are a better measure of location than the mean. Other useful features are the robustness against outliers and that the likelihood estimators are in general more efficient than least square estimators. Besides the technical features,

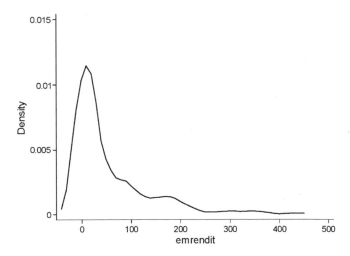

Figure 19.1 Kernel-density estimation of IPO returns. 'Emrendit' is IPO profit, the difference between the first-day stock market price and the fixed price (bookbuilding price)

quantile regressions allow that potentially different solutions at distinct quantiles may be interpreted as differences in the response of the dependent variable, namely the growth rates, to changes in the regressors at various points in the conditional distinction of the dependent variable. Thus, quantile regressions reveal asymmetries in the data that could not be detected by simple OLS estimations.[1]

Let (y_i, x_i), $i = 1, ..., n$, be a sample of firms, where x_i is a $K \times 1$ vector of regressors. Assume that $\text{Quant}_\theta(y_i, x_i)$ devotes the conditional quantile of y_i, conditional on the regressor vector x_i. The distribution of the error term $u_{\theta i}$ satisfies the quantile restriction $\text{Quant}_\theta(u_{\theta i}, x_i) = 0$. Thus, we estimate $y_i = \text{Quant}_\theta(y_i, x_i) + \mu_{\theta i}$ or, with $\text{Quant}_\theta(y_i, x_i) = x_i' \beta_\theta$:

$$y_i = x_i' \beta_\theta + \mu_{\theta i}. \tag{19.3}$$

We analyze different quantiles. The 0.10 quantile includes the less performing firms based on column.[2] The median quantile is based on the 0.50 quantile. This regression is closest to the OLS approach, where the expected mean value is used in the estimation instead of the median. Finally, we use the 0.80 quantile with the higher performing firms. As θ is increased from 0 to 1, the entire conditional distribution of the endogenous variable y is traced conditional on x. The quantile's coefficient could be interpreted using the partial derivative of the quantile of y with respect to one of the regressors, say j. This derivative can be interpreted as the marginal change in the θth conditional quantile due to marginal change in the jth element of x.

19.4   Descriptive statistics and empirical results

First, we provide the descriptive statistics. Table 19.1 shows the different equity holders of the firms before IPO. About 38% of the equity is held by the CEO, mostly the entrepreneur or founder of the firm. In the sample from Ljungqvist and Wilhelm (2003), CEOs on average owned 20.5% of pre-IPO shares, while median ownership is 8.9%. Thus, compared to their sample, the firms in this dataset are more closely held and managed by their founders.

Venture capitalists represent the second largest group of shareholders, followed by other corporations. On average, 13.34% of the stakes are held by venture capitalists. As in Ljungqvist and Wilhelm (2003), about half of the firms in the sample are backed by venture capitalists. In their sample, aggregate venture capital stakes declined over the period from about 44% in 1996 to 40.4% in 2000. This large difference between the two samples clearly demonstrates the different role and impact of venture capitalists in the USA and Germany.

Corporations are the third group of shareholders. On average, 13.2% of the stakes are held by other corporations, in contrast to the Ljungqvist and Wilhelm (2003) sample. In their sample, the average stake is 42.3% in 1996 and about 33% in 2000.

Also in sharp contrast to Ljungqvist and Wilhelm (2003), bank-held stakes are rather low. In their sample, the mean stake held by banks is about 14.5%. However, we did

[1] See Buchinsky (1998) for a survey of the method and some application in the labor markets.
[2] As an example, the 0.20 quantile divides the dataset into two parts, whereas 20% of the included firms have IPO returns less than or equal to the 0.20 quantile and 80% of the firms have higher IPO returns.

Table 19.1 Descriptive statistics of the dataset

Variable	Mean	Standard deviation	Median	Minimum	Maximum
Shareholders					
Venture capitalists	13.34	21.08	0	0	100
Banks	2.01	7.9	0	0	98.6
Firms	13.20	28.07	0	0	100
Friends and family	0.89	4.75	0	0	55.67
CEO	38.61	32.45	33.95	0	100
Rest	2.51	7.53	0	0	66
Firm-specific variables					
IPO returns (%)	51.57	73.27	19.35	−25	433.33
Firm age	9.31	8.038	8	0.1	35
Employees before IPO	185.61	268.44	89	2	1370

not differentiate between commercial banks and investments banks. Friends and family members play only a minor role in controlling the firm. However, as the median values show, more than 50% of the firms have a rather low shareholder concentration.

As seen in Figure 19.1, IPO rents are positive and highly skewed, while, on average, about 50% of the invested money could be earned by the investors at the first day listed on the stock market. The median value is about 20%. Ljungqvist and Wilhelm (2003) reported for their sample that first-day returns on IPOs averaged about 17% in 1996 and then increased to 73% in 1999, before tapering off to 58% in 2000.

The descriptive statistics also show that the firms are strikingly young. The median firm is about 8 years old before listing on the stock market. This is comparable with the patterns found by Loughran and Ritter (2001) and Ljungqvist and Wilhelm (2003). The smallest firm consists of only two employees, while the largest firm employed more then 1300 people before IPO. On average, 185 people are employed before IPO.

Next, we provide the results from the quantile regressions (Table 19.2). First, we consider the median regression. Only the dummy variable indicating the IPO year 1998 is significant and positive. None of the included ownership variables enters the regression in a significant way. Columns 2 and 3 show the results for the low-performing group of firms. Remember that the 10% (and the 20%) quantile divides the dataset into two parts, whereas 10% (20%) of the firms included have IPO returns less than or equal to the 0.10 (0.20) quantile and 90% (80%) of the firms have higher IPO returns. In these columns, the coefficient for venture capitalists is significant and positive.

Summing up, the results clearly show that shareholder ownership has no significant effect explaining IPO rents. This, however, does not necessarily mean that neither ownership concentration nor the type of shareholder has no impact on IPO rents. We interpret from this result that both the costs and benefits of the different shareholders is reflected by the stock prices.

In contrast, the dummy variable for the IPO year 1998 is significant and positive in all regressions. While the first seven firms, which entered the Neuer Market in 1997, increased the demand and interest for the Neuer Markt, the firms which entered the stock market in 1998 could be interpreted as high-quality firms. Most of

Table 19.2 Estimation of the equity held by major shareholders

Variable	10% Q	20% Q	30% Q	50% Q	70% Q	80% Q	90% Q
Venture capitalists	0.173	0.147	0.064	−0.067	0.002	0.137	−0.667
	(2.01)**	(1.88)*	(0.69)	(0.39)	(0.01)	(0.03)	(1.19)
Banks	−0.002	0.012	−0.109	0.003	0.644	1.073	−0.654
	(0.01)	(0.04)	(0.24)	(0.00)	(0.47)	(0.73)	(0.31)
Firms	0.021	0.003	−0.048	−0.117	−0.203	−0.292	−0.395
	(0.49)	(0.08)	(0.97)	(1.29)	(0.67)	(0.74)	(0.89)
Friends and family	−0.074	−0.167	−0.233	−0.474	−0.887	−1.576	−3.175
	(0.15)	(0.37)	(0.69)	(0.76)	(0.80)	(0.349)	(0.97)
Log SIZE	0.931	−0.131	0.711	−0.752	−5.091	−9.171	9.892
	(0.52)	(0.09)	(0.47)	(0.24)	(0.69)	(0.95)	(0.72)
Log AGE	−0.865	0.195	−1.191	−2.333	−1.081	8.001	8.013
	(0.63)	(0.17)	(0.86)	(0.82)	(0.17)	(1.11)	(1.05)
IPO97	7.11	10.46	10.534	23.841	19.423	31.686	−14.312
	(0.78)	(0.70)	(0.77)	(1.21)	(0.53)	(0.80)	(0.33)
IPO98	16.06	18.79	27.658	42.486	64.778	78.518	88.401
	(2.50)**	(2.29)**	(2.73)**	(2.23)**	(2.05)**	(2.08)**	(1.99)**
IPO99	6.79	1.645	−0.105	0.374	5.012	−0.923	−22.862
	(2.32)***	(0.64)	(0.04)	(0.06)	(0.33)	(0.04)	(0.61)
Industry dummies	n.s.	n.s.	Telecom+	n.s.	n.s.	n.s.	Media+
Constant	−11.263	−0.648	1.825	22.667	63.854	107.661	84.858
	(1.45)	(0.10)	(0.25)	(1.31)	(1.66)*	(2.43)**	(1.29)
Pseudo R	0.043	0.034	0.043	0.0643	0.0726	0.079	0.102
N	277	277	277	277	277	277	277

The dependent variable is the IPO performance. t-values are given in parentheses. Asterisks denote statistical significance at the 1% (***), 5% (**), and 10% (*) levels. The technology sector and the IPO dummy for the year 2000 are taken as the control group. n.s. = not significant. x% Q is the x% quantile.

the firms entered the stock market in 1999 and 2000, the so-called IPO wave in Germany. The positive dummy variable for the IPO year 1998 could be interpreted as further evidence for the window of opportunity as found by Ritter (1991) for the USA. Since the coefficient of this dummy variable increases continuously from the lowest to the highest quantiles, the premium for the firms which entered the stock market in 1998 is highest in the upper quantiles, i.e. the firms with the highest IPO returns. These results are in line with those of Ljungqvist and Wilhelm (2003), showing that pre-IPO ownership is a weak predictor for first-day IPO returns.

19.5   Conclusion

In this chapter we analyze the determinants of IPO returns for all 285 German IPOs that entered the Neuer Market from 1997 until 2001. In particular, we analyzed whether ownership variables could explain some of the variations of the IPO returns. Since the endogenous variable, IPO returns, is highly skewed, we applied quantile regression techniques, which is more appropriate than OLS estimation techniques.

However, the results clearly show that shareholder ownership has no significant impact on IPO returns. This finding could be interpreted in such a way that the costs and benefits of the different shareholders on firms is included in the prices, as Demsetz (1983) noted about 20 years ago. In contrast, the results confirm the findings of Ritter (1991) and Ljungqvist and Wilhelm (2003) that in IPO waves the quality of the firms brought to the stock market decreases.

The Neuer Markt was created in 1997 to allow high and innovative firms to receive the necessary financial resources that could not be provided by banks. The experience of the Neuer Markt ended in 2003, when this market segment was closed by the Deutsche Borse AG. During this time, more then 50 firms were delisted from the stock market due to misbehavior, insolvency, and fraud (Audretsch and Lehmann, 2005). In most of the firms that were delisted from the Neuer Markt, venture capitalists were the largest shareholders (Audretsch and Lehmann, 2005), either because of the higher risk of these firms or their self-interest in selling shares of firms with lower quality at the end of the IPO wave. Although the major finding – that pre-IPO ownership cannot explain underpricing – is similar to studies based on US firms, the descriptive statistics clearly show that German IPOs are different.

References

Aghion P. and Bolton, P. (1992). An Incomplete Contracts Approach to Financial Contracting. *Review of Economic Studies*, 59(3):473–494.

Audretsch, D. (1995). Innovation, Growth and Survival. *International Journal of Industrial Organization*, 14(4):441–457.

Audretsch, D. B. and Thurik, R. (2001). What's New about the New Economy? Sources of Growth in the Managed and Entrepreneurial Economies. *Industrial and Corporate Change*, 10(1):267–315.

Audretsch, D. B. and Lehmann, E. E. (2004). Debt or Equity: The Role of Venture Capital in Financing High-Tech firms in Germany. *Schmalenbach Business Review*, 56(3):340–357.

Audretsch, D. B. and Lehmann, E. E (2005). Ownership, Knowledge, and Firm Survival. *Review of Accounting and Finance*, 4 (forthcoming).

Audretsch, D. B., Keilbach, M. and Lehmann, E. E (2005). *Entrepreneurship and Growth*.: Oxford University Press, Oxford (in press).

Barry, Ch. B., Muscarella, C. J., Peavy, J. W., and Vetsuypens, M. R. (1990). The Role of Venture Capital in the Creation of Public Companies: Evidence from the Going-Public Process. *Journal of Financial Economics*, 27(4):447–471.

Bascha, A. and Walz, U. (2001). Financing Practices in the German Venture Capital Industry: An Empirical Assessment. Working Paper, University of Tuebingen.

Becker, R. and Hellmann, T. (2001). The Genesis of Venture Capital – Lessons from the German Experience. Working Paper No. 1705, Stanford University.

Benveniste, L., Ljungqvist, A. P., Wilhelm, W. J., and Yu, X. (2003). Evidence of Information Spillovers in the Production of Investment Banking Services. *Journal of Finance*, 58(3):577–608.

Bergemann, D. and Hege, U. (1998). Venture Capital Financing, Moral Hazard, and Learning. *Journal of Banking and Finance*, 22(6–8):703–735.

Berger, A. N. and Udell, G. (1998). The Economics of Small Business Finance: The Role of Private Equity and Dept Markets in the Financial Growth Cycle. *Journal of Banking and Finance*, 22(6–8):613–673.

Berglöf, E. (1994). A Control Theory of Venture Capital Finance. *Journal of Law, Economics, and Organization*, 10(2):247–267.

Berle, A. A. and Means, G. C. (1932). *The Modern Corporation and Private Property*. MacMillan, New York.

Black, B. and Gilson, R. (1997). Venture Capital and the Structure of Financial Markets: Banks versus Stock Markets. *Journal of Financial Economics*, 47(1):243–277.

Bottazzi, L. and Da Rin, M. (2002). Venture Capital in Europe and the Financing of Innovative Companies. *Economic Policy*, 17(1):229–269.

Buchinsky, M. (1998). Recent Advantages in Quantile Regression Models. *Journal of Human Resources*, 33(1):88–126.

Caves, R. (1998). Industrial Organization and New Findings on the Turnover and Mobility of Firms. *Journal of Economic Literature*, 36(4):1947–1982.

Cumming, D. and MacIntosh, J. G. (2003). A Cross Country Comparison of Full and Partial Venture Capital Exits. *Journal of Banking and Finance*, 27(3):511–548.

Demsetz, H. (1983). The Structure of Ownership and the Theory of the Firm. *Journal of Law and Economics*, 26(2):375–390.

Diamond, D. W. (1984). Financial Intermediation and Delegated Monitoring. *Review of Economic Studies*, 51(3):393–414.

Dittmann, I., Maug, E. G., and Kemper, J. (2001). How Fundamental are Fundamental Values? Valuation Methods and their Impact on the Performance of German Venture Capitalists. Working Paper, Humbold University of Berlin.

Frick, B. and Lehmann, E. E. (2005). Corporate Governance in Germany: Problems and Prospects. In: *Corporate Governance and Labour Management* (Gospel, H. and Pendleton, A., eds), pp. 122–147. Oxford University Press, Oxford.

Gohrman, M. and Sahlman, M. (1989). What Do Venture Capitalists Do? *Journal of Business Venturing*, 4(4):231–248.

Gompers, P. (1995). Optimal Investments, Monitoring, and the Staging of Venture Capital. *Journal of Finance*, 50(5):1461–1489.

Gompers, P. A. (1996). Grandstanding in the Venture Capital Industry. *Journal of Financial Economics*, 42(1):133–156.

Gompers, P. and Lerner, J. (2001). The Venture Capital Revolution. *Journal of Economic Perspectives*, 15(2):145–168.

Hart, O. and Moore, J. (1998). Default and Renegotiation: A Dynamic Model of Debt. *Quarterly Journal of Economics*, 113(1):1–41.

Hellmann, T. (1998). The Allocation of Control Rights in Venture Capital Contracts. *Rand Journal of Economics*, 29(1):57–76.

Hellmann, T. and Puri, M. (2000). The Interaction Between Product Market and Financing Strategy: The Role of Venture Capital. *Review of Financial Studies*, 13(4):959–984.

Hellmann, T. and Puri, M. (2002). Venture Capital and the Professionalization of Start-up Firms: Empirical Evidence. *Journal of Finance*, 57(1):169–197.

Jensen, M. C. and Meckling, W. (1976). Theory of the Firm: Managerial Behavior, Agency Costs, and Ownership Structure. *Journal of Financial Economics*, 3(4):305–360.

Kaplan, S. N. and Stroemberg, P. (2003). Financial Contracting Theory meets the Real World: An Empirical Analysis of Venture Capital Contracts. *Review of Economic Studies*, 70(2):281–315.

Kaplan, S. N. and Stroemberg, P. (2004). Characteristics, Contracts, and Actions: Evidence from Venture Capitalist Analysis. *Journal of Finance*, 58(5):2059–2086.

Lehmann, E. (2005). Does Venture Capital Syndication Spur Growth and Shareholder Value? Evidence from German IPO Data. *Small Business Economics* (forthcoming).

Lehmann, E. E. and Neuberger, D. (2001). Do Lending Relationships Matter? Evidence from Bank Survey Data in Germany. *Journal of Economic Behavior and Organization*, 45(3):339–359.

Lehmann, E. E. and Weigand, J. (2000). Does the Governed Corporation Perform Better? Governance Structures and Corporate Performance in Germany. *European Finance Review*, 4(2):157–195.

Lehmann, E. E., Warning, S., and Weigand, W. (2004a). Efficient Governance Structures, Multidimensional Efficiency, and Firm Profitability. *Journal of Management and Governance*, 8(3):279–304.

Lehmann, E. E., Neuberger, D., and Raethke, S. (2004b). Lending to Small and Medium-Sized Firms: Is there an East–West Gap in Germany? *Small Business Economics*, 23(1):23–39.

Lerner, J. (1994). The Syndication of Venture Capital Investments. *Financial Management*, 23(3):10–27.

Lerner, J. (1995). Venture Capitalists and the Oversight of Private Firms. *Journal of Finance*, 50(1):301–318.

Ljungqvist, A. P. and Wilhelm, W. J. (2003). IPO Pricing in the Dot-Com Bubble. *Journal of Finance*, 58(4):723–752.

Loughran, T. and Ritter, J. (2001). Why Has IPO Underpricing Increased Over Time? Working Paper, University of Florida, FL.

Megginson, W. L. and Weiss, K. A. (1991). Venture Capitalist Certification in Initial Public Offerings. *Journal of Finance*, 46(4):879–903.

Rajan, R. and Zingales, L. (2000). The Governance of the New Enterprise. In: *Corporate Governance* (Vives and Xavier, eds). Cambridge University Press.

Ritter, J. (1991). The Long-Run Performance of Initial Public Offerings. *Journal of Finance*, 46(1):3–27.

Sahlman, W. (1990). The Structure and Governance of Venture Capital Organizations. *Journal of Financial Economics*, 27(2):473–521.

Schefczyk, M. and Gerpott, T. J. (2001). Qualifications and Turnover Managers and Venture Capital-Financed Firm Performance. An Empirical Study of German Venture Capital-Investments. *Journal of Business Venturing*, 16(2):145–163.

Stiglitz, J.E. and Weiss, A. (1981). Credit rationing in markets with imperfect information. *American Economic Review*, 71(3):393–410.

Ueda, M. (2003). Banks versus Venture Capital, Project Evaluation, Screening, and Expropriation. *Journal of Finance*, 59(2):601–621.

20 Ownership structure and initial public offerings in Portugal

José Miguel Almeida and João Duque

Abstract

This chapter aims to answer three questions. First, whether we could observe short-term abnormal return anomaly or long-term underperformance of initial public offerings (IPOs) in a small economy. Second, if these anomalies do appear to exist, whether they are distinct when ownership categories (private versus state owned) are compared. Third, if these categories show different patterns, whether private placements show significantly different under/overpricing phenomena compared with placements made by state-owned companies. In order to do this, we selected the Portuguese market to test whether cumulative abnormal returns (CARs) or the wealth relative (WR) of a set of portfolios were statistically and significantly different from zero.

We found significant short-term abnormal returns both for IPOs placed by private firms and for IPOs placed by state-owned firms. In addition, state-owned IPOs have been more profitable for short-term investments than private IPOs.

We also observed weak signs for 1-year underperformance, but we found new evidence, as reported in the literature, of significant differences for 1-year performance according to the ownership structure. Contrary to what the literature on economic and financial performance of privatized firms would lead us to expect, we found that IPOs placed by private companies tend to perform better in a 1-year term than IPOs placed by state-owned firms. However, our results are quite sensitive to the methodology used.

20.1 Introduction

In a few areas of finance, European financial markets have been the leading field of observation. One such area is the privatization phenomenon. Originating in Germany under the government of Konrad Adenauer in 1957 (Megginson et al., 1994) and initially called the denationalization program, privatization became famous under the Thatcher government in the United Kingdom during the 1980s. While not synonymous, privatization became popular when operated through initial public offerings (IPOs). Therefore, we see why the share price market performance became a standard way of evaluating the performance of newly privatized firms.

Although it does not deal exclusively with privatization, the chapter is dependent on the occurrence of this phenomenon in Portugal. Without it, the current Portuguese capital market would be significantly different. In fact, even though it is still small and marginally significant in terms of the Portuguese economy, without the privatization program it would not exist at all.

The aim of this study is to analyze IPOs in a small economy, using the case of the Portuguese securities market and paying particular attention to the ownership structure of the companies that place the offer. We consider whether the so-called underpricing phenomenon commonly referred to in the literature, and detected in several major markets, is observable in a small security market, such as that in Portugal. Moreover, we investigate whether private companies placing public offers in the market show a different pattern of behavior than state-owned companies doing the same, particularly when executing a governmental privatization program.

If the value of the stock is fairly priced by the issuer in the public offer, the investors should not expect any abnormal returns. Otherwise, statistically strong abnormal returns should be observed.

In Portugal during the 1990s, both government and private companies competed for funds. Although the state-owned IPO processes were more innovative, private companies followed them immediately.

We suspect that the empirical findings of underpricing observed in developed markets are still observable in a small and emerging market. However, in accordance with Megginson et al. (1994), who found privatization programs associated with an increase in economic and financial performance of privatized companies, we would expect a significant difference between state-owned companies and private IPOs. Therefore, we suspect that the underpricing phenomenon is still observable in a small economy, but it is expected to be more pronounced when state-owned companies are involved, serving the national interests of the government in stimulating the use of capital markets by the entire economy. Splitting the analysis into two samples – public offers made by private companies and by state-owned firms – we expect to find differences between them. The study spans a 6-year period, between 1992 and 1998, assuming investors would buy the stocks in the IPO or on the first trading day after it occurred and holding it for a 1-year time period.

We start this chapter by describing briefly the IPO literature in section 20.2. Next we present the data and the methodology in section 20.3. Then we present the empirical results in section 20.4 and conclusions in section 20.5.

20.2 Reasons and findings around initial public offering patterns

Financial theory has been uncovering an IPO pattern where the initial abnormal returns are positive and the long-term abnormal returns are negative. Additionally, the IPO literature has suggested a positive association between IPO activity and the stock market momentum.

Ibbotson (1975), using a small sample and non-normal distribution, concluded that, on average, the IPO abnormal return at the end of the first trading month (bid price) was +11.4%. At the end of 1 year, the average monthly abnormal return was 2.4%. In the long term, however, he did not find statistically strong support to reject the hypothesis of an efficient market. The author justified this market behavior with the hypothesis of a value transfer between investors and issuers through financial intermediaries. This process would guarantee the subscription of all subsequent IPOs placed by the financial intermediary. He also showed that IPO issuers had a higher systematic risk than the market as a whole.

Later, Ibbotson and Jaffe (1975) and Ibbotson et al. (1988) showed the links between market variables such as initial abnormal returns and 'hot-issue markets'.

In the long term, Ritter (1991) provided evidence that IPO issuers underperform other non-issuers in the same economic sector with equal market value. The author concluded that timing for placing an IPO is not random, as the most adequate moment for the market is chosen. Loughran and Ritter (1995) compared two portfolios of IPO issuers and non-issuers through the process that Ritter (1991) called wealth relatives, defined as the ratio between the buy-and-hold IPO portfolio returns and the buy-and-hold non-issuers portfolio returns for the same time period.[1] In a study with 1 year of data after the IPO event, the wealth relatives were estimated as 0.95, implying a negative abnormal return. When changing the non-issuers portfolio for the Standard & Poor's 500 index, the conclusions did not change. Even using a 5-year period abnormal returns remained negative, with the IPO portfolio having higher systematic risk than a non-issuers' portfolio. Following these studies the IPO literature has been abundant in providing evidence of these three phenomena.

From a different perspective, Dewenter and Malatesta (1997) compared the market price behavior of private companies with state-owned companies when both are publicly offered through IPOs. These authors concluded that, while in the UK state-owned companies are significantly underpriced when compared with the degree of underpricing observed for private companies, in other countries, such as Canada and Malaysia, the opposite is observed. This helped Dewenter and Malatesta (1997) to conclude that there is no general tendency to support the hypothesis that state-owned companies are more underpriced than private companies when going public. Furthermore, they showed evidence of other effects. They found the degree of underpricing to be dependent upon the degree of development of the capital market and the degree of industrial sector regulation where the IPO takes place. Also, in Poland, although Aussenegg (2000) and Jelic and Briston (2003) found evidence of IPO underpricing, they find no differences when comparing state-owned versus private IPOs.

Our chapter renews the debate started by Dewenter and Malatesta (1997), testing the issue for Portuguese data. We are concerned with IPO behavior in Portugal as a whole, but we also want to bring some extra light to the question of whether state-owned companies are significantly underpriced when compared to privately owned companies when both go public. The literature has been substantial in providing hypotheses for the patterns presented earlier.

In the winner's curse hypothesis, Rock (1986) supports the idea that IPO returns are a compensation for trading against agents with superior information, showing the possible existence of information asymmetry between market agents. The cost of information acquisition hypothesis supports the theory that initial abnormal returns are the reward for investors who reveal valuable information to the financial firm. This information is vital to price the IPO. In this sense, Benveniste and Spindt (1989) support the investors' discrimination.

Welch (1992) claimed that investors take into account previous buying decisions from other investors in the IPO process. If investors' decisions are sequential, latter investors behave according to previous investment decisions. To avoid initial lack of interest in the IPO, which can affect subsequent investment decisions, the issuer undervalues it. This should capture an important first wave of investors who will attract others, creating the effect of a cascade (the cascades hypothesis).

---

[1] Please refer to equation (20.3).

The information asymmetry hypothesis is based on the presumption that financial firms have superior knowledge of the market over the issuer and benefit from it, reducing the risk. However, Beatty and Ritter (1986) showed a negative relation between financial firms' market share and the fixing of a wrong IPO price. Ibbotson et al. (1988) defended the idea that financial firms avoid behavior that might be construed as misconduct in order to protect their commercial brand name.

Brennan and Franks (1997), supporting the ownership dispersion hypothesis, pointed out that the initial underpricing creates a demand surplus. When it happens, managers can select the investors and sell less stock to each one. On the other hand, shareholders have less power and influence over management.

The signaling hypothesis implies the issuer's management has a high value reference for the company. In order to signal this value over time, they underprice the IPO. Usually, in the long term, the issuer makes a seasoned equity offering to recover the initial underprice. However, Jegadeesh et al. (1993) found supporting evidence to state that initial underpricing is due to lack of market information by the issuer. Nevertheless, Garfinkel (1993) did not find statistical support for either of these hypotheses.

The stabilization hypothesis is based on the presumption that initial underpricing is the effect of an agreement between the issuer and the financial firm to sustain the price at or above the IPO price. This process would create the ideal conditions for subsequent public offers. Ruud (1993) found empirical support for this proposition.

The market incompleteness hypothesis assumes that investors ask a premium (the initial return) for holding IPO stocks instead of listed stocks. Tiniç (1988) suggested a legal hypothesis explaining that issuers underprice the offer to reduce the probability of future legal actions against them, if something goes wrong with the IPO. However, Drake and Vetsuypens (1993), Ibbotson and Ritter (1995), and others did not find support for this hypothesis. Market regulation could be another reason for underpricing, if there are any kinds of rules (or limits) applied in pricing the IPO.

The wealth distribution hypothesis has its roots in the privatization programs of the majority of European governments, which underprice the offers in order to attract small investors to the market.

Ibbotson and Ritter (1995) explained the hot-issue markets with the favorable information hypothesis, where investors buy stocks if a previous IPO has had notable rallies.

Finally, there is the hypothesis based on the changing perception of risk, which considers the concentration of high-risk-stock IPOs within short time periods.

The explanation for the long-term underperformance observed by Loughran (1993) may be obtained from three different theories found in the literature. The opportunity windows hypothesis suggested by Ritter (1991) argues that managers are able to determine the best time to sell the stocks. Usually, they sell overpriced stock, which corrects its price in the long term. However, Jung et al. (1996) did not support this hypothesis.

Shiller (1990) presents another suggestion, known as the impresario hypothesis. He supports the idea of financial firms creating an initial and apparent demand surplus. In the long term the market would correct the price. Issuers have no second chance because financial firms, which do not underprice, would be out of business.

The divergence of opinion hypothesis, presented by Miller (1977), is based on the assumption of the existence of two clusters of investor opinion – the optimistic and the pessimistic – about the IPO's future performance. The former are notorious prone buyers in the IPO but, as time goes by, opinions tend to converge implying a long-term price underperformance.

As a result of the literature, when observing the result of an IPO wave process in a small economy, where a significant number of firms have changed their ownership structure, passing from being state owned to being private, we have no expectations of different behavior. Therefore, we expect to observe the short-term initial abnormal return effect as well as the long-term underperformance.

Moreover, we are expecting to find privatized firms with a better market performance as a result of the significant change in ownership structure, and consequential setting of higher targets and reaching of better economic and financial results. This should be particularly evident if the industry regulatory framework, from which the privatized companies come, is significantly changed.

20.3 Data and methodology

We analyze all the initial public offerings (IPOs) followed by listing that occurred in the main market (Mercado de Cotações Oficiais) of the Euronext Lisbon, from 1992 to 1998.[2] In order to be listed, the exchange requires a firm to have at least 2 years of business activity and 3 years of published accounts. Additionally, the issuer must have a sound economic and financial situation, an estimated minimum market capitalization of 2.5 million euros, representing 500,000 shares, or a 25% free float. This enables small companies, in European terms, to be offered and quoted on the Lisbon Stock Exchange.

The issuer establishes the offering price in the prospectus, which is approved by the securities regulator (CMVM – Portuguese Securities Market Commission). If the issuer agrees, this offering price can be revised (lowered) for an amount no less than 5%. Because the issuer cannot increase the offering price, it sells a call option with a strike price equal to the offering price. Welch (1992) observed that this rule is also common to the US market, in order to prevent issuers from making IPOs with raised prices, which would than fail. In 1995, the Portuguese issuers started initial public offerings based on the bookbuilding system and a price interval to establish the offering price. These changes increased the flexibility to fix the IPO price. Benveniste and Wilhelm (1997) defined the bookbuilding system as the process of gathering information from institutional investors to fix the offering price, quantity, and buyers for the IPO. Under Portuguese law, the issuer can stop the IPO if there is a proper clause previously set in the prospectus.

Figure 20.1 shows the evolution of the BVL All Share (BVL – Geral) index and the number of IPOs in the main market per year.

The IPO activity has not been constant over time, showing some signs of being correlated with price movements. Table 20.1 shows the correlation coefficient between the BVL All Share index return and changes in the number of IPOs per year. It is noticeable that the IPO activity tended to be more aggressive in bull markets. Both

---

[2] Although some issues were observed after this, the criteria used for selection were not fulfilled and could not be included in the sample.

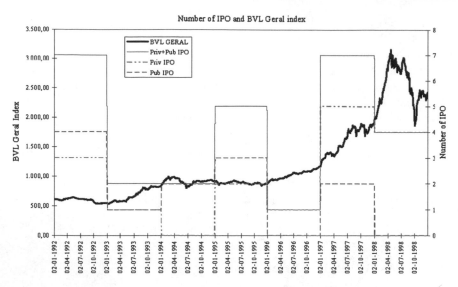

Figure 20.1 The number of IPOs and the BVL All Share stock index

Table 20.1 Correlation coefficient between the BVL All Share index return and the variation in the number of IPOs per year

IPO	Private + State Owned	Private	State Owned
$\rho_{t/t}$	0.41	0.65	0.65
$\rho_{t/(t-1)}$	0.14	0.24	0.13

$\rho_{t/t}$ = correlation coefficient between the variation in the number of IPOs in year t and the BVL All Share index return in year t. $\rho_{t/(t-1)}$ = correlation coefficient between the variation in the number of IPOs in year t and the BVL All Share index return in year $(t-1)$. Private + State owned = sample of private plus state-owned IPOs; Private = sample of private IPOs; State owned = sample of state-owned IPOs.

private companies and state-owned companies follow this general rule. However, recently, as the number of companies already privatized increased, the state-owned IPOs tend to decrease.

Moreover, Figure 20.1 also shows signs of some waving IPO activity, as spotted by Ritter (1991).

There were 28 IPOs in the main market of the Lisbon Stock Exchange (16 placed by private companies and 12 placed by state-owned companies) between 1992 and 1998, with an approximate total value of 5129 million euros. Following the IPO, all these companies were admitted to the listing process. Seventeen of them were made at a fixed price, six as tender offers and five as direct placements. Twelve IPOs used the bookbuilding system. The other markets of the Lisbon Stock Exchange (Second Market and Market without Quotations) had 12 IPOs, but most of them were very illiquid in the aftermarket and therefore were not considered.

In order to avoid other important effects on the companies selected for sampling, we dropped the IPOs that were followed by a seasoned equity offering within a 1-year time period after the IPO event.[3] Whenever a tender offering or an exclusion from the market occurred, we kept the IPO in the sample but the price observations were dropped. Hence, we did not collect prices after the day preceding the event announcement (market exclusion or a subsequent tender offer) until the end of the 247 trading days time window. Although other methods could be used to treat these phenomena, we think this is a more realistic assumption for investors holding IPO portfolios, as was suggested by Loughran and Ritter (1995). Kothari and Warner (1997), for instance, filled the remaining return series after the tender offers with the return earned until the exclusion, and Barber and Lyon (1997) filled them with the return of a reference portfolio.

All stocks considered in the sample have a known offering price and were listed (with a known first-day closing price) immediately after the IPO. Then, we were able to build three different samples: a total sample with 21 observations representing an approximate value of 5069 million euros, a sample with 11 IPOs placed by state-owned companies representing 86% of that value, and a sample of 10 IPOs placed by private companies.

Stock prices were retrieved from the Lisbon Stock Exchange data system and represent daily closing prices. Each price series was corrected for the most relevant events (stock splits, equity issues, and dividends). In the case of dividends, the observed drop in stock prices was assumed to equal the gross dividend paid. Daily instantaneous stock returns were then computed according to $r_{it} = \ln(P_{i,t}/P_{i,t-1})$, where $P_{i,t}$ represents the closing adjusted price of stock i on day t. For the first trading day, ordinary investors would get an instantaneous rate of return of $r_{i1} = \ln(P_{i,1}/P_{i,0})$, where $P_{i,0}$ represents the offering price of the IPO.

We computed the cumulative abnormal returns (CARs) in comparison to the market:

$$CAR_{p,u} = \sum_{t=p}^{u}\left[\sum_{i=1}^{n} x_i(r_{it} - r_{mt})\right],$$ (20.1)

with $CAR_{p,u}$ = the portfolio cumulative abnormal return between day p and day u, with $u > p$, r_{mt} = market (m) return on day t measured by log relative BVL All Share index, and x_i the stock i weighting factor. In order to account for a possible size effect in IPO long-run underperformance, detected by both Brav and Gompers (1997) and Fama (1998), we used two different methodologies to calculate the portfolio CARs: the equally weighted methodology where $x_1 = x_2 = \ldots = 1/n$ and value-weighted methodology. The value weight for a specific stock is:

$$x_i = \frac{N_i P_{i,1}}{\sum_{j=1}^{n} N_j P_{j,1}}$$ (20.2)

where N_i represents the number of stocks listed and $P_{i,1}$ the first closing price of stock i after the IPO.

Choosing the BVL All Share index to compute the abnormal return we encounter three problems. First, the index is a value-weighted index, which creates a mismatch

---

[3] As the average number of trading days per year in the Lisbon Stock Exchange between 1992 and 1998 was 247, we assumed a time window of that range around the IPO as a measure of 1-year time.

when computing the equally weighted CAR (CAR_{eqw}). Second, following the IPO, the new listed stock is one of the index components. And third, we assume $\beta_i = 1$ when Ibbotson (1975) and Ritter (1991) showed that IPO issuers have a systematic risk higher than 1. This means that the sample tends to overvalue abnormal returns.

Although Barber and Lyon (1997) concluded that abnormal returns measured against other non-offering issuers with similar market value and book-to-market ratio show good results, we could not adopt this method because of scarcity of issuers. In the Lisbon Stock Exchange, on average, 28% of the issuers make some sort of public offer each year. Using that method, and a protective time window for keeping data isolated from other effects, would dry up the total sample. Nor could sector indices be used, as Brav and Gompers (1997) proposed, since in some cases the sectors are the result of the new public offers under consideration.[4]

We also used one other method to estimate abnormal returns called the wealth relative (WR) as suggested by Ritter (1991):

$$WR_{p,u} = \frac{1+R_{i,u}}{1+R_{m,u}} = \frac{1+\sum_{i=1}^{n}x_i\left[\prod_{t=p}^{u}(1+r_{i,t})-1\right]}{1+\sum_{i=1}^{n}x_i\left[\prod_{t=p}^{u}(1+r_{m,t})-1\right]} \tag{20.3}$$

If WR > 1, then the return from investing in an IPO portfolio is higher than investing in the market portfolio. If WR < 1, it means the opposite, and if WR = 1, there would be no important difference in returns between the portfolios.

The aim of the study is to answer three different questions. First, whether we could observe short-term abnormal return anomaly and long-term underperformance. Second, if these anomalies do seem to exist in the Portuguese market in general, whether they are distinct when ownership categories (private versus state owned) are compared. And third, if these categories do show different patterns, whether private placements show significantly different under/overpricing phenomena compared with placements made by state-owned companies. In order to achieve this, we tested the null hypothesis (H_0) of the cumulative abnormal returns (CARs) of Portuguese IPOs as well as the wealth relative (WR) being rejected for the total sample, the state-owned companies sample, and the private companies sample. This is:

$H_0: \mu = 0$

$H_a: \mu \neq 0$

A t-test was used to accept/reject the null hypothesis, assuming independent and normally distributed abnormal returns.

20.4 Empirical results

We started by computing the market value of the issue for each sample. In order to do so we used the closing prices after the stock was listed. The average value of the

---

[4] This is the case for the telecommunications, energy, and cement sectors.

state-owned IPOs is greater than the average value of the private IPOs and the total value is almost double. However, the difference between private and public IPOs is not linear when we compare the median and minimum amounts for each in Table 20.2. This is a result of a few, very large, public IPOs (usually utilities).

Usually, neither daily returns nor abnormal daily returns after the IPOs follow normal distributions. They show high values for skewness and kurtosis. Table 20.3 documents the characteristics of the daily returns and the daily abnormal returns determined for equally weighted (eqw) and value-weighted (vw) portfolios for each

Table 20.2 Market value of the issues in each sample computed using the closing price of the first trading day after the IPO

	Market value (euros, million)		
	Private plus state-owned IPOs (21 issues)	Private IPOs (10 issues)	State-owned IPOs (11 issues)
Median	184	169	184
Mean	393	310	467
Maximum	2745	1019	2745
Minimum	18	54	18
Total	8244	3103	5141

Private plus state-owned market values on the first trading day after the IPO are from Almeida (1999).

Table 20.3 Descriptive statistics of daily returns of each sample (a) and daily abnormal returns of each sample (b)

IPO	Period: 247 trading days				
	Mean (%)	Median (%)	Standard deviation (%)	Skewness	Kurtosis
(a) Daily returns of each sample					
Private + state owned (eqw)	0.08	0.09	1.08	2.48	48.16
Private (eqw)	0.16	0.09	1.46	6.19	70.72
State owned (eqw)	0.01	0.06	1.37	−2.57	65.14
Private + state owned (vw)	0.19	0.07	1.32	7.99	98.57
Private (vw)	0.19	0.09	1.59	2.73	20.12
State owned (vw)	0.19	0.01	1.53	7.30	85.96
(b) Daily abnormal returns of each sample					
Private + state owned (eqw)	−0.01	−0.05	1.08	3.18	56.91
Private (eqw)	0.08	0.00	1.31	7.18	85.80
State owned (eqw)	−0.08	−0.06	1.40	−2.17	62.60
Private + state owned (vw)	0.04	−0.02	1.16	10.20	137.44
Private (vw)	0.07	−0.01	1.33	2.35	17.75
State owned (vw)	0.03	−0.12	1.39	10.03	133.25

Private + state owned = sample of private plus state-owned IPOs; Private = sample of private IPOs; State owned = sample of public IPO. Private plus state-owned IPO figures are from Almeida (1999). eqw = equally weighted; vw = value weighted. Normal distribution has a skewness = 0 and a kurtosis = 3.

sample. Brown and Warner (1985) overcame this difficulty in their study by using 250 samples, each one with 50 stocks, but our small sample does not allow such a procedure in this study.

While daily returns show a positive mean and median, we did not find similar results for daily abnormal returns. However, we found that state-owned IPOs show a poorer daily performance than private IPOs, in terms of both average returns and average abnormal returns. Furthermore, although state-owned IPOs show a lower daily performance they also present a higher abnormal returns' standard deviation. In addition, both returns are far from being normally distributed. In spite of this, care must be taken when interpreting statistical results.

The initial returns (observed between the subscription price and the first closing price after the listing) are positive whichever weighting method is used (Table 20.4), but the weighting method makes a difference. Large state-owned IPOs show a higher return than small state-owned IPOs. In the private IPOs we have the opposite situation.

Our sample with equally weighted private plus state-owned IPOs shows smaller initial returns than those reported by Alpalhão (1988) for the Portuguese market. It is the seventh smallest initial return of the 25 countries reported by Loughran et al. (1994), when ranked among their sample.

After studying the initial abnormal return anomaly, we looked to cumulative abnormal returns (CARs) and the wealth relatives (WRs) on the 247th trading day. As described earlier in the chapter, we used CARs and WRs with two methodologies. We started by assuming portfolios were composed of stocks bought at the IPO subscription price (with time period represented by [0;247]). Then, in a second version, we assumed that portfolios were composed of stocks bought at the first trading day closing price after the IPO (time period represented by [1;247]).

The cumulative returns on the 247th trading day, when the stock is bought in the IPO, are shown in Table 20.5. We found the same pattern as in the initial returns, but the value-weighted method in the private IPOs reaches a higher return than the equally weighted method. Once again, the value-weighted methodology makes a positive difference after 247 trading days.

Figures 20.2 and 20.3 document the evolution of the cumulative returns per sample and weighting methodology until the 247th trading day after the IPO.

As observed in Figures 20.2 and 20.3, the weighting method seems to interfere with the results. When using the equally weighted methodology, the cumulative returns of

Table 20.4 Initial returns

IPO$_{0,1}$	Initial returns (%)	
	eqw	vw
Private + state owned	10.55	16.68
Private	16.95	13.33
State owned	4.74	18.70

Private + state owned = sample of private plus state-owned IPOs; Private = sample of private IPOs; State-owned = sample of state-owned IPOs. Private plus state-owned IPO figures are from Almeida (1999). eqw = equally weighted; vw = value weighted.

Table 20.5 Cumulative returns on the 247th trading day

IPO$_{0,247}$	Cumulative returns (%)	
	eqw	vw
Private + state owned	20.48	47.11%
Private	40.30	45.78%
State owned	3.28	46.29%

Private + state owned = sample of private plus state-owned IPOs; Private = sample of private IPOs; State owned = sample of state-owned IPOs. Private plus state-owned IPO figures are from Almeida (1999). eqw = equally weighted; vw = value weighted.

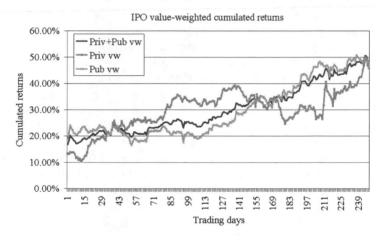

Figure 20.2 IPO value-weighted cumulative returns. Priv + State Own = sample of private plus state-owned IPOs; Priv = sample of private IPOs; and state Own = sample of state-owned IPOs. Private plus state-owned IPOs (Priv + State Own) figures are from Almeida (1999). eqw = equally weighted; vw = value weighted

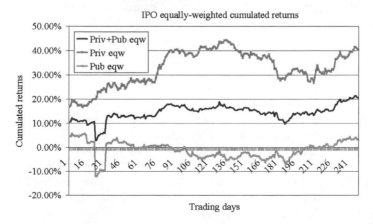

Figure 20.3 IPO equally weighted cumulative returns. Priv + Pub = sample of private plus state-owned IPOs; Priv = sample of private IPOs; Pub = sample of state-owned IPOs. Private plus state-owned IPO figures are from Almeida (1999). eqw = equally weighted; vw = value weighted

the state-owned IPOs are lower than the private IPOs, whatever the time period under observation. When using the value-weighted method the private IPOs' dominance is less obvious and depends on the time period under consideration. In this particular case, we cannot reject the null hypothesis that the mean difference equals zero.

When studying the IPO abnormal returns at the end of 247 trading days, results are dependent on the sample and method under consideration. When observing the entire sample, investors buying stocks in the IPO would obtain positive abnormal returns if compiling a value-weighted portfolio, but negative abnormal returns if choosing an equally weighted portfolio. However, when buying stocks on the first day the results would have been negative whatever the method under consideration.

When comparing the results of private and state-owned IPOs, we found that whatever the method, it has been more profitable, on average, to invest in portfolios composed of private company IPOs rather than state-owned company IPOs. This seems to contradict our forecasts since we were expecting state-owned IPOs to perform better than companies placed in IPOs by private firms. However, as the standard deviations observed in all samples are high and sample sizes are small, the cumulated abnormal returns (CARs) and the wealth relatives (WRs) are not statistically strong enough to reject the null hypothesis of the mean being equal to zero.

Brav and Gompers (1997) and Fama (1998) support the theory that long-term underperformance of IPOs is a size effect observed for small market value issues. Our results for the private plus state-owned IPO and the state-owned IPO samples seem to support the results of these authors. The equally weighted samples show worse results than the value-weighted samples (except for the private IPO samples). For a 5% level of confidence we reject the null hypothesis that the mean of value-weighted samples is lower than the mean of equally weighted samples (except for the private IPO samples). We also reject the hypothesis of the private IPO mean being lower than the public IPO mean, whichever the purchase day (IPO [0;247] or IPO [1;247]).

Aggarwal et al. (1993) showed that in Chile the state-owned IPOs underperfomed the market over 1 year, no matter which methodology was used (CAR or WR and whether stocks are bought in the IPO or on the first trading day). This state-owned IPO sample presented poorer results than the mixed sample of private plus public IPOs. This behavior is consistent with what we found for the Portuguese market.

From Table 20.6, we see that the way investors weight the investment and the day on which they buy the stocks makes a difference. Buying the stocks on the first trading day after the IPO leads to worse performance than buying the stocks in the IPO.

Table 20.7 shows that the first trading day has positive abnormal returns significant at the 5% level, assuming normality and independence.

Contrary to the previous analysis, the state-owned IPO presents a first-day return above the private IPO. This seems to provide us information about the way government and private managers fix the offering price. The state-owned offerings present higher initial abnormal returns and lower 1-year abnormal returns than the private offerings. Also, the initial abnormal returns are a key element to the performance of investing in IPOs (mainly state-owned offerings). The value-weighted methodology outperforms the equally weighted methodology, except in the case of private IPOs. The initial returns behavior is equivalent to that observed by Ibbotson (1975) and many other authors. It seems that investors could take advantage of this market inefficiency by flipping the stocks on the first trading day. Interestingly, the state-owned

Table 20.6 Cumulative abnormal returns (CARs) and wealth relatives (WR) when the investors buy the stocks on: (a) the IPO ([0;247]); or (b) the first trading day after the IPO ([1;247]) and keep it in the portfolio until the 247th trading day

IPO	CAR vw	CAR eqw	WR vw	WR eqw
(a) Investors buy the stock in the IPO [0;247]				
Private + state owned	10.87% (1.34)	−2.80% (−0.18)	110.78% (1.80)	97.04% (−0.19)
Private	17.42% (1.41)	19.46% (1.17)	116.36% (1.49)	126.68% (1.21)
State owned	7.98% (0.80)	−20.50% (−0.83)	107.80% (1.14)	71.07% (−1.56)
(b) Investors buy the stocks on the first trading day after the IPO [1;247]				
Private + state owned	−4.83% (−0.70)	−13.75% (−0.91)	94.16% (−1.17)	83.73% (−1.24)
Private	6.67% (0.62)	3.56% (0.26)	103.36% (0.45)	106.21% (0.41)
State owned	−10.71% (−1.33)	−26.96% (−1.11)	89.36% (−1.69)	64.62% (−1.84)

Private + state owned = sample of private plus state-owned IPOs; Private = sample of private IPOs; State-owned = sample of state-owned IPOs. Private plus state-owned IPO figures are from Almeida (1999). eqw = equally weighted; vw = value weighted. t-statistics are given in parentheses. In the wealth relative (WR) method, the t-statistic is computed by the difference between the return of stock i and its expected return.

Table 20.7 Abnormal returns ($CAR_{1,1}$) and wealth relatives ($WR_{1,1}$) on the first trading day after the IPO ([0;1])

IPO	$CAR_{0,1}$ vw	$CAR_{0,1}$ eqw	$WR_{0,1}$ vw	$WR_{0,1}$ eqw
Private + state owned	15.70%* (36.78)	10.95%* (12.86)	115.55%* (4.70)	111.00%* (2.79)
Private	10.75%* (17.52)	15.90%* (19.50)	110.48%* (2.28)	115.73% (2.21)
State owned	18.69%* (34.54)	6.46%* (4.55)	118.68%* (4.20)	106.57% (1.83)

Private + state owned = sample of private plus state-owned IPOs; Private = sample of private IPOs; State owned = sample of state-owned IPOs. Private plus state-owned IPO figures are from Almeida (1999). eqw = equally weighted; vw = value weighted. t-statistics are given in parentheses. In the wealth relative (WR) method, the t-statistic is computed by the difference between the return of stock i and its expected return.
* Significant at the 5% level, assuming normality and independence.

IPOs initial results with the equally weighted methodology are similar to those presented by Aggarwal et al. (1993) (CAR = 7.6% and WR = 108%).

The analysis of the CAR and WR series between the IPO and the 247th trading day shows that the value-weighted methodology is always positive during this time period. This does not happen with the equally weighted methodology due to small state-owned IPOs underperformance (Table 20.8). Whatever the market value of state-owned IPOs, the initial performance is diluted with time. The rejection rate of the null hypothesis is located in the first half of the series and the statistical results of the private IPO sample are stronger than the state-owned offerings.

Table 20.8 Descriptive statistics of the cumulative abnormal returns (CARs) and wealth relatives (WRs) of the IPO between the offering and the 247th trading day ($t = 0, ..., 247$): maximum, minimum, relevant trading day, frequency of rejection of the null hypothesis, and number of trading days higher than zero

IPO		$CAR_{0,247}$ vw	$CAR_{0,247}$ eqw	$WR_{0,247}$ vw	$WR_{0,247}$ eqw
Private +	Maximum	18.96%	12.22%	119.94%	113.24%
State Owned	[trading day]	[3]	[3]	[3]	[3]
	Minimum	4.35%	−6.37%	104.92%	94.52%
	[trading day]	[184]	[185]	[187]	[226]
	Rejects H_0	130	20	86	6
	[CAR or WR >0]	[247]	[151]	[247]	[151]
Private	Maximum	19.93%	27.38%	121.61%	138.53%
	[trading day]	[245]	[133]	[55]	[116]
	Minimum	1.54%	14.10%	104.80%	115.73%
	[trading day]	[179]	[17]	[179]	[1]
	Rejects H_0	90	110	1	0
	[CAR or WR >0]	[247]	[247]	[247]	[247]
State Owned	Maximum	23.74%	7.27%	125.35%	107.59%
	[trading day]	[3]	[3]	[3]	[3]
	Minimum	4.36%	−23.99%	104.38%	69.17%
	[trading day]	[184]	[185]	[176]	[233]
	Rejects H_0	77	4	33	0
	[CAR or WR >0]	[247]	[23]	[247]	[22]

Private + state owned = sample of private plus state-owned IPOs; Private = sample of private IPOs; State owned = sample of public IPOs. Private plus public IPO figures are from Almeida (1999). eqw = equally weighted; vw = value weighted. The indices in each method represent the period of analysis. The t-statistics are given in parentheses. In the wealth relative (WR) method, the t-statistic is computed by the difference between the return of stock i and its expected return. 'Rejects H_0' = number of trading days in which the null hypothesis is rejected from being equal to zero. The statistical test is continuously repeated over all the trading days $t = 0, 2, 3, ..., 247$. (CAR or WR > 0) = number of trading days in which each method is positive or higher than 100% respectively. (trading day) = sequential number of the first trading day in which the value was registered.

There is another difference between the private and state-owned IPOs. While the private IPOs show a higher result in the second half of the period under consideration, the state-owned IPOs present higher results at the beginning (also associated with the previously reported first-day abnormal return). Figure 20.4 depicts the evolution of cumulative abnormal return (CAR) during 247 trading days.

Figure 20.5 shows a similar evolution for the wealth relative (WR). If investors bought the stock on the first trading day after the IPO, we observe a similar data pattern to that which was previously seen (Table 20.9). However, in this case, every sample registers a larger number of negative results with less positive results. The rejection rate is non-relevant.

Alpalhão (1988), for a sample taken between 1986 and 1987, rejects the null hypothesis that the Portuguese IPO market is efficient. His initial abnormal return was 54.4% when taking the BTA index as the benchmark. Imposing the additional criteria of at least 20 quotes out of 30 initial trading days after the IPO, he found an initial abnormal return of 72.6% and a cumulated abnormal return of 36.2% at the end of 20 quotes.

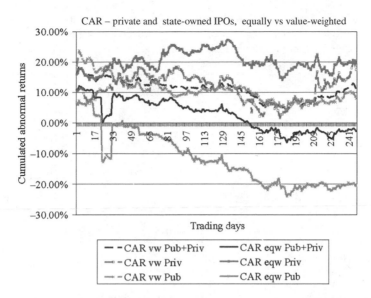

Figure 20.4 Cumulative abnormal returns (CARs) – private and state-owned IPOs, equally vs. value weighted. Pub + Priv = sample of private plus state-owned IPOs; Priv = sample of private IPOs; Pub = sample of state-owned IPOs. eqw = equally weighted; vw = value weighted

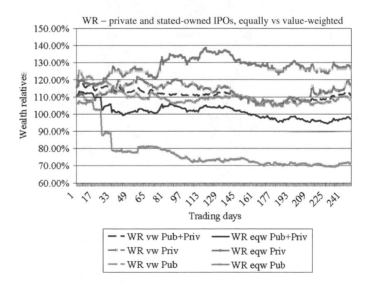

Figure 20.5 Wealth relative (WR) – private and state-owned IPOs, equally vs. value weighted. Pub + Priv = sample of private plus state-owned IPOs; Priv = sample of private IPOs; Pub = sample of state-owned IPOs. eqw = equally weighted; vw = value weighted

Mello (1994), for a sample taken between 1989 and 1993, found that the Portuguese IPO average annual return was +8.3% against a market average return of −8.0%.

Our results go a step further than those reported by both authors. We show that the initial abnormal returns are positive and statistically strong, but over 1 year the

Table 20.9 Descriptive statistics of the cumulative abnormal returns (CARs) and wealth relatives (WRs) of the IPO between the first trading day after the offering and the 247th trading day ($t = 1, ..., 247$): maximum, minimum, relevant trading day, frequency of rejection of the null hypothesis, and number of trading days higher than zero

IPOs		$CAR_{1,247}$ vw	$CAR_{1,247}$ eqw	$WR_{1,247}$ vw	$WR_{1,247}$ eqw
Private +	Maximum	3.27%	1.26%	103.31%	101.26%
State Owned	[trading day]	[3]	[3]	[3]	[3]
	Minimum	−11.35%	−17.32%	89.45%	81.59%
	[trading day]	[184]	[185]	[179]	[226]
	Rejects H_0	4	4	33	0
	[CAR or WR >0]	[10]	[5]	[14]	[9]
Private	Maximum	9.18%	11.48%	108.54%	115.39%
	[trading day]	[245]	[133]	[55]	[116]
	Minimum	−9.21%	−1.80%	93.37%	98.86%
	[trading day]	[179]	[17]	[164]	[17]
	Rejects H_0	0	0	0	0
	[CAR or WR >0]	[154]	[221]	[148]	[234]
State Owned	Maximum	5.05%	0.82%	105.12%	100.74%
	[trading day]	[3]	[3]	[3]	[2]
	Minimum	−14.33%	−30.45%	86.40%	62.59%
	[trading day]	[184]	[185]	[212]	[233]
	Rejects H_0	12	9	44	0
	[CAR or WR >0]	[15]	[7]	[16]	[6]

Private + state owned = sample of private plus state-owned IPOs; Private = sample of private IPOs; State owned = sample of public IPOs. Private plus public IPO figures are from Almeida (1999). eqw = equally weighted; vw = value weighted. The indices in each method represent the period of analysis. The t-statistics are given in parentheses. In the wealth relative (WR) method, the t-statistic is computed by the difference between the return of stock i and its expected return. 'Rejects H_0' = number of trading days in which the null hypothesis is rejected from being equal to zero. The statistical test is continuously repeated over all the trading days $t = 1, 3, ..., 247$. (CAR or WR > 0) = number of trading days in which each method is positive or higher than 100% respectively. (trading day) = sequential number of the first trading day in which the value was registered.

abnormal returns depend on the weighting methodology. After 1 year, we do not prove the market is inefficient.

20.5 Conclusion

This chapter aims to answer three questions. First, whether we could observe the short-term abnormal return anomaly or long-term underperformance in IPOs of a small economy. Second, if these anomalies do exist, whether they are distinct when ownership categories (private versus state owned) are compared. Finally, if these categories do show different patterns, whether private placements show a significantly different under/overpricing phenomenon compared with placements made by state-owned companies. In order to do this, we selected the Portuguese market to test whether cumulative abnormal returns (CARs) or the wealth relatives (WRs) of a set of portfolios were statistically and significantly different from zero.

We started by concluding that there have been significant abnormal returns in the short term for IPOs in the Portuguese market and they seem to be more pronounced if value-weighted portfolios were compiled. These findings seem to support the majority of previous studies in the field, such as that of Ibbotson (1975). In addition, state-owned IPOs have been more profitable for short-term investments than private IPOs, confirming, for Portugal, what Dewenter and Malatesta (1997) found for the UK market.

In a second study using a 1-year time period, we found that abnormal returns obtained from Portuguese IPOs were not statistically different from zero, either for private or for state-owned IPOs. However, we found that there are significant signs that private IPOs perform better in a 1-year term than state-owned IPOs. This seems to confirm the empirical results observed by Aggarwal et al. (1993) for the Chilean market, but seems to reject our pre-expectations about their relative performance based on the research of Megginson et al. (1994). According to these authors, privatized companies significantly improve their economic and financial performance. Therefore, we would expect privatized firms to perform better than private firms after being listed. In addition, these results are also contradictory to the findings of Dewenter and Malatesta (1997). We believe that in small economies (like Portugal or Chile) where privatized firms were basically monopoly utilities, the change in the ownership structure did not affect deeply the firms' environment or its management. For the Portuguese case this is particularly true, since privatized companies were only partly placed in the market, leaving the remaining slides of the share capital to seasoned equity offerings. And on top of that, the State has always guaranteed a Golden Share, particularly significant for large firms and those offering essential products/services, which had a major effect on our value-based methodology. As Huibers and Perotti (1998) maintain, this is a source of political risk with negative impact on price. Additionally, taking into consideration that these privatized monopolies tended to become regulated by recently created regulatory structures, they suffered additional operational restrictions and strong price limits. Therefore, although changing, the new ownership structure did not affect their operational structure, at least not as quickly as the market and regulators would desire. As a consequence, markets seem to have penalized them.

Acknowledgments – The opinions and conclusions in this chapter do not express in any way the opinions of CMVM – Comissão do Mercado de Valores Mobiliários and cannot be used in any circumstances in processes related to CMVM. Financial support granted by the Fundação para a Ciência e a Tecnologia (FCT) and the Programa Praxis XXI is gratefully acknowledged. This chapter was first presented as a paper at the ABN – AMBRO International Conference on Initial Public Offerings, Universiteit van Amsterdam, 2000. The authors are grateful to the participants for their helpful comments on its earlier version.

References

Aggarwal, R., Leal, R., and Hernandez, L. (1993). The Aftermarket Performance of Initial Public Offerings in Latin America. *Financial Management*, 22(1):42–53.
Almeida, M. (1999). A Venda de Acções em Bolsa pelas Entidades Emitentes Portuguesas. Evidência sobre a Eficiência do Mercado Português. Master Thesis, Lisbon: ISEG – Instituto Superior de Economia e Gestão, UTL – Universidade Técnica de Lisboa.

Alpalhão, R. (1988). Ofertas Públicas Iniciais: o Caso Português. Faculdade de Economia, Universidade Nova de Lisboa, Working Paper No. 100, Lisbon.

Aussenegg, W. (2000). Privatization versus Private Sector Initial Public Offerings in Poland. *Multinational Finance Journal*, 4(1–2):69–99.

Barber, B., and Lyon, J. (1997). Detecting Long-Horizon Abnormal Stock Returns: the Empirical Power and Specification of Test Statistics. *Journal of Financial Economics*, 43(3):341–372.

Beatty, R., and Ritter, J. R. (1986). Investment Banking, Reputation and the Underpricing of Initial Public Offerings. *Journal of Financial Economics*, 15(1–2):213–232.

Benveniste, L., and Spindt, P. (1989). How Investment Bankers Determine the Offer Price and Allocation of New Issues. *Journal of Financial Economics*, 24(2): 343–362.

Benveniste, L. and Wilhelm, W. (1997). Initial Public Offerings: Going by the Book. *Journal of Applied Corporate Finance*, 10(1):98–108.

Brav, A. and Gompers, P. (1997). Myth or Reality? The Long-Run Underperformance of Initial Public Offerings: Evidence from Venture and Non-Venture Capital-Backed Companies. *Journal of Finance*, 52(5):1791–1821.

Brennan, M. and Franks, J. (1997). Underpricing, Ownership and Control in Initial Public Offerings of Equity Securities in the UK. *Journal of Financial Economics*, 45(3):391–413.

Brown, S. and Warner, J. (1985). Using Daily Stock Returns. The Case of Event Studies. *Journal of Financial Economics*, 14(1):3–31.

Dewenter, K. L. and Malatesta, P. H. (1997). Public Offerings of State-Owned and Privately-Owned Enterprises: An International Comparison. *Journal of Finance*, 52(4):1659–1679.

Drake, P. and Vetsuypens, M. (1993). IPO Underpricing and Insurance Against Legal Liability. *Financial Management*, 22(1):64–73.

Fama, E. (1998). Market Efficiency, Long-Term Returns, and the Behavioural Finance. *Journal of Financial Economics*, 49(3):283–306.

Garfinkel, J. (1993). IPO Underpricing, Insider Selling and Subsequent Equity Offerings: Is Underpricing a Signal of Quality? *Financial Management*, 22(1): 74–83.

Huibers, F. and Perotti, E. C. (1998). The Performance of Privatization Stocks in Emerging Markets: The Role of Political Risk. CEPR, Working Paper, University of Amsterdam.

Ibbotson, R. (1975). Price Performance of Common Stock New Issues. *Journal of Financial Economics*, 2(3):235–272.

Ibbotson, R. and Jaffe, J. (1975). Hot Issue Market. *Journal of Finance*, 30(4):1027–1042.

Ibbotson, R. and Ritter, J.R. (1995). Initial Public Offerings. In: *Handbooks in Operation Research and Management Science* (Jarrow, R., Maksimovic, V. and Ziemba, W., eds). North-Holland, Amsterdam.

Ibbotson, R., Sindelar, J., and Ritter, R. J. (1988). Initial Public Offerings. *Journal of Applied Corporate Finance*, 1(2):37–45.

Jegadeesh, N., Weinstein, M., and Welch, I. (1993). An Empirical Investigation of IPO Returns and Subsequent Equity Offerings. *Journal of Financial Economics*, 34(2):153–175.

Jelic, R. and Briston, R. (2003). Privatisation Initial Public Offerings: The Polish Experience. *European Financial Management*, 9(4):457–484.

Jung, K., Kim, Y., and Stulz, R. (1996). Timing, Investment Opportunities, Managerial Discretion, and the Security Issue Decision. *Journal of Financial Economics*, 42(2):159–185.

Kothari, S. and Warner, J. (1997). Measuring Long-Horizon Security Price Performance. *Journal of Financial Economics*, 43(3):301–339.

Loughran, T. (1993). NYSE vs NASDAQ Returns Market Microstructure or the Poor Performance of Initial Public Offerings? *Journal of Financial Economics*, 33(2): 241–260.

Loughran, T. and Ritter, J. R. (1995). The New Issues Puzzle. *Journal of Finance*, 50(1):23–51.

Loughran, T., Ritter, J. R., and Rydquist, K. (1994). Initial Public Offerings: International Insights. *Pacific-Basin Finance Journal*, 2(2–3):165–199.

Megginson, W., Nash, R. C., and Van Randenborgh, M. (1994). The Financial and Operating Performance of Newly Privatised Firms: An International Empirical Analysis. *Journal of Finance*, 49(2):403–452.

Mello, S. (1994). A Competitividade do Mercado de Acções Português, Associação da Bolsa de Valores de Lisboa, Lisbon.

Miller, E. (1977). Risk, Uncertainty and Divergence of Opinion. *Journal of Finance*, 32(4):1151–1168.

Ritter, J. R. (1991). The Long-Run Performance of Initial Public Offerings. *Journal of Finance*, 46(1):3–27.

Rock, K. (1986). Why New Issues Are Underpriced. *Journal of Financial Economics*, 15(1–2):187–212.

Ruud, J. (1993). Underwriter Price Support and the IPO Underpricing Puzzle. *Journal of Financial Economics*, 34(2):135–151.

Shiller, R. (1990). Speculative Prices and Popular Models. *Journal of Economics Perspectives*, 4(2):55–65.

Tiniç, S. (1988). Anatomy of Initial Public Offerings of Common Stock. *Journal of Finance*, 43(4):789–822.

Welch, I. (1992). Sequential Sales, Learning, and Cascades. *Journal of Finance*, 47(2):695–732.

Part Four
Bookbuilding, Listing, and Underwriting

21 Bookbuilding and share pre-allocation in IPOs

Nancy Huyghebaert and Cynthia Van Hulle

Abstract

Since the second half of the 1990s, initial public offerings (IPOs) in Continental Europe have increasingly used bookbuilding to market their shares. During this process, a special role is assigned to institutional investors, who frequently – but not always – are pre-allocated a fraction of the offering. But firms going public using other selling methods, such as auctions or fixed price, may also pre-assign shares to retail and institutional investors. This chapter empirically investigates the driving forces behind bookbuilding and share pre-allocation in IPOs. Using data on Belgian IPOs, we find that firms using the stock market as a financing vehicle are more likely to use bookbuilding and pre-allocate shares at the time of IPO. However, information asymmetries are a major determinant of bookbuilding, whereas agency and monitoring considerations only influence the pre-allocation decision. Finally, we find that underpricing is larger with bookbuilding. By contrast, pre-allocating shares is shown to reduce underpricing and enhance post-IPO stock liquidity.

21.1 Introduction

In the second half of the 1990s, the European initial public offering (IPO) market has shown a spectacular increase in the number of firms going public. Ritter (2003) demonstrated that for the first time the Continental European IPO market even exceeded that of the USA, in spite of a high US IPO volume. This upsurge in the number of new listings has coincided with the development of new markets, such as Easdaq and the alliance of European growth markets Euro.NM. These stock exchanges were set up to meet the financing needs of an increasing number of young and high-growth companies. The European IPO market has indeed witnessed a shift in the population of firms going public. Whereas historically firms tended to be much older than those becoming listed in the USA, in the second half of the 1990s there was an explosion in the number of young Internet and technology-related companies going public. Simultaneously, IPOs in Continental Europe have increasingly been marketed through bookbuilding, a method that was originally developed in the USA (Sherman, 2000; Cornelli and Goldreich, 2001). In Belgium, for example, more than 60% of IPOs in the second half of the nineties were sold after a bookbuilding procedure. Before that time, it was rarely used. In essence, bookbuilding involves asking professional investors how many shares they are willing to buy and at what price. On the basis of the resulting demand curve, the firm and its investment bankers determine the IPO offer price. Bookbuilding thus helps to reduce the information asymmetries that surround the IPO decision, thereby allowing young high-growth firms to go public at a fair price.

During the process of bookbuilding, institutional investors play an important role. These investors can submit their indications of demand at any time until the book closes, and are free to change, or even cancel their bids as investment bankers revise the initial price range. Retail investors generally do not participate in this bookbuilding procedure. According to Jenkinson and Ljungqvist (2001), the main reasons for excluding them are the infeasibility of inviting bids and discussing the issue with a large number of small investors, although they also recognize that retail investors typically may be less informed regarding the value of the company than professional investors. While institutional investors have been prominent in Anglo-Saxon countries for a long time, Huyghebaert and Van Hulle (2004) provided evidence that their importance in Continental Europe has increased dramatically, especially since the second half of the 1990s. Simultaneously, they documented that during this time period institutional investors in Continental Europe on average showed a larger appetite for investments in the equity of listed companies.

In exchange for the information that they reveal during the bookbuilding procedure, institutional investors generally are allotted a fraction of the IPO shares. This fraction tends to be large. Aggarwal et al. (2002) reported an average of 72.77% (median 74.26%) in their sample of US IPOs from 1997 to 1998. These authors, among others, therefore suggest that investment bankers favor their own institutional clientele, to the detriment of small retail investors. As a consequence, the interest of retail (and potentially also non-client institutional) investors in IPOs may dwindle, thereby reducing the overall size of the shareholder base when firms go public. Worldwide, there is a growing tendency to limit the discretionary allocation power of investment bankers by having them pre-assign a fraction of the IPO shares to retail investors, thereby restraining the allotment of shares to institutional investors. This pre-allocation decision is typically included in the IPO prospectus and is referred to as the retail and institutional tranche respectively.

Share pre-allocation is not limited to the case when bookbuilding is used to sell the shares. In fact, IPO prospectuses show that in the second half of the 1990s, a – usually somewhat smaller – fraction of the shares may also be reserved for retail investors when shares are sold through auctions or at fixed price. Furthermore, when IPO shares are marketed by means of bookbuilding, the prospectus does not always mention such a share pre-allocation. Hence, bookbuilding and share pre-allocation in IPOs are distinct decisions and this study empirically examines the driving forces behind these. To the best of our knowledge, our research is the first to examine the determinants of share pre-allocation.

Using data on Belgian IPOs, we find that firms using the stock market as a financing vehicle are more likely to use bookbuilding and pre-allocate shares at the time of IPO. These decisions are not influenced by investor sentiment, as measured by the historical stock market return. However, information asymmetries are a major determinant of bookbuilding, whereas agency and monitoring considerations only influence the pre-allocation decision. Specifically, we show that firms where initial owners retain a large stake in the company post-IPO are less inclined to pre-assign a fraction of the offering to retail and institutional investors. By contrast, if post-IPO ownership by initial shareholders is smaller and the stock market is used as a financing vehicle, firms are more likely to pre-allocate shares at the time of IPO. Given that initial owners in our sample on average retain 64.94% (median 69.10%) of the shares post-IPO, these results likely reflect that firms with a really high post-IPO ownership by initial shareholders – and thus a small free float – have only limited opportunities to reduce the discretionary allocation power of investment bankers. Conversely, when firms go public to fulfill possibly important financing needs and initial owners necessarily retain a smaller fraction of the shares post-IPO, they limit the portion of shares that can be allotted to institutions. Besides reducing the conflict of interest with investment bankers, this restriction is likely to enhance the interest of retail investors in the IPO. Brennan and Franks (1997) argued that owners who dislike the monitoring by active institutional shareholders may have an incentive to disperse the shares among a large investor base when their firm becomes listed. In their model, this goal is achieved by means of underpricing, whereas our study suggests that another – potentially cheaper – method such as share pre-allocation may also stimulate retail demand for the IPO. Consistent with these ideas, we document that pre-assigning a fraction of the shares to retail and institutional investors reduces underpricing and enhances post-IPO stock liquidity. By contrast, we find that underpricing is larger when firms use bookbuilding. A positive relation between bookbuilding and underpricing is not consistent with the US literature, but may reflect that agency problems between IPO firms and investment bankers are large in a Continental European context, where the investment bankers' institutional clientele mainly consists of their captives.

The remainder of this chapter is organized as follows. Section 21.2 discusses the role of bookbuilding in reducing information asymmetries and the different motives to restrain the discretionary allocation power of investment bankers by pre-assigning a fraction of the offering to retail and institutional investors. Section 21.3 presents our sample, while Section 21.4 discusses the results of our empirical study on the driving forces behind bookbuilding and share pre-allocation. Section 21.5 subsequently examines the implications of bookbuilding and share pre-allocation for underpricing and post-IPO stock liquidity. Finally, Section 21.6 concludes.

21.2   Theory and hypotheses

In this section, we first discuss the role of bookbuilding in reducing information asymmetries during the IPO process. Then, we argue how agency problems between the IPO firm and its investment bankers, institutional monitoring considerations, and the use of windows of opportunity may affect the decision to pre-allocate shares to retail and institutional investors.

21.2.1   The role of bookbuilding in reducing information asymmetries

Using the example of the used car market, Akerlof (1970) showed that information asymmetries lead to price discounts. If information asymmetries are really important, this discount may become so large that good-quality sellers are driven out of the market. Adverse selection through asymmetric information is also a well-known phenomenon in financial markets. When stock prices are low, managers and company insiders often complain that their firm cannot issue new shares to finance its investment opportunities because the market cannot be convinced that it underestimates the true value of the firm. Consequently, firms may invest in reducing information asymmetries to increase their stock prices.

In the context of going public, the problem of information asymmetries can be reduced by assigning a special role to professional investors in determining the price at which the IPO shares will be marketed. Specifically, when the shares are sold through a bookbuilding procedure, institutional investors are asked how many shares they are willing to buy and at what price. On the basis of the resulting demand curve, the firm and its investment bankers determine the IPO offer price. Usually, book-building is part of a two-stage procedure whereby in the first stage the offer price is determined as described above. A key role of the syndicate of investment bankers in this stage is to provide access to a set of institutional investors who will be invited to offer their bids (Jenkinson and Ljungqvist, 2001). In the second stage, retail investors are allowed to subscribe at the price determined in the first stage.[1] As this subscription price reflects the value professionals are willing to pay, it should reduce the threshold to participate in the IPO for small retail investors, all other things being equal. The method thus uses the fact that as compared to retail investors, institutions generally are better able to evaluate the true worth of a firm. Cohen et al. (2002) indeed found empirical support for this conjecture. Their evidence indicates that institutional shareholders are capable of better evaluating the informational content of cash flow news than retail investors.

For bookbuilding to work in practice, investment bankers should give their institutional customers an incentive to invest in information collection and then truthfully reveal their opinion. This is typically achieved by reducing the subscription price below the true worth of the firm as revealed by the bookbuilding. Subscribers then achieve a positive return when selling out on the first day (in most countries, this return to 'underpricing' amounts to 15% on average).[2] Because of this reduction in price, investors usually ask more shares than are supplied by investment bankers so that rationing has to take place. Classically, the institutions that bid the highest price during the bookbuilding phase are less rationed. This logic has been developed in detail by Benveniste and Spindt (1989), Benveniste and Wilhelm (1990), Welch (1991), and Cornelli and Goldreich (2001), among others. It has also received some empirical support. Indeed, as predicted by these models, institutions collect valuable information and prove to be able to outperform small investors at the time of an IPO (Aggarwal et al., 2002; Ljungqvist and Wilhelm, 2002; Cornelli and Goldreich, 2003; among others). Furthermore, when allocation rules change and the benefits of participating in an IPO are reduced, these professionals collect less information (Ljungqvist and Wilhelm, 2002; Keloharju and Torstila, 2002). Ljungqvist and Wilhelm (2002) also showed that, overall, the indirect issuance costs caused by underpricing are reduced through the process of bookbuilding and hence benefit IPO firms.

Nevertheless, bookbuilding, and in particular the aspect of complete discretionary share allocation by investment bankers, also has received a lot of criticism. For investment bankers may use their decision power in the share allotment process not only to

---

[1] These two stages can occur sequentially (in the USA, for example) or simultaneously, which is often the case in Belgium. In the latter case, retail investors do not know at what price they will buy shares at the time they subscribe to the IPO; they only know that the price will be in a predetermined price range. In cases where the price that institutional investors are willing to pay exceeds the maximum of this price range, retail investors are allowed to cancel their bids.

[2] Alternative explanations have been put forward in the literature to explain IPO underpricing. For an excellent overview of the main underpricing theories, see Jenkinson and Ljungqvist (2001).

optimize information extraction, but also to serve their own interests. A well-known complaint is that when the issue is oversubscribed, share allocation can be used to benefit good customers with promising potential for future business. Consequently, institutional customers may benefit, to the detriment of small retail investors. By contrast, if information collection is the motive guiding the investment bankers' allocation decision, the allotment received by each party should reflect its contribution during the information-gathering process. Not surprisingly, recent research has paid much attention to share allocation in IPOs and the motivations underlying it.

Ljungqvist and Wilhelm (2002), Keloharju and Torstila (2002), and Cornelli and Goldreich (2003) indeed found that IPO share allocation is driven by the investor's contribution during the information collection process. Although Aggarwal et al. (2002) found a positive correlation between contribution and allotment, they also reported that institutional customers receive a larger share of IPO deals than can be explained by information gathering alone. Furthermore, for a set of European IPOs, Jenkinson and Jones (2004) even found no evidence that more informative bids are allocated a larger fraction of the IPO. They did show that investors less likely to flip are better served. In fact, to explain why they favor institutional shareholders, investment bankers themselves often stress that they allocate on the basis of investor quality, whereby the latter is mainly determined by the investor's non-flipping propensity. However, Aggarwal (2003), as well as Jenkinson and Jones (2004), found that institutions flip more than retail shareholders, especially in hot issues. Besides, a number of studies provided evidence on rent-seeking behavior by investment bankers. Reuter (2002) and Loughran and Ritter (2003) reported that investment bankers favor their institutional clientele – for example, mutual funds – in order to generate subsequent trading commissions. Also, Hogan and Ohlson (2004) found, for a sample of equity carve-outs, that companies endured higher underpricing as a result of spinning practices, i.e. investment bankers over-allocate shares to customers that could bring in more future business. In sum, investment bankers in IPOs need not use their discretionary share allocation power to optimize information collection. Rather, other motives, and especially those inspired by self-serving behavior, may come into play. Hence, the idea to restrict the investment bankers' degrees of freedom in the IPO share allocation process by pre-assigning a fraction of the shares to retail investors, thereby restraining the allotment to institutional investors.

21.2.2 Motives underlying share pre-allocation in IPOs

As mentioned in section 21.1, worldwide there is a growing tendency to pre-assign a portion of the IPO shares to retail and institutional investors. An oft-cited reason is that securities regulators and/or stock exchanges wish to protect small shareholders (for example, Ljungqvist and Wilhelm, 2002; Keloharju and Torstila, 2002; Derrien, 2005). However, share pre-allocation in IPOs is not mandatory in most countries (an exception is, for example, France where a minimum of 10% of the offering should be set aside for retail investors). At least at first sight, one could argue that such a policy would likely be detrimental because it limits the role of the better informed in favor of the less informed parties during the information collection process. The cost of an IPO, and especially the underpricing, therefore may rise (Sherman, 2000; Keloharju and Torstila, 2002; Ljungqvist and Wilhelm, 2002). The reason is that share allocation as a reward for information collection may become difficult to implement.

However, as we argue hereafter, there may be several other reasons why pre-assigning a fraction of the offering to retail and institutional investors could be beneficial for IPO firms.

One important benefit of limiting the investment bankers' degrees of freedom in the share allocation process is the reduction of the earlier discussed conflict of interest. By over-allocating shares to their preferred institutional customers, especially when the IPO is oversubscribed, investment bankers reduce the attractiveness of participating in IPOs for retail and other institutional investors. Consequently, the size of the investor base interested in investing in firms going public may decrease, a reduction that may continue to exist for some time afterwards. The price at which IPO shares can be sold therefore may decrease. In a capital market with incomplete information, Merton (1987) indeed showed that stock prices are higher the larger the number of investors aware of the company's securities. Consistent with the idea that attracting more investors in general enhances prices, Kadlec and McConnell (1994) found that when companies listed elsewhere announce their decision to also list in New York, their stock on average yields a positive abnormal return. Furthermore, a larger shareholder base is also associated with improved stock liquidity, which in turn is related to higher stock prices. Although there is no perfect agreement yet about how the interaction between these factors precisely affects value, there is consensus in the literature that liquidity has an impact on share prices. For example, Amihud and Mendelson (1986), Reingaum (1990), Eleswarapu and Reingaum (1993), Brennan and Subrahmanyam (1996), Brennan et al. (1998), and Eckbo et al. (2000) provided evidence that stock liquidity is priced in asset returns. Specifically, they showed that illiquid shares require higher (pre-trading cost) returns, which implies a higher cost of capital. In a more direct test of the consequences of liquidity for value, Loderer and Roth (2003) reported that the least liquid stocks on Nasdaq and the Swiss Stock Exchange suffer a discount on value of about 30%. Finally, Weston et al. (2002) showed for the USA that companies with highly liquid shares suffer less issuance costs at the time they raise new equity. Overall, the preceding arguments suggest that limiting the agency problems between investment bankers and IPO firms by pre-allocating a fraction of the offering to retail and institutional investors should lead to higher initial prices, hence lower underpricing, and higher stock liquidity in the aftermarket.

Another reason why IPO shares may be pre-allocated is to reduce the monitoring by the financial market. Compared to small retail investors, institutional shareholders typically are in a much better position to effectively exercise corporate oversight, given the size of their investments and the resources at their command. Aruğaslan et al. (2004), for instance, found that institutional ownership significantly influences the likelihood of a firm being acquired within 3 years after its IPO. Besides, Pagano and Roëll (1995) argued that large blockholders may even over-monitor the firm, which is not the case when selling to more dispersed shareholders in an IPO. Brennan and Franks (1997) argued that insiders who dislike institutional (over-)monitoring may have an incentive to underprice the IPO of their firm's stock in order to ensure its wide distribution. Another, potentially cheaper, way to achieve this goal could simply be to reduce the institutional stake in the IPO in favor of retail investors. Pre-assigning a fraction of the offering to retail investors could help to stimulate the retail demand for the IPO, as argued before. Although Brennan and Franks (1997) found empirical support for their conjecture on a sample of UK offerings, Aruğaslan et al. (2004) found no evidence consistent with this reduced monitoring hypothesis of underpricing in their sample of US IPOs. However, when pre-assigning shares to retail investors in order to reduce institutional monitoring, there is no need to underprice the IPO, other things being equal. No empirical study so far has addressed the possibility of using share pre-allocation to influence monitoring by the financial market.

A final reason for pre-allocating shares to small investors could simply be to drive up the initial selling price. In the wake of divergence of opinion and short-selling constraints, over-optimistic investors may boost the stock price in the aftermarket above its intrinsic value, thereby creating a positive initial return. Furthermore, in a model where the aftermarket price of IPO shares depends on the information about the firm's intrinsic value and on investor sentiment, Derrien (2005) showed that during hot IPO markets a too high initial selling price may go hand in hand with positive initial returns. As retail shareholders tend to be the worst informed investors, pre-assigning a fraction of the IPO shares to the former in times of positive investor sentiment strengthens this phenomenon of overpricing. Using data on French IPOs where a fraction of the shares is reserved for retail investors, Derrien found empirical support for his model's predictions. Hence, if this window of opportunity motive plays an important role, we expect market conditions to be a significant driver of share pre-allocation. Furthermore, in IPOs with share pre-allocation, we may observe higher underpricing. This motive, however, has no direct implications for the relation between share pre-allocation and post-IPO stock liquidity.

21.3   Sample selection and description

Our sample covers the period 1984 to 2000 and includes all new listings of Belgian firms on the three main exchanges of the country, i.e. the main market of the Brussels Stock Exchange (Euronext Brussels), Euro.NM Belgium, and Easdaq (Nasdaq Europe). Our sample does not include unit offerings, real estate investment trusts (REITs), nor reverse LBOs. For all 95 firms in the sample, we obtained the issue prospectus (containing ownership data before and after the IPO) and have access to their consolidated financial statements as of 2 years before the IPO. In addition, we collected data on the first-day closing price and trading volumes in the 2 years after the company became publicly quoted.

Figure 21.1 reveals a concentration of new listings in the periods 1986 to 1987 and 1996 to 2000. Other studies (for example, Pagano et al., 1998; Arosio et al., 2001) showed that IPO volume also peaks in other Continental European countries during these years. As expected, increased IPO activity coincides with periods in which the stock market indices BASI (Euronext Brussels) and EASI (Easdaq) are booming.

Table 21.1 shows the industry distribution of the 95 sample firms.[3] Similar to Arosio et al. (2001) for Italy, financial IPOs are concentrated in the earlier years of

---

[3] As in Pagano et al. (1998), holding companies that concentrate 75% of their assets in a single industrial firm are reclassified as belonging to the corresponding industrial sector. Financial firms are kept in the sample; as in Belgium, and many other Continental European countries, these companies represent a relatively important subgroup. However, as financial firms may differ from the other sample firms, we have tested the robustness of our results by removing them from the sample. These results, which show that our conclusions are unaffected, can be obtained from the authors upon request.

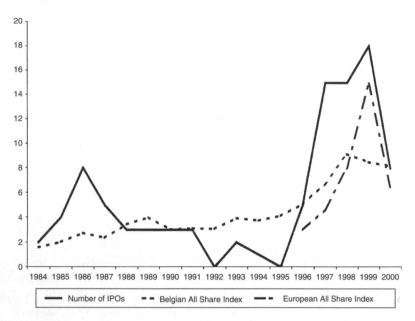

Figure 21.1 Number of IPOs versus stock market returns over the period 1984 to 2000

the sampling period, while high-tech flotations mainly occur during the later years. Despite the creation of new markets, an important fraction of the high-tech firms continues to opt for the main market of the Brussels Stock Exchange. In particular, of the 29 high-tech IPOs since 1996, 14 firms (48.28%) list on the main market, whereas nine firms (31.03%) list on Easdaq and six firms (20.69%) quote on Euro.NM Belgium.

Table 21.2 contains some summary statistics on the IPO firms. Given the length of the sampling period and in view of the high inflation rates during the late 1980s and early 1990s, all absolute statistics are corrected for inflation. Sixty-one firms sell primary shares at the time of IPO. In other words, they create new shares and sell these to the general public at their IPO. Hence, the company receives the proceeds from the sale. Seventy-one firms offer secondary, i.e. existing, shares. This implies that existing shareholders who sell some of their own shares receive the proceeds. In our sample, 34 offerings thus combine primary and secondary shares. The median primary and secondary portions equal 10.50% and 15% respectively. In total, the free float amounts to 25.79% of shares outstanding post-IPO. Thirty-nine firms pre-allocate shares to retail and institutional investors at the time of IPO. Pre-assigning became increasingly popular during the second half of the 1990s, with the spreading use of bookbuilding. Since the beginning of 1996, about 60% of IPOs opted for the book-building procedure; before that time, it was rarely used. Auctions, which were the common IPO selling method before 1996 (6% of IPOs), have become highly unpopular in more recent years (7% of IPOs after 1996). Table 21.2 shows that for the 39 firms with share pre-allocation, on average 60.12% of the offered shares are reserved for institutional shareholders, but the dispersion in this variable is substantial. We were able to collect the effective share allocation data for 47 firms in our sample. For these firms, we find that on average 48.02% (median 54.55%) of the shares placed in

Table 21.1 Industry distribution of sample firms

NACE	Sector	Number of firms
16	Production and distribution of electricity, gas, steam, and hot water	1
22	Production and preliminary processing of metals	1
24	Manufacture of non-metallic mineral products	3
25	Chemical industry	4
31	Manufacture of metal articles (except for mechanical, electrical and instrument engineering, and vehicles)	1
32	Mechanical engineering	1
34	Electrical engineering	7
41/42	Food, drink, and tobacco industry	9
43	Textile industry	2
45	Footwear and clothing industry	2
46	Timber and wooden furniture industry	1
47	Manufacture of paper and paper products; printing and publishing	3
48	Processing of rubber and plastics	3
61	Wholesale distribution (except dealing in scrap and waste materials)	5
64/65	Retail distribution	2
66	Hotels and catering	3
75	Air transport	1
79	Communication	1
81	Banking and finance	14
82	Insurance, except for compulsory social insurance	3
83	Activities auxiliary to banking and finance and insurance; business services	20
84	Renting, leasing, and hiring of movables	1
85	Letting of real estate by the owner	2
97	Recreational services and other cultural services	5
TOTAL		95

public are allotted to institutions.[4] Surprisingly, a few firms allocate no shares to institutional investors at the time of IPO. Institutional share allocation with and without pre-allocation averages 32.46% and 54.63% respectively. This difference is statistically significant (p-value of 0.0040). Also, we find that differences in allocation exist across selling method: for auctions, on average 58.33% of the IPO shares are allotted to institutions. For bookbuilding this value averages 47.18%, whereas it amounts to only 27.81% when the IPO is sold at fixed price. Finally, we find that for firms that pre-allocate shares at the time of IPO, the correlation coefficient between the percentage pre-allocated and the percentage effectively allocated to institutions is 0.7134.

---

[4] The IPO pre-allocation mechanism in Belgium regularly includes a 'claw back' clause. This implies that if the offering is highly successful in attracting small retail investors, the portion of shares allotted to the latter may increase to the detriment of institutional shareholders.

Table 21.2 Summary statistics for the total sample of N = 95 IPOs

Variable	Mean	Median	Std dev.	Min	Max
IPO transaction					
Primary portion	0.3004	0.1050	0.7790	0	6.7568
Secondary portion	0.1704	0.1500	0.1658	0	1
Percentage placed	0.3080	0.2579	0.1629	0.0587	1
Institutional preallocation	0.2468	0	0.3089	0	0.9133
Institutional preallocation if positive	0.6012	0.6000	0.1316	0.3173	0.9133
Institutional allocation	0.4802	0.5455	0.1923	0	0.8500
Underpricing	0.1395	0.0531	0.3429	−0.2153	2.7769
Firm characteristics					
Age	39.4421	18	53.2401	0	283
Total assets (€)	1,348,613,382	44,407,221	9,575,200,000	422,260	92,360,483,771
Equity (€)	106,708,008	11,548,860	306,170,000	−2,597,647	1,783,888,453
Sales (€)	281,596,118	44,588,670	919,420,000	0	6,194,926,469
ROA (EBITD/total assets)	0.1235	0.1452	0.2103	−0.7205	1.1063
ROS (EBITD/sales)	−0.0079	0.1206	0.6423	−3.5983	1
Leverage (debt/total assets)	0.6716	0.7256	0.3421	0.0319	2.8262
Debt mix (bank debt/total debt)	0.4253	0.4186	0.2923	0	1
Interest coverage (interest expenses/EBIT)	22.0540	3.0875	78.4790	−31.8377	461.3582
Market/book	3.9366	1.8992	0.7403	17.9444	4.8245
Assets growth	0.5330	0.2822	0.7407	−0.1541	3.5668
Sales growth	5.1747	0.2143	36.2668	−0.7128	336.4444
Ownership structure					
Blockholders before Ipo	2.46	2	1.4718	1	7
Blockholders after Ipo	1.99	2	1.1439	1	5
Concentration before Ipo	93.31	98.61	11.3780	33.43	100.00
Concentration after Ipo	64.94	69.10	15.9887	11.85	94.13

PRIMARY (SECONDARY) PORTION is the ratio of new (existing) shares sold to the public relative to shares outstanding before the IPO. PERCENTAGE PLACED is the number of new and existing shares sold at the IPO relative to shares outstanding after the IPO. INSTITUTIONAL PREALLOCATION is the percentage of shares that is pre-allocated to institutional investors. INSTITUTIONAL ALLOCATION is the percentage of shares that is effectively allocated to institutional investors at the time of IPO. UNDERPRICING is the initial stock return minus the corresponding market return. The variables measuring firm characteristics are self-contained. BLOCKHOLDERS BEFORE IPO is the number of shareholders whose ownership exceeds 5% before the IPO. BLOCKHOLDERS AFTER IPO equals the number of initial blockholders who retain an ownership stake above 5% after the IPO. CONCENTRATION measures the percentage of shares initial blockholders hold before or after the IPO.

Median underpricing, after correcting for the market return, equals 5.31%. This figure is rather low as compared to the underpricing reported for many other countries (Ritter, 1991; Leleux, 1993; Arosio et al., 2001), but may reflect that a large majority of the sample IPOs are firm-commitment offerings (Jegadeesh et al., 1993).

Firm age at flotation varies between zero and 283 years, with a median of 18 years. Firm size in the year preceding the IPO is also dispersed, independent of the construct used to measure it (total assets, book value of equity, or sales). The median firm has a return on assets of 14.52% and a return on sales of 12.06%, but profitability again differs widely across firms. Companies are highly levered: On average, 67.16% of total assets are debt-financed and bank loans represent 42.53% of total debt (bank debt, leasing, and current liabilities). Despite high leverage, an average coverage ratio of 22.05 indicates that firms can easily meet their debt obligations; the median coverage ratio, however, is much lower (3.09). As some firms have a leverage ratio above 1 and/or a negative coverage ratio, it can be concluded that not all firms are financially sound at the time of IPO. The average market-to-book ratio, calculated using the IPO offer price, is 3.94. The growth rate in total assets and sales in the pre-IPO year amount to 28.22% and 21.43% respectively; these growth rates, however, vary substantially across firms.

Ownership before and after the IPO is highly concentrated. On average, there are 2.46 blockholders (equals ownership above 5%) per firm; together, they own 93.31% of the shares before the IPO. Afterwards, their number and stake are reduced to 1.99 and 64.94% respectively. In only 16% of the cases does initial ownership decrease below 50% after the IPO, but this does not necessarily imply that initial owners lose control once listed. Similar results have been found for Italy (Pagano et al., 1998), Germany (Ljungqvist, 1997; Goergen, 1998), and other Continental European countries.

21.4 Empirical results on bookbuilding and pre-allocation decisions

In this section, we investigate the determinants of choosing bookbuilding to sell the IPO shares. Then, we examine the underlying forces that drive share pre-allocation at the time of IPO. The results are reported in Table 21.3, columns 1 and 2 respectively.

21.4.1 Determinants of using bookbuilding

In this section, we examine the underlying forces behind the decision to use bookbuilding as the selling mechanism at the time of IPO. The dependent variable in our logit regression model, BOOKBUILDING, is a dummy variable that equals 1 when the IPO shares are marketed by means of a bookbuilding procedure and 0 otherwise. Hereafter, we first describe our measurement of explanatory variables and then discuss our results, which are presented in Table 21.3, column 1.

To examine the relation between information asymmetries at the time of IPO and BOOKBUILDING, we use three variables. First, several authors (Megginson and Weiss, 1991; Chemmanur and Fulghieri, 1999) found adverse selection costs to be more serious for young (AGE = logarithm of the firm's age at the time of IPO) and small (SIZE = logarithm of total assets) companies. The reason is that younger and smaller firms typically have a limited track record and low visibility. In addition, firms with large growth opportunities (MARKET/BOOK = number of shares outstanding pre-IPO times the offer price plus book value of debt divided by book value of total assets pre-IPO) also may suffer from severe information problems, since growth opportunities represent investment projects that still have to be converted into cash generation. So, the quality of growth opportunities is uncertain and, as argued in section 21.2.1, firms may find it difficult to communicate that quality. To control for the fact that in carve-outs, information asymmetries are likely smaller, we include a dummy variable (CARVEOUT = dummy variable that is set to 1 when the offering is a carve-out and 0 otherwise).

Second, growth firms planning to use the exchange as a source of future financing may be able to benefit from the reduced information asymmetries produced by the bookbuilding procedure and/or the large allocation of shares to institutions that is associated with this selling method. Conversely, firms that do not intend to tap the stock market in the future gain far less from information production and may even dislike the (over-)monitoring by institutional investors (for example, Brennan and Franks, 1997; Pagano and Roëll, 1998). In fact, when investors who collect more information in the bookbuilding procedure are rewarded with a larger fraction of the IPO shares, the latter firms may prefer selling methods other than bookbuilding. Huyghebaert and Van Hulle (2005) found that firms selling primary shares at the time of IPO (PRIMARY = dummy variable equal to 1 when newly issued shares are sold at the IPO and 0 otherwise) are more likely to raise additional equity in the aftermarket. Furthermore, and consistent with Spiess and Pettway (1997), they found that these firms return rather quickly to the stock market.

Third, to capture the quality of a company's corporate governance, we include the following variables in our regression model. First, Jensen (1986) claims that firms with higher debt ratios (LEVERAGE = total debt to total assets) have a smaller need for capital market disciplining as leverage forces them to regularly pay out free cash flows to meet debt-servicing payments. Second, when initial owners keep an important stake in the company post-IPO (CONCENTRATION = the percentage of shares initial blockholders retain after the IPO), they can exercise sufficient corporate oversight themselves and may even dislike the (over-)monitoring by institutional investors. We also include (1 − CONCENTRATION) × PRIMARY to take into account that firms with a smaller concentration of shares in the hands of initial owners may accept a large institutional ownership and thus monitoring, provided that they gain access to the stock market as a source of future and − because of the monitoring − fairly priced financing.

Fourth, we control for investor sentiment surrounding the IPO (MARKET RETURN = the return on the Belgian All Shares Index (BASI) in the year preceding the IPO). Finally, we include industry dummy variables using the classification of Ritter (1991); the parameter estimates corresponding to these dummy variables are not reported, but can be obtained from the authors upon request.

The regression model thus looks as follows:

$$\text{BOOKBUILDING} = f(\alpha_1\text{AGE} + \alpha_2\text{SIZE} + \alpha_3\text{MARKET/BOOK} + \alpha_4\text{CARVEOUT} + \alpha_5\text{PRIMARY} + \alpha_6\text{LEVERAGE} + \alpha_7\text{CONCENTRATION} + \alpha_8(1 - \text{CONCENTRATION}) \times \text{PRIMARY} + \alpha_9\text{MARKET RETURN} + \gamma_i\text{INDUSTRY})$$

(21.1)

Table 21.3 Logit regression results: determinants of the likelihood of using bookbuilding and share pre-allocation

Variable	Parameter estimate	p-value	Parameter estimate	p-value
Intercept	−14.2152	0.0104	−11.9095	0.0481
Age	−0.4405	0.0827	−0.3093	0.2100
Size	0.6615	0.0054	0.7218	0.0120
Market/Book	0.1431	0.0992	0.0168	0.8433
Carveout	−1.2332	0.1410	−2.1547	0.0234
Primary	2.6676	0.0006	2.9410	0.0003
Leverage	−1.1760	0.2802	0.4018	0.7037
Concentration	0.8444	0.7166	−0.0586	0.0149
(1 − Concentration) × Primary	0.0056	0.8359	0.0535	0.0780
Market Return	0.3946	0.3078	−0.9377	0.4863
Number of observations	95		95	
Log likelihood	−43.3295		−42.9020	
AIC	114.6590		113.804	
Pseudo-R^2 (%)	49.41		47.77	

The dependent (dummy) variable BOOKBUILDING in column 1 equals 1 when IPO shares are marketed through bookbuilding and 0 otherwise. The dependent (dummy) variable PREALLOCATION in column 2 equals 1 when a fraction of the shares is pre-allocated to retail and institutional investors at the time of IPO and 0 otherwise. AGE (SIZE) is measured by the logarithm of the firm's age (total assets) at the IPO. Growth opportunities at the time of IPO are measured by the firm's market-to-book ratio (MARKET/BOOK). CARVEOUT is a dummy variable that is set to 1 when the offering is a carve-out and 0 otherwise. PRIMARY is a dummy variable that equals 1 when primary shares are sold at the time of IPO and 0 otherwise. LEVERAGE is debt to total assets. CONCENTRATION measures the percentage of shares initial blockholders retain after the IPO. MARKET RETURN is the stock market return (Belgian All Share Index) during the 12 months preceding the IPO.

The results in Table 21.3, column 1 show that information asymmetries significantly affect the decision to market IPO shares by means of a bookbuilding procedure. Specifically, we find that young, high-growth firms are significantly more likely to use the bookbuilding selling method. CARVEOUT has the expected negative sign, but is not significant (p-value of 0.1410). The positive and significant coefficient of SIZE is inconsistent with our hypothesis, but may reflect that especially large firms can benefit from the information produced during the bookbuilding exercise, as for these firms the absolute amount of money left on the table because of underpricing likely is large. Overall, our results are consistent with the literature on bookbuilding, which argues that this selling method is highly appropriate for IPO firms that are subject to large information asymmetries.

Next, we find that the coefficient of PRIMARY is positive and significant. So, consistent with our hypothesis, firms using the exchange as a source of (future) financing can benefit from the reduced information asymmetries and/or the large institutional ownership when using bookbuilding to market their shares. Firm leverage and post-IPO ownership by initial blockholders, however, do not affect the decision to sell shares by means of bookbuilding. Investor sentiment, as captured by the variable MARKET RETURN, has no impact either.

21.4.2 Determinants of share pre-allocation

In this section, we investigate the determinants of share pre-allocation. The dependent variable in our logit regression model, PREALLOCATION, is a dummy variable that equals 1 when a fraction of the offering is pre-allocated to retail and institutional investors and 0 otherwise. We use the same model as developed for bookbuilding in Section 21.4.1.

The results in Table 21.3, column 2 show that share pre-allocation is hardly driven by the variables capturing information asymmetries at the time of the IPO. While we do find that carve-outs are significantly less likely to pre-assign shares to retail and institutional investors, we also find that large firms are more likely to pre-allocate a fraction of their offering. The latter result is consistent with the idea that large firms in particular can benefit from an increased shareholder base, through a higher stock liquidity. In large-firm IPOs, institutions may be unable to absorb the entire supply of shares (e.g. Aggarwal et al., 2002). Also, a positive sign for the variable firm size may not be illogical when share pre-allocation helps to reduce the conflict of interest with investment bankers and thus underpricing, as for large firms the absolute amount of money left on the table likely is large. The results in the previous section already revealed that, for large firms, the conflict of interest with investment bankers may be more severe as these firms generally sell IPO shares after a bookbuilding procedure. Finally, AGE and MARKET/BOOK are not significant in explaining the pre-allocation decision.

Consistent with our hypothesis, firms raising new equity at the time of IPO are significantly more likely to pre-assign shares. This finding suggests that firms using the exchange as a source of (future) financing can benefit greatly from the reduced conflict of interest with investment bankers – for instance, through a larger shareholder base and thus liquidity. Consequently, share pre-allocation is likely to reduce the cost of seasoned equity offerings and thus the cost of capital. Huyghebaert and Van Hulle (2005) also concluded that firms using the stock market as a financing vehicle structure their IPO such that a liquid market in their shares can develop. In particular, they document that financing needs at the time of IPO are the main determinant of the size of the primary portion, but that firms with a relatively small portion of primary shares complement their offering with secondary shares in order to realize a sufficiently large free float.

Next, we find support for our conjecture that IPO firms may dislike the monitoring by institutional shareholders. By pre-assigning a portion of their offering to retail investors, firms where initial owners continue to play an important role may then be able to benefit from a larger retail interest in their IPO. On the one hand, we find that CONCENTRATION is significantly negatively related to PREALLOCATION. However, the interaction variable $(1 - \text{CONCENTRATION}) \times \text{PRIMARY}$ has a significantly positive coefficient. Given that initial owners in our sample on average retain 64.94% (median 69.10%) of the shares post-IPO, these results likely reflect that firms with a really high post-IPO ownership by initial shareholders – and thus a small free float – have only limited opportunities to reduce the discretionary allocation power of investment bankers. The reason is that after share pre-allocation to retail investors, the remaining placement would become too small to interest institutional investors. The correlation coefficient between ownership concentration by initial shareholders post-IPO and free float indeed amounts to -0.8732 and is highly significant (p-value < 0.0001). Conversely, when firms go public to fulfill possibly important financing needs and, as a result, initial owners necessarily retain a smaller – but still important – fraction of the shares post-IPO, they limit the portion of shares that can be allotted to institutions. Besides reducing the conflict of interest with investment bankers, this restriction is likely to enhance the interest of retail investors in the IPO and hence increase the overall shareholder base. So, the positive coefficient of the interaction variable likely reflects that firms going public to raise external equity financing and where initial owners continue to play an important role post-IPO structure their IPO in order to reduce agency problems with investment bankers and/or institutional (over-)monitoring. The relation between LEVERAGE and PRE-ALLOCATION is not significant, however.

Finally, we find no support for the model of Derrien (2005), as investor sentiment, which is captured by the variable MARKET RETURN, is not significantly related to share pre-allocation.

Overall, these results reveal that share pre-allocation is driven by forces other than bookbuilding. In particular, our results suggest that reducing the conflict of interest with investment bankers and limiting institutional (over-)monitoring play an important role in the decision to reserve shares for retail investors.

21.5   Effects on underpricing and stock liquidity

In this section, we investigate how bookbuilding and share pre-allocation affect underpricing (section 21.5.1) and post-IPO stock liquidity (section 21.5.2).

21.5.1   Impact of bookbuilding and share pre-allocation on underpricing

In this section, we examine the impact of bookbuilding and share pre-allocation on IPO underpricing, which is defined as the percentage difference between the first-day closing price and the offer price, corrected for the stock market return (BASI) of that day. The results are reported in Table 21.4. In model 1 we include BOOKBUILDING, while PREALLOCATION is included in model 2. Finally, model 3 incorporates both test variables.

In all models, we control for the fact that firms using the stock market as a source of (future) financing may have an incentive to underprice the issue in order to leave a good taste in the investors' mouths (PRIMARY). As in Garfinkel (1993) and Spiess and Pettway (1997), among others, we control for additional factors that are related to IPO underpricing: firm age, firm size, investment opportunities (MARKET/BOOK), whether or not the IPO is a carve-out, a dummy variable that equals 1 when a high-reputation foreign (US) investment bank is part of the syndicate (FOREIGN BANK), the percentage adjustment in the offer price relative to the mid-price of the initial price range (ADJ.PRICE), the historical stock market return (MARKET RETURN), and a measure for hot- versus cold-issue markets (VOLUME = the number of IPOs in the preceding year scaled by the total number of IPOs in the sample). Finally, we include industry dummy variables using Ritter's (1991) classification.

Surprisingly, the results of model 1 show that using bookbuilding generally leads to higher underpricing, other things being equal. This effect continues to hold after

Table 21.4 OLS regression results: determinants of underpricing

Variable	Parameter estimate	p-value	Parameter estimate	p-value	Parameter estimate	p-value
Intercept	−0.1204	0.7982	−0.3866	0.4153	−0.2192	0.6412
Bookbuilding	0.1175	0.0590			0.2348	0.0335
Preallocation			−0.0244	0.7726	−0.1792	0.1040
Primary	−0.1323	0.1425	−0.0924	0.2989	−0.1325	0.1379
Age	−0.0404	0.1131	−0.0446	0.0848	−0.0436	0.0854
Size	0.0047	0.8247	0.0180	0.4013	0.0100	0.6384
Market/Book	0.0209	0.0233	0.0234	0.0103	0.0186	0.0423
Carveout	−0.0662	0.4515	−0.0952	0.2896	−0.0864	0.3268
Foreign Bank	−0.1994	0.0182	−0.2103	0.0146	−0.2161	0.0106
Adj.Price	0.9213	0.0140	0.7830	0.0347	0.9318	0.0122
Market Return	0.3561	0.0310	0.3852	0.0208	0.3514	0.0316
Volume	1.9044	0.0046	2.3167	0.0012	2.2340	0.0015
Number of observations	93		93		93	
Adjusted R^2 (%)	24.07		22.30		25.59	

The dependent variable UNDERPRICING is the percentage difference between the first-day closing price and the offer price, corrected for the stock market return (BASI) of that day. BOOKBUILDING is a dummy variable that equals 1 when IPO shares are marketed through bookbuilding and 0 otherwise. PREALLO-CATION is a dummy variable that equals 1 when a fraction of the shares is pre-allocated to retail and institutional investors at the time of IPO and 0 otherwise. PRIMARY is a dummy variable that equals 1 when primary shares are sold at the time of IPO and 0 otherwise. AGE (SIZE) is measured by the logarithm of firm age (total assets) at the IPO. Growth opportunities at the time of IPO are measured by the firm's market-to-book ratio (MARKET/BOOK). CARVEOUT is a dummy variable that is set to 1 when the offering is a carve-out and 0 otherwise. FOREIGN BANK is a dummy variable that equals 1 when a high-reputation foreign (US) investment bank is part of the syndicate. ADJ.PRICE is the percentage adjustment in the offer price measured relative to the mid-price of the initial price range. MARKET RETURN is the stock market return (Belgian All Share Index) during the 12 months preceding the IPO, while VOLUME is the number of IPOs in that same period scaled by the total number of IPOs in the sample.

controlling for share pre-allocation at the time of IPO (model 3). The positive sign of BOOKBUILDING is inconsistent with the results of other studies that use data on US IPOs. Ljungqvist and Wilhelm (2002), for instance, found that the indirect issuance costs caused by underpricing are reduced through the process of bookbuilding and hence benefit IPO firms. However, Ljungqvist et al. (2003) found that bookbuilding on its own does not lead to lower underpricing, unless the IPO is conducted by US banks and/or targeted at US investors. For Belgium – and other Continental European countries – a positive sign may reflect the conflict of interest between investment bankers and IPO firms, as the institutions that participate in the information production process generally are the investment bankers' captives. We believe that further research is needed to examine in more detail this positive relation between bookbuilding and underpricing.

Next, we find some evidence that firms pre-allocating shares to retail and institutional investors underprice their shares to a smaller extent, even though the variable PREALLOCATION is only marginally significant at the 10% level in model 3 (p-value of 0.1040). This finding is consistent with the idea that limiting the stake of institutional shareholders in advance helps to reduce the conflict of interest between IPO firms and their investment bankers.

The hypothesis that firms using the stock market as a financing vehicle may have an incentive to underprice their offering to a larger extent is not supported by our data. We do find some evidence that information asymmetries are positively related to IPO underpricing. In particular, we document that first-day returns are larger for young firms with a higher market-to-book ratio, other things being equal. However, firm size and the dummy for the IPO being a carve-out do not explain underpricing.

When a high-reputation foreign (US) investment bank is part of the syndicate, IPOs are underpriced to a smaller extent, which is consistent with the findings of Ljungqvist et al. (2003). By contrast, a larger percentage adjustment of the final offer price relative to the mid-price of the initial price range is associated with higher IPO underpricing. The literature (e.g. Aggarwal et al., 2002) considers the latter variable to capture the uncertainty in determining the final price and/or the information that institutional investors reveal when the IPO is marketed by means of bookbuilding; both interpretations should produce a positive coefficient. Finally, when the historical stock market return is large or the IPO takes place in a hot-issue market, offerings are underpriced more. Interestingly, when the latter two variables are removed from model 3, its explanatory power is drastically reduced: the adjusted R^2 drops from 25.59% to 16.08%. Overall, these results thus stress the importance of market conditions in explaining IPO underpricing.

21.5.2 Impact of bookbuilding and share pre-allocation on stock liquidity

In this section, we wish to investigate whether post-IPO stock liquidity is higher for firms that used bookbuilding and/or pre-allocated a fraction of their offering to retail and institutional investors at the time of IPO. Post-IPO stock liquidity (LIQUIDITY) is hereby defined as the number of shares traded during a horizon of 2 years starting 1 month after the IPO divided by the number of shares outstanding after the IPO (see also Eckbo et al., 2000). The reason why we focus on 2-year stock liquidity is that it is easier to explain liquidity over longer horizons (e.g. Huyghebaert and Van Hulle, 2005). The first post-IPO month is disregarded to correct for the fact that early liquidity may be affected by the adopted distribution rules.

The results are reported in Table 21.5. In model 1 we include BOOKBUILDING, while PREALLOCATION is included in model 2. Finally, model 3 incorporates both test variables. In addition, all models include the variable PRIMARY to control for the fact that firms using the stock market as a financing vehicle may also structure their IPO in other ways such that a liquid market in their shares can develop (e.g. Huyghebaert and Van Hulle, 2005). To control for firm age and size, the log of firm age at the IPO and total assets post-IPO respectively are included. As in Brennan and Subrahmanyam (1996), Chordia et al. (2004) and others, we control for additional factors that may affect stock liquidity: investment opportunities (MARKET/BOOK), a dummy that equals 1 when the firm lists on a market for innovative growth companies, i.e. Easdaq or Euro.NM Belgium (MARKET TYPE), a dummy that equals 1 when at least one market maker is appointed (MARKET MAKER), the historical stock market return (MARKET RETURN), and a measure for hot- versus cold-issue markets (VOLUME). Finally, we include industry dummy variables using Ritter's (1991) classification.

Table 21.5 OLS regression results: determinants of post-IPO stock liquidity

Variable	Parameter estimate	p-value	Parameter estimate	p-value	Parameter estimate	p-value
Intercept	0.0130	0.9569	−0.0443	0.8474	−0.0055	0.9814
Bookbuilding	0.1334	0.0078			0.0513	0.4560
Preallocation			0.1574	0.0023	0.1194	0.0969
Primary	−0.0101	0.8186	−0.0088	0.8381	−0.0099	0.8184
Age	0.0111	0.4803	0.0142	0.3633	0.0148	0.3484
Size (post-IPO)	0.0035	0.7338	0.0062	0.5230	0.0042	0.6817
Market/Book	0.0053	0.3267	0.0057	0.2844	0.0051	0.3390
Market Type	0.0959	0.1398	0.1730	0.0166	0.1582	0.0346
Market Maker	0.1082	0.0345	0.0948	0.0621	0.0889	0.0843
Market Return	0.2201	0.0318	0.2182	0.0303	0.2192	0.0301
Volume	−1.2657	0.0012	−1.4741	0.0003	−1.4579	0.0003
Number of observations	77		77		77	
Adjusted R^2 (%)	46.46		48.31		47.96	

The dependent variable LIQUIDITY is the number of shares traded over a window of 2 years following the IPO divided by the number of shares outstanding post-IPO. BOOKBUILDING is a dummy variable that equals 1 when IPO shares are marketed through bookbuilding and 0 otherwise. PREALLOCATION is a dummy variable that equals 1 when a fraction of the shares is pre-allocated to retail and institutional investors at the time of IPO and 0 otherwise. PRIMARY is a dummy variable that equals 1 when primary shares are sold at the time of IPO and 0 otherwise. AGE (SIZE) is measured by the logarithm of firm age at the IPO (total assets post-IPO). Growth opportunities at the time of IPO are measured by the firm's market-to-book ratio (MARKET/BOOK). MARKET TYPE is equal to 1 if the firm lists on a market for innovative growth firms and 0 otherwise. MARKET MAKER equals 1 if at least one market maker is appointed and 0 otherwise. MARKET RETURN is the stock market return (Belgian All Share Index) during the 12 months preceding the IPO, while VOLUME is the number of IPOs in that same period scaled by the total number of IPOs in the sample.

We find that BOOKBUILDING is significantly positively related to post-IPO stock liquidity in model 1. However, this relation proves to be spuriously driven by the positive relation between BOOKBUILDING and PREALLOCATION. Indeed, after controlling for PREALLOCATION, BOOKBUILDING no longer significantly affects post-IPO stock liquidity, whereas PREALLOCATION has a positive and significant coefficient. So, restraining the fraction of shares that can be allocated to institutions positively affects a stock's liquidity in the aftermarket. As argued in section 21.2.2, this effect may manifest when share pre-allocation helps to enlarge the firm's shareholder base, either to decrease the conflict of interest with investment bankers or to reduce monitoring by the financial market.

While firms that use the exchange as a source of (future) financing may also use other mechanisms to develop a liquid market in their shares – for example, complement their offering with secondary shares when the size of the primary portion is relatively small – we find that the dummy PRIMARY is not significantly related to post-IPO liquidity. Huyghebaert and Van Hulle (2005) indeed found that it is the free float that positively affects stock liquidity. Firm age, firm size, and investment opportunities, as captured by the market-to-book ratio, are not significant either.

However, we do find evidence of different levels of stock liquidity depending upon the exchange on which the firm lists. In particular, Easdaq and Euro.NM Belgium, which were established for listing innovative growth companies, have more depth, other things being equal. Hence, as pointed out by Corwin and Harris (2001), the selection of the appropriate stock market is an important consideration for IPO candidates. Appointing a market maker also significantly increases stock liquidity. The latter result is not surprising as the task of a market maker consists mainly of guaranteeing liquidity. Historical stock market performance affects post-IPO liquidity positively. Finally, there is some evidence of reduced liquidity following periods of high IPO volume, which could point at a saturating market.

21.6 Conclusion

In the second half of the 1990s, the European initial public offering market showed a spectacular increase in the number of firms going public. This upsurge in the number of new listings coincided with the development of new markets, which were set up to meet the financing needs of an increasing number of young and high-growth companies. Simultaneously, IPOs in Continental Europe have increasingly been marketed through bookbuilding. For Belgium, for example, more than 60% of IPOs in the second half of the 1990s were sold after a bookbuilding procedure. It was rarely used before that time. Various theoretical models have argued that bookbuilding helps to reduce the information asymmetries that surround the IPO decision, thereby allowing young high-growth firms to go public at a fair price.

Institutional investors play an important role during the process of bookbuilding. In exchange for the information that they reveal, these investors generally are allotted a (rather large) fraction of the IPO shares. However, worldwide there is a growing tendency to limit the discretionary allocation power of investment bankers by having them pre-assign a fraction of the IPO shares to retail investors, thereby restraining the allocation of shares to institutions. But when IPO shares are marketed by means of bookbuilding, the prospectus does not always mention such a share pre-allocation. In addition, share pre-allocation is not limited to the case when bookbuilding is used to sell the shares. Hence, bookbuilding and share pre-allocation in IPOs are distinct decisions and this study empirically examines the driving forces behind them.

Our data on Belgian IPOs during the period 1984 to 2000 largely confirm that bookbuilding is used when firms going public are subject to large information asymmetries. Specifically, we find that firm age is significantly negative, whereas the market-to-book ratio is significantly positive related to the likelihood of using bookbuilding to determine the IPO offer price. Furthermore, firms using the stock market as a financing vehicle are more likely to use bookbuilding. After controlling for information asymmetries, we document that using bookbuilding positively affects IPO underpricing. This relation is inconsistent with the US literature, but may reflect that the conflict of interest between investment bankers and IPO firms is even more serious in a Continental European context. The reason could be that the institutional investors who are invited to participate in the information-gathering process are mainly the investment bankers' captives. Finally, we find no impact of bookbuilding on stock liquidity in the aftermarket, which suggests that reduced information asymmetries through bookbuilding at the time of IPO do not spillover a long time after the firm's stock market introduction.

The decision to pre-assign a fraction of the offering to retail and institutional investors is clearly determined by different variables. On the one hand, we find no relation with the variables capturing information asymmetries. However, we do find that firms using the stock exchange as a financing vehicle are more likely to pre-allocate shares at the time of IPO. Finally, our results suggest that agency and monitoring considerations largely influence the pre-allocation decision. Specifically, we document that firms where initial owners retain a large stake in the company post-IPO are less inclined to pre-assign a portion of the offering to retail and institutional investors. By contrast, if post-IPO ownership by initial shareholders is smaller and the stock market is used as a financing vehicle, firms are more likely to pre-allocate shares at the time of IPO. These results likely reflect that firms with a really high post-IPO ownership by initial shareholders have only limited opportunities to reduce the conflict of interest with investment bankers resulting from the latter's discretionary allocation power. Conversely, when firms go public to fulfill possibly important financing needs and initial owners necessarily retain a smaller fraction of the shares post-IPO, they limit the portion of shares that can be allotted to institutional investors. Besides reducing the aforementioned conflict of interest, this restriction is likely to enhance the interest of retail investors in the IPO. The latter finding may also reflect the owners' dislike of (over-)monitoring by institutional investors, who use share pre-allocation to disperse the shares among retail investors and increase the investor base. In the model of Brennan and Franks (1997), this goal is achieved by means of underpricing, whereas our study suggests that another – potentially cheaper – method such as share pre-allocation may achieve the same result. Consistent with the idea that share pre-allocation can be used to increase the shareholder base – either to reduce agency problems or to decrease monitoring by the financial market – we find that share pre-allocation in IPOs reduces underpricing and enhances post-IPO stock liquidity.

Overall, these results show that when regulators legally enforce share pre-allocation in order to protect the interests of small retail investors, the effects are not one-sidedly negative, especially in a Continental European context. While such a policy is likely to reduce the information production by institutional investors during the bookbuilding procedure and thus increase IPO underpricing, at the same time it helps to reduce the conflict of interest between investment bankers and IPO firms, which could moderate underpricing. So, the impact on underpricing is not clearly a priority, but our data suggest it is negative and thus benefits IPO firms. In addition, the resulting wider distribution of shares is likely to reduce the monitoring incentives of institutional investors, which should negatively affect stock prices. Despite this negative impact on price, pre-allocation may reduce the going public threshold for owners who wish to use the stock market as a source of (future) financing, but dislike financial market (over-)monitoring. Furthermore, as shown by our study, the resulting wider distribution of shares also helps to ensure the stock's liquidity, which should increase its price. Examining whether the positive impact of liquidity on value outweighs the negative impact of reduced monitoring is beyond the scope of this study.

References

Aggarwal, R. (2003). Allocation of Initial Public Offerings and Flipping Activity. *Journal of Financial Economics*, 68(1):111–135.

Aggarwal, R., Prabhala, N., and Puri, M. (2002). Institutional Allocation in Initial Public Offerings: Empirical Evidence. *Journal of Finance*, 57(3):1421–1442.

Akerlof, G. (1970). The Market for Lemons: Qualitative Uncertainty and the Market Mechanism. *Quarterly Journal of Economics*, 84(3):488–500.

Amihud, Y. and Mendelson, H. (1986). Asset Pricing and Bid–Ask Spread. *Journal of Financial Economics*, 17(2):223–249.

Arosio, R., Giudici, G., and Paleari, S. (2001). The Market Performance of Italian IPOs in the Long Run. Working Paper, University of Bergamo, Italy.

Aruğaslan, O., Cook, D. O., and Kieschnick, R. (2004). Monitoring as a Motivation for IPO Underpricing. *Journal of Finance*, 59(5):2403–2420.

Benveniste, L. and Spindt, P. (1989). How Investment Banks Determine the Offer Price and Allocation of New Issues. *Journal of Financial Economics*, 24(2):343–362.

Benveniste, L. and Wilhelm, W. (1990). A Comparative Analysis of IPO Proceeds under Alternative Regulatory Environments. *Journal of Financial Economics*, 28(1–2):173–207.

Brennan, M. and Franks, J. (1997). Underpricing, Ownership and Control in Initial Public Offerings of Equity Securities in the UK. *Journal of Financial Economics*, 45(3):391–413.

Brennan, M. and Subrahmanyam, A. (1996). Market Micro Structure and Asset Pricing: On the Compensation for Illiquidity in Stock Returns. *Journal of Financial Economics*, 41(3):441–464.

Brennan, M., Chordia, T., and Subrahmanyam, A. (1998). Alternative Factor Specifications, Security Characteristics, and the Cross-Section of Expected Stock Returns. *Journal of Financial Economics*, 49(3):354–373.

Chemmanur, T. and Fulghieri, P. (1999). A Theory of the Going-Public Decision. *Review of Financial Studies*, 12(2):249–279.

Chordia, T., Shivakumar, L., and Subrahmanyam. A. (2004). Liquidity Dynamics across Large and Small Firms. *Economic Notes*, 33(1):111–143.

Cohen, R., Gompers, P., and Vuolteenaho, T. (2002). Who Under Reacts to Cash Flow News? Evidence from Trading between Individuals and Institutions. *Journal of Financial Economics*, 66(2–3):409–462.

Cornelli, F. and Goldreich, D. (2001). Bookbuilding and Strategic Allocation. *Journal of Finance*, 56(6):2337–2369.

Cornelli, F. and Goldreich, D. (2003). Bookbuilding: How Informative Is the Order Book? *Journal of Finance*, 58(4):1415–1443.

Corwin, S. A. and Harris, J. H. (2001). The Initial Listing Decisions of Firms that Go Public. *Financial Management*, 30(1):35–55.

Derrien, F. (2005). IPO Pricing in "Hot" Market Conditions: Who Leaves Money on the Table? *Journal of Finance*, 60(1):487–521.

Eckbo, B. E., Masulis, R. W., and Norli, O. (2000). Seasoned Public Offerings: Resolution of the 'New Issues Puzzle'. *Journal of Financial Economics*, 56(2):251–291.

Eleswarapu, V. and Reingaum, M. (1993). The Seasonal Behaviour of the Liquidity Premium in Asset Pricing. *Journal of Financial Economics*, 34(3):373–386.

Garfinkel, J. A. (1993). IPO Underpricing, Insider Selling and Subsequent Equity Offerings: Is Underpricing a Signal of Quality? *Financial Management*, 22(1):74–83.

Goergen, M. (1998). Corporate Governance and Financial Performance: A Study of German and UK Initial Public Offerings. Cheltenham, UK and Northampton, MA.

Hogan, K. M. and Ohlson, G. T. (2004). The Pricing of Equity Carve-Outs During the 1990s. *Journal of Financial Research*, 27(4):521–537.

Huyghebaert, N. and Van Hulle, C. (2004). The Role of Institutional Investors in Corporate Finance. *Tijdschrift voor Economie en Management*, 49(4):689–726.

Huyghebaert, N. and Van Hulle, C. (2005). Structuring the IPO: Empirical Evidence on the Portions of Primary and Secondary Shares. *Journal of Corporate Finance* (forthcoming).

Jegadeesh, N., Weinstein, M., and Welch, I. (1993). An Empirical Investigation of IPO Returns and Subsequent Equity Offerings. *Journal of Financial Economics*, 34(2):153–175.

Jenkinson, T. and Jones, H. (2004). Bids and Allocations in European IPO Bookbuilding. *Journal of Finance*, 59(5):2309–2338.

Jenkinson, T. and Ljungqvist, A. P. (2001). *Going Public: The Theory and Evidence on How Companies Raise Equity Finance*. Oxford University Press.

Jensen, M. J. (1986). Agency Costs of Free Cash Flows, Corporate Finance and Takeovers. *American Economic Review*, 76(2):323–329.

Kadlec, G. and McConnell, J. (1994). The Effect of Market Segmentation and Illiquidity on Asset Prices. *Journal of Finance*, 49(2):611–636.

Keloharju, M. and Torstila, S. (2002). The Distribution of Information Among Institutional and Retail Investors in IPOs. *European Financial Management*, 8(3):357–372.

Leleux, B. F. (1993). Post-IPO Performance: A French Appraisal. *Finance*, 14(2):79–106.

Ljungqvist, A. P. (1997). Pricing Initial Public Offerings: Further Evidence from Germany. *European Economic Review*, 41(7):1309–1320.

Ljungqvist, A. P. and Wilhelm, W. J. (2002). IPO Allocation: Discriminatory or Discretionary? *Journal of Financial Economics*, 65(2):167–201.

Ljungqvist, A. P., Jenkinson, T., and Wilhelm, W. J. (2003). Global Integration in Primary Equity Markets: The Role of U.S. Banks and U.S. Investors. *Review of Financial Studies*, 16(1):63–99.

Loderer, C. and Roth, L. (2003). The Pricing Discount for Limited Liquidity: Evidence from the SWX Swiss Exchange and the NASDAQ. Working Paper, University of Berne, Switzerland.

Loughran, T. and Ritter, J. R. (2003). Why Has IPO Underpricing Changed over Time? Working Paper, University of Florida, Miami, FL.

Megginson, W. and Weiss, K. A. (1991). Venture Capitalist Certification in Initial Public Offerings. *Journal of Finance*, 46(3):879–903.

Merton, R. (1987). A Simple Model of Capital Market Equilibrium with Incomplete Information. *Journal of Finance*, 42(3):483–510.

Pagano, M. and Roëll, A. (1998). The Choice of Stock Ownership Structure: Agency Costs, Monitoring, and the Decision to Go Public. *Quarterly Journal of Economics*, 113(1):187–225.

Pagano, M., Panetta, F., and Zingales, L. (1998). Why Do Companies Go Public. An Empirical Analysis. *Journal of Finance*, 53(1):27–64.

Reingaum, M. (1990). Market Microstructure and Asset Pricing: An Empirical Investigation of NYSE and Nasdaq Securities. *Journal of Financial Economics*, 28(1–2):127–147.

Reuter, J. (2002). Are IPO Allocations for Sale? Evidence from the Mutual Fund Industry. Working Paper, University of Oregon, OR.

Ritter, J. R. (1991). The Long-Run Performance of Initial Public Offerings. *Journal of Finance*, 46(1):3–27.

Ritter, J. R. (2003). Differences between European and American IPO Markets. *European Financial Management*, 9(4):421–434.

Sherman, A. (2000). IPOs and Long-Term Relationships: An Advantage of Bookbuilding. *Review of Financial Studies*, 13(3):697–714.

Spiess, D. K. and Pettway, R. H. (1997). The IPO and First Seasoned Equity Sale: Issue Proceeds, Owner/Managers' Wealth, and the Underpricing Signal. *Journal of Banking and Finance*, 21(7):967–988.

Welch, I. (1991). An Empirical Examination of Models of Contract Choice in Initial Public Offerings. *Journal of Financial and Quantitative Analysis*, 26(4):497–518.

Weston, J., Butler, A., and Grullon, G. (2002). Stock Market Liquidity and the Cost of Raising Capital. Working Paper, Rice University, OH.

22 Costs and benefits in the choice of the audit and underwriting quality in the IPO market: an empirical analysis of competing theories

Joseph Aharony, Ran Barniv, and Chan-Jane Lin

Abstract

This study examines the choice of auditors and underwriters by entrepreneurs prior to initial public offerings (IPOs). The major finding is on the supply side, where we find that the incremental cost of hiring high-quality auditors and underwriters, deflated by the value of the proceeds, increases as firm-specific risk increases. On the demand side, we test the competing hypotheses proposed by Titman and Trueman (1986) and Datar et al. (1991). Partial support is provided for the Titman–Trueman (1986) demand-side proposition that riskier firms have greater incremental benefit from hiring lower-quality auditors or underwriters, rather than the Datar et al. (1991) prediction that riskier firms will gain incremental benefit from higher-quality hirings.

22.1   Introduction

Titman and Trueman (1986) (henceforth referred to as TT) and Datar et al. (1991) (henceforth referred to as DFH) have developed conflicting propositions regarding the value of the audit or underwriting – that is, the demand-side relationship between firm-specific risk and the incremental benefit of hiring a high-quality auditor or underwriter. DFH predicted that entrepreneurs who face greater future cash flow risk will benefit from hiring a high-quality auditor, whereas TT predicted that they will benefit from hiring a low-quality auditor or underwriter.

This study focuses on developing proxy tests to evaluate empirically the supply-side effect of risk – that is, the impact of firm-specific risk on the incremental cost of hiring a high-quality auditor or underwriter – and partially examines the demand-side effect of risk. Recent empirical studies, detailed in the following section, indicate that riskier entrepreneurs may benefit from hiring high-quality auditors, but these studies make no direct empirical examination of the supply-side effect.

We conducted our research on a sample of US initial public offerings (IPOs) confined to firm-commitment share offerings, using regression analyses to test the supply-side effect and the conflicting demand-side hypotheses. Audit fees and underwriting commissions deflated by the IPO proceeds were used as the dependent variables. Four ex-ante variables (firm size, age, financial leverage, and a high-tech indicator) and ex-post variance of daily returns were employed as independent variables representing proxies for firm-specific risk. The ex-post variance of returns, which provides a signal of future cash flow uncertainty, is presumed as a proxy for future payoff risk assessment in TT's and DFH's theoretical analyses.

Regressions with slope dummies indicate that the incremental deflated cost of hiring a high-quality auditor or a prestigious underwriter increases as firm-specific risk increases. This evidence has important implications for testing the demand side, as explained in section 22.3. Similar regression analyses provide some support for TT's proposition of a negative relationship between the risk facing entrepreneurs and the incremental benefit of hiring a high-quality auditor or underwriter. The supply-side and demand-side findings indicate that for high firm-specific risk, the incremental costs exceed the incremental benefits of hiring a high-quality auditor or underwriter.

The remainder of the chapter is organized as follows. Section 22.2 discusses our contribution to the previous literature on the supply-side and demand-side effects. Section 22.3 outlines the testable hypotheses. Data and sample statistics are presented in section 22.4. Section 22.5 describes the research method and in section 22.6 we analyze the empirical results. Section 22.7 provides a summary of the chapter.

22.2 Contribution to the literature

Using US IPOs, Simunic and Stein (1987) and Beatty (1989) reported inverse relations between audit quality and risk factors. These results provide some empirical evidence supporting TT's proposition that firms facing more risk will benefit from hiring lower quality auditors.[1] We provide further evidence to support this proposition. Feltham et al. (1991) (henceforth referred to as FHS) found that ex-ante univariate risk measures from prospectuses and ex-post variances of IPO residual stock returns are statistically nonsignificant across auditor quality subsamples. Whereas this evidence provides insight into the demand-side hypotheses, it supports neither the TT nor the DFH hypotheses, and further results are generally not consistent with the DFH hypothesis. These three studies, however, do not control for supply-side factors in the choice of auditors.

In support of DFH, Clarkson and Simunic (1994) (henceforth referred to as CS) found a positive relationship between auditor quality and firm-specific risk using IPO data from Canada, where the risks and costs of litigation against auditors are significantly lower than in the USA. By drawing data from a legal environment with more constant relation between the incremental cost of hiring a high-quality auditor and firm-specific risk, they were able to control for the supply-side effect of risk on auditor choice, and thus to obtain a more powerful test of the demand-side prediction of DFH (i.e. the positive relation between the incremental benefit of hiring a high-quality auditor and firm-specific risk).[2]

---

[1] Menon and Williams (1991) showed that entrepreneurs with prestigious underwriters are more likely to make the change from low-quality to high-quality auditors. Carter and Manaster (1990) provided evidence that prestigious underwriters are associated with lower-risk offerings.

[2] Also, Lee et al. (2003), using Australian IPO data prior to 1990, provided evidence consistent with DFH's prediction that riskier IPOs demand a higher level of auditor quality. As with the Canadian data used by CS, in Australia during the period prior to 1990, expected litigation costs against auditors were significantly lower than in the USA.

Hogan (1997) examined the tradeoff between the incremental costs and benefits of selecting a Big-Six firm and found that IPOs select the type of auditors that minimize the sum of underpricing and auditing costs. However, she tested neither the DFH hypothesis nor the TT hypothesis.

The current study differs from previous studies in several aspects. First, we provide evidence of the role of supply-side factors in the decision to hire higher-quality or lower-quality auditors or underwriters, whereas previous studies examined the demand side only. Second, whereas FHS and CS tested the DFH demand-side hypothesis, we examine the two conflicting demand-side propositions suggested by TT and DFH.

Third, our research method differs from that used by FHS and CS. We use multivariate regressions with slope dummies for testing the supply-side and the conflicting demand-side hypotheses. Fourth, in contrast to FHS and CS, who both used the residual variance from the market model as the ex-post firm-specific risk measure, we use the actual variance of security returns presumed by TT and DFH to be a proxy for future cash flow uncertainty in their theoretical analysis. Finally, we also examine TT's proposition in the context of the choice of underwriter, whereas CS used underwriter prestige as a right-hand-side (RHS) variable to explain auditor quality (see CS, Tables 22.4 and 22.5). This variable cannot be used as an RHS estimate to test the TT proposition.

22.3 Supply-side and demand-side hypotheses

The supply-side hypotheses examine the impact of firm-specific risk on the incremental cost of choosing high-quality auditors or underwriters. The null hypothesis is that constant costs are expected, i.e.

$H_{S,0}$:   Increasing firm-specific risk does not affect the incremental cost of choosing a high-quality auditor or prestigious underwriter.

The alternate hypothesis is:

$H_{S,A}$:   Increasing firm-specific risk increases the incremental cost of choosing a high-quality auditor or prestigious underwriter.

If the null hypothesis is rejected, it will be more difficult to examine some of the demand-side effects, in particular those suggested by DFH (1991). Nevertheless, a comparison between the demand-side and supply-side effects can still provide some insight into the controversy.

The demand-side hypotheses examine the impact of firm-specific risk on the incremental benefit of choosing high-quality auditors or underwriters. The following competing demand-side hypotheses are examined. The first was proposed by TT and the second by DFH.

$H_{D,TT}$:   Entrepreneurs who face increasing firm-specific risk have lower incremental benefit from hiring a high-quality auditor or prestigious underwriter.

$H_{D,DFH}$:   Entrepreneurs who face increasing firm-specific risk have greater incremental benefit from hiring a high-quality auditor.

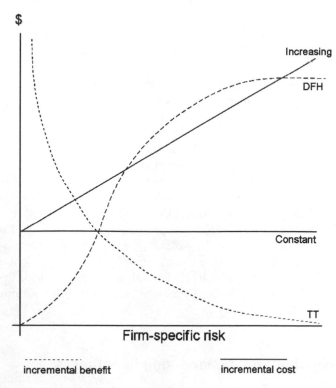

Figure 22.1 Expected relationship between firm-specific risk and the incremental cost and benefit of a high-quality auditor: TT versus DFH hypotheses. Based on Feltham et al. (1991, Figures 1 and 2, pp. 380 and 383)

Figure 22.1 depicts the hypotheses on the relationship between firm-specific risk and the incremental cost and incremental benefit of a high-quality auditor. Figure 22.1 is based on FHS (1991, pp. 380 and 383). According to TT's hypothesis ($H_{D,TT}$), the incremental benefit of hiring a high-quality auditor or prestigious underwriter when firm-specific risk is low is probably above the incremental cost. In this situation, entrepreneurs will tend to hire higher-quality auditors and prestigious underwriters. By contrast, when firm-specific risk is high, entrepreneurs will tend to hire lower-quality auditors and less prestigious underwriters. According to DFH's hypothesis ($H_{D,DFH}$), if the incremental cost of hiring a high-quality auditor increases as firm-specific risk increases, the incremental benefit of hiring a high-quality auditor may be lower than the incremental cost for very high firm-specific risk, but the incremental benefit is expected to be higher than the incremental cost for medium and moderately high firm-specific risk.

22.4   Data and sample statistics

The sample of US IPOs analyzed in this study was taken from Aharony et al. (1993). The final sample consisted of 432 industrial IPOs with firm-commitment share offerings from January 1985 to June 1987. An examination of the industry affiliation of the sample firms shows a wide distribution over 140 three-digit industry categories, and no industry concentration. Table 22.1 presents the choice of auditors and underwriters of the 404 IPOs with complete data. We adopted the commonly used two-tier classification scheme, Big-Eight (for the period we examine there were eight large international auditing firms) versus non-Big-Eight auditing firms, as a proxy for auditor quality. With regard to the quality of the managing underwriters, we followed a classification method suggested by Hayes (1979), who claims that the tombstone style of advertisement placed in financial magazines and in the financial sections of newspapers by prestigious underwriters implicitly signals higher quality.[3] Underwriting is classified as prestigious if it falls into one of three brackets: special, major, and sub-major. It is classified as non-prestigious if it does not belong to any of these brackets. To accommodate changes that have taken place in the underwriting hierarchy over the last decade, the original classification scheme used in this chapter, which was based on Hayes (1979), was updated by (1) examining the tombstone advertisements that appeared in the major financial magazines and newspapers; and (2) referring to surveys in various professional journals. As shown in Table 22.1, there is no obvious concentration of prestigious underwriters: 55.4% of IPOs were taken public by the prestigious group. Overall, 209 firms (51.7% of the sample) selected both Big-Eight auditors and prestigious underwriters, and 37 firms (about 9% of the sample) chose both non-Big-Eight auditors and non-prestigious underwriters when going public.

The financial data were obtained directly from prospectuses filed to the Securities and Exchange Commission (SEC). The initial market prices were gathered from Standard & Poor's Daily Stock Price Record. Table 22.2(A) reports descriptive statistics for the entire sample regarding the dependent variables and the explanatory firm-specific risk variables used in the regressions that examine the supply-side and demand-side effects. For the supply side, two proxies are used as dependent variables: the means (medians) of the deflated audit fees (AUDEXP) and the deflated underwriting commissions (UNDEXP), which are 4.1% (4.8%) and 7.7% (7.3%)

Table 22.1 Sample composition

	Big-Eight auditing firms	Non-Big-Eight auditing firms	Total
Prestigious underwriters	51.7% (209)	3.7% (15)	55.4% (224)
Non-prestigious underwriters	35.4% (143)	9.2% (37)	44.6% (180)
Total	87.1% (352)	12.9% (52)	100.0% (404)

Choice of auditors and underwriters among 404 IPOs with complete data. The number of IPOs is given in parentheses.

[3] The determination of auditor quality and underwriter prestige is based on the analytical and empirical frameworks developed by TT (1986), Simunic and Stein (1987), Krinsky and Rotenberg (1989), Hughes (1989), and FHS (1991). With respect to the determination of underwriter prestige, a comprehensive theory has not yet been developed. However, an underwriter serves as a third party who can certify that the IPO price is consistent with inside information (Booth and Smith, 1986) and can provide information about the firm (Carter and Manaster, 1990).

Table 22.2 Descriptive statistics

	Median	Mean	Std dev.	Max	Min
Total proceeds[a] ($000)	8943	16,352	29,805	350,000	1470
Audit fees as a percentage of total proceeds (AUDEXP)	4.8	4.1	3.4	27.1	0.06
Underwriting commissions as a percentage of total proceeds (UNDEXP)	7.3	7.7	1.1	10.0	5.0
Underpricing as a percentage of market value[b] (BRPR)	1.7	5.3	9.9	53.8	−13.6
Total assests[c] ($000)	16,813	70,622	142,613	1,616,091	92
Net sales[c] ($000)	21,613	70,355	177,407	1,583,769	4
AGE[d]	10.0	19.1	24.3	186	1
Financial leverage[e] (LEVER)	0.037	0.175	0.413	5.46	1
Variance of returns[f] (VARRET)	0.0014	0.0019	0.0019	0.01958	0.00026

Panel B: Partition by choice of underwriters and auditors.

	AUA = 1[g] (n = 158)		AU = 1[g] (n = 209)		AU = 0[g] (n = 37)		t-test[h]	Wilcoxon[h]
	Mean	Median	Mean	Median	Mean	Median		
AUDEXP	0.0539	0.0499	0.0381	0.0314	0.0795	0.0714	−5.63*	−6.92*
UNDEXP	0.0818	0.0784	0.0705	0.0700	0.0894	0.0900	−10.4*	−8.67*
BRPR	0.0665	0.0194	0.0366	0.0137	0.0885	0.0340	−1.96**	−3.05*

Panel B: Partition by choice of underwriters and auditors.

[a] Total shares issued by the company × offering price.
[b] Underpricing is estimated as BRPR = (closing price at the end of first trading date − offering price)/(closing price at the end of first trading date) – see Hogan (1997).
[c] As reported in the latest prospectus filed to the SEC prior to the IPO.
[d] Difference between the year of initial public offering and the year when the firm was founded.
[e] Long-term debt as a percentage of the initial market value of common equity.
[f] Based on 750 trading days subsequent to the initial issue date.
[g] AU = 0 if IPOs select non-Big-Eight auditors and non-prestigious underwriters; AU = 1 if IPOs select Big-Eight auditors and prestigious underwriters; AUA = 1 if IPOs select non-Big-Eight auditors and prestigious underwriters or IPOs select Big-Eight auditors and non-prestigious underwriters, and 0 otherwise.
[h] The t-test (Wilcoxon test) for the difference in mean (median) between IPOs in subgroup AU = 1 and IPOs in subgroup AU = 0.
* Significant at $p < 0.01$. ** Significant at $p < 0.05$.

respectively. For the demand side, underpricing (BRPR), used as a proxy for the benefits from hiring a high-quality auditor (Hogan, 1997), has a mean (median) 5.3% (1.7%) of the IPO closing price at the end of the first trading day. Further analysis of underpricing (not reported) indicates that the sample firms experienced, on average, a market-adjusted abnormal return of 7.2% on the first trading day, which is similar to the 7.8% found in Balvers et al. (1988).

Table 22.2(B) provides comparative statistics for the dependent variables for three subsets grouped by the choice of audit and underwriting quality. AUDEXP and UNDEXP are, on average, significantly smaller for IPOs selecting Big-Eight auditors and prestigious underwriters (AU = 1) than for those selecting non-Big-Eight auditors and non-prestigious underwriters (AU = 0). Similarly, BRPR is, on average, significantly smaller for IPOs selecting AU = 1 than for those selecting AU = 0. AUDEXP, UNDEXP, and BRPR for IPOs selecting Big-Eight auditors and non-prestigious underwriters or non-Big-Eight auditors and prestigious underwriters (AUA = 1) are, on average, higher than for those selecting AU = 1 but lower than for those selecting AU = 0. This three-tier partition enables more precise empirical examination of the effects of the choice of audit and underwriting quality.

22.5 Research method

22.5.1 Firm-specific risk measures

We used five proxies to measure firm-specific risk. These estimates, used as independent variables for testing the supply-side and demand-side hypotheses, are the ex-post variance of common stock returns (VARRET), and four ex-ante variables commonly used in the literature: firm size (ln(TA)), firm age (AGE), financial leverage (LEVER), and high-tech indicator (HT). Other risk-measures –for example, the number of risk factors suggested by Simunic and Stein (1987) and Clarkson and Simunic (1994) – were not available in the database. The correlation coefficients between each pair of firm-specific risk variables, presented in Table 22.3, are statistically significant and range between −0.266 and 0.469 for the entire sample. These correlations among the risk characteristics used as independent variables are relatively high, but further statistical tests (not reported) indicate no violation of the non-collinearity assumptions in our regression analyses.

The variance of common stock returns (VARRET) was estimated from the CRSP files. We report the results on variance of daily returns for 750 trading days subsequent to the initial issue date, but variances of daily returns for other time periods were also estimated and found to be highly statistically significant and positively correlated with the variance reported.

Firm size (TA) was measured by the natural logarithm of total assets reported in the latest prospectus filed to the SEC prior to the IPO (ln(TA)). Large firms were perceived, other things being equal, as less risky than small firms for a number of reasons, such as greater depth of management, better control over the industry's technological development, and lower exposure to bankruptcy risk. As shown in Table 22.3, this variable is negatively and significantly correlated with VARRET.

Table 22.3 Correlation coefficients for the five firm-specific risk variables

Variable[a]	AGE	LEVER	HT	VARRET
Panel A: Entire sample of 404 IPOs[b]				
Ln(TA)	0.469*	247*	−0.266*	−0.229*
AGE		0.177*	−0.241*	−0.210*
LEVER			0.171*	0.098**
HT				0.109*
Panel B: 209 IPOs selecting AU = 1[b]				
Ln(TA)	0.466*	213*	−0.302*	−0.187*
AGE		0.147**	−0.248*	−0.116
LEVER			0.173*	0.171**
HT				0.143**
Panel C: 37 IPOs selecting AU = 0[c]				
Ln(TA)	0.369**	0.549*	−0.189	−0.076
AGE		−0.079	−0.176	−0.202
LEVER			0.221	0.286
HT				0.154

[a] Ln(TA) = log of total assets; AGE = firm age; LEVER = long-term debt/initial market value of equity; HT = 1 if the IPO is a high-tech firm and 0 otherwise; VARRET = variance of daily returns for 750 trading days subsequent to the initial issue date.
[b] AU = 1 if IPOs select Big-Eight auditors and prestigious underwriters.
[c] AU = 0 if IPOs select non-Big-Eight auditors and non-prestigious underwriters.
* Significant at $p < 0.01$.** Significant at $p < 0.05$.

Firm age (AGE) was measured as the difference between the year of the IPO and the year when the firm was founded. Older firms have a longer operating history and are expected to have lower bankruptcy risk (see Dun and Bradstreet statistics) and larger net cash flows. This variable is also negatively and significantly correlated with VARRET.

Financial leverage (LEVER) is measured as the ratio of long-term debt to the initial market value of common equity. This variable is commonly used as a measure of the firm's financial risk. The more highly leveraged the firm, the greater the riskiness of the new issue to investors (e.g. bankruptcy risk). Empirically, this variable is positively and significantly correlated with VARRET.

The high-tech indicator (HT) equals 1 if the IPO firm is in a high-tech industry and 0 otherwise. High-tech IPOs are considered more risky than IPOs in non-high-tech industries, an assertion corroborated by interviews with 10 SEC partners of Big-Eight and non-Big-Eight CPA firms. This variable is positively and significantly correlated with VARRET.

22.5.2 Testing the supply-side and demand-side hypotheses

Slope dummies in multivariate regressions were used for testing the impact of firm-specific risk on the incremental cost of hiring high-quality auditors and prestigious underwriters. Restricted (equations (22.1a) and (22.2a)) and unrestricted (equations

(22.1b) and 22.2b)) regression models (Johnston, 1984; Judge et al., 1988; Kennedy, 1992) were used as follows:

$$\begin{aligned}
\text{AUDEXP}_i = {} &a_{R0} + a_{R1}\cdot\text{LN(TA)}_i + a_{R2}\cdot\text{AGE}_i + a_{R3}\cdot\text{LEVER}_i + a_{R4}\cdot\text{HT}_i \\
&+ a_{R5}\cdot\text{VARRET}_i + \gamma_{Ri}
\end{aligned} \qquad (22.1\text{a})$$

$$\begin{aligned}
\text{AUDEXP}_i = {} &a_{U0} + a_{U0*}\cdot\text{AU} + a_{U1}\cdot\text{ln(TA)}_i + a_{U2}\cdot\text{AGE}_i + a_{U3}\cdot\text{LEVER}_i + a_{U4}\cdot\text{HT}_i \\
&+ a_{U5}\cdot\text{VARRET}_i + a_{U1*}\cdot(\text{ln(TA)}\cdot\text{AU})_i + a_{U2*}\cdot(\text{AGE}\cdot\text{AU})_i \\
&+ a_{U3*}\cdot(\text{LEVER}\cdot\text{AU})_i + a_{U4*}\cdot(\text{HT}\cdot\text{AU})_i \\
&+ a_{U5*}\cdot(\text{VARRET}\cdot\text{AU})_i + \gamma_{Ui}
\end{aligned} \qquad (22.1\text{b})$$

and separately,

$$\begin{aligned}
\text{UNDEXP}_i = {} &b_{R0} + b_{R1}\cdot\text{ln(TA)}_i + b_{R2}\cdot\text{AGE}_i + b_{R3}\cdot\text{LEVER}_i + b_{R4}\cdot\text{HT}_i \\
&+ b_{R5}\cdot\text{VARRET}_i + \lambda_{Ri}
\end{aligned} \qquad (22.2\text{a})$$

$$\begin{aligned}
\text{UNDEXP}_i = {} &b_{U0*} + b_{U0*}\cdot\text{AU} + b_{U1}\cdot\text{ln(TA)}_i + b_{U2}\cdot\text{AGE}_i + b_{U3}\cdot\text{LEVER}_i + b_{U4}\cdot\text{HT}_i \\
&+ b_{U5}\cdot\text{VARRET}_i + b_{U1*}\cdot(\text{ln(TA)}\cdot\text{AU})_i + b_{U2*}\cdot(\text{AGE}\cdot\text{AU})_i \\
&+ b_{U3*}\cdot(\text{LEVER}\cdot\text{AU})_i + b_{U4*}\cdot(\text{HT}\cdot\text{AU})_i \\
&+ b_{U5*}\cdot(\text{VARRET}\cdot\text{AU})_i + \lambda_{Ui}
\end{aligned} \qquad (22.2\text{b})$$

where:

AUDEXP_i = audit fees deflated by total proceeds for firm i

UNDEXP_i = underwriting commissions deflated by total proceeds for firm i

Ln(TA)_i = log of total assets at year end prior to the IPO for firm i

AGE_i = age of firm i

LEVER_i = ratio of long-term debt to initial market value of common equity for firm i

HT_i = 1 if the IPO firm is in a high-tech industry and 0 otherwise

VARRET_i = ex-post variance of common stock returns for firm i

γ and λ = random error terms for firm i.

The interaction elements (LN(TA)·AU), (AGE·AU), (LEVER·AU), (HT·AU), and (VARRET·AU) are formed as the product of AU and the respective independent variable. Equation (22.1a) reflects the restriction that the estimated coefficients are the same for the two IPO subgroups, those selecting high-quality auditors and prestigious underwriters (AU = 1; n = 209 observations), and those selecting low-quality auditors and non-prestigious underwriters (AU = 0; n = 37 observations). Adding the interactions as explanatory variables in equation (22.1b) enabled us to test the differences in slopes of the two subgroups of IPOs. A Chow F-test was used to test the hypothesis that $a_{U0*} = a_{U1*} = \ldots a_{U5*} = 0$, and standard t-tests were used to examine hypotheses such as $a_{U0*} = 0$, $a_{U1*} = 0$, etc. Similar analyses were performed on equations (22.2a) and (22.2b). In addition, we analyzed the entire sample of 404 IPOs adding an additional dummy variable (AUA) for those IPOs making a mixed auditor and underwriter quality selection, where AUA = 1 if IPOs selected high-quality auditors and non-prestigious underwriters or low-quality auditors and prestigious underwriters, and 0 otherwise.

We tested the demand-side proposition of TT ($H_{D,TT}$) against DFH's proposition ($H_{D,DHF}$) using a similar multivariate regression technique with slope dummies. These OLS regressions were used to test the impact of firm-specific risk on the incremental benefit of hiring a high-quality auditor and a prestigious underwriter. The under-pricing variable, BRPR, our proxy for benefits, was used as the dependent variable in the regressions. Note that as it is not possible to obtain a precise measure of incremen-tal benefit, we used the variable suggested by Hogan (1997): BRPR = (closing price at the end of the first trading date − offering price)/(closing price at the end of the first trading date). See also Beatty (1989) and Balvers et al. (1988) on the association between these benefits and underpricing.

22.6 Results

22.6.1 Supply-side indicators

Univariate supply-side indicators are shown in Table 22.4. We examined the impact of proxies for firm-specific risk on the deflated cost of audit and underwriting, AUD-EXP and UNDEXP respectively. For each firm-specific risk variable, the sample of IPOs was split into two subgroups using the median of each respective variable as a cutoff point, except for HT, which was partitioned into high-tech and non-high-tech firms. The results indicate that larger IPOs pay significantly lower deflated audit fees and underwriting commissions than smaller IPOs, and IPOs with lower ex-post VAR-RET pay significantly lower deflated audit fees and underwriting commissions than those with higher VARRET. For example, the mean (median) of AUDEXP is 0.041 (0.036) for IPOs with lower VARRET, compared with 0.055 (0.048) for IPOs with higher VARRET. For AGE, LEVER, and HT, the differences in AUDEXP between less risky and more risky IPOs are not statistically insignificant. However, younger IPO firms and IPOs from high-tech industries have significantly higher UNDEXP com-pared with older and non-high-tech IPOs respectively. In summary, the univariate analysis roughly indicates that the cost of audit or underwriting increases with firm-specific risk.

Tables 22.5 and 22.6 present the impact of firm-specific risk on the incremental deflated cost of hiring high-quality auditors and prestigious underwriters. In Table 22.5 slope dummies are estimated using AUDEXP as the dependent variable, whereas in Table 22.6 UNDEXP is used as the dependent variable.

First, we analyzed the results using the dummy variable AU = 1 for the 209 IPOs selecting Big-Eight auditors and prestigious underwriters and AU = 0 for the 37 IPOs selecting non-Big-Eight auditors and non-prestigious underwriters. The results in Table 22.5 for the restricted OLS estimates of equation (22.1a) show that the model is highly significant and has moderate explanatory power (adjusted R^2 of 0.226). The estimated coefficients for ln(TA), AGE, and HT are statistically significant and the signs of all coefficients are as expected.

The unrestricted model includes the five firm-specific risk variables, the dummy vari-able (AU), and the five interaction variables. This unrestricted regression tests the hypothesis of no coefficient change. The Chow F reported in Table 22.5 is statistically significant, suggesting that at least one interaction coefficient has changed. To examine the statistical significance of the individual coefficients we use the standard t-test. The

Table 22.4 Supply-side indicators: cost of audit (underwriting) for lower and higher firm-specific risk

	Mean	Median	Standard deviation	Mean	Median	Standard deviation	t-test	Wilcoxon Z
Panel A[a]:	Larger IPOs			Smaller IPOs				
Audit fees[b]	0.037	0.029	0.029	0.061	0.055	0.035	−7.72*	−8.84*
Underwriting commissions[b]	0.070	0.070	0.006	0.083	0.080	0.035	−13.5*	−11.3*
Panel B[c]:	Lower VARRET			Higher VARRET				
Audit fees	0.041	0.036	0.034	0.055	0.048	0.033	−4.02*	−4.95*
Underwriting commissions	0.074	0.070	0.010	0.079	0.075	0.011	−4.76*	−5.22*
Panel C[d]:	Older AGE			Younger AGE				
Audit fees	0.046	0.039	0.034	0.050	0.043	0.034	−1.33	−1.76
Underwriting commissions	0.074	0.072	0.009	0.080	0.075	0.013	−5.63*	−4.23*
Panel D[e]:	Lower LEVER			Higher LEVER				
Audit fees	0.049	0.041	0.037	0.047	0.041	0.032	0.62	0.22
Underwriting commissions	0.078	0.073	0.011	0.075	0.070	0.010	1.20	1.18
Panel E[f]:	Non-HT			HT				
Audit fees	0.048	0.041	0.036	0.047	0.041	0.027	0.46	−0.25
Underwriting commissions	0.076	0.073	0.011	0.079	0.073	0.012	−2.30**	−1.60

[a] Size is measured by log of total assets, ln(TA); the median of ln(TA) is used as a cutoff point. Smaller IPOs are perceived as riskier than larger IPOs.

[b] Audit fees and underwriting commissions deflated by the total proceeds, denoted in the text by AUDEXP and UNDEXP respectively.

[c] Variance of daily returns (VARRET); the median of VARRET is used as a cutoff point. Low VARRET for IPOs indicates lower ex-post risk.

[d] The median AGE is used as a cutoff point.

[e] The median LEVER is used as a cutoff point.

[f] IPOs in eight high-tech (HT) industries classified by three-digit SIC codes.

* Significant at $p < 0.01$. ** Significant at $p < 0.05$.

Table 22.5 Supply-side effect: the impact of firm-specific risk on the incremental cost of high-quality auditors and prestigious underwriters (slope dummies for OLS regression equations (22.1a) and (22.1b); AUDEXP as a dependent variable)

Independent variables	Restricted[a] $n = 246$ IPOs[b]	Unrestricted	Restricted[a] $n = 404$ IPOs[c]	Unrestricted
Intercept	0.1574*	0.2411	0.1539*	0.2411*
AU[d]		−0.1325*		−0.1325*
AUA[e]				−0.1056*
Ln(TA)	−0.0117*	−0.0199*	−0.0091*	−0.0199*
AGE	−0.0003*	−0.0128**	−0.0002*	−0.00002
LEVER	0.0045	0.00002	0.0075**	0.0442
HT	0.0128*	0.0169	0.0092	0.0169
VARRET	1.2007	1.9117	0.5868	1.9117
AU·ln(TA)[f]		−0.0128**		−0.0128*
AU·AGE[f]		−0.0002**		−0.0002**
AU·LEVER[f]		−0.0402		−0.0402
AU·HT[f]		0.0069		0.0070
AU·VARRET[f]		1.1612		1.1612
AUA·LN(TA)[g]				−0.0106
AUA·AGE[g]				0.00005
AUA·LEVER[g]				−0.0245
AUA·HT[g]				0.0129
AUA·VARRET[g]				1.5465
F-value	15.3*	10.4*	20.6*	9.41
Chow F		3.54*		2.56**
Adj. R^2	0.226	0.296	0.254	0.262

[a] Restricted regressions without interactions.
[b] 209 IPOs selecting Big-Eight auditors and prestigious underwriters and 37 IPOs selecting non-Big-Eight auditors and non-prestigious underwriters are included in the regressions.
[c] All 404 IPOs of the sample are included in the regressions.
[d] A dummy variable, AU = 1 for IPOs selecting Big-Eight auditors and prestigious underwriters, 0 otherwise.
[e] A dummy variable, AUA = 1 for IPOs selecting non-Big-Eight auditors and prestigious underwriters, or IPOs selecting Big-Eight auditors and non-prestigious underwriters, 0 otherwise.
[f] These variables are formed as the products of AU and the respective independent variables.
[g] These variables are formed as the products of AUA and the respective independent variables.
* Significant at $p < 0.01$ (two-sided t-test).** Significant at $p < 0.05$ (two-sided t-test).

highly significant estimated negative coefficient for the dummy variable (AU) in Table 22.5 suggests that, at the intercept, AUDEXP for zero firm-specific risk is significantly lower for IPOs selecting AU = 1 than for those selecting AU = 0. The significant estimated negative coefficients for the interaction of AU with ln(TA) and AGE respectively indicate changes in the expected direction for the slopes of the two variables. The changes in the slope coefficients of the other three risk variables are not significant (at $p < 0.05$). Thus, the results indicate increasing incremental deflated audit costs of hiring high-quality auditors and prestigious underwriters as firm-specific risk increases.

Table 22.6 Supply-side effect: the impact of firm-specific risk on the incremental cost of high-quality auditors and prestigious underwriters (slope dummies for OLS regression equations (22.2a) and (22.2b); UNDEXP as a dependent variable)

Independent variables	Restricted[a] $n = 246$ IPOs[b]	Unrestricted	Restricted[a] $n = 404$ IPOs[c]	Unrestricted
Intercept	0.1145*	0.1306*	0.1224*	0.1305*
AU[d]		−0.0362*		−0.0362*
AUA[e]				0.0003
Ln(TA)	−0.0042*	−0.0050*	−0.0042*	−0.0050*
AGE	−0.000005	−0.0001**	−0.00005	−0.0001
LEVER	0.0026*	0.0095	0.0028*	0.0095
HT	0.0019	0.0024	0.0008	0.0024
VARRET	0.3575**	0.6635	0.3687**	0.6635
AU·ln(TA)[f]		−0.0027*		−0.0027*
AU·AGE[f]		−0.0009**		−0.0002**
AU·LEVER[f]		−0.0069		−0.0069
AU·HT[f]		0.0015		0.0024
AU·VARRET[f]		0.5848**		0.5847
AUA·ln(TA)[g]				−0.0006
AUA·AGE[g]				0.0001
AUA·LEVER[g]				−0.0064
AUA·HT[g]				0.0032
AUA·VARRET[g]				0.0151
F-value	43.9*	51.3*	102.2*	52.1*
Chow F		28.6*		18.5*
Adj. R^2	0.468	0.693	0.637	0.683

[a] Restricted regressions without interactions.
[b] 209 IPOs selecting Big-Eight auditors and prestigious underwriters and 37 IPOs selecting non-Big-Eight auditors and non-prestigious underwriters are included in the regressions.
[c] All 404 IPOs of the sample are included in the regressions.
[d] A dummy variable, AU = 1 for IPOs selecting Big-Eight auditors and prestigious underwriters, 0 otherwise.
[e] A dummy variable, AUA = 1 for IPOs selecting non-Big-Eight auditors and prestigious underwriters, or IPOs selecting Big-Eight auditors and non-prestigious underwriters, 0 otherwise.
[f] These variables are formed as the products of AU and the respective independent variables.
[g] These variables are formed as the products of AUA and the respective independent variables.
* Significant at $p < 0.01$ (two-sided t-test). ** Significant at $p < 0.05$ (two-sided t-test).

Second, we analyzed the entire sample of 404 IPOs, including those 158 IPOs that made mixed selections of audit quality and underwriting prestige (AUA). The results in Table 22.5 resemble those for the 246 IPOs. In particular, the slope coefficients of ln(TA) and AGE remain significantly smaller for IPOs selecting AU = 1 than for those selecting AU = 0. The estimated coefficient for AUA is statistically significant, indicating that, at the intercept, for zero firm-specific risk, AUDEXP is significantly lower for IPOs selecting AUA = 1 than for IPOs selecting AU = 0, but significantly higher than for IPOs selecting AU = 1. However, all interactions of the respective risk variables with AUA are statistically insignificant, suggesting that the estimated slope coefficients for IPOs selecting AUA = 1 are similar to those for IPOs selecting AU = 0.

The results in Table 22.6, using UNDEXP as the independent variable, are even more significant than those reported for AUDEXP in Table 22.5. The results for the restricted and unrestricted OLS estimates of equations (22.2a) and (22.2b) respectively show that both models have more explanatory power (adjusted R^2 of 0.468 and 0.693 respectively), and that the reported Chow F is also more statistically significant than that reported in Table 22.5. The highly significant estimated negative coefficient for the dummy variable (AU) suggests that, at the intercept, UNDEXP for zero firm-specific risk is significantly lower for IPOs selecting AU = 1 than for those selecting AU = 0. The significant estimated coefficients for the interaction of AU with ln(TA), AGE, and VARRET respectively indicate changes in the expected direction for the slopes of the three variables. The changes in slope coefficients of the other two risk variables are statistically insignificant. Thus, the results indicate increasing incremental deflated underwriting cost of hiring high-quality auditors and prestigious underwriters as firm-specific risk increases.

An analysis of the entire sample of 404 IPOs provides results similar to those reported in Table 22.5. In particular, all interactions of the respective risk variables with AUA are statistically insignificant, suggesting that the estimated slope coefficients for IPOs selecting AUA = 1 are similar to those for IPOs selecting AU = 0. Thus, the findings in both tables suggest that the impact of firm-specific risk on the incremental cost of auditing or underwriting for firms making mixed selections is similar to that of firms selecting both non-Big-Eight auditors and non-prestigious underwriters for their IPOs.

In sum, the tests for the supply-side effect, using slope dummies in multivariate regressions, suggest an increase in the incremental deflated costs of hiring high-quality auditors and prestigious underwriters as firm-specific risk increases. From the interviews with 10 SEC partners of Big-Eight and non-Big-Eight firms that we conducted to gain more insight into the supply-side effect, we learned that a number of risky entrepreneurs decided not to go public after being turned down by Big-Eight auditors. No fee discounts were offered to IPOs by any of the partners interviewed, and it seems that lowballing has not been an issue for auditing IPOs. Risky entrepreneurs have also utilized more partner hours as opposed to hours provided by managers and other staff, and have been charged higher fees relative to the total proceeds, than have the less risky IPOs. Altogether, these interviews confirm the empirical results reported in Tables 22.5 and 22.6.

22.6.2 Demand-side indicators

The findings from the supply-side analyses indicate that examination of the demand side should be interpreted with caution, particularly when the DFH hypothesis ($H_{D,DFH}$) is supported. As in the supply-side analyses, we used only proxies for firm-specific risk for testing the demand side and the underpricing ratio (BRPR) as a proxy for benefits (see Hogan, 1997). Moreover, precise measures of benefits were unobtainable. Test results of the demand-side hypotheses are presented in Table 22.7. The analysis with slope dummies suggests a statistically significant moderate decrease in the incremental benefit of hiring high-quality auditors or prestigious underwriters as firm-specific risk increases.

Table 22.7 Demand-side effect: the impact of firm-specific risk on the incremental benefit of high-quality auditors and prestigious underwriters (slope dummies for the OLS regressions; BRPR as a dependent variable)

Independent variables	Restricted[a]	Unrestricted	Restricted[a]	Unrestricted
	$n = 246$ IPOs[b]		$n = 404$ IPOs[c]	
Intercept	0.1439*	0.0890	0.1162	0.0890
AU[d]		0.0026		0.0026
AUA[e]				-0.0332
Ln(TA)	-0.0085*	-0.0080	-0.0026	-0.0080
AGE	-0.00006	-0.0026**	-0.0002	-0.0026**
LEVER	0.0142	0.0522	0.0242**	0.0522
HT	0.0152	0.0165	0.0095	0.0165
VARRET	6.2425**	9.6808**	1.4837	9.6808**
AU·ln(TA)[f]		-0.0126**		-0.0126
AU·AGE[f]		-0.0027**		-0.0027**
AU·LEVER[f]		0.0375		0.0375
AU·HT[f]		0.0408		0.0408
AU·VARRET[f]		17.798**		17.7968**
AUA·ln(TA)[g]				-0.0071
AUA·AGE[g]				0.0022
AUA·LEVER[g]				0.0050
AUA·HT[g]				0.0193
AUA·VARRET[g]				3.0047
F-value	2.80**	2.33*	3.60*	2.32**
Chow F		2.84**		2.91**
Adj. R^2	0.055	0.099	0.059	0.093

[a] Restricted regressions without interactions.
[b] 209 IPOs selecting Big-Eight auditors and prestigious underwriters and 37 IPOs selecting non-Big-Eight auditors and non-prestigious underwriters are included in the regressions.
[c] All 404 IPOs of the sample are included in the regressions.
[d] A dummy variable, AU = 1 for IPOs selecting Big-Eight auditors and prestigious underwriters, 0 otherwise.
[e] A dummy variable, AUA = 1 for IPOs selecting non-Big-Eight auditors and prestigious underwriters, or IPOs selecting Big-Eight auditors and non-prestigious underwriters, 0 otherwise.
[f] These variables are formed as the products of AU and the respective independent variables.
[g] These variables are formed as the products of AUA and the respective independent variables.
* Significant at $p < 0.01$ (two-sided t-test). ** Significant at $p < 0.05$ (two-sided t-test).

The results for the OLS estimates show that the three models are statistically signifi-cant but have low explanatory power (adjusted R^2 between 0.055 and 0.093). The reported Chow F-values are statistically significant, suggesting that the slope coefficients for IPOs selecting AU = 1 are different than those selecting AU = 0. The statistically insignificant estimated coefficients for the dummy variable (AU) suggest that, at the intercept, BRPR for very low firm-specific risk is generally similar for IPOs selecting AU = 1 and for those selecting AU = 0. The significant estimated coefficients for the interaction of AU with ln(TA), AGE, and VARRET respectively indicate changes in the expected direction for the slopes of the three variables. The changes in the slope coefficients of the other two risk variables are statistically insignificant. All interactions of the respective risk variables with AUA are statistically insignificant, suggesting that the estimated slope coefficients for IPOs selecting AUA = 1 are similar to those for IPOs selecting AU = 0. Given that an increase in BRPR indicates a decrease in benefits, the results suggest a moderate decrease in the incremental deflated benefits of hiring high-quality auditors or prestigious underwriters as firm-specific risk increases, providing some support for the TT hypothesis $(H_{D,TT})$.

In summary, the empirical results moderately support TT's proposition, that entrepreneurs who face increasing firm-specific risk have lower incremental benefit from hiring a higher-quality auditor or prestigious underwriter. The findings indicate that when the IPO firm-specific risk is low, the incremental benefit of hiring a high-quality auditor and a prestigious underwriter is higher than the incremental cost, but the incremental cost may outweigh the incremental benefit when the firm-specific risk is high. These findings should be interpreted cautiously because of the increasing deflated incremental costs of hiring high-quality auditors or prestigious underwriters as firm-specific risk variables increase. The lack of precise ex-ante firm-specific risk variables in the database and the relatively low explanatory power of the regressions presented in Table 22.7 are yet further reasons for caution.

22.7 Conclusion

In this study we develop tests to examine empirically the impact of firm-specific risk on the incremental costs and benefits of choosing high-quality auditors and prestigious underwriters by entrepreneurs prior to initial public offerings (IPOs). In our tests we distinguish between two supply-side (incremental costs) hypotheses and the competing demand-side (incremental benefits) hypotheses proposed by Titman and Trueman (1986) (TT) and Datar et al. (1991) (DFH). Previous studies (Feltham et al., 1991; Clarkson and Simunic, 1994) have examined the demand-side effect. In particular, Clarkson and Simunic (1994), using data from Canada (where the legal environment enabled them to control for the supply-side effect of risk on auditor choice), suggest that riskier entrepreneurs may gain incremental benefit from hiring high-quality auditors. We differ from these empirical studies by examining both the supply-side and the demand-side effects.

Restricting the study to firm-commitment share offerings for which prospectuses were filed to the SEC, we analyzed a sample of 404 US IPOs for which complete data were available. The results indicate that the incremental costs (deflated by the IPO proceeds) of hiring high-quality auditors and prestigious underwriters increase as firm-specific risk increases. We then provide evidence in support of the TT demand-side proposition that riskier firms gain incremental benefit from hiring lower-quality auditors or underwriters, rather than of the DFH prediction that higher-quality hirings are more beneficial. These demand-side results should, however, be interpreted with caution for several reasons, such as the absence of precise measures of benefits, the lack of precise ex-ante firm-specific risk variables in the database, and increasing incremental deflated cost as firm-specific risk increases.

Acknowledgments – Financial support for this study was provided by the Joseph Kasierer Institute for Research in Accounting, Faculty of Management, Tel Aviv University, Israel.

References

Aharony, J., Lin, C., and Loeb, M. (1993). Initial Public Offerings, Accounting Choices, and Earnings Management. *Contemporary Accounting Research*, 10(1):61–81.

Balvers, R., McDonald, B., and Miller, R. (1988). Underpricing of New Issues and the Choice of Auditor as a Signal of Investment Banker Reputation. *Accounting Review*, 63(4):605–622.

Beatty, R. (1989). Auditor Reputation and the Pricing of Initial Public Offerings. *Accounting Review*, 64(4):693–709.

Booth, J. R. and Smith. R. L. (1986). Capital Raising, Underwriting and the Certification Hypothesis. *Journal of Financial Economics*, 15(1–2):261–281.

Carter, R. and Manaster, S. (1990). Initial Public Offerings and Underwriter Reputation. *Journal of Finance*, 45(4):1045–1067.

Clarkson, P. and Simunic, D. (1994). The Association between Audit Quality, Retained Ownership, and Firm-Specific Risk in U.S. vs. Canadian IPO Markets. *Journal of Accounting and Economics*, 14(1–2):207–228.

Datar, S. M., Feltham, G. A., and Hughes, J. S. (1991). The Role of Audits and Audit Quality in Valuing New Issues. *Journal of Accounting and Economics*, 14(1):3–49.

Feltham, G. A., Hughes, J. S., and Simunic, D.A. (1991). Empirical Assessment of the Impact of Auditor Quality on the Valuation of New Issues. *Journal of Accounting and Economics*, 14(4):375–399.

Hayes, S. (1979). The Transformation of Investment Banking. *Harvard Business Review*, 57(1):153–170.

Hogan, C. E. (1997). Costs and Benefits of Audit Quality in the IPO Market: A Self Selection Analysis. *Accounting Review*, 72(1):67–86.

Hughes, J. S. (1989). Discussion of Valuation of Initial Public Offerings. *Contemporary Accounting Research*, 5(2):514–535.

Johnston, J. (1984). *Econometric Methods*. McGraw-Hill, New York.

Judge, G. G., Hill, R. C., Griffths, W. E., Lutkepohl, H., and Lee, T.-C. (1988). *Introduction to the Theory of Econometrics*. John Wiley, New York.

Kennedy, P. (1992). *A Guide to Econometrics*. MIT Press, Cambridge, MA.

Krinsky, I. and Rotenberg, W. (1989). The Valuation of Initial Public Offerings. *Contemporary Accounting Research*, 5(2):501–515.

Lee, P., Stokes, D., Taylor, S., and Walter, T. (2003). The Association Between Audit Quality, Accounting Disclosures and Firm-Specific Risk: Evidence from Initial Public Offerings. *Journal of Accounting and Public Policy*, 22(4):377–400.

Menon, K. and Williams, D. (1991). Auditor Credibility and Initial Public Offerings. *Accounting Review*, 66(2):313–322.

Simunic, D. and Stein, M. (1987). Product Differentiation in Auditing: Auditor Choice in the Market for Unseasoned New Issues. Research Monograph #13, Canadian Certified General Accountants' Research Foundation, Vancouver, BC.

Titman, S. and Trueman, B. (1986). Information Quality and the Valuation of New Issues. *Journal of Accounting and Economics*, 8(2):159–172.

23 Siamese twins and virtual mergers: dual-listed companies in Australia

Paul Ali

Abstract

Three of Australia's largest corporations – BHP Billiton, Brambles Industries, and Rio Tinto – are 'dual-listed companies' (DLCs), with listings on the Australian and London Stock Exchanges. DLCs can be distinguished from the conventional multiple listing of shares, for example, via American depository receipts. DLCs are a novel corporate structure that enable the 'virtual merger' of corporations without the need for a conventional takeover. There is no change in the ownership of the business assets or the shares of the merging corporations in a DLC structure. Instead, the merging corporations enter into contractual arrangements under which they agree to operate their businesses as if they were a single, legally merged entity. This chapter examines the structure of DLCs and the key legal issues that arise when corporations merge using DLCs.

23.1 Introduction

One of the more remarkable developments in corporate affairs of the last hundred years has been the use of the 'Siamese twins' (Licht, 2000) or 'dual-listed companies' structure to effect the 'virtual' merger and consolidation of transnational enterprises. Unlike conventional mergers, the execution of a merger via the creation of dual-listed companies does not involve the absorption of the target company by the bidder or the shareholders of the target company cashing out their shares or exchanging those shares for shares in the bidder. Instead, the companies participating in such a structure retain their separate existence, their own boards of directors and shareholders, and separate listings, but, through a series of complex contractual arrangements, the companies are managed as if they were a single company. Thus, while dual-listed companies, as the nomenclature indicates, involve listings on multiple exchanges, they bear little resemblance to conventional multiple listings of securities, for example via American or Global Depository Receipts.

Dual-listed companies have, however, maintained a surprisingly low profile in scholarly studies of corporate law, despite the fact that some of the world's largest transnational businesses are organized using the dual-listed companies structure. These businesses include Royal Dutch Shell and Unilever, and BHP Billiton and Rio Tinto, the world's two largest diversified resources companies. This chapter examines the different types of dual-listed companies, with particular emphasis on the Anglo-Australian experience. The separate entities structure used by three Anglo-Australian dual-listed companies is the dominant structure for dual-listed companies. This chapter also identifies some of the key legal issues that arise when corporations merge using that structure.

23.2 Dual-listed companies

23.2.1   A brief history of dual-listed companies

Dual-listed companies originated in the Netherlands and UK in the early twentieth century and, for almost 60 years, the only two examples of dual-listed companies were Royal Dutch Shell and Unilever. From the late 1980s, there has been renewed interest in the use of dual-listed companies to effect mergers but, in the vast majority of cases, the templates used have been substantially similar to the templates pioneered by the two Anglo-Dutch transnational businesses.

Of the nine dual-listed companies in existence today, the majority have used the separate entities structure (six), while two have used the combined entities structure, and only one has used the 'stapled securities' structure. These structures will be explained below.

The above list will shortly be reduced by the abandonment of the dual-listed companies structure by Royal Dutch Shell (Royal Dutch Shell Group, 2004) and possibly also Unilever. In the case of the former, if the proposal is accepted by the shareholders of Royal Dutch Petroleum and Shell Transport and Trading Company, the two companies will be united in a single company, Royal Dutch Shell, with the shareholders of the two companies exchanging their shares for shares in the new company. In addition, Unilever is coming under increasing investor pressure to simplify its corporate structure, which would necessarily involve the abandonment of the dual-listed companies structure (Tomlinson, 2005).

Table 23.1 summarizes the development of dual-listed companies and identifies the particular structures employed. This table is based on work undertaken by Bedi et al. (2003) and de Jong et al. (2004), and, in the case of the four most recent dual-listed companies, the author's review of the explanatory memoranda issued by the companies in soliciting shareholder approval for the implementation of the particular structure.

23.2.2   The dual-listed companies structure

The dual-listed companies that have been created to date have all involved the virtual merger of companies incorporated in two different jurisdictions with separate primary listings. Having said that, there is, in principle, no reason why two companies incorporated in the same jurisdiction and having the same primary listing could not also utilize the dual-listed companies structure, or why three or more companies in different jurisdictions could not utilize such a structure (Hume, 2003).

In each case, the effect of implementing the dual-listed companies structure has been to reconstitute the businesses of the merging companies as a single enterprise. While the companies retain their separate legal personalities and, consequently, retain their own boards of directors and shareholders, the intention is that the shareholders of each company should, as a general rule, be indifferent as to which of the companies they hold shares in (although, for many shareholders, the decision may be dictated by the different tax treatment of dividends for resident and non-resident shareholders). Indeed, the contractual arrangements used to implement a dual-listed companies structure have as their purpose the creation of a de facto single economic entity and, accordingly, these arrangements will explicitly provide for the separate companies to be managed as if they were a single company with a single body of shareholders.

Table 23.1 Dual-listed companies

Dual-listed companies	Structure employed	Implementation	Status
Royal Dutch Petroleum (Netherlands)/ Shell Transport and Trading Company (UK)	Combined entities	1907	Announced proposal to unify companies (28 October 2004)
Unilever (Netherlands and UK)	Separate entities	1930	Continuing
ABB (Sweden and Switzerland)	Combined entities	1988	Companies unified (1999)
Euro Tunnel (France and UK)	Stapled securities	1989	Continuing
Smithkline Beecham (UK and USA)	Stapled securities	1989	Companies unified (1996)
Fortis (Belgium and Netherlands)	Combined entities	1990	Companies unified (2001)
Elsevier (Netherlands)/ Reed International (UK)	Combined entities	1993	Continuing
Rio Tinto (Australia and UK)	Separate entities	1995	Continuing
Dexia (Belgium and France)	Combined entities	1996	Companies unified (1999)
Merita (Finland)/ Nordbanken (Sweden)	Combined entities	1997	Companies unified (2000)
Allied Zurich (UK)/Zurich Allied (Switzerland)	Combined entities	1998	Companies unified (2000)
BHP Billiton (Australia and UK)	Separate entities	2001	Continuing
Brambles Industries (Australia and UK)	Separate entities	2001	Continuing
Investec (South Africa and UK)	Separate entities	2002	Continuing
Carnival Corporation (Panama)/ P&O Princess Cruises (UK)	Separate entities	2003	Continuing

As noted in Table 23.1, three different structures have been used in establishing dual-listed companies.

23.2.3 Combined entities structure

This is the oldest type of dual-listed companies structure. Only two of the dual-listed companies now in existence utilize this structure (Royal Dutch Shell and Reed Elsevier).

In this structure, the business assets of the merging companies are transferred to one or more intermediate holding companies (Panel on Takeovers and Mergers, 2002). These holding companies are owned jointly by the two merging companies. Thus, while the two companies retain, as is the case with all dual-listed companies, their separate legal personalities (and separate boards of directors and shareholders), their business assets are consolidated in common holding companies.

23.2.4 Separate entities structure

This is the most common type of dual-listed company. Three of the dual-listed companies employing the separate entities structure are Anglo-Australian businesses: BHP Billiton, Brambles, and Rio Tinto. The others are Investec, P&O Princess Carnival, and Unilever.

The merging companies retain their separate legal personalities (and separate boards of directors and shareholders) but, in contrast to the combined entities structure, there is no transfer of business assets (Panel on Takeovers and Mergers, 2002; Harding, 2002). Instead, the separately owned assets are managed jointly by the two companies.

23.2.5 Stapled securities structure

Only one of the dual-listed companies now in existence uses this structure: Euro Tunnel. Again, the two merging companies retain their separate legal personalities but, unlike the other two structures, the shares in the two companies cannot be separately traded (by stapling the shares together) and there is thus a single body of shareholders common to both companies (Panel on Takeovers and Mergers, 2002).

It has been contended that the stapled securities structure cannot properly be categorized as a dual-listed companies structure due to the absence of separate tradability of the shares (Bedi et al., 2003). The existence of a single body of shareholders also simplifies the legal issues confronting the directors of the individual companies.

23.2.6 Contractual arrangements

Looking at the prevalent form of dual-listed companies, in which the separate entities structure has been employed, there are four key contractual arrangements:

- Sharing agreement between the two companies
- Amendments to the constitution or articles of association of the two companies
- Special voting arrangements
- Cross-guarantees by each company.

The above list is based on Smith and Cugati (2001) and the author's review of the explanatory memoranda for the BHP Billiton and Brambles dual-listed companies.

The sharing agreement provides the basis for the merger of the two companies. The two companies, pursuant to this agreement, undertake to operate as if they are a single merged economic entity, through the appointment of the same persons as directors of the two companies and the creation of a unified, senior management team comprising the same persons as the senior executives of the two companies. In addition, the directors of each company are required, in the discharge of their duties to the company, to take account of the shareholders of both companies as if the companies are a single legal entity and those shareholders comprise the shareholders of that single entity.

The sharing agreement also sets out the relative economic and voting rights (the economic rights comprise rights to dividends, a return of capital, and the distribution of any surplus in a liquidation) attaching to the ordinary shares (or common stock) in the two companies. A share in one company will have, in respect of the single economic entity constituted by the combination of the two companies' businesses, economic and voting rights relative to a share in the other company, in proportion to the equalization ratio stipulated in the sharing agreement. The equalization ratio is the ratio of the economic and voting rights conferred by one share in the first company relative to the corresponding rights conferred upon one share in the second company. This ratio will normally be 1:1, as is the case with BHP Billiton and Brambles. In that situation, the shareholders of the two companies will enjoy equivalent economic and voting rights.

The constitution (or articles of association) of each of the companies must also be amended to give effect to the terms of the sharing agreement. These constitutional amendments will, moreover, stipulate in detail the circumstances in which matters must be voted on by shareholders of both companies (e.g. election of directors, appointment of an auditor). Also, a person cannot take over one company without making a takeover bid on equivalent terms to the shareholders of the other company). Under these voting arrangements, the shareholders of the two companies effectively vote as a single body of shareholders. The votes cast by the shareholders of one company are aggregated with the votes cast by the shareholders of the other company via the mechanism of special voting shares. Resolutions in relation to matters on which both groups of shareholders are entitled to vote can thus only be passed by an overall majority of the shareholders (Glanz and Sanderson, 2001).

The special voting arrangements are designed to give effect to the provisions in the sharing agreement and the constitutional amendments regarding the casting of votes by shareholders. Special voting shares in each company are issued either to an independent trustee (in the case of Brambles) or to separate special voting companies (in the case of BHP Billiton). These shares are used to transmit the votes cast at a meeting of shareholders of one company to the meeting of shareholders of the other company, thus resulting in the aggregation of votes when the shareholders of the two companies are voting on matters that affect both companies. Each company is required to notify the trustee or relevant special voting company of the votes cast at meetings of the first company and the trustee or special purpose company is, in turn, obligated to attend and vote its special voting shares at the meeting of the second company to reflect the votes cast at the meeting of the first company.

Finally, each of the companies in the dual-listed companies structure guarantees the performance of obligations by the other company. The purpose of the cross-guarantees is to create joint and several liability to the creditors of each company and thus place the creditors of one company on an equal footing with the creditors of the other company. From the perspective of the creditors, it is as if the guaranteed obligations of each company are owed by a single, common debtor.

23.2.7 Why use the dual-listed companies structure?

Given the complexity of the dual-listed companies structure relative to a conventional merger of companies and the consequent investor confusion, the obvious question is whether there are any countervailing advantages for the participants in such a structure.

First, in a dual-listed companies structure, the companies retain their primary listings and access to capital in their home markets. The inclusion of the companies in the share indices of their home markets will also be unaffected, thus avoiding the flow-back or selldown risk common to conventional cross-border mergers where the bidder's weighting in its home market indices rises but the target is removed from its home market indices. The selling pressure in the latter market from index-tracking mutual funds (as well as mutual funds and pension funds whose performance is benchmarked against the same indices) may overwhelm the increase in demand in the former market, thus eroding shareholder value (Freshfields Bruckhaus Deringer, 2003).

Secondly, effecting a virtual merger via a dual-listed companies structure generally does not, in contrast to a conventional merger, involve one party paying a 'takeover premium' for the acquisition of control of the other.

Also, such a virtual merger should, unlike a conventional merger, be tax neutral for both the shareholders (there is no disposal of their shares and thus no crystallization of a taxable gain, and the shareholders also retain their current treatment in respect of dividends) and the companies (the companies retain their current tax domiciles and, in the case of the separate entities and stapled securities structures, there is no disposal of business assets).

Moreover, as a dual-listed companies structure does not involve a transfer of shares or, depending on the structure employed, a transfer of business assets, the merging companies can minimize 'change of control' risks. A change in the majority ownership, or a disposal of the main undertaking, of a company will usually trigger preemption rights under joint venture agreements and permit early termination of leases and acceleration of financing agreements.

Finally, the fact that both companies are preserved as separate entities means that a merger via a dual-listed companies structure is an expedient way of avoiding the political concerns, and the application of laws restricting foreign investment, that often accompany the cross-border takeover of 'national icons' or companies that operate in strategically important or politically sensitive sectors.

Balanced against these advantages is the fact that the complexity of the structure and the retention of the separate legal personalities of the two merging companies may make it difficult to integrate the businesses of the two companies (notwithstanding the statements as to joint management in the sharing agreement) and achieve the synergies obtainable in a conventional merger of businesses. In addition, because the shares in the two companies retain their primary listings in different markets, there are likely to be significant pricing disparities between the two shares, despite the allocation of fixed economic and voting rights to the shares in each company (Rosenthal and Young, 1990; Froot and Dabora, 1999; Bedi et al., 2003; de Jong et al., 2004; Scruggs, 2004).

23.3 Some legal issues

Dual-listed companies raise a number of unique legal issues (Harding, 2002). The discussion that follows is based on the general principles of Anglo-Australian corporate law (all nine of the dual-listed companies now in existence involve a UK company, and three of these involve pairings with Australian companies).

The Anglo-Australian law on directors' duties and the norms of corporate governance that have developed in the UK and Australia, as a general rule, envisage the paradigmatic scenario of a single company and thus only a single body of shareholders and a single board of directors. It is trite law to state that, in these circumstances, the directors owe their duties to the company, and their particular duty to act in good faith and in the best interests of the company means that the directors must have regard to interests of the shareholders as a whole (at least when the company is solvent and the risk of insolvency is remote).

The dual-listed companies structure challenges the assumptions on which these principles are based. Even though the companies in that structure are intended to be managed as a single economic entity (and to that end have identical boards of directors and senior executives), the legal reality is that the companies remain legally distinct and each has its distinct body of shareholders, regardless of the common directorships and the degree of overlap created by persons holding shares in both companies.

Accordingly, can a director who sits on the board of two companies managed as a single enterprise disregard their separate legal personality and behave as if the single economic entity constituted by the dual-listed companies structure represents a single legal entity? This involves an examination of two separate issues. First, to what extent can the director take into account the interests of the single economic entity? Second, to what extent can the director take into account the interests of the other company in the dual-listed company structure?

For the first of these issues, it is possible to obtain guidance from the Anglo-Australian law on directors' duties in the context of corporate groups. It is recognized that, as a matter of economic reality, the directors of companies that are members of a corporate group will, when making decisions, have regard to the interests of the group. A director is therefore permitted to have regard to the extraneous interests of the group provided that there is a reasonable basis for believing that having regard to such interests would result in derivative benefits flowing to the company (Harding, 2002). It is critical to note here that the director's duties to the company on whose board he or she sits retain their primacy, and the director cannot, in paying heed to the interests of the group, ignore the interests of the company. Applying this to the dual-listed companies structure, a director is permitted to take account of the interests of the single economic entity (and thus act as if that single economic entity is coeval with the individual companies on whose boards the director sits) provided that there is some benefit to the individual companies. This equates to circumstances where what is in the interests of the single economic entity, constituted by the joint operation of the separate businesses of the individual companies, is consistent with the separate interests of the individual companies.

Equally, as regards the second of the above issues, the director of one company can legitimately take into account the interests of the other company in a dual-listed companies structure, where having regard to the interests of the single economic entity involves taking into account the interests of that other company. Again, this necessarily involves a situation where the interests of that other company are consistent with the interests of the single economic entity.

It is, however, possible to posit a situation in which the interests of one company in a dual-listed companies structure diverge from the interests of the single economic entity or even where the interests of the two companies are inconsistent, if not opposed. This is not unlike the situations involving corporate groups where the interests of a group member may be subordinated (or sacrificed) to the interests of the group as a whole. Here, as in the context of the first issue, the directors must be cognizant of the centrality of the single company to Anglo-Australian corporate law.

In terms of a divergence between the interests of one of the companies in a dual-listed companies structure and the interests of the single economic entity, the absence of either any actual derivative benefits or any reasonable basis for believing that such benefits will flow to the company would preclude a director from taking into account the interests of the single economic entity. Subordination of the interests of the company to that of the single economic entity or indifference towards the former interests will place the director in breach of his or her duty to act in good faith and in the best interests of the company.

Where the interests of the two companies in a dual-listed companies structure diverge, the directors will be confronted with conflicting loyalties. A director must not, as a general principle of the Anglo-Australian law on directors' duties, place him or herself in a position where there is a real or substantial possibility of a material conflict between the director's duty to the company and the director's duty to some other company. This particular conflict seems only capable of resolution, in a dual-listed companies structure, where the divergence in the interests of the two companies can be subsumed within the interests of the single economic entity (Haddy, 2002). That, in turn, requires that there must be actual derivative benefits flowing to the individual companies or a reasonable basis for believing that such benefits will eventuate. Absent such benefits or such a basis for belief, the director will be viewed as having failed to discharge his or her duty of loyalty (of which the duty to avoid conflicts of interests is one aspect) to the individual companies.

The above discussion of directors' duties is predicated on the 'interests' of the company and 'interests' of the single economic entity. What then are these 'interests'? Each company in a dual-listed companies structure retains its separate legal personality and therefore also its original body of shareholders. The shareholders of one company in this structure may, of course, also acquire shares in the other company, but that does not make them any less shareholders of the former or lead to the extinguishment of the separate bodies of shareholders. Yet, as stated above, the single economic entity created in a dual-listed companies structure is managed as if the individual companies had become subsumed within a single legal personality.

In terms of the interests of the individual companies, this, while the company is neither insolvent nor at risk of insolvency, equates to the interests of the shareholders of that company as a whole. In acting in the interests of these shareholders, the directors may legitimately have regard to the interests of the single economic entity and the interests of the shareholders of the other company in the structure, but the former interests have primacy. However, the interests of the single economic entity, and its fiction of a single legal entity, do not fit comfortably with the concept of the primacy of the interests of the shareholders of a company. The single economic entity embraces two separate companies each with their own separate bodies of shareholders and interests of each body of shareholders has primacy vis-à-vis the directors of the companies in which the shares are held.

The closest analogy under Anglo-Australian corporate law for interpreting the intermingled interests of the separate bodies of shareholders in a dual-listed companies structure is a company with different classes of shareholders. Directors are under a duty to act fairly as between the different classes of shareholders. However, this principle is again based upon the paradigm of the single company and, further, assumes a commonality of interest on the part of all classes of shareholders. The distinction between the classes of shareholders may be based upon different legal liabilities to the company (as between fully paid and partly paid ordinary shares), different voting rights (as between different classes of ordinary shares), and different entitlements to dividends and capital (as between ordinary shares and preference shares). Irrespective of the differing rights attaching to shares, the law nonetheless assumes that there is a commonality of interest in that the interests of all the shareholders relate to the entirety of the company's business and undertaking (Ali and Stapledon, 2000).

That is not the case in a dual-listed companies structure. The shareholders of one company do not have a commonality of interest with the shareholders of the other company, since they are shareholders in different companies. In addition, the shareholders of the two companies may have different economic interests in the combined business and undertaking of the single economic entity, as the structure adopted may provide for different relative rights (for example, an equalisation ratio other than 1:1) (Hume, 2003). As such, it is difficult to accommodate the interests of the single economic entity within the general principles of Anglo-Australian law concerning the fair treatment of different classes of shareholders of the same company.

The inability to state with precision what the interests of the single economic entity require in terms of treatment of the potentially disparate interests of the separate bodies of shareholders of the individual companies means that the content of the duties imposed upon the directors of the individual companies cannot also be stated with precision or certainty.

23.4 Conclusion

The dual-listed companies structure can be used to effect a virtual merger of two or more companies where a conventional merger is not feasible – for example, for investment, taxation, or even political reasons. To date, the structures that have been implemented and remain in existence have concerned the cross-border combinations of two companies. In each of these cases, one of the merging companies has been a UK-based company.

However, the dual-listed companies structure is complex. The fact that the merging companies retain their separate legal identities (and separate boards of directors and bodies of shareholders) means that the responsibilities of the directors of those companies cannot readily be accommodated within the existing principles of Anglo-Australian corporate law. This leaves the directors (as well as the shareholders) in an invidious position, as the boundaries between compliance and transgression are even more blurred for directors in a dual-listed companies structure than they are for the directors of other companies.

Investor confusion and the lack of trading parity between the shares in the merging companies are other material disadvantages associated with the dual-listed companies structure.

The amorphous nature of directors' duties, investor confusion, and the price performance of the shares are all likely to have a deleterious effect on the ability of the companies to raise capital in the public markets. Indeed, these matters have been decisive in persuading a number of companies to abandon the dual-listed companies structure (de Jong et al., 2004).

Acknowledgments – The author wishes to thank Phil Spathis for kindly providing him with a copy of the research paper on dual-listed companies commissioned by the Australian Council of Superannuation Investors.

References

Ali, P. U. and Stapledon, G. (2000). Virtual Flotations, Tracking Shares and Corporate Governance. *Company and Securities Law Journal*, 18(6):429–433.

Bedi, J., Richards, A., and Tennant, P. (2003). The Characteristics and Trading Behaviour of Dual-Listed Companies. Research Discussion Paper, International Department, Reserve Bank of Australia, Sydney, Australia.

Cohn, S. R. (2004). The Non-Merger Virtual Merger: Is Corporate Law Ready for Virtual Reality? *Delaware Journal of Corporate Law*, 29:1–42.

de Jong, A., Rosenthal, L., and van Dijk, M. A. (2004). The Limits of Arbitrage: Evidence from Dual-Listed Companies. Working Paper, Erasmus University Rotterdam, Rotterdam, the Netherlands.

Freshfields Bruckhaus Deringer (2003). The Future for DLCs after P&O Princess/Carnival/Royal Caribbean. *New Issues*, March/April:1–3.

Froot, K. A. and Dabora, E. M. (1999). How are Stock Prices Affected by the Location of Trade? *Journal of Financial Economics*, 53(2):189–216.

Glanz, S. and Sanderson, G. (2001). *Dual Listed Companies*. Baker & McKenzie, Sydney, Australia.

Haddy, S. (2002). A Comparative Analysis of Directors' Duties in a Range of Corporate Group Structures. *Company and Securities Law Journal*, 20(3):138–159.

Harding, M. (2002). Dual Listed Companies: Understanding Conflicts of Interest for Directors. *University of New South Wales Law Journal*, 25(2):594–610.

Hume, S. E. K. (2003). Implications of Dual-Listed Companies for their Shareholders. Research Paper, Australian Council of Superannuation Investors, Melbourne, Australia.

Licht, A. N. (2000). Genie in a Bottle? Assessing Managerial Opportunism in International Securities Transactions. *Columbia Business Law Review*, 2000(1):51–120.

Panel on Takeovers and Mergers (2002). Dual Listed Company Transactions and Frustrating Action: Revision Proposals relating to the Definition of an Offer and Rule 21.2 of the Takeover Code. Consultation Paper, Code Committee, Panel on Takeovers and Mergers, London, UK.

Rosenthal, L. and Young, C. (1990). The Seemingly Anomalous Price Behaviour of Royal Dutch/Shell and Unilever NV/PLC. *Journal of Financial Economics*, 26(1):123–141.

Royal Dutch Shell Group (2004). Joint Announcement by NV Koninklijke Nederlandsche Petroleum Maatschappij and the "Shell" Transport and Trading Company, Public Limited Company. News and Media Release, London, UK.

Scruggs, J. T. (2004). Noise Trader Risk: Evidence from the Siamese Twins. Working Paper, Terry College of Business, University of Georgia, Athens, GA.

Smith, C. and Cugati, V. (2001). Innovative Structures – Dual Listed Companies. *Focus – Mergers & Acquisitions*, No. 1. Allens Arthur Robinson, Sydney, Australia.

Tomlinson, R. (2005). One Company, Two Bosses, Many Problems. *Fortune*, 151(2):70–75.

24 Equity issuance trends in Australia's listed investment fund markets

Martin Gold

Abstract

Buoyant equity market conditions in Australia have underpinned investor demand for initial public offerings (IPOs) and new equity raisings. A recent phenomenon observed in Australia has been the emergence of listed investment funds as a vibrant and discrete sector of the Australian Stock Exchange. In contrast to open-ended mutual funds, listed investment funds have traditionally offered investors lower operating costs and portfolio turnover. Although REITs dominate the sector, more recent listed investment funds offer strategies targeting infrastructure, absolute returns, and private equity.

This chapter includes an overview of the institutional features of Australia's listed investment fund market, the demand and supply-side factors driving growth in this sector, and the investment characteristics of the funds available.

24.1 Introduction

The Australian listed investment fund market currently comprises 138 entities with a market value of approximately \$129.3 billion, or about 14% of the market capitalization of domestic stocks listed on the Australian Stock Exchange (ASX).[1] The listed investment fund market has experienced a strong level of interest from mutual fund promoters, investors, and regulators, especially within the nascent sectors such as absolute return products, private equity, infrastructure, and exchange-traded funds. A recent phenomenon observed has been the resurgence of so-called 'cash boxes' – investment vehicles marketed without a specific investment charter.

This chapter provides an overview of the Australian listed investment fund market's institutional structure, examines the demand and supply factors which have driven the recent growth in issuances, and finally reviews the investment proposition offered by Australian share funds in terms of their absolute returns and performance relative to conventional mutual funds.

24.2 Institutional details and market structure

As shown in Figure 24.1, the dominant sectors of the Australian listed investment fund market are listed property trusts (REITs), infrastructure funds, investment companies

---

[1] ASX, *Listed Managed Investment Monthly Update*, January 2005.

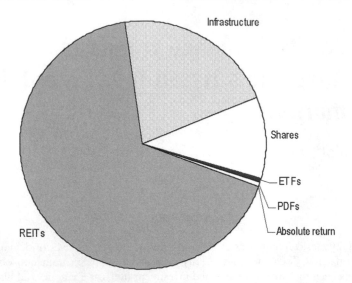

Figure 24.1 Listed investment fund strategies

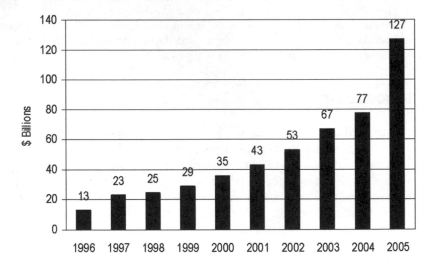

Figure 24.2 Listed fund market asset growth

and trusts, with the balance comprised of exchange-traded funds (ETFs), pooled development funds (PDFs), and absolute return funds (also known as hedge funds).

REITs are the predominant form of fund strategy, with $87.3 billion of assets comprising approximately 68% of the total market. Listed property vehicles became the dominant route of real estate investment for institutional and personal investors in the aftermath of the property bubble of the late 1980s and early 1990s. This episode reflected the dangers of overpaying for assets and the use of excessive leverage, but significantly it highlighted the inability of unlisted real estate vehicles to provide adequate liquidity and marketability to investors, especially institutions and pension funds, which prefer the flexibility offered by exchange-traded instruments to alter portfolio asset allocations.

The growth in the REIT listings, therefore, was underpinned by the transition of unlisted vehicles to public quotation. In recent years, the sector has experienced significant asset growth as a result of consolidation activity, itself a function of the M&A activity amongst the fund managers, the preferences of pension fund consultants and trustees, and the desire of fund managers to extract portfolio scale efficiencies and diversification. More recently, within the REIT sector there has been a marked increase in the number of vehicles stapling together the fund's property assets, and the fund manager.

The Australian infrastructure sector comprises 13 funds with a total value of $27.4 billion, or approximately 21% of the overall market. Infrastructure is a relatively new asset class in Australia, and the growth in the asset size and listings is governed both by the preferences of investors and by the availability of suitable infrastructure projects. The main investments by Australian infrastructure funds have been in toll roads, airports, bulk transport and handling facilities, communications, and energy utilities. The relatively recent development of this asset class, and investor preferences for demonstrable specialist skills, has seen concentration of fund management in a relatively small number of firms. The sector has delivered strong economic returns to investors, and growth in the sector is expected to be underpinned by investment partnership opportunities arising within federal and state jurisdictions.

Listed investment companies are the oldest type of Australian collective managed investments[2] and the ASX estimates more than 300,000 investors own shares in these vehicles. Currently there are 53 funds with total assets of $13.1 billion (or approximately 10% of the total listed funds market). It is significant to note that the funds which have historically dominated the sector are primarily conservative long-term investors that favor profitable, dividend paying firms, and offer low management costs and portfolio turnover. More recent offerings in the sector, by contrast, have emphasized active investment charters and long-term management contracts.

The remainder of the listed investment fund market comprises ETFs (nine funds with $0.8 billion market value), PDFs (nine funds with $0.6 billion market value), and absolute return funds (two funds with $0.2 billion). ETFs were launched in Australia in 2001 and this fund category has experienced steady growth in assets. The growth of ETFs as a sector is constrained by the availability of suitable indices, however. State Street Global Advisors gained first-mover advantage by securing the key domestic equity benchmarks for its streetTRACKS series, which track the S&P/ASX200 Accumulation Index, S&P/ASX Top50, and S&P/ASX200 Listed Property Trust Index respectively.

PDFs were created in 1992 by the Australian Federal Government to facilitate venture capital investment by institutional and professional investors. These funds provide generous tax incentives; however, portfolio investments are regulated and must provide bona fide funding for small, unlisted firms (the value of investee firms must be smaller than $50 million, and minimum shareholding of 10%). The venture capital sector has experienced increasing interest in conjunction with global trends to

---

[2] The first listed investment company was the Australian Foundation and Investment Corporation (AFIC), which gained its ASX listing in 1928.

increase private equity allocations by institutional investors, and recent changes to the taxation of venture capital investment vehicles to enhance their investor appeal.[3]

24.2.1 Demand factors

The principal demand drivers of the growth in listed investment funds have been the disappointing performance track records of conventional mutual funds, the strong growth of private superannuation funds (which typically invest their funds directly into the stock market), and renewed investor appetite for the specialized investment strategies and expertise promised by these products.

24.2.2 Poor absolute performance of mutual funds

In the three successive financial years to 30 June 2003, most Australian superannuation funds delivered negative returns. These performance outcomes have demonstrated the 'herding' effect within conventional mutual funds. This phenomenon reduced the diversity of investment strategy choices (and portfolio diversification) and reinforced negative investor perceptions regarding accountability for investment performance (most mutual funds pay fund managers according to fund size but not performance).

The strong rebound in Australian stocks in the 2004 calendar year also encouraged a renewed investor risk appetite for equity issuances generally. The buoyancy of the general equity market saw 175 new stock market listings in the year to 30 June 2004, and improving valuations lead to increased M&A activity, including several private equity-backed re-listings. These conditions have emphasized the shrinking availability of quality industrial companies, and this momentum for the raisings has coincided with the emergence of private equity vehicles and structured finance products.

24.2.3 Growth of self-managed pension funds

In Australia, private superannuation funds – investment vehicles established by individuals taking direct responsibility for their retirement assets – have experienced very strong growth and now represent approximately 21% of the assets of Australia's entire retirement system.[4] This profound structural change in the financial services market has created strong demand for listed investment funds and other exchange-traded securities.

Research into the growth of private superannuation funds undertaken by the ASX and fund managers has confirmed anecdotal evidence that wealthier investors are dissatisfied by the substantial fee levels levied by public offer funds and disappointing absolute returns. These investors have significant involvement in the investment policy of their funds, and are likely to consult a stockbroker or financial adviser to make portfolio choices from the stock market and other major asset classes. Additionally, these investors are also attracted to the control over taxation liabilities afforded by these structures, making it possible to manage their portfolios on an after-tax return basis: this is not possible for conventional mutual funds which operate a generic investment objective and strategy.

---

[3] These vehicles are known as Venture Capital Limited Partnerships (VCLPs).
[4] Over the past decade, the number of private superannuation funds has nearly tripled. See further: Australian Prudential Regulatory Authority, *Superannuation Insights*, June 2004.

24.2.4 Strategy differentiation and effective diversification

Listed investment funds offer this strongly growing segment of investors an effective route to gaining a diversified exposure to chosen markets, and the promise of specialized management skills (and therefore tangible portfolio diversification). Many listed investment funds provide more concentrated portfolio bets, in contrast to conventional funds, which typically, as a function of their size, are compelled to track broad market and peer fund averages. Another attractive feature of recent listed investment fund offerings is that they offer performance-based fees that more closely align the pecuniary interests of the managers with returns received by investors.

24.2.5 Choice and investor-directed platforms

In Australia, investment advisers are increasingly embracing platform investment structures such as wrap accounts and master trusts. Research conducted by AC Neilsen on behalf of the ASX has confirmed that wrap accounts and other investor-directed administration vehicles are the most popular route of listed investment fund ownership, and that financial advisors use listed investment funds rather than referring clients to stockbrokers to make individual stock selections.[5] Listed investment funds therefore provide investment advisers with an opportunity to generate transaction- and fee-based income streams by offering clients' choice and differentiation. Listed investment funds make ideal candidates for investment selection as advisers seek to unbundle the portfolio decision from multi-asset mutual funds into separately managed portfolios offering customized exposures. From an investment administration perspective, listed investment funds are also ideally suited for platforms because they are priced in real time (versus mutual funds, which are typically valued once a day), and continuous market pricing also offers significant transparency, liquidity, and marketability benefits.

24.2.6 Fees and expenses – distribution costs of mutual funds industry model

In addition to the fees and expenses levels of mutual funds, which have attracted considerable interest in the context of lacklustre returns, listed investment funds have benefited from consumer concerns and misapprehensions about the mutual funds industry's distribution model, especially the structure of remuneration for sales intermediaries. Industry regulators and consumer groups have focused on the existence of trailing and soft dollar commissions, which have highlighted investing costs and the disclosure of mutual funds (although these commissions and benefits are generally paid from the fund managers fees, not the investors' accounts). By contrast, the distribution of listed investment funds is relatively transparent: stockbrokers and financial advisers typically do not receive trailing commissions or other benefits from secondary market transactions. The absence of ongoing distribution costs (in most retail mutual funds, trailer commissions typically equate to 0.2–1.0% of assets) allows listed investment funds to charge significantly lower management fees, further emphasizing their value proposition compared with conventional mutual funds.

---

[5] For more details on the use of listed investment funds by financial advisers, see further: ASX, *Financial Planners Market Research – Key Highlights*, March 2005.

24.2.7 Increasing investor emphasis on post-tax economic returns

Another factor encouraging growth of listed investment funds has been increasing investor awareness of the after-tax economic returns, and the direct and indirect costs of portfolio turnover. Unlike mutual funds, which typically have an open-ended structure, most listed investment funds (with the exception of ETFs) operate a closed-end structure. In addition to providing a captive portfolio, this structure provides the fund manager with the ability to manage the portfolio tax-effectively, including netting capital gains, to deliver an optimal post-tax return.

Because listed investment funds are effectively insulated from investors' transactions, fund managers can focus their efforts exclusively on making their judgements within the portfolio, and this also allows the fund manager to directly control turnover and the associated transaction costs. Interestingly, more recent initial public offerings (IPOs) have emphasized active investment charters, which are more likely to result in more frequent and larger income distributions incorporating realized capital gains and trading income, and thus higher dividend yields.

24.3 Supply factors

The key supply factors behind the growth in the listed funds market include strong stock market returns, the limited availability of conventional industrial company IPOs (as noted above), rationalization and diversification within the funds management market, the emergence of so-called boutique investment firms, and active promotion of the listed investment fund market growth by the ASX.

24.3.1 Rationalization, scale building, and business model diversification by fund managers

The Australian funds management market has undergone significant consolidation, and money managers have sought to diversify their business models beyond conventional mutual fund offerings. Within the REITs segment, for example, a number of the funds managed by one of Australia's largest institutions, AMP Limited, were subject to takeover, which resulted in merging of these funds within their own fund families. Although within-industry mergers between large REITs have reduced the number of funds, their portfolio sizes and diversification have increased, creating enlarged fee revenues for fund managers.

Although many fund managers are reluctant to buy listed investment funds because they prefer to undertake security selections, financial institutions have created listed investment funds to capitalize on investor demand. Investment banks and bank owners of large institutional funds managers have been highly active in creating listed investment funds. For example, Babcock & Brown, Macquarie Bank, and Westpac Banking Corporation have sponsored large investment vehicles (especially focused in the infrastructure, private equity, and debt hybrid categories). These vehicles are expected to be in a highly advantageous position because they will have direct access to the primary deal flows generated by the sponsoring institutions. The formation of listed investment funds also provides an opportunity for these firms to create alternative, potentially captive financing sources, which also allow for greater margin retention (including the placement fees from IPOs and deal sourcing fees for these vehicles).

24.3.2   The increasing popularity of boutique fund managers

A number of listed investment funds have been created by 'boutique' fund managers whose primary concern is to grow funds under management, but do not have any internal sales and distribution infrastructure. These firms have been able to distribute listed investment funds via traditional stockbroking and broker/dealer groups, which have experienced strong client demand for differentiated and specialized investment strategies. Many investment boutiques have been established by investment professionals who have become frustrated within the relatively constrained environment of institutional investment firms whose offerings have traditionally been constructed with reference to competitor funds. The majority of newer generation listed investment funds incorporate flexible investment mandates, innovative and alternative strategies, and an absolute return focus. The profusion of these listed investment funds has been assisted by increasing acceptance from the pension fund consulting community – the industry gatekeepers who control the bulk of wealth flows – who have recognized the need for effective portfolio diversification.

24.3.3   Good market timing and statistical fillips

The supply and acceptance of listed investment funds has been aided by the fact that several funds have recorded strong returns, which can be attributed to both specialized skills and the benefit of establishing these vehicles during an opportune period of rising stock prices. In contrast to traditional mutual funds, whose portfolios are typically constructed with direct reference to market benchmarks, recent IPOs have significantly greater flexibility of investment policies and have adopted concentrated portfolios that have delivered strong returns in the generally buoyant conditions. Many listed investment funds have focused on smaller capitalization issues, which are generally not actively pursued by conventional funds due to investment style and benchmark limitations (including the imposition of tracking error constraints), and their own business risk considerations.

   Additionally, because these funds are measured off a smaller capital base, their incremental returns are more readily visible than the selections made by managers of conventional mutual funds, which are effectively disguised within the returns of these large portfolios.

24.3.4   Concerted efforts to expand the listed investment fund market

The ASX has actively encouraged the development of the listed investment funds market as a discrete sector of the stock market. It has provided selective waivers of its listing rules, which were originally introduced in the 1980s to discourage the formation of cash box companies that do not have any operating business, certainty of profitability, or certainty of investment program. Cash box companies were primary used by entrepreneurs aggregating funds for speculative takeovers, and were blamed for the market volatility of that era.

   It is important to note that the ASX has not changed its listing rules, but has exercised its discretion to waive these rules; however, onerous disclosure requirements still apply to fund raisings by cash box investment companies under Australian securities regulations.[6] In particular, where cash boxes do not provide any factual information about where or how the funds raised by these companies will be invested, they must explicitly discuss this in the prospectus. In these circumstances, heavy reliance is placed on the skills and expertise of the company officers and investment managers.

24.4   Recent issuance trends

Over the past 18 months, the Australian listed investment fund markets have experienced strong support from investors, with approximately $6.4 billion in new capital raisings; however, as shown in Figure 24.3, the momentum in IPOs increased sharply in early 2005, with over $5.6 billion raised or committed. In the 2005 financial year to date, more capital has been raised by listed investment funds than conventional operating companies.

During the calendar year 2004, 24 LIC IPOs raised approximately $3.2 billion; however, the momentum of capital raisings increased dramatically in the first half of 2005, with approximately $3.2 billion committed from only nine IPOs.

Figures 24.4 and 24.5 show the marked changes in issuance patterns between 2004 and 2005, with private equity-oriented cash box funds dominating recent IPO issuances by sector.

In the current financial year, several cash box funds have been readied for market listing, specifically focusing on private equity and hybrid securities. They are notable for their size and the strong investor demand for these issues. These include a $300 million junk bond fund managed by Hastings Funds Management (a subsidiary of Westpac Banking Corporation), and private equity vehicles (including $517 million Allco Equity Partners, $1 billion Babcock & Brown Capital managed by investment bank Babcock & Brown, and the $1 billion Macquarie Capital Alliance managed by Macquarie Bank).

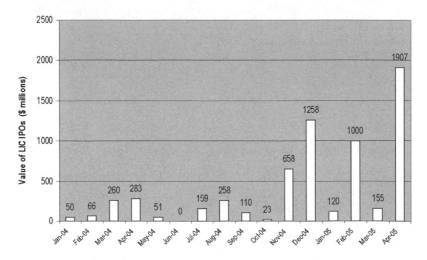

Figure 24.3 Issuance patterns of Australian listed investment funds

---

[6] For further information regarding cash box capital raisings, refer to: Australian Securities and Investments Commission, *Practice Note 70: Prospectuses for Cash Box and Investment Companies*, June 1999.

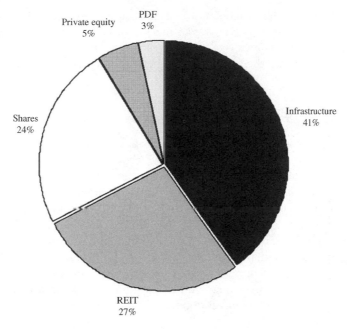

Figure 24.4 Value of IPOs by investment strategy (financial year 2004)

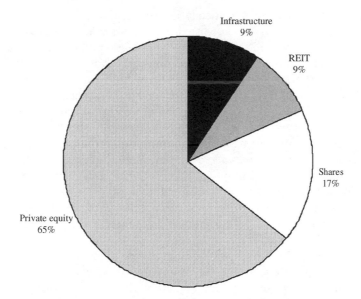

Figure 24.5 Value of IPOs by investment strategy (financial year 2005)

24.5   Performance of listed funds sector, including recent fund IPOs

Listed investment funds can be assessed using cross-sectional analysis of total shareholder returns (incorporating market price and dividends to shareholders), their performance relative to the broader stock market, and existence of premiums or discounts to net tangible assets (NTAs) versus market price. This section briefly analyzes the performance of Australian share listed investment funds, trends in NTA performance, and finally examines the absolute price performance of recent fund IPOs across the sector.

24.5.1   General performance characteristics of Australian share funds

The most relevant yardstick for many investors is a comparison of the returns of listed investment funds with the performance of the broad stock market and traditional mutual funds. According to Aegis Research,[7] for the year ended 31 December 2004, Australian equity-focused listed investment funds significantly underperformed the broad market (proxied by the S&P/ASX All Ordinaries Accumulation Index), providing an average return of 24.7%, compared with the market return of 27.6%. Over the 3 years to 31 December 2004, however, the average annual return from this sample was 11.6% compared to a market average return of 10.7%, reflecting outperformance (after fees and dividends were taken into account). Over this extended period, however, this cohort of listed investment funds marginally underperformed the median return of 12.3% generated by conventional Australian equity mutual funds.

24.5.2   NTA discount and premiums of the Australian shares listed funds sector

For any quoted investment, it is critically important that it trades at, or above, the fair value of its underlying assets. For listed investment funds, the NTA differential is a function of market cyclicality, the quality and marketability of the fund's investments, and investor confidence in the fund manager's abilities. A number of mechanisms can be incorporated into listed investment funds to mitigate sustained NTA discounts – including contestable fund management contracts, capital management initiatives, and continuous disclosure of portfolio composition and taxation provisioning. It can be observed that the majority of recent IPOs in the sector, in contrast to most existing listed investment funds, employ externalized fund management arrangements with long-term management contracts of 25 years. From the perspective of contestability and accountability, therefore, these arrangements are more likely to ensure the entrenchment of the manager rather than provide accountability for performance. As noted above, however, a number of these funds use performance-based fees, and a minority have featured stapling, whereby fund investors are offered a stake in the fund's external manager.

Capital management initiatives, including payment of tax-advantaged dividends or share buy-backs, usually encourage the narrowing of NTA discounts. Capital management initiatives are an increasingly common feature of Australian stocks; however, their application within the context of listed funds is more problematic. Unlike conventional listed firms, managers of listed funds can reasonably argue that surplus cash should be retained and invested in the portfolio over the long term, rather than being returned to shareholders in response to short-term NTA discounts. This is particularly pronounced with the recent listed investment fund IPOs that raised cash in buoyant market conditions; however, fund managers have remained unwilling to

[7] Source: Aegis Research, *Australian Research Managed Investments Analysis*, February 2005.

Table 24.1 NTA discounts for IPOs within the Australian shares sector

	Listing date	Fund size ($ million)	NTA discount (%)
Contango MicroCap	25 March 2004	42	−17.8
Wilson Leaders	10 February 2004	40	−16.9
Van Eyk Three Pillars	28 January 2004	51	−16.3
Clime Capital	3 February 2004	24	−9.4
Century Australia	8 April 2004	185	−8.7

As at 28 February 2005. *Source*: ASX.

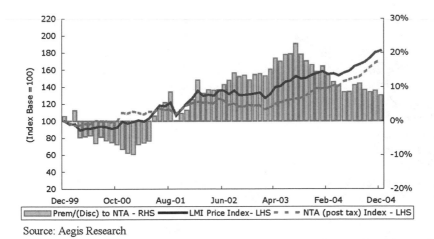

Source: Aegis Research

Figure 24.6 NTA discount/premiums for Australian share listed investment funds.
Source: reproduced by kind permission of Aegis Equities Research.

deploy the cash raised in the short term, resulting in significant NTA discounts (see Table 24.1).

The broader trend of NTA differentials for leading Australian shares funds is shown in Figure 24.6. This reveals a changing trend, with the largest listed investment funds generally trading at a premium to their NTA, although during 2004 this premium contracted, primarily as a result of IPOs satiating excess investor demand. This figure also illustrates the cyclicality in NTA differentials, making it virtually impossible to identify clear trends in the sector, especially when smaller, illiquid issues are included.

24.6 Return performance of recent listed investment fund IPOs

Although listed investment funds are intended to represent long-term investments, investor support of the listed funds market is affected to some extent – at least in the short term – by the performances of recent IPOs. For inexperienced investors expecting stag profits, the short-term performance of recent fund IPOs has been relatively disappointing; however, this pattern is not unexpected. For promoters of listed investment funds, explaining the technical factors contributing to these outcomes is an important educational issue.

Unlike conventional operating companies, there is generally no reason why IPOs of listed investment funds should deliver stag profits. For many listed investment funds, the investment portfolio is not seeded at the time of the IPO; unlike conventional capital raisings, which are dictated by immediate and specified opportunities, the implementation of the investment policy will depend on factors that are outside of the fund's control – especially market sentiment.

As noted above, several listed investment funds floated on the market recently have retained the bulk of the portfolio invested in liquid assets. In the case of private equity funds, the dearth of suitable transaction opportunities has been particularly pronounced. The convergence of these factors means that listed investment funds, in the short to medium term, are likely to experience a cash drag on returns, as a result of not being exposed to the stock market, but instead earning cash parking yields.

Figure 24.7 tracks the price returns for the 10 largest IPOs floated in 2004 as a general indicator of listed investment fund IPOs and their ongoing absolute returns. Of this cohort, the average return earned on their first trading day was 1.11%; however, only one performed strongly, seven closed at their issue prices, and two delivered losses to investors.

This chart reveals a mixed trend in returns of the larger IPOs, which was also evident across the sector overall. In terms of short-term performance, Figure 24.8 shows the dispersion of returns from the IPOs for the calendar year. Of the 24 IPOs in 2004, only seven remained below their issue price at the end of the year, after taking into account the value of stapled securities.

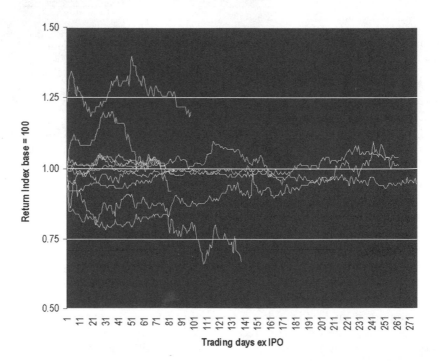

Figure 24.7 Price performance of fund IPOs

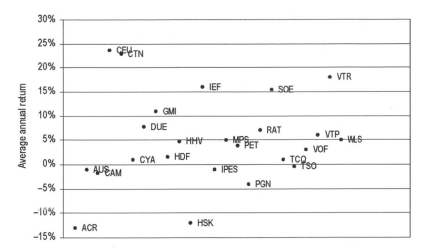

Figure 24.8 Returns of all listed investment fund IPOs in 2004

24.7 Conclusion

The Australian listed funds sector has experienced a resurgence of interest driven by favorable cyclical market conditions and investor preferences for targeted strategies. Many mutual fund managers and specialist investment boutiques have entered this market, employing the distribution infrastructure of stockbrokers to grow asset scale and to diversify their business models.

The supply of recent investment vehicles has reflected strong demand from investors and opportunism by fund promoters. Many offerings have featured lucrative long-term management contracts; however, they have also incorporated performance-based remuneration, thereby ameliorating some investor concerns about the governance of these funds. The recent trend of private equity formations has significant implications for the broader stock market, with mobilization of capital likely to propel significant corporate actions and to increase competition for deal flows.

Investors, however, need to be cognizant of the longer-term nature of these offerings, with many funds unable to deploy their capital in the short term, subsequently creating prolonged return dilution from the cash drag in those portfolios. Overall, however, the listed investment funds market is expected to continue to provide diversified and cost-effective exposure for investors, especially the growing numbers directing their own retirement funds seeking innovative strategies and portfolio diversification. Disappointing IPO results and significant NTA discounts are likely to present excellent opportunities for long-term investors, provided that their fund managers adhere to their valuation disciplines throughout the market cycle.

Bibliography

Aegis Equities Research (2005). *Managed Investments Analysis*, February. Aegis Equities Research, Sydney.

Australian Prudential Regulatory Authority (2004). *Superannuation Insights*, June. Australian Prudential Regulatory Authority, Sydney.

Australian Securities and Investments Commission (1999). *Practice Note 70: Prospectuses for Cash Box and Investment Companies*. Australian Securities and Investments Commission, Sydney.

Australian Stock Exchange (2005). *Listed Managed Investment Monthly Update*, January. ASX, Sydney.

Australian Stock Exchange (2005). *Financial Planners Market Research – Key Highlights*. ASX, Sydney.

Bell Potter Securities (2004). *Listed Investment Companies*. Financial Services Research, Melbourne.

Cotter, J., Goyen, M., and Hegarty, S. (2005). Offer Pricing of Australian Industrial Initial Public Offers. *Accounting and Finance*, 45(1):95–126.

Ferguson, R. and Leistikow, D. (2004). Closed-End Fund Discounts and Expected Investment Performance. *Financial Review*, 39(2):179–202.

Mercer Investment Consulting (2004). Guide to New Listed Investment Companies. Discussion Paper, Sydney.

Shaw Stockbroking (2004). *Listed Investment Companies: Preferred LICs and Relative Performance*. Shaw Stockbroking, Sydney.

25 Do underwriters create value for issuers by subjectively determining offer prices?

Steven Dolvin

Abstract

Many existing theories attempt to explain initial public offering (IPO) underpricing by suggesting that underwriters purposefully set offer prices below market value. These theories implicitly assume that underwriters have perfect foresight and can, with complete accuracy, place a value on issuing firms. I evaluate this assumption by comparing offer prices set by underwriters to prices from three objective, valuation-based approaches. Relative to these estimates, the offer prices chosen by underwriters result in lower levels of underpricing, suggesting that the prices underwriters select are actually value creating for issuing firms in that they reduce the opportunity cost of issuance.

25.1 Introduction

Several potential explanations have been given for the historically positive level of initial public offering (IPO) underpricing, which is defined as the percentage change from the offer price to the market price at the end of the first trading day. Many of these explanations implicitly assume that underwriters are sufficiently informed so as to set the offer price equal to the market value of an issue, thereby implying that underpricing, which is also known as initial return, is intentional. In fact, Chen and Mohan (2002) stated, 'Most of the [existing] theoretical and empirical studies hold that initial underpricing is undertaken deliberately.' As a specific example of an existing explanation that makes this assumption, Benveniste and Spindt (1989) suggested that underwriters knowingly partially adjust offer prices in order to compensate investors for truthfully revealing information regarding the market demand for an issue.

Within these existing theories, there is an implicit assumption that underwriters possess perfect foresight, meaning they are able, with certainty, to determine the fundamental, or market, value of an issue. It is also commonly believed, and admitted, that underwriters make subjective adjustments to estimated values in order to select a final offer price. If the assumption of perfect foresight is correct, then these adjustments, given the average positive levels of underpricing that exist, suggest that underwriters actually reduce proceeds to issuing firms (for example, a higher opportunity cost) by purposefully offering issues at below market value. The goal of this chapter is to evaluate the implicit assumption of perfect foresight. Thus, I study offer prices selected by underwriters relative to offer prices estimated using three objective, valuation-based approaches.

First, I obtain a full information price, which is a comparison approach that determines a price, based on the characteristics of previously issued IPOs. Second, I apply the Residual Income Model, which is an economic value added approach whose derivation is based on accounting relations and the standard dividend discount model. Third, I utilize a standard price ratio analysis of comparable firms in the same industry as the issuing firm.

If the implicit assumption that underwriters purposefully set offer prices below fundamental value is correct, then actual underpricing should be larger than the underpricing that would result from using the objective pricing methods mentioned above. However, if this assumption is not correct and underwriters, in fact, create value for issuers through the offer prices they select and the subjective adjustments they make, then actual underpricing should be lower than the underpricing that would result from using these objective approaches.

I find that in comparison to the objective valuation approaches employed, offer prices set by underwriters, particularly once the risk of undersubscription is controlled, result in the lowest average level of underpricing. This suggests that underwriters do not purposefully set prices below fundamental value. Rather, the findings indicate that true value is difficult to determine, and the prices set by underwriters reflect this uncertainty. Additionally, the relatively low level of underpricing also suggests that underwriters capture value for issuers by subjectively adjusting offer prices away from (i.e. in the upward direction) the estimates obtained from objective pricing models.

I also find cursory evidence that suggests the amount of value captured for issuers is increasing in underwriter reputation (up to a point), which implies that higher quality underwriters apply more subjective criteria for selecting offer prices and/or that the criteria employed are of higher quality. Thus, I conclude that underwriters do create value for issuers, and this value is generally increasing in reputation.

The rest of this chapter proceeds as follows. Section 25.2 presents background information on the role of the underwriter and methods for determining offer prices. Section 25.3 describes my data. Section 25.4 compares objectively determined offer prices to those actually set by underwriters, and section 25.5 concludes.

25.2 Background

25.2.1 The role of the underwriter

Although there have been a handful of firms that have attempted to take their own shares public, the vast majority employ an underwriter, which suggests that the services received are worth the added cost. The primary services rendered by an underwriter can be classified into three categories: (1) legal and administrative, (2) certification and market building, and (3) pricing.

Legal and administrative duties involve activities such as developing the prospectus and overseeing registration of the securities with the Securities and Exchange Commission (SEC) and the market or exchange where the security will be listed. Certification and market building include performing due diligence activities that certify the issue as reputable and also conducting the roadshow to build demand for the issue.

The third category of service provided by the underwriter is pricing, which is the primary focus of this study. Pricing generally involves setting the offer price for an issue, and this process entails utilizing pricing models, and to some extent subjective criteria, to determine underlying market value. As discussed earlier, existing IPO underpricing theories suggest that underwriters can precisely determine the value of an issue and any underpricing that exists is due to purposeful actions by the underwriter. However, this assumption of perfect foresight, particularly given the high volatility of IPO prices, seems to be unreasonable, especially when the underlying incentive to price an issue appropriately, which I discuss next, is considered.

Because the majority of recent IPOs are conducted on an underwritten, rather than a best effort, basis, the offer price represents the contracted gross amount issuers will receive (i.e., the risk of sale is borne by the underwriter rather than the issuer). In exchange for this guarantee, and also to cover direct costs, underwriters receive a gross spread, which for most offerings is fixed at 7% (Chen and Ritter, 1999) of total gross proceeds.

Given the prevalent structure of the underwriting market, underwriters face two conflicting objectives. First, assuming a predetermined number of shares to be issued, the spread (in dollars) received by the underwriter is positively related to the offer price. Thus, other things being equal, there is an incentive to push the offer price as high as possible. Second, the underwriter wants to insure the offer is not undersubscribed. The risk of undersubscription declines with the offer price, creating an incentive to reduce offer prices. Given the conflicting objectives, the final offer price chosen by the investment bank must be such that the tradeoff between the two risks is optimized (Booth and Smith, 1986).

Theoretically, the price that would minimize the risk tradeoff and serve as the optimum for both the issuer and the underwriter is the fundamental (market) value of the issue. If the underwriter sets the offer price exactly at this value, then underpricing is equal to zero, which implies that issuers raise the maximum proceeds and underwriters receive the maximum gross spread. Additionally, at this price all shares are sold, eliminating the risk of undersubsciption. At an offer price above fundamental value, the issue is undersubscribed, resulting in a gain for issuers (for example, higher guaranteed proceeds) and a loss for underwriters (for example, unsold shares due to undersubscription). At a price below fundamental value, issuers receive lower proceeds and underwriters receive a lower gross spread, although the risk of undersubscription is minimized since shares are offered at a discount. Given that the optimal price is fundamental value, the historically large, positive level of underpricing suggests that underwriters cannot with certainty determine fundamental value and that the assumption of perfect foresight is unjustified.

25.2.2 Objective pricing methods

The entire process of security analysis is predicated on finding the fundamental value of an investment; however, particularly for equities, analysts would probably agree that this is a daunting task. As such, there is no single method that provides the most accurate value for an equity security, rather there are two primary methods employed, each having different strengths and applications.

First, standard pricing theory states that the price of any asset, including equity, is the present value of future cash flows generated by the asset. As such, valuation generally involves applying the standard dividend discount and free cash flow models, forecasting each of these to some horizon period then applying a terminal value calculation. For IPOs, these models are extremely problematic. For example, at issuance IPO firms rarely pay a dividend and cash flows are generally negative, and these situations are unlikely to change for some period of time. Thus, determining the fundamental value of an IPO using these models is virtually impossible.

Second, market efficiency suggests that similar firms should have similar pricing characteristics, thus most analysts employ price ratios, determining prices based on comparable firm multiples. This approach is much more easily and broadly applied, particularly to IPOs. As such, the standard conception is that underwriters apply price ratio analysis in the process of setting offer prices, although the final offer price is subjectively adjusted to reflect certain firms or other subjective criteria.

The use of the comparable firm method for pricing IPOs has been previously studied. Kim and Ritter (1999) found that price ratios have only modest predictability, and they also found that price–earnings ratios are less accurate than other ratios due to the variability in these figures. Yetman (2001) and Purnanandam and Swaminathan (2004) also studied the use of price ratios in setting offer prices, finding that price ratios are not effectively compounded into offer prices and that, even with positive underpricing, IPOs actually appear to be overvalued, rather than undervalued as previous studies suggest.

A primary contribution of this chapter is to consider two additional pricing methods that, to my knowledge, have not been previously applied to IPOs. First, I calculate what I refer to as a full information price (FIP). This price is a type of comparison firm valuation, in that the value is based on the market's valuation of other IPO firms; however, the approach is not as simplistic as standard price ratios. To calculate the FIP, I regress IPO market prices at the end of the first trading day on characteristics (for example, size, venture capital backing, etc.) that previous IPO studies have found to be significant in predicting underpricing. I then use the estimated regression coefficients to forecast offer prices based on the characteristics of the IPO of interest. A more detailed discussion of this approach is included in section 25.4.

Second, I estimate offer prices using the Residual Income Model (RIM). The RIM is an economic value added model that, with the clean surplus accounting assumption, which assumes changes in book value come only from earnings and dividends, is a rearrangement of the standard dividend discount model. The RIM has not been broadly applied in the finance literature; however, accounting researchers have demonstrated its usefulness. For example, Ohlson (1995) and Feltman and Ohlson (1995) discussed and applied the RIM. Lundholm and O'Keefe (2001) illustrated that the RIM is equivalent to the dividend discount model, assuming clean surplus accounting; therefore, the choice of which model to use is based on the type of information that is available. For IPOs, book values are readily attainable, and earnings estimates are also available for a subset of the issues. Thus, I am able to apply the RIM to IPO valuation.

25.3 Data and summary statistics

I collect data on all original firm-commitment IPOs for the period 1986 to 1998 from Thompson Financial's Securities Data Company (SDC) database. SDC began reporting data on lockup periods and CUSIP numbers in 1986; therefore, I begin with this year. I eliminate 1999 and 2000 due to the general market bubble, during which time prices are believed to have deviated widely from fundamental values. Although I collect data beginning in 1986, my primary results cover the period 1990 to 1998. I use the 1986 to 1989 period, particularly for the full information price analysis, as the base period by which to begin the pricing comparison.

For calculation of initial returns, I collect closing prices on the first day of trading using the Center for Research in Security Prices (CRSP) database. Additionally, I collect earnings forecasts in place at the time of the initial offering from Zacks Earnings Database. I obtain monthly risk-free (for example, T-bill) rates from the St Louis Federal Reserve, and other company-specific information comes from Compustat.

Elimination of closed-end funds, spinoffs, real estate investment trusts, American depositary receipts, mutual to stock conversions, unit issues, and IPOs with offer prices below $5 produces a final sample of 3092 IPOs over the 1990 to 1998 period. Table 25.1 provides basic descriptive statistics for the full sample of IPOs. The average IPO has an offer price of $11.40, and issuers receive average proceeds of $38.89 million. The average initial return is 15.85%, and the average amount of money (Money) left on the table is $7.27 million.

On average, 42% of issues are venture capital (VC) backed, and the typical firm is taken public by an underwriter with a Carter–Manaster Rank (CM Rank), as updated by Loughran and Ritter (2004), of 6.79 and a market share of 3.17%. Additionally, the average firm's management must refrain from trading in the IPO for a lockup period of 220.60 days. Finally, as would be expected based on the findings of Chen and Ritter (1999), the average spread is clustered around 7%. Overall, these statistics are comparable to those reported in other studies examining similar time periods.

Table 25.1 Firm and offering characteristics

Variable	N	Mean	Std dev.
Offer	3092	11.40	4.51
Proceeds	3092	38.89	47.40
Initial	2926	15.85	24.69
Money	2926	7.27	17.72
VC	3092	0.42	0.49
CM Rank	3076	6.79	2.29
Share	3092	3.17	4.58
Lockup	2917	220.60	126.12
Spread	3091	7.34	1.03

This table provides firm and offering characteristics for the full sample of IPOs over the 1990 to 1998 time period. 'Offer' is the average offer price. 'Proceeds' is the dollar size of the offer in millions. 'Initial' is initial return in percent, calculated as the change in price from offer to the market price at the end of the first trading day. 'Money' is money left on the table in millions, calculated as the dollar difference between the end of first-day market price and the offer price, multiplied by the number of shares offered. 'VC' is a dummy variable equal to 1 if the offer is venture capital backed; thus, the value reported represents the fraction of the firms that have venture capital backing. 'CM Rank' is based on the Carter and Manaster (1990) ranking system, which ranges from 1 (worst) to 9 (best), as updated by Loughran and Ritter (2004). 'Share' is the market share in percent of the lead underwriter. 'Lockup' is the number of days spent in lockup. 'Spread' is the spread charged by the underwriter, in percent. Data are from the SDC and CRSP databases.

25.3.1 Statistics by underwriter quality level

In this study, I examine whether offer prices chosen by underwriters outperform (result in lower underpricing) objectively based values. This analysis is indirectly a test of the pricing ability of underwriters, and therefore I also address the question of whether or not higher quality underwriters are more capable of selecting offer prices. Based on the findings of Dolvin (2005), I identify three distinct groups of underwriters: low quality (Rank 1–3), medium quality (Rank 4–6), and high quality (Rank 7–9). Table 25.2 presents summary statistics for these three groups, as well as a difference of means test for each variable.

The results reported in Table 25.2 are generally consistent with Dolvin (2005). As underwriter rank increases, so do offer prices, proceeds, and underwriter market shares. Lockup times and spreads decrease as underwriter quality increases, which is consistent with a certification effect and/or higher quality underwriters dealing in higher quality issues. Additionally, also consistent with Dolvin (2005), there appears to be a U-shaped relation between rank and underpricing. Underpricing is smallest for medium-quality underwriters as compared to both low- and high-quality underwriters; however, there is no difference between high- and low-quality underwriters. This suggests that medium-quality underwriters may be the best judges of values, and

Table 25.2 Descriptive statistics by underwriter quality level

Variable	Descriptive statistics			t-statistics		
	Low (1–3)	Medium (4–6)	High (7–9)	Low vs med.	Low vs high	Med. vs high
N	468	533	2091			
Offer	5.98	9.60	13.11	−20.58	−56.60	20.20
Proceeds	8.67	20.91	50.34	−14.23	−35.05	20.74
Initial	16.44	11.30	15.98	3.56	0.35	−4.69
Money	1.66	2.44	9.18	−2.91	−16.19	13.57
VC	0.13	0.31	0.52	−7.00	−20.37	9.09
Share	2.34	5.15	8.18	−61.05	−166.58	81.82
Lockup	382.05	219.07	184.14	−9.92	−42.49	38.44
Spread	9.09	7.45	6.91	23.84	40.91	−12.02

This table provides firm and offering characteristics for the full sample of IPOs over the 1990 to 1998 time period by underwriter quality level, as based on the Carter and Manaster (1990) ranking system, where a higher rank indicates higher prestige. The sample is split into low-quality (Rank 1–3), medium-quality (Rank 4–6), and high-quality (Rank 7–9) underwriters. The table also provides a t-statistic from difference of means tests between each group. 'Offer' is the average offer price. 'Proceeds' is the dollar size of the offer in millions. 'Initial' is initial return in percent, calculated as the change in price from offer to the market price at the end of the first trading day. 'Money' is money left on the table in millions, calculated as the dollar difference between the end of first-day market price and the offer price, multiplied by the number of shares offered. 'VC' is a dummy variable equal to 1 if the offer is venture capital backed; thus, the value reported represents the fraction of the firms that have venture capital backing. 'CM Rank' is based on the Carter and Manaster (1990) ranking system, which ranges from 1 (worst) to 9 (best), as updated by Loughran and Ritter (2004). 'Share' is the market share in percent of the lead underwriter. 'Lockup' is the number of days spent in lockup. 'Spread' is the spread charged by the underwriter, in percent. Data are from the SDC and CRSP databases.

I address this in more detail in a later section. Although money left on the table (in dollars) increases with rank, this reflects the size of the issue, not necessarily underwriter quality.

25.3.2   Residual Income Model sample

The RIM is a measure of economic value added, and the model prices a security as its current book value plus the present value of all future economic profit (revenue in excess of a charge for equity). To implement the model, I require book values after the offer and earnings forecasts, rather than dividends or cash flows. As with other growth models, forecasts of growth rates (in earnings) and discount rates are also needed. Book values are readily available from SDC and CRSP for almost all IPOs; however, earnings forecasts and growth rates are only available for a subset (approximately 550) of the IPOs. To draw inferences based on the RIM sample, I determine if there are significant differences between the full sample and the sample of firms used to calculate values based on the RIM.

Table 25.3 presents summary statistics for the RIM sample and compares them to the full sample results replicated from Table 25.1. Since earnings forecasts, which come from Zacks Earnings Database, are more likely to be available for larger, more closely followed companies, I expect the RIM sample to contain larger firms than the

Table 25.3 Sample comparison: Full vs RIM

Variable	Full sample			RIM sample			t-statistics
	N	Mean	Std dev.	N	Mean	Std dev.	
Offer	3092	11.40	4.51	551	12.91	4.91	−6.73
Proceeds	3092	38.89	47.40	551	97.41	406.75	−3.37
Initial	2926	15.85	24.69	531	16.78	30.02	0.69
Money	2926	7.27	17.72	551	13.20	95.96	−1.45
VC	3092	0.42	0.49	551	0.29	0.45	6.16
CM Rank	3076	6.79	2.29	551	7.39	1.90	−6.58
Share	3092	3.17	4.58	529	4.00	5.19	−3.52
Lockup	2917	220.60	126.12	527	194.91	78.04	6.35
Spread	3091	7.34	1.03	551	6.96	0.76	−10.19

This table provides firm and offering characteristics for the full sample of IPOs over the 1990 to 1998 time period, as well as for the partial sample used for valuation employing the Residual Income Model. Additionally, the table provides t-statistics from a difference of means test between the two samples. 'Offer' is the average offer price. 'Proceeds' is the dollar size of the offer in millions. 'Initial' is initial return in percent, calculated as the change in price from offer to the market price at the end of the first trading day. 'Money' is money left on the table in millions, calculated as the dollar difference between the end of first-day market price and the offer price, multiplied by the number of shares offered. 'VC' is a dummy variable equal to 1 if the offer is venture capital backed; thus, the value reported represents the fraction of the firms that have venture capital backing. 'CM Rank' is based on the Carter and Manaster (1990) ranking system, which ranges from 1 (worst) to 9 (best), as updated by Loughran and Ritter (2004). 'Share' is the market share in percent of the lead underwriter. 'Lockup' is the number of days spent in lockup. 'Spread' is the spread charged by the underwriter, in percent. Data are from the SDC and CRSP databases.

full sample. The table confirms this expectation. Also, because the RIM sample contains larger issues, it is likely to be associated with larger, higher quality underwriters. Thus, any conclusions drawn from the RIM analysis may be specific to larger, higher priced issues.

25.4 Determining offer prices

Underpricing is determined by two factors: the end of first-day market price and the offer price. Typically, the market price is assumed to be the fundamental value, and underpricing is therefore attributed to the offer price selected by the underwriter. As discussed earlier, prior research appears to assume that underwriters have perfect foresight and should be able to correctly judge what the market is willing to pay for an issue (i.e. identify fundamental value). I address this assumption by considering three methods for determining the offer price: (1) a full information price that uses current and past information available at the time the offer price is selected to predict what the market is willing to pay for an issue; (2) the Residual Income Model as popularized by Ohlson (1995); and (3) a standard price ratio forecast using all firms in the same industry, as measured by three-digit SIC code.

These three methods represent purely objective choices for the offer price. If the actual offer price set by the underwriter outperforms (i.e. creates a lower average level of underpricing) these objective values, then the underwriter, even in the presence of positive average underpricing, has created value for issuers. If these objective prices, on the other hand, would produce lower levels of underpricing, then the implicit assumption that underwriters purposefully set offer prices too low may be correct.

25.4.1   Full information price

Prior research reveals that there are certain issue characteristics that affect underpricing. Having observed the historical relation between these factors and underpricing, underwriters could set an issue's offer price based on its characteristics and the known relations to underpricing (i.e. to the market's perceived value). Using this rationale, I attempt to find the offer price that would produce zero underpricing, and I refer to this offer price as the full information price (FIP).

To estimate the FIP, I use the end of first-day market price as the dependent variable. Observing the relationships between IPO characteristics and the market's price, I predict what offer price will minimize underpricing and therefore maximize proceeds. I could use the entire sample period (1986 to 1998) to estimate the relationship between IPO characteristics and market prices, but this would present look-ahead bias. Additionally, it would not be an applicable approach for underwriters since these future data would not be available at the time the offer price is set. Therefore, I use only data that would be available prior to setting the offer price. Offer prices can be adjusted as late as the day prior to, or even the day of, the offering. Thus, to insure data are available when the final offer price is selected, I only use data available at least 1 day prior to the offering.

Beginning 1 January 1990, I estimate a regression at the beginning of every quarter, using all available data since 1986. The regression coefficients are then used to estimate full information offer prices for the subsequent quarter. As an example, the regression for the third quarter of 1995 would include all data from 1 January 1986 to 30 June 1995. The estimated relations would then be used during July, August, and September of 1995. The following represents the regression used to estimate full information offer prices:

$$Market_i = \alpha + \beta_1 LnPre + \beta_2 VC + \beta_3 Overhang + \beta_4 HT$$

$$+ \beta_5 Secondary + \beta_6 EInt + \beta_7 IPOLag_{-1} + \beta_8 NasLag_{-1}$$

$$+ \beta_9 Multiple + \beta_{10} AmUp + \beta_{11} AmDown + \beta_{12} CMRank \qquad (25.1)$$

$$+ \beta_{13} Volatility + \beta_{11} Midfile + \beta_{12} Range + \ldots_i,$$

where:

$Market_i$ = the market price at the end of the first trading day for issue i

LnPre = natural log of the expected proceeds in millions, where expected proceeds are equal to shares filed multiplied by the amended midfile price (or original midfile price if no amendment)

VC = dummy variable equal to 1 if the issue is venture capital backed, 0 otherwise

Overhang = pre-IPO shares retained divided by total shares filed

HT = dummy variable equal to 1 if the issuer is classified as a high-technology firm, 0 otherwise

Secondary = the percentage of shares filed that are secondary shares

EInt = dummy variable equal to 1 if all original and amended file prices (high, low, and mid) are integers

IPOLag = an underpricing index defined as the average initial return in percent for all IPOs in the sample on calendar days −1 to −30 before the issue date

NasLag = the cumulative return, in percent, on the Nasdaq composite for the 21 trading days (1 month) prior to issue

Multiple = dummy variable equal to 1 if the issue has more than one class of common shares, 0 otherwise

AmUp = percentage change from the original midfile price to the amended midfile price if the amendment is positive and if the amendment takes place at least 1 day prior to offer, 0 otherwise

AmDown = percentage change from the original midfile price to the amended midfile price if the amendment is negative and if the amendment takes place at least 1 day prior to offer, 0 otherwise

CMRank = underwriter quality as measured by updated Carter and Manaster (1990) ranks

Volatility = volatility of NasLag

Midfile = the original midfile price

Range = the range (i.e. highest − lowest) of the initial high and low file prices.

The variables used are similar to those applied in previous studies examining IPO underpricing (Bradley and Jordan, 2002; Smart and Zutter, 2003; Dolvin, 2005; Bradley et al., 2005).

I run the above regression for each quarter and use the results to predict offer prices and to calculate initial returns that would have resulted had offer prices been set using the predictions. I then compare these results to actual offer prices and underpricing.

I perform this comparison for the overall sample, as well as by underwriter quality level. Table 25.4 presents the results of these comparisons.

Looking at the overall sample, the average underpricing is 15.85%; however, if underwriters were to price issues at the FIP, the underpricing falls to an average of 2.93%. Thus, it appears that underwriters do not adjust offer prices to reflect market information and therefore purposefully set offer prices too low. However, this difference is not statistically significant due to the high variability of the forecasted FIP and its associated underpricing. Additionally, this conclusion fails to consider the number of issues that would be undersubscribed (for example, have a negative initial return).

Using the original offer price set by underwriters, only 317 issues (10.25% of all issues) have negative underpricing. However, using the FIPs would result in 1694 issues (54.8% of all issues) having negative underpricing. Given that over half of all issues would have a negative return, demand for IPOs would dramatically decline as a result of the winner's curse, thereby increasing the risk of an undersubscribed issue and limiting the use of the FIP without any adjustments.

To control for the risk of undersubscription, I also consider the underpricing that would result if the FIPs were objectively adjusted such that the exact number of issues in the original sample had negative underpricing (AdjInitial). Thus, I adjust the FIPs

Table 25.4 FIP offer prices vs actual offer prices

Variable	Actual	Forecasted FIP	t-statistic
Full sample			
Offer price	11.40	13.78	−15.15
Initial return	15.85	2.93	1.28
AdjInitial	15.85	46.35	−3.43
Ranks 1–3			
Offer price	5.98	8.11	−8.11
Initial return	16.44	1.25	7.11
AdjInitial	16.44	9.78	1.71
Ranks 4–6			
Offer price	9.60	11.66	−6.27
Initial return	11.30	27.96	−0.58
AdjInitial	11.30	62.85	−2.42
Ranks 7–9			
Offer price	13.11	15.07	−15.10
Initial return	15.98	−2.14	1.76
AdjInitial	15.98	51.44	−1.92

This table compares initial returns using actual offer prices to those using forecasted full information prices (FIPs). Additionally, comparisons are provided for initial return versus adjusted initial return (AdjInitial), which is forecasted initial return adjusted for the risk of undersubscription (i.e. adjusting so that only 10% of issues have negative underpricing). The results are given for the full sample, as well as by underwriter quality level. t-statistics from difference of means tests are also reported. Full information prices (FIPs) are forecasted using all information available at least 1 day prior to actual issuance. Data are from SDC and CRSP for the period 1986 to 1998, although data from 1986 to 1989 are used for forecasting purposes. Offer prices and returns are strictly from 1990 to 1998.

such that only 317 issues would have a negative initial return. I find that this process entails an adjustment to the full information price of 0.7033. That is, for an issue that had an FIP price of, say, $10.00, the adjusted FIP would be $7.03. Because issuers would not necessarily know beforehand which issues would produce negative returns, all forecasted full information offer prices would be adjusted.

I apply this adjustment and find the mean level of underpricing is 46.35%, which is significantly higher than the actual level of underpricing (for example, *t*-statistic of 3.43). Thus, I conclude that, although average underpricing is dramatically reduced using the FIP, the number of issues with negative underpricing involves too high a risk of undersubscription. I also conclude that after adjusting the FIP to minimize negative returns, the underpricing based on FIPs is much higher than that based on actual offer prices. Thus, once the risk of undersubscription is controlled for, underwriters appear to outperform the full information price, thereby creating value for issuers, even in the presence of positive underpricing.

To address the influence of underwriter quality, I repeat the above analysis by underwriter quality level. As Table 22.4 indicates, the results by underwriter quality level exhibit two differences worth noting. First, the difference in actual and predicted initial returns for lower quality underwriters is highly significant, and I find that this difference remains even after controlling for the risk of undersubscription. Second, similar to the full sample, actual and forecasted initial returns for medium- and high-quality underwriters are not statistically different; however, once undersubscription is controlled for, actual initial returns are lower than predicted initial returns.

These findings suggest that medium- and high-quality underwriters capture more value for issuers and that lower quality underwriters either (1) purposefully misprice issues, which is consistent with fraud in the penny stock market as discussed by Bradley et al. (2005) or (2) are unable to accurately value issuing firms. Thus, it appears that underwriters as a whole create value for issuers by subjectively adjusting offer prices away from objective estimates; however, the value created is likely increasing in underwriter quality level, at least in comparing medium- and high-quality underwriters to those in the lowest category.

25.4.2 Residual Income Model valuation

Determining fundamental value is difficult, but most analysts and researchers would likely agree that the current price of a stock should be equal to the present value of all future cash flows received. Forecasting to infinity is difficult, so most valuation analyses use some form of the dividend discount model with a terminal value and/or the Gordon growth model. However, since most IPO issuers do not pay a dividend, these models are essentially useless in this context. Fortunately, recent work by Ohlson (1995) has brought a renewed focus to the Residual Income Model (RIM), which is an algebraic manipulation of the dividend discount model that facilitates use of accounting information and earnings forecasts rather than dividends and cash flows. The RIM is derived in the Appendix.

Ohlson (1995) illustrated that, with the clean surplus accounting assumption, the RIM is algebraically equivalent to the dividend discount model. Thus, analysts may choose the valuation model for which the data are most readily available. For IPOs, accounting data are more prevalent than dividends. Therefore, I apply the RIM to the IPOs in my sample; however, recall the sample size is much smaller for the RIM sample relative to the full sample and is composed of larger IPOs, which is due to the availability of earnings forecasts.

Using the RIM, I estimate the value of each issue for which data are available. As discussed previously, the RIM requires current book value, current and forecasted earnings (or an expected growth rate), and a discount rate (required return). Application of the RIM then involves adding current book value to the discounted value of expected future economic profit (forecasted earnings in excess of the cost of equity). These earnings go to infinity, thus a terminal value calculation is required. For this terminal value, I choose to use the Gordon growth formula, replacing abnormal earnings for dividends. Thus, the model I use for estimating value is as follows:

$$\text{RIM}(P) = \sum_{t=1}^{T} \frac{E[x_{a,t}]}{(1+r)^t} + \frac{E[x_{a,T+1}]}{(r-g)(1+r)^T} + BV_0, \qquad (25.2)$$

where $\text{RIM}(P)$ is the estimated value; $E[x_{a,t}]$ is expected abnormal earnings per share in time t, where abnormal earnings represent net income less a charge for equity; BV_0 is beginning book value per share after the offering; T is the number of periods prior to the terminal value calculation; r is the required return on equity capital; and g is the forecasted long-term growth rate in earnings.

Book values after the offer come from SDC and CRSP, and they represent values in place after proceeds are collected. Current EPS come from SDC, and forecasted values come from Zacks Earnings Database. Zacks provides earnings forecasts for 2 subsequent years, as well as a long-term growth forecast thereafter. Bradshaw and Sloan (2002) show that street earnings typically exceed GAAP income; thus, my estimates are conservative in that they overstate value. Additionally, Francis et al. (2000) showed that, using forecasted earnings, rather than realizations, is more realistic and also produces better measures of the current price.

Because changes in discount rates and expected growth rates can have large impacts on price estimates, I test a variety of values for each. For discount rates, I calculate company-specific values by applying the capital asset pricing model to industry averages, which I obtain by both value- and equal-weighted averages of Compustat data, where I use three-digit SIC codes to define industries. Additionally, based on the findings of Sougiannis and Yaekora (2001), I apply fixed discount rates of 12% and 15%. For growth rates, I use Zacks earnings forecasts, which implies a terminal value is calculated at the end of period 2. Also, I examine a 5-year abnormal growth period, in which the growth rates in periods 3, 4, and 5 linearly regress toward the long-term growth rate given by Zacks, with the terminal value calculated at the end of period 5.

In all cases, the estimated value, on average, is well below the actual offer and market prices, and, in fact, the average estimated value across all samples is approximately 75% below the actual offer price. To bias against rejecting my hypothesis, I choose to report results based on the valuation that represents the smallest average difference between calculated values and offer prices. Thus, I use estimated values calculated using a standard 12% discount rate and a 5-year abnormal earnings period. This specification gives an undervaluation of estimated prices relative to offer prices of 57% and forecasted underpricing of 148.82%, which is much higher than the actual level of underpricing.

Historically, IPO research has focused specifically on the relation between underwriter prestige and underpricing. However, I conjecture that decomposing underpricing may provide additional insight into this relationship. Underpricing can be decomposed into two components: market mispricing and underwriter mispricing. Market mispricing refers to the market's valuation of an IPO relative to its RIM value, and underwriter mispricing refers to the underwriter's valuation of an IPO relative to its RIM value. Note that market mispricing minus underwriter mispricing is equal to initial return. This decomposition is given as follows:

$$\text{Underpricing} = \text{Market Mispricing} - \text{Underwriter Mispricing}$$

$$\text{Underpricing} = \frac{P_1 - \text{OP}}{\text{OP}} = \frac{P_1 - \text{RIM}}{\text{OP}} - \frac{\text{OP} - \text{RIM}}{\text{OP}} \qquad (25.3)$$

where P_1 is the market price at the end of the first trading day, OP is the offer price, and RIM is the estimated value from the residual income model.

I would generally expect that higher quality underwriters would have lower underwriter mispricing, meaning they are better at determining value; however, this ignores the true role of the underwriter, which is to capture value for issuers. Thus, I hypothesize that if an issue has positive market mispricing, then higher quality underwriters would actually have higher underwriter mispricing. Thus, they are able to capture a higher percentage of the market's misvaluation for the issuers they represent.

Table 25.5 presents means and difference tests for market mispricing, underwriter mispricing, and underwriter mispricing as a percentage of market mispricing (Captured) for all issues in the RIM sample that have positive underpricing, as well as by high (Rank 7–9), medium (Rank 4–6), and low (Rank 1–3) quality underwriters. Both market mispricing (MktErr) and underwriter mispricing (UnderErr) are

Table 25.5 Pricing errors from initial return decomposition

Variable	Full	Descriptive statistics			Difference of means test		
		Low (1–3)	Medium (4–6)	High (7–9)	Med. vs low	High vs low	High vs med.
N	413	28	56	329			
MktErr	0.78	0.31	0.61	0.85	3.33	6.42	4.72
UnderErr	0.56	0.18	0.46	0.61	3.41	5.73	3.88
Captured	0.72	0.55	0.75	0.71	1.89	1.72	−0.66

This table presents pricing errors relative to forecasted values, as calculated using the Residual Income Model (RIM), for the market and for underwriters. 'MktErr' is equal to the end of first-day market price less the forecasted residual income value, relative to the offer price. 'UnderErr' is equal to the offer price less the forecasted residual income value, relative to the offer price. MktErr less UnderErr is equal to initial return. 'Captured' is UnderErr as a percentage of MktErr. The analysis is done for the complete RIM sample, as well as by underwriter quality level. The table also provides a t-statistic from difference of means tests between each group. Statistics are calculated using data from SDC, CRSP, and Zacks Earnings Database over the period 1990 to 1998. Only issues that had positive initial returns are included.

increasing in underwriter rank and are significantly different among all three quality levels. However, this relationship does not hold for the amount of mispricing captured. Medium- and high-quality underwriters capture a larger portion of mispricing than low-quality underwriters, but high-quality underwriters do not capture a larger portion than medium-quality underwriters. Thus, it appears that underwriters in general capture value for issuers, and that underwriters of medium-to-high quality are able to capture the largest percentage of market mispricing.

25.4.3 Price ratio analysis

It is commonly agreed that underwriters use ratio comparisons as the primary method for pricing an IPO. Thus, they take the market's valuation of comparable firms as a best estimate of the true value of the issuing firm. However, rather than using the price ratios of the entire market or even of the specific industry as a whole, the underwriters apply specifically chosen comparable firms. Additionally, upward and downward adjustments are made on a subjective basis.

As an additional study of the potential value of underwriters, I consider the offer prices and associated underpricing that would result from using the price ratio of the entire industry, rather than those chosen and adjusted by the underwriter. As such, I retrieve quarterly data on all Nasdaq listed firms from Compustat. I then calculate industry-specific average price-to-book ratios by three-digit SIC code. Each IPO is then matched to the industry average price-to-book ratio in place at the time of offering. Finally, I estimate an offer price based on the price-to-book ratio.

If underwriters do indeed create value for issuers, the offer prices they choose should result in reduced underpricing in comparison to that which would result from an objective selection of the industry average price ratio. The average underpricing across all issues using the actual offer price is 15.85%. However, if issuers were to use offer prices based on industry price-to-book ratios, mean underpricing would be 60.34%. Additionally, approximately 46% of the issues would be undersubscribed, since the offer price would be above the end of first-day market price. If I eliminate those issues with negative underpricing based on the price-to-book forecasted offer price, the difference in underpricing is even more pronounced: 15.63% versus 186.12%. Thus, overall, the offer price set by underwriters appears to reduce the risk of sale and also decrease money left on the table, both of which are value creating for issuers.

I also examine the differences by underwriter quality level. I find, consistent with earlier results, that the differences between forecasted returns and actual returns are greatest for medium- and high-quality underwriters. Because actual returns are lower than forecasted, the larger differences imply more value captured. These results are consistent with the lowest quality underwriters capturing the least value for issuers.

25.5 Conclusion

Many existing theories attempt to explain the historically positive level of underpricing by suggesting that underwriters purposefully set offer prices too low. These theories implicitly assume that underwriters are able to determine fundamental values with complete accuracy. I test this assumption by comparing actual levels of underpricing to those that would result if offer prices were set using objective estimates of value.

If the implicit assumption that underwriters purposefully set offer prices below fundamental value is correct, then actual underpricing should be larger than the underpricing that would result from using objective pricing methods. However, if this assumption is not correct and underwriters, in fact, create value for issuers through the offer prices they select, then actual underpricing should be lower than the underpricing that would result from using these objective approaches.

I calculate objective offer prices using three different methods. First, I calculate a full information price, which is based on the market's apparent valuation of specific IPO characteristics. Second, I estimate value using the Residual Income Model, which is essentially an accounting derivation of the standard dividend discount model. Third, I apply a standard price ratio analysis.

I find that in all cases, particularly once the risk of undersubscription is controlled for, the actual level of underpricing is much less than the underpricing that would result from setting offer prices using the objective methods employed. I also examine if higher quality underwriters capture more value for issuers, and I find that the lowest quality underwriters do the poorest job. However, there is little difference between medium- and high-quality underwriters. Thus, I conclude that underwriters do create value for issuers, and that the value captured increases with underwriter quality, at least up to a point.

References

Benveniste, L. and Spindt, P. (1989). How Investment Bankers Determine the Offer Price and Allocation of New Issues. *Journal of Financial Economics*, 24(2):343–361.

Booth, J. and Smith, R. (1986). Capital Raising, Underwriting and the Certification Hypothesis. *Journal of Financial Economics*, 15(2):261–281.

Bradley, D. and Jordan, B. (2002). Partial Adjustment to Public Information. *Journal of Financial and Quantitative Economics*, 37(4):595–616.

Bradley, D., Cooney, J., Dolvin, S., and Jordan, B. (2005). Penny Stock IPOs. Working Paper.

Bradshaw, M. and Sloan, R. (2002). GAAP Versus the Street: An Empirical Assessment of Two Alternative Definitions of Earnings. *Journal of Accounting Research*, 40(1):41–66.

Carter, R. and Manaster, S. (1990). Initial Public Offerings and Underwriter Reputation. *Journal of Finance*, 45(4):1045–1067.

Chen, C. and Mohan, N. (2002). Underwriter Spread, Underwriter Reputation, and IPO Underpricing: A Simultaneous Equation Analysis. *Journal of Business Finance and Accounting*, 29(3–4):521–540.

Chen, H. and Ritter, J. R. (1999). The Seven Percent Solution. *Journal of Finance*, 55(3):1105–1131.

Dolvin, S. (2005). Market Structure, Changing Incentives, and Underwriter Certification. *Journal of Financial Research*, 28(3):403–419.

Feltham, G. and Ohlson, J. (1995). Valuation and Clean Surplus Accounting for Operating and Financial Activities. *Contemporary Accounting Research*, 11(2):689–731.

Francis, J., Olsson, P., and Oswald, D. (2000). Comparing the Accuracy and Explainability of Dividends, Free Cash Flow, and Abnormal Earnings Equity Value Estimates. *Journal of Accounting Research*, 38(1):45–69.

Kim, M. and Ritter, J. R. (1999). Valuing IPOs. *Journal of Financial Economics*, 53(3):409–437.

Loughran, T. and Ritter, J. R. (2004). Why Has Underpricing Changed Over Time? *Financial Management*, 33(3):5–38.

Lundholm, R. and O'Keefe, T. (2001). Reconciling Value Estimates from the Discounted Cash Flow Model and the Residual Income Model. *Contemporary Accounting Research*, 18(2):311–335.

Ohlson, J., (1995). Earnings, Book Values, and Dividends in Security Valuation. *Contemporary Accounting Research*, 11(2):661–687.

Purnanandam, A. and Swaminathan, B. (2004). Are IPOs Really Underpriced? *Review of Financial Studies*, 17(3):811–848.

Smart, S. and Zutter, C. (2003). Control as a Motive for Underpricing: A Comparison of Dual- and Single-Class IPOs. *Journal of Financial Economics*, 69(1):85–110.

Sougiannis, T. and Yaekura, T. (2001). The Accuracy and Bias of Equity Values Inferred from Analysts' Earnings Forecasts. *Journal of Accounting, Auditing, and Finance*, 16(3):331–362.

Yetman, M. (2001). Accounting-Based Value Metrics and the Informational Efficiency of IPO Early Market Prices. Working Paper (http://www.ssrn.com).

Appendix: Derivation of the Residual Income Model

Standard asset pricing theory suggests that the price of any asset is the present value of all future cash flows, which is represented by dividends for common equity securities. As such, the price of an IPO, or any common stock, is represented by the following:

$$P = \sum_{t=1}^{\infty} \frac{E[d_t]}{(1+r)^t},$$

(25.A1)

where P is the estimated value of the security, $E[d_t]$ is the expected dividend per share in time t, and r is the discount rate.

Clean surplus accounting suggests that changes in book value are completely determined by earnings and dividends. As such, the following holds true:

$$BV_t = BV_{t-1} + x_t - d_t,$$

(25.A2)

where BV is the book value per share, x_t is the earnings per share in time t, and d_t is the dividends per share in time t. Equation (25.A2) can be rearranged as follows:

$$d_t = BV_{t-1} - BV_t + x_t.$$

(25.A3)

Let time T be a terminal date at which time a liquidating dividend is paid. After the liquidating dividend, book value is equal to zero. At time T, the following holds true:

$$d_T = (BV_{T-1} - BV_T + x_t) + BV_T.$$

(25.A4)

Rewriting equation (25.A1) produces the following equivalent statement:

$$P = \lim_{T \to \infty} \sum_{t=1}^{T} \frac{E[d_t]}{(1 + r)^t}.$$

(25.A5)

Replacing terms provides the following:

$$P = \lim_{T \to \infty} \left(\sum_{t=1}^{T} \frac{E[x_t + BV_{t-1} + BV_t]}{(1+r)^t} + \frac{E[BV_T]}{(1+r)^T} \right).$$

(25.A6)

The dividend discount model assumes that net income, dividends, and earnings all grow at the same rate (e.g. at rate r). The clean surplus assumption implies that book value also grows at rate r. Thus, the following holds:

$$E[BV_t] = E[BV_{t-1}](1+r).$$

(25.A7)

Substituting equation (25.A7) into equation (25.A6) and simplifying yields the following:

$$P = \lim_{T \to \infty} \left(\sum_{t=1}^{T} \frac{E[x_t - BV_{t-1}^* r]}{(1+r)^t} + \frac{BV_0(1+r)^T}{(1+r)^T} \right).$$

(25.A8)

Abnormal earnings (i.e. $E[x_a]$) are defined as earnings less the cost of equity, which implies the following:

$$E = [x_{a,t}] - E[x_t - BV^*_{t-1}r].$$
(25.A9)

Substituting equation (25.A9) into equation (25.A8) and simplifying produces the following:

$$P = \sum_{t=1}^{\infty} \frac{E[x_{a,t}]}{(1+r)^t} + BV_0.$$
(25.A10)

Equation (25.A10) is the Residual Income Model.

Index

Page numbers in *italics* refer to figures and tables